UFAS Retrofit Guide

Accessibility Modifications for Existing Buildings

designed to be used in conjunction with

the Uniform Federal Accessibility Standards for Compliance with

- Title II of the Americans with Disabilities Act
- Section 504 of the Rehabilitaion Act of 1973
- the Architectural Barriers Act of 1968

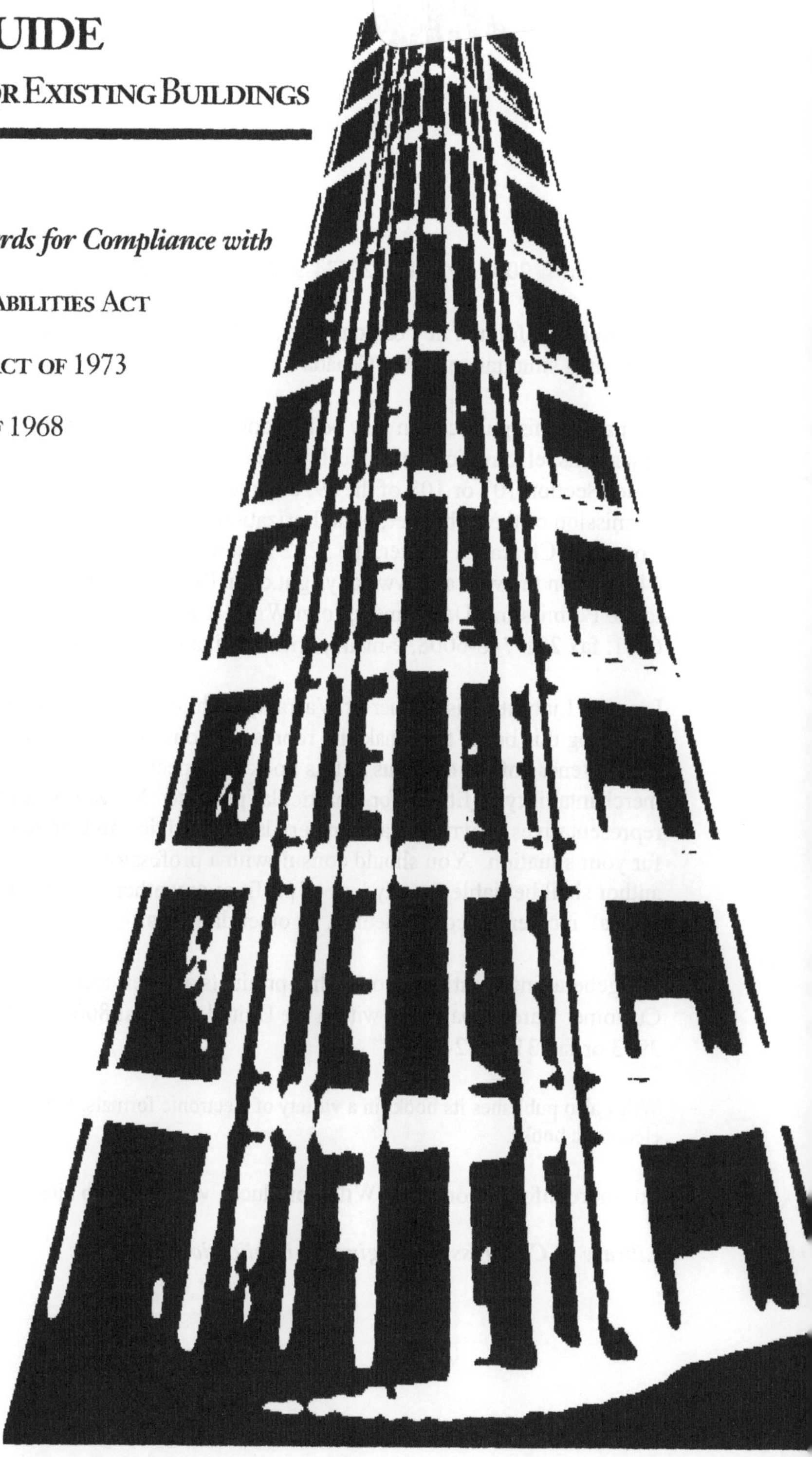

Designed and Developed by

Barrier *free* Environments Incorporated

Raleigh, North Carolina

Published by John Wiley & Sons, Inc., Hoboken, New Jersey
Published simultaneously in Canada

For general information on our other products and services, or technical support, please contact our Customer Care Department within the United States at 800-762-2974, outside the United States at 317-572-3993 or fax 317-572-4002.

Wiley also publishes its books in a variety of electronic formats. Some content that appears in print may not be available in electronic books.

For more information about Wiley products, visit our web site at www.wiley.com.

Library of Congress Cataloging-in-Publication Data:

10 9 8 7 6 5 4 3 2 1

CONTENTS

INTRODUCTION

In this era of economic turbulence influenced by the development of world markets, the environmental crisis, increasing construction costs, land saturation, and resource depletion, recycling of materials and buildings is becoming commonplace. Adaptive reuse, preservation, restoration, and renovation projects now outnumber new construction projects. The Americans with Disabilities Act (ADA) has mandated unprecedented attention to the needs of people with disabilities in new and existing buildings. This new law can affect all buildings nationwide regardless of other local, state, or federal laws and codes. Never has the emphasis on retrofitting existing buildings for accessibility been of such magnitude.

The far reaching impact of the ADA is creating an enormous need for information and technical assistance on accessibility. To date, however, few publications examine building elements and spaces and offer detailed advice for making modifications to provide access for people with disabilities. Most have focused on new construction and how to meet current codes and standards of lesser scope.

In 1973 the passage of the Rehabilitation Act forbid discrimination against people with disabilities in all programs that received federal funding. The ADA extends the prohibition against discrimination on the basis of disability into the private sector and guarantees equal opportunity for people with disabilities in the areas of employment, public accommodations, transportation, state and local government services, and telecommunications; with compliance no longer being based on whether entities receive federal funds.

Because physical barriers prevent access to services, programs, and activities, their presence is one form of discrimination. Several standards existed prior to the passage of the ADA that describe how buildings and facilities should be designed to provide access to people with disabilities. Of these the Uniform Federal Accessibility Standards (UFAS), has been the most widely utilized. Since 1984 UFAS has been the mandatory standard for all federal agencies and has been the minimum standard that recipients of federal funds must use when meeting their obligations under Section 504 of the 1973 Rehabilitation Act. The ADA design standard known as the ADA Accessibility Guidelines (ADAAG) is an outgrowth of UFAS and contains most of the same topics presented in the same order as UFAS.

Title II of the ADA covers State and local governments including all departments, agencies, special purpose districts, or other instrumentalities, as well as certain commuter authorities and AMTRAK. The Title II regulations allow State and local government agencies to choose between one of two design standards. When planning alterations or new construction, either UFAS or ADAAG may be used for compliance. (If ADAAG is the standard selected, the elevator exemption allowed for Title III public accommodations is not allowed for Title II entities.) Title II permits a government entity to use one standard throughout their facility or to select one standard for one building and another standard for another building. State or local government agencies may wish to select UFAS when developing their transition plans, especially if the agency used UFAS for earlier Section 504 compliance efforts. Agencies that provide housing or have facilities that are not currently covered by specifications in the ADAAG should also consider using UFAS until ADAAG is expanded to include housing.

Unlike State and local governments, private companies providing a place of public accommodation (Title III entities) must comply exclusively with ADAAG or an equivalent state code certified by the US Department of Justice. Many of the requirements from UFAS have been adopted into ADAAG, but some differences do exist between the two standards. Occasionally the UFAS specification for an element or a scoping provision exceeds the ADAAG requirement. In other cases, the reverse is true. It also should be noted that many states have adopted all or parts of the UFAS Standard since it was first published in 1984.

The *Retrofit Guide* was originally developed in 1991 out of a need for information on UFAS in retrofitting situations. Since much of the technical information in ADAAG and UFAS overlap, the *Retrofit Guide* is a highly versatile document that presents generic solutions useful during the planning process for any building renovation or alteration which may require accessibility improvements under either standard. For further information regarding the differences between the two standards see the Department of Justice's *Americans with Disabilities Act Title II Technical Assistance Manual* available from the Civil Rights Division, US Department of Justice, PO Box 66118, Washington, DC, 20035-6118.

The *Retrofit Guide* is keyed to the Uniform Federal Accessibility Standards. UFAS is organized principally around the specification of requirements for providing accessibility in new construction. In the standard many retrofit issues are discussed as "exceptions" to the new construction requirements. This manual illustrates many of those exceptions and offers recommended design solutions and alternative approaches to access problems in existing buildings. It provides the reader with the rational for why a particular element should be installed in a certain way. Highlighting all relevant UFAS requirements, one of the most valuable portions of the manual is the section that describes and illustrates "distinct site and building spaces" and "occupancy specific spaces." The UFAS reference index at the end of each presentation of technical information provides a valuable cross referencing tool to guide the reader through the overlapping requirements for each topic.

This manual is a complement to and in no way replaces UFAS. It is intended to provide advice when meeting the requirements of UFAS and offers the reader suggestions on effective measures when complying with the standard. While the manual does not specifically apply to private companies and their facilities, many of the recommendations are appropriate for Title III barrier removal activities or for alterations of existing facilities. The reader must refer to all applicable regulations and design standards when attempting to meet the requirements of either UFAS or ADAAG.

CREDITS

PRODUCED BY
Barrier Free Environments, Inc.
Raleigh, North Carolina

AUTHORS
Lucy Harber
Ronald Mace, FAIA
Peter Orleans, AIA

GRAPHIC ARTIST
Kelly Houk

ILLUSTRATORS
Robert Graham
Rex Jefferson Pace
Stephen Wald

PREPARED UNDER CONTRACT TO
United States Architectural and
Transportation Barriers Compliance Board
Washington, DC

ACKNOWLEDGMENTS

Barrier Free Environments, Inc. wishes to extend special thanks to the following members of the Architectural and Transportation Barriers Compliance Board for their invaluable technical assistance: Ruth Lusher, Ellen Harland AIA, and Dennis Cannon.

We wish to thank the following members of the advisory panel for their contributions:

Ms. Barbara Allan
Easter Seal Society of Washington
Seattle, WA

Mr. Eric Dibner
Alpha One
South Portland, ME

Mr. Roger Goldstein
Goody, Clancy & Associates, Inc.
Boston, MA

Ms. Mary Ann Hiserman, AIA
Architectural Associate
Office of Physical Resources
University of California at Berkeley
Berkeley, CA

Mr. Richard Hudnut
Products Standards Coordinator
Building Hardware Manufacturers Association
New York, NY

Mr. James Keane
President
Keane Monroe Corporation
Monroe, NC

Mr. Robert Dale Lynch, AIA
United Cerebral Palsy Association
Coraopolis, PA

Mr. Peter Margen
Access California
Oakland, CA

Mr. Terence Moakley
Eastern Paralyzed Veterans Association
Jackson Heights, NY

Ms. Roxane Offner
New York State Office of Advocate
for the Disabled
New York, NY

Ms. Elaine Ostroff
Executive Director
Adaptive Environments Center
Boston, MA

Mr. Walter Park
Independent Housing Services
San Francisco, CA

Mr. John Salmen, AIA
The American Hotel and Motel Association
Washington, DC

Dr. Lawrence A. Scadden
Director
Rehabilitation Engineering Center
Washington, DC

Mr. Elliot Schreier
Director
National Technology Center of the
American Foundation for the Blind
New York, NY

Ms. Katrinka Sloan
Senior Program Specialist
The American Association of Retired Persons
Washington, DC

Mr. William Smith
Preservation Planner
Massachusetts Historical Commission
Boston, MA

Mr. Robert Spangler
Program Manager
Council of American Building Officials
Falls Church, VA

Dr. Ed Steinfeld
Associate Professor of Architecture
State University of New York at Buffalo
Buffalo, NY

U N I T 1

Philosophical Approach to Design

Overview

In our society, almost every aspect of human activity is influenced by the built environment. The ability to live independently, to receive an education, to find a job, to travel, to participate in religious, social, athletic, and recreational activities, and to choose where to live is affected. Indeed, one can easily say that life, liberty, and the pursuit of happiness is affected by the designed environment.

For people with disabilities this is even more true. The environment can support or prohibit participation as people with disabilities seek access to the same facilities and services as other people. Housing, shopping, employment, education, travel, recreation, sports, and health care are just as important, if not more important, to disabled people as they are to others.

There are millions of disabled people in America. Their disabilities range from impaired vision to blindness, from a slight loss of hearing to deafness, and from minor mobility impairments to the need for a power wheelchair at all times. Children are continually disadvantaged in "adult-size" environments by elements such as light switches which are too high and doors which are too heavy. Many people are temporarily disabled as a result of a sports accident or even a muscle strain that limits reaching. From childhood to old age, every person is at some time inhibited by inaccessibility. The varieties and degrees of disabling conditions are so extensive that some people believe that the majority of people have some form of disabling condition and that the exact number will never be known.

Recent trends and legislation are helping to change the face of the built environment. Legislation has been passed at both the federal and state levels recognizing that people with disabilities are active human beings capable of participating in all of life's activities and deserving of the rights and opportunities to do so. These laws, through the application of new and more uniform building standards and codes, are requiring access to almost all new and renovated buildings in localities across the country.

GENERAL DESIGN CONSIDERATIONS

FUNCTIONAL LIMITATIONS CREATED BY DISABILITIES

When referring to accessibility most people think immediately of an environment that would accommodate a wheelchair user. However, there are various types of disabilities that require specific accommodations in the environment. Most design standards, including UFAS, are based on the needs of ambulatory people with mobility impairments who may use crutches, canes or walkers, people with visual or hearing impairments, and wheelchair users.

■ Wheelchair Users

People who cannot walk and others who walk with difficulty use wheelchairs to move about. It is important to remember that many people who use wheelchairs may have limited strength and movement in their upper bodies as well.

Recent technology has facilitated new developments in the design and manufacture of wheelchairs. There is a wide variety of manually operated and power operated chairs in a multitude of shapes and sizes. These chairs can be custom designed to allow the user to stand with support, recline, be seated at various levels, transport packages, and remotely operate other elements in the environment. The three wheel cart/scooter is a variation on the power wheelchair which has become quite popular with people who have difficulty walking.

■ Ambulatory Mobility Impairments

People who walk with difficulty or who lack coordination also have needs which should be accommodated in the environment. They often do not have use of their arms or hands while walking because they may use crutches, canes, or walkers to facilitate mobility. Use of braces, artificial limbs, or orthopedic shoes may also cause them to be unsteady on their feet.

■ Visual Impairments

People with visual impairments are those with limited vision or total vision loss. Many people with impaired vision can distinguish light and dark, sharply contrasting colors, or large print but cannot read small print, negotiate dimly lit spaces, or tolerate high glare.

Many blind individuals depend on their senses of touch and hearing to perceive their environment and communicate with others. Many use a long cane or have a guide dog to facilitate wayfinding.

■ Hearing Impairments

People with hearing impairments use a variety of methods to compensate for their inability to hear sound. People with partial hearing often use a combination of speech reading and hearing aids, which amplify the available sounds, to obtain information or communicate in the environment. Echo, reverberation, and extraneous background noise can distort hearing aid transmission. Totally deaf people who rely on lip reading for information must be able to clearly see the face of the individual who is speaking. Those who use sign language to communicate may also be adversely affected by poor lighting.

Many deaf people use sign language to communicate. As with other dialogues that occur between people who speak different languages, hearing people who learn sign language can communicate with deaf people.

■ Other Impairments

There are other impairments, both temporary and permanent, which may affect an individual's ability to independently use a site or facility. People with cognitive and learning disabilities may have difficulty using facilities, especially if the signage system is unclear and very complicated. There are others who may have a temporary condition which affects their usual abilities. Broken bones, pregnancy, illness, trauma, or surgery, all may affect people's use of the built environment for a short time.

In addition, people have diseases which limit their overall physical ability. Diseases of the heart and lung, neurological diseases, arthritis, or rheumatism may reduce physical stamina or cause pain and numbness. Reductions in overall ability are also experienced by many older persons. People of extreme size or weight often need special accommodations as well.

ACCOMMODATING "ABILITIES" THROUGH DESIGN

A major part of understanding design for people with disabilities is comprehending the ranges in the total population – whether designing for able-bodied or disabled, children or adults, men or women, infants or elderly – the range of ability is vast. In designing for the wide ranges of abilities, one must rely upon the minimum specifications of the building standards, anthropometric data from various groups of people, common sense, and design experience.

Like other building standard dimensions and specifications which are based upon research and testing with adult males, the access standards also are skewed because the data are derived from limited research conducted primarily with adult males using more traditional mobility devices. For this reason, "minimum" standards and dimensions are not adequate to accommodate the range and variety of abilities and equipment used by all people to achieve independent mobility. In addition to the "minimum" specifications and information provided in building codes and standards, designers must develop a thorough understanding of human factors to learn why and how certain specifications and tolerances work. After one has developed a foundation of understanding, the basic concepts can be incorporated into designs which are truly universally usable.

Wheelchair users present some of the most obvious access needs. Additional maneuvering space must be provided; steep paths must be reduced in grade; rough surfaces require smoothing; vertical access must be provided by lifts, ramps or elevators; doors and other features must be easily operable with one hand; mounting heights of wall mounted fixtures must be lowered, and toilet rooms/fixtures need to be carefully configured. However, these same "access" features accommodate people with wide ranges of ability. Children and people who walk with difficulty or have reduced stamina due to a variety of conditions are assisted by these improvements and options in the environment. Actually, almost everyone benefits from the "built-in" features that accompany design for access. For example, larger toilet stalls which are required for wheelchair users also benefit parents who must assist small children, travelers or shoppers who must carry luggage or packages into the rest room, and people needing to change clothes.

Even very specific requirements that appear to benefit only a small portion of society make the environment safer and easier to use for everyone. Signage and alarms designed to meet the access requirements for deaf people and blind people make emergency communications easier for everyone.

In recent years, the experience gained from designing facilities and products to meet mandated access requirements has established a direction toward a new era of a universally usable environment. What follows is a brief history of the evolution of the design philosophy which spawned the current concept of universal design.

DESIGN FOR ACCESS

HISTORICAL OVERVIEW

■ Barrier Free (separate and special)

The building accessibility codes include minimum requirements and specifications which, when implemented, provide basic access for people with disabilities. Because many designers and builders were unfamiliar with the rationale for these minimum specifications, they tended to create spaces and use elements which met code but weren't well integrated into the fabric of the building or site. This lack of understanding was particularly apparent in renovated buildings where access features were often not included at all and in new buildings where they were included after the fact, giving them an "added on" appearance. Building aesthetics were further compromised by the use of "hospital-type" hardware and fixtures which were clinical looking and expensive. Understandably "design for access" was often perceived as expensive and ugly.

■ Adaptable/adjustable

The problem was particularly apparent in housing where accessible rental units, if not leased to wheelchair users, became more difficult to rent to people without disabilities because of the apartments' "different" appearance. To solve this problem, the concept of adjustable/adaptable design was formulated. Using this concept, designers were given the flexibility to create building elements that looked no different and could be used in a "traditional" manner or adjusted to suit the requirements of an individual with different needs.

■ Life-Span/universal

The adjustable/adaptable concept has further evolved into the concept of life-span or universal design. The intent of the universal design concept is to incorporate characteristics for access into products, elements, and spaces designed for use by everyone. The universal design concept considers the changes that are experienced by everyone during his or her lifetime. Children, pregnant women, older persons, people with visual and/or hearing impairments, those with heart conditions or any of a variety of temporary disabilities, and anyone who deviates from the mythical "average" can benefit from environments that are universally designed. In universal design, "mere aesthetics" do not alter the form and function of the end product. Buildings and facilities incorporating universal design can be aesthetically appealing and used safely and effectively by almost everyone. They need not be "labeled", cost more, or look different.

AWARENESS

■ Need for Increased Understanding

Many people are now surviving catastrophic accidents or illness which render them permanently disabled. The average lifespan is longer with each generation, increasing the percentage of older persons in our society. It seems logical that as society changes to accommodate the differences associated with a changing population that the design and construction industry will do likewise. As greater numbers of designers, builders, and manufacturers become aware of the broader needs of society, it is inevitable that new design solutions will continue to be developed to accommodate the entire spectrum of the population. Economics also dictates that for the efforts of industry to be rewarded, the trend will be away from expensive one-of-a-kind solutions to practical, more universally usable products and spaces.

■ Implications for the Future

Universal design succeeds because it goes beyond specialization. The concept promotes designing every product and building so that everyone can use them to the greatest extent possible– every faucet, light fixture, shower stall, public telephone, or entrance. Universal design is an appealing and practical leap forward in the evolution of building and design procedures. As designers and manufacturers further cultivate new insights, legislation, information, technologies, and sensitivities, universal design will become common, convenient, and profitable.

FRANKFURTERS
UNIT 2

Regulatory Issues

Overview

The issue of design for accessibility became a regulatory matter because people with disabilities were routinely denied equal opportunity. Like other civil rights movements, the disability rights movement was led by people with disabilities and their membership organizations who were frustrated with the status quo. These individuals and groups lobbied at the federal and state level for legislation which would allow them equal access to public facilities and programs.

The persistent lobbying by disabled veterans, disability groups, and advocacy organizations, which increased dramatically after World War II, has continued to the present day. Successful efforts to improve opportunities for education, employment, housing, and later, recreation and transportation, brought increased pressure for more accessible buildings and facilities. Advocacy groups pressed for mandatory requirements for accessibility through legislation, building codes, local ordinances, and government agency regulations. Industry responded through cooperative efforts to develop national and federal standards. Local and statewide access requirements also became common. Separate and differing codes and standards created confusion and conflicts from state to state in technical specifications. Unfortunately, these conflicts prevented many practitioners from learning good design principles and prevented manufacturers from producing more accessible building products that could be specified rather than custom built.

New standards and revisions in the 70's and 80's sought to eliminate conflicts and create greater nationwide uniformity. Although there are still small differences between access codes, much has been done to improve their overall uniformity. Continuing efforts in this area improve the likelihood for eventual nationwide uniformity.

STANDARDS AND CODES

ANSI A117.1(1980)

AMERICAN NATIONAL STANDARD SPECIFICATIONS FOR MAKING BUILDINGS AND FACILITIES ACCESSIBLE TO AND USABLE BY PHYSICALLY HANDICAPPED PEOPLE

The American National Standards Institute (ANSI) is a professional non-partisan accrediting body with no governmental status which sets voluntary design standards in a variety of areas. In 1960, an ad hoc group, lead by the Easter Seal Society and the President's Committee for Employment of the Handicapped, held a conference in conjunction with ANSI, for the purpose of certifying a set of design criteria for access as "standard". The ANSI A117.1 Standard, which was approved by consensus of the ANSI committee in 1961, was the first national standard describing design for access. ANSI A117.1(1961) was six pages in length and described some very minimal design criteria which had been field tested at the University of Illinois at Champaign/Urbana.

The Standard contained only minimal "scope" provisions: an "appropriate number" or "at least one" were the only directives provided by the Standard regarding the number of features and where they should be implemented. The Standard also did not provide any specifications for housing, or facilities which were being altered/renovated, or guidelines as to how the Standard might be applied in historic structures.

The Standard was endorsed by many organizations representing the concerns of people with disabilities. These organizations promoted use of the Standard on a voluntary basis among federal, state, and business organizations. Some federal agencies incorporated some or all of the design criteria in their construction criteria. In 1971, the ANSI A117.1 Standard was reviewed and reaffirmed with no changes in the content.

In 1974, the Department of Housing and Urban Development, contracted with the University of Syracuse to revise and expand the ANSI Standard. After a long and arduous review and approval process, the results of the study were published in a much expanded version of ANSI in 1980. The technical provisions of ANSI A117.1(1980) were greatly expanded and illustrated, and information on housing was included.

ANSI A117.1(1980) technical provisions and structure were modified slightly and made part of the Minimum Guidelines and Requirements for Accessible Design (MGRAD). The Minimum Guidelines were mandated by Congress and developed by the Architectural and Transportation Barriers Compliance Board (ATBCB or Access Board) for use by federal agencies in developing improved and consistent federal standards. In addition to ANSI's technical provisions, MGRAD added broad scope requirements based on building types and occupancies stipulating how many accessible features are required and where. The ATBCB was and still is a member of the ANSI committee, and its representation provides an avenue for sharing research results and developing consistency between federal government and private sector standards.

In 1986, the ANSI Standard was again reviewed and revised, based on the same research that led to the Uniform Federal Accessibility Standards (UFAS), making the Standard's technical provisions more consistent with the recently introduced UFAS requirements (see UFAS below). The illustrations were improved and the language was altered to clarify some of the technical provisions. All references to scoping or the number of accessible elements were deleted to allow adopting authorities to specify scoping provisions suitable for their constituencies. The technical provisions of ANSI A117.1 (1986) were also incorporated into MGRAD with certain changes to make them consistent with UFAS.

In 1989-90 the ANSI committee, as part of the regular ANSI review cycle, began meeting to review the Standard and determine which, if any, provisions should be changed or added to allow use of changing or improved technology.

UNIFORM FEDERAL ACCESSIBILITY STANDARDS (UFAS)

The four federal standard-setting agencies, the General Services Administration, the Department of Defense, the Postal Service, and the Department of Housing and Urban Development developed the Uniform Federal Accessibility Standards (UFAS) to be consistent with the Minimum Guidelines and Requirements for Accessible Design (MGRAD). As such, when introduced in 1984, UFAS was the most comprehensive standard to date and is still the mandatory standard for all buildings designed, constructed, altered, or leased with federal funds. The UFAS scope provisions and the technical requirements meet or exceed the comparable provisions of MGRAD.

STATE AND LOCAL CODES

Cities, counties or states develop their own building construction regulations, and most have added accessibility provisions by adopting in whole or in part the technical specifications of ANSI 117.1(1980), (1986), UFAS, MGRAD, or those in one of the model codes (see following section). Most state and local codes modify or develop their own scoping provisions to match local preferences or conditions. All states have some form of access standards. Some states such as North Carolina and California have developed their own access codes from scratch, and they differ both in technical as well as scope provisions from ANSI and UFAS Standards. When local scope or technical specifications differ from national specifications there are often questions as to which specification to follow. As a general rule, the more stringent specification should be followed. Questions about facilities which may have federal funding should be addressed to the Access Board or the federal funding agency. The Access Board gives technical assistance to all agencies and organizations that must comply with UFAS as well as to any individual requesting information or technical assistance.

If no federal money is used in the design, construction, or renovation of the facility, then the Architectural Barriers Act (1968) does not apply. Information on which requirements should be met are available from the local/state office or agency which grants building permits or the Access Board.

Similar to the national standards, if local and state codes require modifications to provide access to existing buildings, they almost always restrict the requirements to wide-scale projects by applying a "trigger" provision. For example, a common trigger provision states that renovated buildings will have to meet certain access requirements if the project cost exceeds a threshold based on the cash value of the building or if there is a change of occupancy type such as converting a house to a restaurant.

MODEL CODES

Model code organizations develop, promote, and support voluntary regional/local building codes that reflect differing construction methods, climates, and local practices. Codes apply to buildings constructed in areas where a legal authority for enforcement has been established and where a model code has been amended and adopted by the jurisdiction. Many local jurisdictions adopt one of the model codes, amending the document to be consistent with local practice and need. All model codes have some access provisions that are usually based upon ANSI or UFAS.

There is work underway through the Board for the Coordination of Model Codes, consisting of the International Conference of Building Officials (ICBO), the Building Officials Code Administrators International (BOCA), the Southern Building Code Congress International (SBCCI), and the National Fire Protection Association (NFPA) representatives, to bring all model codes closer together if not to move toward one nationwide code.

RELATED TOPICS IN ENFORCEMENT AND APPLICATION OF RETROFIT REQUIREMENTS

ARCHITECTURAL BARRIERS ACT (1968)

Architectural Barriers Act P.L.90-480 and amendments have stipulated that all buildings designed, constructed, altered, and (later) leased with federal financial assistance must be accessible according to a standard issued by federal agencies. The first standard applied was the early ANSI or equivalent. Today, UFAS is the applicable federal standard. Retrofit requirements are as specified in UFAS under "alterations", "additions", or "historic structures".

REHABILITATION ACT (1973)

In **Section 502** of the Rehabilitation Act of 1973 (P.L.93-112), the ATBCB was established to ensure compliance with the standards issued under the 1968 Architectural Barriers Act. The Board is comprised of a unique mix of government agency representatives and private citizens, some with disabilities. The Access Board and technical staff members investigate and examine alternative approaches to the architectural, transportation, communication, and attitudinal barriers confronting people with disabilities. The Access Board seeks voluntary compliance with the standards from all federal agencies. If voluntary compliance is not forthcoming, the Board follows an administrative process and a set of enforcement rules to settle the dispute.

Authority was also given to the ATBCB to develop minimum guidelines for the federal agencies to use in developing standards (see reference to MGRAD in ANSI/UFAS topics above).

Section 504 of the Rehabilitation Act of 1973 (P.L.93-112) stipulated that any program or activity receiving any form of federal financial assistance had to be accessible to everyone. Section 504 and further amendments to the Rehab Act of 1973 have resulted in some building modifications for accessibility because recipients of federal funds are required to make their programs accessible for people with disabilities by modifying the existing facility to make it accessible, by moving the program to an accessible facility, or by making other accommodations.

The early ANSI (or an equivalent standard), and its applicable retrofit provisions for access modifications, were initially "adopted" by many agencies. Now almost all Federal agencies have identified (or are in the rulemaking process) adherence to UFAS as the design standard to be followed for physical modifications which may be needed to achieve Section 504 compliance.

HISTORIC STRUCTURES

It is a frequent misconception that projects involving renovation or alteration of historic structures are exempt from accessibility mandates. However, in most cases, historic structures fall under federal, state, and local accessibility mandates and must therefore comply with a variety of specifications for access. Several states exempt historic structures from compliance with access mandates while other states and the federal government have adopted clear guidelines and procedures to ensure that access is provided. Thorough research should be undertaken to determine which procedures and regulations should be followed for each project.

The general approach to application of standards is to require a cooperative analysis of each renovation/alteration to a "qualified structure" by interested parties, state and local advisory councils on historic preservation, and others to determine the extent and methods for compliance. The procedures for completing this analysis are described in Section 106 of the National Historic Preservation Act of 1966, as amended, 16 USC 470 (including Executive Order 11593, Protection and Enhancement of the Cultural Environment), and "Protection of Historic and Cultural Properties," 36 CFR Part 800.

In the provision of access to historic structures, careful planning and design are necessary to avoid adverse effects and damage to the structure's historic fabric. Federal agencies are required to operate programs and activities which are readily accessible to people with disabilities; and to the maximum extent feasible, without impairing significant historic features of facilities, or causing undue financial or administrative burdens for the program, they are also required to make each existing facility accessible. The agency can use alternate means to create program access by redesign of equipment, reassignment of services to accessible buildings, assignment of aides to beneficiaries, alteration of facilities, construction of new facilities, or use of rolling stock. Some specific methods of obtaining program access include: using audio visual materials and devices to depict those portions of an historic property that otherwise cannot be made accessible, assigning persons to guide disabled persons into or through portions of historic properties that cannot otherwise be made accessible, or adopting other innovative methods. The agency is also mandated to take appropriate steps to ensure effective communication (including auxiliary aids and appropriate signage) with applicants, personnel, and participants of sponsored programs. Nevertheless, those historic buildings covered by the Architectural Barriers Act must adhere to the provisions of UFAS when renovations are undertaken.

Americans with Disabilities Act

The landmark Americans with Disabilities Act (ADA) is the most important piece of federal legislation ever to prohibit discrimination against over 43 million people with disabilities. This law gives civil rights protections to people with disabilities that are like those provided to all other members of our society on the basis of race, sex, national origin, and religion. The ADA now guarantees equal opportunity in the areas of employment, public accommodations, transportation, State and local government services, and telecommunications.

State and local government agencies are required to "provide an equal opportunity for people with disabilities to participate in and benefit from a public entity's services, programs, and activities." In existing facilities this does not mandate total physical accessibility, but requires the entity to review its facility to determine if physical barriers are preventing access to services, programs, or activities. Steps must be taken to either relocate services into accessible facilities or remove physical barriers.

The ADA also covers all private establishments/facilities which are considered "places of public accommodation" such as restaurants, hotels, retail establishments, private hospitals or schools, doctors' offices, and theaters. These establishments may not refuse to serve people with disabilities or deny them an opportunity to participate in, or to benefit equally from, an opportunity. Establishments must remove barriers or otherwise make services available. Commercial facilities and privately operated public transit systems including rail and bus services are also covered by the law.

State and local government employers and most private employers are prohibited from discriminating against people with disabilities who are otherwise qualified for a job. Employers must also provide "reasonable accommodations" to people with disabilities which may include making existing facilities accessible, providing special equipment and training, arranging modified work schedules, or providing readers.

The effective dates for compliance with the ADA are staggered to avoid creating financial hardships for business and industry. The requirements for State and local government entities as well as existing places of public accommodation went into effect on January 26, 1992. Privately owned and operated new buildings and facilities are covered if first occupied after January 26, 1993.

When planning new construction or making alterations to existing facilities the ADA regulations allow State and local governments to choose between one of two design standards: the Uniform Federal Accessibility Standards (UFAS) or the Americans with Disabilities Act Accessibility Guidelines (ADAAG). Private companies providing a place of public accommodation, however, must comply exclusively with the ADAAG or an equivalent state code certified by the US Department of Justice. ADA creates an immediate need to modify many existing buildings and an ongoing mandate for all future construction to be accessible for all citizens.

U N I T 3

SCOPE AND OCCUPANCY

OVERVIEW

This unit describes how the *Retrofit Guide* is organized and keyed to the Uniform Federal Accessibility Standards (UFAS) and characterizes how the scoping requirements apply to projects involving access modifications in a variety of existing buildings and facilities. Before proceeding, the user should have a clear understanding of the definitions of scope and occupancy as they pertain to the UFAS document. These terms are defined below:

Scope is the set of directives which provide information about "where", "when", and "how many" elements and spaces must comply. The occupancy-type further defines scope by providing the big picture of "where" through descriptions of the types of facilities which must comply. Other more detailed information about "where" is provided in the description of individual spaces.

The "why" is explained, in part, through the human factors information contained in UFAS and further described in this unit, along with the regulatory issues described in Unit Two. The "what" and "how" are provided via technical specifications throughout the UFAS document and are usually very explicit. "What" and "how" will also be illustrated and elaborated upon (in the context of renovation projects) in Units Four and Five of this manual.

Scope and Occupancy

where, when, how many

Human Factors and Regulatory Requirements

why

Technical Specifications

what, how

ORGANIZATION OF THE UNIFORM FEDERAL ACCESSIBILITY STANDARDS

INTRODUCTION

Generally, UFAS is described as a document containing two types of information: scoping information which indicates how many of a particular item should be included and where, and technical information which describes how these items, including features, elements and spaces should be designed and installed to make them accessible. In UFAS, scoping information is contained in Section 4.1 Minimum Requirements, and technical information is contained in the remaining parts of Section 4. There are a few places where there are minor inconsistencies, but for the most part this organization holds true. It is especially important that the UFAS user know where to locate specific information on both the scoping and the technical requirements of particular elements and features when designing facilities required to comply with UFAS. Users are encouraged to familiarize themselves with the different types of information provided in these sections.

One goal of this *Retrofit Guide* is to provide the user with a deeper understanding of the "how" and "why" of the UFAS requirements. For the purposes of achieving this goal, the UFAS scoping and technical information may be couched in a slightly different manner. In the *Retrofit Guide*, information will be discussed in terms of: (a) that which is contained in sections focusing on human factors and performance specifications data, and (b) specific technical information which is contained in sections pertaining to elements and spaces of buildings, facilities, and sites.

Human factors data are primarily contained in UFAS sections dealing with Space Allowances and Reach Ranges (4.2) and Protruding Objects (4.4). Performance specifications data are contained in UFAS sections dealing with: Ground and Floor Surfaces (4.5), Handrails, Grab Bars, Tub and Shower Seats (4.26), and Controls and Operating Mechanisms (4.27).

All other parts of Section 4, 4.3 through 4.33, provide information about the components of individual buildings, entire facilities, and the sites on which they are located. These other sections provide information which, for discussion purposes in this manual, have been categorized into 1) elements and 2) spaces.

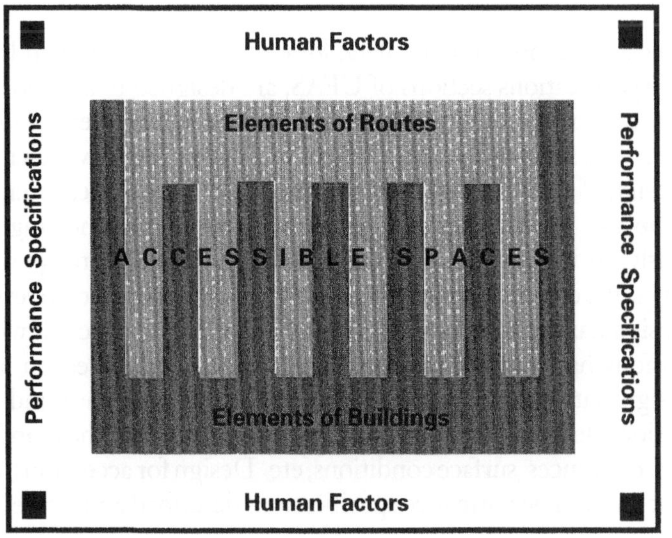

Human factors and performance specifications influence all aspects of accessible/universal design. Specifications for "elements" include "route" and "building" features which are combined to create accessible spaces.

In order to use UFAS effectively, it is necessary to understand how the human factors and performance specifications sections affect the remaining sections. The human factors and performance specifications are incorporated either directly or by cross-reference in the information provided in all the other sections. The structure of the UFAS document does not necessarily make this fact obvious. However tedious and time consuming this cross-referencing may be, it is essential if UFAS is to describe explicitly for each application the conditions required to achieve accessibility. The interrelatedness of all the specifications is not and should not be explained within the standards document itself. Manuals such as this one provide information on the application of the standards and provide users with the basic rationale for why a particular element should be installed in a certain way.

To clarify some of the confusion experienced by users unfamiliar with the UFAS document, the organization of this manual focuses on describing the human factors and performance specifications at the outset and then demonstrating how these factors and specifications affect the design of components of buildings, facilities, and sites. In doing so, it illustrates how retrofit projects involving alterations and/or additions to existing buildings, facilities, and sites can achieve accessibility for everyone through compliance with the particular UFAS specifications. It is also important to note that all of the specifications contained in UFAS are minimum requirements. Greater accessibility is always permitted and encouraged throughout the *Retrofit Guide* in the "Practical Plus" segments included in Units Four and Five.

HUMAN FACTORS AND PERFORMANCE SPECIFICATIONS

Ergonomic and anthropometric data, located in both the human factors and the performance specifications sections of UFAS, are designed to address the needs of a significant portion of the general population in the establishment of design criteria/ requirements. The most significant changes in design criteria, which are required to permit the design of environments that are accessible to everyone, pertain to the needs of people who use wheelchairs and people with vision and hearing impairments. Serendipitously, in the process of accommodating a broader range of people with various abilities, the designed environment is made safer and easier for everyone to use.

Like all design standards developed to assure accessibility for people with disabilities, UFAS provisions have been developed from design data based on averages. The resulting design data represent **minimum** acceptable clearance and maneuvering space dimensions, level changes, slopes, operating pressures, shear and tensile force requirements, clearances, surface conditions, etc. Design for access must conform with the human factors and performance specifications described and referenced throughout UFAS.

Throughout the UFAS document, specifications which are relevant to a particular situation are cross-referenced in the narrative and annotated on the accompanying drawings. This manual will incorporate similar cross-referencing techniques. The incorporation of cross-referencing between the manual and UFAS document should make the provisions and requirements of UFAS more understandable and accessible to the reader. Supplementary descriptive information, indicated by an * throughout the UFAS document, is contained in the UFAS Appendix and in other publications listed in the *Retrofit Guide* Bibliography.

■ Human Factors Specifications

An understanding and acceptance of human factors information is essential to appropriate design for human use. This, perhaps, is why *Architectural Graphic Standards* begins with a section which illustrates "Dimensions of the Human Figure." UFAS expands upon human factors data to provide information to assist in the accommodation of needs of people with various disabilities. It does so, in part, by presenting dimensional data describing space allowances required for maneuvering a "standard" wheelchair. This maneuvering and space allowance data also applies to the spatial allowances required to accommodate ambulatory adults who must rely on aid devices such as canes, walkers, and crutches. Just as *Architectural Graphic Standards* presents information describing reach ranges for a typical standing adult, UFAS describes reach ranges for a seated adult who uses a wheelchair.

In addition to maneuvering space and reach range data, UFAS also presents human factors data pertaining to other dimensional tolerances which must be met if unimpeded movement through the environment is to be facilitated. This information, listed in the UFAS Section 4.4 Protruding Objects, is akin to the more commonly understood, and accepted, dimensional characteristic of door height. [The standard door height of 6'-8" is intended to accommodate the majority of the population, even as it excludes a small number of tall people]. The protruding object information presented in UFAS is intended to eliminate obstacles and hazardous conditions which are particularly difficult for visually impaired people to detect and avoid. The UFAS requirements regarding protruding objects also benefit people who are distracted, or who just may be inattentive to their surroundings.

Human factors information can be found in two sections of the UFAS document: (a) Space Allowances and Reach Ranges, Section 4.2 and (b) Protruding Objects, Section 4.4. There is also some additional worthwhile information on these topics in the Appendix of the UFAS document.

[4.2] Space Allowances and Reach Ranges

The two matters taken up in UFAS Section 4.2 are interrelated. Though the extent of a person's reach is dependent upon whether the person is seated or standing, it is also dependent upon the relationship of the reached-for object to the person who is doing the reaching. *Architectural Graphic Standards* describes the minimum clear floor space occupied by the average standing adult to be 20" by 27". UFAS describes the minimum clear floor space for the average seated adult in a wheelchair to be 30" by 48". By comparison *Architectural Graphic Standards* indicates the minimum clear floor space occupied by an average seated adult, not in a wheelchair, to be 29 1/2" by 32".

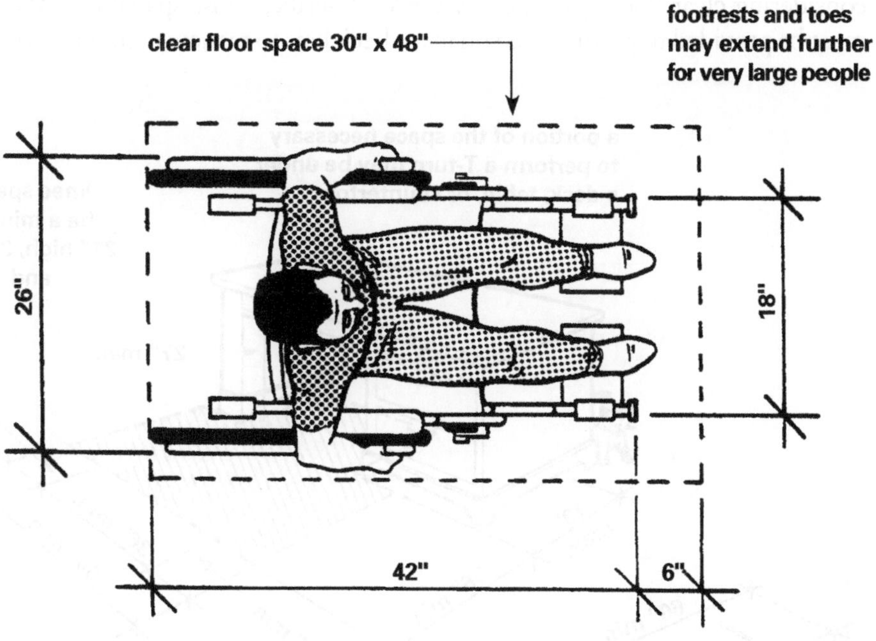

Space Allowances and Approximate Dimensions of Adult-Sized Wheelchairs

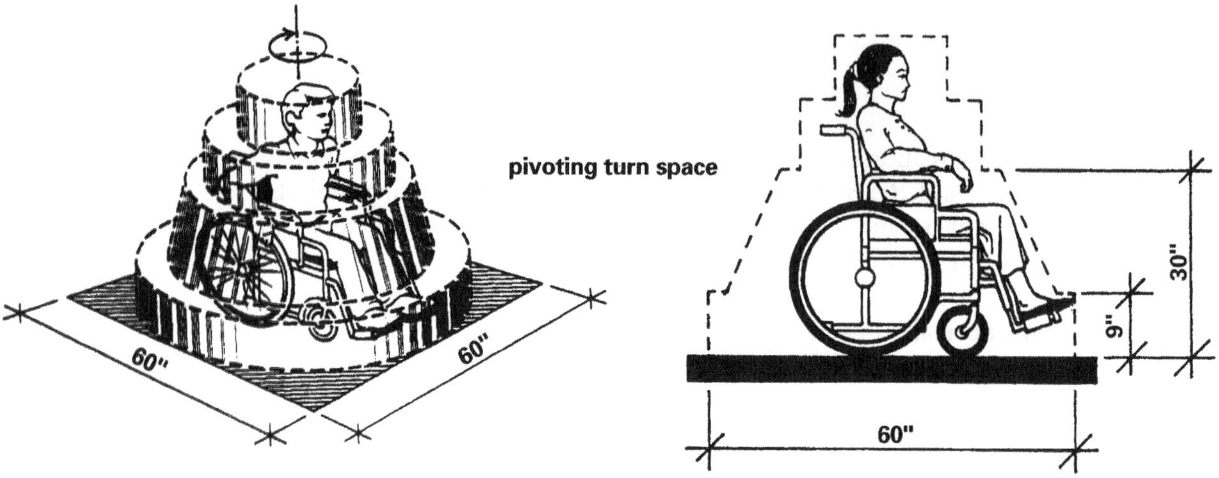

Space Allowances for Movement of Wheelchairs

Architectural Graphic Standards, in presenting dimensional information about the average adult, does not take up the matter of movement (e.g., typical gait, etc.). UFAS differs in this respect. Because many disabled people use wheelchairs to achieve mobility and wheelchairs cannot "side-step" obstacles, the maneuvering characteristics of the wheelchair become an important consideration in design. Thus, in addition to considering clear floor space per se, UFAS describes those spatial tolerances which must be provided to permit a person in a wheelchair to maneuver in the environment.

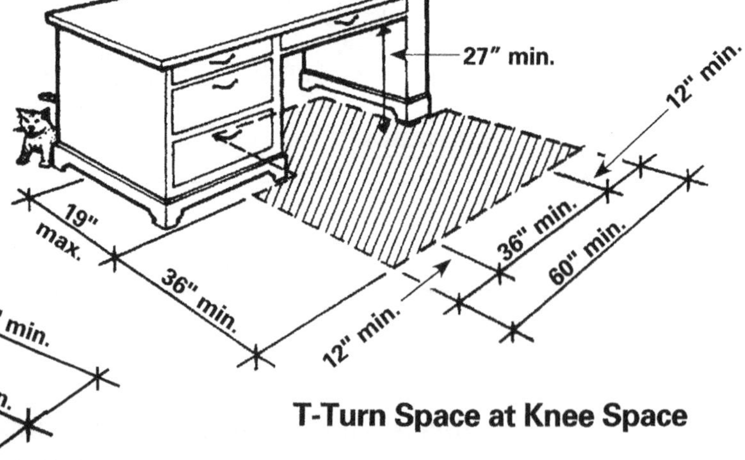

T-Turn Space at Knee Space

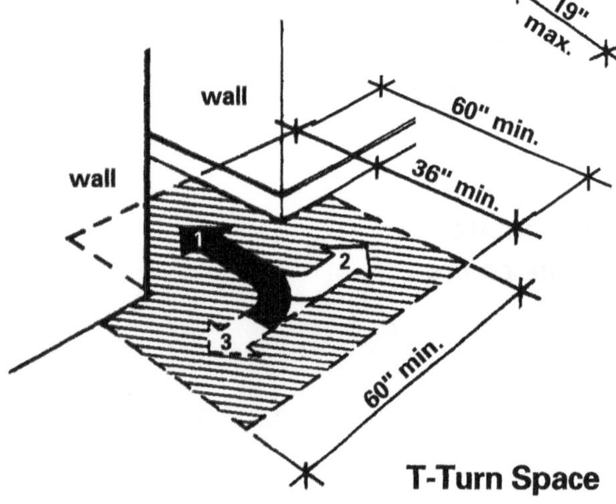

T-Turn Space

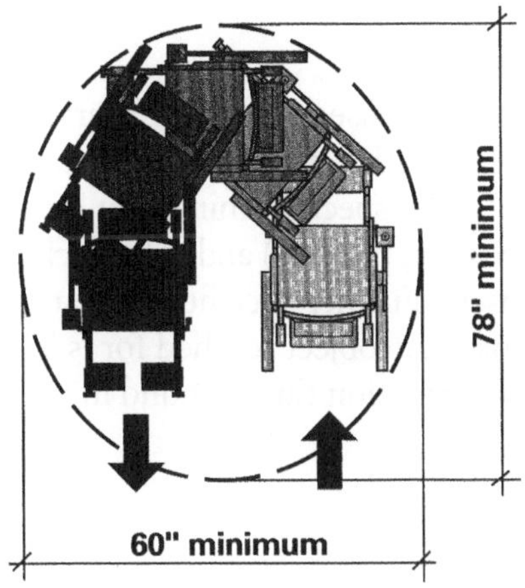

Space Needed for Smooth U-Turn in a Wheelchair

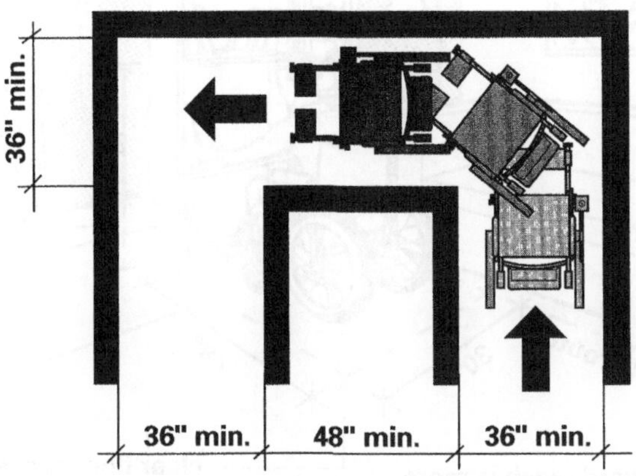

90 Degree Turn

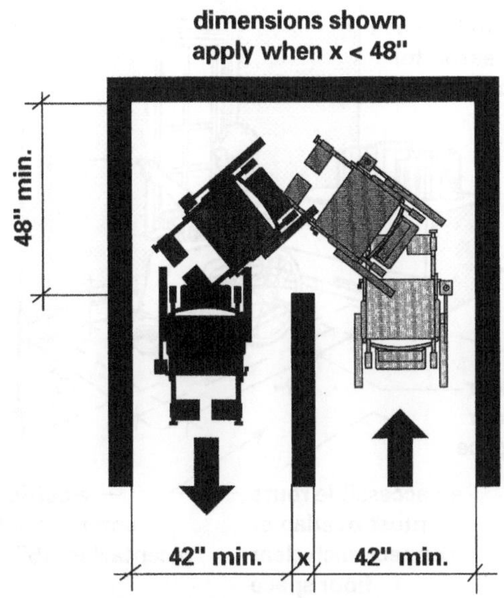

Turns Around an Obstruction

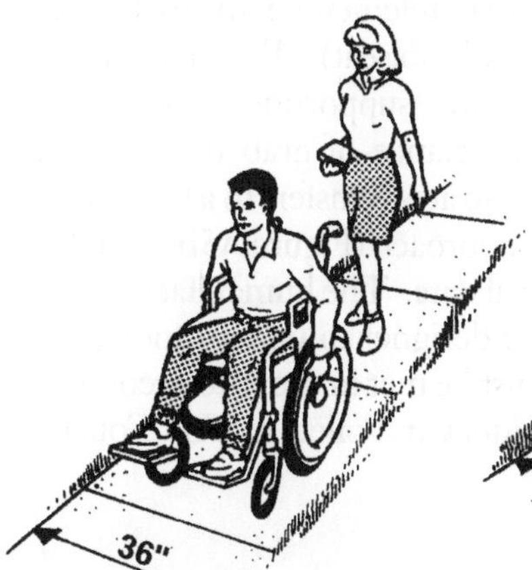

One-Way Passage

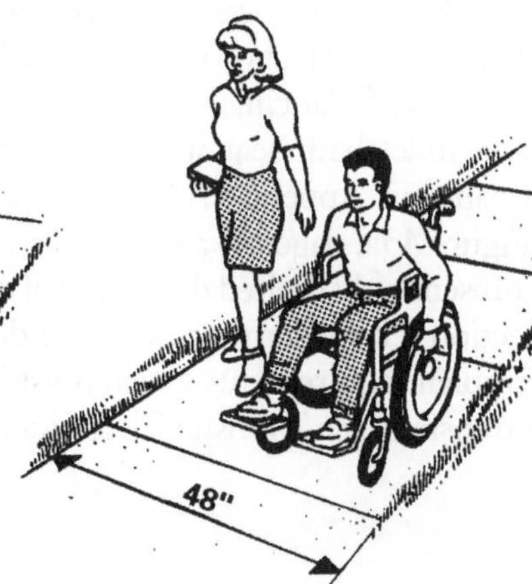

Wheelchair and Walking Passage

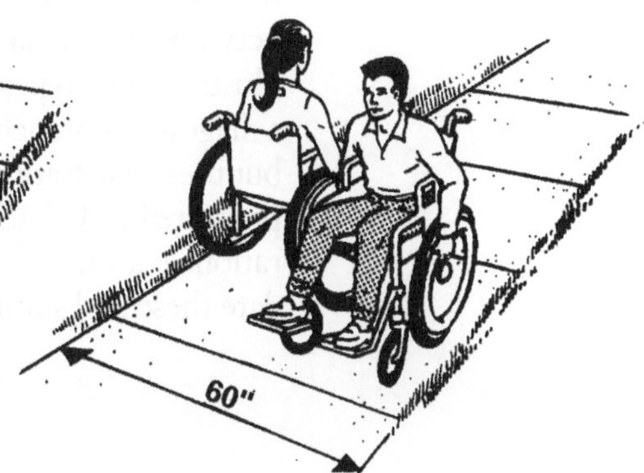

Two-Way Wheelchair Passage

Additionally, because the reach of a person using a wheelchair is limited both by that person's seated position and by the orientation of the wheelchair to the object being reached for, UFAS specifies minimum dimensional tolerances involved in forward reach (UFAS 4.2.5, page 15) and side reach (UFAS 4.2.6, page 15) by a typical adult wheelchair user. Further specifications are included if the user must reach over an obstruction or if the object reached for is in an alcove. Additional dimensional and reach range information can be found in the UFAS Appendix, page 61.

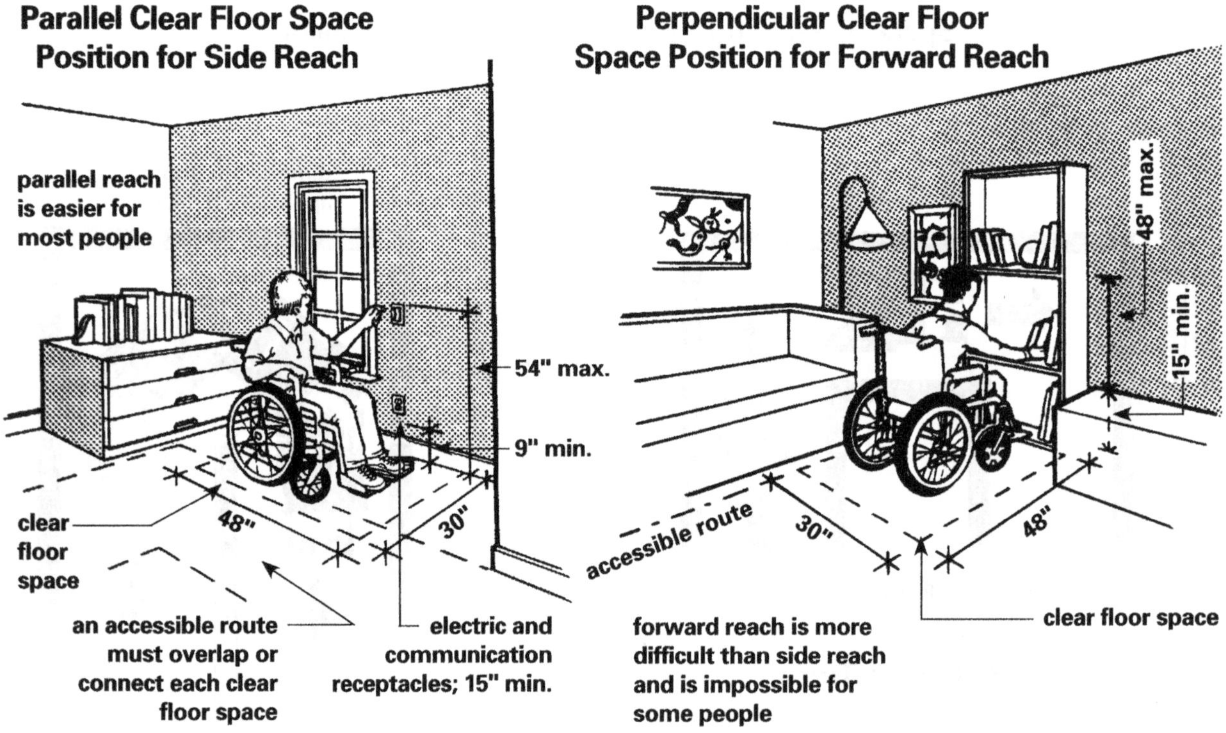

Another aspect of clear floor space necessary to approach elements involves transfers from the wheelchair (e.g., to a toilet, shower seat or bathtub seat). Transfers involve maneuvering the wheelchair, balancing, steadying, and supporting body weight between wheelchair and toilet/bath seat with the assistance of grab bars. UFAS illustrates two types of transfers. Appendix A4.16.4 illustrates transfers to a toilet using a diagonal approach (Figure A5a, page 64) and a side approach (Figure A5b, page 64), but these illustrations present only limited dimensional data. The human factors data presented in UFAS Section 4.2 can further assist the designer in understanding the rationale for the dimensional requirements which must be met in order to accommodate these and similar transfers (see Transfer Techniques at Toilets in Unit Four).

[4.4] Protruding Objects

In the most general sense, human factors data describe average human physical characteristics which help to define our use of the environment. With this information, we then design the environment to accommodate these abilities and limitations. Thus, for example, the more or less standard height (3'-0") and depth (2'-0") of work surfaces is determined by the stature and reach of a typical person. Similarly, tread/riser ratios for indoor and outdoor stairs are determined by the gait of the average person. These and other dimensional properties of the built environment are predicated on the idea that the average user is an able-bodied adult with some assumed "normal" sensory capacity (i.e., someone whose vision and hearing are not limited).

However, the environment may pose distinct hazards unless it is designed to accommodate people whose capacity differs from the assumed average in stature, gait, stamina, sensory acuity, etc. Most environmentally-caused accidents and injuries result from designed elements which fail to account for these individual differences. For example, protruding objects present a particularly hazardous problem for people who are not visually attentive to their surroundings, as well as for visually impaired people using a cane along a "shoreline" to orient themselves and detect objects in their path.

UFAS Section 4.4 presents dimensional information designed to eliminate the hazards posed by undetectable protruding objects. The dimensional data contained in this UFAS section are based on both conventionally accepted headroom requirements (UFAS 4.4.2, page 20) and typical cane detection tolerances (UFAS 4.4.1, page 20).

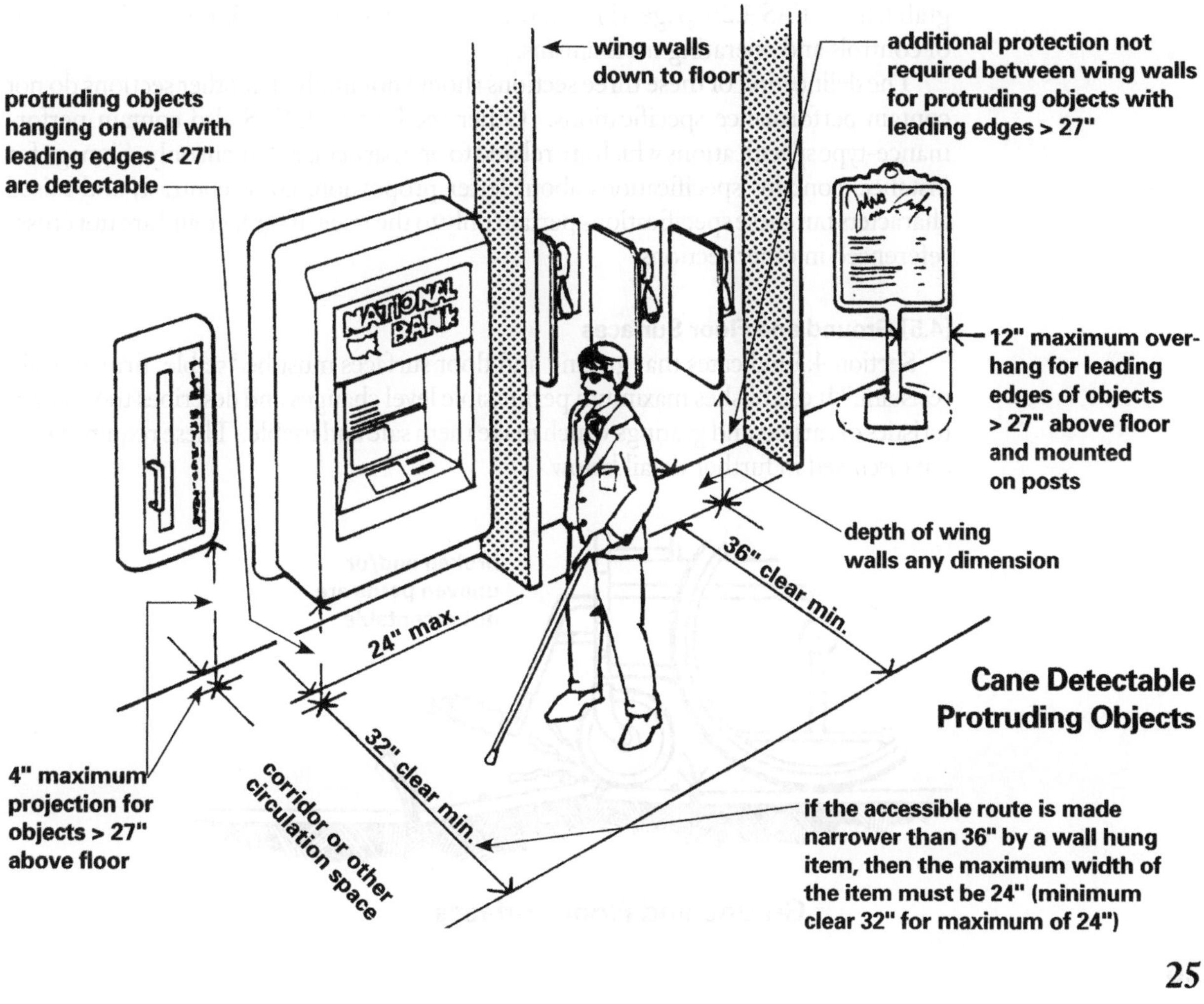

Cane Detectable Protruding Objects

■ Performance Specifications

The Construction Specification Institute defines a performance specification as "a statement of required results verifiable as meeting stipulated criteria and free from unnecessary process limitations" (CSI, Manual of Practice, MP-1-12, 3/80, page 1). Further, CSI suggests that a performance specification is most appropriately used when "no single, distinct, solution is recognized as (the) exclusive choice in a given situation in terms of material, configuration, or technique (as well as when) a project element embodies a technology where state-of-the-art has not yet evolved a standard or commonly accepted solution for a given situation" (page 9).

Access, particularly in terms of use of distinct elements, depends upon the extent to which the features of these elements permit, or impede, manipulation or use. Performance specifications incorporated in UFAS generally describe those conditions or characteristics which must prevail if a person is to be able to use, which is to say, manipulate elements or maneuver easily through spaces in the environment. Typically such UFAS specifications pertain to situations in which "no single, distinct, solution is recognized as (the) exclusive choice," but in which a certain minimum result (performance) is required.

Three parts of Section 4 of UFAS contain performance specifications which are referenced frequently in other sections of UFAS. Understanding the full implications of the requirements contained in these sections is imperative because of the relationship of these basic requirements to many other requirements for access. Specifically, these sections pertain to ground and floor surface characteristics and level changes (UFAS 4.5, page 22), the configuration, size, spacing and structural strength of handrails and grab bars (UFAS 4.26, page 45), and the location and usability (UFAS 4.27, page 45) of controls and operating mechanisms.

The delineation of these three sections should not imply that other sections do not contain performance specifications. Other sections of UFAS also contain performance-type specifications which are related to one particular element only. Signage for instance, contains specifications about letter proportion, color contrast, and raised characters but these specifications pertain only to the issue of signage and are not cross-referenced in other sections.

[4.5] Ground and Floor Surfaces

Section 4.5 indicates that ground and floor surfaces must be "stable, firm and slip resistant." It establishes maximum permissible level changes and describes the characteristics of carpets and gratings which make them safe and usable. These requirements are discussed in further detail below.

Ground and Floor Surfaces

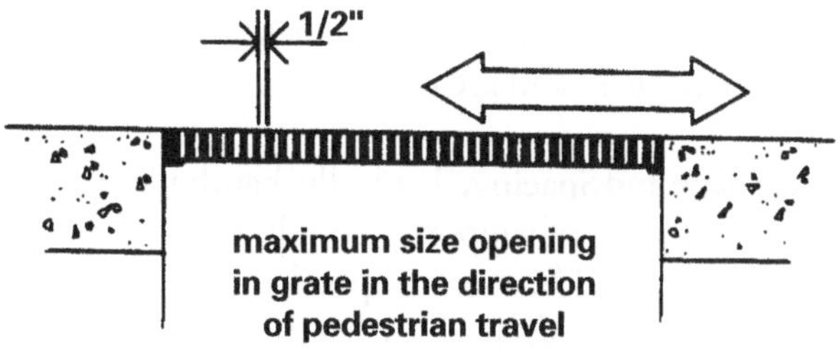

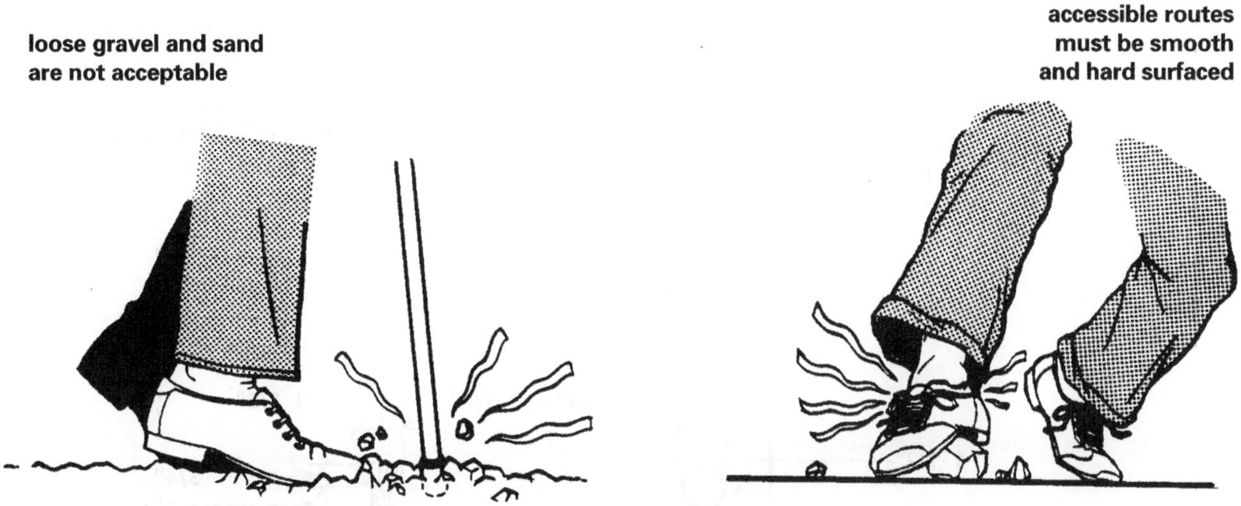

Ground and Floor Surfaces

Surface Treatment. Surface treatment is critical to the safety and ease of ambulation of all people. For this reason UFAS requires that ground and floor surfaces must be "firm, stable and slip resistant." Additionally, however, ground and floor surfaces must be clear of obstructions which pose hazards to persons using canes, crutches, walkers, wheelchairs and other assistive devices, as well as for people who wear spiked athletic or high-heeled dress shoes. It is for these reasons that UFAS requires: (a) that ground and floor surface mounted grates have openings (parallel to the direction of travel) no greater that 1/2", and (b) that carpet pile and pad depth not exceed 1/2".

Level Changes. Minor changes in level (e.g., at thresholds, where there is a change in surface materials, etc.), because they are small and unnoticed, become hazards for all people. All too frequently they are the cause of tripping and falling accidents. Such minor changes in level are especially onerous for people with poor balance, unsteady gait, or who have trouble lifting their feet, as well as those negotiating the environment in wheelchairs, because they are often difficult to surmount. To minimize the hazards and difficulties such minor level changes pose for all people, UFAS requires that changes in level up to 1/4" "may be vertical and without edge treatment," but that ground and floor surface level changes between 1/4" and 1/2" "shall be beveled with a slope no greater than 1:2. (UFAS Subsection 4.13.8, page 36 includes an exception to the 1/2" measurement by allowing 3/4" level change at exterior sliding doors).

[4.26] Handrails, Grab Bars, Etc.

The configuration, size, spacing and structural strength of these elements typically used as aids to manipulating, or maneuvering in, the environment are indicated in UFAS 4.26, page 45 and are described in detail below.

Size, Shape and Spacing. Typically, handrails and grab bars are installed to provide a convenient means of support. To fulfill this purpose the user must be able to get a good grip on them. The user's grip is dependent largely upon the shape and size of the gripping surface. UFAS specifies that the diameter, or width, of handrails and grab bars shall be between 1 1/4" and 1 1/2" or that the shape of a non-circular element shall be equivalent in gripping surface area. A user, particularly an unsteady user, may lose his/her grip in such a way that an arm falls toward the wall on which the handrail or grab bar is mounted (catching the arm between the element and the wall). To minimize the hazard posed by such an occurrence, the handrail or grab bar must be installed so that a person's arm cannot get wedged between it and the wall but ample space is allowed for the knuckles of the hand. To insure that this is the case UFAS requires that the space between the handrail or grab bar and the wall on which it is mounted be precisely 1 1/2".

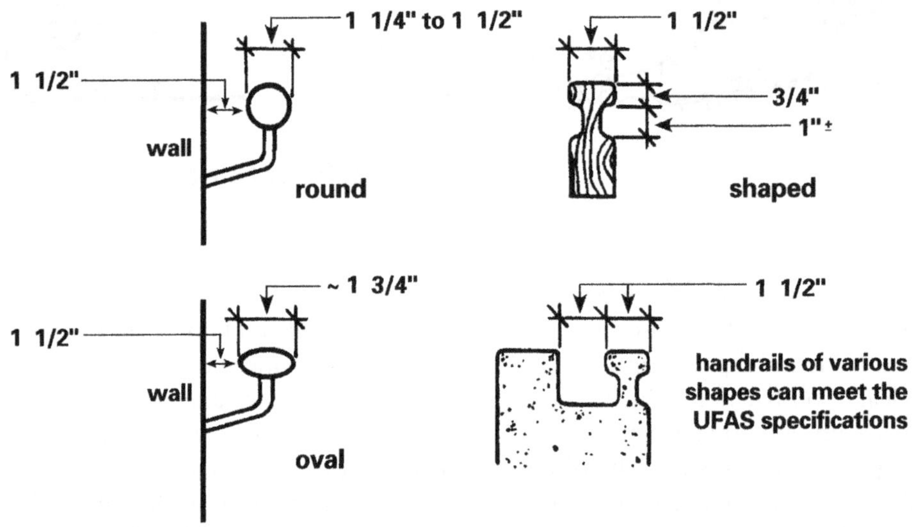

Handrail Shapes

Structural Strength. In normal use, as people push against and pull at handrails and grab bars, they are subjected to certain bending, shear and tensile stresses. Proper "seating" of the connective hardware is essential, and adjustments may have to be made for different types of wall (and floor) construction. UFAS establishes bending, shear and tensile stresses which must be accommodated in the installation of handrails and grab bars. It is particularly important in retrofit applications to consult both the manufacturers' specifications and the manufacturers' installation recommendations to determine whether the UFAS minimum requirements can be met.

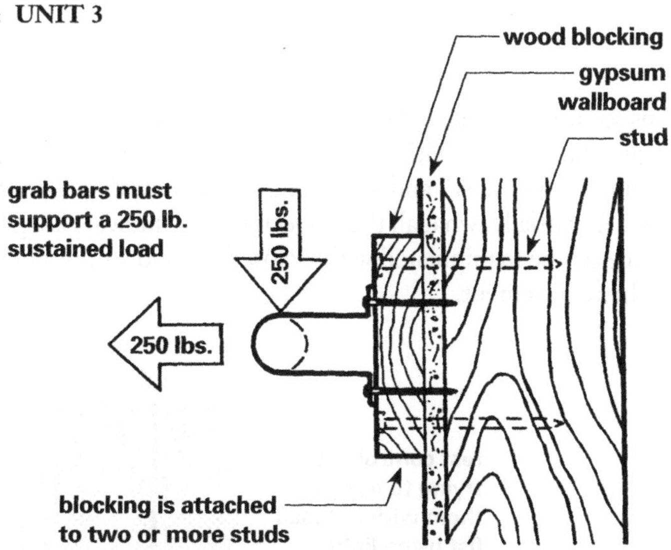

Inexpensive Surface Reinforcing for Grab Bars on Stud Walls

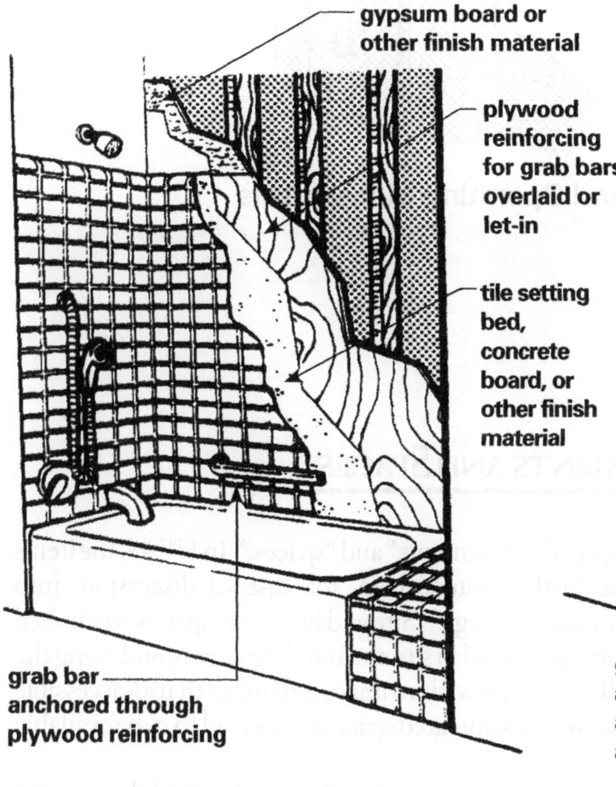

Whole Wall Plywood Reinforcing for Grab Bars on Stud Walls

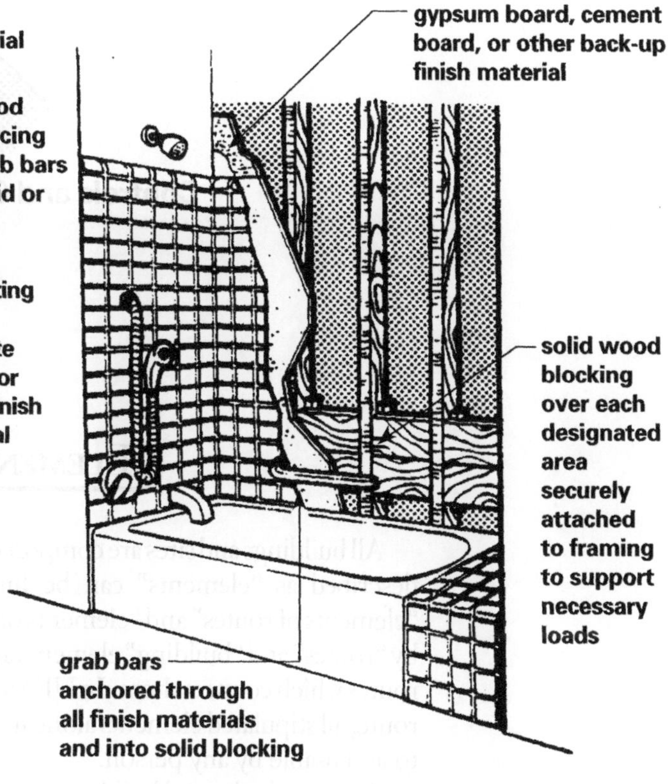

Solid Wood Reinforcing for Grab Bars on Stud Walls

[4.27] Controls and Operating Mechanisms

The usability of controls and operating mechanisms depends upon (a) physical access as determined by the maneuvering space and reach requirements, and (b) method of operation. For this reason, UFAS Section 4.27, which describes controls and operating mechanisms, references UFAS Section 4.2 Space Allowance and Reach Ranges which includes descriptions of forward and parallel approaches.

This section also establishes the requirement that "controls and operating mechanisms shall be operable with one hand and shall not require tight grasping, pinching, or twisting of the wrist" and shall require an activation force no greater than 5 lbf (22.2N). Essentially, what all these specifications indicate is a general test of usability: if a device can be manipulated with a closed fist and a minimum of effort, it probably meets the requirement.

Controls and Operating Mechanisms

ELEMENTS AND SPACES

All buildings and sites are composed of "elements" and "spaces." In UFAS, the items described as "elements" can be further categorized, for ease of discussion, into "elements of routes" and "elements of buildings." Site and building "spaces" are linked by "routes" and "building" elements are found in site and building spaces, and along the routes which connect them. In UFAS, the provision of access requires that an accessible route, all stipulated elements along it, and stipulated spaces connected to it, be available to and usable by any person.

To provide site and building access the designer must first understand the concept of accessible route. However, to extend the concept of access to include facility use, the designer also must understand what constitutes an accessible element and how these elements should be combined in creating an accessible space. A route which provides access to inaccessible elements or spaces will not permit their use. Accessible elements and spaces cannot be used if they cannot be reached via a route which provides access.

All aspects of elements and spaces must conform with the human factors and performance specifications of UFAS. It is for this reason that each UFAS section describing a component of an element or a space incorporates by reference the human factors and performance specifications.

■ Elements

UFAS defines an element as "an architectural or mechanical component of a building, facility, space or site, e.g., telephone, curb ramp, door, drinking fountain, seating, water closet."

Elements of Routes

"Accessible routes" are pathways which can be used by anyone. They are a specific case: a particular kind of route. An accessible route is defined in UFAS as "an unobstructed path connecting all accessible spaces and elements in a building or facility. Interior accessible routes may include corridors, floors, ramps, elevators, lifts, and clear floor space at fixtures. Exterior accessible routes may include parking access aisles, curb ramps, walks, ramps and lifts."

For buildings or facilities and sites to be accessible, they must incorporate, and be linked by, an accessible route. Thus, the accessible route, as described in UFAS Section 4.3, serves as a key organizing principle for the provision of access. UFAS sections which are specifically related to components of accessible routes include (with the exception of stairs*):

- **4.3 Accessible Route**
- **4.7 Curb Ramps**
- **4.8 Ramps**
- **4.9 Stairs (*not part of an accessible route but a route element useful to many)**
- **4.10 Elevators**
- **4.11 Platform Lifts**

Elements of Buildings

The organization of the *Retrofit Guide* departs from the UFAS definition of elements only insofar as it characterizes route specific elements as "elements of routes" and all other elements as "elements of buildings." Indicated below are those sections of UFAS which pertain specifically to elements of buildings:

- **4.12 Windows**
- **4.13 Doors**
- **4.15 Drinking Fountains**
- **4.16 Water Closets**/Toilets**
- **4.17 Toilet Stalls**
- **4.18 Urinals**
- **4.19 Lavatories/Mirrors**
- **4.20 Bathtubs**
- **4.21 Shower Stalls**
- **4.24 Sinks**
- **4.25 Storage**
- **4.28 Alarms**
- **4.29 Tactile Warnings**
- **4.30 Signage**
- **4.31 Telephones**
- **4.32 Seating/Work Surfaces**

** Water closet is the technical name for the toilet fixture. For clarity, the more common term, toilet, is used throughout this manual.

■ **Spaces**

The inclusion of specifications for distinct spaces in design standards may create confusion. Design standards are written with the intention that the designer will apply the general rules for elements and features to create a total space, in this case an accessible space. Some distinct spaces, however, have properties that are peculiar to the functions they are intended to serve. The UFAS standards have included some "distinct spaces" sections, which really are cross-reference sections, to ensure that requirements for all elements and features of these distinct spaces are encompassed in the design.

To assist users, UFAS identifies the following distinct site and building spaces:

- **4.3.10 Egress/Safe Refuge**
- **4.6 Parking/Passenger Loading**
- **4.14 Entrances**
- **4.22 Toilet Rooms**
- **4.23 Bath/Shower Rooms and Bathing Facilities**
- **4.33 Assembly Spaces**

UFAS also contains several "spaces" sections which are set apart by occupancy-type for the purpose of clarifying access to elements and features which are specific to certain types of facilities. These "occupancy specific spaces" include:

- **5.0 Restaurants and Cafeterias**
- **6.0 Health Care**
- **7.0 Mercantile**
- **8.0 Libraries**
- **9.0 Postal Facilities**

PROJECT TYPE AND OCCUPANCY

ORGANIZATION OF UFAS SECTION 4.1

The various subsections of UFAS Section 4.1 describe the minimum scoping requirements involved in assuring access in a number of different situations including: sites and exterior facilities (4.1.1), accessible buildings (4.1.2), accessible housing (4.1.3)*, various types of facilities depending on occupancy classifications (4.1.4), additions (4.1.5), alterations (4.1.6) and historic preservation (4.1.7).

The applicability of scoping requirements in UFAS for both new construction and renovations varies with the occupancy classification of particular buildings and facilities. Scoping considerations based on these various occupancy classifications are discussed below in Occupancy.

*This manual is intended to cover retrofit in non-residential facilities only. Because accessibility in housing is not discussed in this manual the retrofit application of the provisions of Subsection 4.1.3 Accessible Housing will not be included.

PROJECT TYPE

The UFAS document is organized principally around the specification of requirements for providing accessibility in new construction. The scope of the application of these requirements in new construction for "Sites and Exterior Facilities" is described in Subsection 4.1.1 of the UFAS document. The scope of new construction requirements for "Buildings" is described in Subsection 4.1.2.

To understand access issues as they relate to retrofit projects, one must first fully understand new construction requirements. This base of knowledge is necessary because, in the UFAS document, many retrofit issues are discussed as "exceptions" to the new construction requirements. Retrofit projects involving additions, alterations, and historic preservation, and the applicable scope provisions for each, are discussed in detail later in this unit.

OCCUPANCY

Users are encouraged to familiarize themselves with the various occupancy types described in the UFAS document. Occupancy types are described in UFAS as 1) general exceptions, 2) military exclusions, 3) military housing, 4) assembly, 5) business, 6) educational, 7) factory/industrial, 8) hazardous, 9) institutional, 10) mercantile, 11) residential, 12) storage, and 13) utility and miscellaneous. This section is located on pages 7-11 of the UFAS document.

■ Occupancy in General

With the noted exceptions, the requirements of UFAS apply to all buildings and facilities* irrespective of occupancy classification. Therefore, in this manual no distinction is made regarding various occupancy classifications. The retrofit conditions described and illustrated in this manual apply regardless of the occupancy being accommodated.

* Note: A facility is defined in UFAS as: "All or any portion of a building, structure, or area, including the site on which such building, structure, or area is located, wherein specific services are provided or activities performed."

■ Exclusions

With the exception of a few occupancy types, UFAS provisions apply to "**all areas** of those buildings and sites for which the intended use will require **public access,** or in which physically handicapped persons may be **employed.**" For ease of review, exceptions to this statement of the scope of application of UFAS requirements have been "culled out" and are listed below:

General Exceptions

Accessibility is not required to elevator pits, elevator penthouses, mechanical rooms, piping or equipment catwalks, lookout galleries, electrical and telephone closets, and general utility rooms.

Military Exclusions

Access is recommended but not required in facilities which are intended for use or occupancy by able-bodied military personnel only, or in those portions of Reserve and National Guard Facilities not open to the public, which are not likely to be used by physically handicapped persons employed or seeking employment, but which are used primarily by able-bodied military personnel.

Military Housing

Common areas, and at least five percent of the total, but at least one unit (on an installation-by-installation basis), are required to be accessible or easily adapted.

Educational Facilities

All areas of buildings and structures used by six or more people at any time for educational purposes (through the twelfth grade) are required to be accessible. Schools for business or vocational training are required to conform with requirements of the trade, vocation or business taught.

Institutional Facilities

Long Term Care Facilities: At least 50% of patient toilets and bedrooms, all public use, common use, or areas which may result in employment of physically handicapped persons are required to be accessible.

Outpatient Facilities: All patient toilets and bedrooms, all public use, common use, or areas which may result in the employment of physically handicapped persons are required to be accessible.

General Purpose Hospitals: At least 10% of patient toilets and bedrooms, all public use, common use, or areas which may result in the employment of physically handicapped persons are required to be accessible.

Hospitals Treating Conditions That Affect Mobility: All patient toilets and bedrooms, all public use, common use, or areas which may result in the employment of physically handicapped persons are required to be accessible.

Jails, Prisons, Reformatories and Other Detention or Correctional Facilities: 5% of residential units available or at least one unit, whichever is greater, all common use, visitor use, or areas which may result in the employment of physically handicapped persons are required to be accessible.

MINIMUM REQUIREMENTS FOR EACH PROJECT TYPE

As indicated above, the minimum UFAS requirements applicable in retrofit projects are indicated in separate subsections of 4.1 where for the most part they are described as "exceptions" to the requirements for new construction.

NEW CONSTRUCTION

The user is encouraged to review the minimum requirements for new construction in UFAS to get an overview of the types of items covered in the requirements.

■ Accessible Sites and Exterior Facilities

The minimum requirements for accessible sites and exterior facilities are described in detail in Subsection 4.1.1 of the UFAS document, pages 4-5.

■ Accessible Buildings

The minimum requirements for accessible buildings are described in detail in Subsection 4.1.2 of the UFAS document, pages 5-7.

ADDITIONS TO EXISTING BUILDINGS

Any addition itself is to be treated as new construction. Existing spaces and elements in the original building or facility, not provided in the new addition, may be substituted for new construction insofar as it is feasible and practicable to modify them to achieve accessibility in the facility as a whole. Basically, there are three methods of achieving accessibility in projects involving additions.

■ Self-Contained Entity

An addition can be a "self-contained entity" with an accessible entrance/exit and full access to all amenities and programs provided in the new construction/addition.

■ Partially-Contained Entity

This type of addition relies on the access to it being provided via the entrances/exits in the existing building. The new addition either includes all amenities or provides access to accessible amenities in the existing building.

■ Not Self-Contained

This type of addition does not have a separate accessible entrance or amenities provided as part of the addition/new construction. In this case, the addition relies totally on the existing building's entrances/exits and amenities for compliance with access specifications.

"Exceptions" to the new construction requirements applicable for projects involving new additions to existing buildings are detailed in Subsection 4.1.5 of UFAS, pages 11-12. These "exceptions" cover the topics of: Entrances, Accessible Route, Toilet and Bathing Facilities, and Elements, Spaces and Common Areas.

Alterations

UFAS distinguishes among several kinds of alteration situations. The scope or extent of required compliance depends upon: (a) the extent of the modifications to be made (e.g. whether they are limited to electrical, mechanical and plumbing systems, whether they are "substantial" or minor, etc.), (b) whether the facility is vacated during alteration, and (c) whether accessibility modifications have been made already to bring the building or facility into compliance with earlier standards of the Architectural Barriers Act of 1968. As a general rule, if existing elements, spaces, essential features or common areas are altered, then each shall comply with access provisions for new construction. Often, when a building or facility is altered to provide access, certain exceptions to the applicable minimum requirements apply. These "exceptions" to the new construction requirements for projects involving alterations to existing buildings are detailed in Subsection 4.1.6 of UFAS, pages 12-13.

■ General Alterations

As mentioned above, if elements, spaces, or essential features are altered, then each altered element, space, or feature shall comply. However, there is no requirement in UFAS to provide accessibility which would be greater than that required for new construction. Also, if the alteration work is limited solely to the electrical, mechanical, or plumbing system(s) or involves mechanical rooms and other spaces not frequented by the general public or required to be accessible, then it is exempted from the provisions of UFAS.

■ Vacated Buildings

"Where a building or facility is vacated and it is totally altered, then it shall comply with 4.1.1 to 4.1.5 of the Minimum Requirements, except to the extent where it is structurally impracticable". Structural impracticability is defined in UFAS as "changes having little likelihood of being accomplished without removing or altering a load-bearing structural member and/or incurring an increased cost of 50 percent or more of the value of the element of the building or facility involved."

■ Substantial Alterations

Alteration to a building or facility is considered substantial if the total cost for the alterations in any twelve month period amounts to 50 percent or more of the full and fair cash value of the building. Under UFAS guidelines, "full and fair cash value is calculated for the estimated date on which the work will commence on a project and means: (1) the assessed valuation of a building or facility as recorded in the assessor's office of the municipality and as equalized at one hundred percent (100%) valuation, or (2) the replacement cost, or (3) the fair market value."

Each element or space that is altered (or added) must comply with the applicable minimum requirements established by UFAS for new construction except to the extent where it is structurally impracticable, and at a minimum, the completed building or facility must contain the elements and spaces described in Subsection 4.1.6 (3), page 12 of the UFAS document.

Technical Exceptions

Occasionally, difficulties are encountered in making existing buildings and facilities accessible. Because modification costs can be limited and basic (though less than optimal) access provided by adjusting some of the UFAS requirements, the exceptions from UFAS are permitted but not encouraged. These special technical provisions involve: ramps, stairs, elevators, doors, toilet rooms, and assembly areas and are discussed in detail in Subsection 4.1.6 (4) of the UFAS document on pages 12-13.

HISTORIC BUILDINGS, FACILITIES, AND SITES

In the special case of historic buildings the requirements for providing access are detailed in Subsection 4.1.7 of UFAS, pages 13-14. The general approach to application of standards at historic sites is to require a cooperative analysis of each renovation/alteration to a "qualified structure" to determine the extent and methods for compliance. The procedures for completing this analysis are described in Section 106 of the National Historic Preservation Act of 1966, as amended, 16 United States Code 470 (including Executive Order 11593, Protection and Enhancement of the Cultural Environment), and "Protection of Historic and Cultural Properties", 36 CFR Part 800.

Each federal agency is responsible for taking into account the effect of an undertaking on any property included (or eligible for inclusion) in the National Register of Historic Places. As a general rule, an official from the federal agency will work with the State Historic Preservation Officer and other interested parties to identify potential conflicts and propose methods for resolving the conflicts during the early planning stages of the project. The goal of this initial planning is to determine what effects (either none, not adverse, or adverse), the proposed undertaking will have on the property.

If it is determined that there will be some effect on the property, the Advisory Council on Historic Preservation reviews and comments on the proposed plans and either amends or accepts the plan. If it is determined that some adverse effect will occur, it is necessary to draw up a Memorandum of Agreement outlining how the effects will be taken into account. An undertaking is considered to have an adverse effect when the effect on a historic property may diminish the integrity of the property's location, design, setting, materials, workmanship, feeling, or association. Only after the Council has determined that accessibility requirements for accessible routes, ramps, entrances, toilets, parking, displays, and signage have an adverse effect can the special application provisions of Subsection 4.1.7(2), page 14, be utilized. And even then, all requirements which do not have an adverse effect must be met.

U N I T 4

Technical Information
Modifications to Elements

Overview

UFAS defines an element as "an architectural or mechanical component of a building, facility, space or site, e.g., telephone, curb ramp, door, drinking fountain, seating, water closet." The organization of the *Retrofit Guide* departs from the UFAS definition of elements only insofar as it characterizes route specific elements as "elements of routes" and all other elements as "elements of buildings".

Elements of Routes

UFAS sections which are specifically related to components of routes include:

- **4.3 Accessible Route**
- **4.7 Curb Ramps**
- **4.8 Ramps**
- **4.9 Stairs (not part of an accessible route but a route element useful to many)**
- **4.10 Elevators**
- **4.11 Platform Lifts**

Elements of Buildings

UFAS sections which pertain specifically to elements of buildings include:

- **4.12 Windows**
- **4.13 Doors**
- **4.15 Drinking Fountains**
- **4.16 Water Closets/Toilets**
- **4.17 Toilet Stalls**
- **4.18 Urinals**
- **4.19 Lavatories/Mirrors**
- **4.20 Bathtubs**
- **4.21 Shower Stalls**
- **4.24 Sinks**
- **4.25 Storage**
- **4.28 Alarms**
- **4.29 Tactile Warnings**
- **4.30 Signage**
- **4.31 Telephones**
- **4.32 Seating/Work Surfaces**

What to Look For

The topic areas contained in Unit Four parallel the UFAS Sections pertaining to elements of routes and buildings. Under each topic area several types of information are provided. The key below describes each type of information included and how they are related.

Introduction

Topic

Contains a brief overview of the technical issues and minimal scoping information specific to renovations, additions, or historic properties.

Basic Design Considerations

Sub-topic

Describes each design issue or group of related issues to explain the characteristics which must be considered for a particular element to be accessible.

Problem Example

Describes a particular problem related to the design consideration. One or more problems may be included.

Solution Example

Describes one or more possible solutions to a particular problem. Generally, solutions are presented in the order of least intrusive/expensive to more involved and generally more expensive. The appropriate solution will depend on the particular retrofit situation.

Illustrations are used throughout each section to explain the design considerations, show problems, and demonstrate solutions which meet or exceed UFAS (Practical Plus).

PRACTICAL PLUS

It is often possible to implement solutions which go beyond the UFAS requirements. These solutions tend to make the element more universally usable and are presented here as additional "options" which may be useful in some situations.

IDEAL CONDITIONS

Several topic areas contain many design issues which must all be considered and addressed if the element is to be usable. For further clarification, these issues are presented together as an "ideal solution" to the myriad of problems which may be encountered.

REFERENCE INDEX TO UFAS DOCUMENT

TOPIC

The *UFAS Retrofit Guide* relies heavily on references between related topic areas. The reference index is provided to facilitate joint use of the UFAS document and this manual.

ACCESSIBLE ROUTE

UFAS 4.3

INTRODUCTION

The accessible route is the critical element involved in the good design of any site or building. As such, the initial evaluation/planning of a site or building should revolve around the goal of providing access to all elements/features via a path of travel which meets the criteria for an accessible route. An accessible route is defined in UFAS as "a continuous unobstructed path connecting all elements and spaces of a building or facility." Such a path is one that can be negotiated safely by anyone, including persons with a broad range of disabilities.

To provide access to a facility, an accessible route must link all elements and features within a building, all buildings on the site, and the site amenities required to be accessible. In any given facility, there may be several "routes" to any given feature, at least one of the "routes" must meet the criteria for an accessible route and adjoin the clear floor space at accessible elements and features. Interior accessible routes may include corridors, floors, ramps, elevators, platform lifts, and clear floor space at fixtures and elements. Exterior accessible routes may include parking access aisles, passenger drop-off areas, curb ramps, walks, ramps, platform lifts, and clear floor space at entries.

Section 4.3 of UFAS describes the attributes of an accessible route and the technical requirements which must be met for any path of travel to be considered an accessible route. Many of the requirements are similar to commonly accepted code provisions (exiting requirements, clear headroom, corridor width, etc.) designed to ensure safe and convenient use of the facility. Included in the requirements for an accessible route are specifications for a minimum clear width, vertical clearance, protruding objects, passing spaces, ground and floor surfaces, level changes, slope, and cross slope.

In new construction it is generally easier to plan for access by making the entire facility universally usable. In renovations it is usually more difficult because many existing facilities have no provisions for basic access. Regardless of the obstacles, when an alteration to a facility or building occurs, at least one accessible route to all altered elements/spaces must be provided. In facilities earmarked for historic preservation, at least one accessible route from a site access point to an accessible entrance must be provided, as well as an interior route to all publicly used spaces on at least one level. If the only accessible route to a planned addition is located in the existing building or facility, then at least one accessible route shall provide access through the existing building or facility to all rooms, elements, and spaces in the new addition.

BASIC DESIGN CONSIDERATION

HEIGHT AND WIDTH

Corridors within and sidewalks approaching most public use buildings will likely be wide enough to meet the 36 inch minimum width requirement for an accessible route. However, it is not uncommon that such paths will fail to include either a T-intersection or a 60 inch by 60 inch area every 200 feet to meet wheelchair passing area requirements. The accessible route can narrow to 32 inch minimum width at a doorway but must increase to provide maneuvering space at doors or to allow turning around an obstruction. A minimum of 80 inches of vertical clearance must also be provided on an accessible route. Often, especially in older buildings, public telephones, signage, drinking fountains, etc. project into corridors diminishing the effective minimum width and posing a hazard to unobservant and visually impaired users. Occasionally, at stairs which are often located in lobby and corridor areas of older buildings, the required headroom is not provided below which poses a hazard for all users.

PROBLEM INSUFFICIENT WIDTH

SOLUTION WIDEN PATHWAY

If a walkway or corridor is not wide enough along its entire length, then it must be at least 36 inches wide with passing spaces included at least every 200 feet. This may entail moving water coolers, telephones, trash receptacles, benches, etc. out of the path of travel.

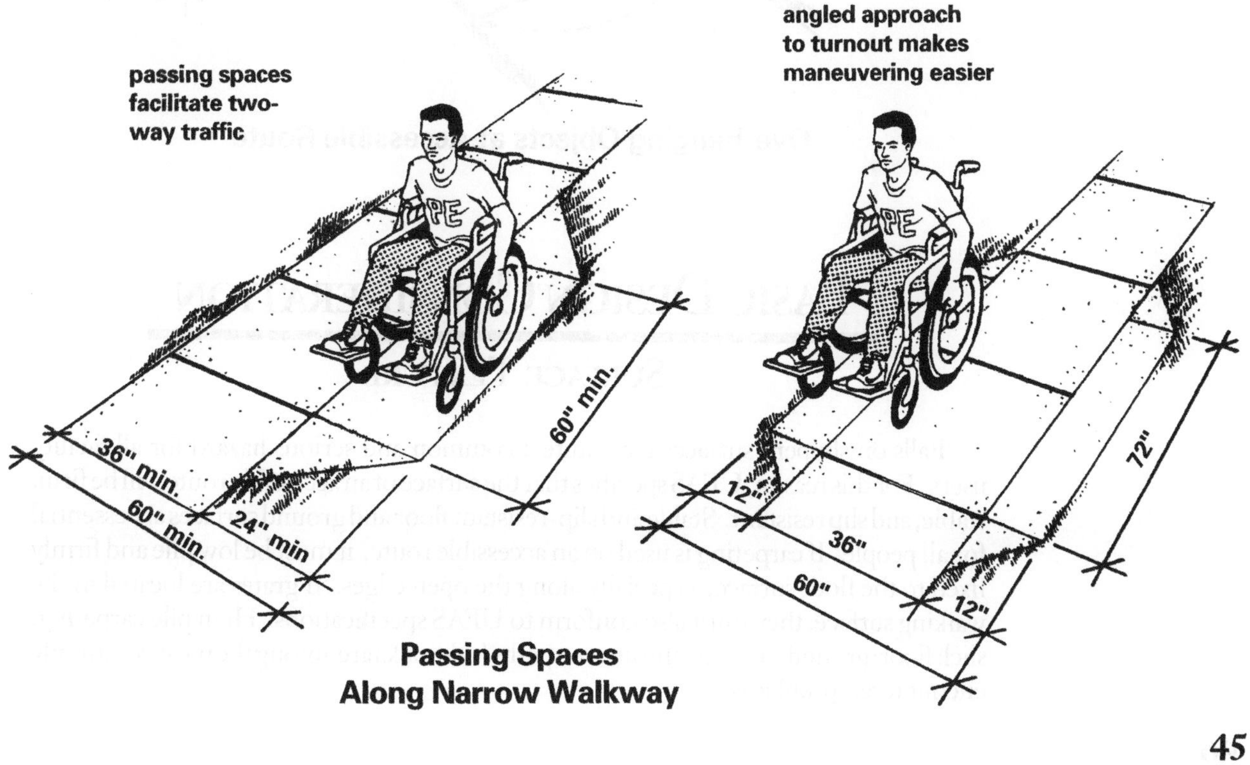

Passing Spaces Along Narrow Walkway

PROBLEM — INSUFFICIENT VERTICAL CLEARANCE

SOLUTION — REMOVE OR RELOCATE OVERHANGING OBJECTS

Signs, tree limbs, and other elements which overhang the path of travel may need to be removed or relocated. Protruding objects present similar problems, especially for visually impaired people (see Protruding Objects in Unit Three).

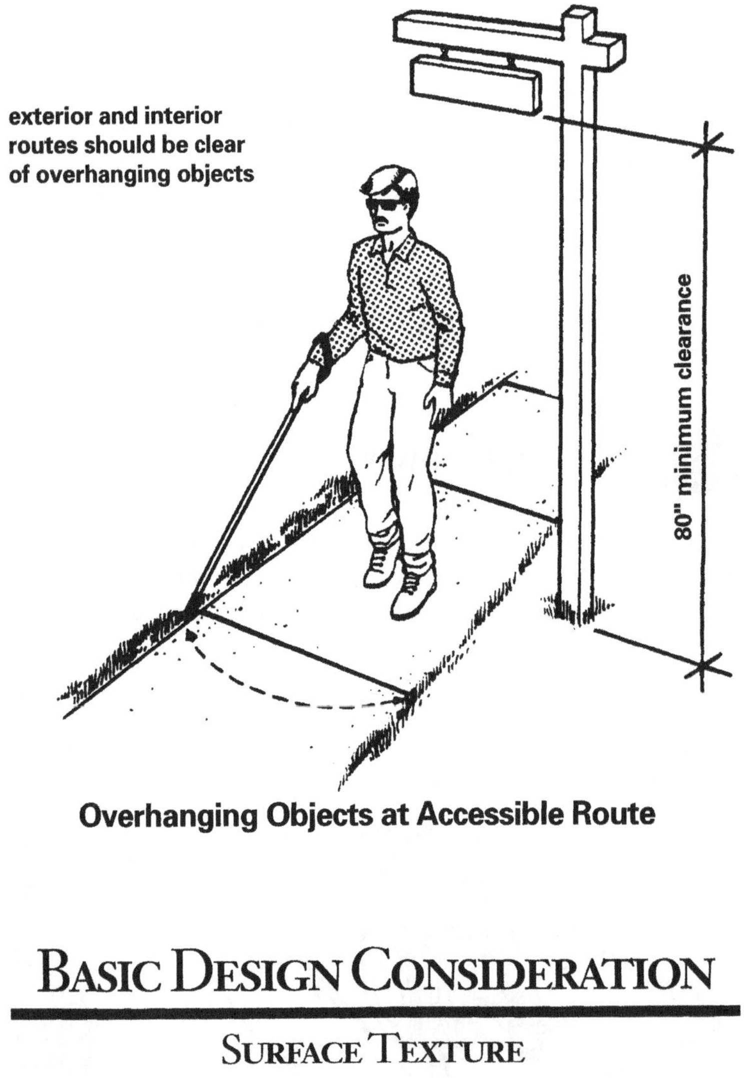

Overhanging Objects at Accessible Route

BASIC DESIGN CONSIDERATION

SURFACE TEXTURE

Falls on slippery surfaces constitute a common and serious hazard for all facility users. For this reason, UFAS specifies that the surface of an accessible route will be firm, stable, and slip resistant. Stable and slip-resistant floor and ground surfaces are essential for all people. If carpeting is used on an accessible route, it must be low pile and firmly fixed to the floor surface, especially along the open edges. If grates are located in the walking surface, they must also conform to UFAS specifications. High pile carpeting, slick floor/ground surfaces, and uneven paths/sidewalks are among the most commonly encountered problems.

PROBLEM SIDEWALK/PATHWAY SURFACE UNEVEN

SOLUTION REPAIR OR REPLACE SIDEWALK

Older sidewalks, particularly those which are located close to tree roots, tend to be uneven and may need repair or replacement. If the existing surface material is loose sand or gravel, it should be replaced with a more suitable material.

PRACTICAL PLUS

In parks and outdoor areas where a natural appearance is desired, it may be possible to utilize one of the recently developed bonding materials to create an appropriate path surface. These surfaces are generally applied to more traditional paving materials to mimic the natural look of the surrounding terrain.

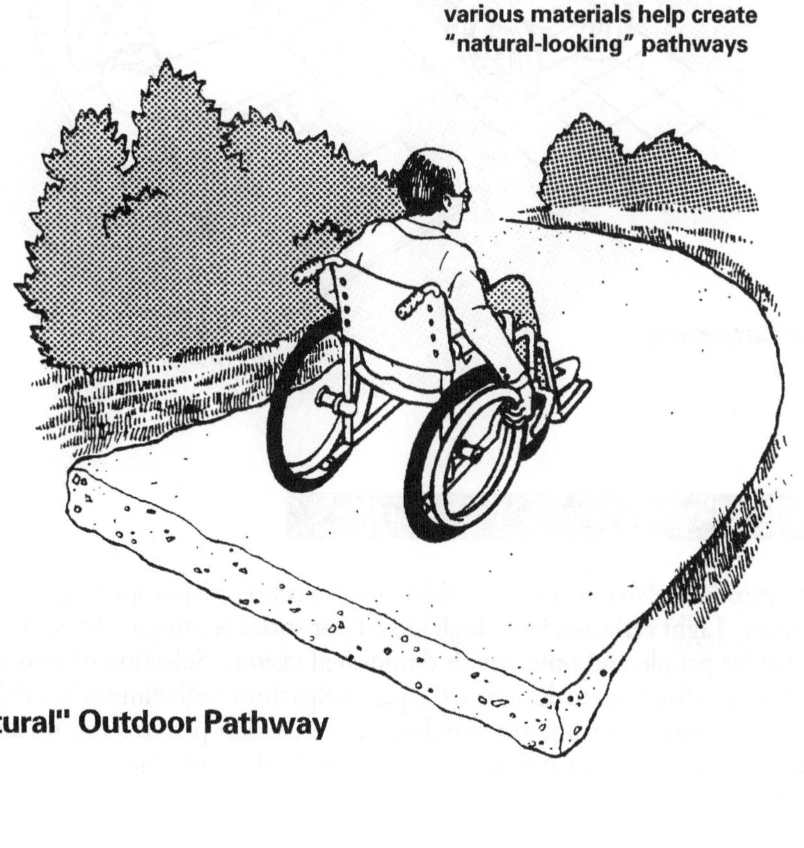

"Natural" Outdoor Pathway

PROBLEM — EXISTING CARPETING NOT ACCEPTABLE TYPE

SOLUTION — REPLACE CARPET WITH APPROPRIATE SURFACE

If existing carpeting has thick pile and padding, it should be replaced with a more appropriate surface. It may not be necessary to replace all of the carpeting if "access pathways" of tile or low pile carpet can be provided to all features and elements.

"Pathway" of Tile or Carpeting

PRACTICAL PLUS

There are other related issues to consider in the selection of appropriate ground and floor surfaces. Light reflected from high gloss floor surfaces can pose a visual hazard for many older people and others with diminished vision. Selection of non-glossy contrasting colors/surfaces to designate the path helps those with diminished vision to discriminate the path from the surrounding area. Certain patterns (high contrast, checkerboards, or small repeats), also tend to cloud edge definition and can cause disorientation.

PROBLEM SLIPPERY FLOOR/GROUND SURFACE

SOLUTION INSTALL NON-SLIP SURFACE

Carborundum adhesive strips can be installed on slick floor surfaces to improve their safe use. There are also permanent treatments which can be applied to the entire surface to create a non-slip surface. If excessive wetness is a constant problem, the floor or ground may need to be resurfaced and drainage installed.

PRACTICAL PLUS

In colder climates with extreme winter weather, it is often helpful to install snow/ice melting equipment on walkways, ramps, and entrances. This feature improves safe use of the facility for all users.

devices installed under side-walks, loading areas, and door mats keep outdoor pedestrian pathways free of ice and snow

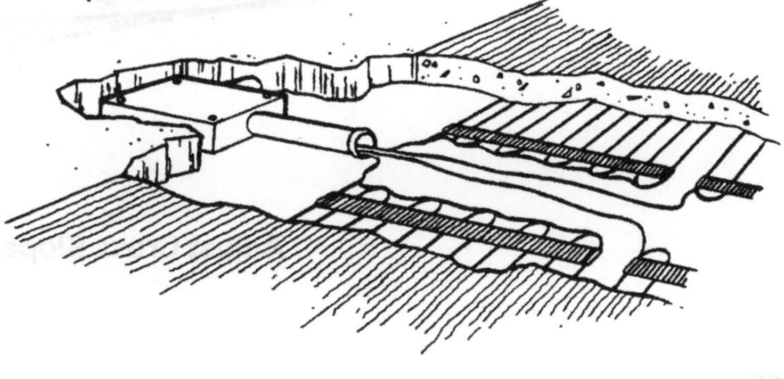

Snow Melting Equipment

BASIC DESIGN CONSIDERATION

MAXIMUM SLOPE AND CROSS SLOPE

The maximum slope and cross-slope tolerances prescribed by UFAS are based on averages designed to accommodate the needs of the majority of both wheelchair users and ambulatory people. A gradual incline with a slight cross slope for drainage minimizes the need for the wheelchair user to continually compensate for side slipping as he/she attempts to maintain a straight path. A cross slope greater than 1:50 can also be disorienting for many pedestrians. Although UFAS allows steeper slopes on ramps because of their limited length and level resting places, the maximum slope for an unlimited walkway is 1:20. For many wheelchair users and those who walk with difficulty, when sloped surfaces exceed 1:20, the effort required to travel along the path increases significantly.

PROBLEM CROSS SLOPE EXCEEDS 1:50

SOLUTION REGRADE AND RESURFACE WALKWAY

If a sidewalk or pathway exceeds the maximum 1:50 cross slope, it should be leveled with only a slight slope to provide drainage.

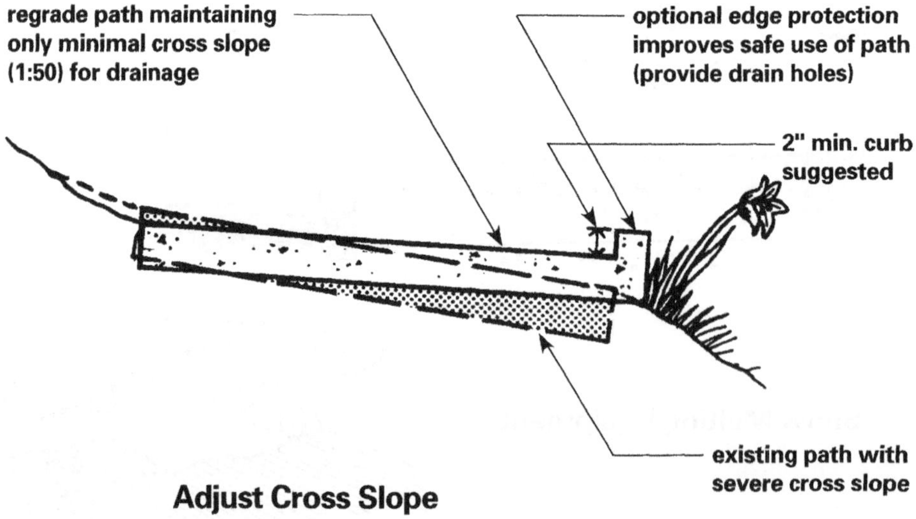

Adjust Cross Slope

PROBLEM SLOPE EXCEEDS 1:20

SOLUTION REGRADE AND/OR REROUTE WALKWAY

If an existing pathway exceeds the 1:20 slope, then, by definition, it becomes a ramp and must meet the multiple requirements for ramps. If there is ample space on the site, it may be possible to regrade and/or reroute the pathway to keep the slope under 1:20. In many situations the earthwork to regrade a pathway will be less expensive than bringing a non-complying pathway into compliance with ramp requirements. An alternate solution may be to include short ramps in the steeper parts of the path while maintaining less than a 1:20 slope for the majority of the walkway.

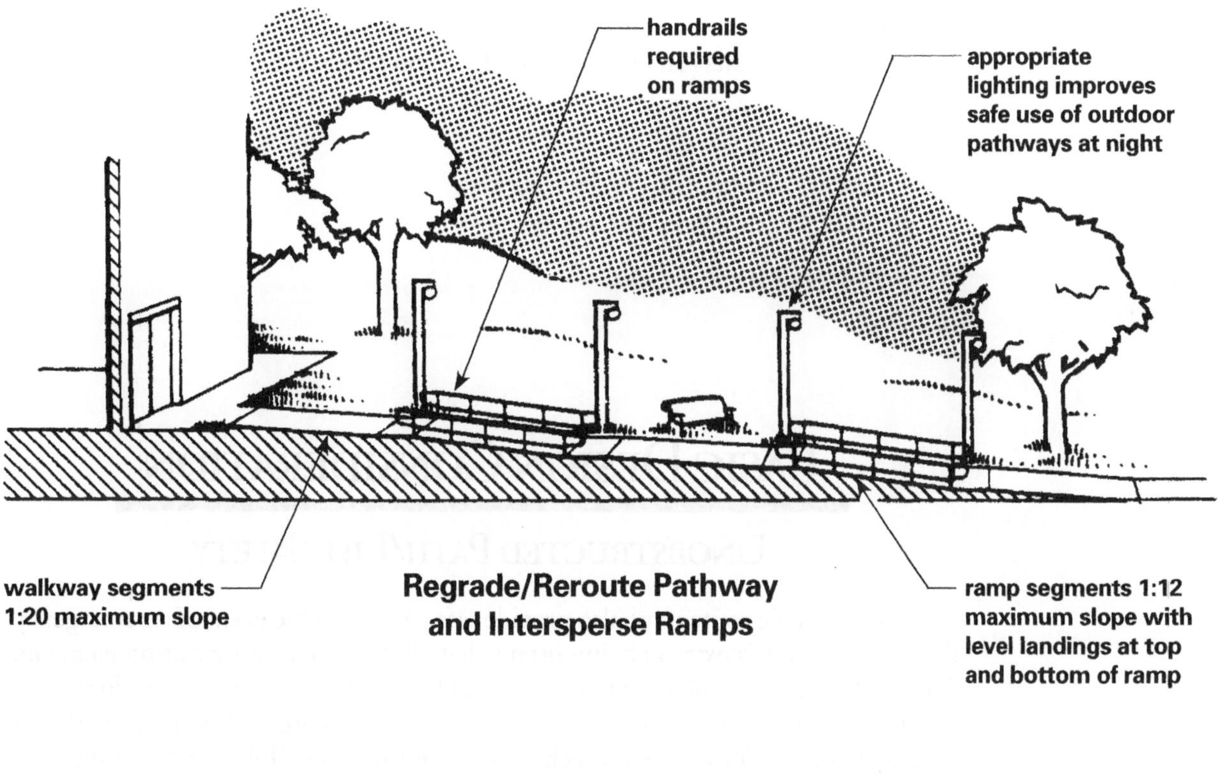

Regrade/Reroute Pathway and Intersperse Ramps

BASIC DESIGN CONSIDERATION

CHANGES IN LEVEL

Small abrupt changes in elevation are especially hazardous and account for most tripping accidents in buildings. Larger changes in elevation pose insurmountable obstructions for people who use wheelchairs or have difficulty walking. For this reason, according to UFAS, no level change greater than 1/2 inch (unless ramped) is permitted on an accessible route. Ramps, curb ramps, elevators and platform lifts, all discussed in detail in other sections of this manual, are acceptable means of accommodating large or small changes in level along an accessible route.

PROBLEM LEVEL CHANGE GREATER THAN 1/2"

SOLUTION 1 REGRADE PATHWAY

If the level change is a few inches or less, it may be possible to regrade and/or reroute the pathway, as suggested above.

SOLUTION 2 INSTALL CURB RAMPS, RAMPS, ELEVATORS, PLATFORM LIFTS

If the level change is too large to be addressed by regrading the path, then a ramp, elevator, or platform lift will need to be installed. Specifications and detailed information on these elements can be found in UFAS and other sections of this manual.

BASIC DESIGN CONSIDERATION

UNOBSTRUCTED PATH/LIFE SAFETY

The accessible route must also provide safe passage in the event of an emergency. For this reason it is extremely important that all doors and other exiting elements/devices along an accessible route be designed for independent operation. Fire doors which are located on corridors to help contain smoke and fire are frequently part of an accessible route. These doors, which are exempt from the UFAS door opening force requirements, may function as obstructions to many disabled people when left in the closed position. If allowed by the authority having jurisdiction, alarm activated magnetic door closers which hold the doors in the open position until required to close in an emergency, make day-to-day use of the doors easier for everyone (see Doors section of *Retrofit Guide*).

Accessible routes are also required to places of safe refuge. Further information on the design of places of safe refuge can be found in Unit Five of the *Retrofit Guide*.

REFERENCE INDEX TO UFAS DOCUMENT

GENERAL REQUIREMENTS FOR AN ACCESSIBLE ROUTE

CURB RAMPS
UFAS 4.7

INTRODUCTION

Curb ramps are intended to provide a smooth transition between sidewalks and roadways. As part of an accessible route, curb ramps are required to facilitate movement of wheelchairs and eliminate the need for pedestrians to climb steps. When properly installed, curb ramps reduce tripping accidents and are a great convenience for those using baby strollers, hand carts, and bicycles. There are several different types of curb ramps which are appropriate in a number of different settings. Careful placement and construction are required to ensure safe movement of pedestrian and automobile traffic and to facilitate drainage of rainwater and snow removal.

UFAS requires a curb ramp whenever an accessible route crosses a curb. This requirement is true in new construction, additions, and alterations, including historic properties. There are, however, some provisions for existing sites which allow steeper slopes if space does not allow installation of a conventional curb ramp.

BASIC DESIGN CONSIDERATION

TYPES OF CURB RAMPS

There are three types of curb ramps allowed by UFAS: flared ramp, returned ramp, and the built-up ramp. All three types of curb ramps must be at least 36 inches wide, provide a smooth transition from the walk to the street with no abrupt level change, and have a slope no greater than 1:12. The surface of the curb ramp must be stable, firm, and slip resistant to facilitate passage of pedestrians and wheeled devices. Although curb ramps do not require level landings, the adjoining slope of the sidewalk or street should not exceed 1:20. When the ramp slope is perpendicular to the direction of traffic on the sidewalk, there must be sufficient space on the sidewalk to allow a person using a wheelchair to turn at the top of the ramp and proceed along the walk.

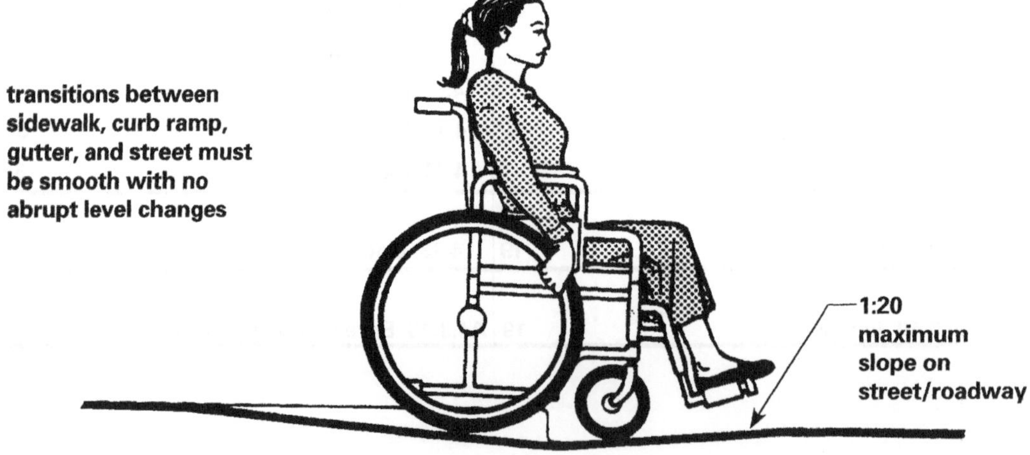

Smooth Transition Between Sidewalk and Street

Although not required by UFAS, warning textures and/or color distinctions on curb ramp surfaces, designed to alert visually impaired or inattentive pedestrians of vehicular crossings, are required by some state and local codes. Warning textures on curb ramps have been reserved and removed from the UFAS standards because research to support their effectiveness has been inconclusive. Many "detectable" textured surfaces are quite pronounced, create tripping hazards for pedestrians, and require additional maintenance, particularly in the winter when water collects and freezes on the surface.

Flared curb ramps are the most versatile type of curb ramp and are safest to use when pedestrian traffic must walk across the ramp. To maintain a safe walking surface, the maximum slope of the flared sides must not exceed 1:10. However, if the space on the sidewalk at the top of the ramp is less than 48 inches wide then the slope of the flared sides may not exceed 1:12.

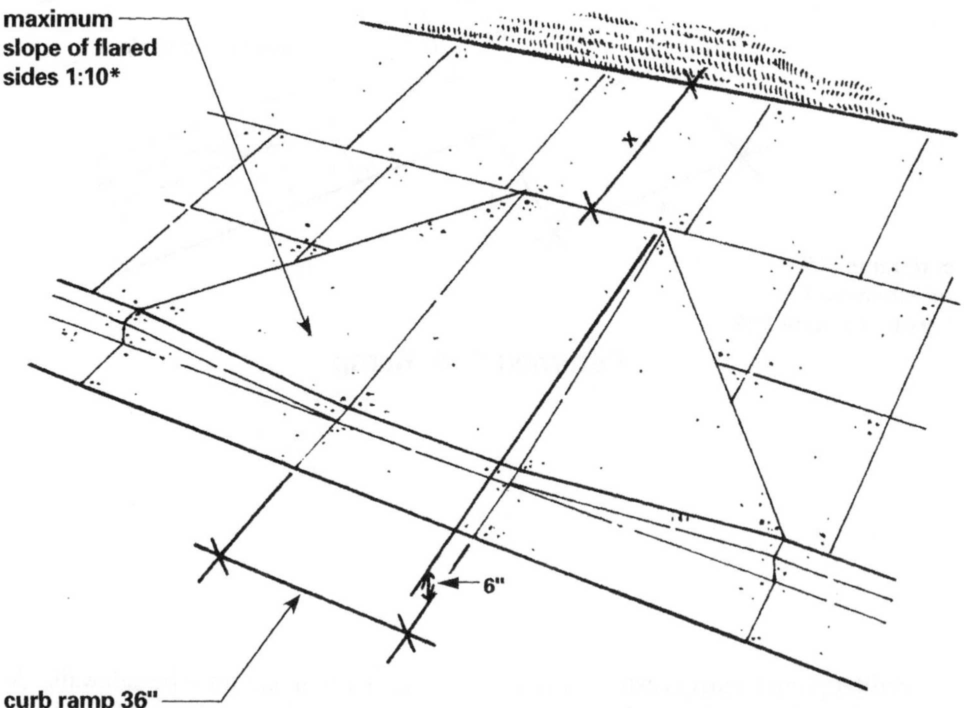

Flared Curb Ramp

* if space at the top of the curb ramp (x) is less than 48", then the slope of the flared sides must not exceed 1:12

Returned curb ramps may only be used when pedestrian traffic does not cross the ramp. Returned curbs must therefore be located adjacent to non-walking surfaces such as grass, shrubs, benches, and planters. Local and state codes should be consulted before installing this type of curb ramp because some prohibit their use.

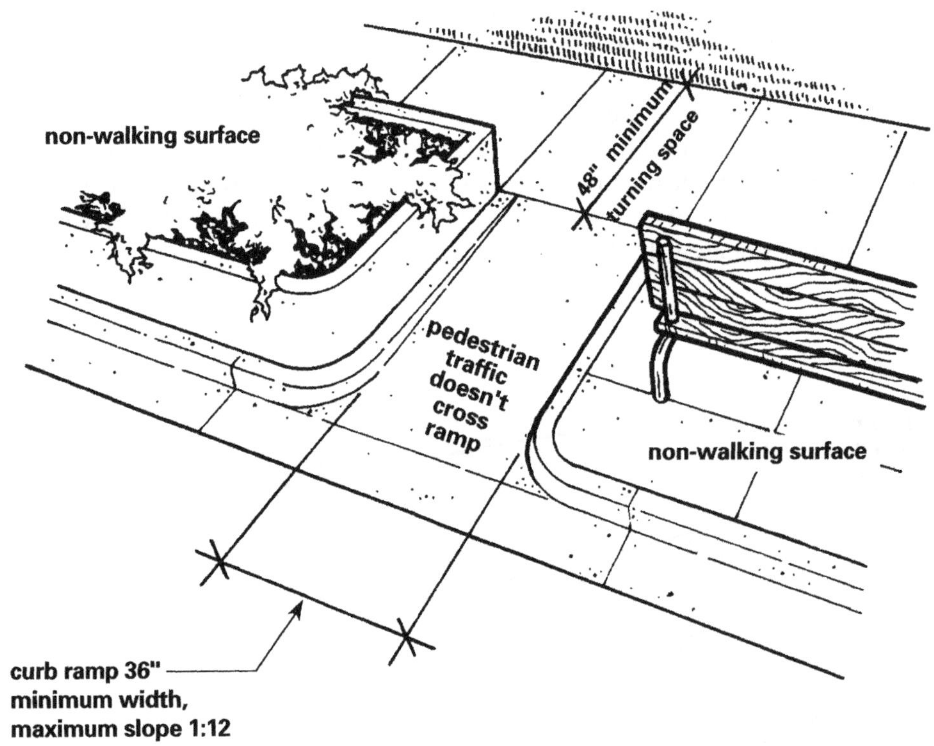

Returned Curb Ramp

Built-up curb ramps extend into the street rather than cut into the sidewalk. As with the flared ramp, the maximum running slope of the built-up ramp is 1:12 and 1:10 on the flared sides. Built-up ramps can only be installed if they do not project into vehicular traffic lanes or into parking access aisles.

This type of curb is least preferred and is used primarily in renovation situations where other options are limited. Built-up curbs are frequently installed improperly and as a result tend to interfere with vehicular traffic, restrict drainage of rainwater, and create obstructions for snow removal equipment. Many state and local codes prohibit the use of built-up curb ramps.

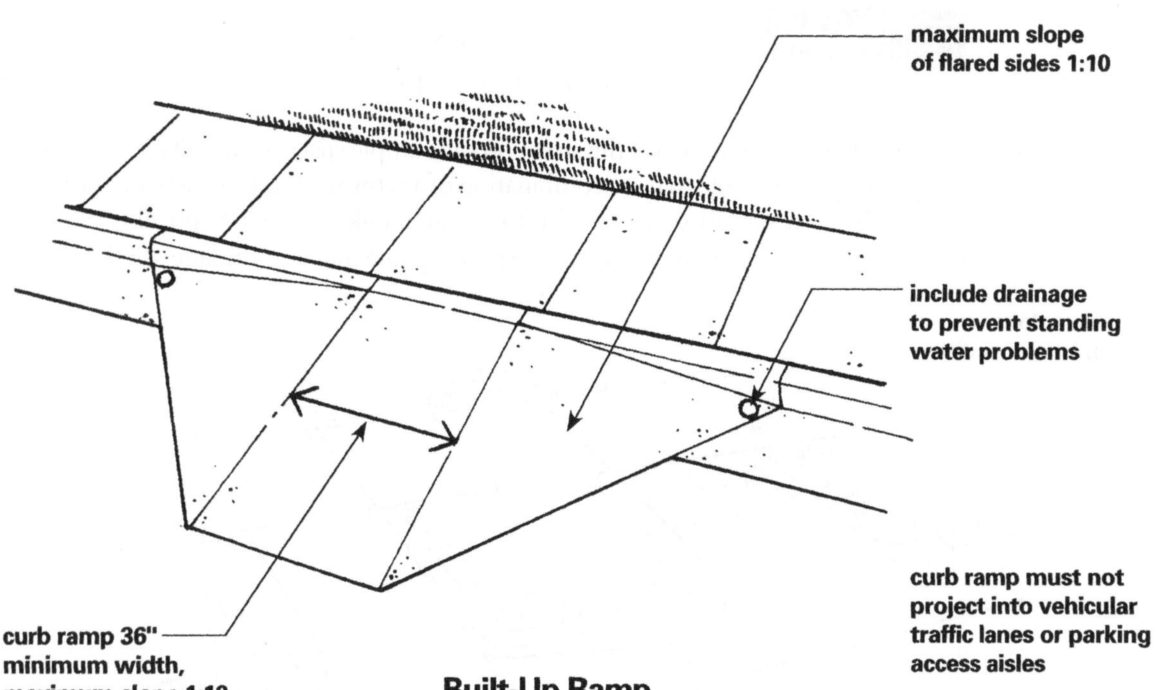

Built-Up Ramp

PROBLEM CURB RAMP NOT INSTALLED OR IMPROPERLY INSTALLED

SOLUTION ALTER EXISTING OR INSTALL NEW CURB RAMP

Usually the conditions of the existing site will dictate which type of curb ramp is best suited for a particular installation. However, if major site renovations are planned, it should be possible to provide space for installation of the preferred flared or returned curb ramp. If an existing curb ramp does not meet the requirements, it should be modified to bring it into compliance.

PROBLEM HIGH CURB WITH LIMITED SIDEWALK SPACE

SOLUTION 1 INSTALL CURB RAMP WITH STEEPER SLOPE

If space limitations on the sidewalk and/or in the street prohibit the use of a 1:12 slope on the curb ramp, then steeper slopes as specified in UFAS Table 2, page 13 may be used (note that a 1:8 slope is limited to a 3 inch maximum rise, half the height of a typical curb). The minimum possible slope which allows maneuvering space at the top and bottom of the curb ramp should be used.

SOLUTION 2 COMBINE A RETURNED CURB RAMP AND A BUILT-UP CURB

If neither the sidewalk nor the street provide ample space for installation of a curb ramp, it may be possible to use a combination of a returned ramp and a built-up ramp. The curb ramp should be recessed into the sidewalk as much as possible and the remainder of the ramp extended into the parking lane (not a traffic lane) on the street.

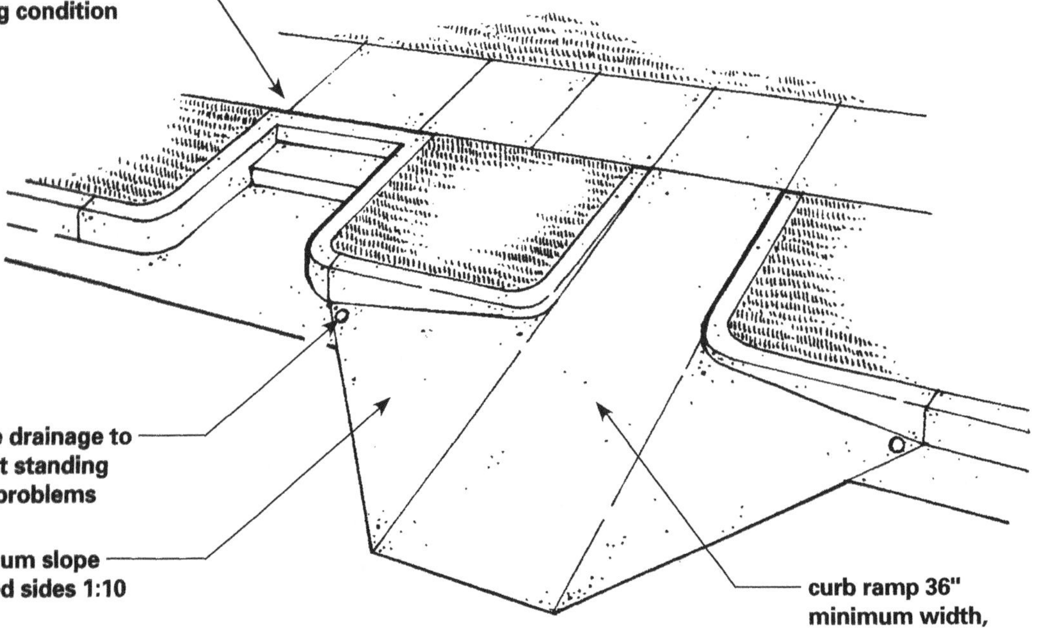

Combination Returned and Built-Up Ramp

BASIC DESIGN CONSIDERATION

PLACEMENT OF CURB RAMPS

As mentioned above, curb ramps are required at all curbs along accessible routes. At large sites and facilities this may include street corners, parking lots, drop-off zones, driveways, and pedestrian crosswalks. Curb ramps must be protected or located away from moving vehicular traffic and obstruction by parked cars. At marked pedestrian crossings, curb ramps must be completely contained within the markings, excluding the flared sides, to ensure safety of the users. A simple but important consideration on curbed streets is the provision of curb ramps on all corners so that sidewalk access is continuous.

Corner type curb ramps reduce the number of curb ramps required at an intersection. However, the lack of a curb on the corner increases the likelihood that vehicles will encroach upon the sidewalk while turning the corner. Strategically placed planters and posts, that don't obstruct access to the ramp, can help reduce the possibility that a pedestrian will be struck by a vehicle while waiting to cross the street. UFAS requires that returned curbs and well defined edges of diagonal/corner type curb ramps be parallel to the direction of pedestrian flow to reduce the likelihood of creating a tripping hazard and provide an extended detectable shoreline for blind people. Diagonal/corner type curb ramps with flared sides must also have a straight curb on each side of the curb ramp, within the marked crossing. The straight curb segment provides a more level alternate path for pedestrians and serves as an orientation cue for blind people, UFAS Figure 15 (b & c), page 26.

Curb ramps can also be placed away from the immediate corners at intersections. Curb ramps in these locations tend to be safer and facilitate the smooth flow of pedestrian traffic. UFAS Figure 15 (a & b) illustrates two possible placements for curb ramps. Option (b) provides the most versatile and safe alternative for a wide variety of users. When the curb ramp is offset from the main flow of pedestrian traffic, it gives users the choice of using the curb ramp or stepping directly from the sidewalk to the street. Visually impaired and inattentive people are less likely to unknowingly walk down a curb ramp and into vehicular traffic when the ramp is set out of the direct flow of pedestrian traffic.

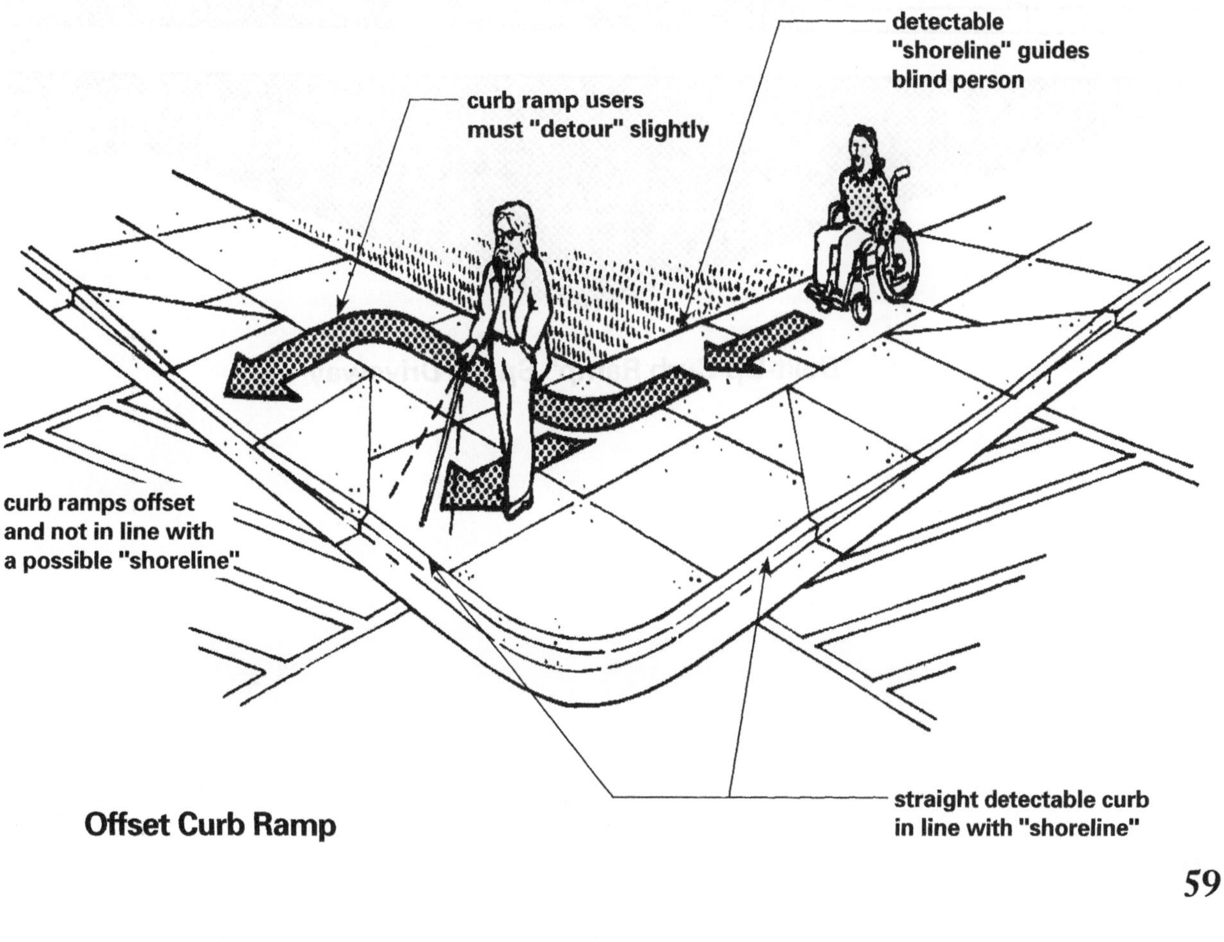

Offset Curb Ramp

At pedestrian crosswalks where vehicular traffic is slow moving, it may be possible to incorporate a built-up curb ramp into a "raised crosswalk" which spans the entire width of the street. This technique is frequently used at shopping centers, airports, bus terminals, and hotels where pedestrian traffic must cross vehicular traffic without benefit of a traffic signal.

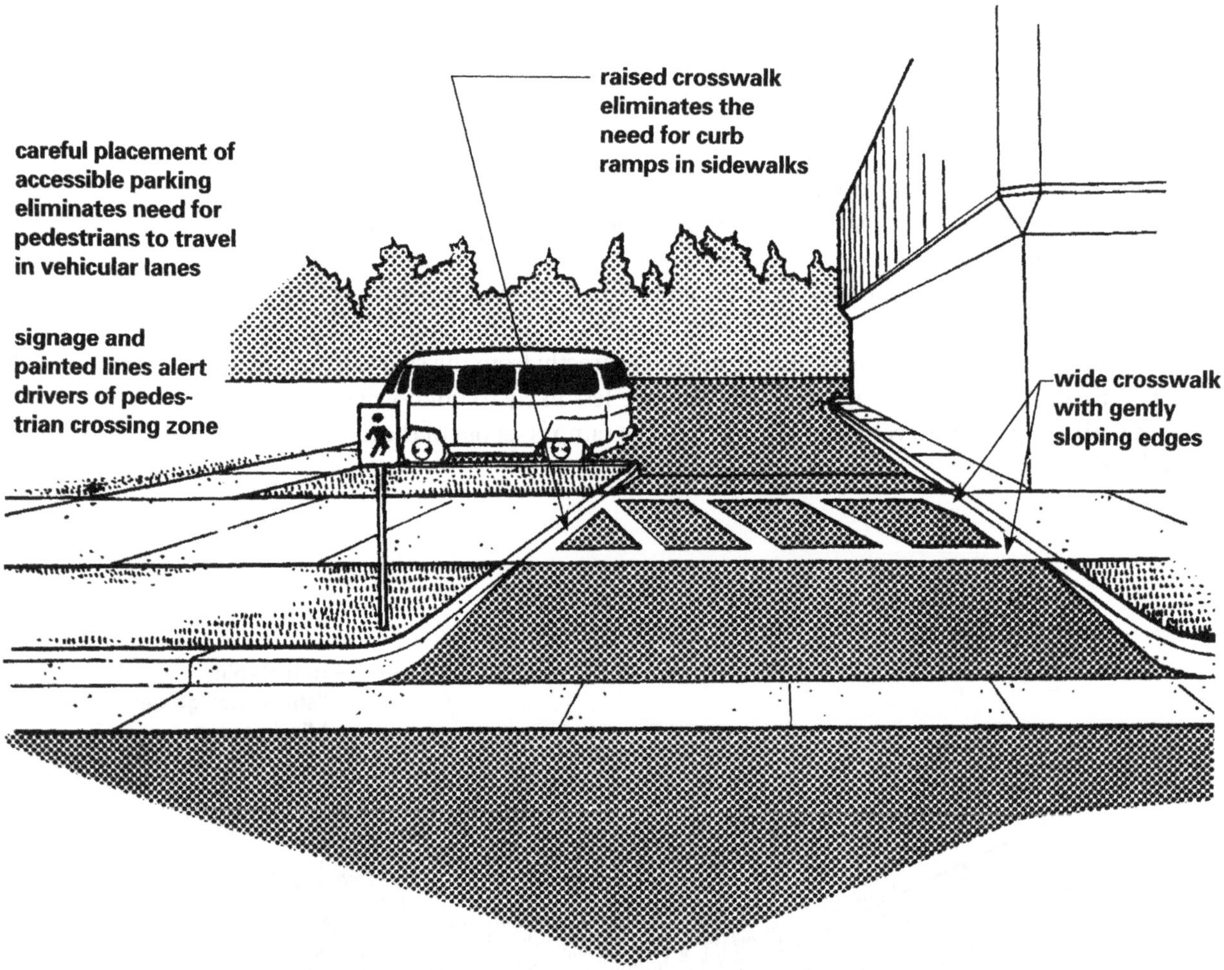

"Built-Up Curb Ramp" Spans Driveway

Traffic islands are required to be cut through level with the street or have curb ramps on both sides. The island must have a level area at least 48 inches long to accommodate pedestrians who may not be able to traverse a large intersection in a single traffic light change. Additional safety measures such as strategically-placed posts or planters provide supplemental protection from vehicles.

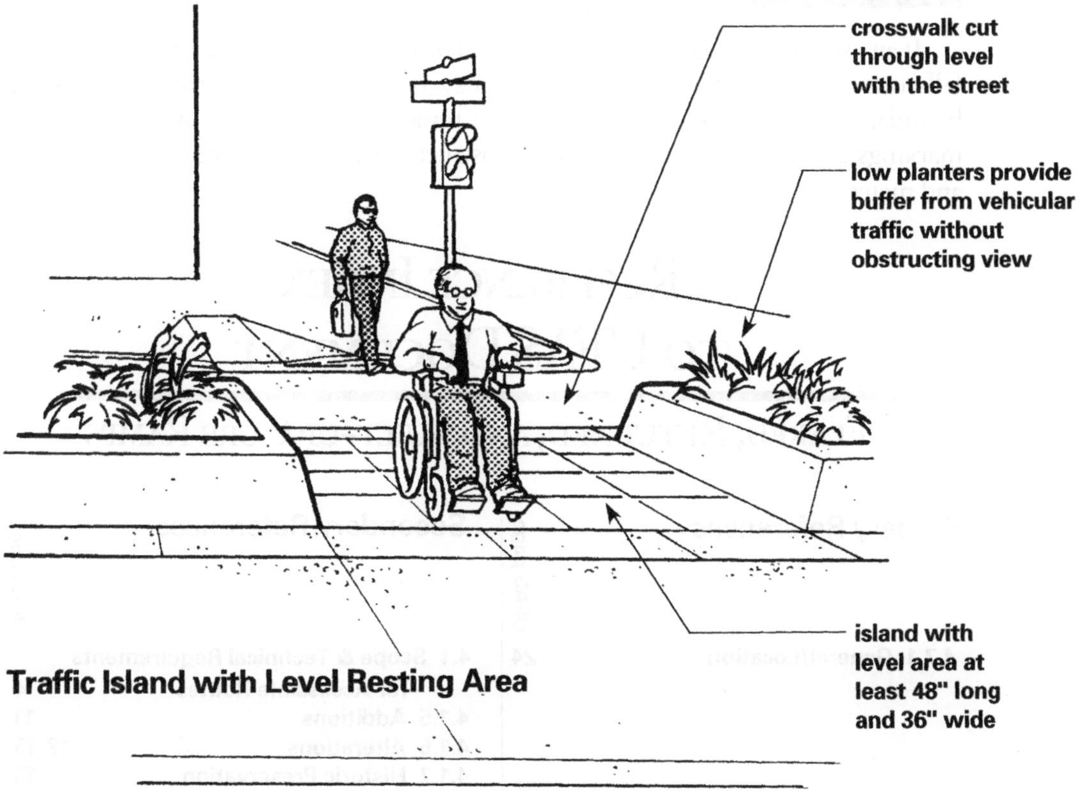

Traffic Island with Level Resting Area

Side streets and driveways which intersect sidewalks should also contain curb ramps if necessary. Sidewalks are often continuous over driveways, but curb ramps may be necessary for smooth passage over side streets and alleys. As with all transitions, passage over driveways, side streets, and alleys should be as smooth as possible with no abrupt level change greater than 1/4 inch.

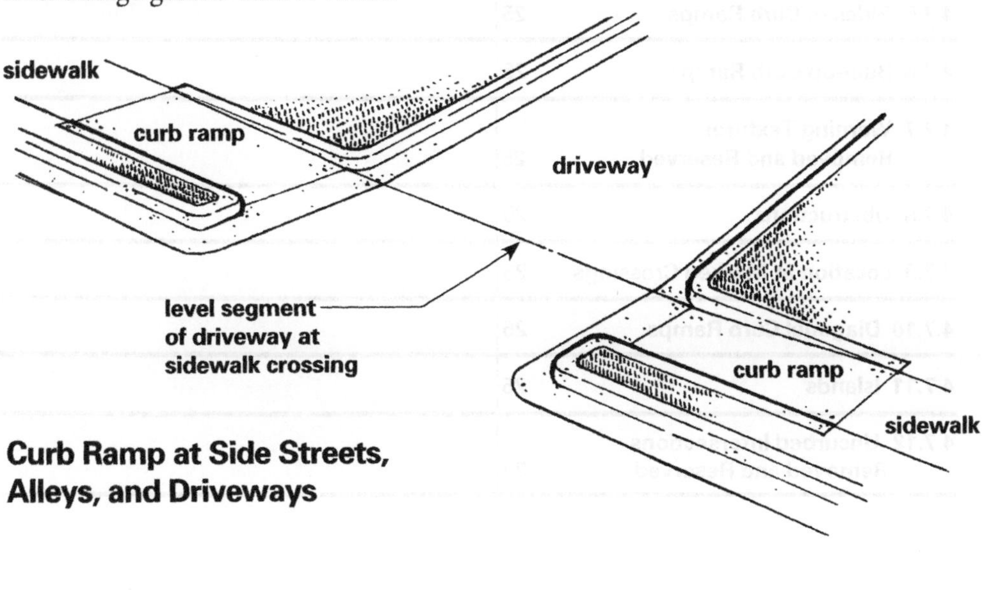

Curb Ramp at Side Streets, Alleys, and Driveways

PROBLEM — CURB RAMP IMPROPERLY PLACED

SOLUTION — REDRAW MARKED CROSSING BOUNDARIES

If an existing curb ramp complies with all other requirements for a curb ramp but falls outside of the marked crossing, it may be possible to relocate the crossing boundaries. This procedure may involve removing or painting over the present markings and removing other existing obstructions such as marked parking spaces and meters.

REFERENCE INDEX TO UFAS DOCUMENT

FLARED, RETURNED, AND BUILT-UP CURB RAMPS

Primary References	UFAS page	Secondary References	UFAS page
4.7.1 General/Location	24	4.1 Scope & Technical Requirements for Accessible Routes 4.1.5 Additions 4.1.6 Alterations 4.1.7 Historic Preservation	4 11 12-13 13
4.7.2 Slope	24	4.8.2 Slope and Rise 4.1.6(4)(a) Alterations - Ramps/Table 2	25 13
4.7.3 Width	25		
4.7.4 Surface	25	4.5 Ground and Floor Surfaces	22
4.7.5 Sides of Curb Ramps	25		
4.7.6 Built-up Curb Ramps	25		
4.7.7 Warning Textures Removed and Reserved	25		
4.7.8 Obstructions	25		
4.7.9 Location at Marked Crossings	25		
4.7.10 Diagonal Curb Ramps	25		
4.7.11 Islands	25		
4.7.12 Uncurbed Intersections Removed and Reserved	25		

Introduction

UFAS defines a ramp as a walking surface in an accessible space that has a running slope greater than 1:20. Ramps are most often used in renovations of sites and on the exteriors and interiors of existing buildings as a means of providing limited vertical access. They are typically installed in combination with steps to accommodate the preferences and needs of a variety of users. Ramps provide the only non-mechanical means of vertical access for wheelchairs and other wheeled vehicles and may also be preferred by pedestrians who have difficulty climbing steps. Others who use crutches and/or leg braces often cannot get the "proper swing" and may have trouble maintaining their balance while walking on inclined surfaces. People with stamina problems may find climbing several steps preferable to walking the entire distance of a ramp.

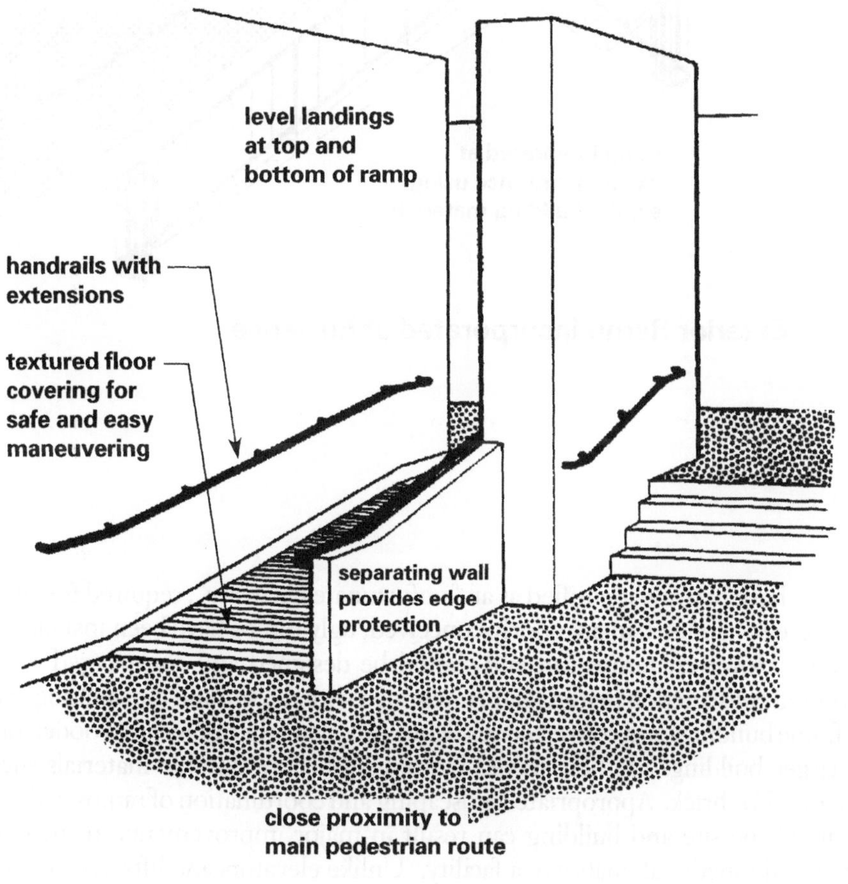

Interior Ramp Provides Access to Sunken Lobby

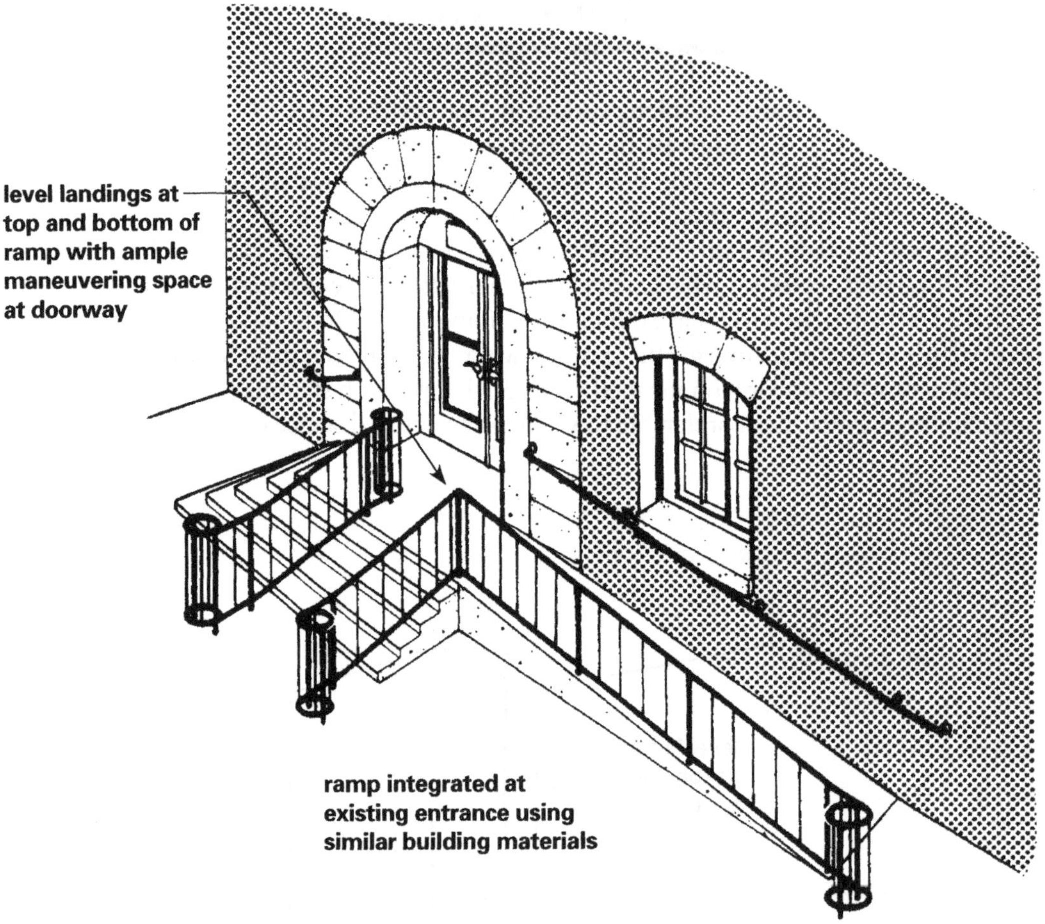

Exterior Ramp Incorporated at Entrance

Ramps have become identified as an "unfortunate necessity", required for "handicapped access." Indeed, many poorly conceived, ugly ramps have been installed over the years. However, ramps can and should be designed and constructed so their location and construction materials are integrated with the site and the building. Small wood frame buildings and converted residences may lend themselves to wooden ramps while larger buildings are best served by ramps of more durable materials such as concrete and/or brick. Appropriate landscaping and coordination of ramps with other elements of the site and building can result in major improvements to the overall aesthetic and functional quality of a facility. Unlike elevators and lifts, ramps are not subject to mechanical failure and are always available for emergency egress.

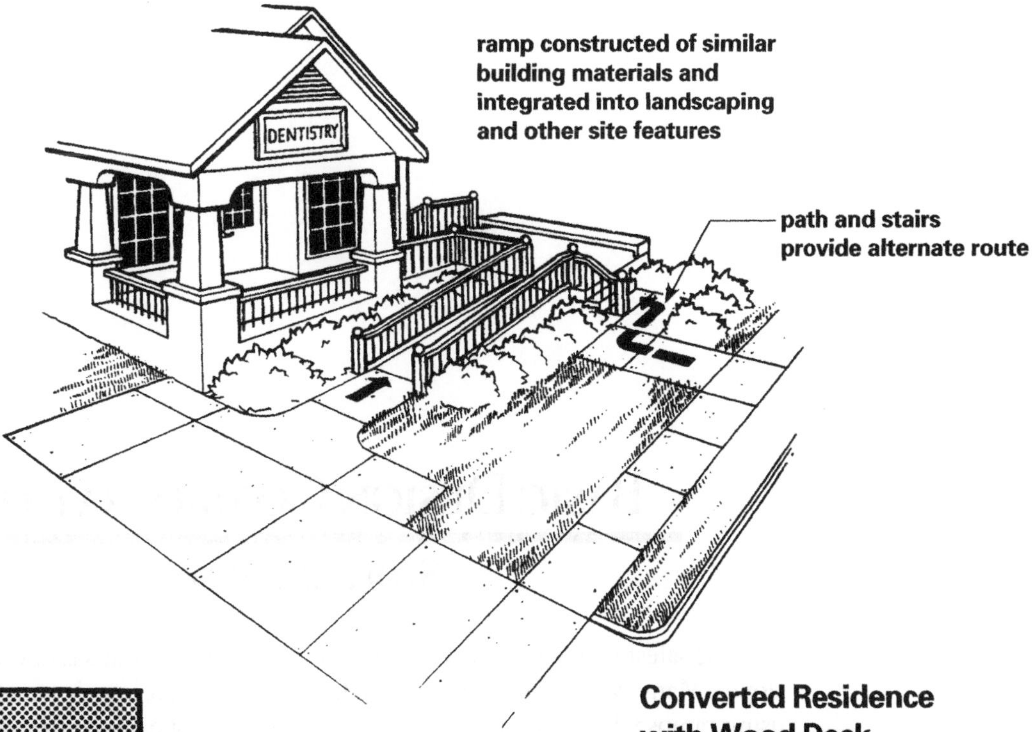

Converted Residence with Wood Deck

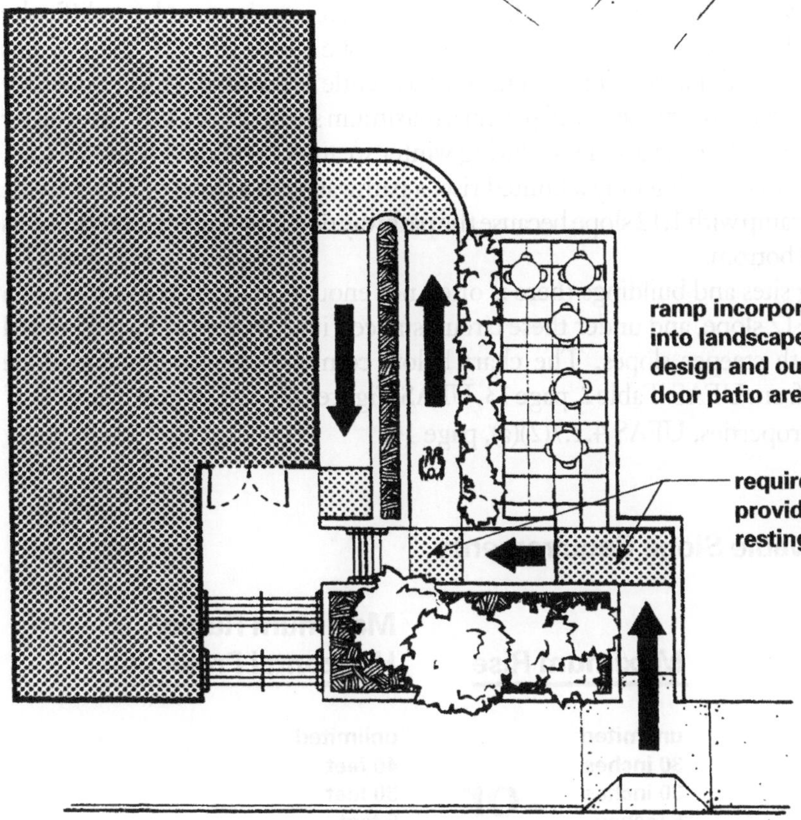

Larger Building with Patio, Planters, and Shrubbery Incorporated at Ramped Entrance

UFAS states that any part of an accessible route with a slope greater than 1:20 must comply with the requirements for ramps. There are some exceptions to the slope requirements for ramps in alterations to existing facilities and historic properties. In addition to slope specifications, UFAS defines requirements for other features of ramps including the width, landings, handrails, cross slope, surface, and edge protection.

BASIC DESIGN CONSIDERATION

SLOPE AND RISE

The safest and generally preferred path for all pedestrians is one with little or no slope. Many wheelchair users and pedestrians with gait impairments have difficulty using ramps which are built at the 1:12 maximum slope allowed by UFAS. For this reason, it is preferred that the slope of ramps be as gentle as possible. Also, some state and local codes in northern states will permit a maximum slope of only 1:20 on exterior ramps to reduce pedestrian accidents during winter weather. It should be noted that, in some instances involving only a limited rise, a pathway with a slope of 1:20 may be shorter than a ramp with 1:12 slope because the pathway does not require level landings at the top and bottom.

At existing sites and buildings there is often not enough space to accommodate a ramp with a 1:12 slope, and under these circumstances, it is possible to install limited rise ramps with steeper slopes. The chart below combines information on slope requirements from UFAS Table 2, page 13, UFAS Figure 16, page 27, and "exception" for Historic Properties, UFAS 4.1.7(2)(a), page 14.

UFAS Allowable Slope Requirements

Slope	Maximum Rise		Maximum Run or Horizontal Projection
Less than 1:20	unlimited	or	unlimited
1:20 to 1:16	30 inches	or	40 feet
1:16 to 1:12	30 inches	or	30 feet
1:12 to 1:10*	6 inches	or	5 feet
1:10 to 1:8*	3 inches	or	2 feet
No Greater than 1:6**	4 inches	or	2 feet

*Exception for use in alterations to existing sites and buildings only.
**Exception for use at an entrance (not a threshold) to historic property only.

PRACTICAL PLUS

If use of a short, steep ramp is necessary because of limited space, it is best to keep the horizontal projection/run at 18 inches or less.This length will allow most wheelchair users to keep at least one set of wheels on level ground and eliminate the need to maintain the entire chair on a steep slope at one time. From this balance point, users can generally negotiate the rise in one push.

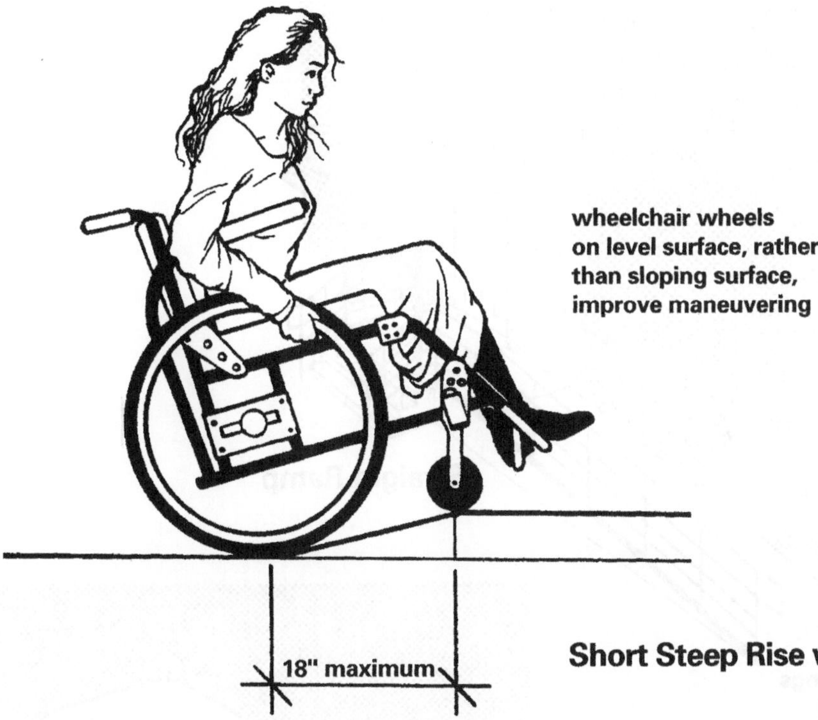

Short Steep Rise with Limited Run

The concern for many users is that they may become exhausted climbing up a lengthy ramp or may lose control while coming down. UFAS specifies that landings be located a minimum of every 30 - 40 feet (depending on the slope of the ramp) to provide level resting areas. Landings must be included at the bottom and top of each run, at least as wide as the ramp, and 60 inches in length. If ramps change direction, the minimum landing size shall be 60 inches by 60 inches. If a doorway is located at the landing, then ample maneuvering space must be allowed at the front and side of the door.

PROBLEM — EXISTING RAMP TOO STEEP AND SPACE IS LIMITED

SOLUTION 1 — INSTALL LIFT OR RELOCATE ACCESSIBLE ROUTE

If the slope of an existing ramp is steeper than allowed, it may be necessary to consider other options. If permitted by the local authorities, platform lifts provide vertical access and require less space than ramps (see Lifts). It may also be possible to move the accessible route to a location with a less steep grade.

SOLUTION 2 RECONFIGURE RAMP

Ramps can be configured in many ways to take advantage of existing space on a site or in a building. Often the immediate location will accommodate a ramp of a different shape, allowing installation of the required length of ramp to surmount the existing rise. Straight, L-shaped, or U-shaped (switchback) ramps are commonly used configurations.

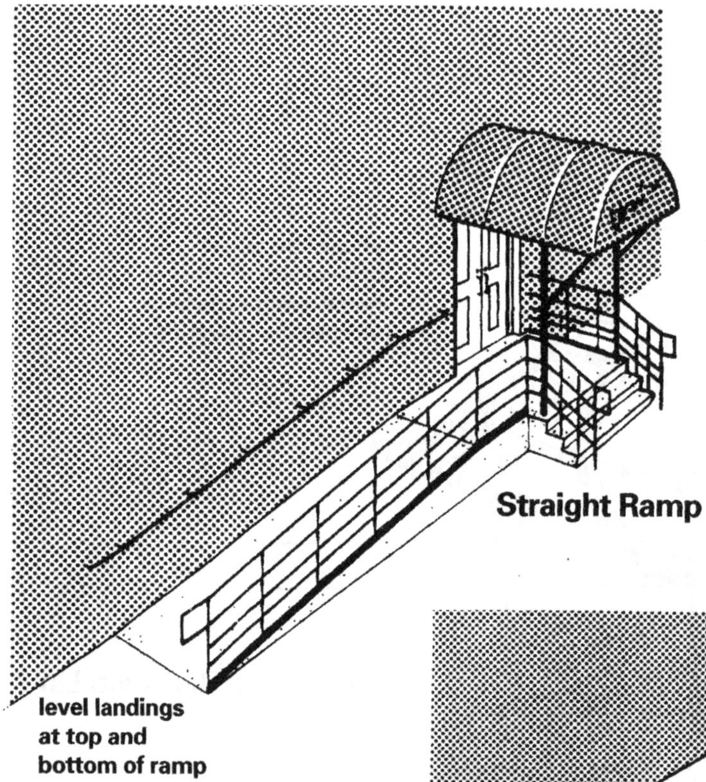

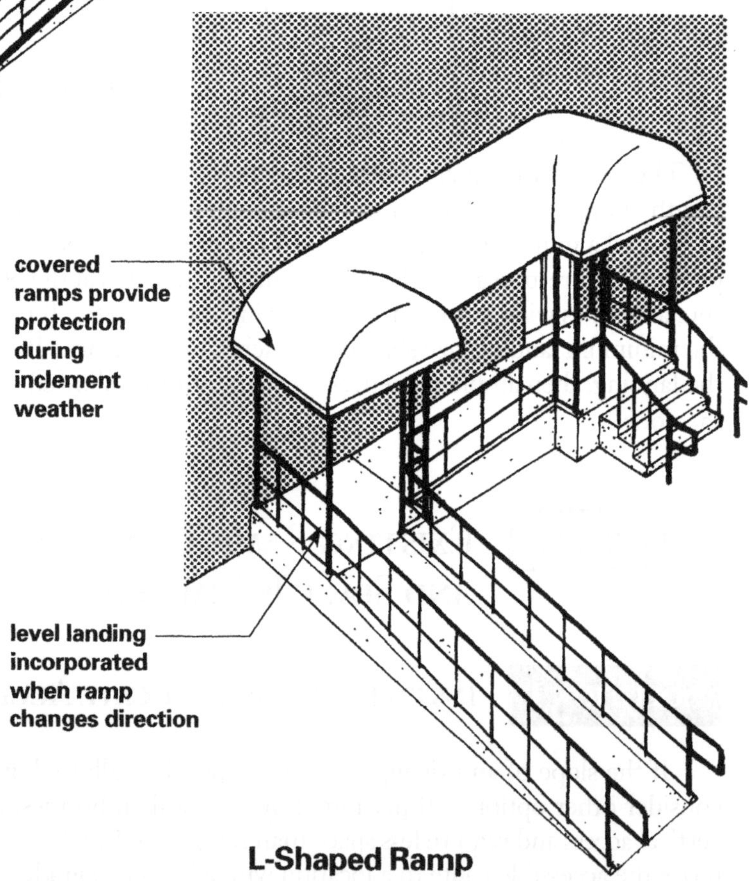

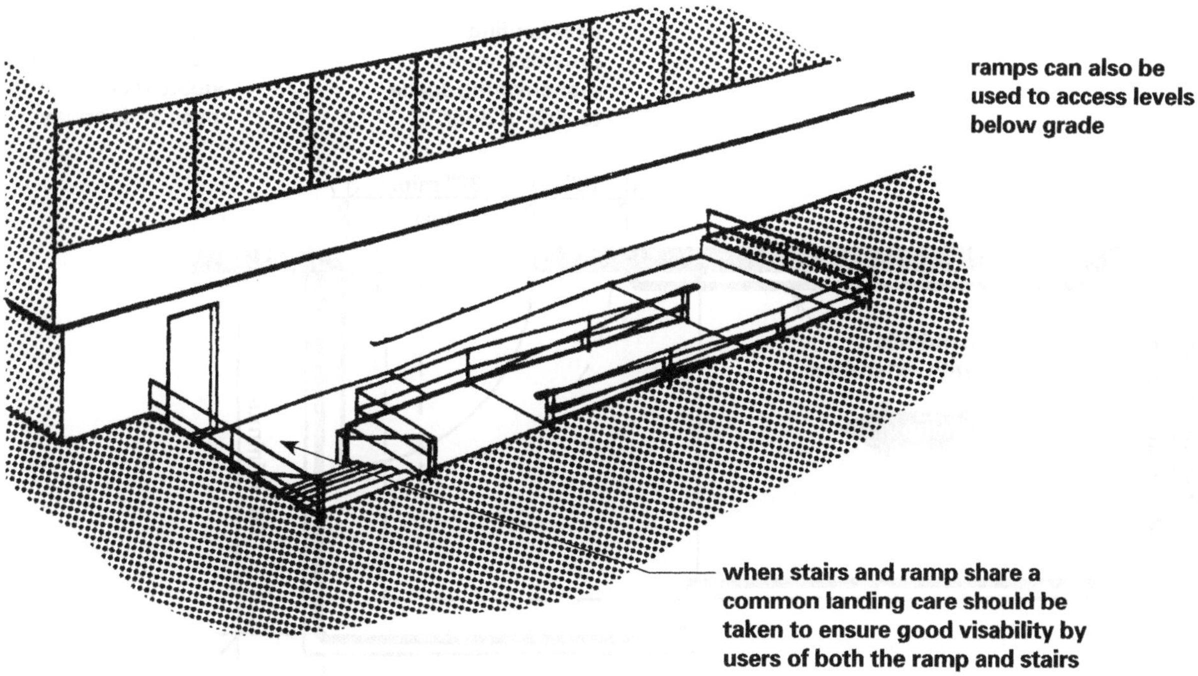

Switchback Ramp

PROBLEM

NO LANDINGS OR LANDINGS TOO SMALL IN EXISTING RAMP

SOLUTION

INSTALL LANDINGS AT APPROPRIATE INTERVALS

If the slope of the existing ramp is within the range established by UFAS, it may be possible to regrade the ramp and add landings at the appropriate intervals while maintaining the minimum slope requirements. If an existing ramp is already at the maximum allowable slope, then corrective action is almost impossible without demolition or extension of the ramp. If existing landings are too small, especially in locations where doors exit onto the landing, then the size of the landing should be increased.

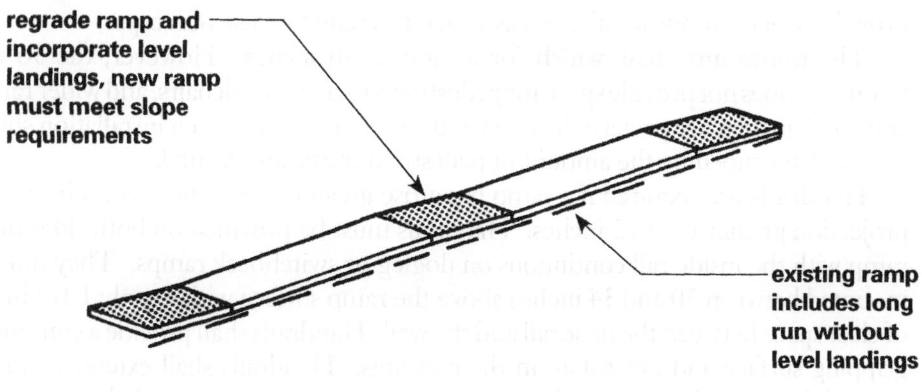

Regrade Ramp to Include Level Landings

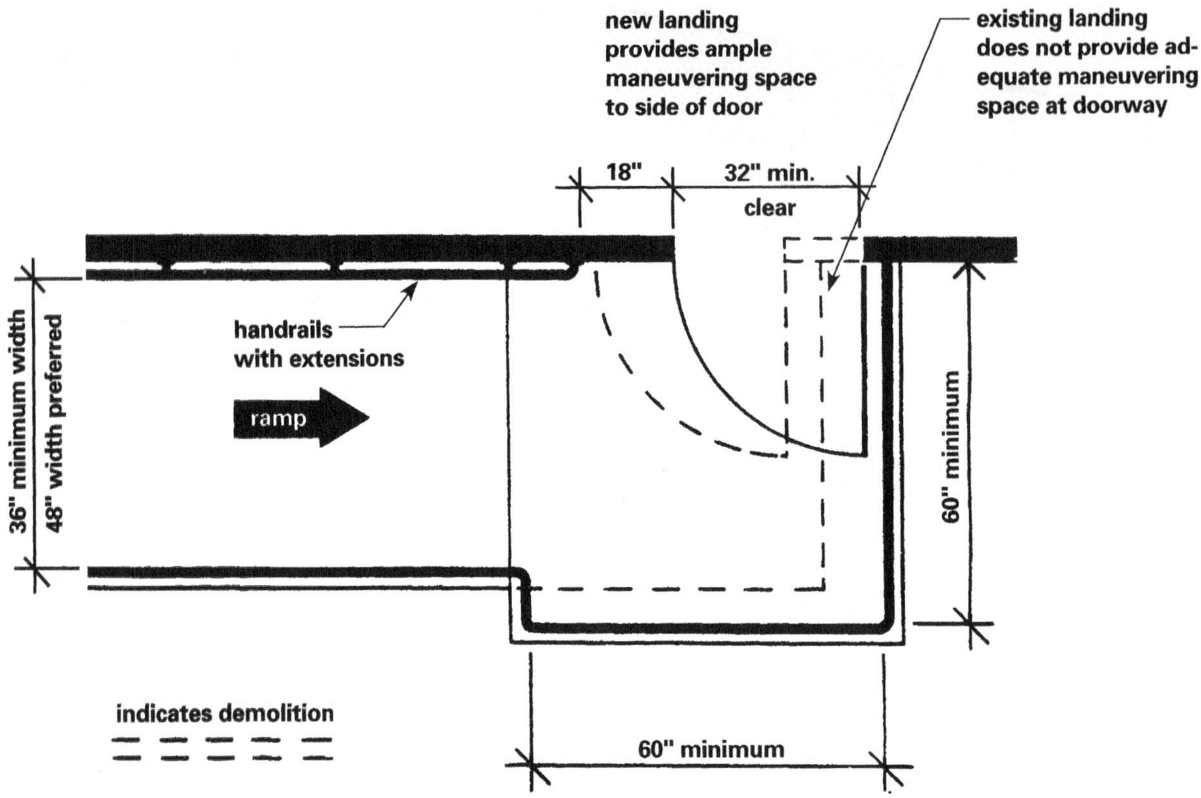

Enlarge Landing to Include Maneuvering Space

BASIC DESIGN CONSIDERATIONS

OTHER REQUIRED FEATURES

In addition to slope requirements and the provision of intermittent landings, UFAS provides specifications in other areas which facilitate safe use of ramps.

The **minimum clear width** for a ramp is 36 inches. However, the 36 inch minimum does not provide space for pedestrians to pass wheelchairs, and wider ramps, at least 48 inches, are preferred. The width of a ramp in any given installation should also be determined by the amount of pedestrian traffic anticipated.

Handrails are required if a ramp has a rise greater than 6 inches or a horizontal projection greater than 72 inches. Handrails must be provided on both sides of the ramp with the inside rail continuous on dogleg or switchback ramps. They must be mounted between 30 and 34 inches above the ramp surface with exactly 1 1/2 inches of clear space between the handrail and the wall. Handrails shall provide a continuous gripping surface and not rotate in their fittings. Handrails shall extend 12 inches beyond the top and bottom of the ramp segment with the ends rounded and returned smoothly to the floor, wall, or post.

In addition to the particular specifications for handrails at ramps, handrails must also comply with the additional performance specifications of UFAS 4.26 Handrails, Grab Bars, and Tub and Shower Seats, page 45. This section includes requirements for the shape and size of the handrail and structural strength.

PRACTICAL PLUS

A second set of handrails mounted at approximately 24 inches provides a convenient gripping surface for children and wheelchair users of small stature.

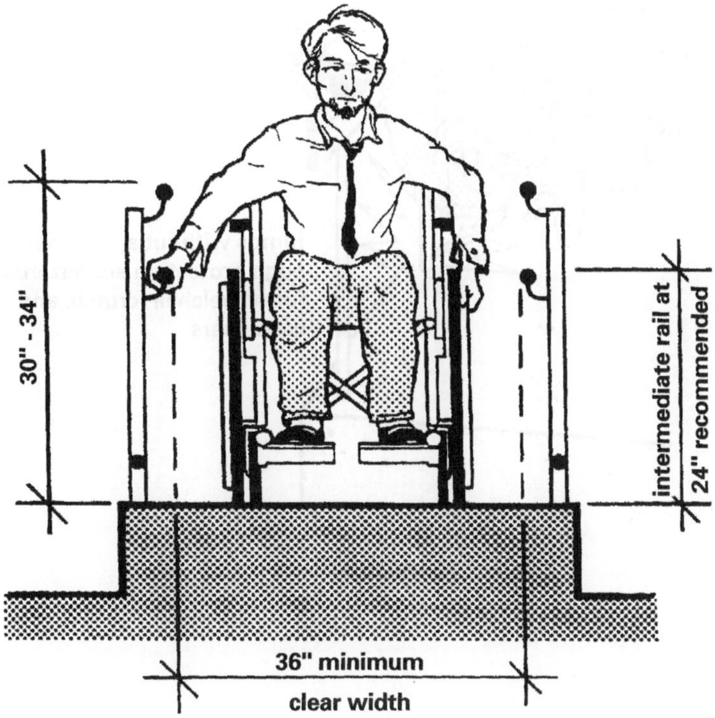

Intermediate Handrails Facilitate Use of Ramp

The **cross slope** of ramps and landings must be no greater than 1:50. This will allow drainage of water from the surface without presenting a hazard to pedestrians. Cross slopes greater than 1:50 are difficult for pedestrians and wheelchair users to navigate. To further enhance the navigability of the ramp, the surface of the ramp must be firm, stable, and slip resistant as required by UFAS 4.5 Ground and Floor Surfaces, page 22. The surface should be easy to maintain and kept free of snow, ice, and debris.

Edge protection is required on ramps and landings with drop-offs. Curbs, walls, railings, or projecting surfaces which prevent people from slipping off the ramp qualify as edge protection. If curbs are used, they shall be a minimum of 2 inches high. Solid walls on each side of a ramp with wall-mounted handrails or very high curbs are the safest edge protection since a wheelchair gone off course will be gently guided down the ramp rather than colliding with the railing.

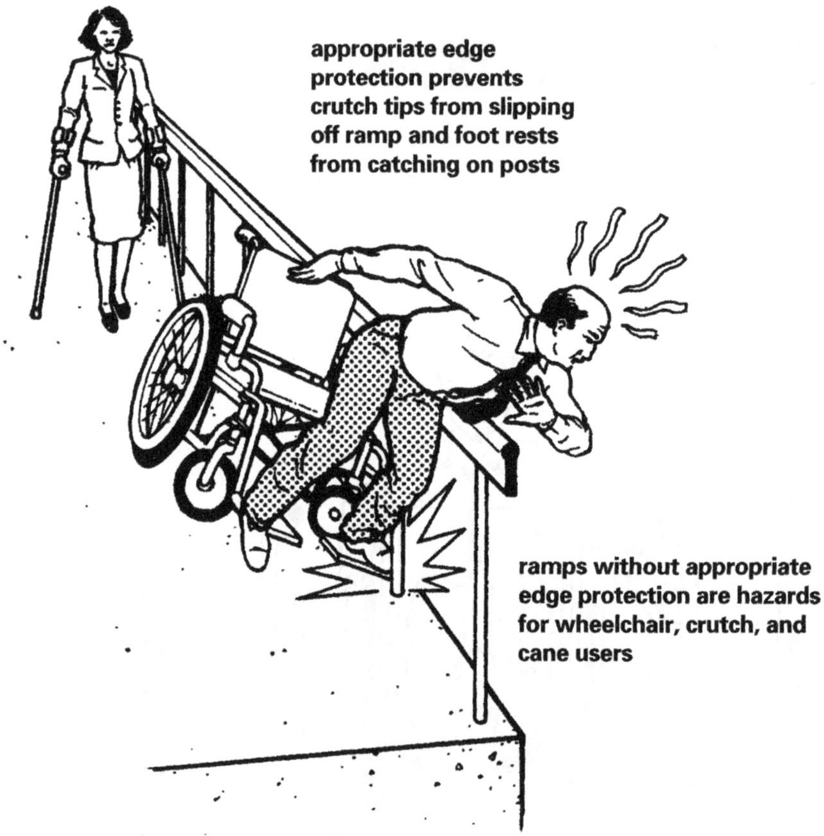

Edge Protection

PROBLEM

APPROPRIATE HANDRAILS AND/OR EDGE PROTECTION NOT PROVIDED

SOLUTION

HANDRAILS AND/OR EDGE PROTECTION AS REQUIRED

If existing handrails and edge protection are either missing or improperly installed, then action should be taken to remedy the situation. Some of the most common problems with existing handrails are handrails with improper shapes, loose fittings, non-continuous gripping surfaces, improper mounting heights or distance from the wall, and handrails with no extensions in the railing at the top or bottom of the ramp. Edge protection is often completely omitted and needs to be installed.

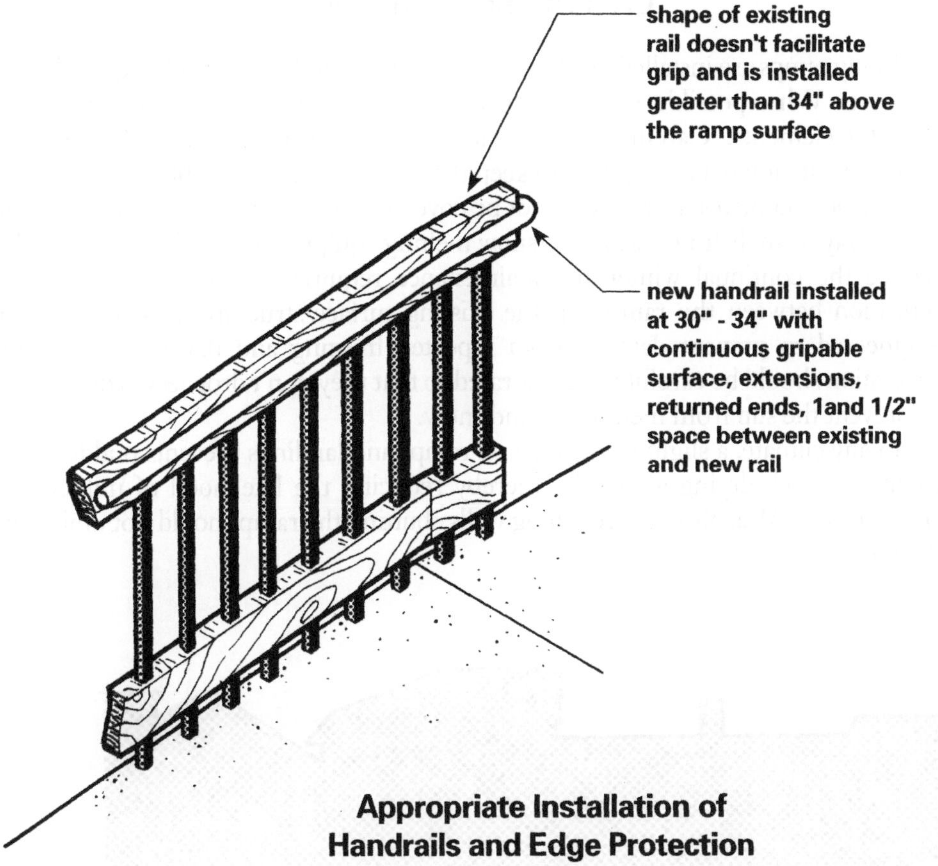

Appropriate Installation of Handrails and Edge Protection

PROBLEM SURFACE OF RAMP IS SLIPPERY

SOLUTION REFINISH EXISTING SURFACE

If the existing surface does not provide adequate traction or gets slippery when wet, it should be possible to refinish the surface by adding carborundum strips or a treatment over the entire surface. The existing surface should be thoroughly cleaned and prepared according to the installation requirements specified by the manufacturer.

BASIC DESIGN CONSIDERATIONS

OUTDOOR CONDITIONS

Many ramps are installed outdoors where they are fully or partially exposed to the elements. When possible, ramps should be covered and placed in a location protected from the elements. Careful planning and installation can improve the function and reduce the maintenance required to keep the ramps safe and passable.

In colder climates, if ramps cannot be covered, they should be located in a sunny place away from drifting snow. Ice/snow melting equipment may also be installed to reduce the continual wintertime maintenance required in snowy climates. The transition between the ramp and the existing surface/structure must be carefully engineered to prevent damage from repeated freezing and thawing. Plants and vegetation should be carefully incorporated so that they don't drop leaves on the path or prevent the sun from melting ice and snow.

In any climate, a slight cross slope on ramps and landings prevents puddling and facilitates quick drying after rain, thereby reducing the likelihood of mildew and algae growth. Weepholes in retaining walls abutting the ramp should not drain onto the ramp.

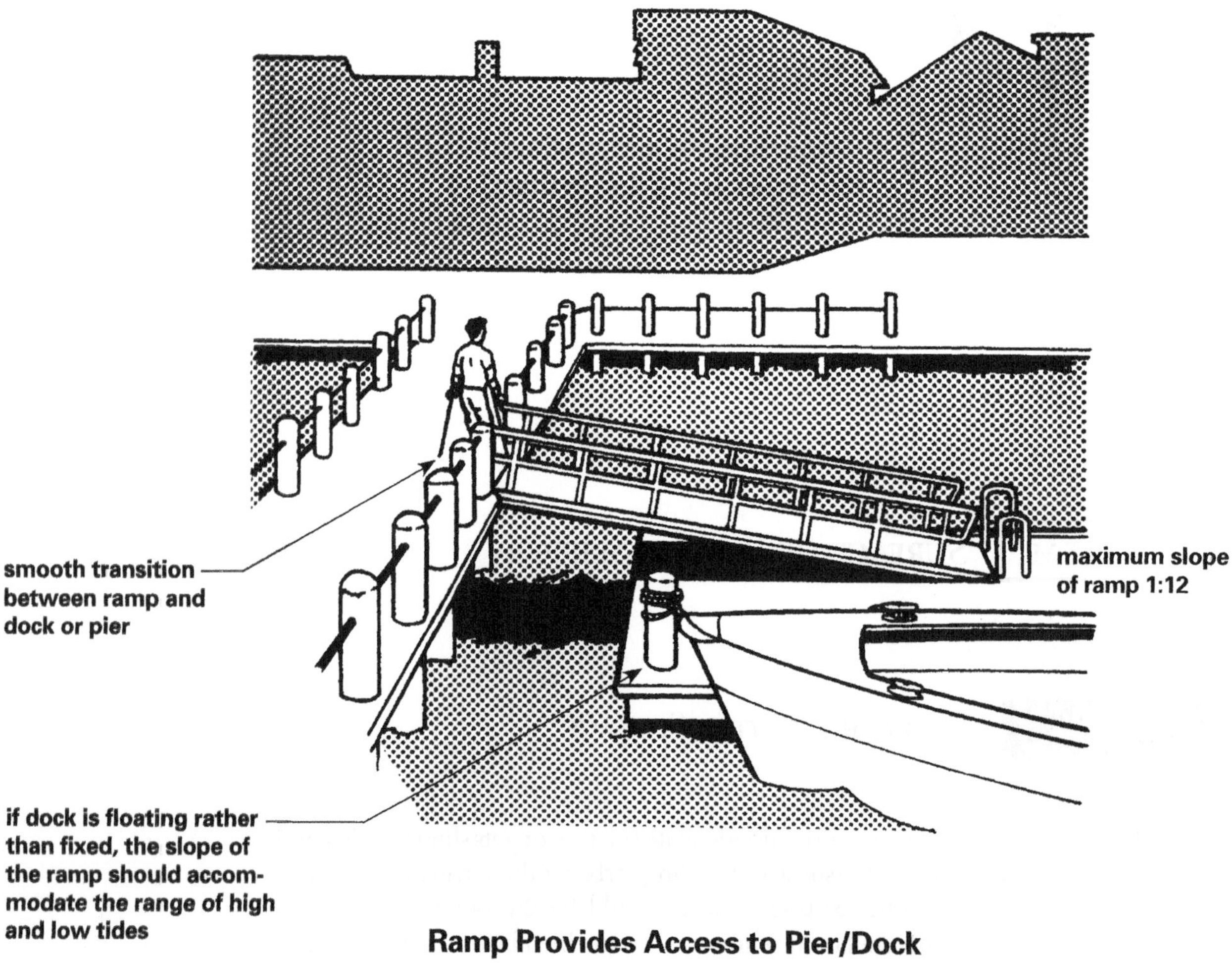

Ramp Provides Access to Pier/Dock

On existing sites with fully developed facilities, pronounced grade level changes are generally more difficult to accommodate because of limitations of available space. Very often, some combination of rerouting the path, regrading, and ramping can provide suitable vertical access in a variety of different settings. In addition to the more common applications, ramps are frequently used to provide access to piers, docks, and swimming pools. At piers and docks, particular attention must be given to maintaining an appropriate slope and smooth transition from the ramp to the pier/dock at all tide levels. Ramped access is sometimes provided at swimming pools, although pool lifts are more commonly used, particularly in retrofit situations.

REFERENCE INDEX TO UFAS DOCUMENT

EXTERIOR AND INTERIOR RAMPS

Primary References	UFAS page	Secondary References	UFAS page
4.8.1 General/Location	25	4.1 Scope & Technical Requirements/ Accessible Route	4
		4.1.5 Additions	11
		4.1.6 Alterations	12-13
		4.1.7 Historic Preservation	13
		A4.8.1 General/Location	63
4.8.2 Slope and Rise	25	4.1.6(4)(a) Alterations - Ramps/Table 2	13
		4.1.7(2)(a) Historic Preservation	14
		A4.8.2 Slope and Rise	63
4.8.3 Clear Width	25		
4.8.4 Landings	25	4.13.6 Maneuvering Clearances at Doors	36
4.8.5 Handrails	25	4.26 Handrails, Grab Bars, and Tub and Shower Seats	45
		A4.8.5 Handrails	63
4.8.6 Cross Slope and Surfaces	27	4.5 Ground and Floor Surfaces	22
4.8.7 Edge Protection	27		
4.8.8 Outdoor Conditions	27		

STAIRS

UFAS 4.9

INTRODUCTION

It is a common misconception that stair design has nothing to do with the provision of access. On the contrary, many ambulatory people who walk with difficulty and/or with the aid of crutches, canes, and braces prefer the use of steps to ramps, and often to escalators. Improperly designed stairs, both exterior and interior, cause falls which often result in personal injury. Proper design and regular maintenance help reduce the likelihood of accidents and improve safe use for all people; especially on steps and stairs which are used for emergency egress.

Traditional stair design has focused on the manner in which people walk/climb up stairs. However, it has been documented that most accidents occur during descent. Contrary to common belief, it is more difficult biomechanically to go down stairs than to go up. In climbing stairs the upward foot is in contact with the higher tread before support is released from the lower leg. However, coming down stairs, support must be released, by flexing the knee, before the downward foot reaches the tread and support can be transferred.

While climbing up steps, a person may place all or part of the foot on the tread and lean forward, with or without the aid of the handrail. As a result, tripping up the steps usually results in a shorter fall which may be broken by grabbing onto the handrail. In descent, a person must attempt the more difficult movement of placing all of the foot on the tread to maintain proper balance. People often use the handrail for additional support and to maintain balance. Slipping on steps while descending may result in a backward fall, which limits the ability of the user to grab the handrail to break the fall. Far more dangerous are tripping accidents which cause a person ascending the steps to tumble backward or someone descending the steps to fall forward.

Proper design of steps and stairs including treads, risers, nosings, handrails, lighting, surface, and maintenance can reduce the probability of accidents for all users. UFAS contains requirements which address most of these safety features. These requirements are to be met on all stairs connecting levels that are not connected by an elevator.

BASIC DESIGN CONSIDERATIONS

TREADS, RISERS, AND NOSINGS

UFAS requires that all steps on any given set of stairs have uniform riser heights and uniform tread widths. Treads shall be no less than 11 inches wide, measured from riser to riser, and open risers are not permitted. Tread depths of approximately 11–12 inches are deep enough to allow a user to place the entire foot on the tread while descending and are shallow enough to facilitate a normal gait/stride. Although not specified in UFAS, risers of 6–7 inches maximum are generally preferred.

UFAS specifies that the undersides of nosings shall not be abrupt, and the radius of the curvature of the leading edge of the tread shall be no greater than 1/2 inch. Risers are also required to be sloped or the underside of the nosing shall have an angle not less than 60 degrees from the horizontal. Nosings shall not project more than 1 1/2 inches.

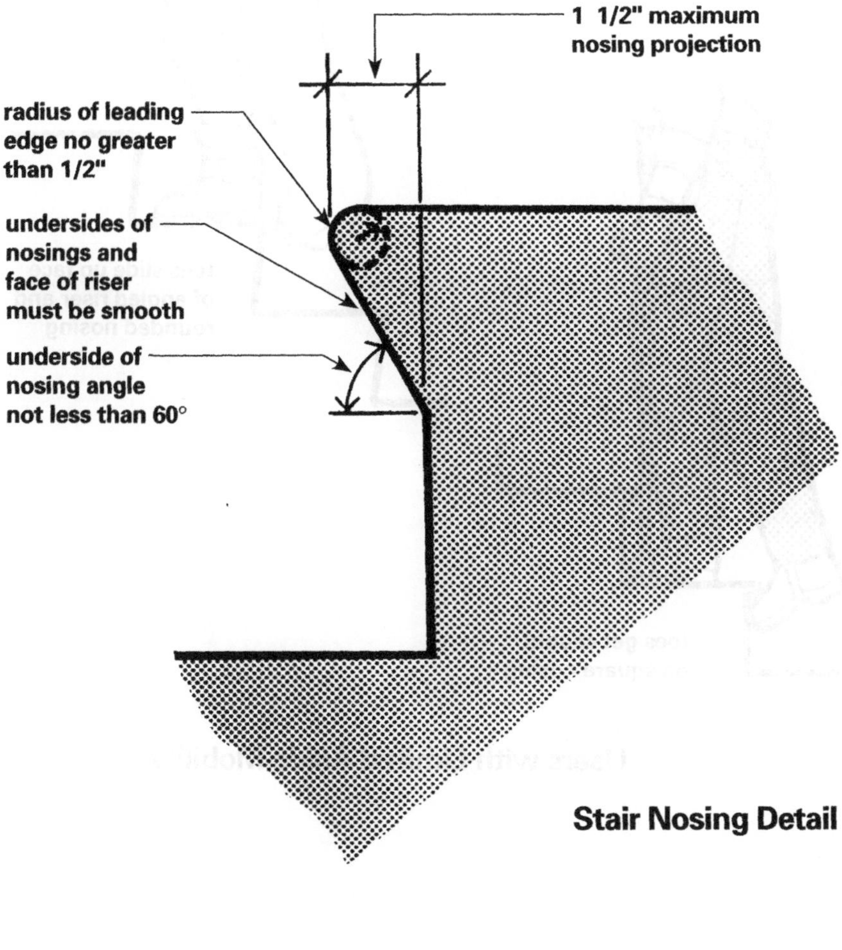

Stair Nosing Detail

Treads, risers, and nosings which don't comply with these requirements create unnecessary difficulties. Irregular treads and risers, steps with risers which are too high or low, and treads which are too shallow create hazards for users. If the risers are not uniform (as is often the case with the first riser at the top or the bottom of a flight) or the treads are too shallow, the body's natural rhythm is disturbed or interrupted, and frequently a fall takes place. Protruding square nosings and open risers are tripping hazards for all users but make stairs impassable when the toes of a user with limited ankle mobility become caught on the edge of the nosing. Extremely rounded nosings may cause users to slip off the edge, particularly during descent. Some users may place their crutches or canes against the riser of a step above them to provide additional stability while they mount the step.

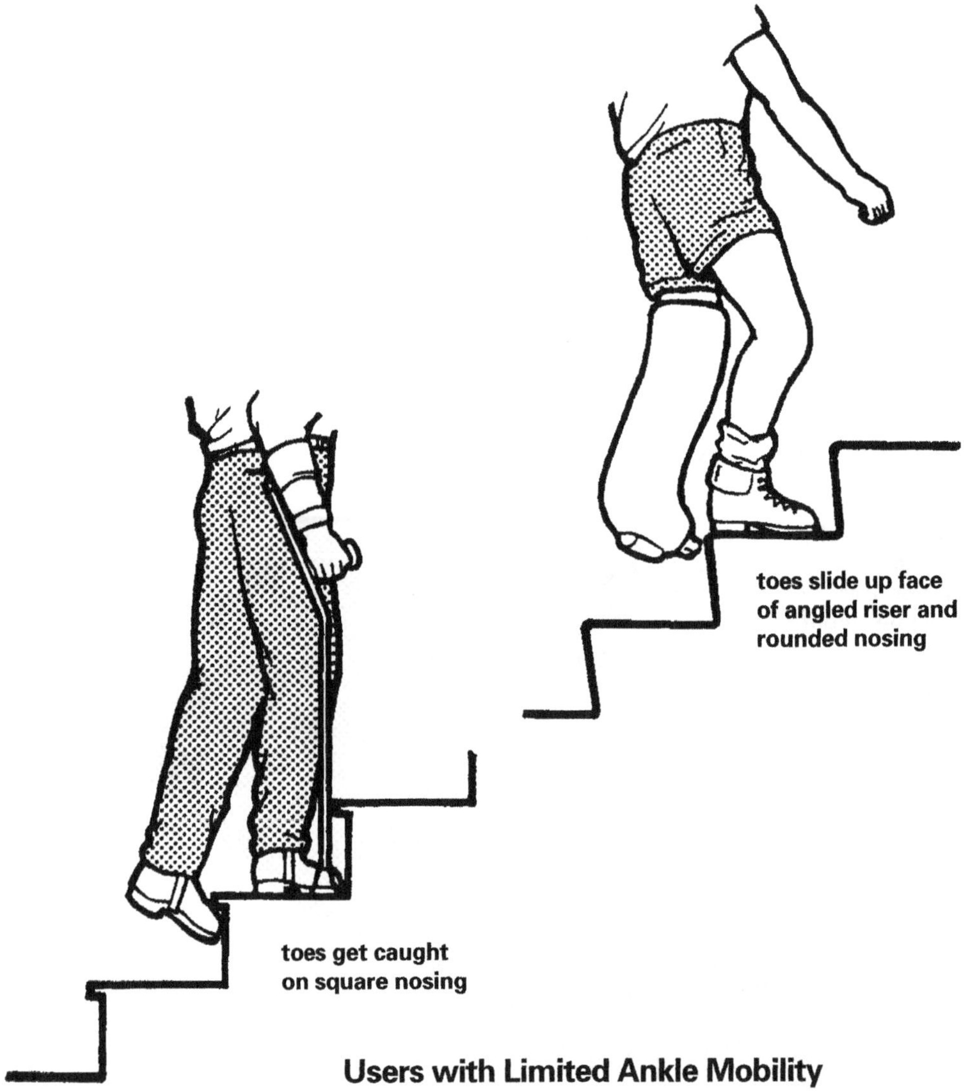

Users with Limited Ankle Mobility

Although not specified in UFAS, some codes include recommendations for maximum vertical displacement for a flight of stairs and requirements for landings of a particular size. These are valid concerns because extremely long flights of steps are fatiguing, and if landings are not interspersed, there is no place for people to rest while climbing. Steep stairways are also dangerous for people with vertigo, heart ailments, and those prone to seizures. The switchback stair is used frequently because it is an efficient use of space and consolidates entry and exit.

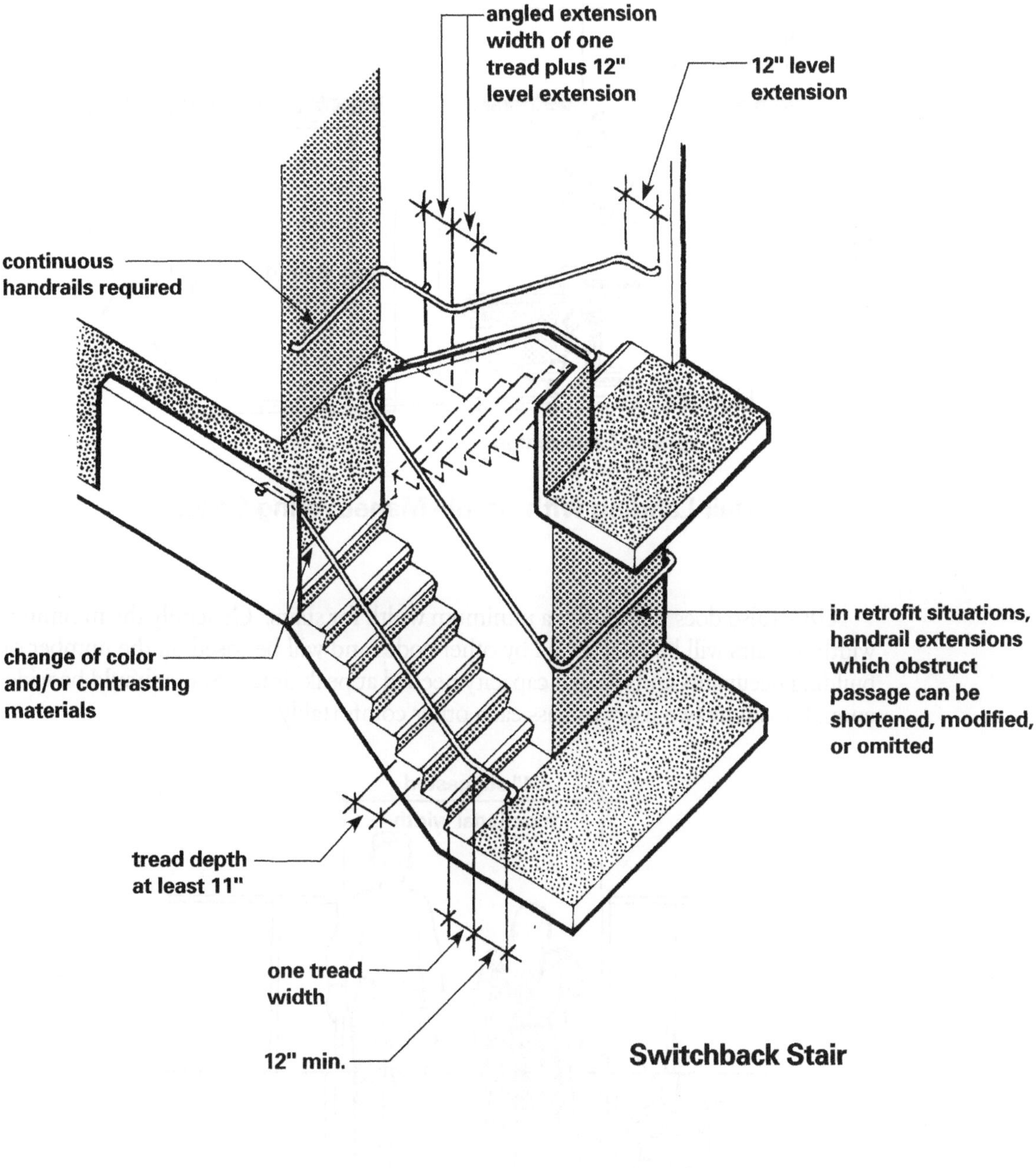

Switchback Stair

Although UFAS does not specifically address the size of landings, if a doorway opens into a stairwell (as in the case of egress stairs), then the requirements for maneuvering clearances at doors will help establish a minimum size landing. Also, if landings/stairwells are established as places of safe refuge, landings must be large enough to accommodate building occupants who may wait there for assistance (see

Egress, Unit Five). As a general rule, doors which do not interfere with the flow of traffic are safer for all users. When possible, glass inserts/view panels in the doors or sidelights make door use safer.

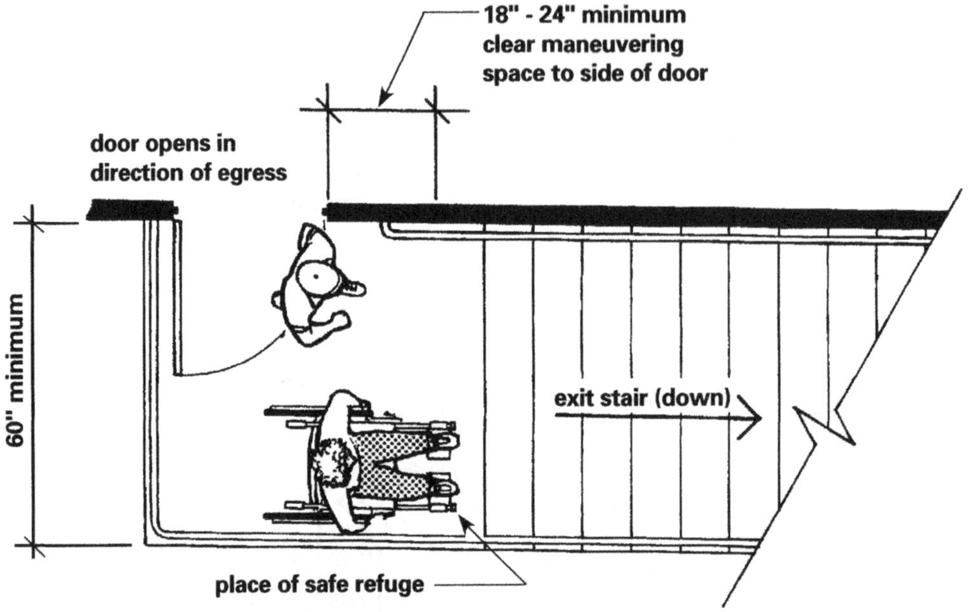

Stair Landing with Ample Maneuvering Space

UFAS also does not specify a minimum width for stairs. Generally the minimum width of stairs will be established by other codes and will be based on the number of building occupants and the exit capacity needed at peak times. Stairs should be wide enough to allow two users to pass each other comfortably.

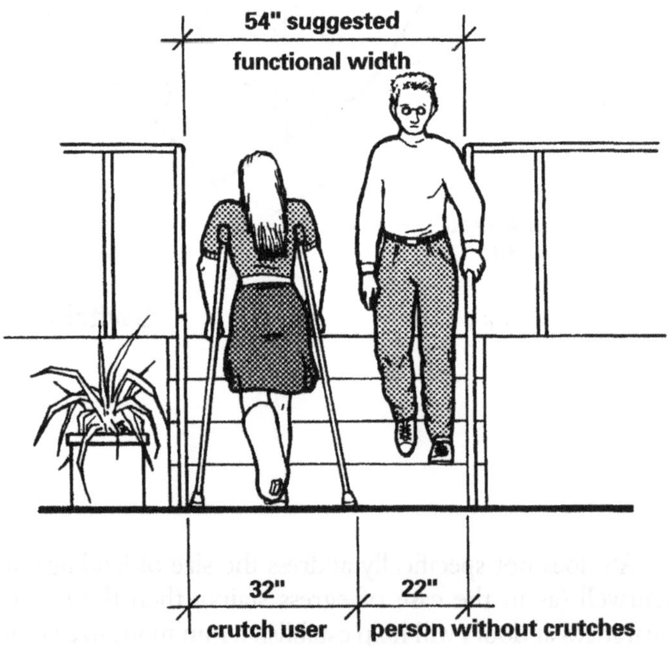

Stair Width

PROBLEM Nosings Don't Comply

SOLUTION Modify Nosings

If existing steps have nosings which don't comply, or open risers, it may be possible to modify the nosings or fill in the risers. Modifications must be accurately detailed and coordinated with the existing stair installation. Also, modifications must be carefully installed so they do not come loose and cause tripping hazards on the stairs.

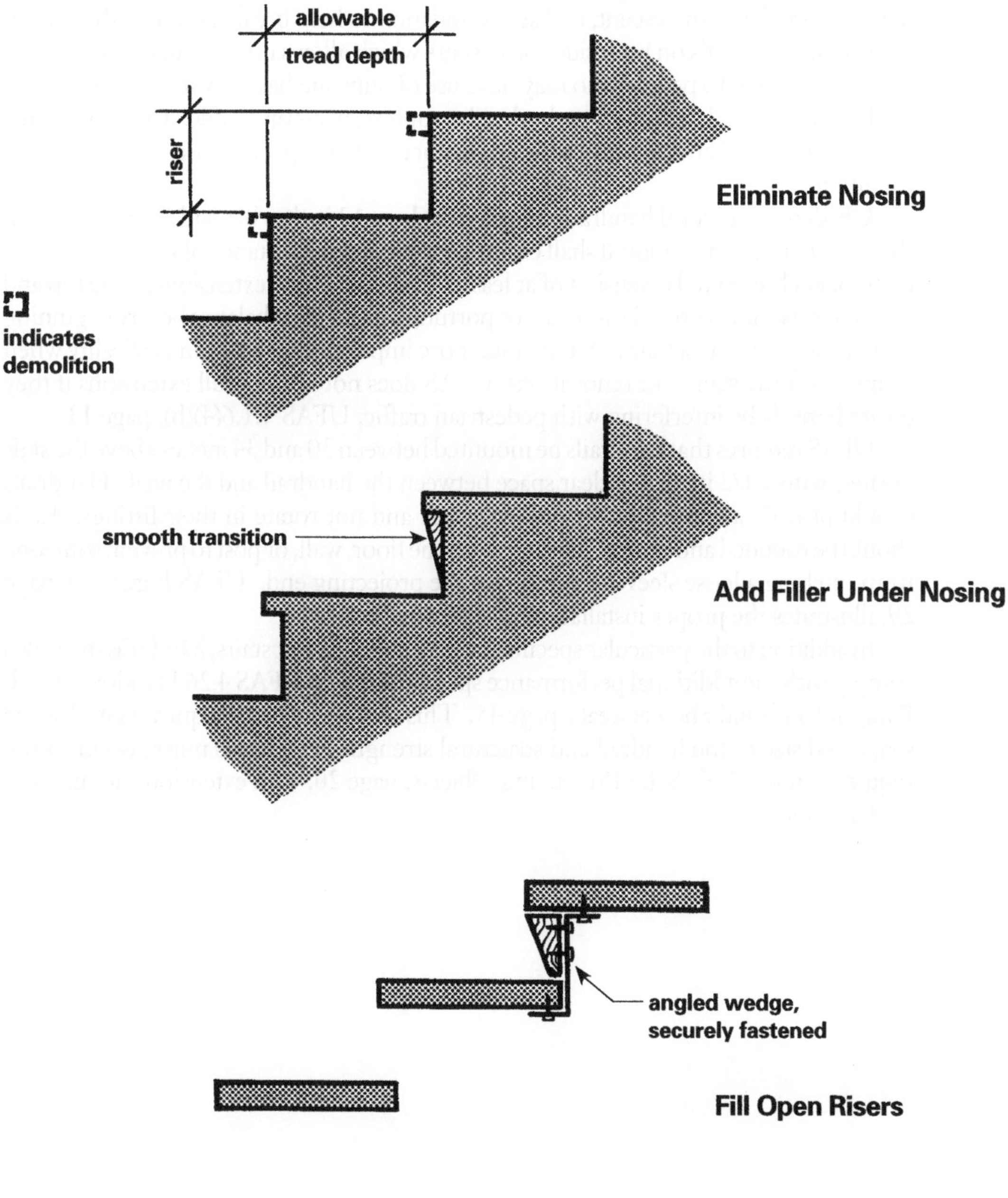

Nosing Modifications

BASIC DESIGN CONSIDERATIONS

HANDRAILS

Proper design and installation of handrails improve safe use of stairs for all people. Handrails serve several purposes including: assistance in maintaining balance, support in ascent, guidance in descent, and as a foundation to help break falls. UFAS requires continuous handrails on both sides of all stairs which allows use of either hand. This is especially helpful to people who may have use of only one hand. Also, on stairs which are heavily traveled, handrails on both sides support two-way traffic. On wide flights of stairs, intermediate handrails provide easy access to support for users who prefer or require it.

UFAS requires level handrail extensions at least 12 inches beyond the top riser. At the bottom riser, the handrail shall continue to slope for a distance of the width of one tread plus a horizontal extension of at least 12 inches. These extensions at the top and bottom of handrails provide users the opportunity to get their balance before beginning to descend or ascend a flight of steps and, more importantly, to regain verticality when stepping off the stairs. In renovations, UFAS does not require full extensions if they create hazards by interfering with pedestrian traffic, UFAS 4.1.6(4)(b), page 13.

UFAS requires that handrails be mounted between 30 and 34 inches above the stair nosings with 1 1/2 inches of clear space between the handrail and the wall. Handrails should provide a continuous gripping surface and not rotate in their fittings. Ends should be rounded and returned smoothly to the floor, wall, or post to prevent someone from catching a loose sleeve or pocket on the projecting end. UFAS Figure 19, page 29, illustrates the proper installation of handrails at stairs.

In addition to the particular specifications for handrails at stairs, handrails must also comply with the additional performance specifications of UFAS 4.26 Handrails, Grab Bars, and Tub and Shower Seats, page 45. This section includes requirements for the shape and size of the handrail and structural strength. Handrails must also meet the requirements of UFAS 4.4 Protruding Objects, page 20, with extensions designed to be detectable.

PRACTICAL PLUS

A second set of handrails mounted at approximately 24 inches provides a convenient gripping surface for children. Handrails mounted at this height may also be useful to adults who have fallen and are reaching out for a stable surface to help break their fall. In facilities where children are frequently present, walls, tightly spaced intermediate rails, or mesh keep children from crawling under the railing and falling.

intermediate handrails, ornamental grilles, and panels serve as guardrails to prevent users from falling off stairs

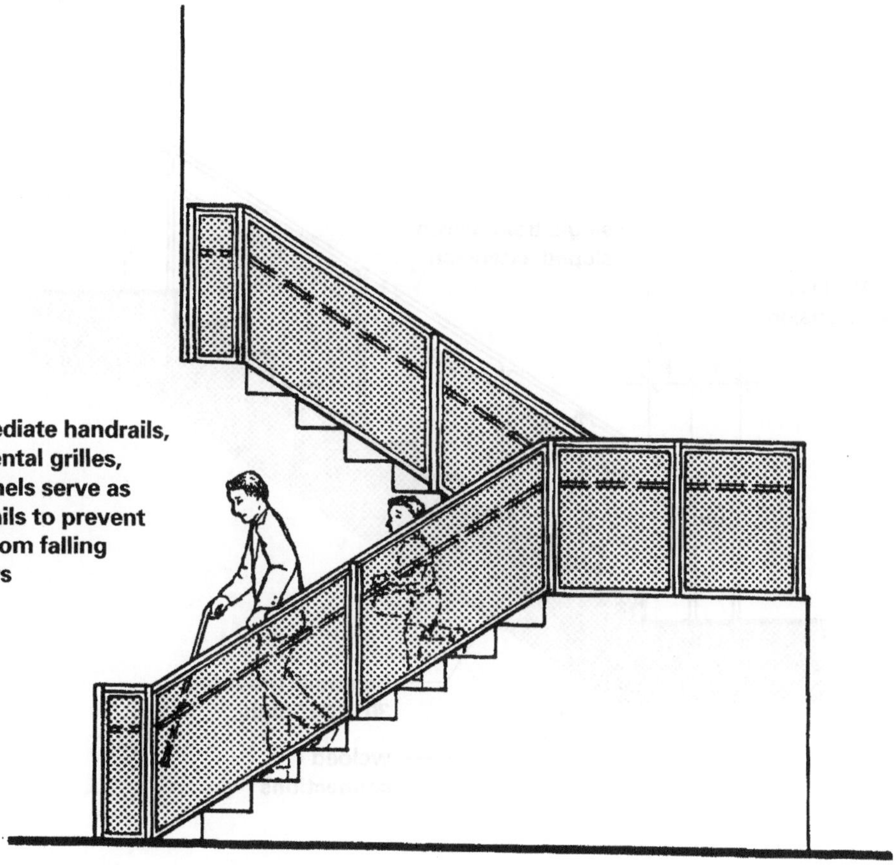

Intermediate Handrails Improve Safe Use of Stairs

PROBLEM APPROPRIATE HANDRAILS AND/OR EXTENSIONS NOT PROVIDED

SOLUTION INSTALL HANDRAILS AND/OR EXTENSIONS AS REQUIRED

If existing handrails or extensions are either missing or improperly installed, then action should be taken to correct the situation. Some of the most common problems with existing handrails are improper shapes, loose fittings, non-continuous gripping surfaces, improper mounting heights or distance from the wall, and no extensions in the railing at the top or bottom of the stairs.

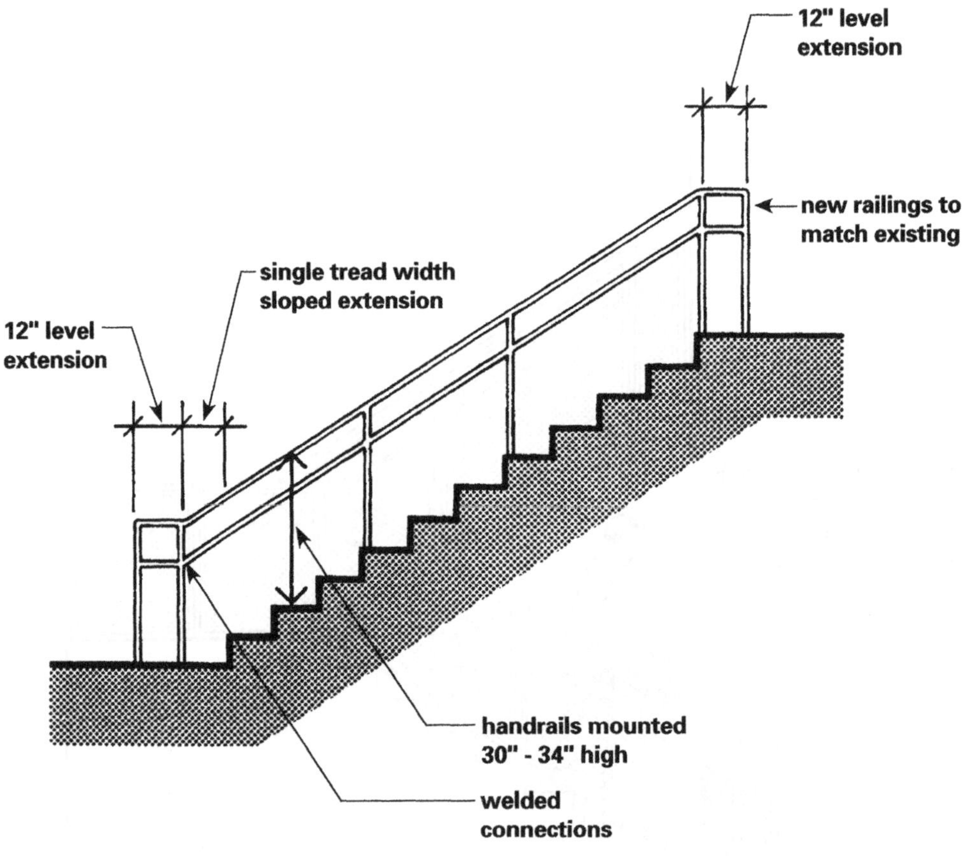

Add Extensions to Handrails

BASIC DESIGN CONSIDERATIONS

TACTILE WARNINGS

Although required by some state and local codes, UFAS does not include requirements for tactile warnings at stairs. At the present time, this topic has been removed from the standard because research data did not demonstrate that a specific surface could be used and detected under all circumstances. The topic has been reserved for future inclusion in the event that new research and product development demonstrates that tactile warnings at steps are effective.

PRACTICAL PLUS

There are several tactile and visual design features which can improve safe use of stairs. The most common and obvious feature is the use of contrasting colors and materials on treads and risers or color strips on nosings to visually and tactilely orient the user. For instance, heavily patterned carpeting makes treads and risers difficult to discriminate while contrasting colors on treads, risers, and stringers provide orientation cues for people with visual impairments. The use of contrasting colors on escalators is especially important because the edge of the tread "disappears" and can create visual confusion for many users.

Proper lighting is extremely important at stairs. Strong artificial or natural lights which cast shadows on treads make negotiating steps difficult for all people. Stairways should be evenly lit with diffuse lighting which eliminates glare. Visual distractions, such as video screens, "moving" signs, or flashy displays, which come into view at the top of a flight of stairs can be particularly disorienting if they redirect a user's attention before the user reaches the top of the steps. Such elements should be located to reduce or eliminate this hazard as much as possible.

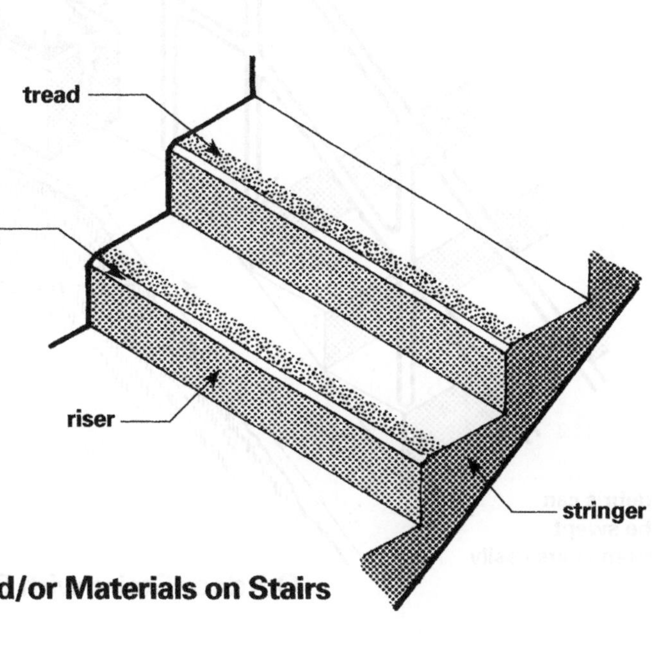

use of contrasting colors and materials makes steps visually and tactilely detectable

Contrasting Colors and/or Materials on Stairs

BASIC DESIGN CONSIDERATIONS

OUTDOOR CONDITIONS

Stairs in outdoor locations pose a particular set of safety concerns for users and facility managers. A major design concern for outdoor steps is the elimination of standing water from the surface of the steps and the landings. Standing water is hazardous in the winter, when ice forms on the surface, and in the summer, when surfaces which are continually damp become slimy with algae growth. To alleviate this problem, stairs should be designed with slight slopes on treads and landings to prevent standing water from accumulating. The allowed slope of 1:50 is usually sufficient for this purpose.

Stairs should also be designed to facilitate proper maintenance. Recessed cheek walls which are properly designed can make removing/sweeping of debris from the surface much easier. Careful placement of the handrails prevents users from sliding off the edge of the steps.

In bright sunlight or in heavily patterned shadows cast by trees, short flights of stairs can be mistaken for ramps or even completely overlooked. Handrails at steps and ramps, as required by UFAS, provide a visual cue which can be observed from a distance alerting the user of some type of grade level change. Even on short flights of two to three steps, handrails can provide much needed support, especially to people carrying bundles and those trying to navigate steps coated with ice and snow. Contrasting colors and materials should be used on treads and risers to provide further visual cues.

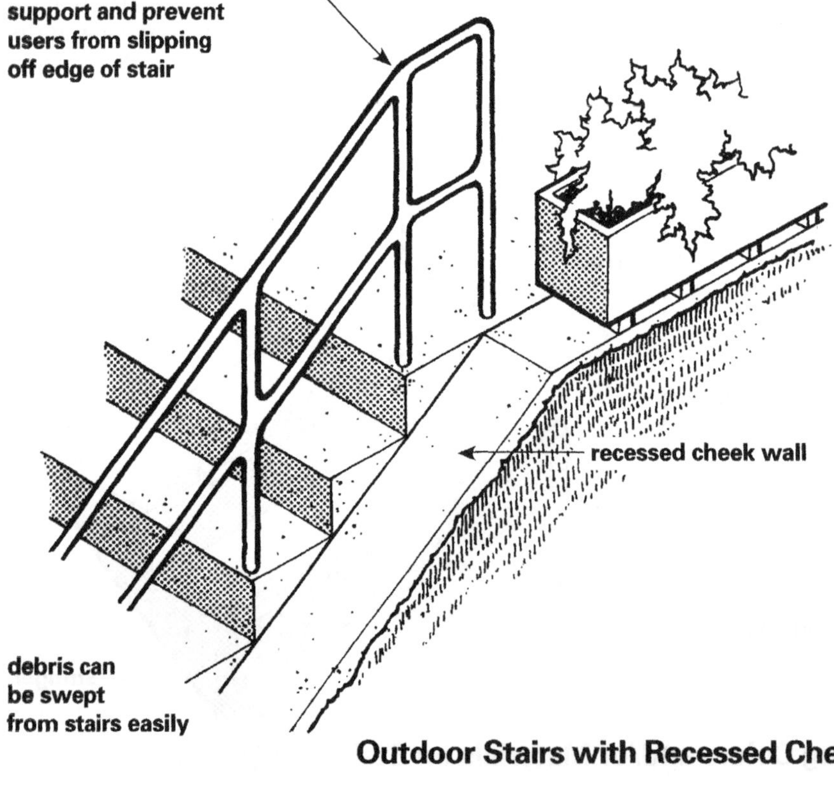

Outdoor Stairs with Recessed Cheek Walls

REFERENCE INDEX TO UFAS DOCUMENT

EXTERIOR AND INTERIOR STEPS

Primary References	UFAS page	Secondary References	UFAS page
4.9.1 Minimum Number/Location	27	4.1 Scope & Technical Requirements/ Accessible Route	5
		4.1.5 Additions	11
		4.1.6 Alterations	12-13
		4.1.7 Historic Preservation	13
4.9.2 Treads and Risers	27		
4.9.3 Nosings	27		
4.9.4 Handrails	27	4.4 Protruding Objects	20
		4.26 Handrails, Grab Bars, and Tub and Shower Seats	45
		4.1.6(4)(b) Alterations-Stairs	13
4.9.5 Tactile Warnings at Stairs Reserved	27		
4.9.6 Outdoor Conditions	27		

ELEVATORS
UFAS 4.10

INTRODUCTION

Elevators provide the most common means of interior vertical movement between levels in multi-story buildings. As an allowable element of an accessible route, elevators must be accessible to people with disabilities. To facilitate use of an elevator by people with various levels of ability, UFAS provides specifications which address the user's ability to perceive signage and signals, reach and manipulate controls, and enter and leave the elevator car. The redundant cueing of signs and signals and specific tolerances for controls and other features are consistent with general elevator safety and use requirements and improve safe use of elevators for all facility users.

In new construction, additions, and alterations, UFAS requires that one passenger elevator shall serve each level of multi-story buildings and facilities. If more than one elevator is provided, then each one shall comply. Accessible ramps or, if no other alternative is feasible, accessible platform lifts may be used in lieu of an elevator. In addition to the particular accessibility issues described in UFAS, elevators are also required to comply with the American National Standard Safety Codes for Elevators, Dumbwaiters, Escalators, and Moving Walks, ANSI A17.1.

BASIC DESIGN CONSIDERATION

SUITABLE ELEVATOR LOCATION

As a general rule, elevators should be located as close as possible to the primary (accessible) entrance. However, in renovation situations where no elevator previously existed, the location of the elevator may be determined by unique characteristics of the existing structure and site.

The existing structure and site characteristics may also determine the type of elevator which can be installed. Traction or cable-operated elevators require installation of a hoist beam and penthouse, and the structure must be able, through modification in some cases, to support the weight and operation of the elevator assembly.

Hydraulic elevators, which are generally used in mid- and low-rise multi-story buildings, are supported from below by the plunger and place no vertical load on the building structure. No penthouse is required, and hoistways can be of lighter construction. Most hydraulic elevators require a jack hole, drilled to a depth equivalent to the distance which the elevator travels, to accommodate the plunger when the elevator is on the lowest level. Several manufacturers produce hydraulic elevators for low-rise buildings which require either no hole or a small hole, making them ideal for installation in existing buildings where hole drilling would be difficult.

For both hydraulic and traction/cable elevators, provisions must also be made for an equipment or mechanical room, an elevator pit, main and back-up power supplies, accessible elevator lobbies on each level, and a structurally sound hoistway with proper fire protection and venting. Local and/or state building codes may contain additional installation and use requirements which must be considered during the design and implemented during construction.

PROBLEM NO VERTICAL ACCESS PROVIDED

SOLUTION 1 INSTALL INTERIOR ELEVATOR

Elevator shafts can be placed inside the building if a common accessible space can be located on each floor, the floors and roof can be remodeled to accommodate the shaft, and the location does not interfere with structural framing of the building.

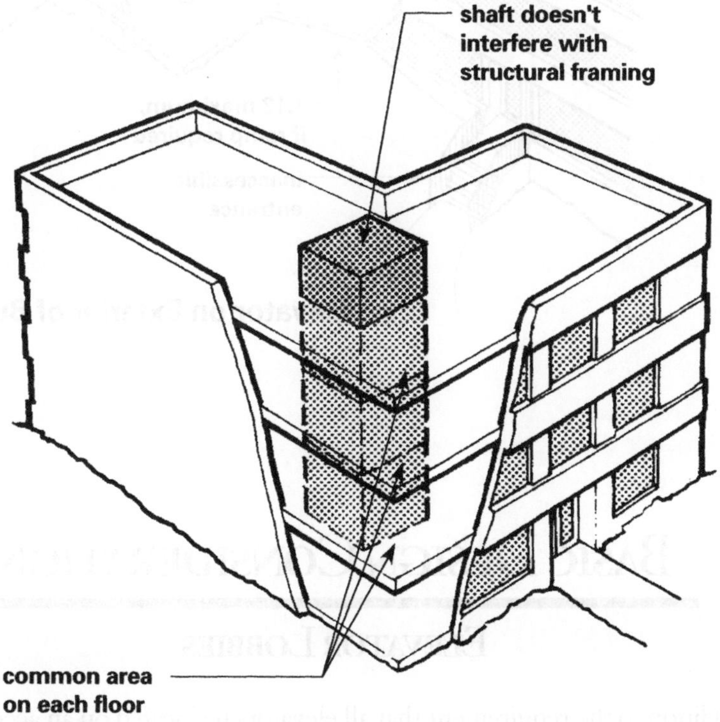

Elevator Installed in Interior of Building

SOLUTION 2 INSTALL EXTERIOR ELEVATOR

If interior space cannot be located but common accessible space can be found along an outside wall, then it may be possible to install an elevator shaft attached to an outside wall of the building. If two adjacent buildings lack provisions for vertical access, then it may be possible to locate a single elevator tower between the two buildings connected by bridges. Similarly, if an adjacent building uses an elevator to provide access to different levels, it may be possible to use connector walkways/ramps to provide horizontal access between the similar levels of the two buildings. When possible, elevators should be configured to facilitate emergency evacuation from buildings, see Unit Five, 4.3.10 Egress.

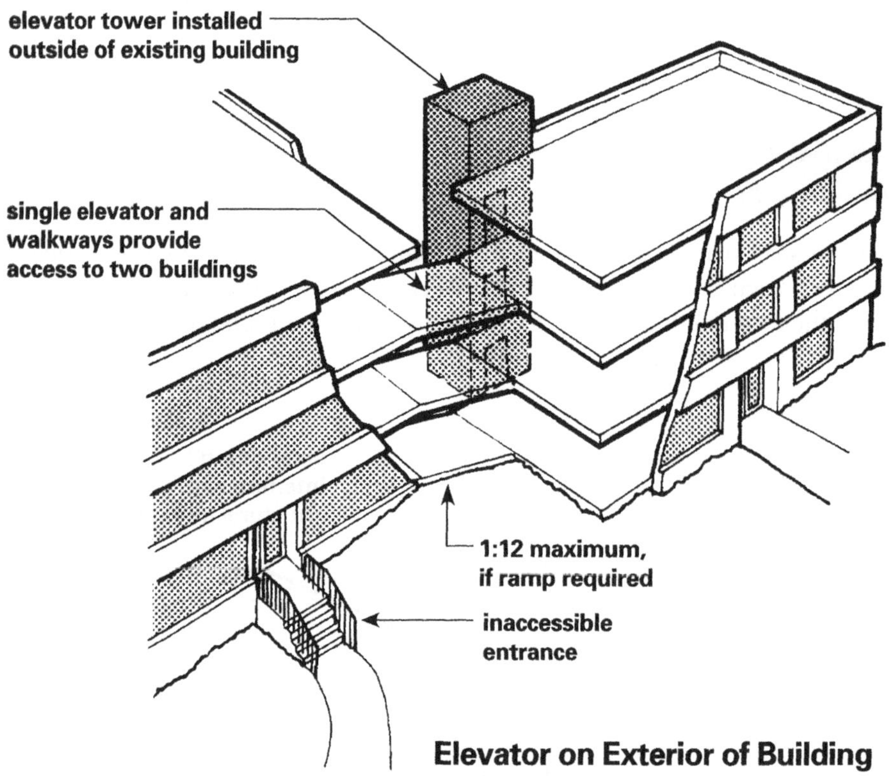

Elevator on Exterior of Building

BASIC DESIGN CONSIDERATION

ELEVATOR LOBBIES

In addition to the requirement that all elevators be located on an accessible route, hall call buttons, hall lanterns, and raised characters on hoistway entrances must be installed according to the requirements specified in UFAS and outlined below.

Call buttons must be mounted vertically and centered at 42 inches above the floor with the up button on top and the down button on the bottom. The call buttons must also have a visual signal to indicate when a call is registered and answered. Buttons can be raised or flush but must be at least 3/4 inch in the smallest dimension with the top button designating upward travel. Objects, such as ash trays which are frequently mounted beneath the call button, should not project into the lobby more than 4 inches.

Hall lanterns must provide a visible and audible signal at each hoistway entrance to indicate which car is answering the call. Audible signals must sound once for the up direction and twice for the down direction or have verbal annunciators which indicate the direction of travel. The accompanying visual signal shall be visible from the vicinity of the hall call button and mounted with its centerline at least 72 inches above the floor. The visual elements shall be at least 2 1/2 inches in the smallest dimension. Although not required by UFAS, several codes require that hall lanterns be arrow-shaped, consistent with the direction of travel, and color coded, with white indicating "up" and red indicating "down".

Raised characters on hoistway entrances provide helpful visual and tactile information about the location of the elevator without requiring the passenger to leave the elevator car. The characters must be permanently mounted with center-lines 60 inches from the floor. The raised characters must be 2 inches high and comply with UFAS specifications, 4.30 Signage, page 47.

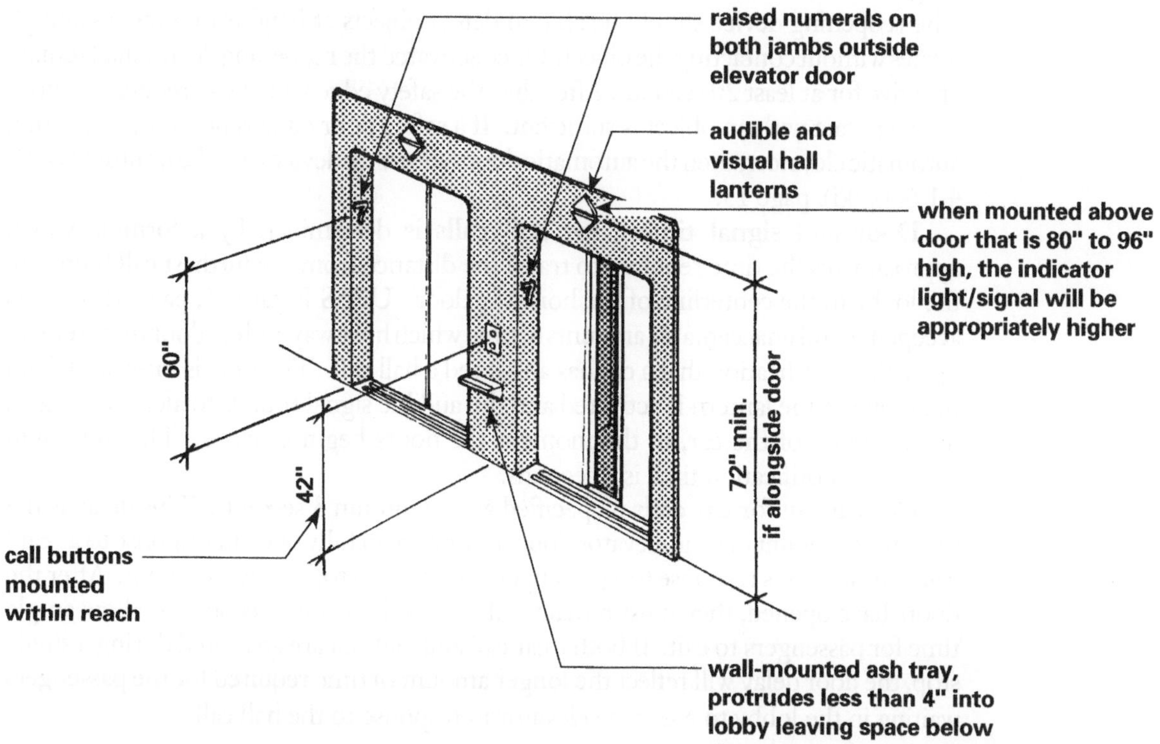

Elements Elevator Lobby

PROBLEM NON-COMPLYING ELEMENTS IN EXISTING ELEVATOR LOBBY

SOLUTION RELOCATE, REPLACE, OR INSTALL APPROPRIATE ELEMENTS

If hall call buttons, hall lanterns, or raised characters on the hoistway do not conform with one or several requirements of UFAS, they should be brought into compliance. The elevator manufacturer and/or contractor should be consulted for information on the particular system involved to ensure that the most appropriate and cost effective techniques are used.

BASIC DESIGN CONSIDERATIONS

MOVEMENT AND OPERATION OF THE ELEVATOR

UFAS includes several requirements which address automatic operation of leveling devices and elevator doors:

Automatic operation is required including self-leveling features that automatically bring the car to within 1/2 inch of the floor landing.

Door protective and reopening devices shall function to automatically stop and reopen both car and hoistway doors should either be obstructed by a person or object. The reopening device should be able to detect objects at heights of 5 inches and 29 inches without contacting the object. Once activated the reopening device shall remain effective for at least 20 seconds. After this, the safety edge which will reopen the door upon contact with an object is sufficient. If a safety door edge is provided in existing automatic elevators, then the automatic door reopening devices may be omitted UFAS 4.1.6(4)(c)(i), page 13.

Door and signal timing for hall calls is determined by a formula which approximates the time required to travel the distance from the furthest call button in the lobby to the centerline of the hoistway door. UFAS Figure 21, page 31, depicts acceptable and unacceptable amounts of time which hoistway and car doors may remain open after notification that a car has answered a hall call. The time is measured from the moment the lantern is activated and the audible signal sounds to alert passengers to the arrival of the car, to the moment the doors begin to close. The minimum acceptable notification time is 5 seconds.

Door delay for car calls is specified at a minimum 3 seconds. This delay is the minimum amount of time elevator doors must remain fully open in response to a "car" call, the elevator's response to a passenger's request to stop at a certain floor. After the doors have opened, they must remain fully opened for three seconds to allow ample time for passengers to exit. If both a car call and hall call are answered during a single stop, the door delay will reflect the longer amount of time required for the passengers waiting in the lobby to enter the elevator in response to the hall call.

PROBLEM AUTOMATIC OPERATION FEATURES ARE INAPPROPRIATE OR NOT INSTALLED

SOLUTION ADJUST EXISTING FEATURES OR INSTALL NEW ONES

In older model elevators some of the automatic features may not be sufficiently sophisticated to meet the tolerances specified. The elevator manufacturer and/or contractor should be contacted regarding possible options which could be used to bring the existing elevator into compliance.

BASIC DESIGN CONSIDERATIONS

ELEVATOR CAR

There are several specific features of elevator cars which must meet the UFAS requirements. These requirements are described in UFAS and outlined below:

Floor plan of elevator cars must allow space for a person using a wheelchair to enter the car, maneuver within reach of the controls, and exit from the car. As shown in UFAS Figure 22, page 31, the elevator doors can be located in the center or to the left or right side of the longer dimension of the car. In alterations where existing shaft or structural elements prohibit strict compliance with these dimensions the minimum floor area dimensions may be reduced by the minimum amount necessary, but in no case shall they be less than 48 inches by 48 inches, UFAS 4.1.6.(4)(c)(ii), page 13. The door opening must be 36 inches minimum, and the distance from the car platform sill to the hoistway landing can be no greater than 1 1/4 inches.

Hoistway Platform to Car Sill Opening

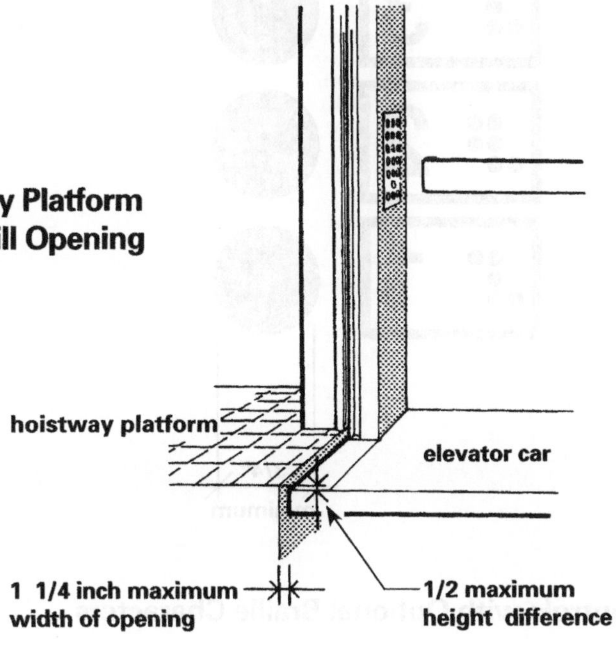

Floor surfaces are required to comply with UFAS 4.5 Ground and Floor Surfaces, page 22, which designates, among other things, that floor surfaces be stable, firm, and slip resistant. Floor surfaces in public use elevators must be easy to walk or roll over, securely fastened to prevent tripping, and durable enough to withstand heavy pedestrian traffic.

Illumination levels at car controls, platform, car threshold, and landing sill are required to be at least 5 foot candles. Proper lighting of these features will reduce the likelihood of tripping accidents as users enter and exit the elevator and facilitate use of the controls by all people. Additional lighting and reinforced glass panels are often incorporated at exterior elevators to reduce vandalism and augment security measures at the facility.

Car controls shall be designed to facilitate easy use for all passengers. Buttons on the control panel shall be at least 3/4 inch in their smallest dimension and shall be raised or flush with the panel. The buttons shall be designated by raised standard alphabet characters for letters, Arabic characters for numerals, or standard symbols as shown in UFAS Figure 23(a), page 32, and detailed in UFAS 4.30 Signage, page 47. All raised designations shall be placed immediately to the left of the button to which they apply. Floor buttons shall be provided with visual indicators which indicate when a call has been registered and extinguish when a call has been answered.

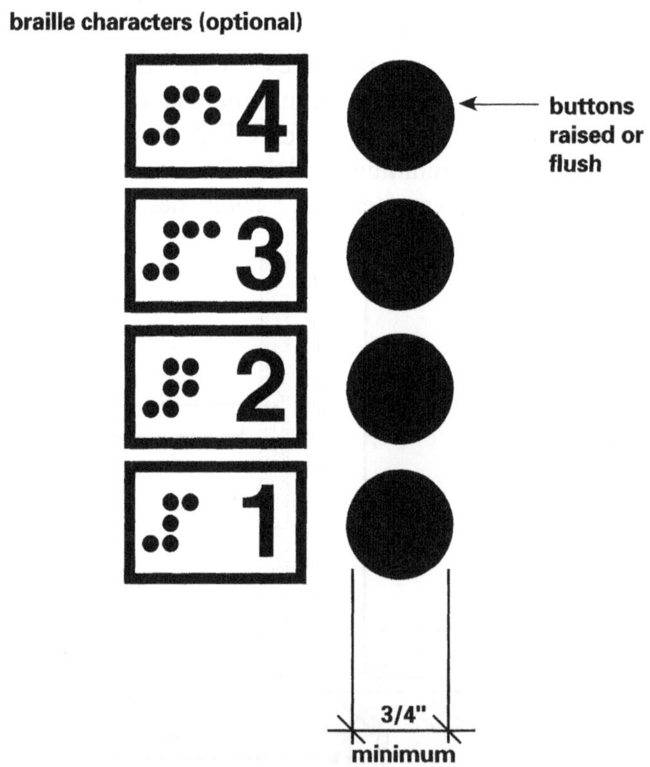

Car Controls with Optional Braille Characters

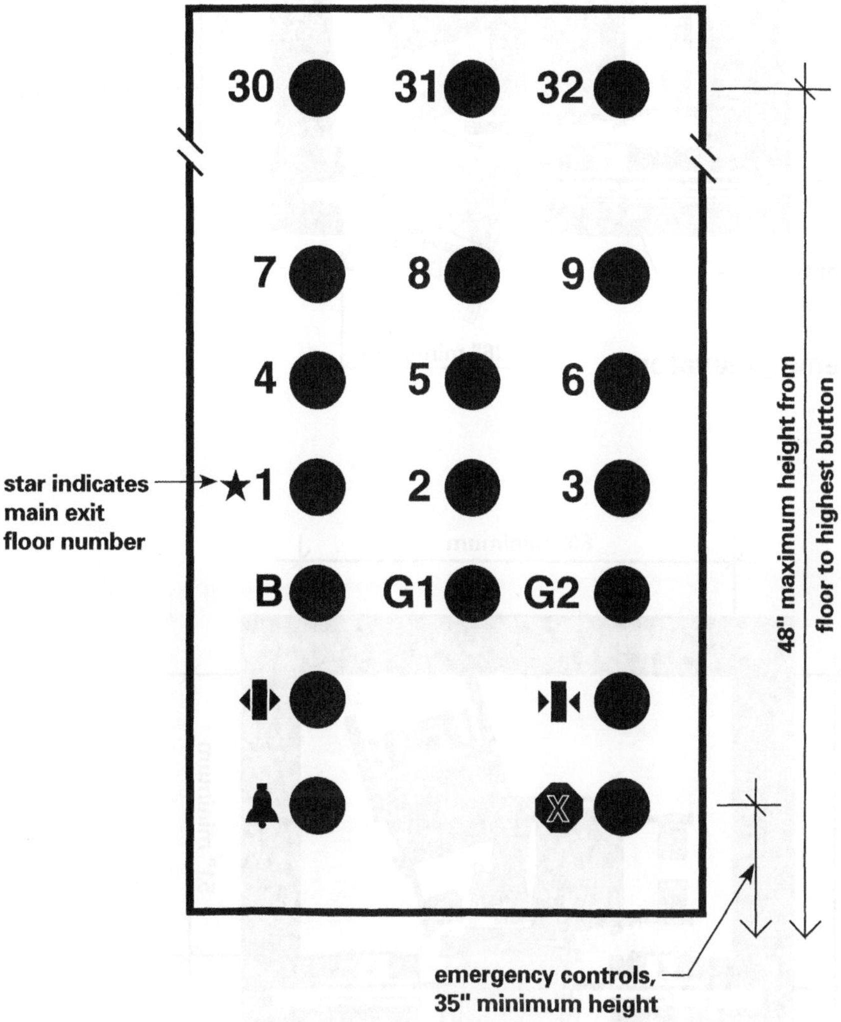

Detail of Car Control Panel

All floor buttons shall be mounted no higher than 48 inches unless there is a substantial increase in cost, in which case the maximum mounting height may be increased to 54 inches. Emergency controls, including the alarm and the stop, shall be grouped at the bottom of the panel with their centerlines no less than 35 inches above the floor. The panels shall be located on the front walls if cars have center opening doors and on the side wall or front wall next to the door if cars have side opening doors.

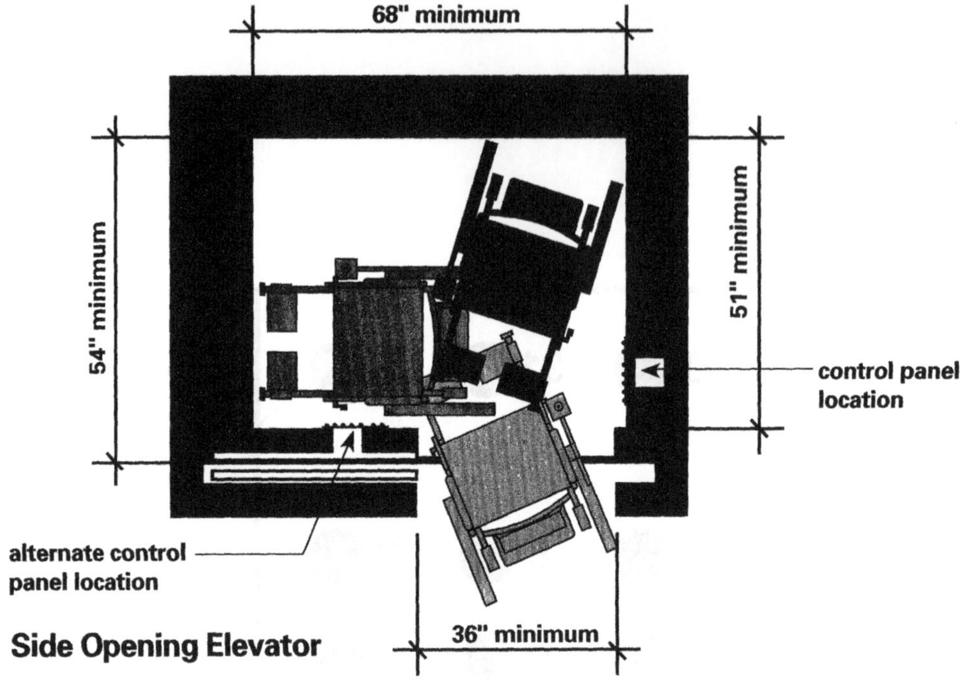

Side Opening Elevator

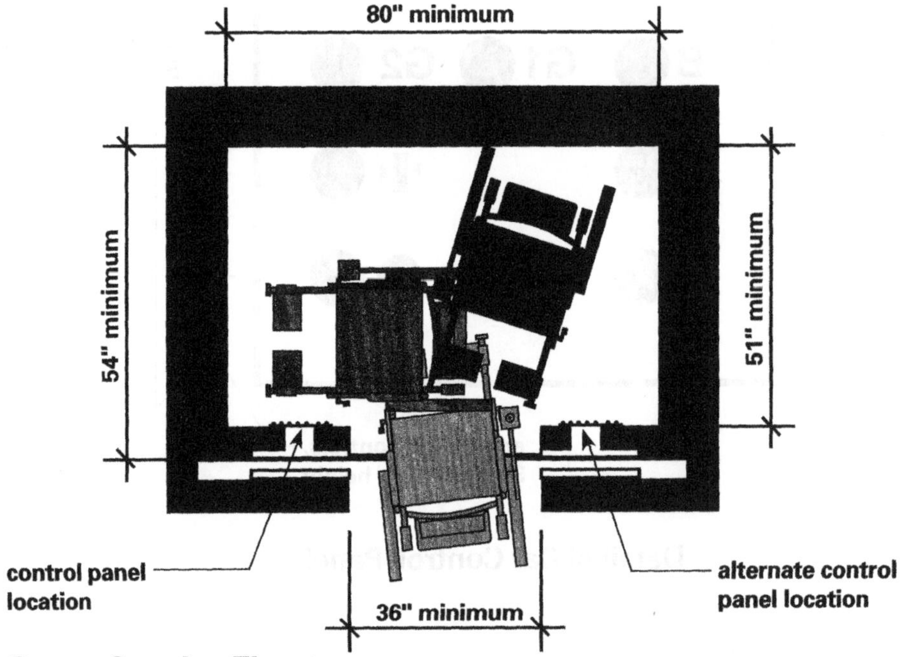

Center Opening Elevator

Maneuvering Space/Approach and Use of Control Panel

Car position indicators provide visual and audible signals/tones indicating the floor level location of the car in the hoistway. Visual indicators shall be located above the control panel or above the door with numerals a minimum of 1/2 inch high. An automatic verbal announcement of the floor number may be substituted for the audible signal.

Emergency communications must be provided between the elevator car and a location outside the hoistway. The system must be mounted no higher than 48 inches from the floor and meet the requirements of 4.27 Controls and Operating Mechanisms, page 45. An emergency system which requires no handset is best. Although the intercommunication system may offer voice communication, it shall not require voice/spoken communication for notification of an emergency.

PROBLEM NON-COMPLYING ELEMENTS IN EXISTING ELEVATOR CAR

SOLUTION RELOCATE, REPLACE, OR INSTALL APPROPRIATE ELEMENTS

If the existing elements do not comply with the requirements, they should be relocated or replaced. If a required feature is not included in the current installation, it should be installed to meet the specifications.

PRACTICAL PLUS

Although not required by UFAS, some codes do require or recommend handrails. Handrails are often included on side and rear walls of elevators to provide passengers with a surface to grasp or lean against while the elevator is in motion. Some people are uneasy or unsteady on their feet and require additional support (particularly on express elevators), while others may use the handrails to support baggage or packages.

REFERENCE INDEX TO UFAS DOCUMENT

ELEVATOR CARS, LOBBIES, AND OPERATING MECHANISMS

INTRODUCTION

Platform lifts are electrically-operated mechanical devices designed to transport a person who cannot use stairs over a short vertical distance. They can be used by wheelchair users and people with limited mobility and are sometimes equipped with folding seats for those not using wheelchairs. Generally they are appropriate for use in low traffic settings where the change of elevation is less than one story and installation of a ramp would be an awkward or impossible alternative.

There are two kinds of platform lifts, vertical lifts and inclined lifts, which can be installed in a variety of situations. Vertical lifts are similar to elevators in that they travel only up and down in a fixed vertical space. Some vertical lifts are also "weatherproof" and can be installed outdoors in unprotected areas. Inclined platform lifts travel along the slope of the stairs. Inclined lifts are useful for installation on long flights of stairs where a vertical platform lift is not practical, where headroom is tight, or ceilings are low. The installation of both vertical and inclined lifts can be designed to be both attractive and safe.

Use of lifts is incorporated in UFAS as an "exception" in cases where elevators, ramps, and other alternatives are not feasible. UFAS does not specify in detail the minimum acceptable features and characteristics of platform lifts although Sections 4.2.4 Clear Floor or Ground Space for Wheelchairs, 4.5 Ground and Floor Surfaces, and 4.27 Controls and Operating Mechanisms are included by reference. UFAS also incorporates the applicable safety regulations of the American National Standard Safety Codes for Elevators, Dumbwaiters, Escalators, and Moving Walks, ANSI A17.1

Some codes limit or prohibit the installation of platform lifts and often include additional requirements for features such as safety enclosures, interlocking gates which prevent anyone from entering the lift area unless the platform is at that level, platform edges and guardrails of a specific dimension, operating controls requiring constant contact (dead man control), keyed operation to limit access, automatic cut-off controls in the event that an obstruction is contacted, a manual override for use in the event of a power failure, a positive locking mechanism which holds the lift in place in the event of a mechanical or power failure, and protection of the space below the lift. In addition, platform lifts may not provide ample space to accommodate three and four wheeled scooters and individuals accompanied by service or guide dogs. Careful research should be conducted to ensure that pre-manufactured devices and recommended installation configurations meet the necessary requirements.

BASIC DESIGN CONSIDERATION

UFAS REQUIREMENTS

As mentioned above, UFAS does not specify in detail the minimum acceptable features and characteristics of platform lifts. However, the sections, 4.2.4 Clear Floor or Ground Space for Wheelchairs, 4.5 Ground and Floor Surfaces, and 4.27 Controls and Operating Mechanisms, which are included by reference, do contain specific requirements which are applicable to platform lifts. UFAS also requires that the lift's design facilitate independent use, including entry and exit. These requirements are described in further detail below.

Clear Floor or Ground Space. The clear floor space, required for use of a platform lift by a person using a wheelchair or other mobility device, must be a minimum of 30 inches by 48 inches and must adjoin an accessible route. Depending upon the type of lift entry/platform, the type of entry gate or door, and the direction of entry/exit in relation to the controls and gate, it may be necessary to provide additional maneuvering clearances appropriate for alcoves, UFAS 4.2.4, page 16, Figure 4(e) and maneuvering clearances at doors, UFAS 4.13.6, page 34, Figure 25. Where the load capacity of the lift allows more than one passenger, use of a larger lift platform will allow an aide to accompany the disabled user, if necessary.

Ground and Floor Surfaces. Use of a platform lift involves crossing a threshold between the existing floor surface, or a "bridge" surface, and the lift platform. The level change at the lift threshold must be less than 1/2 inch and if it is between 1/4 inch and 1/2 inch it must be beveled with a slope of no more than 1:2. The "bridge" and platform surface should be stable, firm, and slip resistant. In some cases, the lift platform (or the "bridge" to the lift platform) is made of a grating material. If it is used, grating should have spaces no greater than 1/2 inch in one direction with elongated openings placed so that the long dimension is perpendicular to the direction of travel.

Controls and Operating Mechanisms. Lift controls and call buttons should be configured to accommodate either a forward or side reach from a wheelchair so that the lift can be used without assistance. Lift controls, whether integral to the lift device itself or placed in a remote (detached) location, must comply with the requirements of UFAS 4.27 Controls and Operating Mechanisms, page 45. The controls must be easy to use with one hand and must not require tight grasping, pinching, or twisting to activate. In addition, lift controls must be placed within the reach ranges specified in UFAS 4.2 Space Allowance and Reach Ranges, page 14.

PROBLEM RAMP AND ELEVATOR CANNOT BE USED TO PROVIDE VERTICAL ACCESS

SOLUTION 1 INSTALL VERTICAL PLATFORM LIFT

If the existing stairs are wide enough, a vertical platform lift can be installed over the stairs by bridging the span between the landing and the elevated lift platform. This bridging technique can be accomplished in several ways depending on permanence of the solution and the desired aesthetics. Local codes should be consulted to ensure that the lift installation does not encroach upon the minimum required exit width.

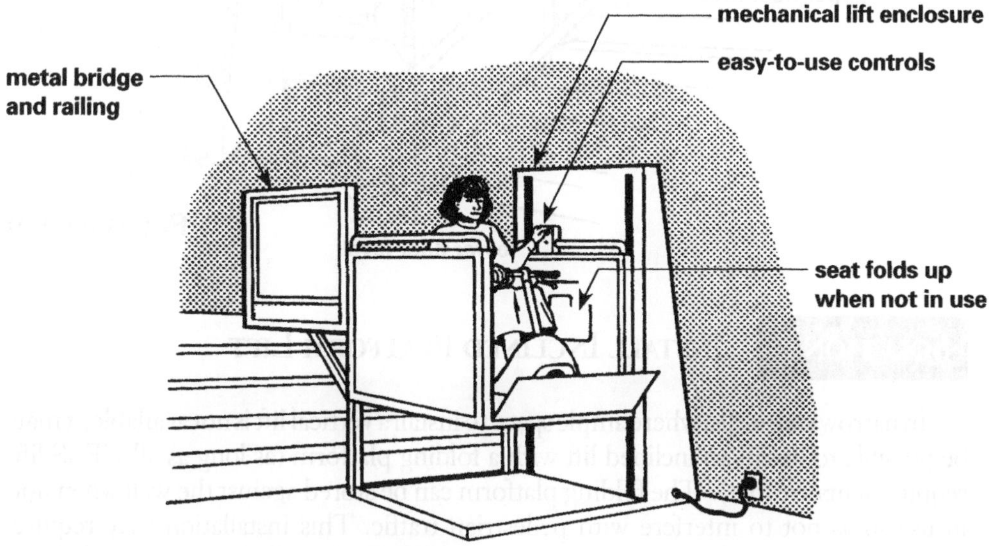

Temporary or Portable Installation

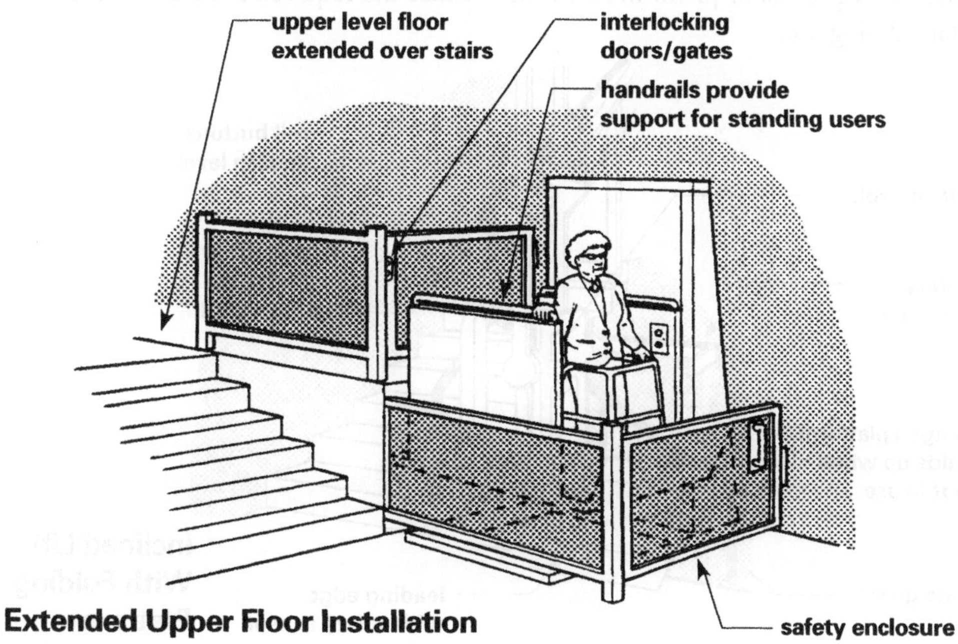

Extended Upper Floor Installation

If space allows and a more permanent solution is desired, a segment of the stairs can be removed and the vertical lift installed in the alcove. A safety enclosure with interlocking doors can protect people from contacting the lift mechanism during operation and improve the aesthetic quality of the installation. Specially designed "weatherproof" vertical platform lifts can be installed outdoors in unprotected areas.

Recessed Lift

SOLUTION 2 INSTALL INCLINED PLATFORM LIFT

In narrow stairwells, where ample space to install a vertical lift is not available, it may be possible to install an inclined lift with a folding platform (as long as all UFAS lift requirements are met). The folding platform can be stored against the wall when not in use so as not to interfere with pedestrian traffic. This installation may require supervised use and/or key operated use since the lift is not installed in a safety enclosure. Some building codes will not allow installation of unenclosed lifts, lifts without interlocking gates, or platform lifts which reduce the required fire exit width of the stairs during use.

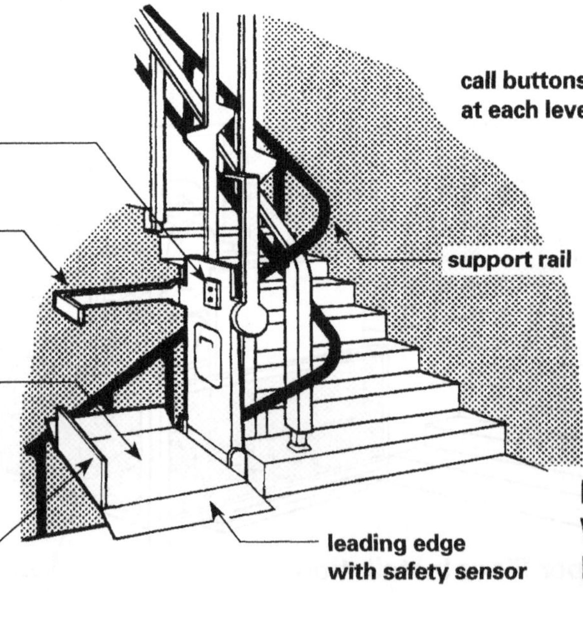

Inclined Lift With Folding Platform

If the stairs are wide enough, it may be possible to install a safety rail or wall to separate the lift path from the pedestrian path. Gates or doors, installed at the top and bottom of the lift enclosure, prevent pedestrians from entering the lift pathway while the lift is in use.

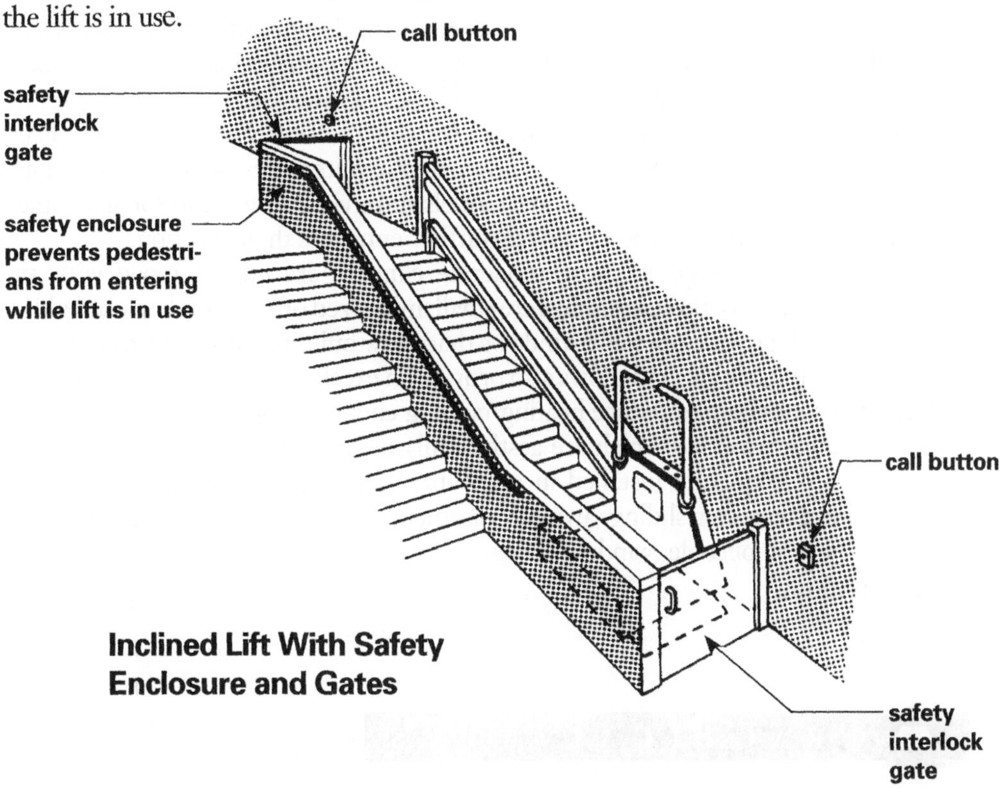

Inclined Lift With Safety Enclosure and Gates

REFERENCE INDEX TO UFAS DOCUMENT

VERTICAL AND INCLINED PLATFORM LIFTS

Primary References	UFAS page	Secondary References	UFAS page
4.11.1 General/Location	33	4.1 Scope & Technical Requirements	6
		4.1.5 Additions	11
		4.1.6(1)(b) Alterations	12
		4.1.7 Historic Preservation	13
		A4.11 General/Location	63
4.11.2 Other Requirements	33	4.2.4 Clear Floor or Ground Space for Wheelchairs	14
		4.5 Ground and Floor Surfaces	22
		4.27 Controls and Operating Mechanisms	45
4.11.3 Entrance	33	4.11.2 Other Requirements	33

WINDOWS

UFAS 4.12

INTRODUCTION

Windows is a reserved topic because research in the design and use of windows had not produced a conclusive set of specifications for "universally usable windows" which could be adopted in the current version of UFAS. However, ANSI A117.1(1986) incorporates requirements for window hardware which will likely be included in UFAS in the next update. Although UFAS has no current requirements for windows, certain features of available windows make some models and styles more usable for all people. Careful installation of easy-to-use models further enhances their function.

Quite often, buildings in more moderate climates are not equipped with air conditioning. Many of these buildings are small, mid-sized office complexes and older structures which provide operable windows that allow building occupants to ventilate the space with outside air. Windows also provide an excellent source for natural light, and thermal panes help to reduce heating/cooling energy costs.

Replacement windows which are aesthetically compatible with various architectural styles are frequently installed in renovations of older buildings. If operable, these windows, whether sliding, awning, casement, or double-hung, should be easy to use. Some applicable window design and installation recommendations are described below.

PRACTICAL PLUS

Although not required by UFAS, there are several performance and human factors specifications described in UFAS which can easily be applied to the design and installation of windows. As with other building elements, windows should be installed on an accessible route with ample clear floor space to allow for a parallel or forward approach. Controls, including cranks and locks, should be within reach and easy to operate.

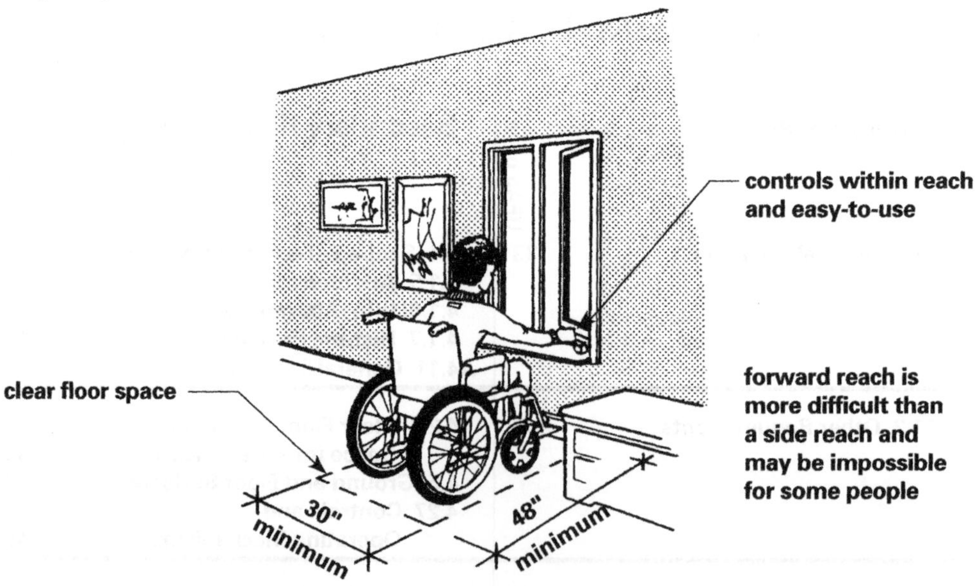

Perpendicular Approach for Forward Reach

Parallel Approach for Side Reach

Easy-to-Use Features

PRACTICAL PLUS

Power window operators are commonly used to control opening and closing of difficult to reach windows. Other devices including electronic locks, crank extensions, auxiliary handles, add-on linkages, and replacement locks can also make window use easier for all people.

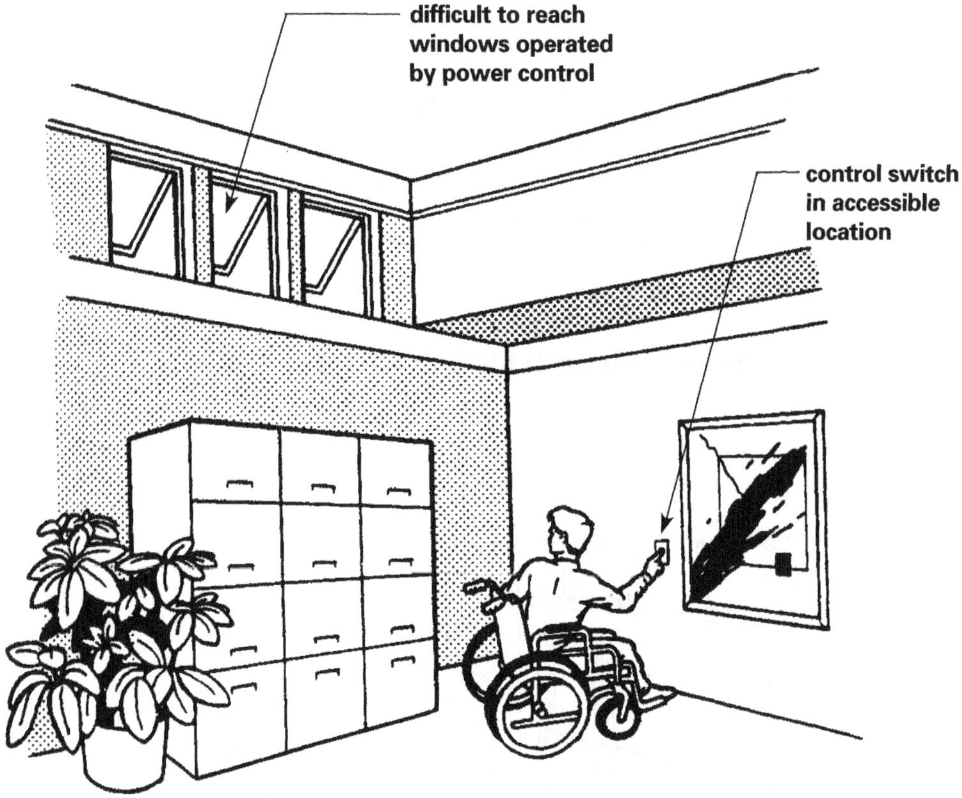

Power Operators Control Hard-to-Reach Windows

PRACTICAL PLUS

Windows can also serve as a means of escape in the event of an emergency. The *Life Safety Code NFPA 101* suggests that windows used for fire/emergency rescue purposes should be a minimum of 20 inches wide, 24 inches high, 5.7 square feet in area, with lower edges no more than 44 inches above the floor. Window sills which are 24 inches or less from the floor and window openings at least 30 inches wide may be more usable to wheelchair users and other people with limited mobility as an assisted means of egress at grade level. At upper levels, lower and larger windows also make it easier for rescue personnel to assist building occupants. If screens are included, they should be easy to remove.

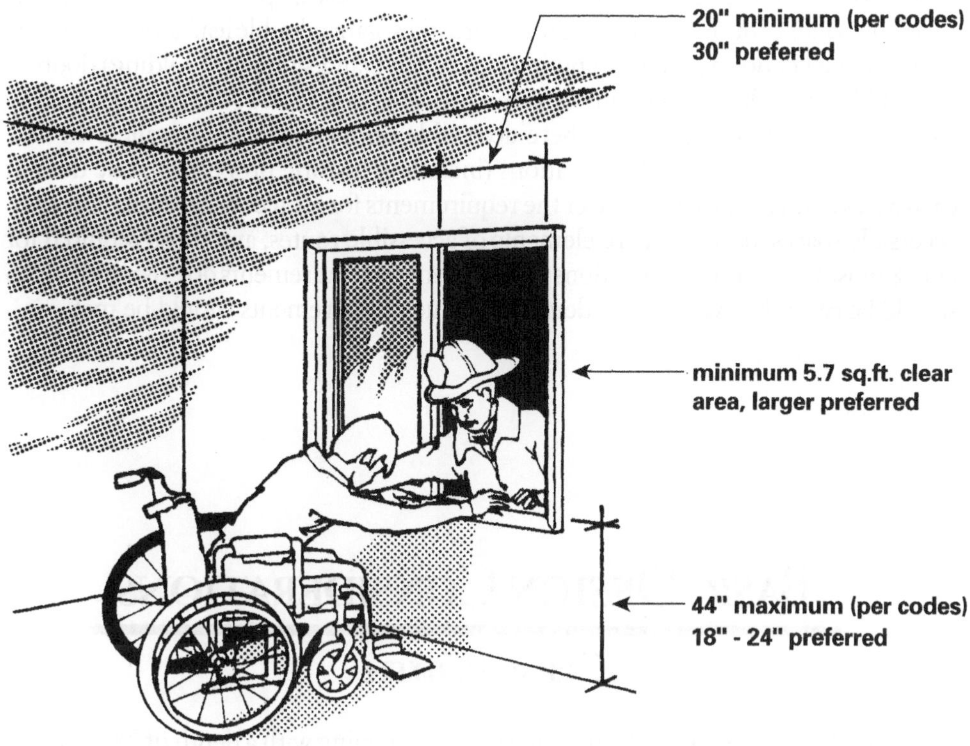

Window as a Means of Egress

INTRODUCTION

The use of a door involves positioning oneself appropriately in relation to the door and manipulating the door to open and pass through it. The location and type of each door involved affects each of these factors. UFAS makes specific reference to the following kinds of doors: revolving doors, turnstiles, gates, double leaf doors, two doors in series, pocket doors, exterior and interior hinged, and sliding (or folding) doors.

In addition to the technical information provided in 4.13, UFAS also provides very specific information regarding where accessible doors should be installed. In new construction, additions, and renovations (including historic properties), one door at each accessible entrance must meet the requirements for an accessible door. Doors to accessible spaces, doors that are elements of accessible routes, and those required for egress must also comply. Exceptions to these general requirements do exist, and UFAS should be carefully examined to determine which requirements should be met.

BASIC DESIGN CONSIDERATIONS

CLEAR WIDTH

As specified in the UFAS document, any door opening with a depth of 24 inches or less must have a minimum clear width of 32 inches (UFAS Figures 24a - 24e, page 33). The 32 inch minimum door opening allows passage of most wheelchairs. Adult wheelchairs vary in width from 27 to 32 inches. Walkers which are approximately 32 inches wide can be accommodated in this door width, and this is also the distance between crutch tips of an average adult male using crutches.

Provision of the minimum 32 inch clear opening usually requires installation of at least a 34 inch wide door. Full 36 inch doors are generally available as stock inventory items and are often less costly than less commonly used 34 inch doors. The 36 inch doors provide ample space for the user's hands and elbows, allow passage through the doorway at an angle, and passage by users of the increasingly popular, and larger power vehicles.

The 32 inch opening is measured from the stop on the door jamb on the latch side to the face of the door when standing open in the 90 degree position. Push bars and panic type hardware may protrude into this space if they are mounted high enough to allow the wide part of the wheelchair to pass below. In alterations, where existing elements prohibit strict compliance with the clearance requirements, a projection of 5/8 inch maximum is permitted on the latch side doorstop (UFAS 4.1.6(4)(d)(i), page 13).

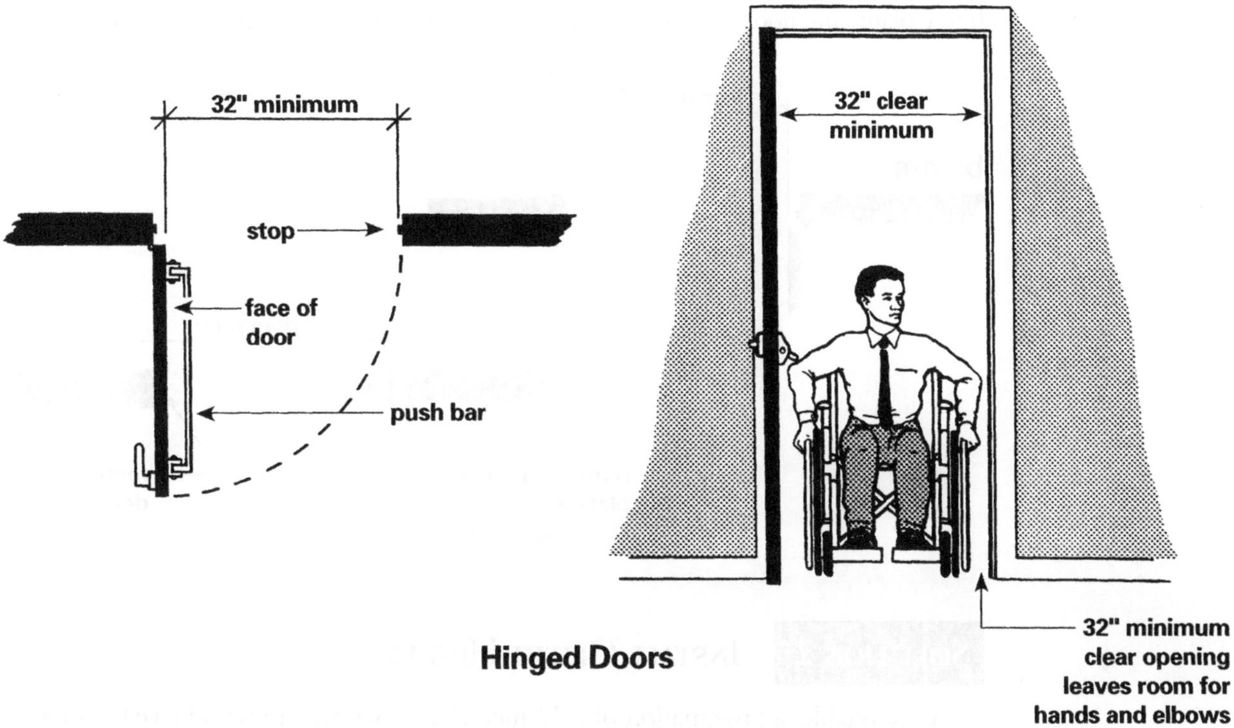

Hinged Doors

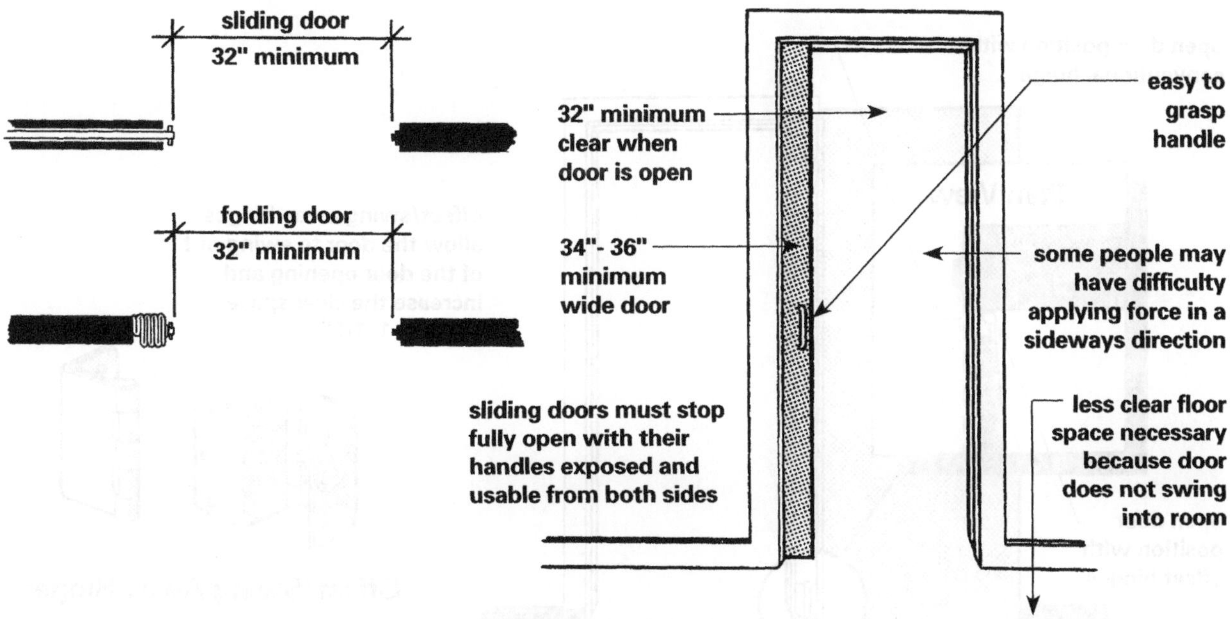

Sliding and Folding Doors

PROBLEM — DOORWAY TOO NARROW

SOLUTION 1 — REMOVE DOOR

Some interior doors can simply be removed to provide a 32 inch clear opening. Fire and security doors cannot be removed. To improve the "look" of this solution, the hinge plates and door stop should be removed and the molding repaired and painted.

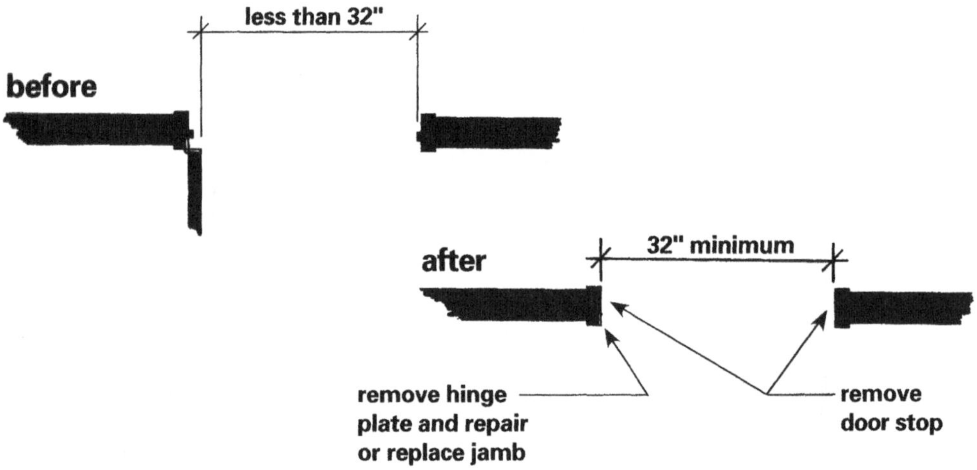

SOLUTION 2 — INSTALL OFFSET HINGES

A reasonable approximation of a 32 inch clear opening can be achieved with an existing 32 inch door by refitting it with offset hinges. Offset hinges allow the door to swing clear of the frame, thereby increasing the usable opening width.

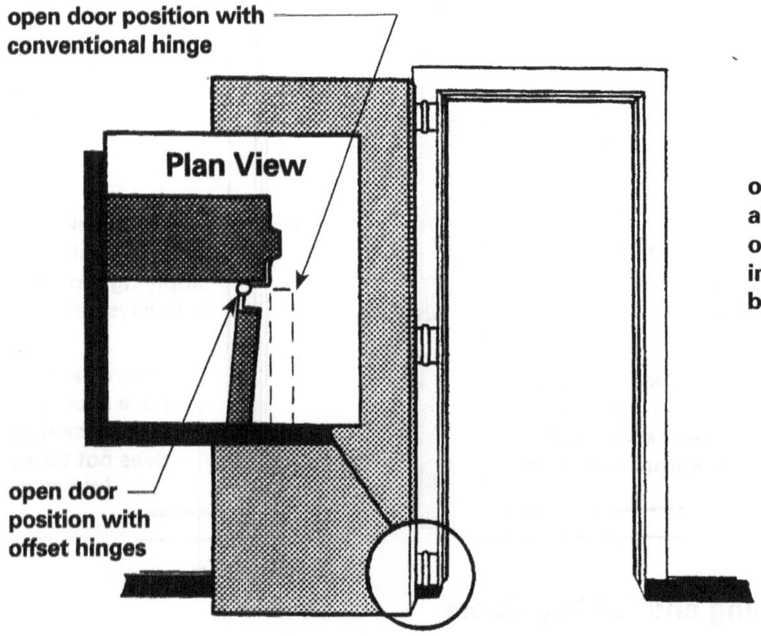

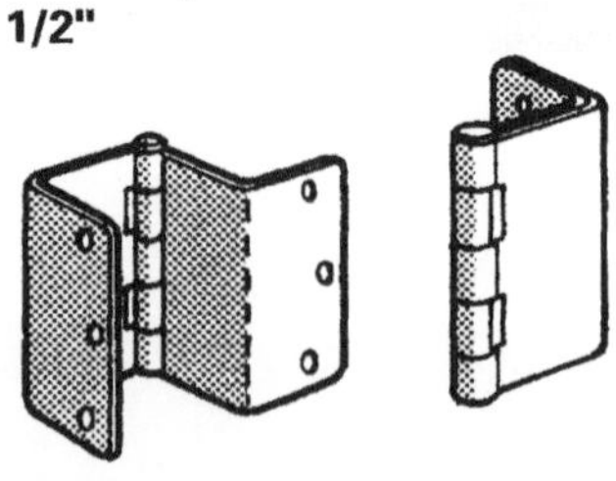

Offset/Swing Away Hinges

SOLUTION 3 INSTALL ALTERNATE DOOR

In some cases, a separate new door can be installed elsewhere in the space to provide access. This alternative may be most practical when a general rerouting of traffic is desired as part of the solution.

SOLUTION 4 DOOR WIDENING/SINGLE LEAF HINGED

Widening of existing doors to provide access varies widely in cost and complexity depending on the type of door, wall material, and location. In some types of construction, it may be possible to achieve the necessary clear opening by removing the stop or reshaping the jamb without cutting the wall.

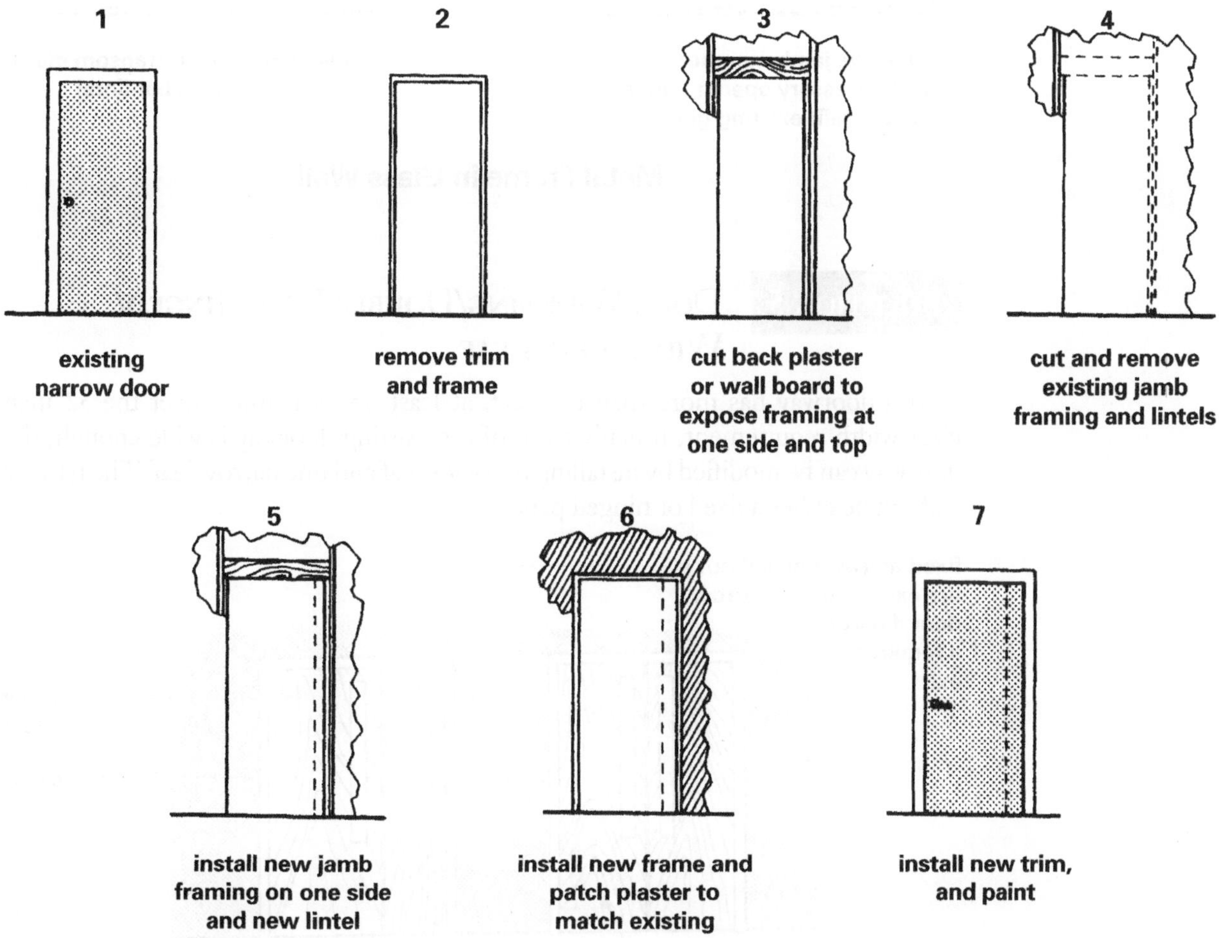

Wood Frame Wall

1

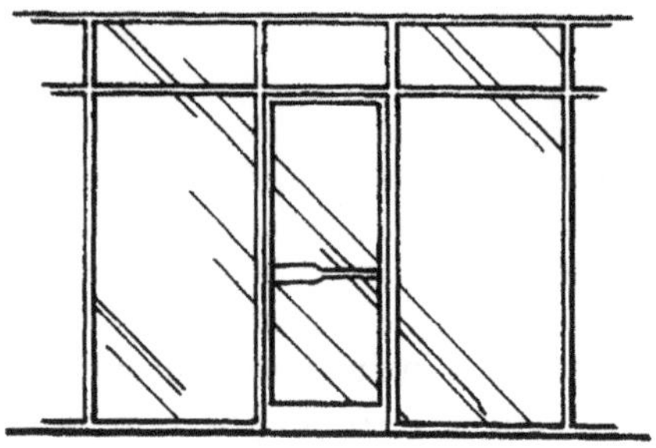

existing narrow door

2

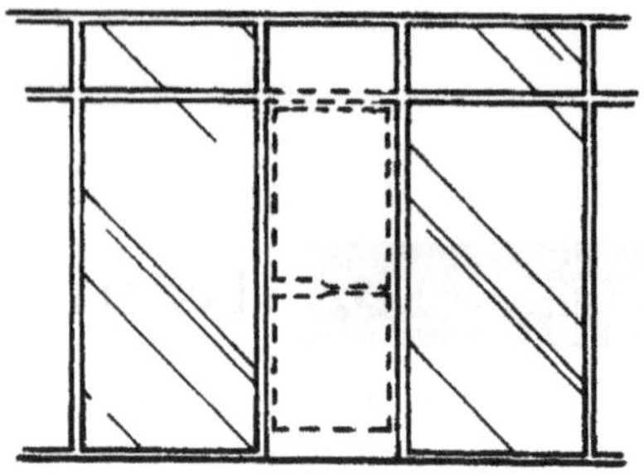

remove door, cross bar, and transom glass

3

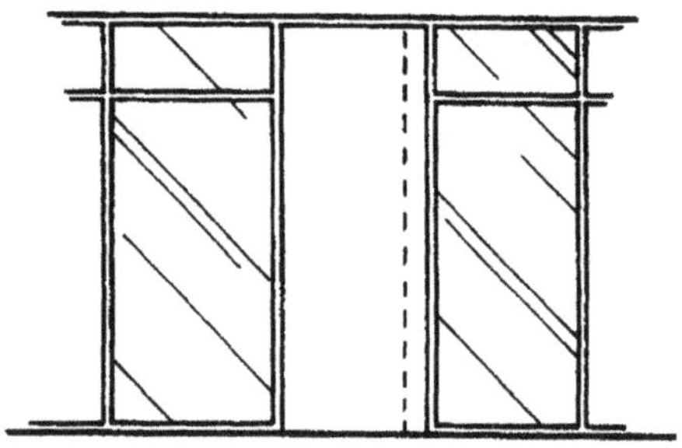

move one jamb member to provide necessary opening, then cut and refit existing glass

4

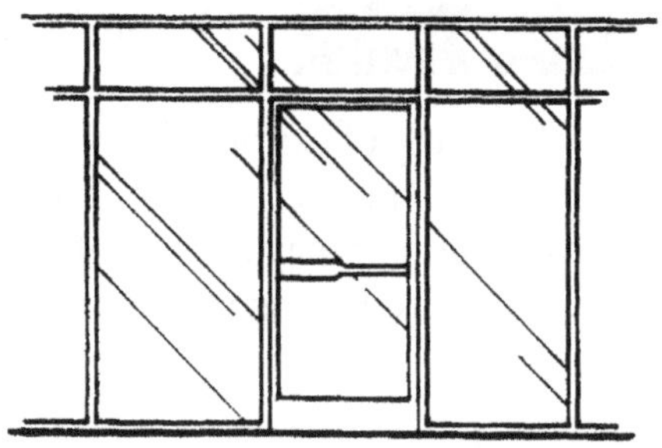

install new door, transom glass, and cross bar lintel

Metal Frame in Glass Wall

SOLUTION 5 DOOR WIDENING/DOUBLE LEAF HINGED/ WIDEN ONE LEAF

If a doorway has more than one leaf, at least one leaf must meet the 32 inch clear width requirement. If neither leaf of the existing doorway is wide enough, the doorway can be modified by installing one wide leaf and one narrow leaf. The narrow leaf can be either a fixed or hinged panel.

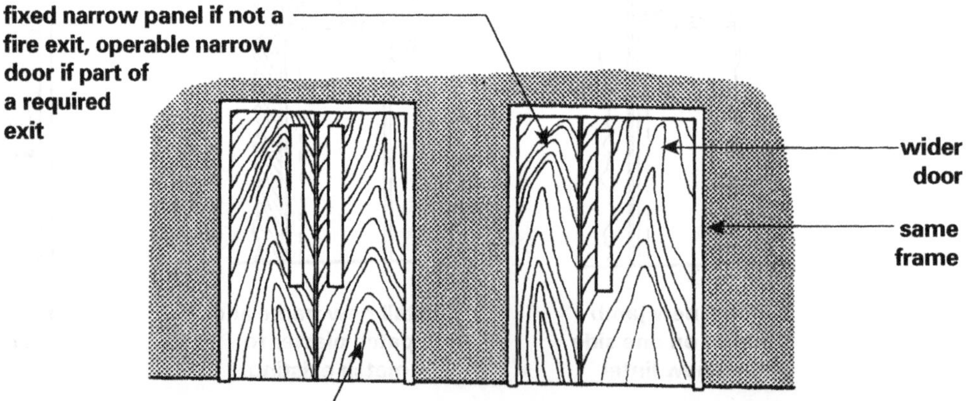

Modified Door With One Wide Leaf and One Narrow Leaf

SOLUTION 6 DOOR WIDENING/DOUBLE LEAF HINGED/ INSTALL AUTOMATIC OPENER

An automatic opener which operates both doors simultaneously can be installed (see Install Automatic Door Operator Solution below). In most cases the existing doors may be used. However, if the existing installation uses a center door stop/mullion, it will need to be removed and the doors reframed.

BASIC DESIGN CONSIDERATIONS

MANEUVERING CLEARANCES

The floor area required to manipulate an element is referred to in UFAS as maneuvering clearance or clear floor space. When referring to doorways, the dimensions and locations of the clear floor space vary with the direction of approach (front or side approach) and with the face of the door being approached (push or pull side). The various dimensions and locations are intended to assure accommodation of maneuvers by wheelchair, walker, and crutch users, or someone with an unsteady gait, while opening and passing through a door– when they are either pushing or pulling the door from front or side approaches.

Space to the side of the door on the pull side is extremely important to many people. People who use wheelchairs, walkers, or crutches often cannot hold onto the door knob and move backward to pull the door open because they use their hands for mobility. Providing space to the side of the door on the pull side allows users to position themselves and their mobility aids out of the path of the door while they pull it open. This is also important in a solid door without a view panel, to prevent users on the pull side from being hit if the door is pushed open from the other side. The clear space to the side of the door on the pull side must be a minimum of 18 inches although 24 inches is preferred.

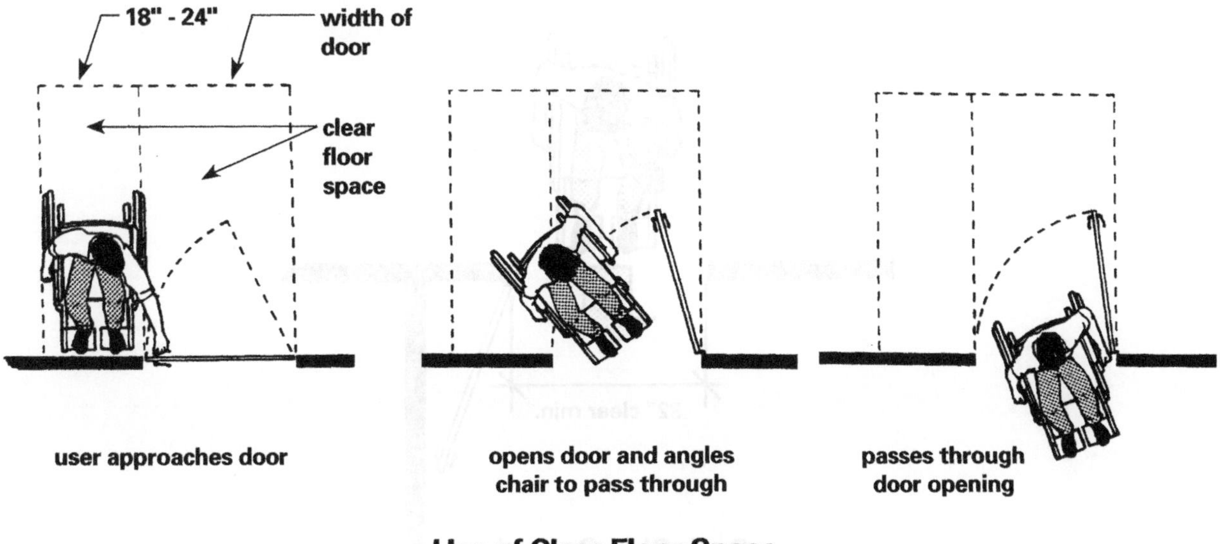

Use of Clear Floor Space

All complying manually-operated doors must have level and clear floor spaces adjoining an accessible route. The clear floor space required for doors to be usable varies with each door configuration. UFAS specifies the minimum acceptable dimensions. However, as a "rule of thumb", a 60 by 60 inch clear floor space on both sides of the door, with the required maneuvering space to the latch side of the doorway, is acceptable. To reduce these dimensions but still ensure sufficient maneuvering space, the designer must comply with the minimum maneuvering clearances (UFAS Figures 25 - 26, page 34-35).

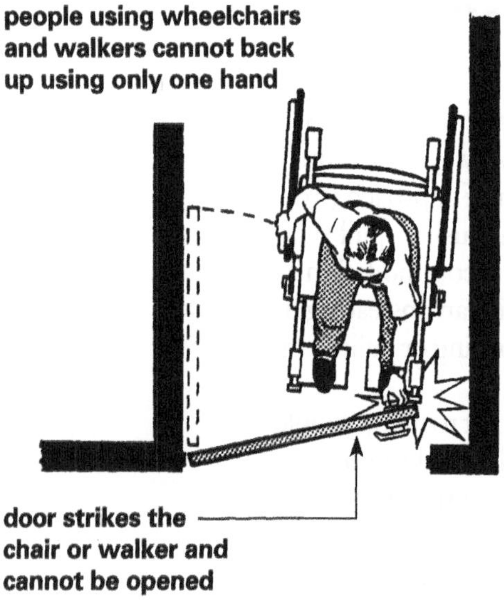

Inadequate Space to the Side of the Door

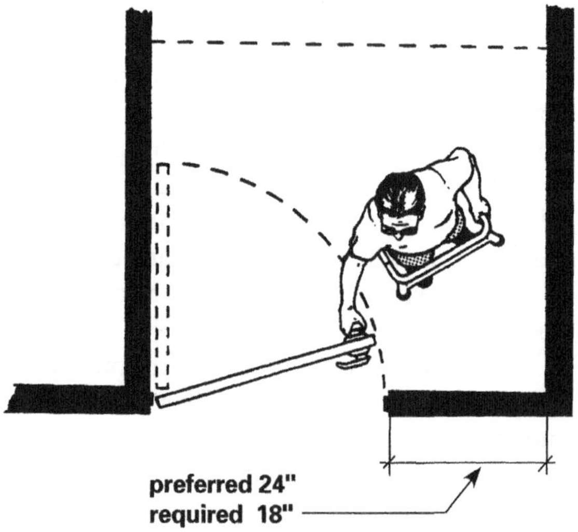

Adequate Space to the Side of the Door

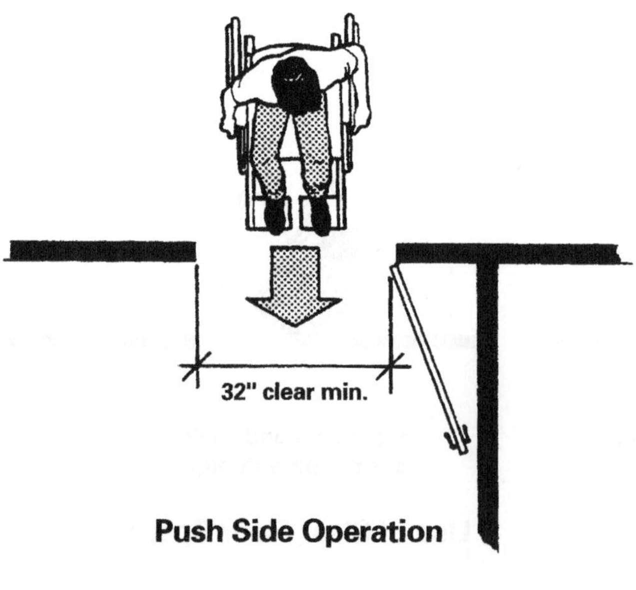

Push Side Operation

PROBLEM INSUFFICIENT CLEAR FLOOR SPACE ON THE PULL SIDE OF THE DOOR

SOLUTION 1 REVERSE THE SWING OF THE DOOR

In some situations, ample clear floor space exists on the push side of the door but not on the pull side where it is required. Reversing the swing of the door takes advantage of the existing clear floor space by allowing it to be used on the pull side. Check local code requirements before reversing the swing of a door used as an exit from a room or building.

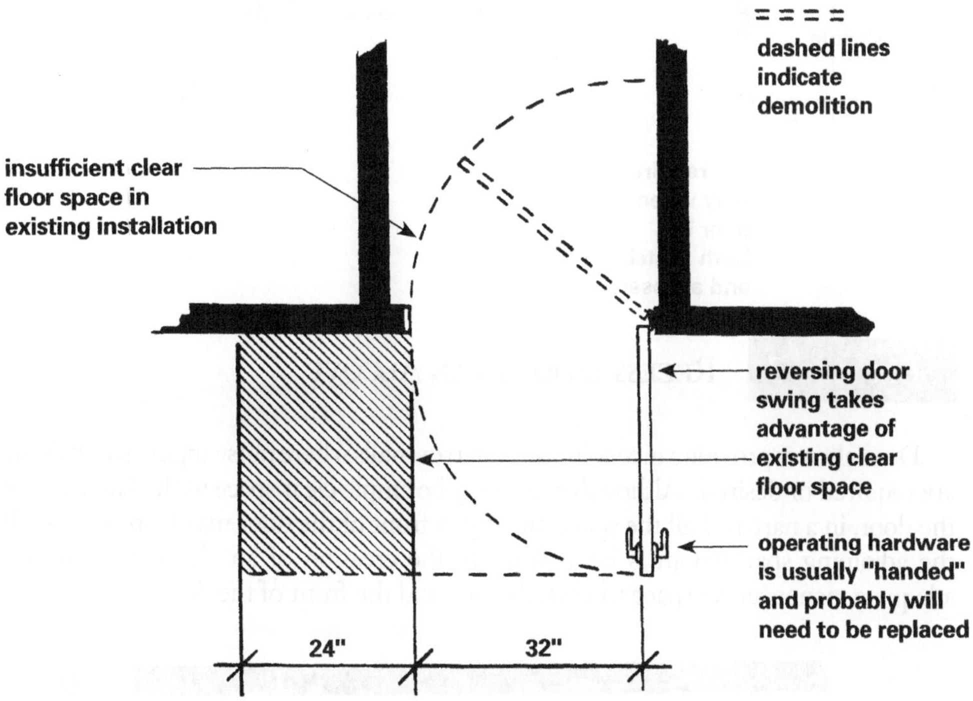

Install a Double Action Door

SOLUTION 2 INSTALL A DOUBLE ACTION DOOR

If insufficient clear space exists to the side of the door on either the push or the pull side, it may be possible to install a double action door. A double action door can be used in the push mode from both sides, eliminating the requirement for 18-24 inch clear space to the side of the door on the pull side. In this situation, windows or sidelights should be installed to ensure the safety of users on either side and eliminate the possibility of being struck by the outswinging door. Local requirements should be checked before implementing this solution at an exit door because most building codes will not allow a double-acting door to be used in this situation.

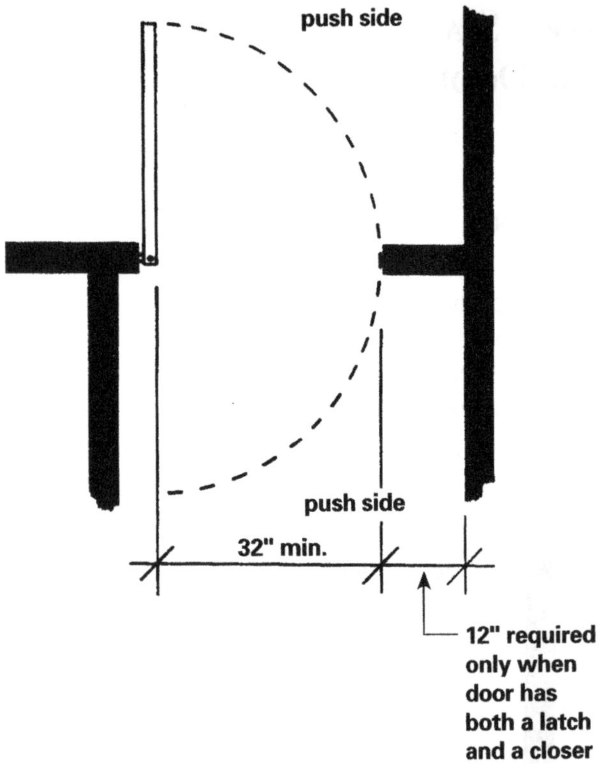

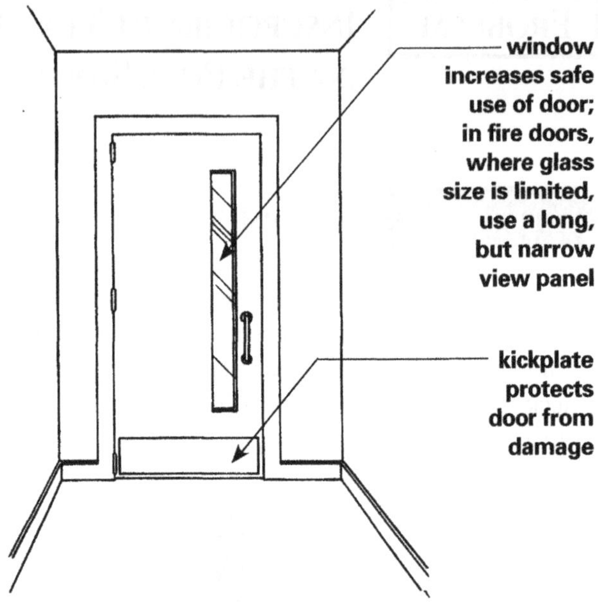

SOLUTION 3 RECESS DOOR IN AN ALCOVE

Door alcoves provide a nice solution in narrow halls where outswinging room doors are required or desired. Although there may be ample clear space to the latch side of the door, in a narrow hall the space directly in front of the door may be too small. If the adjoining space/room is large enough, the creation of an alcove can provide adequate maneuvering space to both the side and the front of the door.

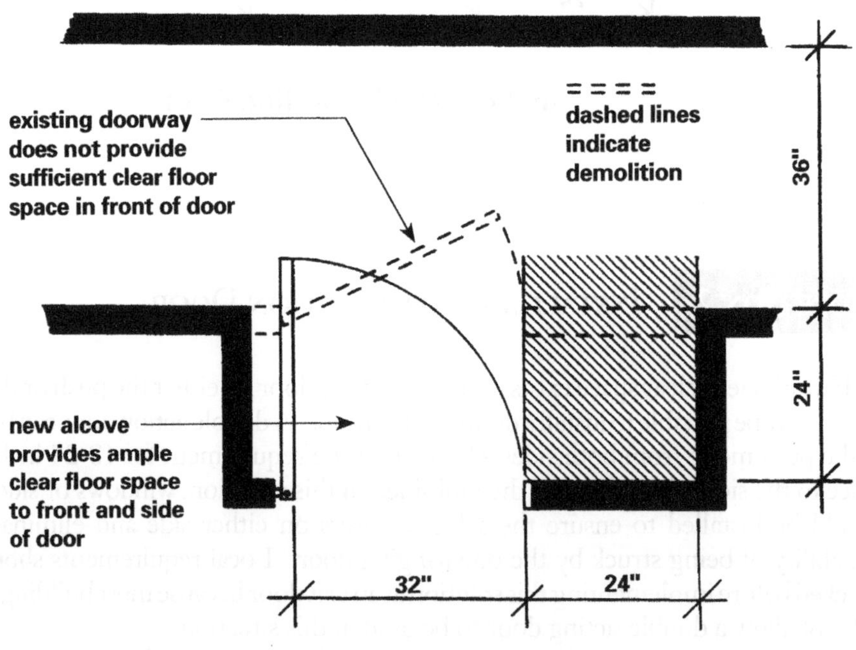

SOLUTION 4 NARROW ALCOVE/REVERSE DOOR SWING OR WIDEN ALCOVE

If an existing door opens into a narrow alcove, rehang the door to swing in the opposite direction. As an additional safety measure, a window could be cut into the door so users on the push side can avoid bumping a person approaching from the other side. The existing alcove could also be widened to provide clear floor space to the side and eliminate the need to reverse the door swing.

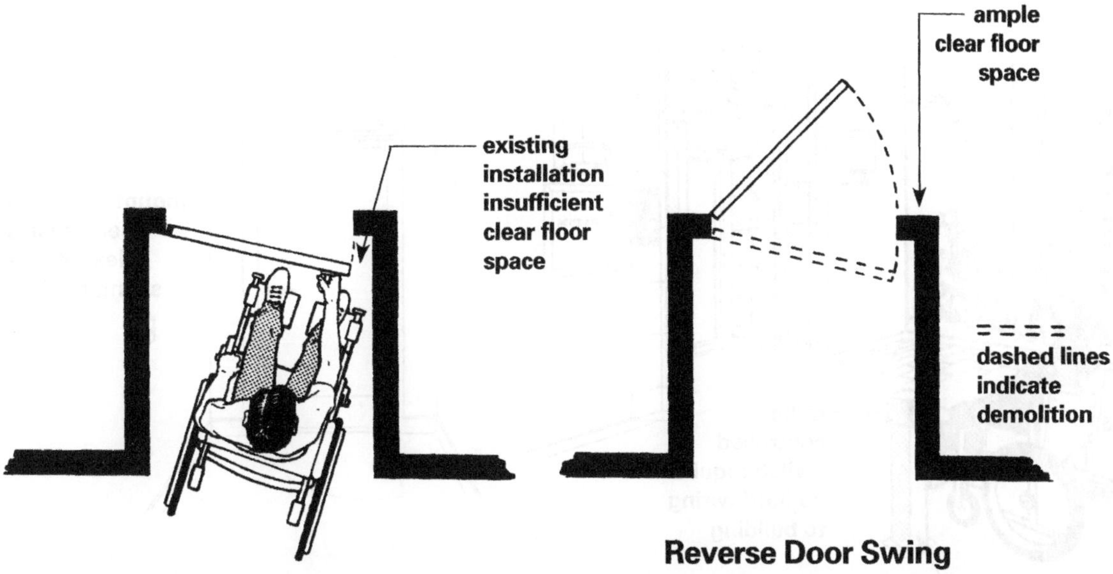

Reverse Door Swing

SOLUTION 5 INSTALL LOW-FORCE OR FULL-POWER AUTOMATIC DOOR OPERATOR

When maneuvering space to the side of the door is not adequate, a low-force or full-power door operator can be used, in lieu of maneuvering space, to provide access to both interior and exterior doors. A properly installed low-force or full-power operator eliminates the requirement for clear floor space on the pull side of the door. Assuming the door width is adequate, this solution can eliminate the need for costly modifications to doors and entrances. Full-power doors are more expensive and may require more space for the control mats and sensing devices (see Installation of Full-Power Door Opener Solution later in this section).

Low-force power doors move very slowly in the power mode and therefore, do not require the space consuming safety features necessary for full-power doors. To activate the power mode, the user presses a switch which causes the door to open slowly with little force and then to close automatically. If something obstructs the movement of the door, the door stops or reverses, thus eliminating the need for safety mats and sensing devices. The door also functions as a manually-operated door for users who do not activate the power switch. A low-power operator can be installed to operate existing door(s) if they are wide enough.

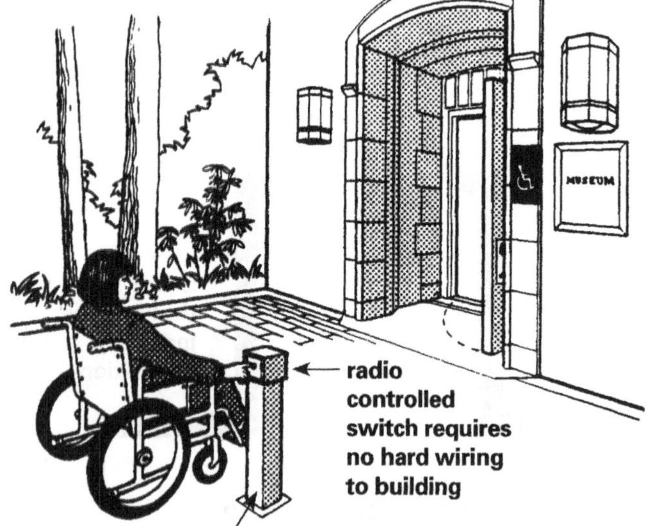

Exterior Door

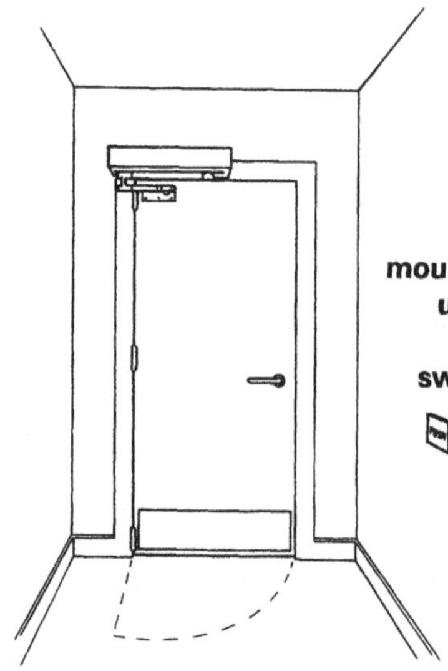

Interior Door

BASIC DESIGN CONSIDERATIONS

FORCE REQUIRED TO OPEN DOORS

Many disabled and older people and children cannot operate a door requiring a sustained force of more than 5 lbf. For this reason, UFAS specifies that interior or sliding doors should not require more than 5 lb. of force to open. Fire doors are an exception to this requirement. No force minimums have been established for exterior doors because the 5 lb. force is often too little to hold a door closed against the counter forces of wind pressures, or the pressures created by ventilation and air conditioning systems.

Door closers are often required to close doors completely in buildings where breezes and drafts would otherwise hold them open. Unfortunately, the force of a door closer must be overcome when opening a door. Large heavy doors pose similar problems which must be overcome.

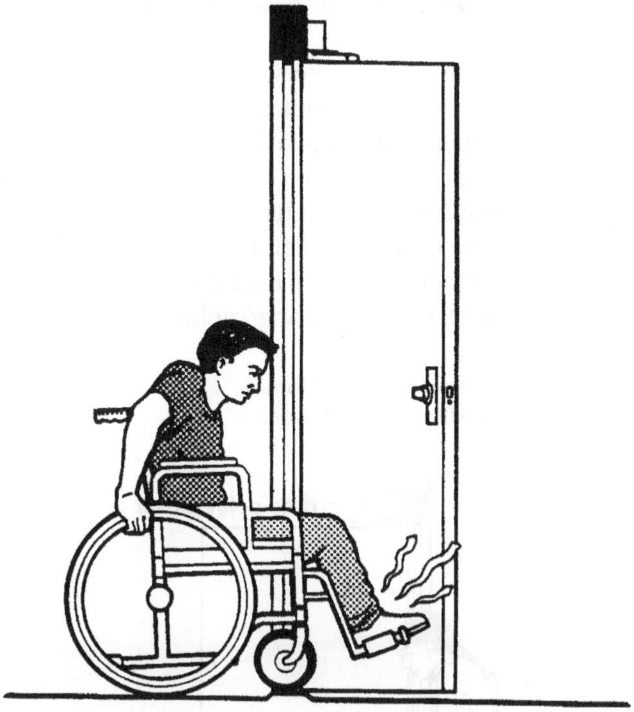

pressure of door against bumper of chair pushes chair backwards

Heavy Doors/Difficult Closers

PROBLEM TOO MUCH FORCE REQUIRED TO OPEN DOORS

SOLUTION 1 ADJUST/REMOVE EXISTING CLOSER OR INSTALL NEW CLOSER

Some closers are adjustable, and a simple adjustment may greatly improve their use. Often, closers on interior doors are not really necessary and may be removed without compromising the use of the space. If a closer is necessary and the existing installation is non-adjustable, it can be replaced with an adjustable type.

PRACTICAL PLUS

Time delay closers offer an additional assist for difficult doors. Some users, although they cannot sustain 5 lbf. of pressure, can apply that force initially to push/pull a door open by bracing themselves against the adjoining wall. The time delay closer then holds the door open long enough for users to collect themselves and pass through without having to hold the door open in the process. Time delay closers may be installed in lieu of low pressure closers and are useful on both interior and exterior doors. When used on exterior doors, time delay closers are best if included at vestibules where heating/cooling losses can be minimized.

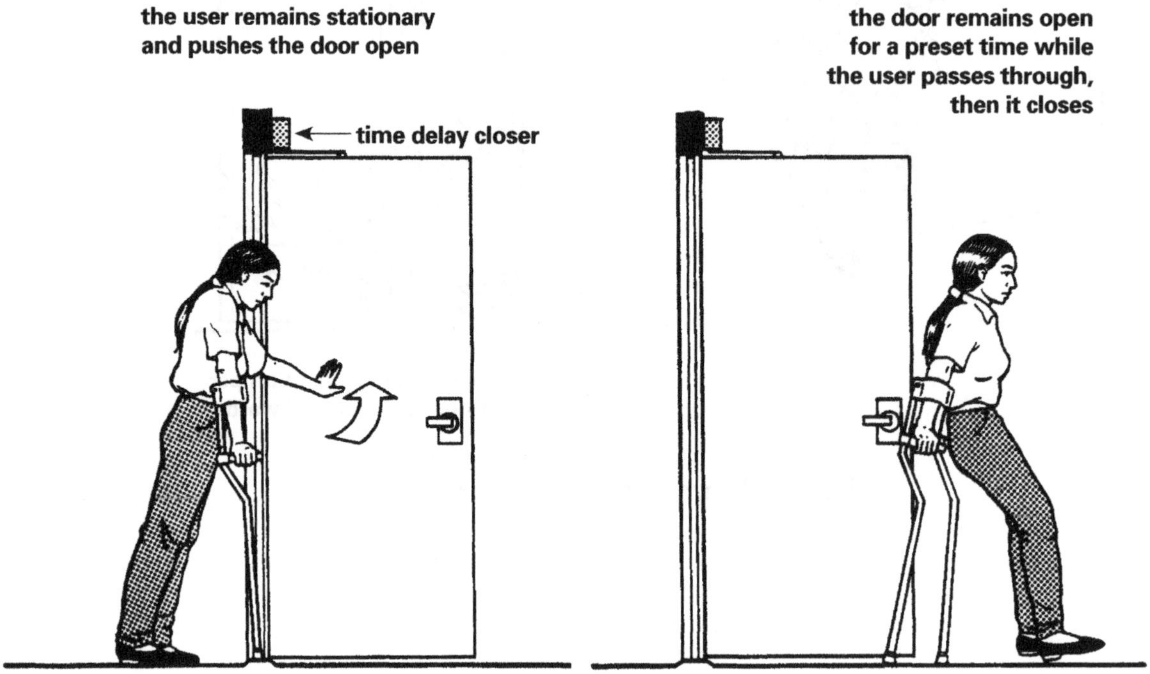

Use of Time Delay Closer

PRACTICAL PLUS

Fire doors are excluded from the UFAS door opening force requirements but are still required to meet the minimum opening force allowable by the appropriate administrative authority. This minimum allowable force may still cause access problems for disabled users. Electromagnetic fire door holders, if allowed by the administrative authority, may alleviate the access problems by holding the doors in the open position during general daily use.

SOLUTION 2 INSTALL POWER-ASSISTED DOOR OPENER

Power-assist door openers help heavy and difficult doors meet the requirement to provide doors which can be opened with little force. This solution is particularly useful in historic structure renovations because the original doors can be used. Power-assisted doors use pneumatic or hydraulic pressure to release the closing pressure while the user is opening the door. The user controls the opening of the door by providing some minimal force but is relieved of the requirement to provide all of the force necessary to open the door. Often the "assist" needs to be activated by the user by pressing a button near the door handle. Adequate clear floor space must be provided when using this solution because the user must still be able to approach and operate the door.

SOLUTION 3 INSTALL LOW-FORCE OR FULL-POWER DOOR OPENER

Low-force door openers, described earlier in this section, are also useful for overcoming the obstacles created by heavy doors or doors which require closers. Full-power automatic door openers, although not required by UFAS, are frequently used in commercial applications to facilitate use of doors, especially in high traffic areas, and are usually appreciated by everyone. Sliding automatic doors are often safer than swinging automatic doors, particularly for use by people with visual impairments who may not be able to detect a door swinging toward them. Swinging automatic doors can be made safe if space is available to install the necessary guard rails and safety mats. However, activating mats are only one method of activating a powered door. Other options include infrared sensors, and photo cells.

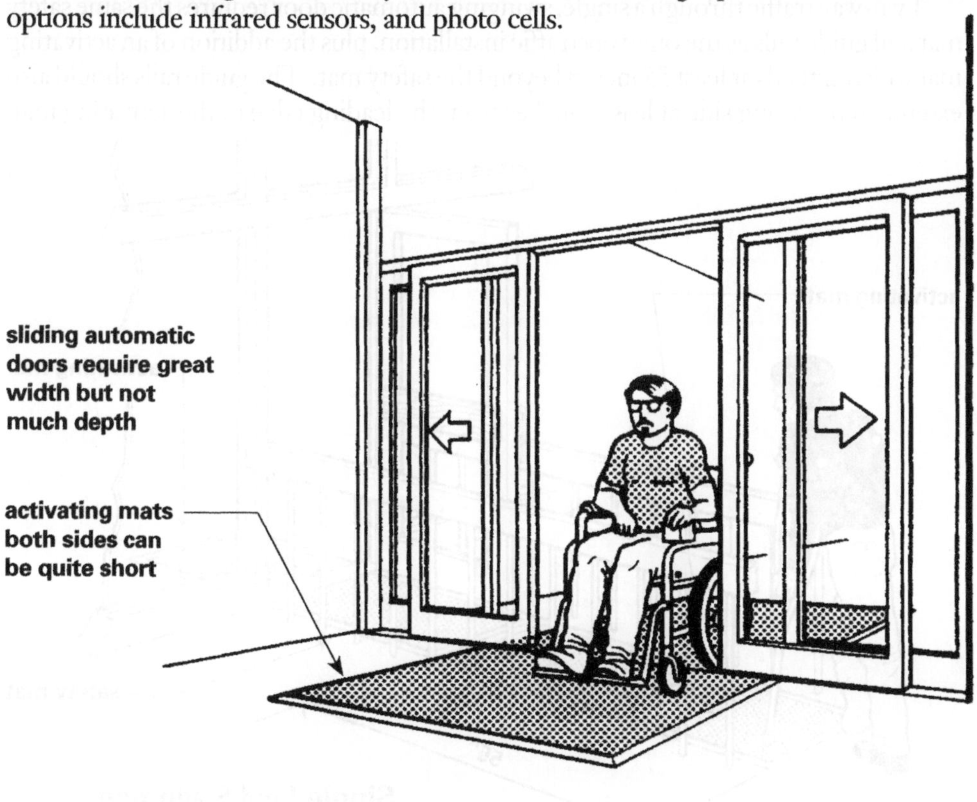

Sliding Automatic Doors

A single, swinging automatic door may be used for both one-way and two-way traffic. If traffic is designated as one-way only, the installation will require a safety mat on the swing side to prevent operation if someone is standing within the door swing area. Standards require that safety mats be narrower than the door width and at least five inches longer than the door width. Guide rails prevent people from approaching from the side of the safety mat where they would be struck by the moving door.

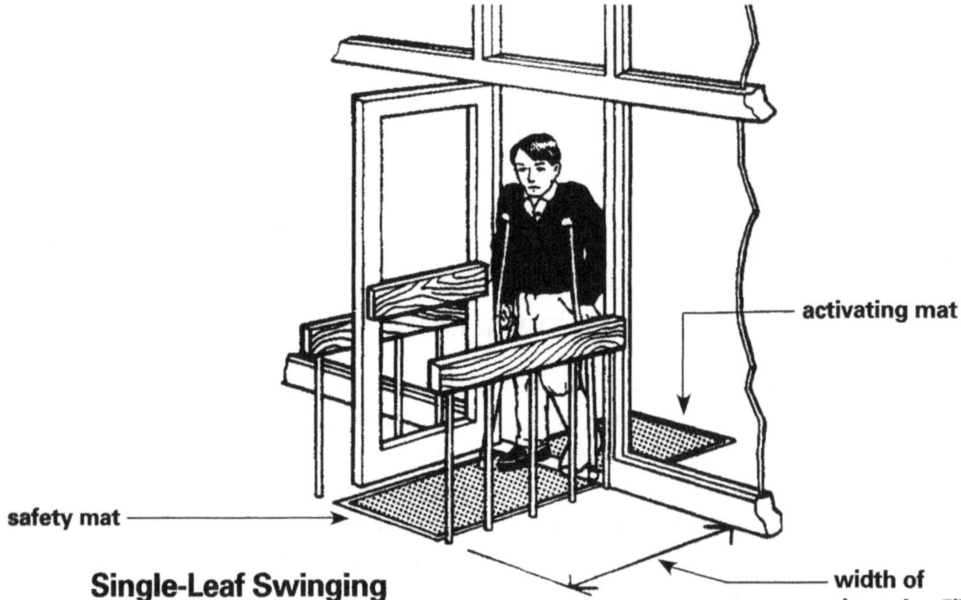

Single-Leaf Swinging Automatic Door (One-Way Traffic)

Two-way traffic through a single, swinging automatic door requires the same safety mat and guide rails as the one-way traffic installation, plus the addition of an activating mat which extends at least 55 inches beyond the safety mat. The guide rails should also extend on the swing side at least 5 inches from the leading edge of the activating mat.

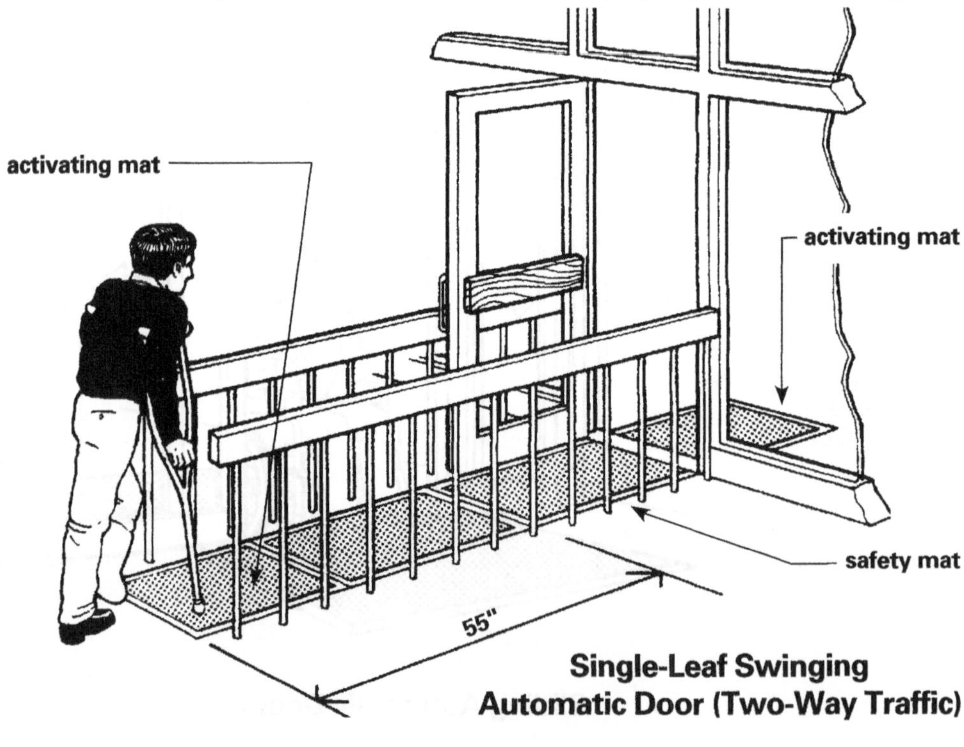

Single-Leaf Swinging Automatic Door (Two-Way Traffic)

In retrofit situations, existing power doors should be evaluated to ensure that they comply with current operational standards (refer to American National Standard for Power-Operated Doors, ANSI A156.10).

BASIC DESIGN CONSIDERATIONS

DOORS IN SERIES

Two doors used in a series to form an air lock or privacy vestibule can be a potential trap for wheelchair users. If the vestibule is too small and proper maneuvering space is not provided, wheelchair users may not be able to open the second door and get out of the vestibule. For this reason, the clear floor space requirements apply to each door separately for doors in a series.

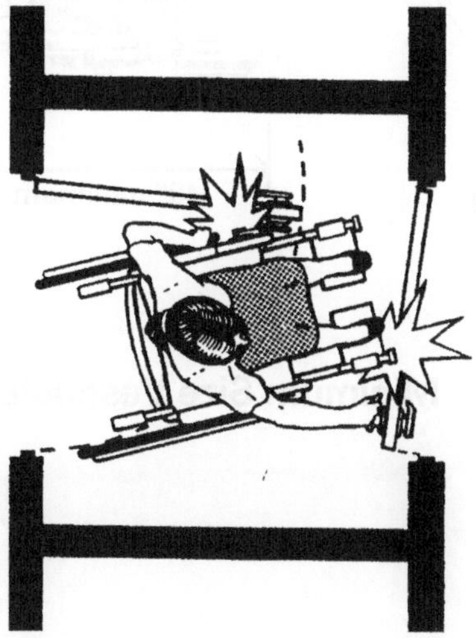

after maneuvering to get around the first door, the user cannot open the second door

Inadequate Space in Vestibule

A vestibule can be as small as 48 inches provided both doors swing out of the vestibule (UFAS Figure 26, page 35). This configuration prevents wheelchair users from becoming trapped because both doors can be pushed open from inside the vestibule. However, under most codes, such a vestibule cannot be used as a fire exit because one door swings against the flow of traffic.

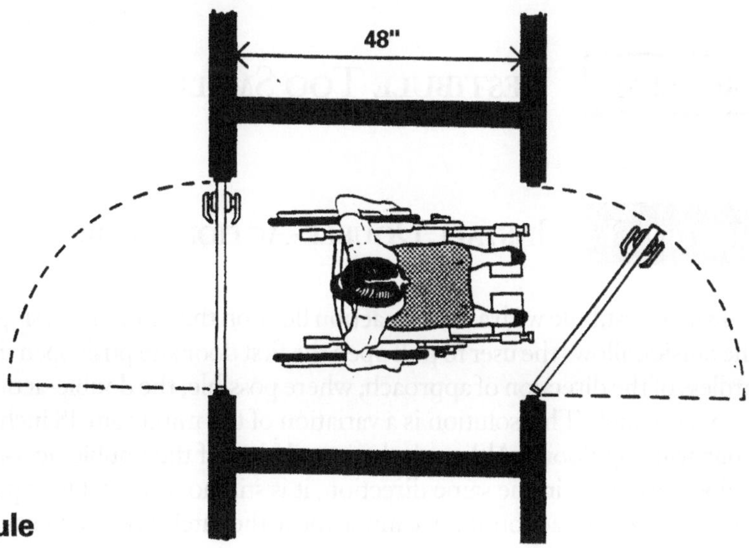

not acceptable as fire exit

both doors swing out

Minimum Size Vestibule

If both doors swing in the same direction, the vestibule must be at least 48 inches plus the width of any door swinging into the vestibule.

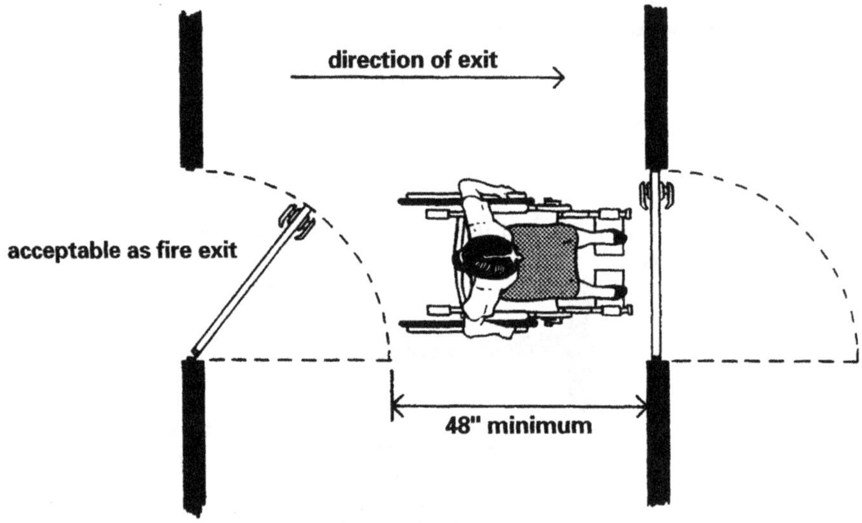

Minimum Size Vestibule

PROBLEM — VESTIBULE TOO SMALL

SOLUTION 1 — INSTALL DOUBLE-ACTION DOOR

A 48 inch vestibule with a double-action door on the inside and a single-action door on the outside allows the user to pull open the first door and push open the second door regardless of the direction of approach; where possible, the double-action door should have a view panel. This solution is a variation of the minimum 48 inch vestibule with two outswinging doors. Although the installation of the double-action door permits both doors to swing in the same direction, it is still not acceptable as part of a fire exit because the double-action door cannot meet the latch requirements for fire doors.

However, this solution may be useful in locations such as entries to group toilet rooms where the double-action door serves a different function.

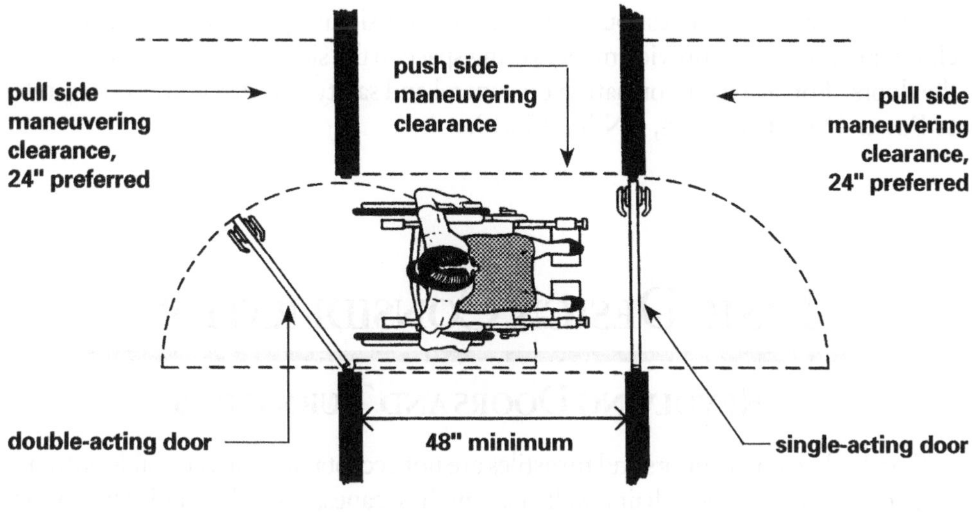

Alternate Small Vestibule
not acceptable as fire exit

SOLUTION 2 OFFSET DOOR IN AN EXISTING WIDE VESTIBULE

In an existing vestibule where width but not depth is available, offset doors and maneuvering clearances may provide a space saving alternative. Maneuvering clearances to the side of each door are determined by the direction of approach. If the primary approach is from the side rather than the front, additional clearance to the side of the door is required (UFAS Figure 25, page 34).

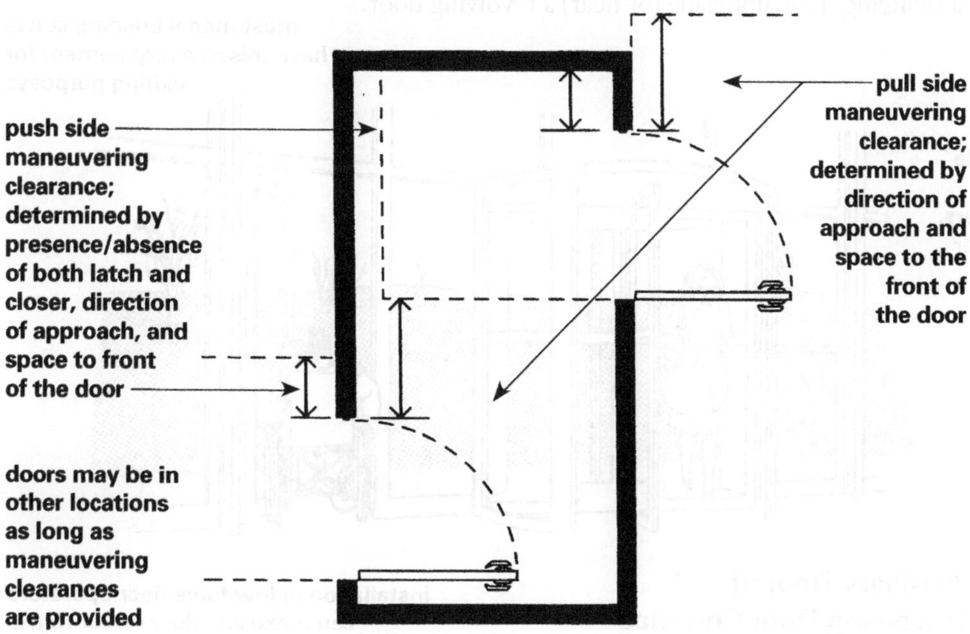

SOLUTION 3 INSTALL POWER DOOR OPERATOR

In an existing, small vestibule, installation of a sliding power door and operator eliminates the need to provide maneuvering space to the side of the doors and between the doors. For specific information on control and safety mats for power doors, refer to Power Operated Doors, ANSI A156.10.

BASIC DESIGN CONSIDERATIONS

REVOLVING DOORS AND TURNSTILES

Standard revolving doors and turnstiles are not acceptable as an accessible entrance for people who use wheelchairs, walkers, crutches, canes, and other mobility devices.

PROBLEM REVOLVING DOOR AT ENTRANCE

SOLUTION 1 INSTALL AUXILIARY DOOR

An auxiliary door installed in close proximity to the revolving door provides an alternate means of entry and exit. This doorway must include appropriate maneuvering spaces in front of and to the side of the door to allow independent use by mobility impaired users. The auxiliary door also provides convenient entry/exit for people using handcarts, pushing strollers, and carrying bulky packages. Many building codes require a swinging door alongside (or near) a revolving door.

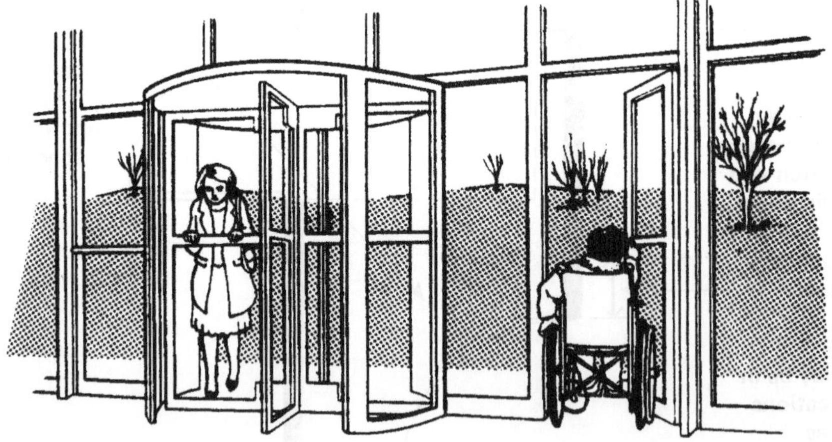

Auxiliary Door at Revolving Door Entrance

SOLUTION 2 INSTALL ACCESSIBLE REVOLVING DOOR

A relatively recent addition to the market are revolving doors which are accessible by UFAS requirements. These doors are approximately 12'+ in diameter and have three, rather than four leaves. "Longitudinal" revolving doors, sometimes called moving vestibules, are also available. The accessible revolving doors have enhanced safety features, heating and cooling loss controls, security options, and are motor driven to eliminate the requirement for the user to push the door around. However, because they are power driven, they pose a hazard to people who walk or move slowly or who have poor balance. Use of these revolving doors appears to require a degree of coordination not possible for some mobility impaired people. If the existing doors are to be replaced and space is adequate, then this solution may be viable. Accessible revolving doors may not necessarily be used in lieu of the auxiliary/hinge-type doors which are frequently required by life safety/fire codes for the provision of emergency egress.

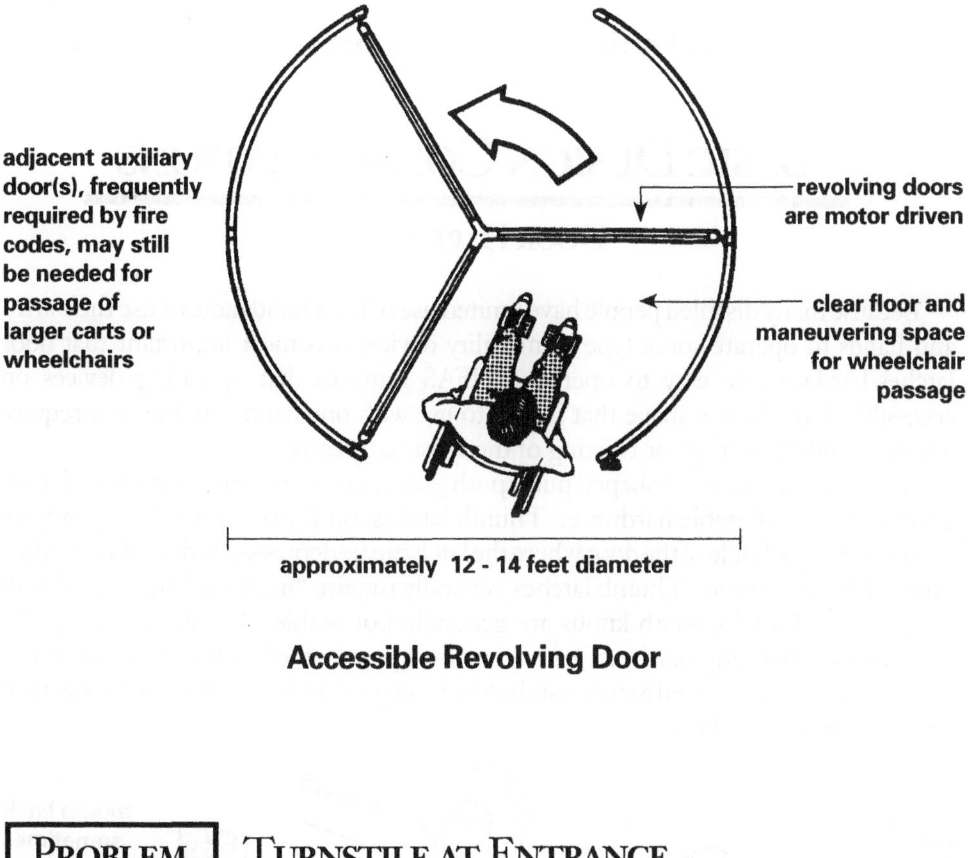

Accessible Revolving Door

PROBLEM TURNSTILE AT ENTRANCE

SOLUTION INSTALL AUXILIARY GATE OR REPLACE WITH ACCESSIBLE TURNSTILE

An auxiliary gate or accessible turnstile installed in close proximity to a traditional turnstile provides an alternate means of entry and/or exit. This gate should provide appropriate maneuvering spaces in front of and to the side of the latch to allow independent use by mobility impaired users.

If traffic control is required at the turnstile, electronically-operated auxiliary gates which serve this purpose can be installed. In some cases, security cameras/monitors and guards may need to be stationed nearby to control use of the gate.

Install Auxiliary Gate at Turnstile

BASIC DESIGN CONSIDERATIONS

DOOR HARDWARE

Because many disabled people have limited use of their hands and/or use their arms and hands to operate some type of mobility device, it is most important that door latches/hardware be easy to operate. UFAS requires that operating devices on accessible doors have a shape that is easy to use with one hand and does not require grasping, tight pinching, or twisting of the wrist to operate.

Lever handles, large U-shaped pulls, push plates, push bars, and toggle handles are good examples of usable hardware. Thumb latches, on the other hand, may only be usable on the push side of the door where the latch can be depressed and the door pushed open with one motion. Thumb latches generally require "pinching" and are difficult to operate. Round smooth knobs are generally not usable. On sliding doors, the handles and operating hardware must remain exposed whether the door is open or closed. Hardware required for accessible door passage must be mounted no higher than 48 inches above the floor.

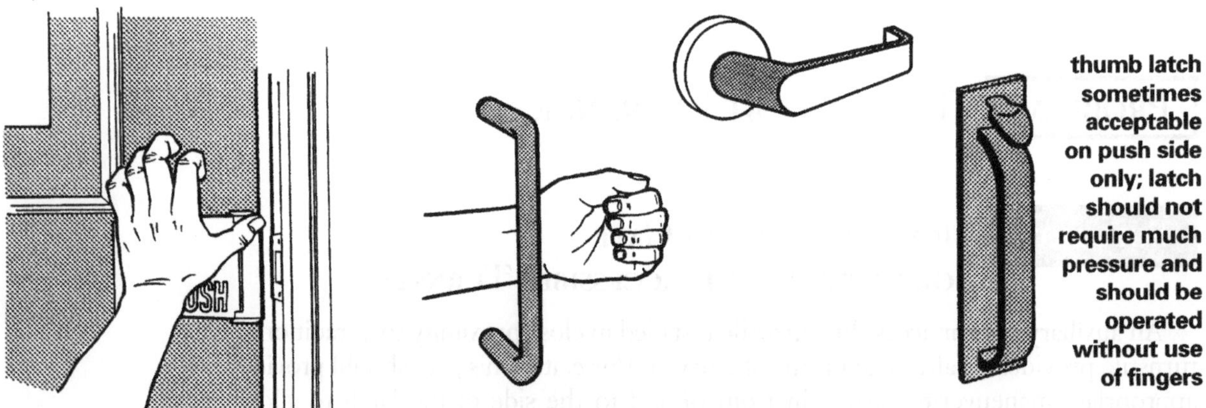

Acceptable Door Hardware

PRACTICAL PLUS

Many disabled users, after passing through the door opening, cannot reach the handle/knob to pull the door closed. Auxiliary handles, mounted near the hinge side of the door, can provide a solution to this problem. Once through the door, the disabled user can pull alongside of the door and close it using the auxiliary handle rather than the unreachable door handle/knob.

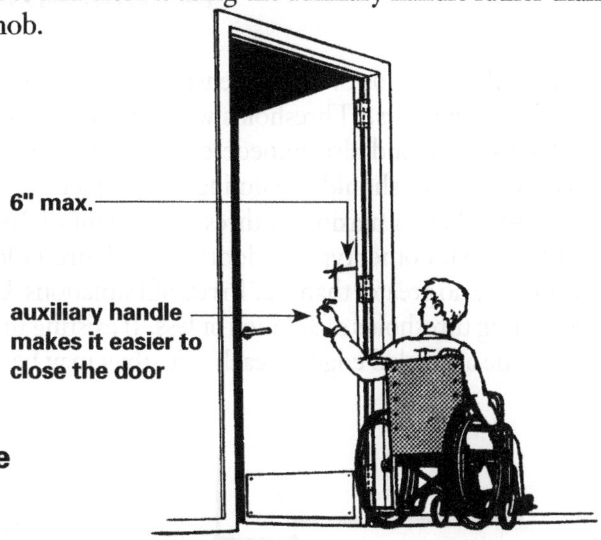

Auxiliary Handle

PRACTICAL PLUS

Self-closing door hinges are also a viable option to assist with door closing. These hinges use gravity to initiate the door closing rather than some additional closing pressure which must be overcome upon door opening.

PROBLEM NON-COMPLYING DOOR HARDWARE

SOLUTION 1 MODIFY HARDWARE

Several specialty manufacturers make add-on lever handles which can be installed over existing knobs.

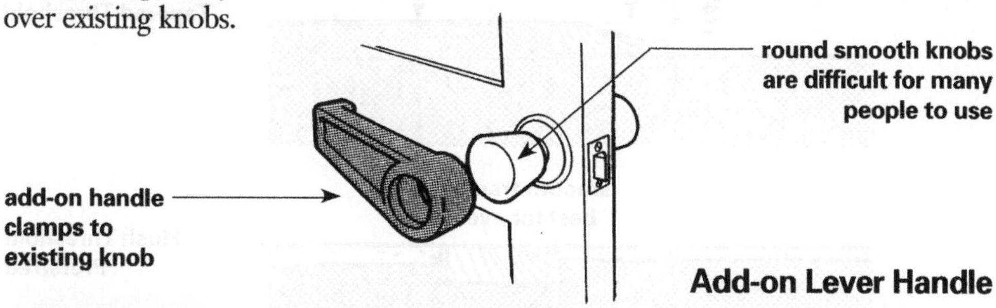

Add-on Lever Handle

SOLUTION 2 REPLACE HARDWARE

Some manufacturers provide an assortment of knobs or handles which can be used interchangeably with the same basic lockset. If alternate lever-type handles are not available, the entire lockset may need to be replaced.

BASIC DESIGN CONSIDERATIONS

THRESHOLDS

Raised thresholds of any dimension greatly increase the difficulty disabled people have in using doors. Thresholds with abrupt level changes are a tripping hazard for walking people and also impede easy passage for wheelchairs. Whenever possible, raised thresholds should be eliminated completely.

UFAS allows a maximum threshold height of 3/4 inch for exterior sliding doors and 1/2 inch for other types of doors. Raised thresholds are also required to be beveled with a slope no greater than 1:2. In retrofit situations, UFAS does provide an exemption for existing thresholds of 3/4 inch or less. If existing thresholds are beveled or modified to provide a beveled edge on each side, they may be retained.

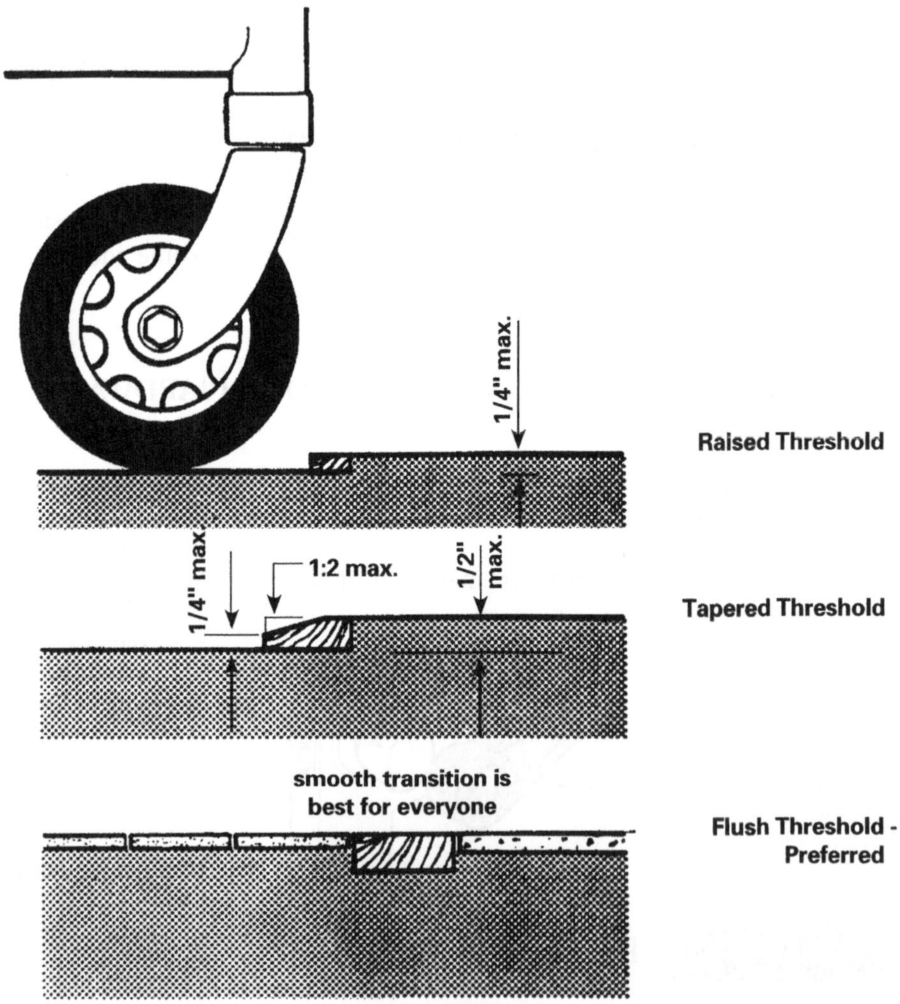

Acceptable Thresholds

PROBLEM NON-COMPLYING THRESHOLD

SOLUTION MODIFY THRESHOLD

Thresholds can be modified using a wedge to minimize the level change. If a new platform or floor is to be installed, it can be raised to eliminate the level change.

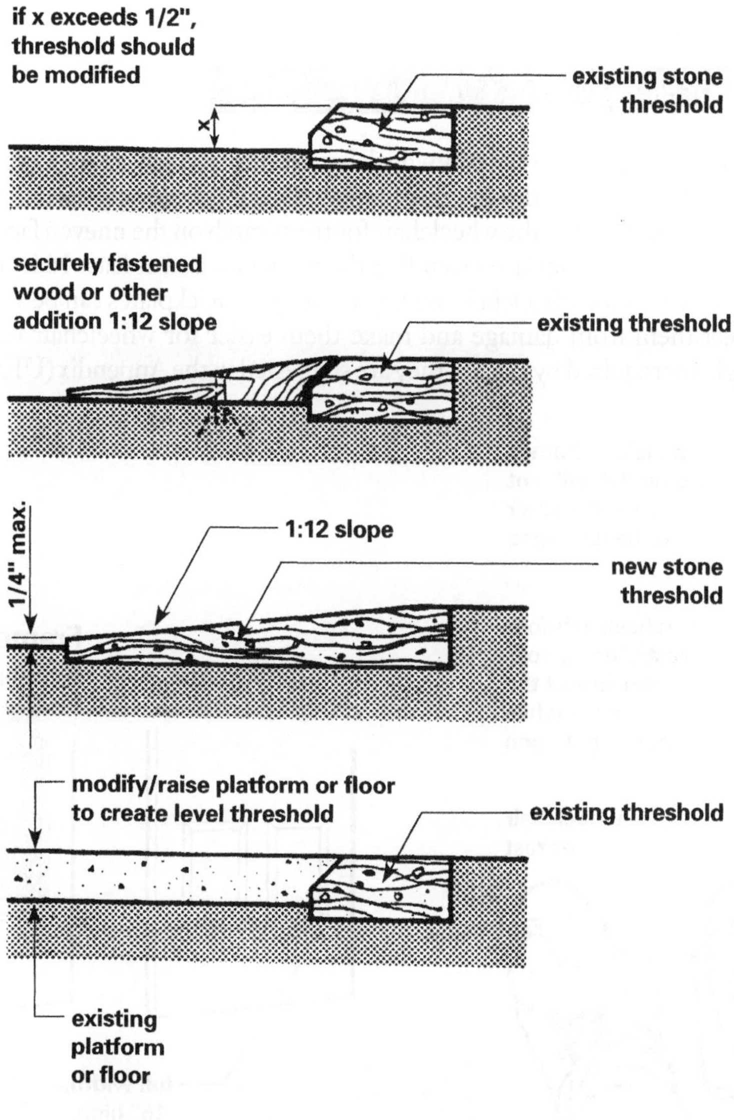

Threshold Modifications

PRACTICAL PLUS

If used, door mats should be recessed into the floor and/or firmly fixed to provide an even surface to walk or roll over. Snow and sand catchers should be similarly installed and comply with the specifications for level changes and gratings (UFAS 4.5.2 and 4.5.4, page 22).

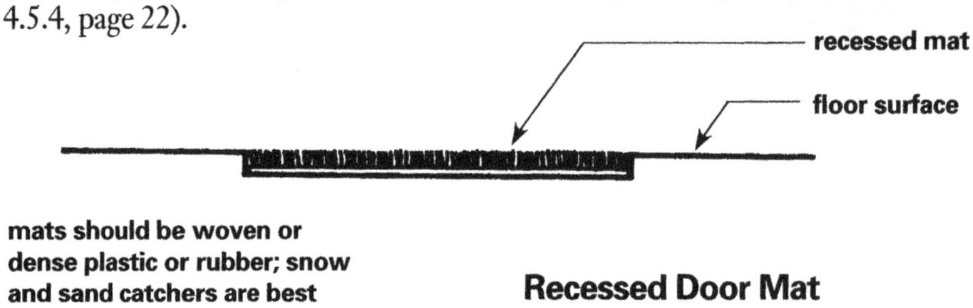

Recessed Door Mat

PRACTICAL PLUS

Doors are subject to damage by wheelchair footrests which are used to push the door open. Panel doors, framed glass doors, and screen doors generally sustain more damage than flush doors because the wheelchair footrests catch on the uneven face of the door. Doors with a smooth surface extending the full width and at least 16 inches from the bottom are easier for wheelchair users to push open. Kickplates can be added to doors to protect them from damage and make them easier for wheelchair users to open. Although not required by UFAS, they are suggested in the Appendix (UFAS, page 63).

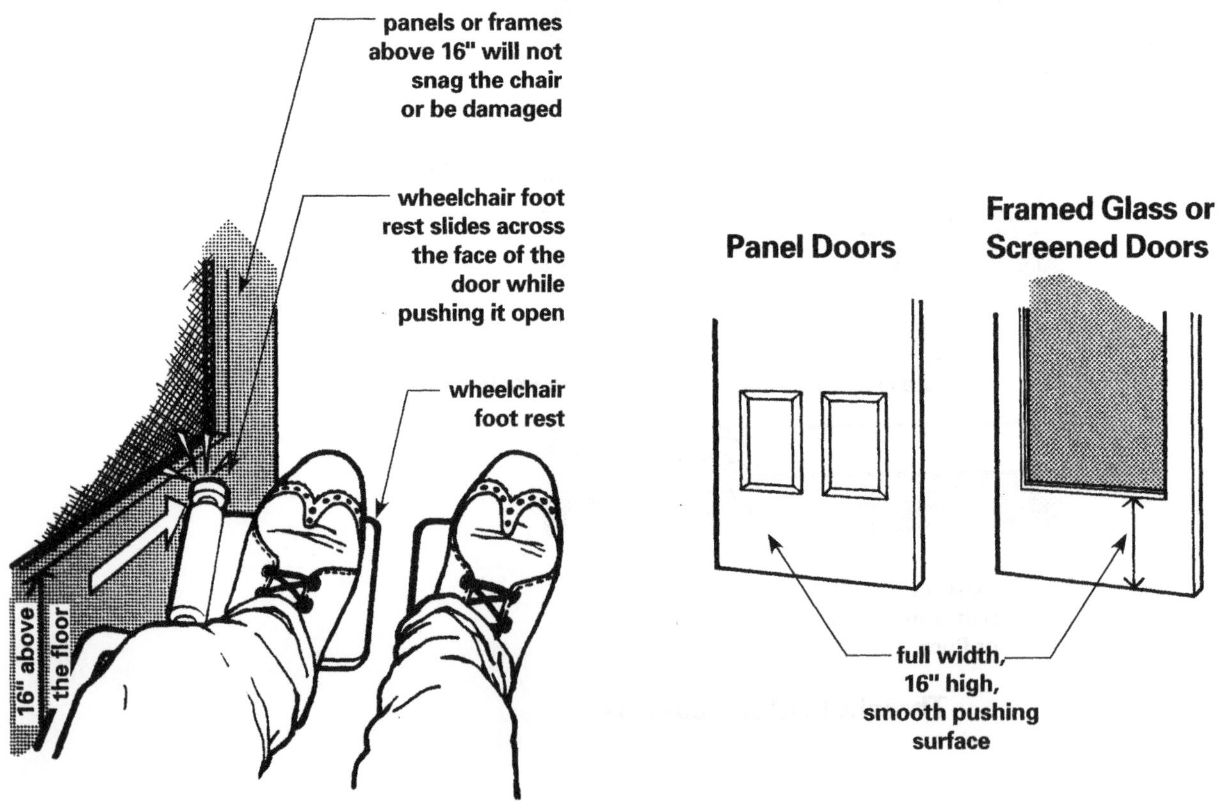

IDEAL CONDITIONS

- ❑ Ample clear width for passage
- ❑ Ample maneuvering space to side and front on pull side of the door
- ❑ No threshold or minimal level change
- ❑ Lever-type hardware; mounted no higher than 48"
- ❑ Door swings easily with no closer or with a time delay closer
- ❑ Kickplate across the lower part of door
- ❑ Auxiliary handle to aid in closing the door if door does not automatically close
- ❑ Non-slip floor surfaces and/or mat recessed into floor
- ❑ Sidelight or glass panel in door to improve lighting and allow view of oncoming traffic
- ❑ Signage should be high contrast, tactile, and mounted on wall on latch side of the door

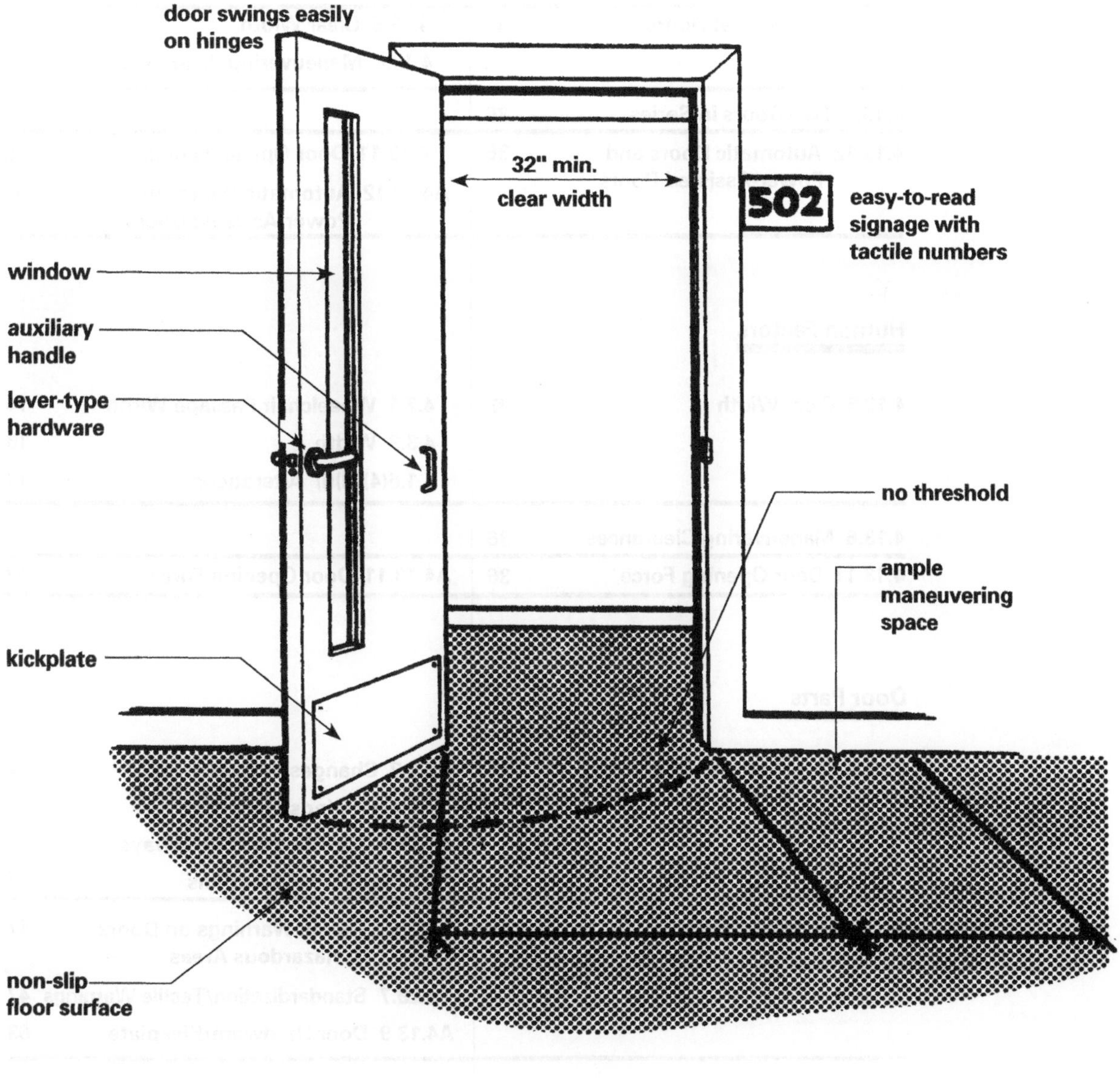

Ideal Door

REFERENCE INDEX TO UFAS DOCUMENT

EXTERIOR/INTERIOR HINGED, POCKET, SLIDING, FOLDING, AND AUTOMATIC/POWER-ASSISTED DOORS

Primary References	UFAS page	Secondary References	UFAS page
Door Types/Location			
4.13.1 General/Location	33	4.1 Scope & Technical Requirements	6
		4.1.5 Additions	11
		4.1.6 Alterations	12
		4.1.7 Historic Preservation	13
4.13.2 Revolving Doors and Turnstiles	33		
4.13.3 Gates	33		
4.13.4 Double-Leaf Doors	33	4.13.5 Clear Width	33
		4.13.6 Maneuvering Clearances	36
4.13.7 Two Doors in Series	36		
4.13.12 Automatic Doors and Power-Assisted Doors	36	4.13.11 Door Opening Force	36
		A4.13.12 Automatic Doors and Power-Assisted Doors	63
Human Factors			
4.13.5 Clear Width	33	4.2.1 Wheelchair Passage Width	14
		4.3.3 Width	18
		4.1.6(4)(d)(i) Alterations	13
4.13.6 Maneuvering Clearances	36		
4.13.11 Door Opening Force	36	A4.13.11 Door Opening Force	63
Door Parts			
4.13.8 Thresholds at Doorways	36	4.5.2 Changes in Level	22
		4.5.4 Gratings/Door Mat	22
		A4.13.8 Thresholds at Doorways	63
		4.1.6(4)(d)(ii) Alterations	13
4.13.9 Door Hardware	36	4.29.3 Tactile Warnings on Doors to Hazardous Areas	47
		4.29.7 Standardization/Tactile Warnings	47
		A4.13.9 Door Hardware/Kickplate	63
4.13.10 Door Closers	36	A4.13.10 Door Closers/Time Delay	63

INTRODUCTION

Drinking fountains are an important amenity found in the public spaces of many buildings and must be carefully installed to accommodate the needs of a variety of people. Tall adults, children, and people who use wheelchairs have difficulty using the same water fountain. Blind people, using canes for mobility, may have difficulty detecting some cantilevered drinking fountains which protrude from the wall. People using free-standing water coolers in corridors may hamper passage of other people. Many buildings now include several fountains with different features to accommodate the needs of many users. Although UFAS allows for several types of water fountains, if properly installed, those which provide knee space for wheelchair users are the most universally usable.

When drinking fountains are furnished, UFAS requires that at least fifty percent of those provided be accessible and located on an accessible route. If only one drinking fountain is provided on any floor, then it must be accessible. In facilities scheduled for alteration, drinking fountains and other basic elements should be considered high priority items for inclusion after other "requirements" are met, UFAS 4.1.6(3)(d)(ii), page 12.

BASIC DESIGN CONSIDERATION

ACCESSIBLE UNIT DESIGN

Several of the UFAS requirements for drinking fountains pertain directly to the design of the unit although installation concerns are more important in many instances. For a drinking fountain to be accessible, the spout outlet should be located at the front edge and should be no higher that 36 inches above the floor. The spout must direct the flow of water at least four inches high and parallel or nearly parallel to the front edge of the unit. The controls for the drinking fountain must be front- or side-mounted near the front and easy to use without gripping or twisting.

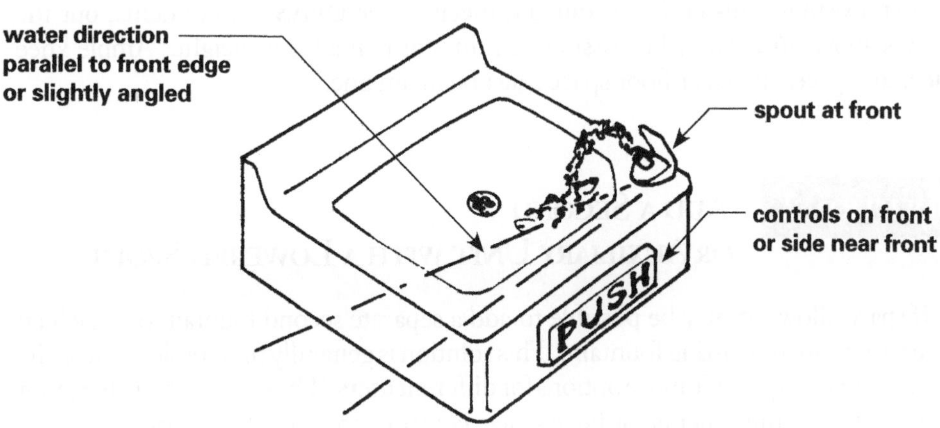

Spout Location

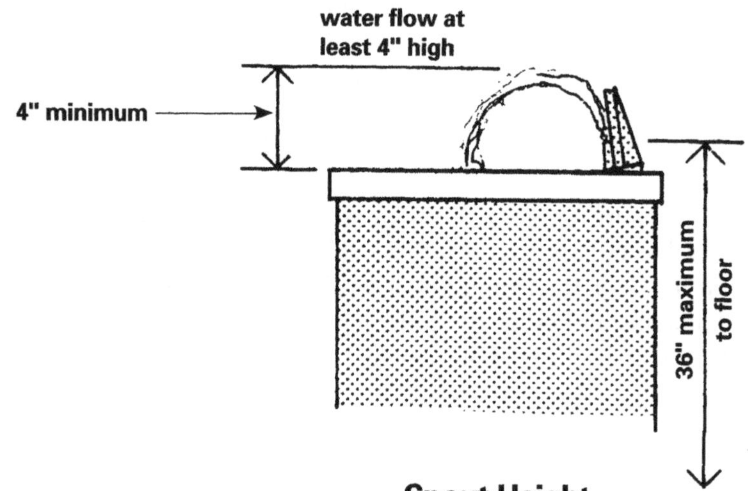

Spout Height

PROBLEM — DRINKING FOUNTAIN SPOUT IS TOO HIGH

SOLUTION 1 — LOWER DRINKING FOUNTAIN

If an existing wall-mounted fountain meets other UFAS requirements, but the spout is above 36", it may be possible to remount it at a lower height. Ample knee space, toe space, and clear floor space must be maintained.

SOLUTION 2 — ADD A SECOND OR AUXILIARY UNIT WITH A LOWERED SPOUT

If space allows, it may be possible to add a separate second fountain or attach an auxiliary unit to the existing fountain. This solution is generally preferable because the two spout heights provide more options for different users. The second or auxiliary unit must meet the requirements for knee space, controls, and clear floor space.

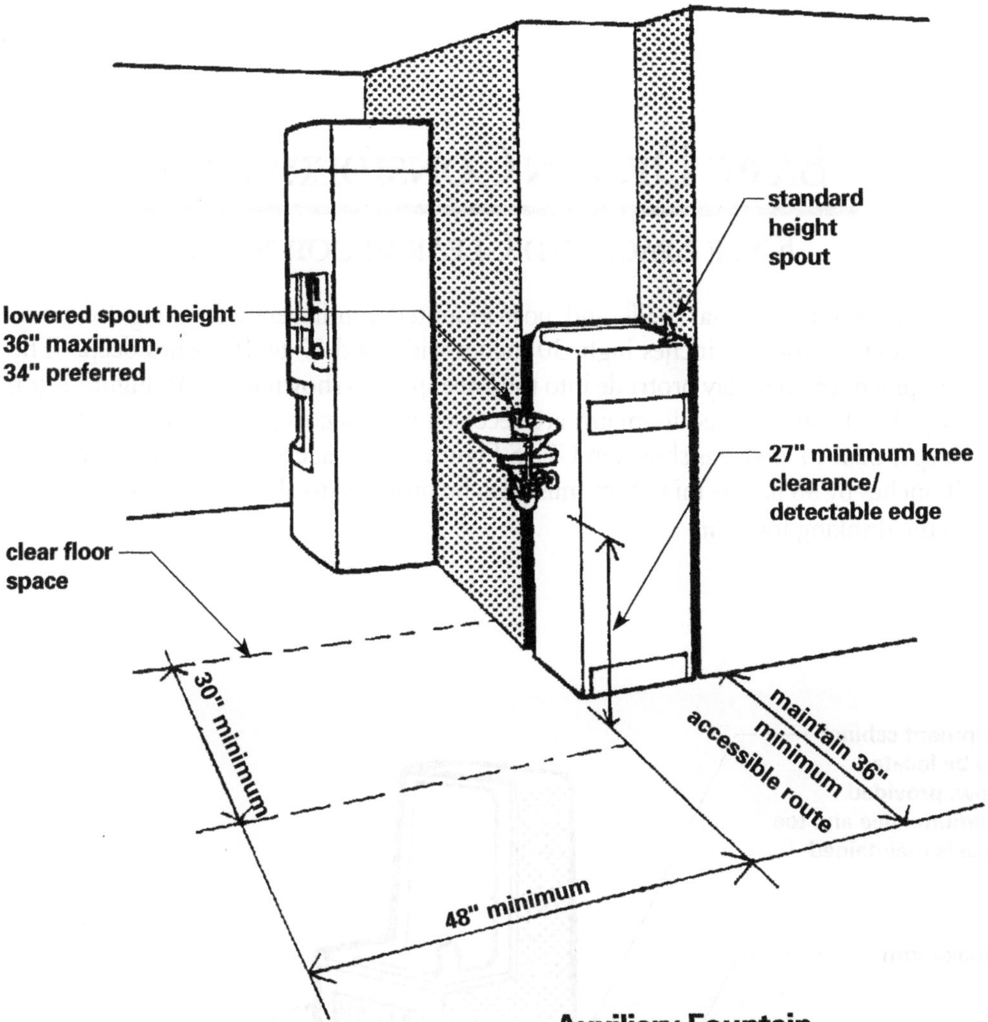

Auxiliary Fountain

PROBLEM CONTROLS DON'T MEET REQUIREMENTS

SOLUTION INSTALL AUXILIARY CONTROLS

If the existing fountain has foot controls or hand controls which are difficult to use or mounted near the back of the fountain, it may be possible to install auxiliary controls which meet the UFAS requirements. Electronic valves and metered flow valves which offer "hands-free" use after activation are easier for many people to use.

BASIC DESIGN CONSIDERATION

KNEE SPACE AND CLEAR FLOOR SPACE

UFAS requires that wall- and post-mounted cantilevered drinking fountains have a knee space 27 inches high, 30 inches wide, and 17 to 19 inches deep. The equipment cabinet may protrude into the knee space as shown in UFAS Figure 27(a), page 37. If cantilevered fountains are recessed in an alcove, the alcove may not be deeper than 24 inches as shown in UFAS Figure 27(b), page 37. A clear floor space of 30 inches by 48 inches minimum must also be provided to allow a forward approach to the drinking fountain.

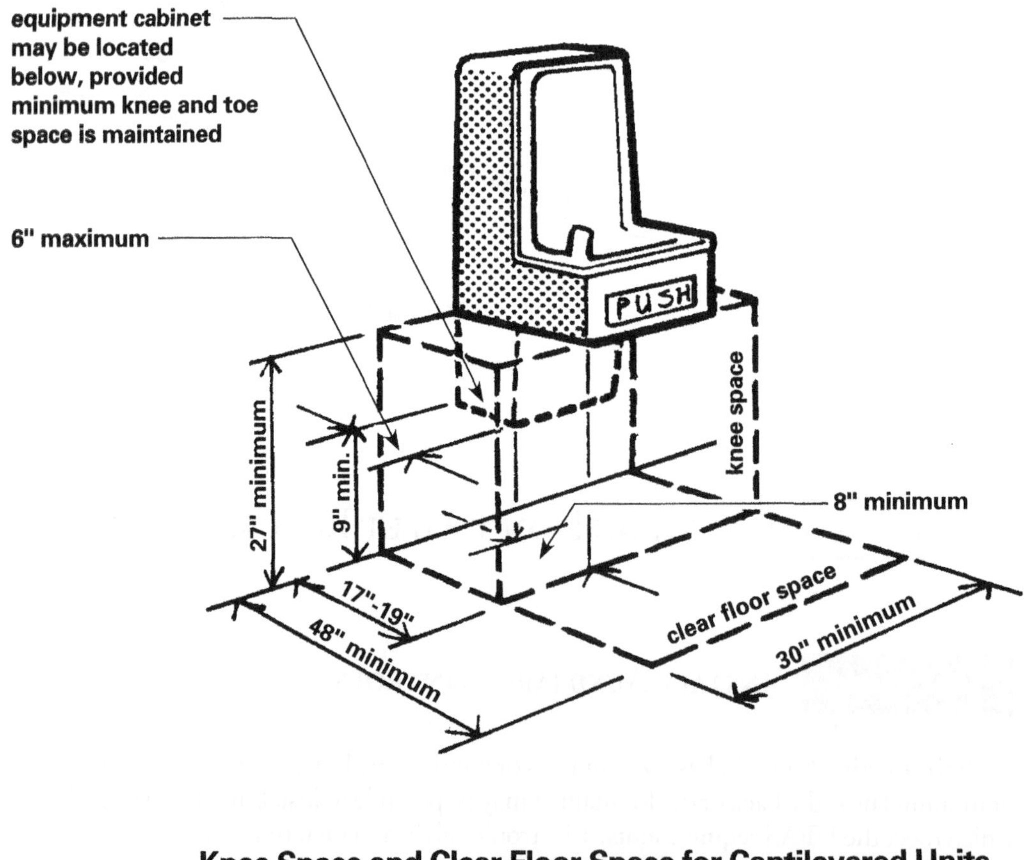

Knee Space and Clear Floor Space for Cantilevered Units

Free-standing and built-in wall units do not have to meet the requirements for knee space. However, clear floor space to allow parallel approach by a wheelchair user must be provided. The clear floor space should be centered on the water fountain.

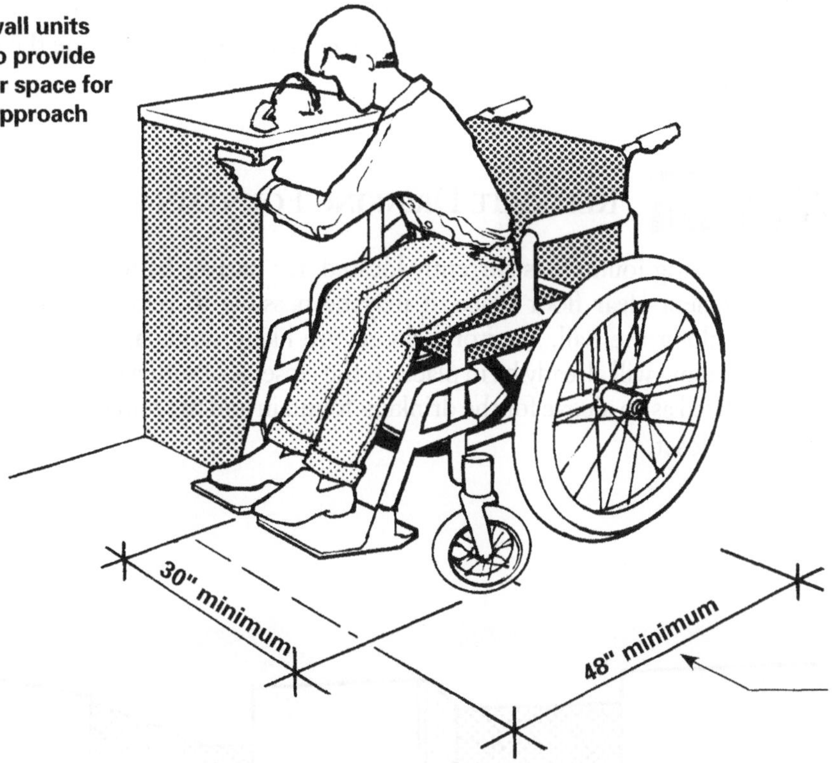

Clear Floor Space for Free-Standing or Built-In Unit

PROBLEM INSUFFICIENT KNEE SPACE

SOLUTION RELOCATE OR REPLACE UNIT

This situation is most likely to occur when the drinking fountain is 1) located in an alcove which is not wide enough or 2) when the actual dimensions of the wall-hung unit preclude the provision of proper knee and toe space. In the first instance, it may be possible to either make the alcove wider or relocate the fountain to provide appropriate maneuvering space. In the second situation, if the location of the fountain provides space for a parallel approach, it meets the UFAS requirements; if not, the fountain should be relocated or replaced.

PROBLEM — INSUFFICIENT CLEAR FLOOR SPACE

SOLUTION 1 — REMODEL SPACE AROUND DRINKING FOUNTAIN

If the drinking fountain is located in an alcove that can be enlarged, or next to a wall that can be removed, these external features can be modified to provide the required clear floor space.

SOLUTION 2 — RELOCATE DRINKING FOUNTAIN

If the drinking fountain is currently located in a narrow hallway which does not provide sufficient clear floor space, it may be possible to relocate it in an alcove somewhere along the hall. Janitor's closets are likely candidates for this solution because plumbing will already be in place. If the closet is of sufficient size, a portion of it can be utilized as an alcove for the drinking fountain and the remainder reserved for the janitor's closet.

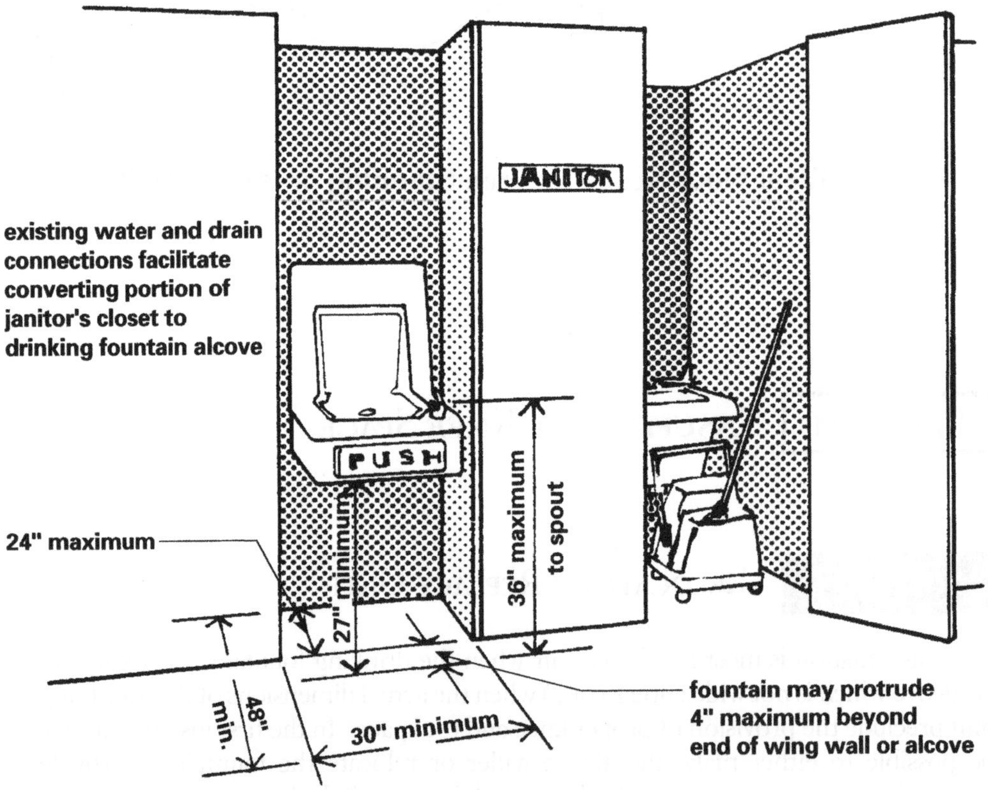

Create Alcove for Drinking Fountain

BASIC DESIGN CONSIDERATION

PLACEMENT

Wall-mounted drinking fountains must be configured so that they do not constitute a hazard by protruding into the lane of pedestrian traffic. This is particularly true of fountains which are installed in hallways. Although cantilevered drinking fountains are preferred by wheelchair users, they can be a menace to blind people if not properly installed. For a cantilevered water fountain to be detectable by a blind person using a cane, the lower edge must be at or less than 27 inches above the floor. Since the standards also require a 27 inch knee space, special attention must be given to the installation of fountains.

Drinking Fountains Can Be Hazardous Protruding Objects

PROBLEM — DRINKING FOUNTAIN PRESENTS A PROTRUDING OBJECT HAZARD

SOLUTION — INSTALL WING WALLS

If the existing drinking fountain has a lower edge greater than 27 inches above the floor but meets all other UFAS requirements, it may be possible to eliminate the protruding object hazard by enclosing the fountain between two wing walls. Clear floor space and ample knee space will need to be provided between the wing walls. This installation is usable by wheelchair users and safer for all pedestrians who pass by.

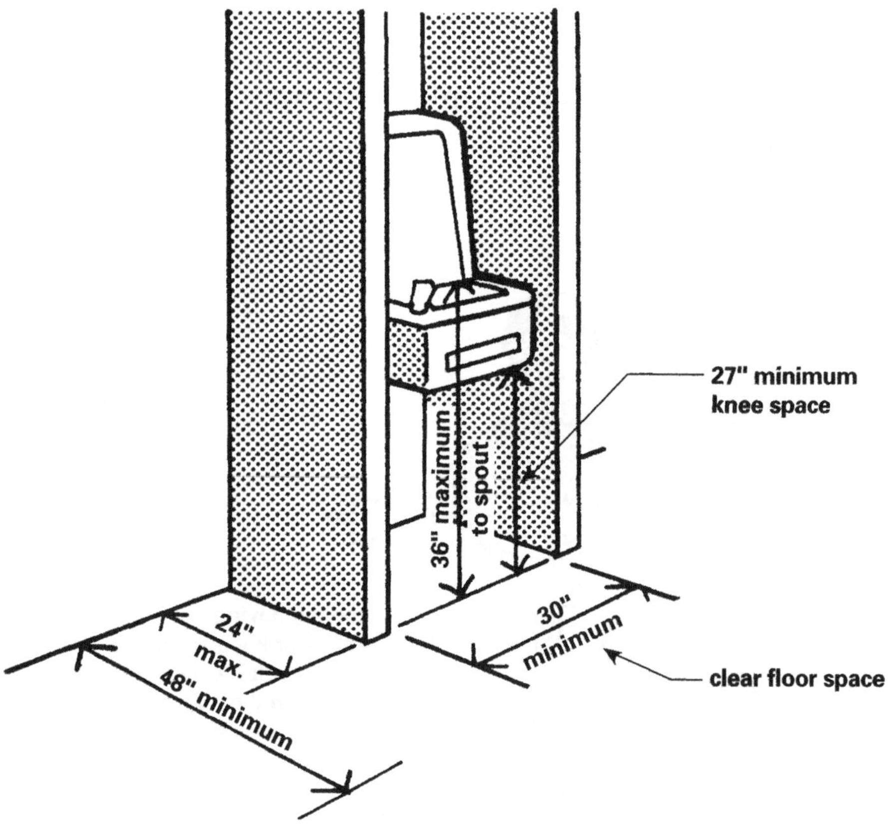

Install Wing Walls Around Drinking Fountain

REFERENCE INDEX TO UFAS DOCUMENT

WALL- AND POST-MOUNTED CANTILEVERED FREE-STANDING/BUILT-IN WATER FOUNTAINS & WATER COOLERS

Primary References	UFAS page	Secondary References	UFAS page
4.15.1 Minimum Number	**36**	**4.1 Scope & Technical Requirements** **4.1.5 Additions** **4.1.6(3)(d)(ii) Alterations - Special Consideration** **4.1.7 Historic Preservation**	**6** **11** **12** **13**
4.15.2 Spout Height	**36**	**A4.15.2 Spout Height**	**64**
4.15.3 Spout Location	**36**		
4.15.4 Controls	**36**	**4.27.4 Operation - Controls and Operating Mechanisms**	**45**
4.15.5 Clearances	**36**	**4.2.4 Clear Floor or Ground Space for Wheelchairs** **4.4 Protruding Objects**	**14** **20**

INTRODUCTION

Access to and safe use of toilets* depends on proper seat height, appropriately placed grab bars and toilet paper dispensers, and usable easy-to-reach flush controls. Access is also dependent upon the provision of sufficient and properly located clear floor space to allow approach and transfer onto the toilet. When the toilet is enclosed in a toilet stall, as is the case in multi-fixture, public rest-rooms, clear floor space considerations change and are expanded to include access to the toilet stall itself (see Toilet Stalls and Toilet Rooms in later sections of this manual). Specific information on where accessible toilets must be located in new construction, additions, and renovations (including historic properties) can be found throughout UFAS under provisions for Toilet Rooms.

* Water closet is the technical name for the toilet fixture. For clarity, the more common term, toilet, will be used throughout this manual.

BASIC DESIGN CONSIDERATIONS

TOILET SEAT HEIGHT

Seat heights from 17 inches to 19 inches are easier for both standing mobility impaired people and wheelchair users to use. An 18 inch seat height is generally recommended because most wheelchair seats are approximately 18 inches high. The 18 inch seat height is also convenient for people who may have difficulty sitting down and getting up from standard toilets. In addition, toilet seats must not be spring loaded to return to a lifted position.

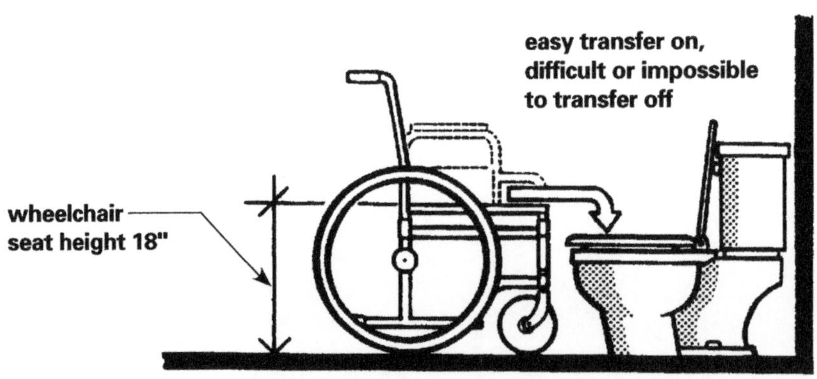

Seat Height Too Low

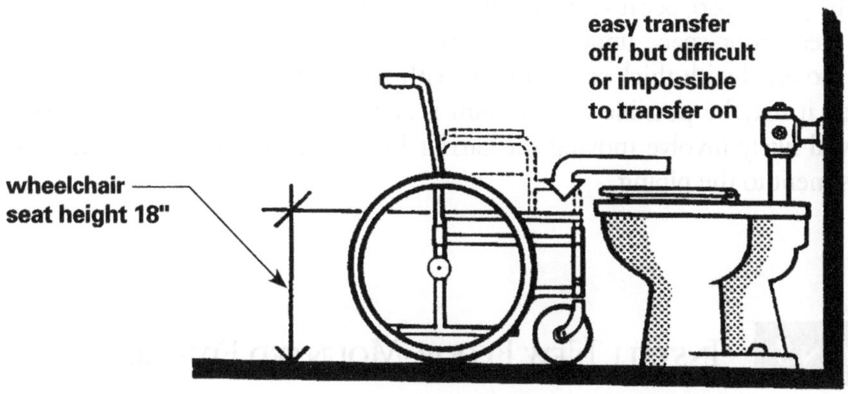

Seat Height Too High

PROBLEM SEAT HEIGHT LESS THAN 17 INCHES

SOLUTION 1 INSTALL THICK SEAT OR SEAT WITH SPACER

Seat height on both wall-and floor-mounted toilets can be adjusted by installing special order "thick seats" or "combination seats with spacers" to raise the seat height to the required level.

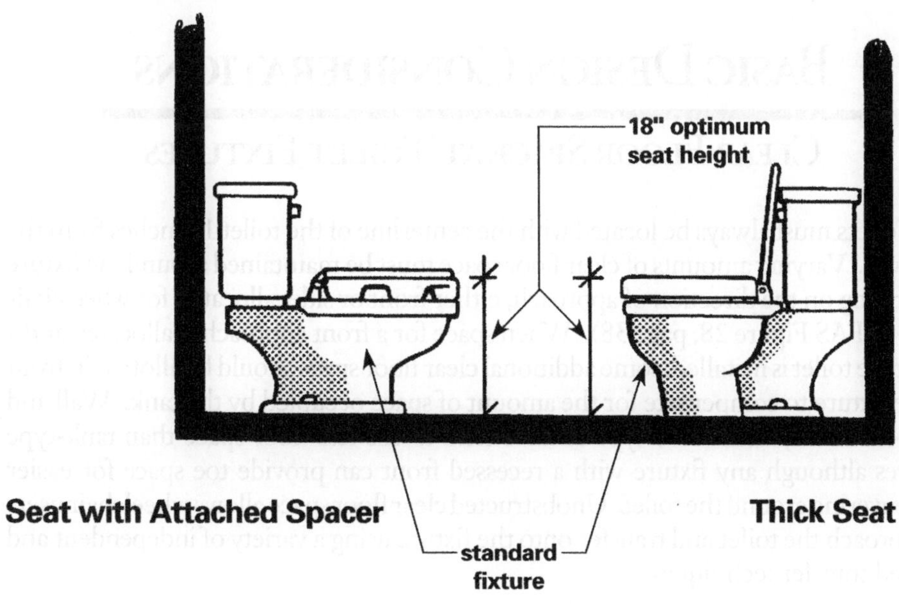

SOLUTION 2 RE-INSTALL WALL-MOUNTED FIXTURE AT PROPER HEIGHT

Wall-mounted fixtures provide the greatest flexibility for the provision of appropriate seat heights. Also, because there is no base, wall-mounted toilets provide some additional clear floor space under the fixture. If an existing wall-mounted toilet cannot be modified with thick seats or seats with spacers to achieve the proper seat height, then it may be possible to re-mount it at a more appropriate height. This approach will likely involve moving the carrier iron which supports the toilet and some adjustment to the piping.

SOLUTION 3 INSTALL NEW FLOOR-MOUNTED FIXTURE

Many toilet manufacturers carry toilets with rims which are approximately 18 inches from the floor. If the existing fixture is a floor-mounted type and the center line of the waste pipe is 18 inches from the side wall, then the fixture can simply be replaced with a higher toilet.

BASIC DESIGN CONSIDERATIONS

CLEAR FLOOR SPACE AT TOILET FIXTURES

Toilets must always be located with the centerline of the toilet 18 inches from the side wall. Varying amounts of clear floor space must be maintained around the fixture depending on the direction of approach, either front or side, allocated for wheelchair users (UFAS Figure 28, page 38). When space for a front approach is allocated and a tank type toilet is installed, some additional clear floor space should be allotted in front of the fixture to compensate for the amount of space occupied by the tank. Wall and floor-mounted, flush valve-type fixtures tend to use less floor space than tank-type fixtures although any fixture with a recessed front can provide toe space for easier maneuvering around the toilet. Unobstructed clear floor space allows wheelchair users to approach the toilet and transfer onto the fixture using a variety of independent and assisted transfer techniques.

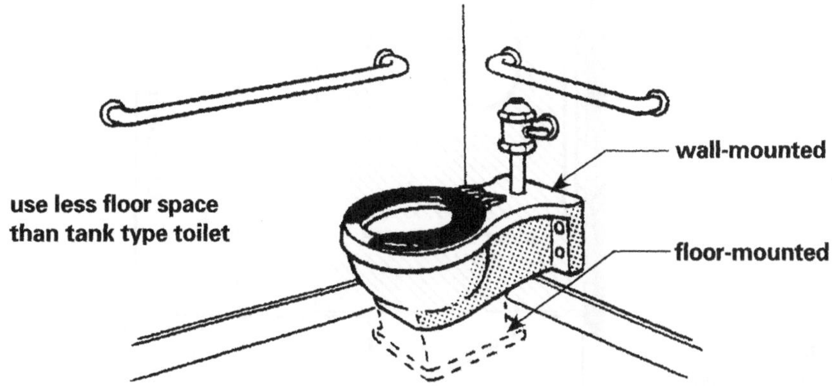

Flush Valve Fixture

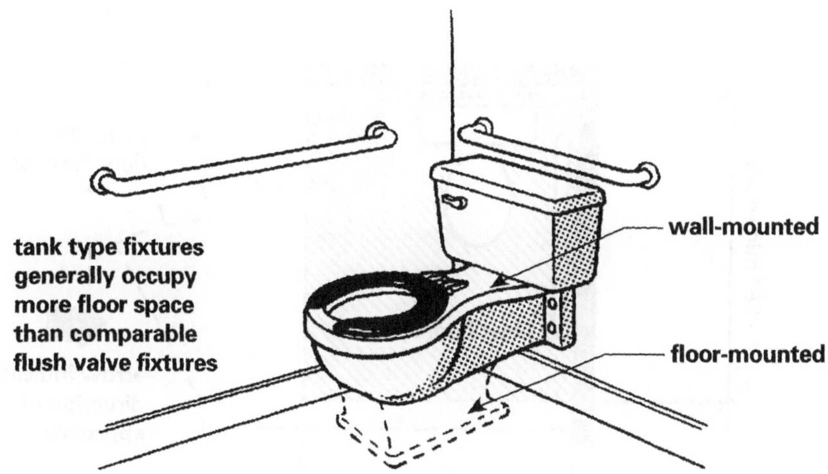

Tank Type Fixture

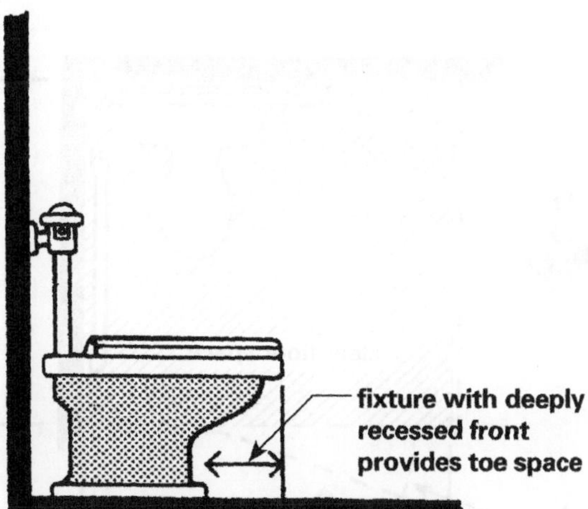

Fixture with Recessed Front

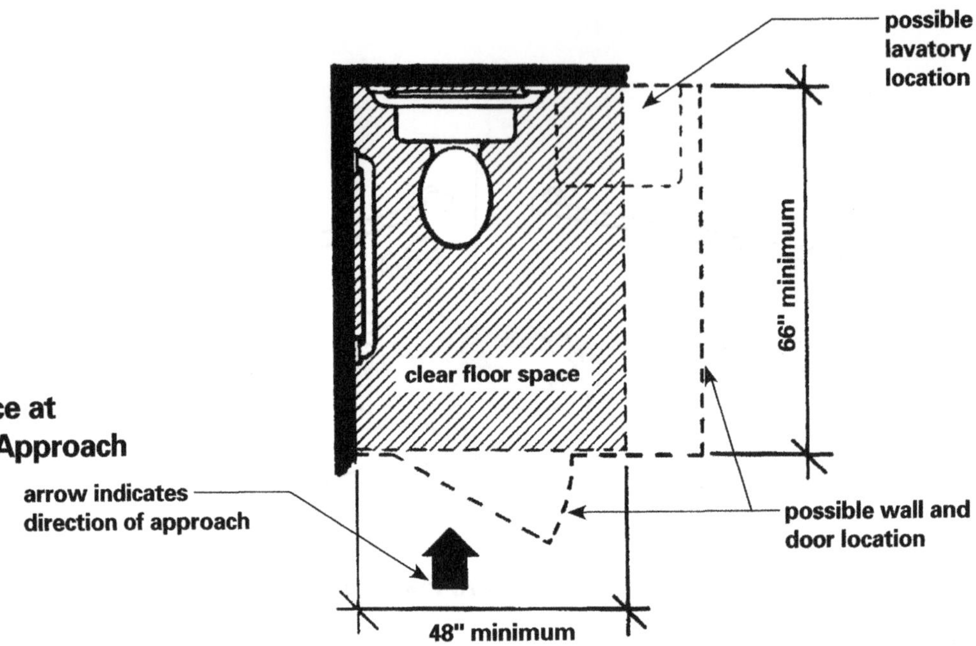

Clear Floor Space at Toilet for Front Approach

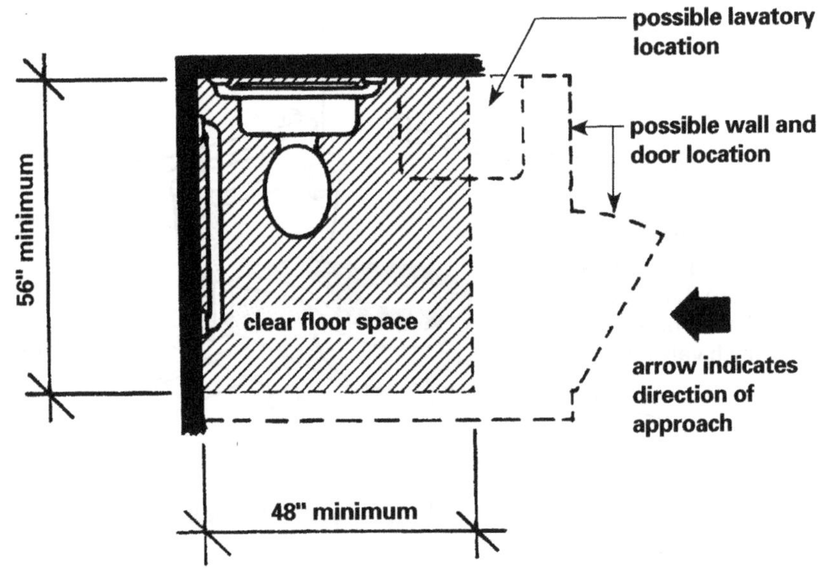

Clear Floor Space at Toilet for Side Approach

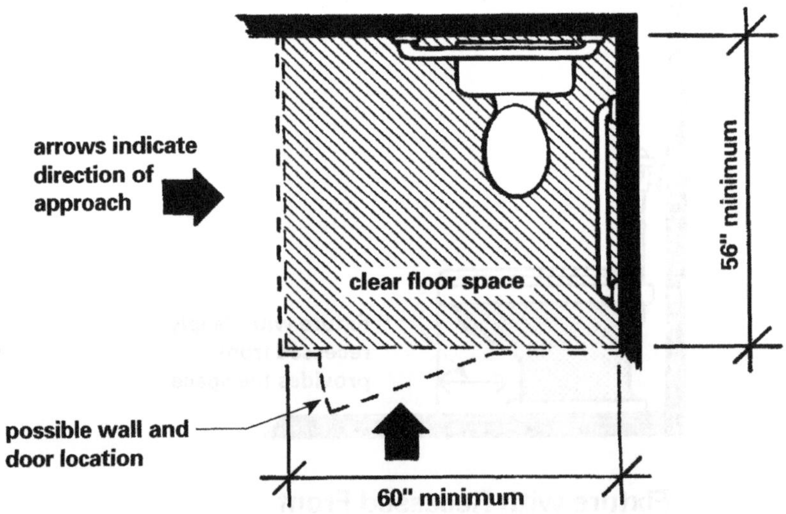

Clear Floor Space at Toilet for Both Front and Side Approach

PROBLEM INSUFFICIENT MANEUVERING SPACE AT TOILET FIXTURE

SOLUTION RELOCATE TOILET FIXTURE

If sufficient space exists in the toilet room to provide the clear space required, then the fixture should be relocated appropriately. If ample space does not exist, then it may be necessary to provide wheelchair accessible toilets in a different space (see Toilet Stalls and Toilet Rooms in later sections of this manual).

BASIC DESIGN CONSIDERATIONS

GRAB BARS AT TOILETS

As with all grab bar installations, the general issues of location, secure mounting, appropriate size, and spacing must always be considered (see Unit Three, Performance Specifications and UFAS 4.26, page 45). Grab bars at toilets are strategically located to provide assistance to users during transfers to the toilet (also see UFAS Appendix, Figure A5(a) and (b), page 64).

Transfer Techniques

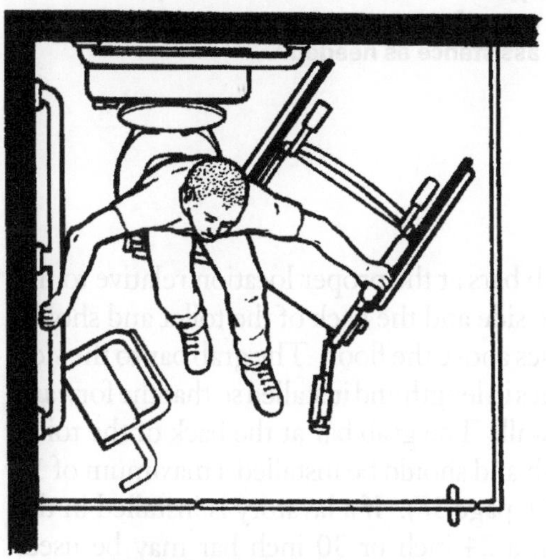

Diagonal Approach

The chair is placed at a comfortable diagonal angle to the fixture. The armrest on the chair may or may not be removed. The user slides onto the toilet seat using the grab bar and the chair for support.

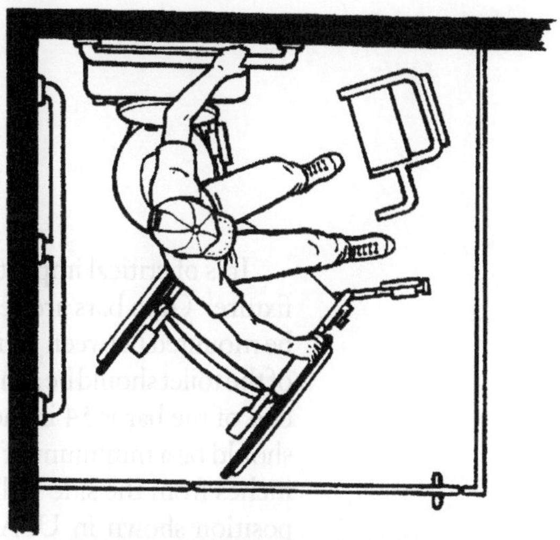

Reverse Diagonal Approach

Due to the nature of their disability, many people can only transfer on one side. One of the major advantages of the 60 inch wide stall is that it allows individuals to transfer using either their left or right side, depending upon the approach to the fixture. In the reverse diagonal approach, the chair is placed at a comfortable diagonal position facing the back wall rather than forward. The armrest is removed and the individual slides onto the toilet seat using the rear grab bar and the chair for support.

Transfer Techniques

Perpendicular Approach

The chair is placed at right angles to the fixture and the individual uses the wheelchair and the grab bar for support while making the transfer.

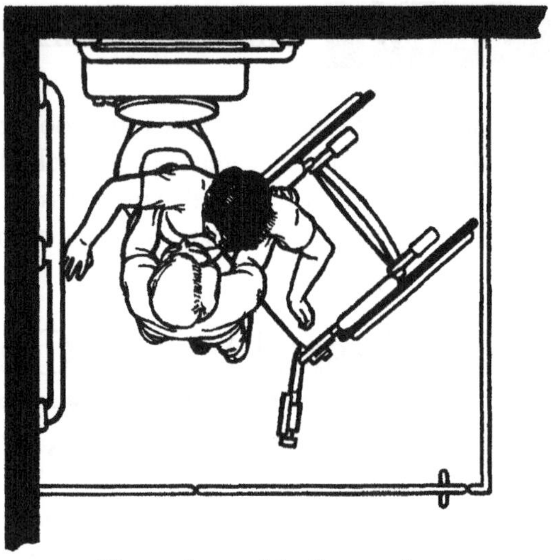

Transfer with Attendant

The 60 inch wide stall is usable by most people but not all individuals can transfer independently. Some people must have an attendant to help them make any type of transfer. The wider stall provides space for an attendant to provide assistance as needed.

It is of critical importance to install grab bars at the proper location relative to the fixture. Grab bars are required to both the side and the back of the toilet and should be mounted between 33 inches and 36 inches above the floor. The grab bar to the side of the toilet should be a minimum of 42 inches in length and installed so that the forward end of the bar is 54 inches from the back wall. The grab bar at the back of the toilet should be a minimum of 36 inches in length and should be installed a maximum of 12 inches from the side wall (UFAS Figure 29, page 38). If a lavatory is installed in the position shown in UFAS Figure 28, then a 24 inch or 30 inch bar may be used. "L-shaped" grab bars of the appropriate length are also suitable. If flush controls or flush valves are located in a position that conflicts with the location of the rear grab bar, then the grab bar may be split or shifted to the side. Grab bars should be installed so they do not interfere with the installation of shorter easy-to-reach flush valves.

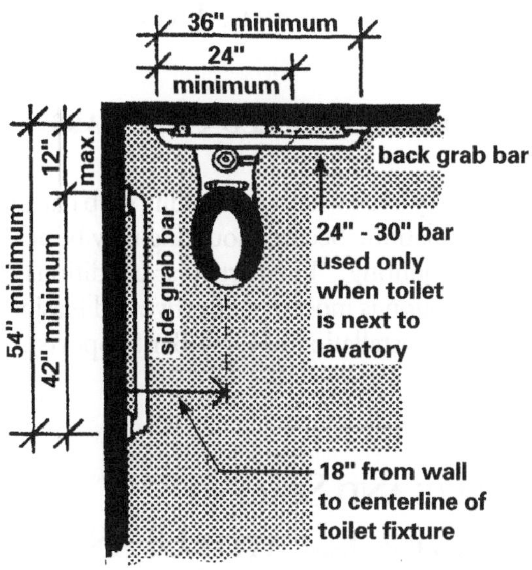

Separate Side and Back Grab Bars

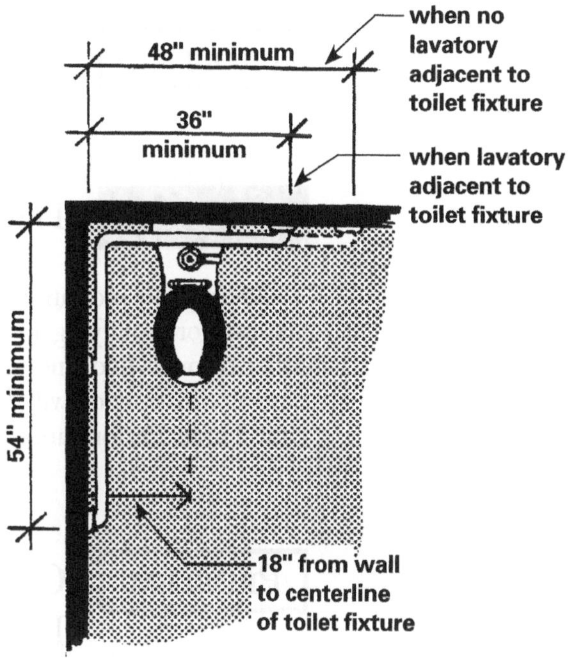

"L-Shaped" Grab Bar

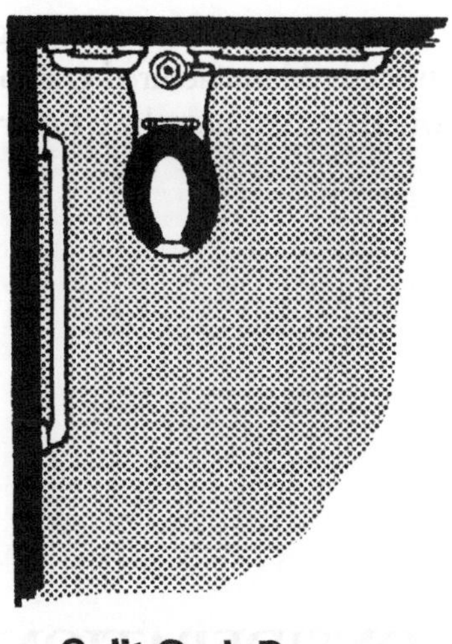

Split Grab Bar

Split "L-Shaped" Grab Bar

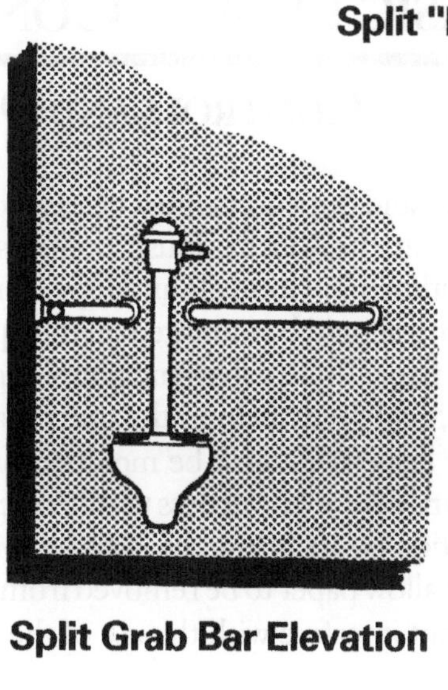

Split Grab Bar Elevation

PROBLEM NO GRAB BARS OR GRAB BARS IMPROPERLY INSTALLED

SOLUTION PROVIDE PROPERLY INSTALLED GRAB BARS

Appropriate mounting support is the key issue whether installing grab bars for the first time or modifying an improper installation. Secure mounting may be achieved either through floor mounting or wall mounting. The particular conditions of the existing construction will dictate which option is most cost effective and feasible (see Unit Three, Performance Specifications - Installation of Grab Bar Supports).

PROBLEM GRAB BAR SIZE AND SPACING DOES NOT CONFORM WITH UFAS

SOLUTION REPLACE WITH SUITABLE GRAB BARS

If existing grab bars do not meet the UFAS requirements for length, strength, diameter, and/or shape, they should be replaced. Manufactured grab bars should be evaluated before installation to determine whether they meet the UFAS requirements.

BASIC DESIGN CONSIDERATIONS

CONTROLS AND DISPENSERS

Flush controls and dispensers must be easy to operate and located within reach of a person seated on the toilet. Flush controls should be automatic or meet the specifications outlined in Controls and Operating Mechanisms (UFAS 4.27.4, page 45). Flush controls should be mounted on the open side of the toilet no more than 44 inches above the floor. Flush valves and plumbing can be located behind walls or to the side of the toilet, or directly behind the toilet if a toilet seat lid is provided.

Toilet paper dispensers must be mounted on the side wall within easy reach and with the horizontal center line no less than 19 inches above the floor. Usually the most convenient location is just below the grab bar but above the height of the toilet seat. Dispensers must allow paper to be removed from the roll easily and should be mounted so that they do not interfere with the use of the grab bar.

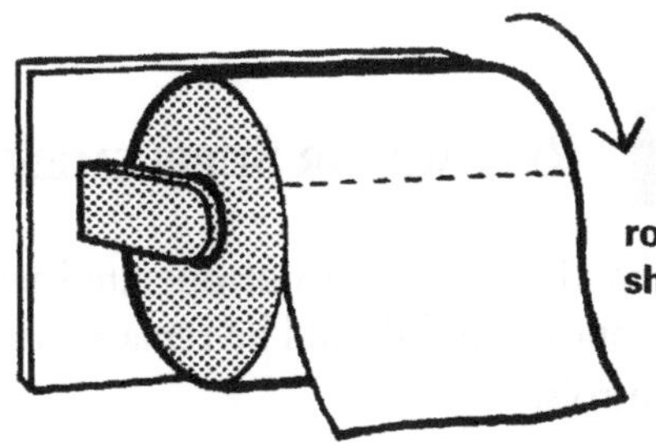

Toilet Paper Dispenser

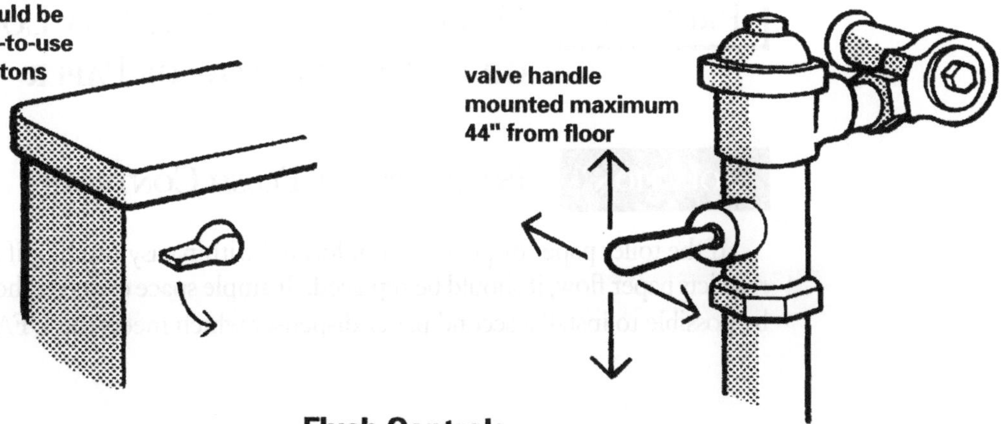

Flush Controls

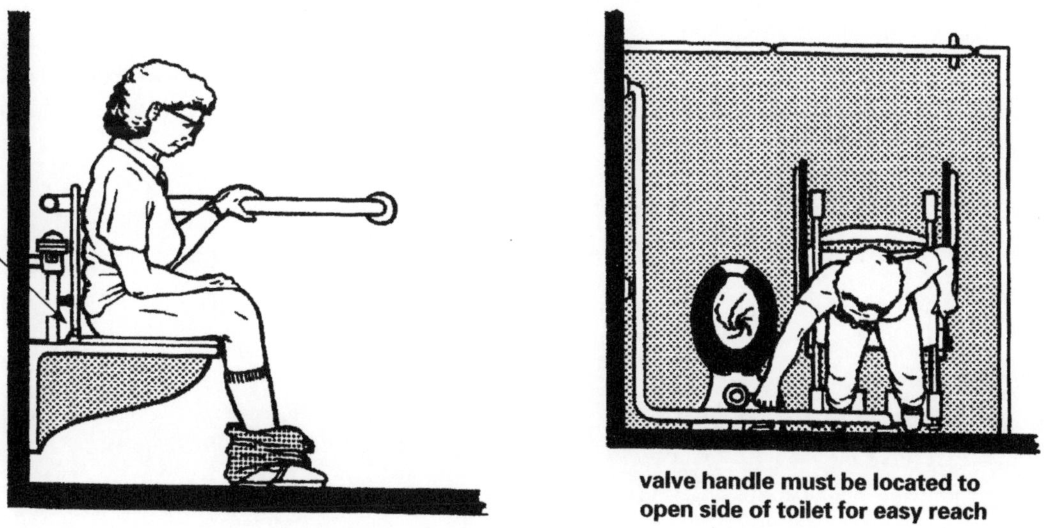

Location of Flush Controls

PROBLEM INAPPROPRIATE FLUSH CONTROLS

SOLUTION REPLACE OR SUPPLEMENT FLUSH CONTROLS

Inappropriate hand controls and foot-operated pedals do not meet the performance specifications for controls and should be replaced or supplemented with appropriate hand-operated controls.

PROBLEM DISPENSER INAPPROPRIATELY LOCATED OR RESTRICTS FLOW OF PAPER

SOLUTION INAPPROPRIATE FLUSH CONTROLS

If the toilet paper dispenser is not located within easy reach or if it is a type which restricts paper flow, it should be replaced. If ample space exists on the side wall, it may be possible to install a second paper dispenser which meets the UFAS requirements.

REFERENCE INDEX TO UFAS DOCUMENT

WALL-MOUNTED, FLOOR-MOUNTED, FLUSH VALVE AND TANK TYPE TOILETS

Primary References	UFAS page	Secondary References	UFAS page
Toilet Types/Location			
4.16.1 General/Location	37	4.1 Scope & Technical Requirements for Toilet Rooms	5-6
		4.1.5(3) Additions	11
		4.1.6(3)(c)(i) Alterations	12
		4.1.6(3)(c)(ii) Alterations	12
		4.1.6(4)(e) Alterations	13
		4.1.7(2)(c) Historic Preservation	14
		4.22.4 Toilet Rooms/Water Closets	44
		4.23.4 Bathing Facilities/Water Closets	44
Human Factors			
4.16.2 Clear Floor Space	37		
4.16.3 Height	37	A4.16.3 Height	64
4.16.4 Grab Bars	37	4.26 Grab Bars	45
		A4.16.4 Grab Bars	64
Toilet Parts			
4.16.5 Flush Controls	38	4.27.4 Controls and Operating Mechanisms	45
		A4.16.5 Flush Controls	65
4.16.6 Dispensers	38		

INTRODUCTION

Toilet stalls are enclosures provided to facilitate privacy in public toilet facilities. An accessible toilet stall must comply with all the UFAS requirements for toilets, including clear floor space, seat height, length of grab bars, flush controls, and dispensers (see Toilets section), and some additional requirements, including the arrangement of the stall, toe clearance, doors, and grab bar locations.

UFAS describes three types of accessible toilet stalls, the standard stall and two alternate stalls. The standard toilet stall is required in all instances, including retrofit installations, unless it can be demonstrated that either 1) it is structurally impracticable or 2) removal of an existing fixture to provide access would violate the plumbing code minimum fixture count. If either of these conditions is present in an existing facility, then one of the alternate stalls may be substituted. Specific information on where accessible toilets must be located in new construction, additions, and renovations (including historic properties) can be found throughout UFAS under provisions for Toilet Rooms.

BASIC DESIGN CONSIDERATION

60 INCH STANDARD STALL

The standard stall is a minimum of 60 inches wide and at least 56 inches deep when the toilet is wall-mounted and 59 inches if it is floor-mounted. A standard stall can be located wherever adequate access can be provided to the stall door. If approach to the stall door is from the latch side, the access aisle must be a minimum of 42 inches wide. If approach is from the hinge side or front of the door, a minimum of 48 inches must be allowed.

In the standard stall, the minimum width door must be outswinging, located in either the front or side partition diagonally across from the toilet fixture (to facilitate front and side approaches to the toilet), and no more than 4 inches from the corner. The "end of row" standard fixture can have an inswinging door provided a 36 inch minimum access aisle is allocated behind the door which does not overlap the clear floor space for the toilet fixture. Typically, standard accessible stalls are located at the end of the row in configurations similar to those shown in UFAS Figure 30(a) and 30(a-1), page 39.

The latching hardware on partition doors frequently does not meet the UFAS performance requirements because the small knobs, latch bolts, and locks require gripping and twisting to operate. Also, when there is no automatic door closer, this type of hardware is difficult to grasp to pull the door closed. To facilitate use, easy-to-grasp hardware and/or auxiliary handles should be installed in all accessible stalls.

The standard stall is designed to provide clear floor space and grab bars to facilitate a variety of transfers (see Grab Bars at Toilets in Toilets section). At least 9 inches of toe clearance under the front partition and one side partition is required for the minimum size standard stall to be fully accessible. If toe clearance cannot be provided then the stall depth must be increased to at least 60 inches.

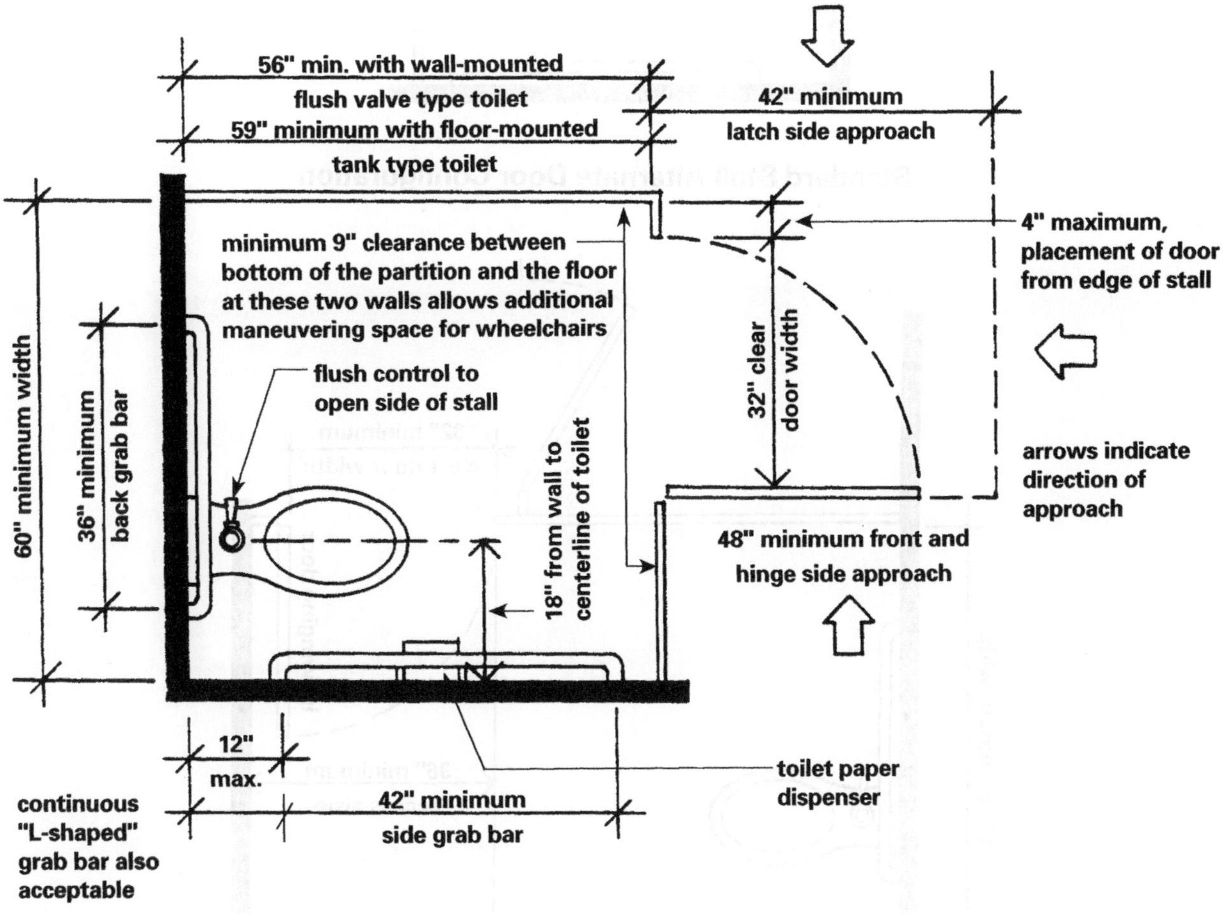

Standard 60 Inch Stall

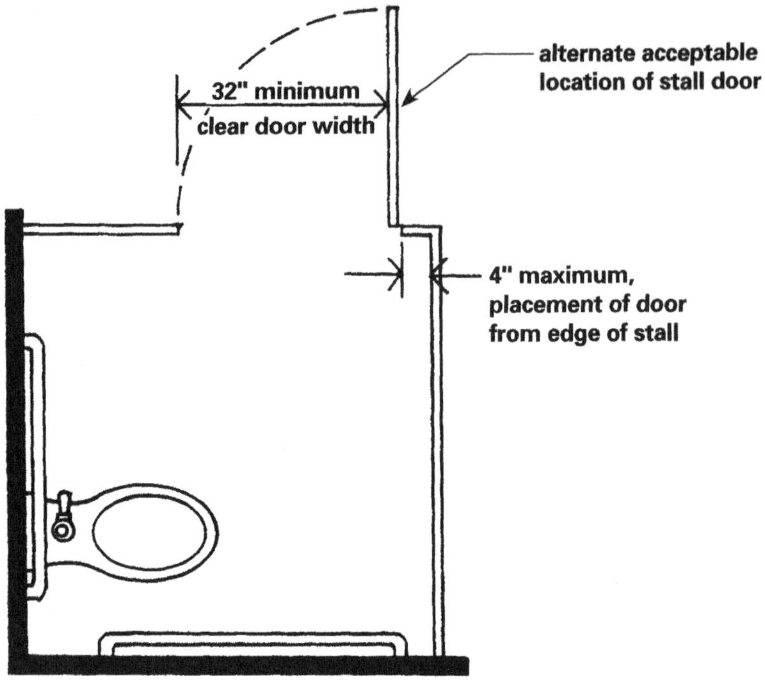

Standard Stall Alternate Door Configuration

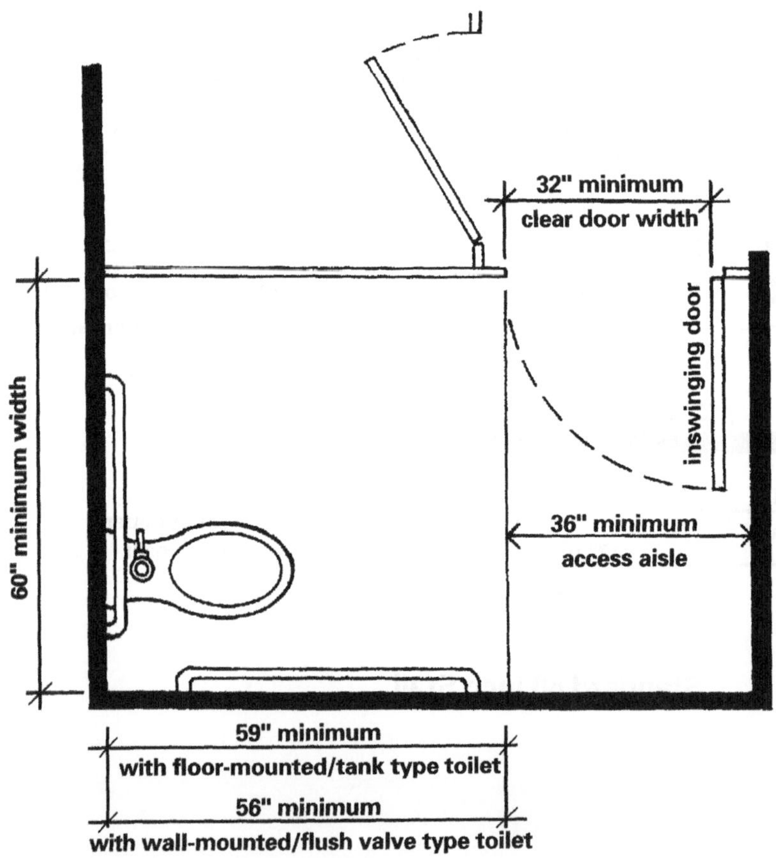

Standard Stall End-of-Row Configuration

PROBLEM NO STANDARD WHEELCHAIR ACCESSIBLE STALL IN EXISTING TOILET ROOM

SOLUTION COMBINE TWO EXISTING STALLS TO CREATE STANDARD 60 INCH STALL

Many older facilities were constructed without provisions for wheelchair access and lack accessible toilet facilities. In these situations, a common solution is to combine two existing 30 inch stalls by removing one toilet, rearranging the partitions, installing grab bars, and replacing the stall door. This solution is only possible when the number of fixtures remaining after renovation meet the minimum plumbing code requirements (see Unit Five: Toilet Rooms for more options).

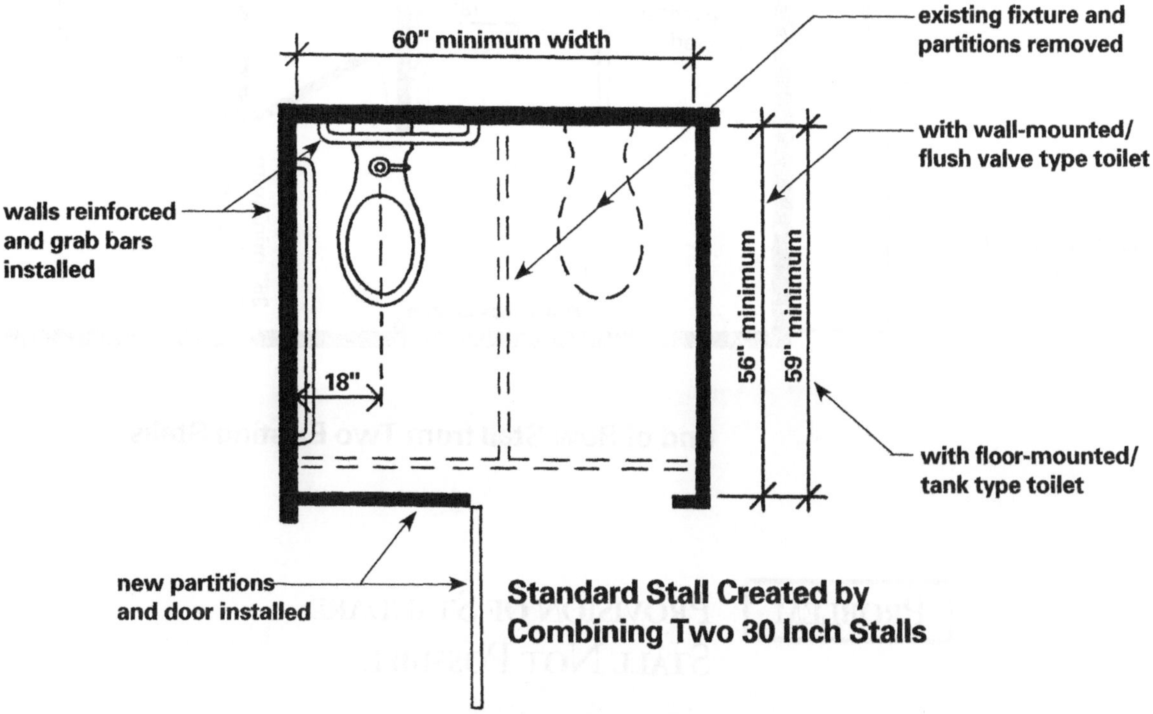

Standard Stall Created by Combining Two 30 Inch Stalls

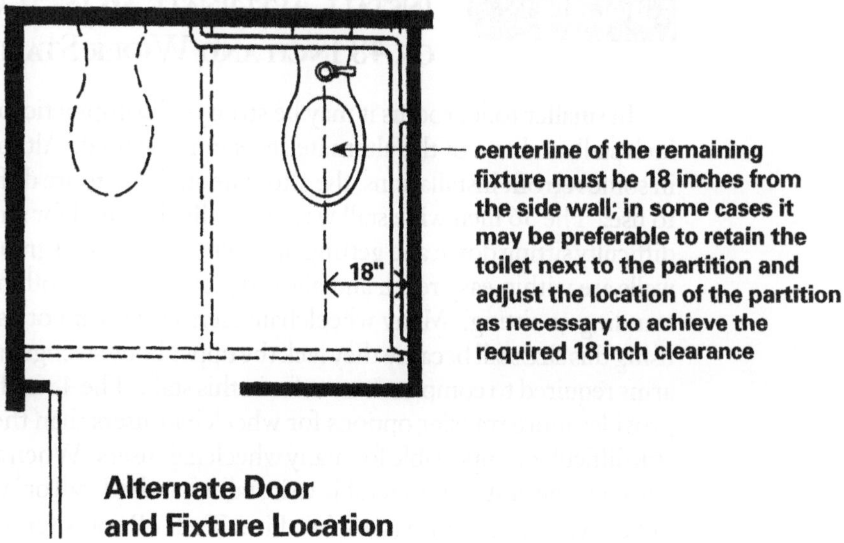

Alternate Door and Fixture Location

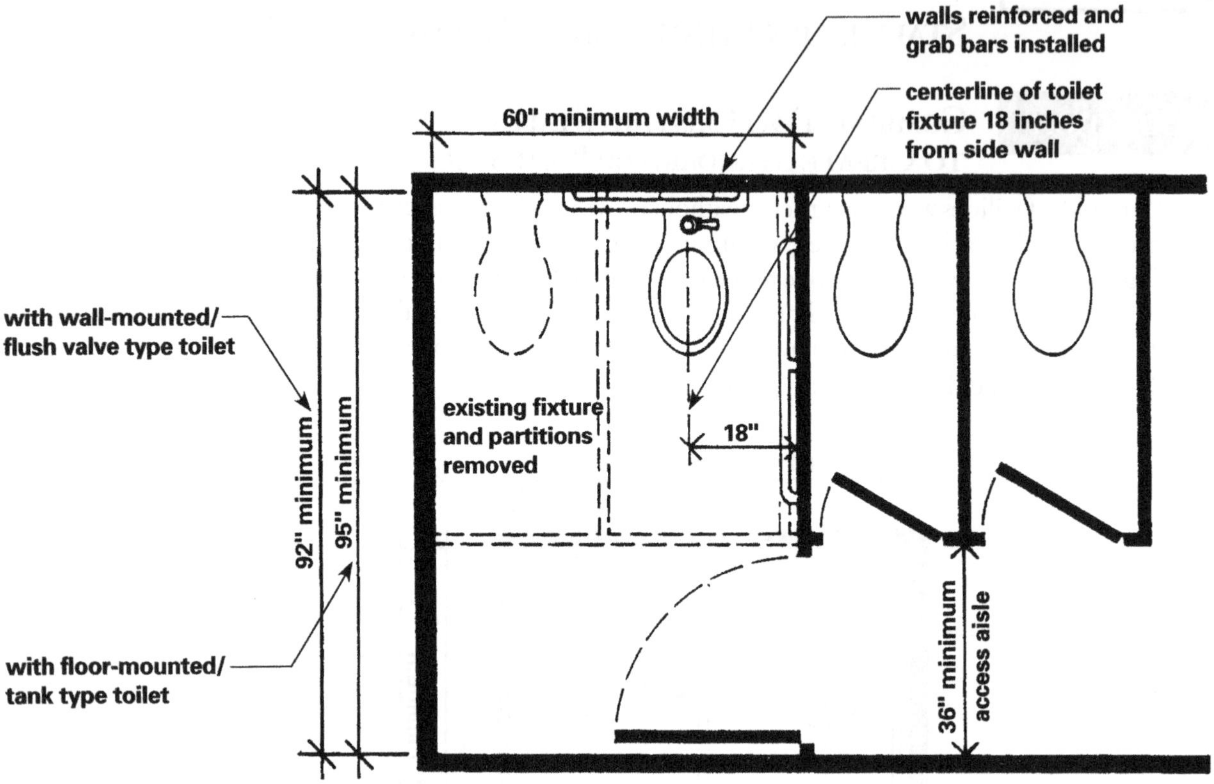

End of Row Stall from Two Existing Stalls

PROBLEM — PROVISION OF STANDARD STALL NOT POSSIBLE

SOLUTION — INSTALL ALTERNATE 36 INCH WIDE OR 48 INCH AND WIDER STALL

In smaller toilet rooms it may be structurally impracticable to install a standard 60 inch stall, and one of the alternate stalls must be used. Although permitted by UFAS in some retrofit installations, the alternate stalls are more difficult for wheelchair users to use. The 36 inch wide stall was originally designed for ambulatory users who have difficulty sitting down and getting up again. The parallel grab bars mounted on the side walls are within easy reach and allow the user to grab both bars simultaneously while standing or sitting. Many wheelchair users either cannot use or have great difficulty using this size stall because they lack the upper body strength and use of their hands and arms required to complete a transfer in this stall. The 48 inch minimum alternate stall provides more transfer options for wheelchair users than the 36 inch wide stall but is still difficult or impossible for many wheelchair users. When alternate space is available and codes permit, it is preferable to install a standard stall or "unisex toilet" in a different but convenient location (see Unit Five: Toilet Rooms for more options).

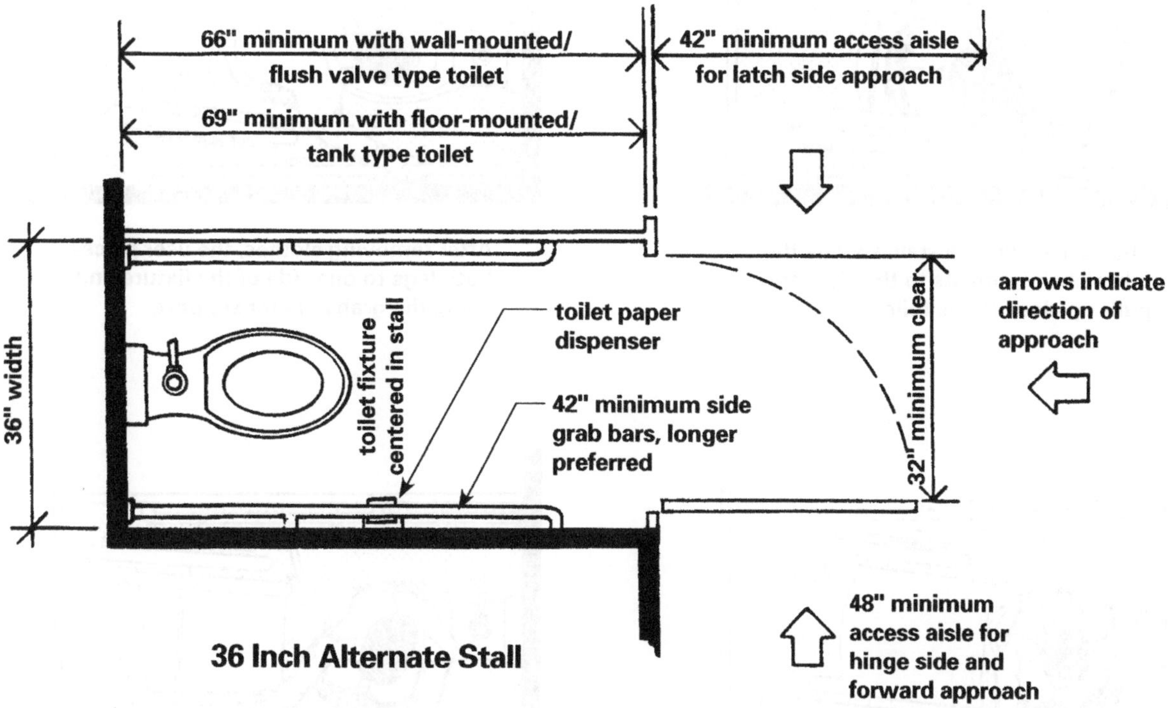

36 Inch Alternate Stall

The 36 inch and 48 inch alternate toilet stalls must be 66 inches deep if a wall-mounted/flush valve type toilet is used and 69 inches deep if a floor-mounted/tank type toilet is used. Grab bars must be installed as shown in UFAS Figure 30(b). If approach to the stall door is from the latch side, the access aisle must be a minimum of 42 inches wide. If approach is from the hinge side or front of the door, a minimum of 48 inches must be allowed. Spring-loaded hinges, which pull the door closed automatically, provide privacy for wheelchair users who may be able to get into the stall but not reach behind themselves to fasten the latch.

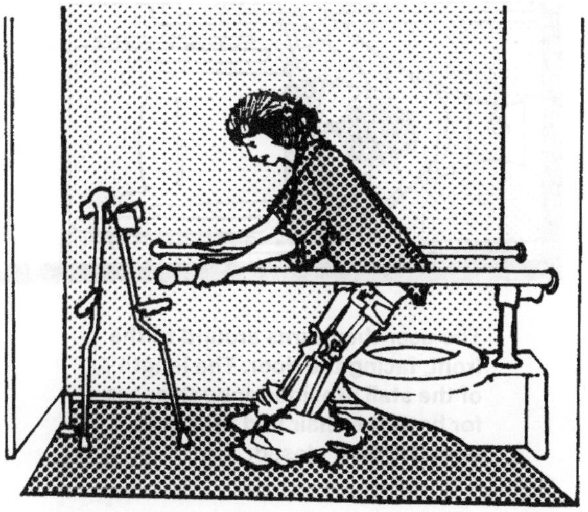

The 36 inch wide toilet stall with two long grab bars was originally designed for people who have difficulty sitting down and rising again to a standing position. The stall is an excellent design for people with arthritis or those who walk with braces or crutches because they can use both grab bars to lean on and to pull on while sitting down or getting up.

36" Alternate Stall for Ambulatory User

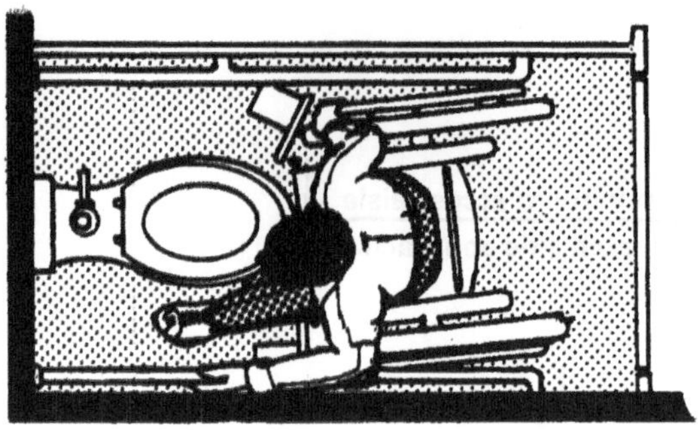

The user enters the stall, swings the wheelchair footrests to the side, and pulls up close to the toilet.

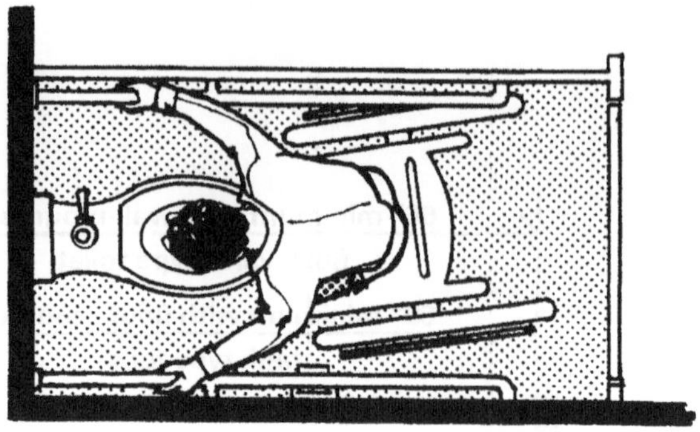

After removing clothes, the user places both legs to one side of the fixture and, using the grab bars for support,

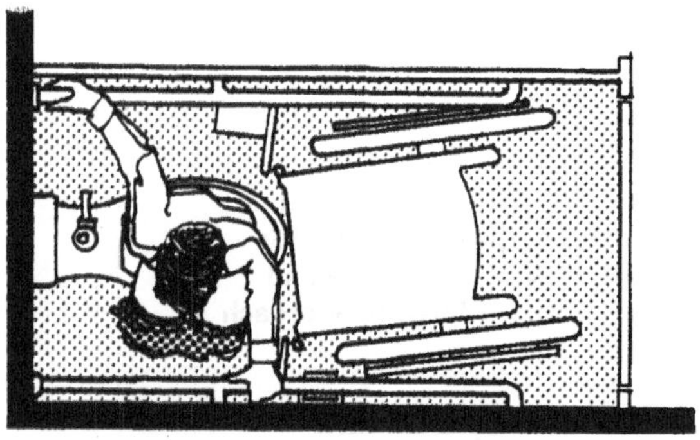

the user pulls forward and slides onto the toilet seat in a sideways position.

After placing both hands on the facing grab bar, the user releases the wheelchair brakes and pushes the chair back out of the way.

36 Inch Alternate Stall Forward Approach for Wheelchair User

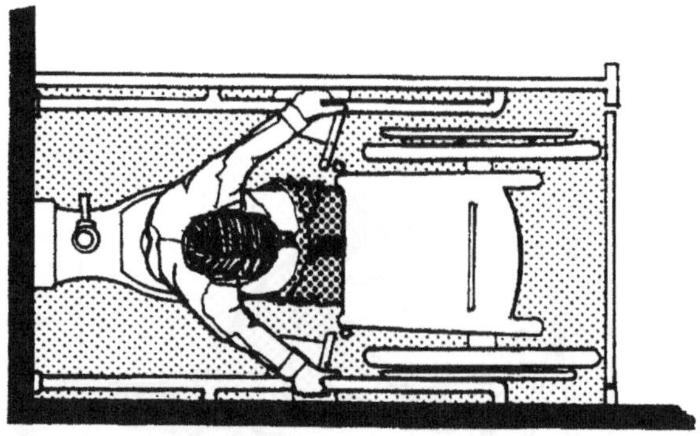

The user then turns around to the front, facing the door. The length of the stall provides enough space for both the chair and the user with the door closed.

Most stalls in existing toilet rooms are approximately 30 inches wide and do not easily lend themselves to conversion to the 36 inch width required by the alternate stall. Although the 36 inch width can be achieved by simply moving one of the side partitions, this solution is not acceptable because it makes the adjacent stall very cramped and the toilet fixture is off center in each stall. If space exists at the end of the row, both partitions can be adjusted/moved to create a 36 inch width stall or 48 inch minimum width stall, with the toilet fixture located 18 inches from the side partition. In most cases the 36 inch and 48 inch alternate stalls will need to be deeper than existing stalls and the protrusion into circulation space may be unacceptable, especially in small toilet rooms.

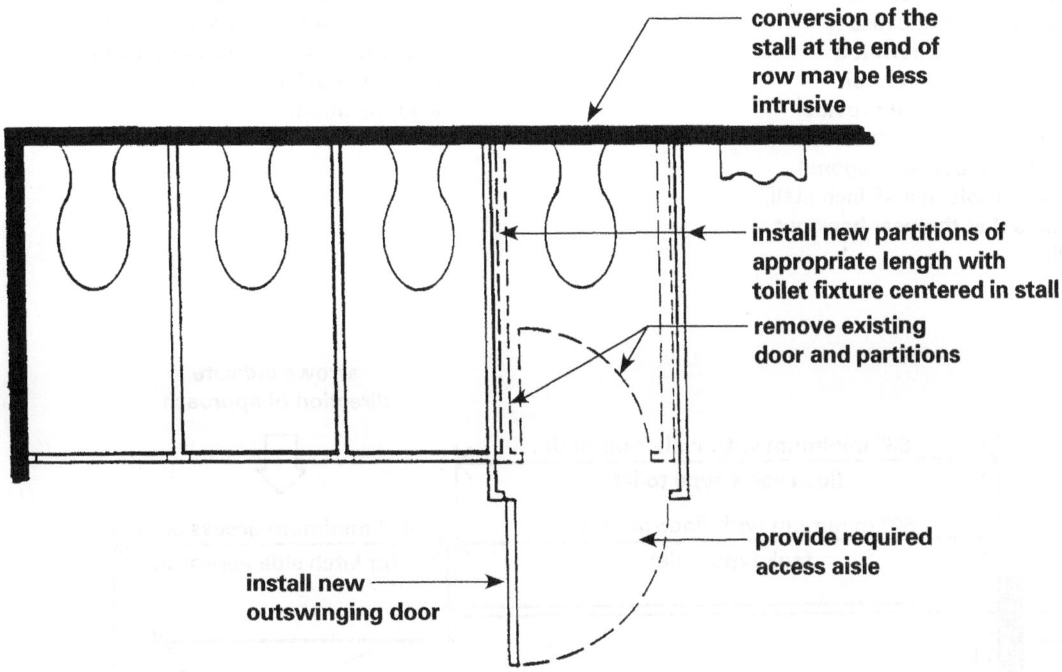

Conversion of 30 Inch to Alternate 36 Inch Stall

Use of 48" Wide Stall

The 48 inch stall is less usable than the 60 inch stall because it is not wide enough to permit a parallel or diagonal wheelchair approach. It also does not provide enough space for a wheelchair user to turn around. A reverse diagonal approach is possible in a 48 inch stall, but it requires that the user back out of the stall.

Use of Wider Stall

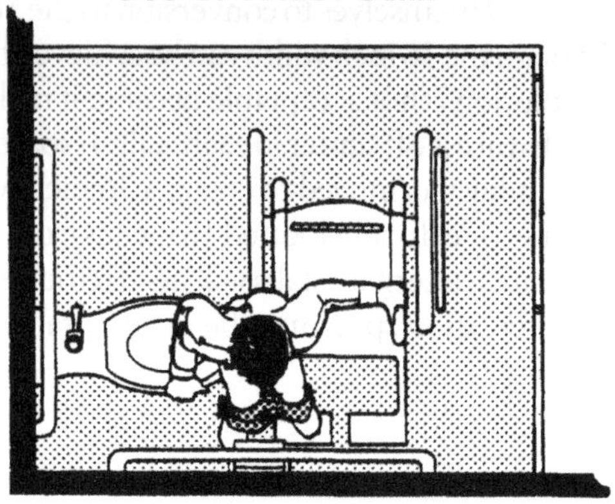

A perpendicular approach may be possible for some users if the stall is wider than 48 inches; permitting the user to back in and turn into the 90° position.

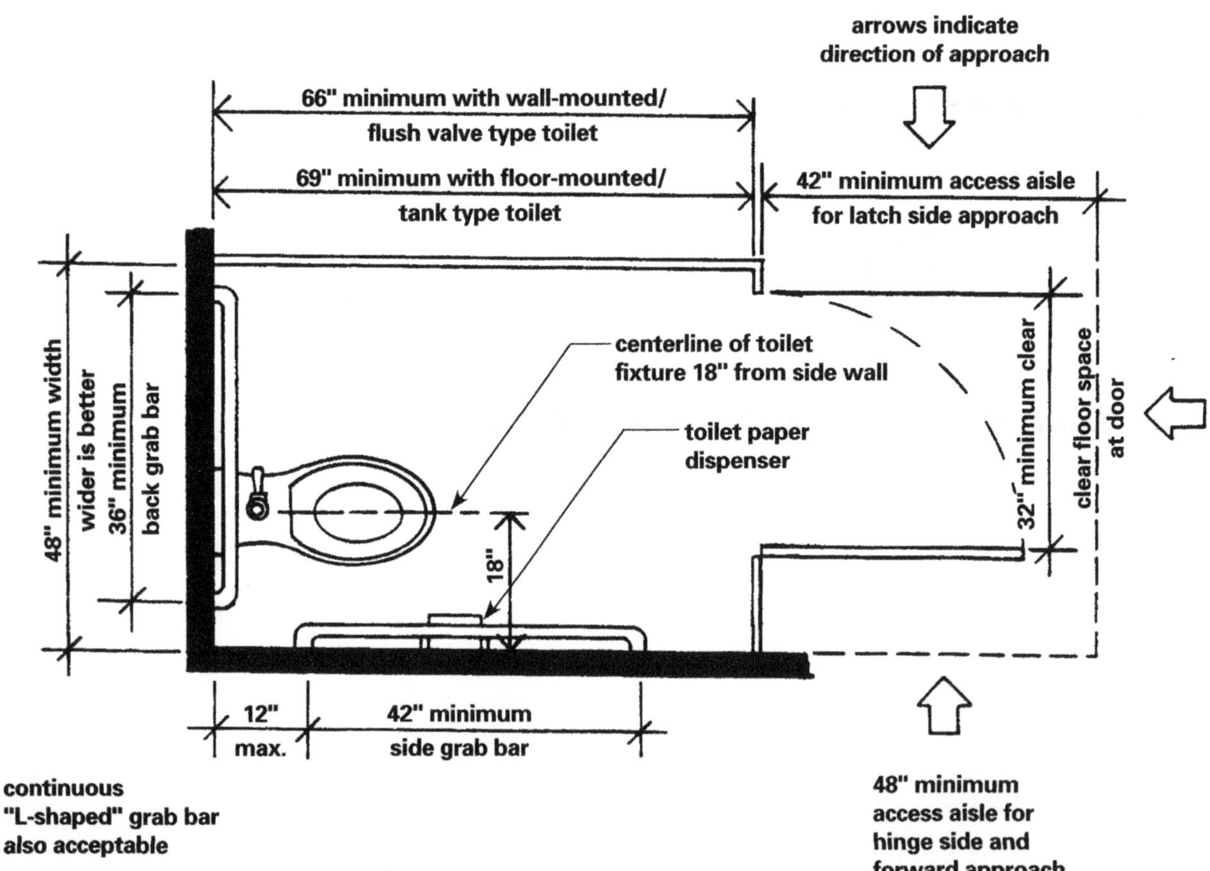

48" Minimum Alternate Stall

REFERENCE INDEX TO UFAS DOCUMENT

STANDARD 60 INCH AND ALTERNATE 36 INCH AND 48 INCH TOILET STALLS

URINALS

UFAS 4.18

Introduction

A properly installed urinal eliminates the necessity for male wheelchair users to either transfer onto the toilet to urinate or to make an awkward attempt to straddle the toilet fixture and use it as though it were a urinal. Also, because accessible urinals are mounted at lower heights, they are more easily used by young boys who may have difficulty using standard height urinals. Furthermore, the lower height urinals are more convenient for men who may use the fixture to empty a leg bag.

UFAS requires that, if urinals are provided, at least one must be accessible (see UFAS Subsections 4.22.5 and 4.23.5 under Toilet Rooms and Bathing Facilities, page 44). Although some state access codes do not require an accessible urinal if an accessible stall is provided, the only exception allowed by UFAS involves existing toilet rooms which are structurally impracticable to renovate. In these situations, a unisex toilet room may be installed at a nearby location.

Basic Design Considerations

Urinal Types and Installation Requirements

UFAS requires that urinals be either stall-type/floor-mounted or wall-mounted with an elongated rim. UFAS also requires that the rim be mounted no higher than 17 inches from the floor, several inches lower than the "standard" mounting height for urinals. Some state codes require rim heights even lower, at a maximum of 15 inches. The lower rim height allows wheelchair users to pull in close, with the leading edge of their wheelchair seat over the top of rim, while the elongated lip permits the user's legs to straddle the fixture. Although UFAS does not define elongated, ANSI A117.1(1986) and some state codes require that the urinal project a minimum of 14 inches from the wall. Floor-mounted urinals should have rims level with the floor (drains below floor level) to allow close approach by wheelchair users. Some state codes do not consider floor-mounted urinals to be accessible.

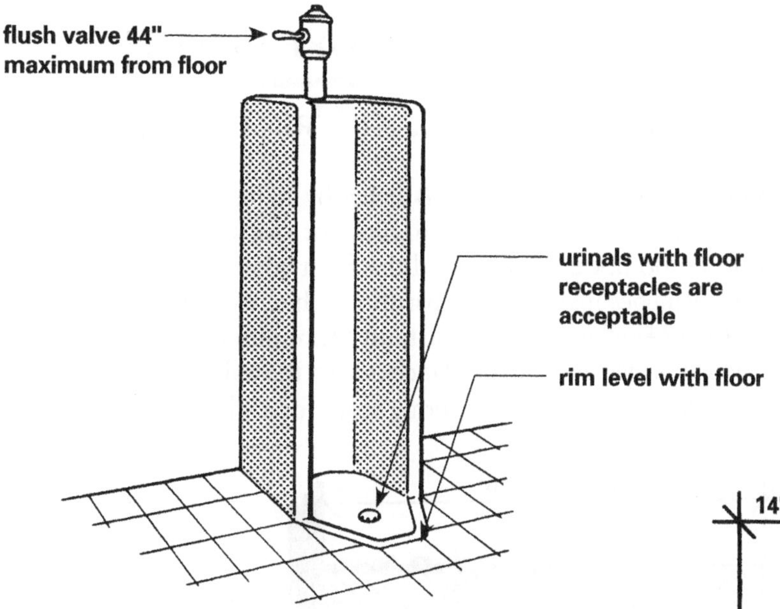

Stall Type/Floor-Mounted

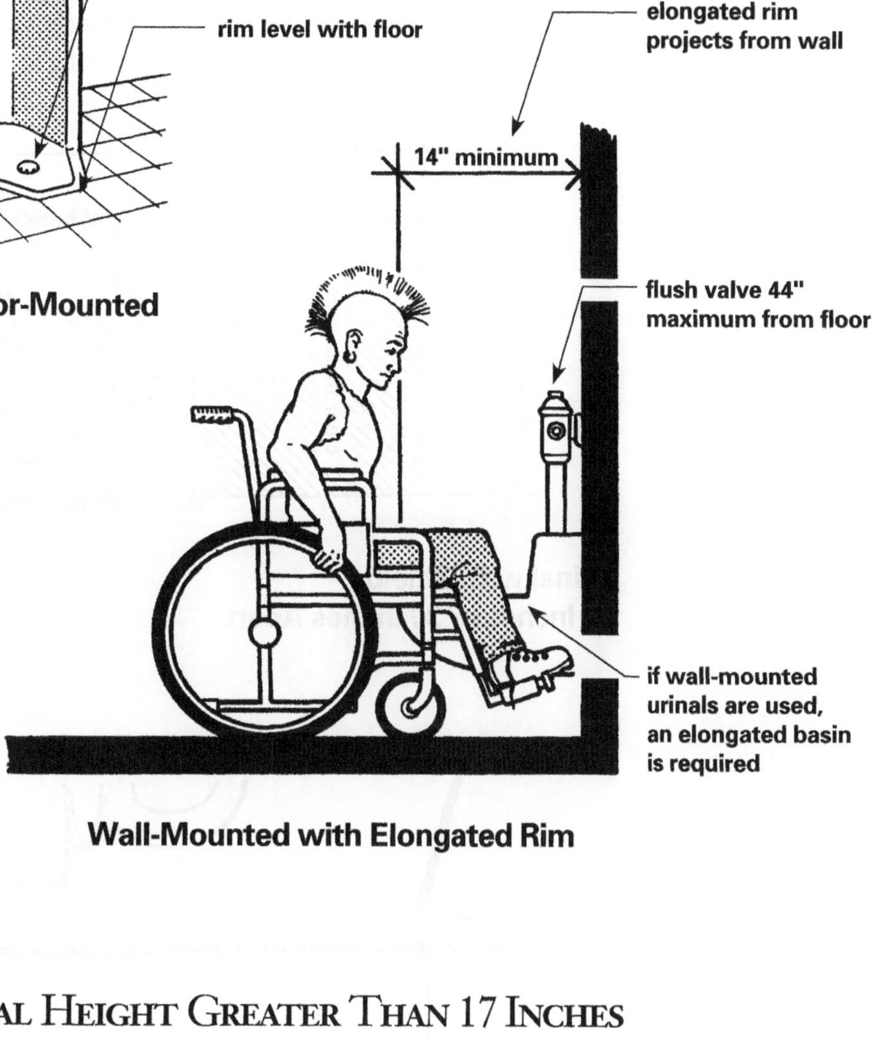

Wall-Mounted with Elongated Rim

PROBLEM URINAL HEIGHT GREATER THAN 17 INCHES

SOLUTION RE-INSTALL OR REPLACE WALL-MOUNTED URINAL AT PROPER HEIGHT

If an existing wall-mounted fixture is mounted too high, it may be possible to reinstall the fixture within the range required by UFAS. This approach will likely involve moving the carrier iron which supports the fixture and some adjustment to the piping. If the design of the existing fixture is not appropriate, then it may be best to replace the unit with a more suitable model.

BASIC DESIGN CONSIDERATIONS

CLEAR FLOOR SPACE AT URINALS

UFAS requires that a clear floor space of 30 inches by 48 inches, which adjoins an accessible route, be provided in front of urinals to allow for a forward approach. Urinal shields/partitions which do not extend beyond the front edge of the urinal may be spaced a minimum of 29 inches apart. Shields/partitions which extend beyond the front of the urinal but less than 24 inches from the wall must be a minimum of 30 inches apart. Shields/partitions which project more than 24 inches from the wall must be a minimum of 36 inches apart to allow adequate maneuvering space for a wheelchair user.

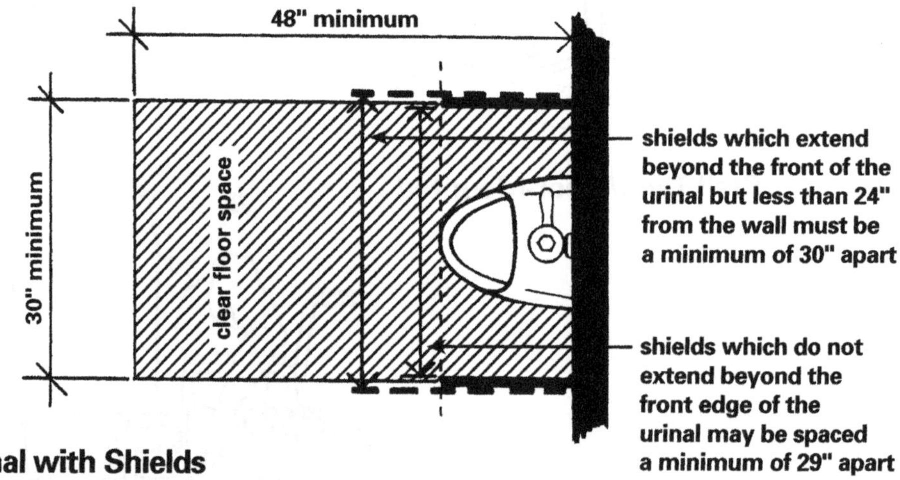

Urinal with Shields
29 Inches or 30 Inches Apart

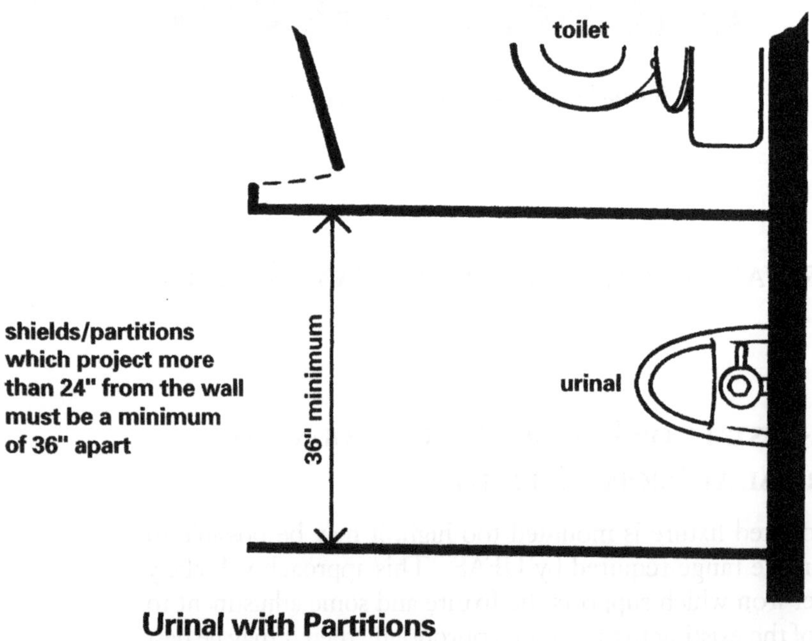

Urinal with Partitions
36 Inches Apart

PROBLEM INSUFFICIENT MANEUVERING SPACE AT URINAL

SOLUTION REMOVE OR RELOCATE SHIELDS

If the existing shields do not meet the UFAS requirements, then they should be relocated or removed. If the shields are 29 inches apart but extend beyond the rim of the urinal, then they should be shortened.

BASIC DESIGN CONSIDERATIONS

FLUSH CONTROLS

Flush controls can be automatic or manual, mounted no more than 44 inches above the floor. The flush controls must be easy to operate with one hand and not require gripping or twisting or more than five pounds of force to operate, as specified in UFAS 4.27.4, page 45.

PROBLEM INAPPROPRIATE FLUSH CONTROLS

SOLUTION REPLACE OR SUPPLEMENT FLUSH CONTROLS

Inappropriate hand controls and foot-operated pedals do not meet the performance specifications for controls and should be replaced or supplemented with suitable hand-operated controls.

PRACTICAL PLUS

Some state codes require the installation of vertical grab bars on both sides of urinals. These grab bars are designed to serve as auxiliary support for ambulatory men who use a mobility aide such as crutches, leg braces, canes, and walkers, or wheelchair users who prefer to stand with support. As with all grab bar installations, the general issues of location, secure mounting, appropriate size, and spacing must always be considered.

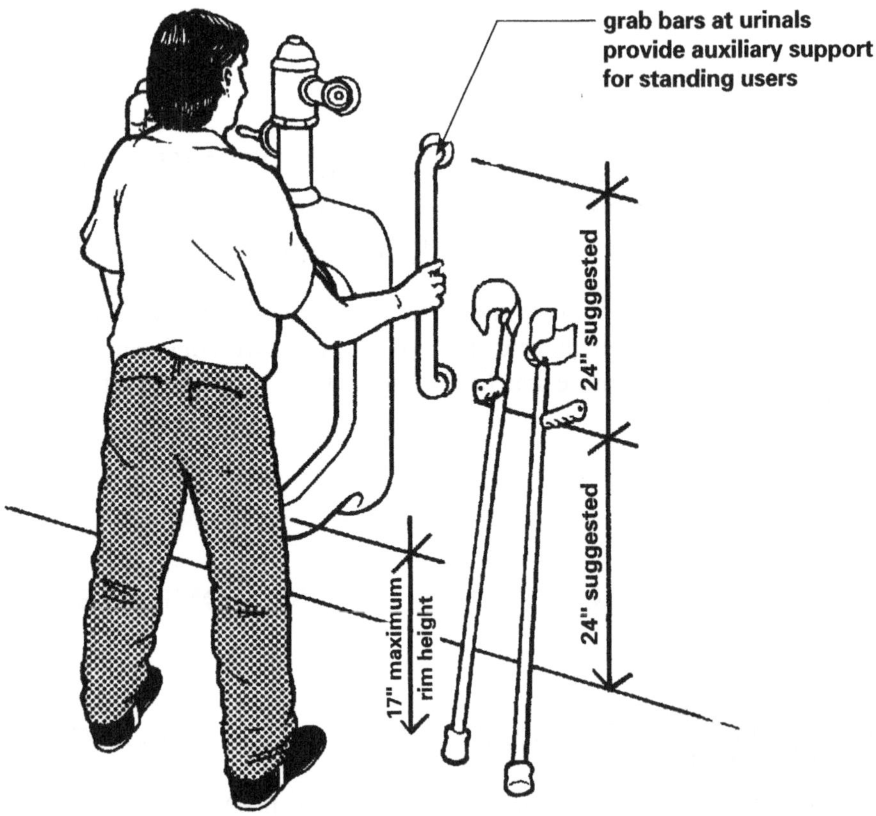

Grab Bars at Urinal

REFERENCE INDEX TO UFAS DOCUMENT

WALL-MOUNTED AND FLOOR-MOUNTED URINALS

Primary References	UFAS page	Secondary References	UFAS page
4.18.1 General/Location	40	4.1 Scope & Technical Requirements for Toilet Rooms	5-6
		4.1.5(3) Additions	11
		4.1.6(3)(c)(i) Alterations	12
		4.1.6(3)(c)(ii) Alterations	12
		4.1.6(4)(e) Alterations	13
		4.1.7(2)(c) Historic Preservation	14
		4.22.5 Toilet Rooms/Urinals	44
		4.23.5 Bathing Facilities/Urinals	44
4.18.2 Height	40		
4.18.3 Clear Floor Space	40	4.2.4 Clear Floor or Ground Space for Wheelchairs	14
4.18.4 Flush Controls	40	4.27.4 Controls and Operating Mechanisms	45

Introduction

As with other building elements and features, lavatories and mirrors must be designed and installed to provide adequate space for users to approach and maneuver about the fixtures. Additionally, in the case of lavatories, the controls must be easy to reach and operate. For the most part, the requirements for use by people with disabilities do not differ significantly from those of other users. Proper installation involves several features including the provision of appropriate clear floor space adjacent to an accessible route, sufficient knee space, and usable controls. In addition, for the safety of wheelchair users, a protective covering must be provided at lavatories when waste and hot water lines are exposed.

The scoping requirements for lavatories and mirrors are described in UFAS Subsections 4.22.6 and 4.23.6 under Toilet Rooms and Bathing Facilities, page 44. As with other toilet room fixtures, UFAS requires that, if lavatories and mirrors are provided, at least one of each must be accessible. The accessible lavatory can be included as part of a "unisex" toilet room if alterations to existing toilet rooms are structurally impracticable.

Basic Design Considerations

Mounting Height and Knee Clearance for Lavatories

Mounting Height and Knee Clearance. UFAS requires that the front edge of the lavatory be a minimum of 17 inches from the back wall. Lavatories must be mounted with the rim or counter surface a maximum of 34 inches and the bottom of the apron a minimum of 29 inches above the finished floor. Additionally, a 27 inch minimum vertical knee space must be allotted below the lavatory which may slope down and back a minimum of 8 inches from the front edge of the apron. From this point, the knee space further slopes down and back a minimum of 3 inches to a point at least 9 inches above the floor. The drain and pipes may occupy space from this line back to the wall, provided toe space, a maximum of 6 inches deep and a minimum of 9 inches high, is left unobstructed. The provision of knee and toe space is necessary for wheelchair users to make a close front approach to the lavatory without their knees or chairs bumping the lavatory and pipes and without foot rests hitting the wall.

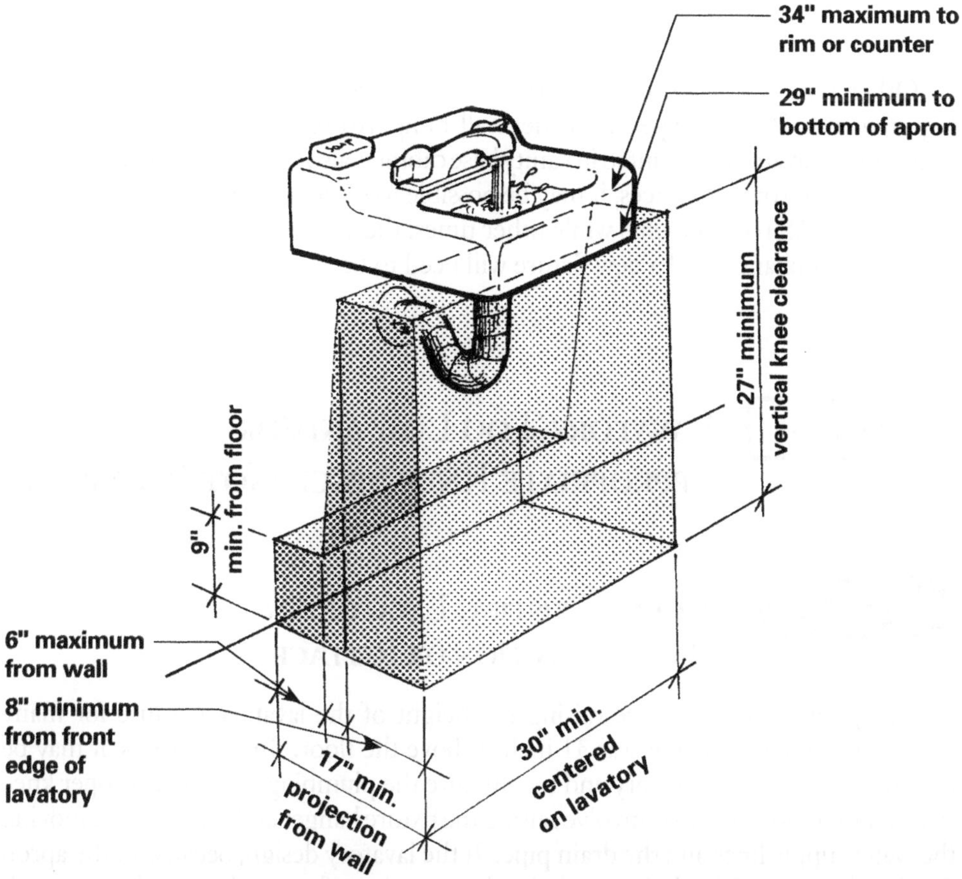

Knee Space and Toe Space at Lavatories

Some state codes may not require knee space if clear space for side approaches is allotted. In this instance, UFAS is the more stringent requirement, and knee space meeting the UFAS specifications must be provided. Some state codes also differ from UFAS in the mounting height and knee space requirements for lavatories. If the state code requires a mounting height no higher than 32 inches, then the state requirement should be met since, in this instance, the state code is more stringent than the UFAS requirement for a 34 inch maximum height.

Type of Fixtures. The UFAS requirements apply to all types of lavatories including wall-hung, countertop, pedestal, vanity, and special combination models. In most cases, appropriately designed standard fixtures can be carefully installed or modified to meet the UFAS requirements. For example, there are many standard model, wall-hung lavatories with narrow aprons which have front edges which project a minimum of 17 inches from the back wall. However, several manufacturers carry special "accessible hospital-type" models with elongated basins. Some lavatories with elongated basins are actually more difficult to use because the faucets are hard to reach. Although these "accessible hospital-type" fixtures may meet the UFAS requirements, they are not required and are usually more expensive, unattractive, and unnecessary.

Other types of lavatories, by virtue of their designs, do not meet the UFAS requirements. Pedestal type and corner wall-hung fixtures may not provide sufficient knee space. Lavatories mounted in vanity base cabinets also do not provide the required knee space. In some instances, it may be possible to modify an existing installation to meet the UFAS requirements while other times, the actual design of the fixture may preclude compliance, and a new fixture will need to be installed.

PROBLEM — LAVATORY TOO LOW AND/OR APPROPRIATE KNEE SPACE NOT PROVIDED

SOLUTION 1 — MOUNT EXISTING LAVATORY IN HIGHER POSITION OR REPLACE

Many renovations require raising the height of the lavatory because for many years the "standard" height was 31 inches above the floor. In some cases, it may be possible to rehang the lavatory and reconfigure the plumbing to provide proper knee space. This renovation may involve raising the fixture hanger and extending or moving the water supply lines and the drain pipe. If the lavatory design, because of the apron depth or location of the drain, precludes the provision of proper knee and toe space, it may be necessary to replace it.

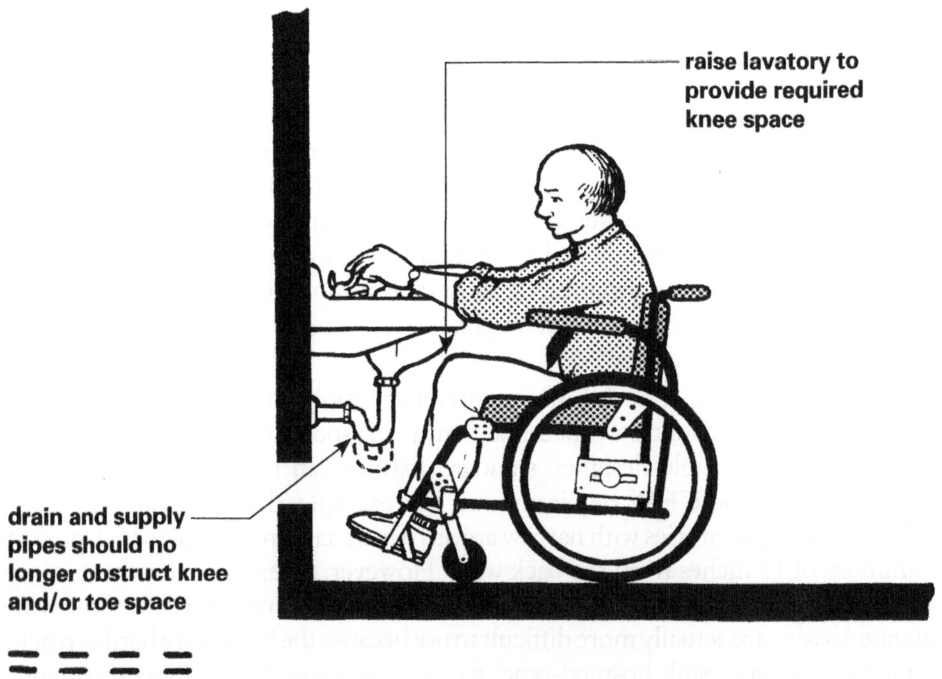

Raise Lavatory

SOLUTION 2 ADAPT COUNTERTOP AND VANITY CABINET

Countertops and vanity cabinets can usually be adapted to meet the UFAS requirements. If the front apron of the countertop obstructs the knee space, then it may be possible to trim out a segment of the apron to allow close approach for wheelchair users. Vanity base cabinets can be removed to provide knee space and the vanity top/ lavatory can be reinstalled by securely mounting it to the wall as a cantilevered unit mounted on brackets. The knee space must meet the requirements described above, and exposed surfaces and pipes must be covered.

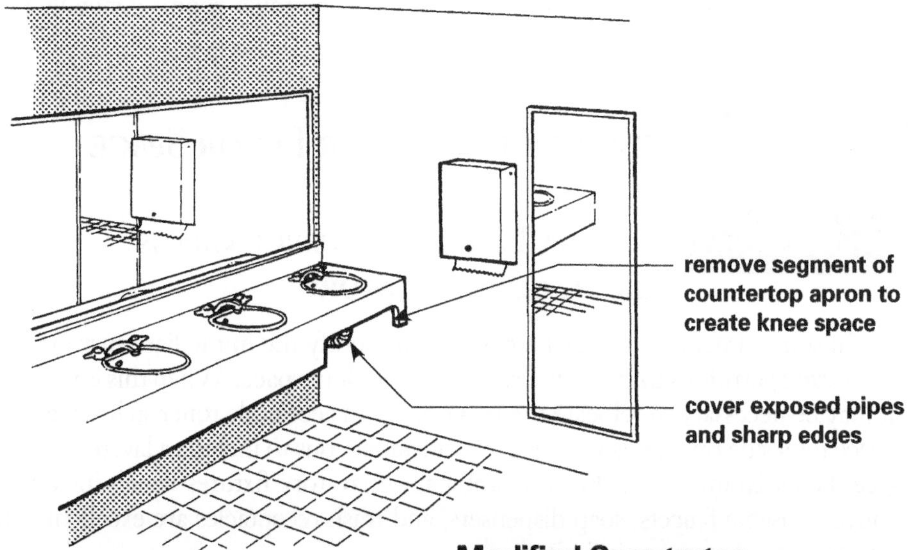

Modified Countertop

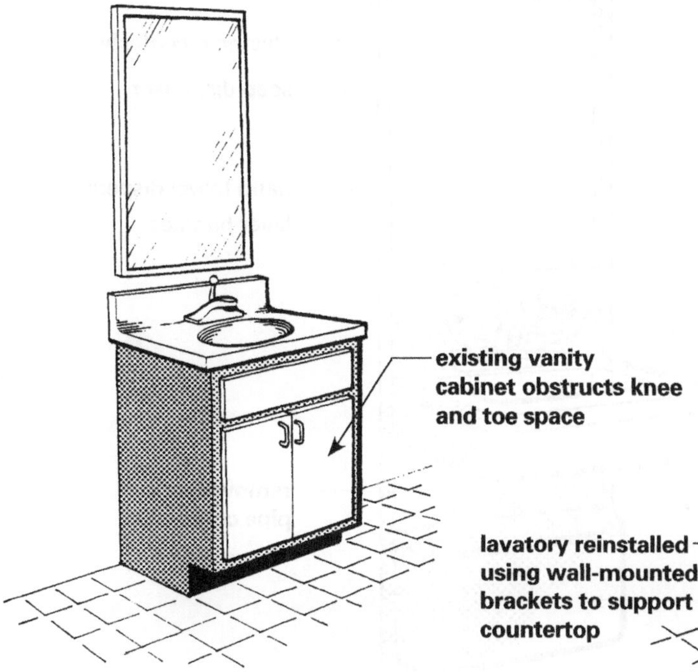

Lavatory with Vanity Base Cabinet

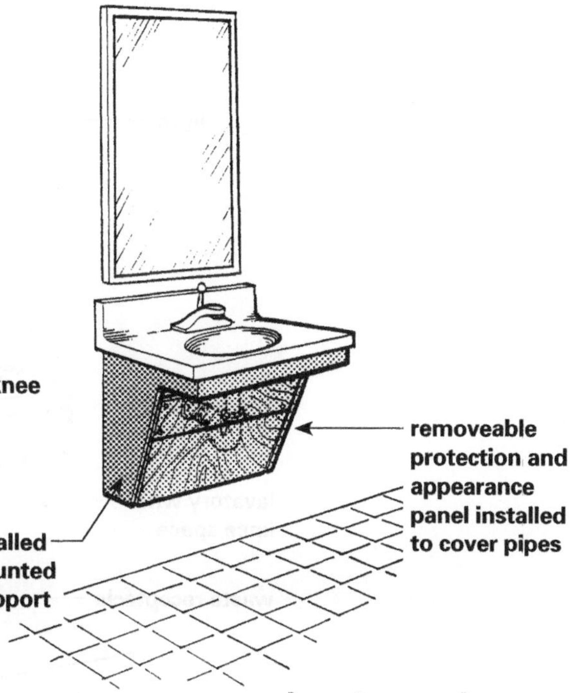

Lavatory and Countertop Reinstalled

BASIC DESIGN CONSIDERATIONS

CLEAR FLOOR SPACE AT LAVATORIES

Clear floor space is required at lavatories to allow for a forward approach to the fixture. The space must adjoin an accessible route and be 30 inches by 48 inches minimum which may extend under the lavatory a maximum of 19 inches. If a lavatory is mounted in an alcove, between walls or partitions which are greater than 24 inches in length, then the clear floor space must be widened to 36 inches. With the exception of very small rest rooms, most multi-fixture, public toilet rooms generally provide adequate clear floor space in front of lavatories.

PROBLEM — INSUFFICIENT CLEAR FLOOR SPACE

SOLUTION — MODIFY IMMEDIATE SURROUNDINGS OR RELOCATE LAVATORY

In some situations, it may be possible to modify the immediate surroundings by relocating partitions to create the required clear floor space. When this is not possible, it may be necessary to relocate the lavatory. If an accessible toilet stall is planned and space for a side transfer is included, it is advantageous to include a lavatory in the stall (see Toilet Rooms, Unit Five). Combination lavatory fixtures which include lights, mirrors, usable faucets, soap dispensers, and trash receptacles are excellent compact alternatives when space is limited.

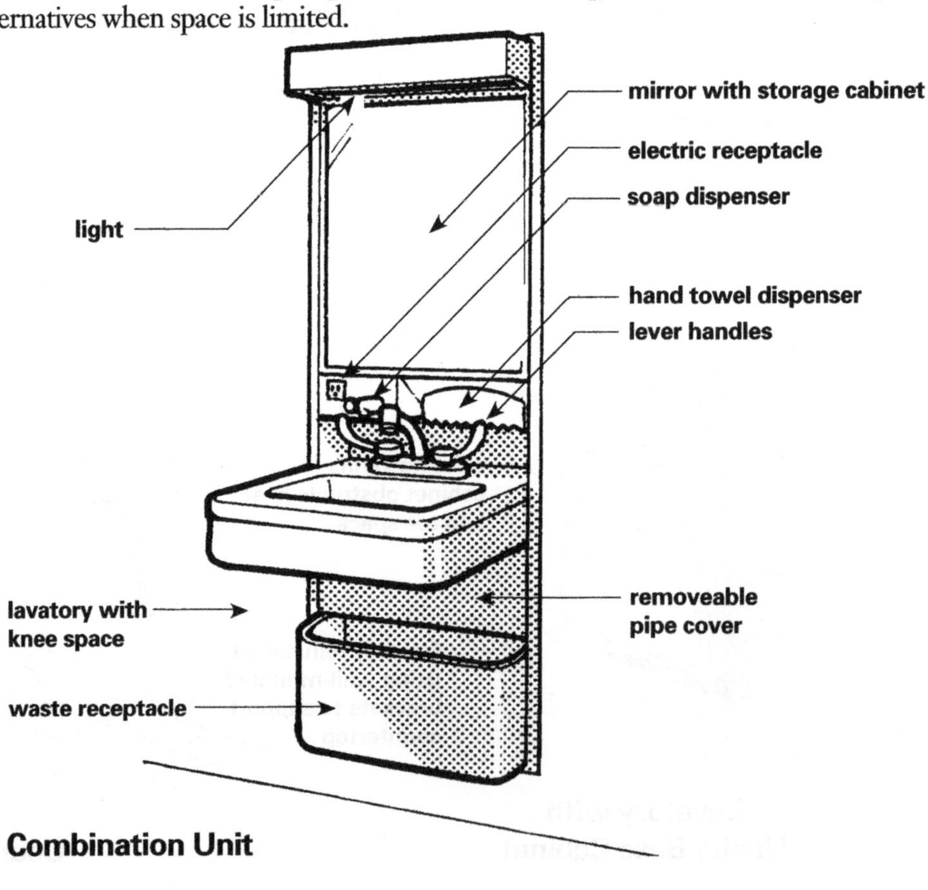

Combination Unit

BASIC DESIGN CONSIDERATIONS

PIPE PROTECTION FOR LAVATORIES

UFAS requires that hot water and drain pipes under lavatories be insulated or covered and that there be no sharp or abrasive surfaces under it. These measures ensure that wheelchair users, who may have little or no sensation in their legs, do not come in contact with hot or sharp surfaces. Although not required by UFAS, some designers and building managers prefer to use PVC or ABS plastic pipes in addition to protective covers, because they give off less heat than metal pipes. Protective covers, panels, or wraps must not encroach on the required knee and toe space.

PROBLEM NO PIPE PROTECTION

SOLUTION WRAP PIPES WITH INSULATION OR INSTALL COVER

The least expensive method of providing protection from hot pipes and sharp surfaces is to wrap them with insulation. Although this solution is effective, it is often difficult to maintain the insulation in good repair, and it may be removed completely and not replaced when repairs are made. A reasonably-priced, aesthetic and functional improvement may be possible with the installation of a commercially available or custom-made pipe cover. These pipe covers should be designed and installed so they are easy to remove and replace when the drain trap or valves need repair.

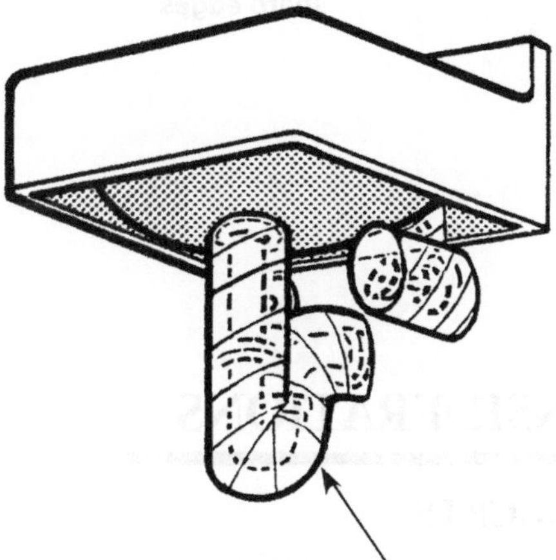

foam or fiber insulation with protective overwrap on drain, hot water supply, and sharp edges

Insulation Wrap

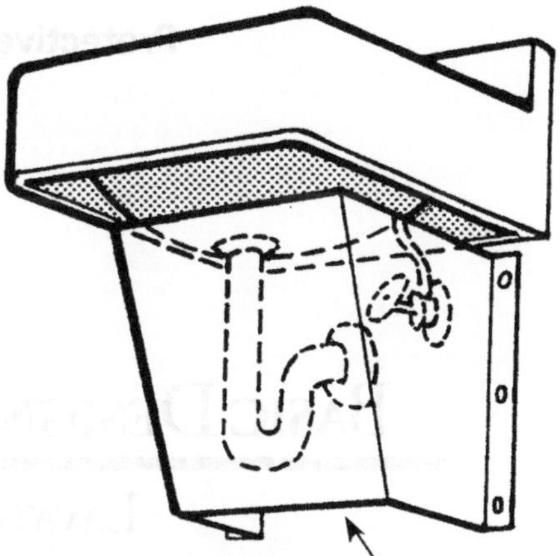

commercially available or custom-made pipe cover; easily removable for plumbing repairs

Pipe Cover

SOLUTION 2 INSTALL PROTECTIVE PANEL AT COUNTERTOP LAVATORIES

The supply pipes and drains for lavatories located in countertops can frequently be hidden with a panel which both protects wheelchair users and improves the aesthetic quality of the installation. Many cabinet manufacturers offer countertops with lavatories which meet the UFAS requirements for knee and toe space. Existing installations can often be modified to include protective panels. The panels should be removable to allow for easy repair.

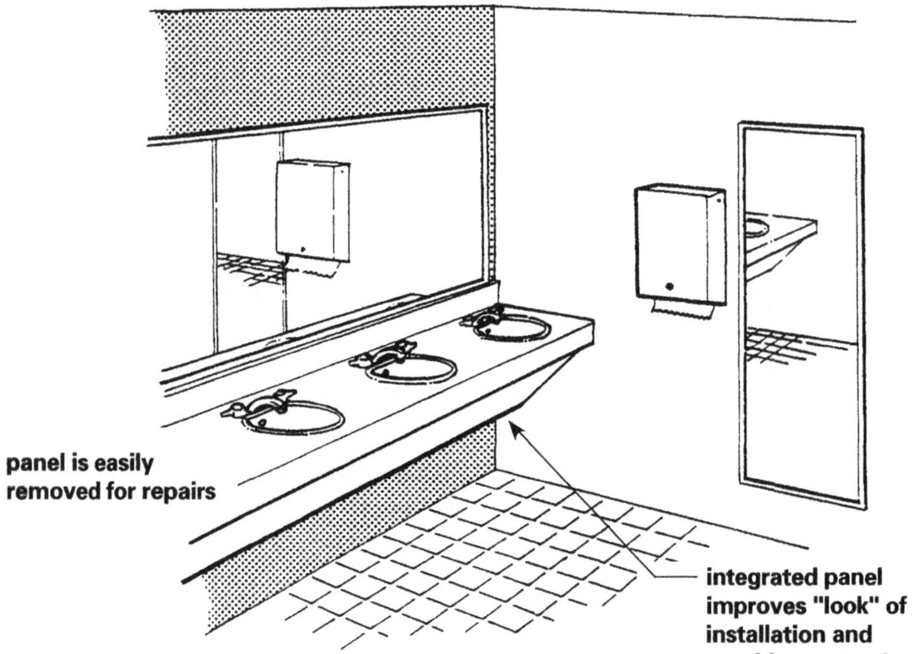

Protective Panel

BASIC DESIGN CONSIDERATIONS

LAVATORY FAUCETS

UFAS requires that controls at lavatories meet the operating requirements established in 4.27.4 of Controls and Operating Mechanisms, page 45. The faucets may be lever-operated, push-type, or electronically controlled provided they are operable with one hand and do not require gripping, twisting, or excessive force to operate. Self-closing valves are allowed if the faucet remains open for at least 10 seconds.

An additional requirement of some state codes is that the faucets be located no more than 17 inches from the front edge of the lavatory. Although not included in UFAS, the intent of this specification is to ensure that the faucets are easy to reach. Some of the "accessible/elongated" models will not meet this requirement and cannot be installed under codes containing this requirement. Some state and local codes specify temperature maximums for hot water and include requirements that the hot water faucet be located on the left-hand side and the cold water faucet be located on the right-hand side, as is common practice. As a rule, if both temperature and volume can be controlled by one hand, the control is probably acceptable.

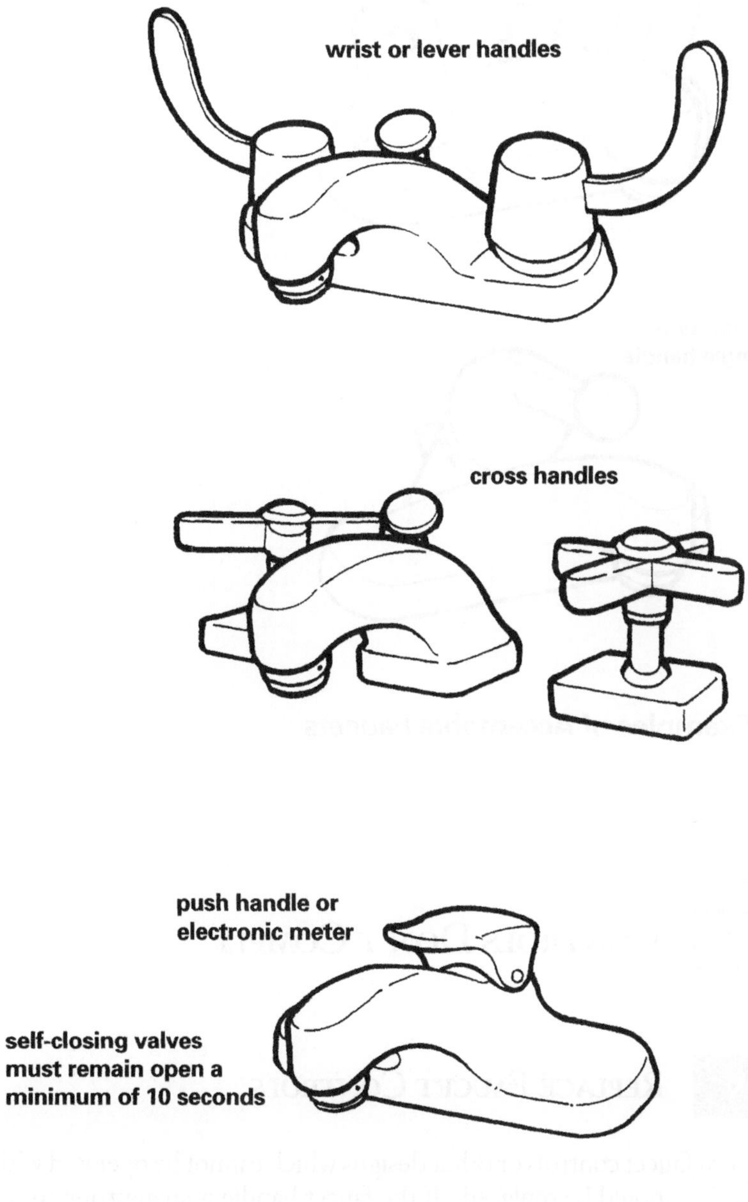

Examples of Acceptable Faucets

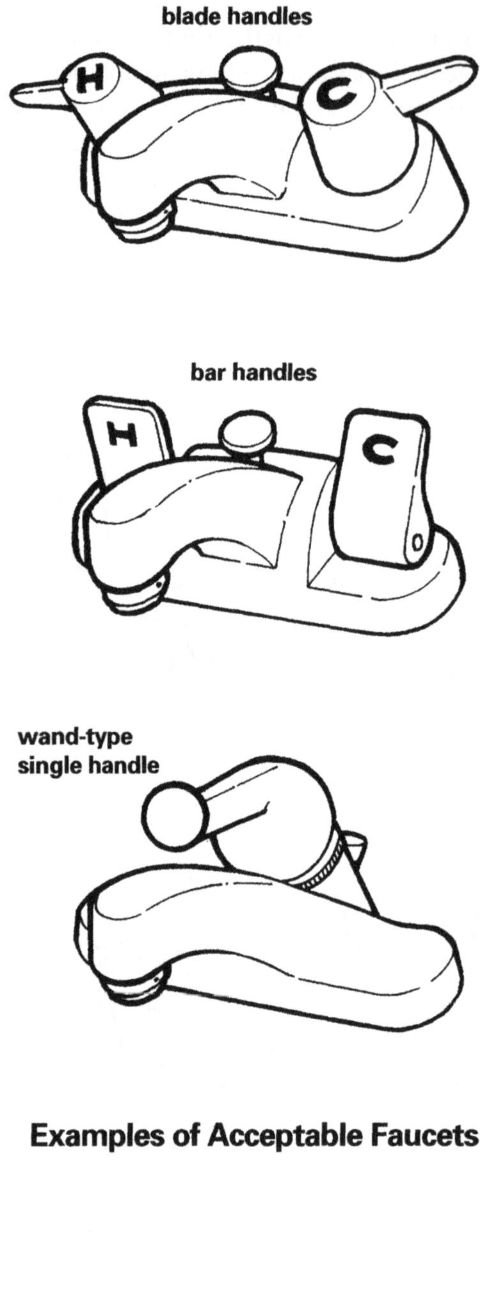

Examples of Acceptable Faucets

PROBLEM — CONTROLS DON'T COMPLY

SOLUTION — REPLACE FAUCET CONTROLS

Round smooth faucet controls or other designs which cannot be operated without gripping or twisting should be replaced. If the faucet handle is an appropriate shape but is difficult to turn, it should be adjusted so it works easily.

BASIC DESIGN CONSIDERATIONS

MIRRORS

To be usable by most people, including children, people of short stature, and those using wheelchairs, UFAS requires that the lower edge of the reflecting surface be not more than 40 inches above the floor. This height was established for mirrors which are typically installed on the wall behind the lavatory. Some state codes are more stringent than UFAS and require lower edges at 38 inches.

Several manufacturers offer supposedly useful, fixed- and/or adjustable- tilt mirrors which provide short users with an oddly distorted image of themselves and standing people with a view of their legs and feet. A more universally usable solution is a full length mirror installed nearby which gives all users a full view of themselves. The UFAS Appendix suggests that, if mirrors are to be used by standing people, the top most edge should be at least 74 inches high.

PROBLEM INAPPROPRIATE MIRROR HEIGHT

SOLUTION LOWER EXISTING MIRROR OR INSTALL FULL LENGTH MIRROR

Frequently, existing mirrors can be lowered to the required height without much difficulty. If existing mirrors are mounted to the doors of a medicine or storage cabinet, it may be may difficult to lower the mirrored doors further without conflicting with faucets or faucet controls. If the lavatory installation prohibits lowering the mirror, then it may be best to simply add a full length mirror nearby.

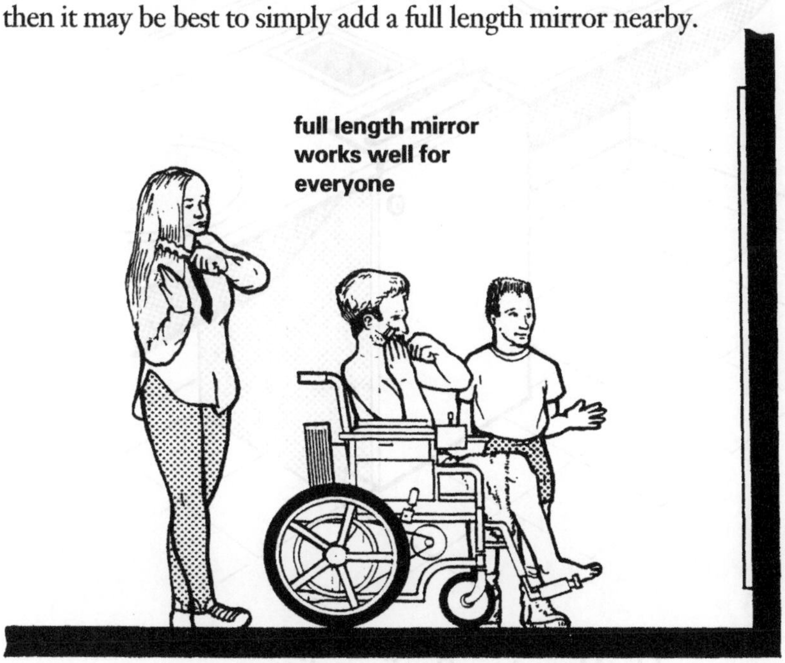

Universally Usable Full Length Mirror

IDEAL CONDITIONS

- ❑ Lavatory mounted at universally usable height
- ❑ Drain located to back of basin to minimize obstruction of knee space
- ❑ Ample knee and toe space with protective panel to prevent accidents
- ❑ Basin installed as close as possible to front edge of counter to minimize reach to faucet controls
- ❑ Clear floor space for maneuvering and forward approach
- ❑ Mirror at appropriate height
- ❑ Countertop provides ample space for resting parcels and purses while using lavatory
- ❑ Lever handles on thermostatically controlled faucets are easy and safe to use
- ❑ Soap and towel dispensers within reach and easy to use
- ❑ Built-in trash receptacle provides maximum clear floor space

Ideal Lavatory Configuration

REFERENCE INDEX TO UFAS DOCUMENT

LAVATORIES AND MIRRORS

Primary References	UFAS page	Secondary References	UFAS page
4.19.1 General/Location	40	4.1 Scope & Technical Requirements for Toilet Rooms	5-6
		4.1.5(3) Additions	11
		4.1.6(3)(c)(i) Alterations	12
		4.1.6(3)(c)(ii) Alterations	12
		4.1.6(4)(e) Alterations	13
		4.1.7(2)(c) Historic Preservation	14
		4.22.6 Toilet Rooms/Lavatories and Mirrors	44
		4.23.6 Bathing Facilities/Lavatories and Mirrors	44
4.19.2 Height and Clearances	40		
4.19.3 Clear Floor Space	40	4.2.4 Clear Floor or Ground Space for Wheelchairs	14
4.19.4 Exposed Pipes and Surfaces	40		
4.19.5 Faucets	40	4.27.4 Controls and Operating Mechanisms	45
4.19.6 Mirrors	40	A4.19.6 Mirrors	65

Introduction

Three distinct types of bathing fixtures are described in UFAS including bathtubs, transfer showers, and roll-in showers. Bathtubs are perhaps the most versatile type of fixture, offering the user the choice of a soaking bath, a standing shower, or with the addition of a removable tub seat, a seated shower. UFAS also describes a second type of seat/transfer surface which is built in at the head of the tub. Additional features including grab bars, maneuvering space, appropriate controls, and shower units, which make tubs easier and safer to use for everyone, are also described in UFAS .

In new construction, additions, and renovations (including historic properties), UFAS requires that, if tubs or showers are provided, then at least one accessible tub or one accessible shower must be provided. Some state codes are more stringent than UFAS and require both accessible tubs and showers if both are provided. Additional information on bathtubs and bathroom layout can be found in Unit Five, Bathing Facilities and Shower Rooms.

Basic Design Considerations

Accessible Tub Features

Bathtubs which meet the UFAS specifications can be fabricated from a variety of materials including acrylic, plastic, fiberglass, or porcelain enamel. Several fixture manufacturers carry molded units, complete with grab bars and portable/integral seats, which when properly installed meet the UFAS requirements and performance specifications. The UFAS design and installation requirements are described in further detail below.

Floor Space. UFAS describes floor space in terms of a wheelchair user's approach to the bathtub fixture and the type of seat installed. If space for a parallel approach is planned, it should be a minimum of 30 inches by 60 inches for an in-tub seat and 30 inches by 75 inches minimum if the seat is included at the head of the tub. If a forward approach is planned, a minimum space of 60 inches by 48 inches should be allowed. The lavatory can overhang the clear floor space provided proper knee and toe space are allocated under the lavatory and it is located so it does not interfere with access to the seat.

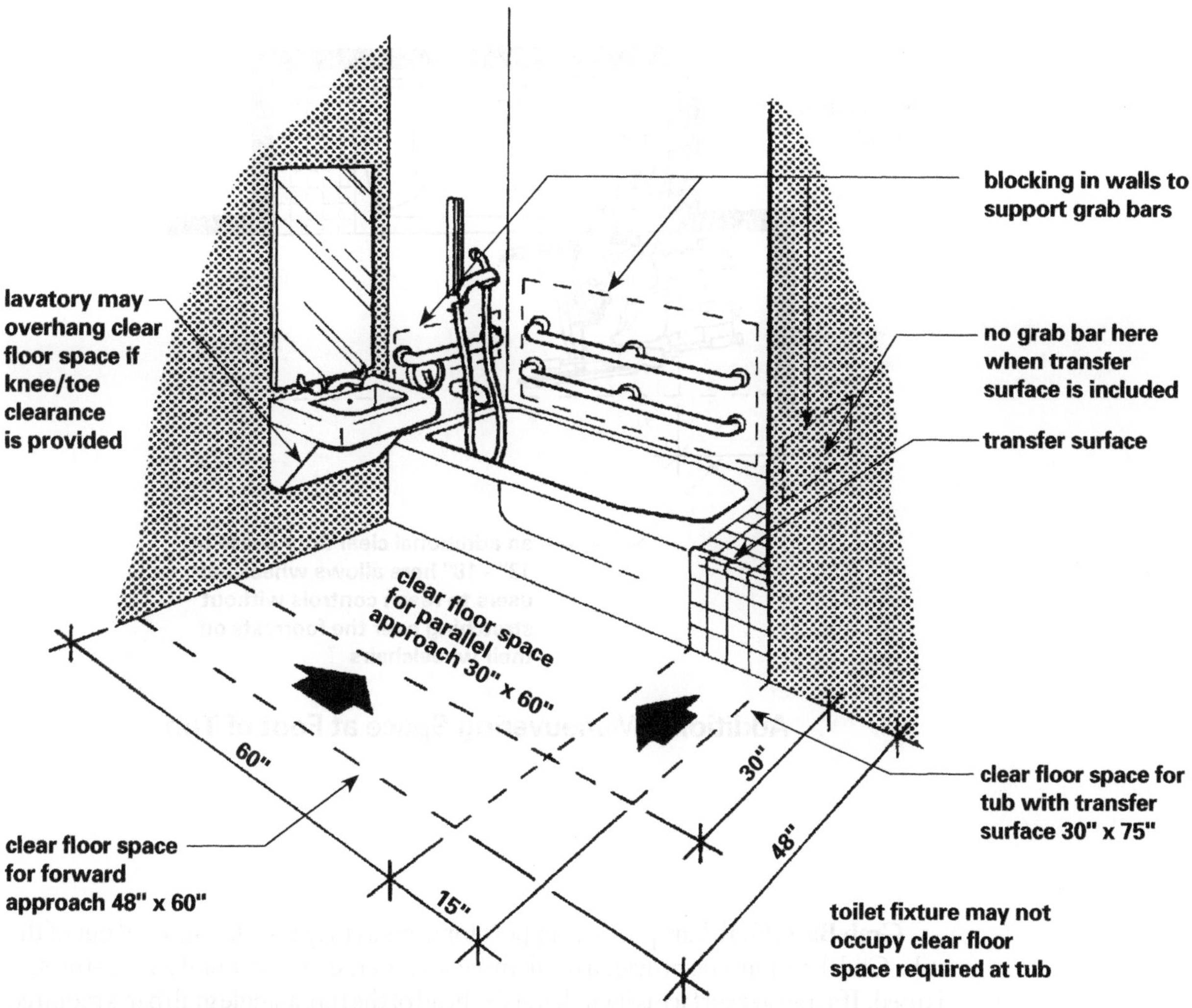

Maneuvering Space at Bathtubs

PRACTICAL PLUS

If possible, the inclusion of additional clear floor space forward of the tub near the controls makes reaching the controls easier for wheelchair users who may have difficulty leaning forward to operate the controls.

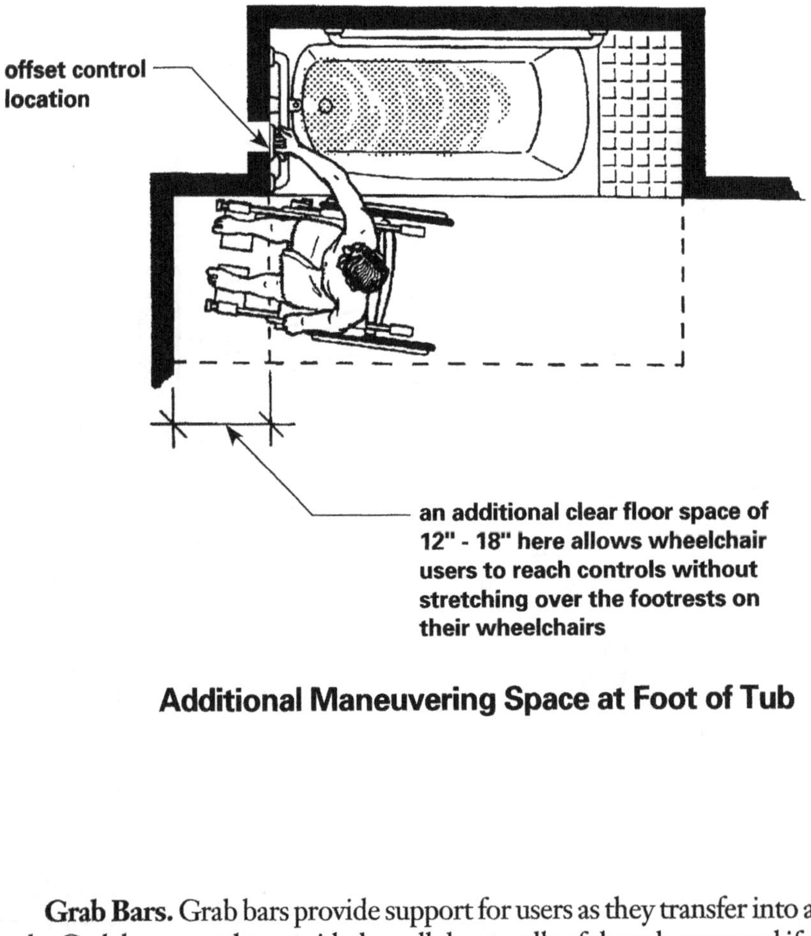

Additional Maneuvering Space at Foot of Tub

Grab Bars. Grab bars provide support for users as they transfer into and out of the tub. Grab bars must be provided on all three walls of the tub surround if an in-tub seat is used. If a transfer surface is included at the head of the tub, a single grab bar is required on the wall at the foot of the tub and dual grab bars are required along the length of the back wall, but no grab bars are required at the head of the tub where they would interfere with the use of the transfer surface. The lower grab bar along the back wall is used for support and leverage while lowering oneself down into or out of the tub. The upper grab bar is used while standing. Grab bars should be carefully selected and installed to comply with UFAS 4.26 Handrails, Grab Bars, and Tub and Shower Seats, page 45.

PRACTICAL PLUS

A vertical or L-shaped grab bar near the controls on the outside edge of the tub surround can provide support for ambulatory users as they step over the rim of the tub. It may also serve to provide support to standing users who may bend over to adjust the controls while showering.

Vertical Grab Bar Provides Support for Ambulatory Users

In-Tub Seat or Transfer Surface. Portable in-tub seats which can be readily installed and easily removed allow the tub fixture to be used in a variety of ways. With the seat removed, the tub is available for standing showers and soaking baths. When the seat is installed, wheelchair users and others, who may be unsteady on their feet in a wet environment, can sit down while showering. Some hydraulically-powered seats provide users with the option of being lowered into the tub for a soaking bath. Seats which include a small transfer surface outside the tub are generally easier for people to use because they eliminate the need for the user to balance on the rim of the tub before transferring to the seat. Since a small free-standing stool rarely offers sufficient stability, UFAS requires that seats comply with the specifications of 4.26.3 Structural Strength for Tub and Shower Seats, page 45. For sanitary reasons, the surface of the seat should be impervious to water and easy to clean. When not installed, the seat should be stored in an accessible cabinet nearby.

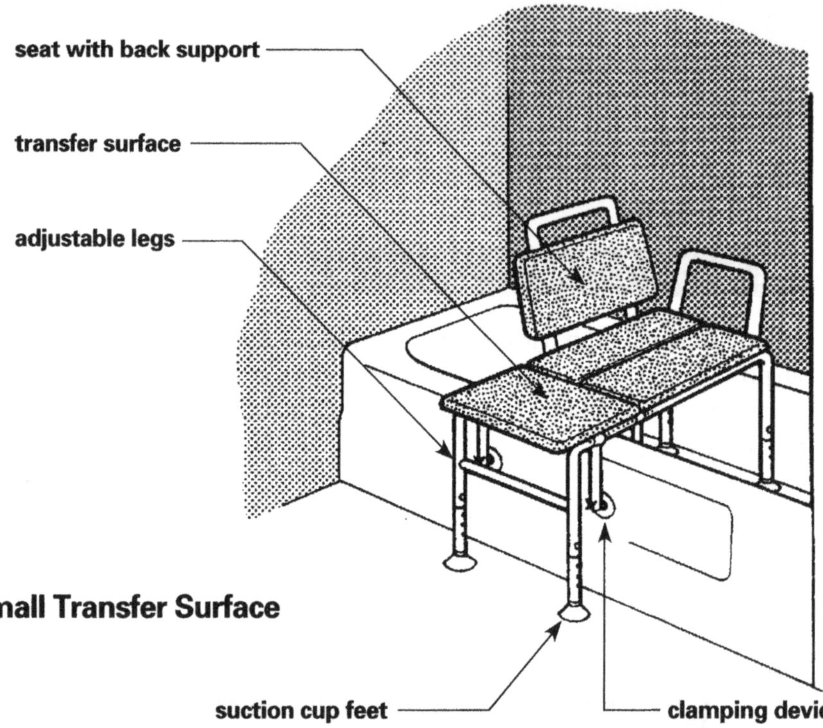

In-Tub Seat with Small Transfer Surface

Unlike the in-tub seat, the transfer surface at the head of the tub is not designed to be used as a shower seat but rather as a surface to facilitate transfer into the tub for a soaking bath. The surface is designed to be used by both wheelchair users and ambulatory users. The transfer surface should be as wide as the tub, 15 inches deep, and flush with the rim of the tub. Ideally the rim of the tub/transfer surface should be approximately the same height as a wheelchair seat to facilitate transfers. Although UFAS does not specify a rim height, some state codes specify tub rim heights between 16-20 inches from the floor.

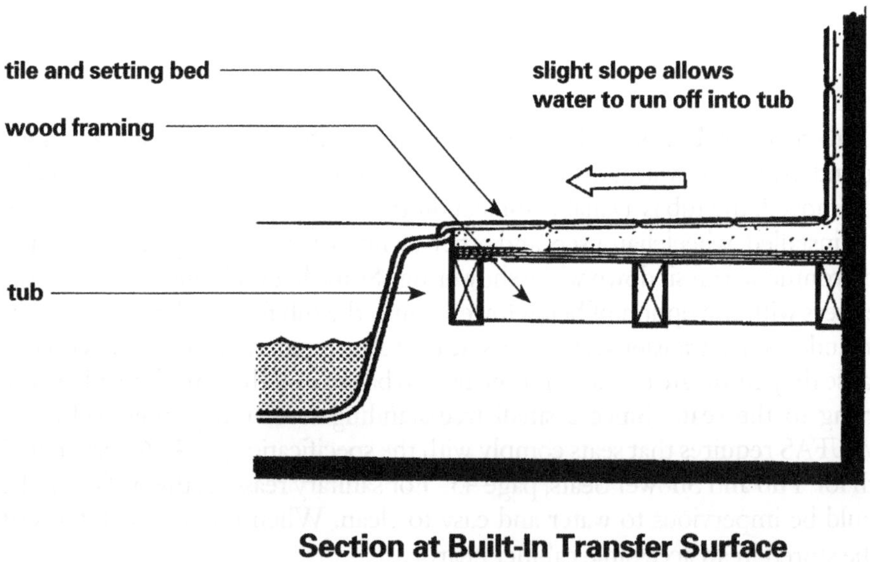

Section at Built-In Transfer Surface

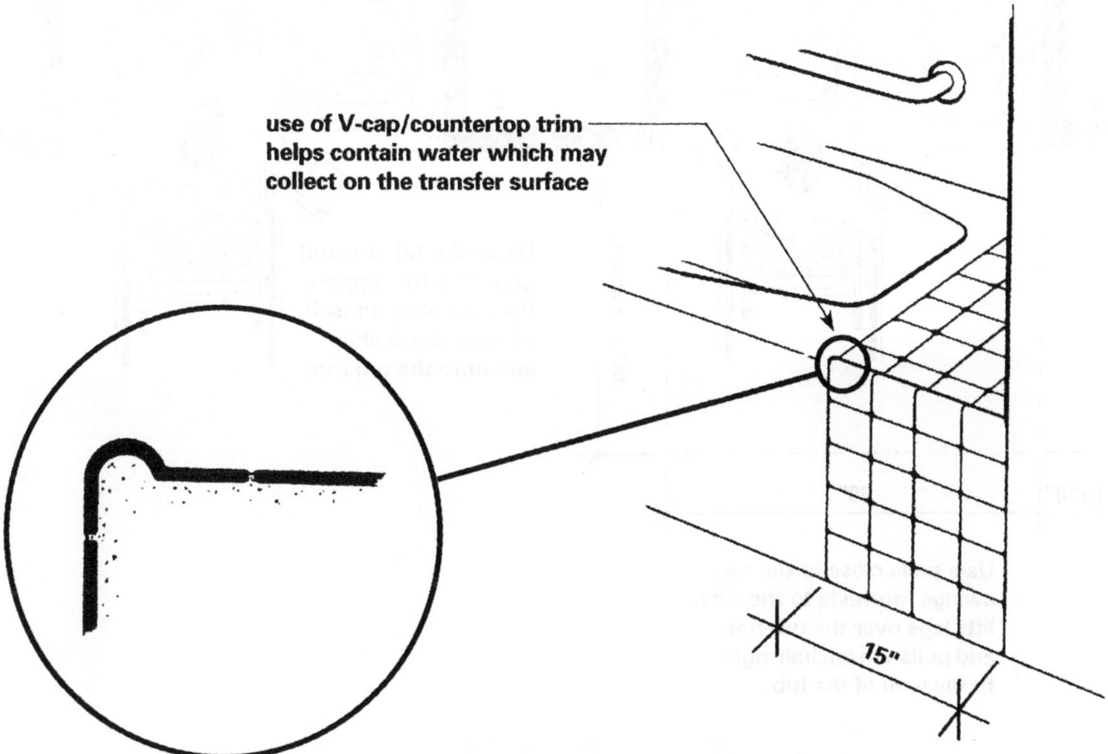

Edge Detail at Transfer Surface

Tub Enclosure. UFAS requires that, if tub enclosures are included, they must not obstruct controls or interfere with transfers. Enclosures which require tracks mounted to the tub rim are not allowed. Shower curtains are probably the most versatile and frequently used enclosure as they can be easily moved out of the way when necessary and replaced when damaged.

Many people require some combination of grab bars, seats, transfer surfaces, lift devices, and a clear floor area around the tub. Inclusion of these features makes safe use of bathtubs possible for many people who otherwise would not be able to use the fixture. The following series of illustrations depict users approaching and using the various safety features included at bathtubs.

Forward Transfer Into Tub

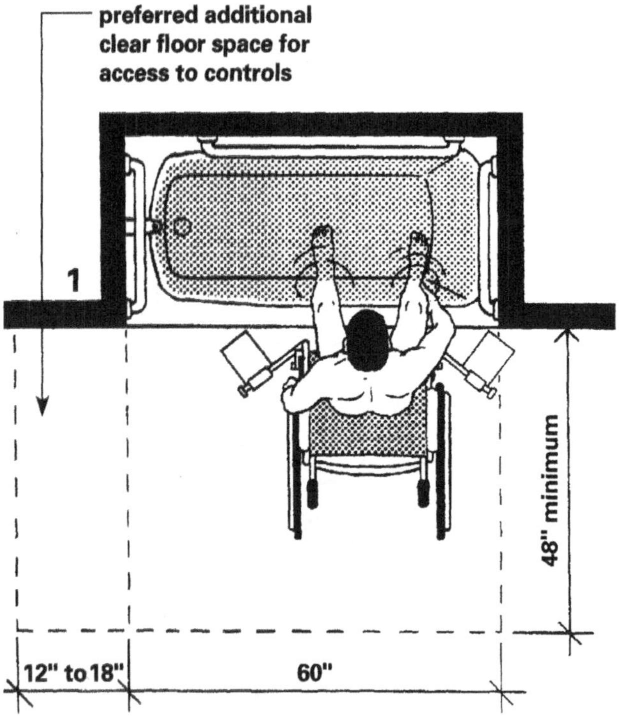

User pulls close to the tub, swings footrests to the side, lifts legs over the tub rim, and pulls wheelchair tight to the wall of the tub.

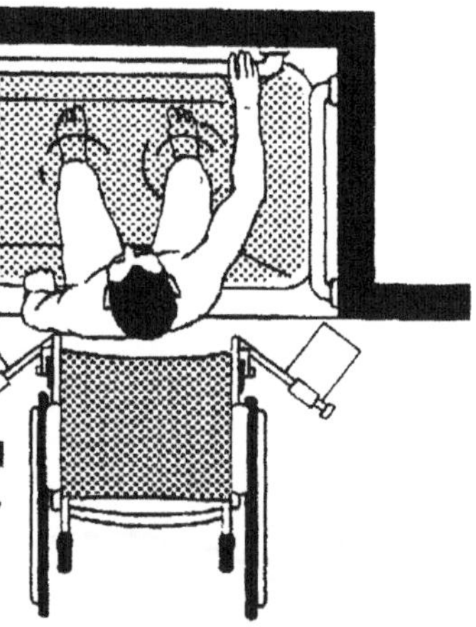

Using the tub rim and grab bars for support, the user pulls himself forward in his chair and onto the tub rim.

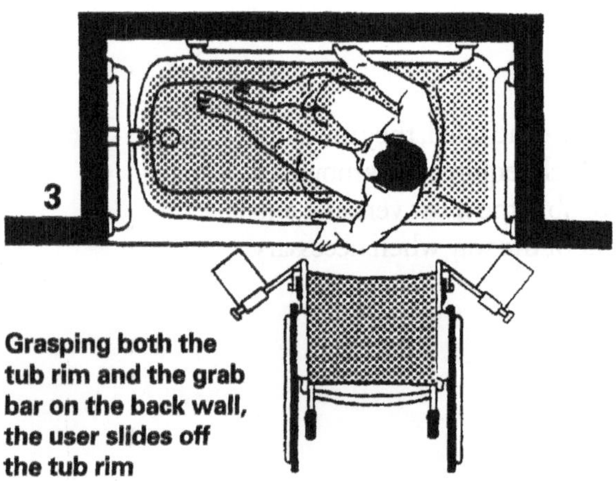

Grasping both the tub rim and the grab bar on the back wall, the user slides off the tub rim

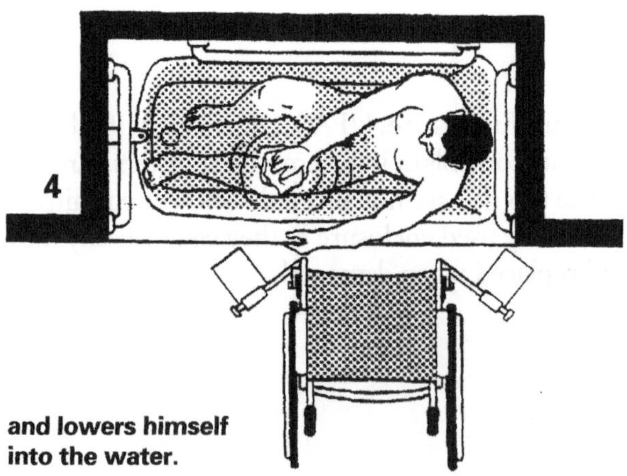

and lowers himself into the water.

Parallel Approach to Transfer Surface

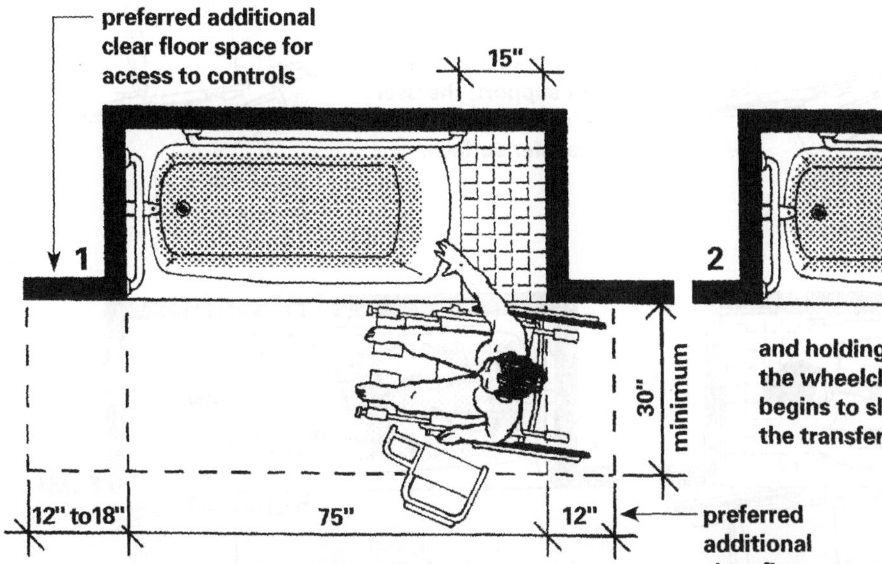

User pulls parallel to transfer surface at head of tub, removes arm rest,

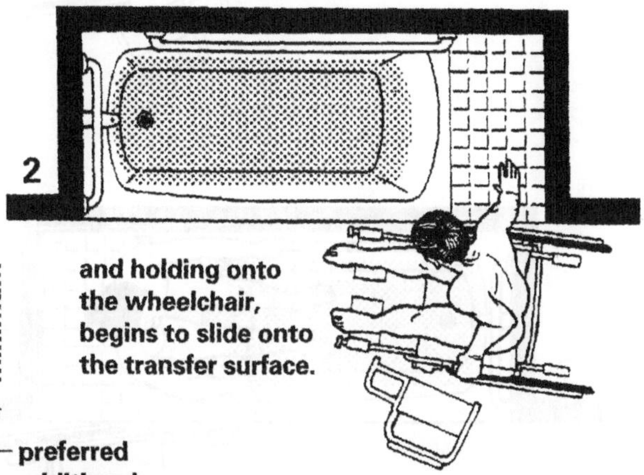

and holding onto the wheelchair, begins to slide onto the transfer surface.

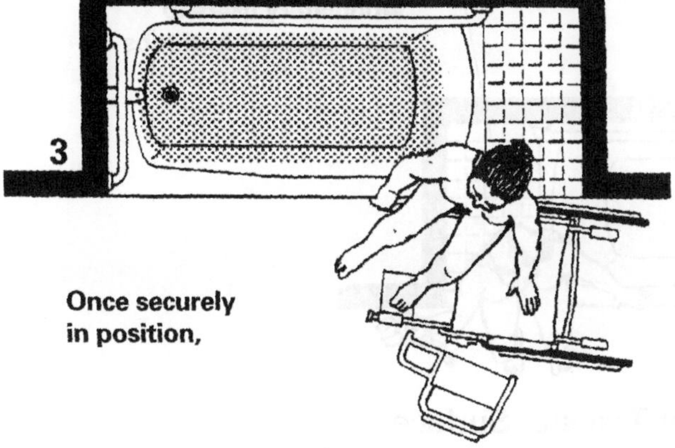

Once securely in position,

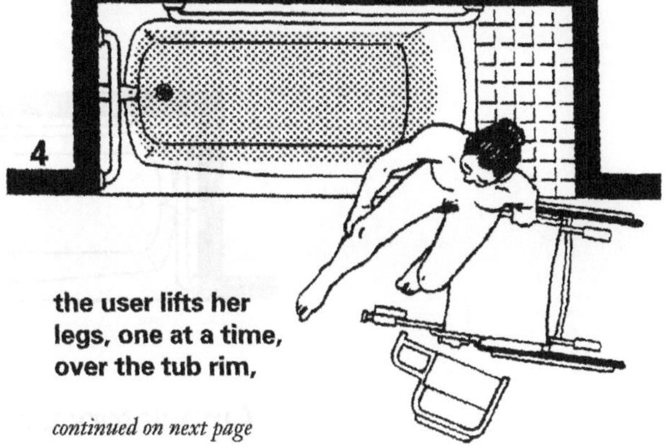

the user lifts her legs, one at a time, over the tub rim,

continued on next page

Parallel Approach to Transfer Surface

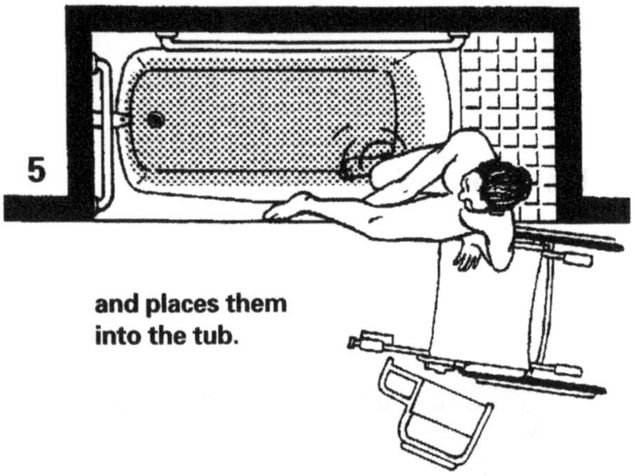
5

and places them into the tub.

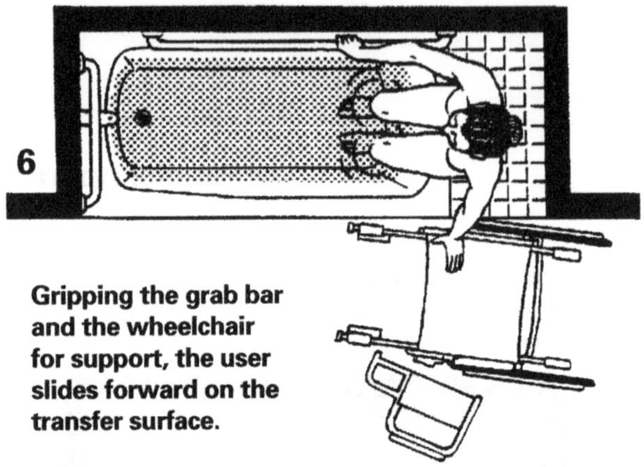
6

Gripping the grab bar and the wheelchair for support, the user slides forward on the transfer surface.

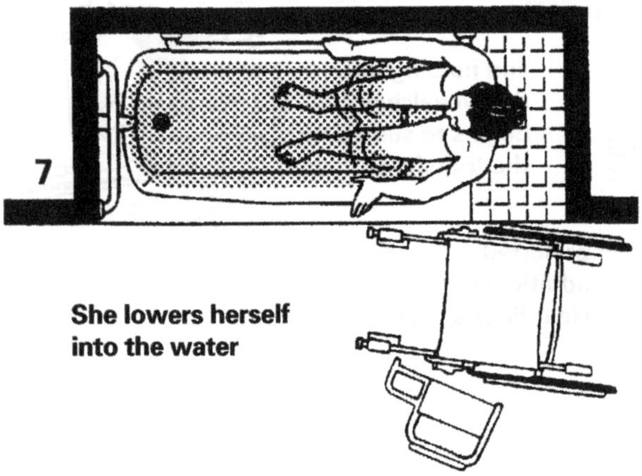
7

She lowers herself into the water

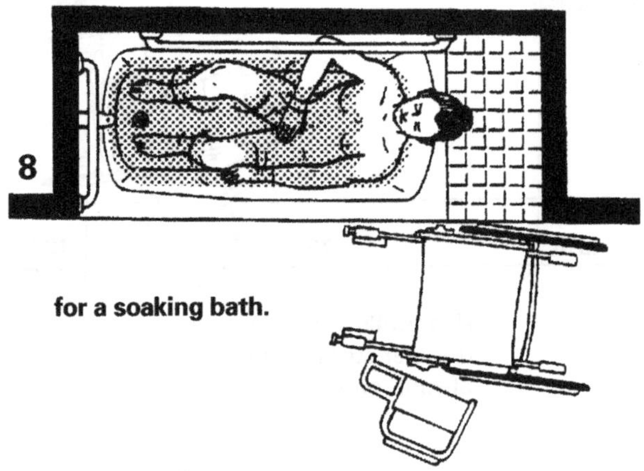
8

for a soaking bath.

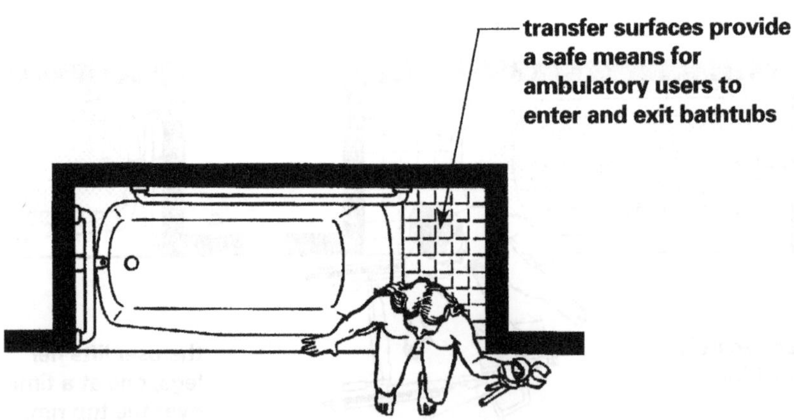

Ambulatory User at Transfer Surface

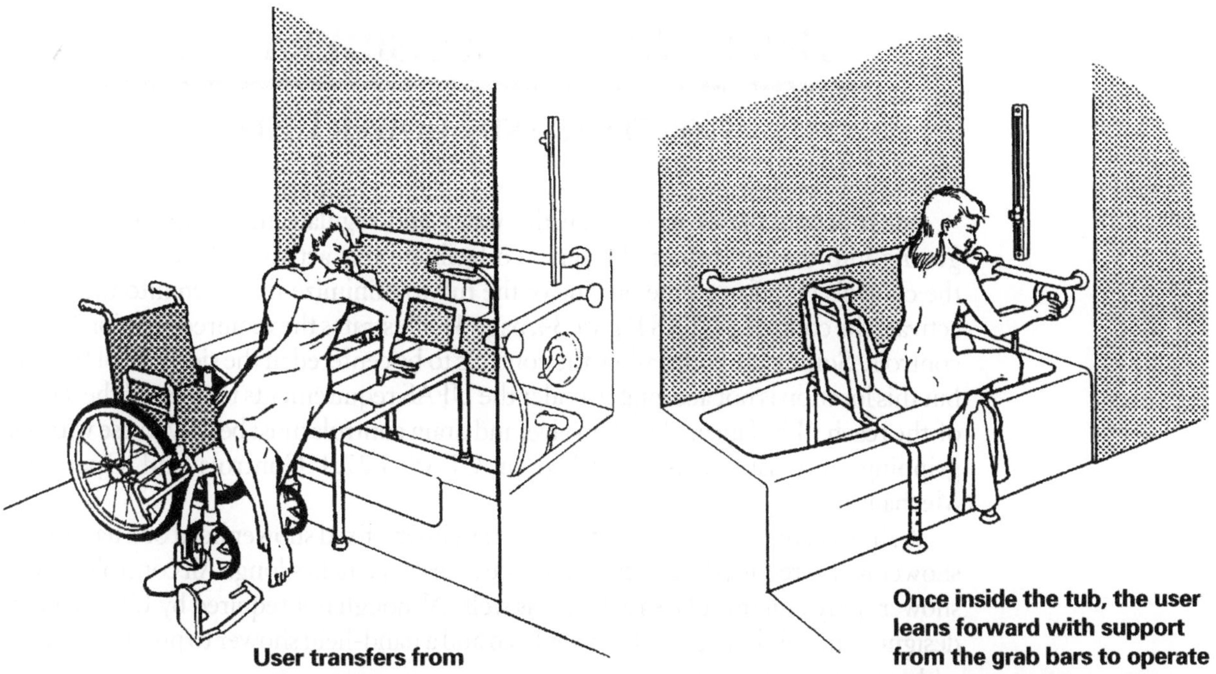

User transfers from wheelchair to tub seat.

Once inside the tub, the user leans forward with support from the grab bars to operate the water controls and the shower unit.

Parallel Approach and Transfer to Tub Seat

PROBLEM — EXISTING TUB /INSTALLATION DOESN'T COMPLY

SOLUTION — MODIFY EXISTING TUB OR REPLACE IT

If the existing tub doesn't comply with one or several of the UFAS requirements, steps should be taken to bring it into compliance. The most frequent and demanding problems with existing tubs are the lack of grab bars, and controls located in the wrong place. In both instances, walls must be opened up so plumbing can be moved and additional blocking installed to support grab bars. This process is rather time consuming and complicated. If the necessary renovations are very extensive and exterior walls must be removed, it may be possible to replace the existing tub with a new one-piece molded fixture, complete with built-in grab bars and removable seat. However, in most renovations, it is not possible to bring the one-piece units through existing construction, and multi-part fixtures must be used. Regardless of the type of fixture used, ample supports must be provided in the wall to anchor the grab bars (see Unit Three, Performance Specifications - Installation of Grab Bar Supports for more detail).

If a seat or transfer surface is not included in the existing installation, in-tub seats can usually be purchased and adjusted to fit most tubs. In-tub seats must be the type which securely clamp onto the tub to form a very stable surface.

BASIC DESIGN CONSIDERATIONS

CONTROLS AND SHOWER UNIT

Most people prefer to turn on the water and regulate the temperature before getting into the bathtub or shower. To facilitate this activity, UFAS requires that the controls be offset to the outside of the tub to minimize the reach into the tub to activate the controls. UFAS Figure 34, page 41, illustrates the required location for the controls. Some state codes allow the controls to be centered in the side wall of the tub, but this location is not acceptable under the UFAS requirements because of the length of the reach. The faucet, diverter valve, and drain controls must be easy to use without gripping or twisting, as described in UFAS 4.27.4 Controls and Operating Mechanisms.

A shower spray unit which can be used as either a fixed shower head or a hand-held shower is also required. The hose must be at least 60 inches long. All controls for the shower spray unit must be easy to use as well. Although not required by UFAS, many designers include both a fixed shower head and a hand-held shower to provide the user with a range of options.

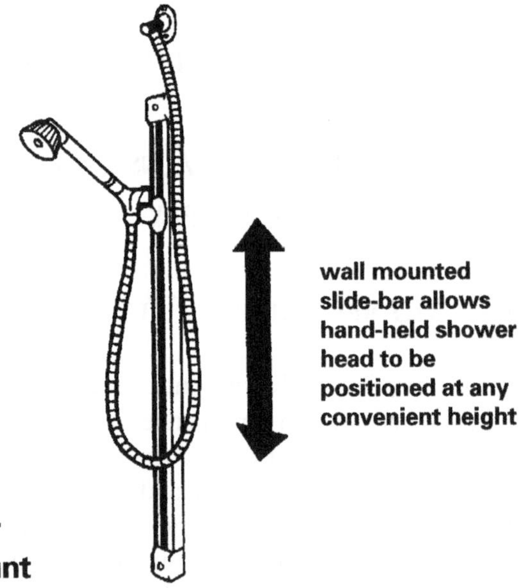

Hand-Held Shower Head on Slide Mount

PRACTICAL PLUS

Thermostatically controlled faucets which can be preset at a maximum temperature improve safe use for all users. These anti-scald devices are particularly helpful to disabled users who may have limited ability to detect hot and cold.

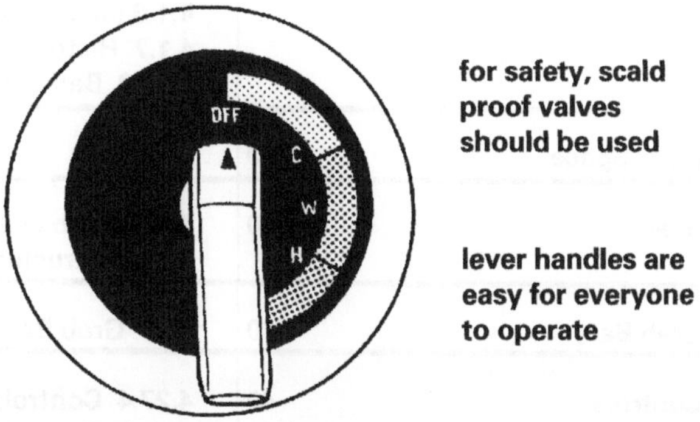

Thermostatically Controlled Valve

PROBLEM CONTROLS NOT OFFSET TO OUTSIDE OF TUB AND/OR SHOWER UNIT NOT INCLUDED

SOLUTION MOVE CONTROLS

If the controls are not offset to the outside of the tub, they will need to be moved. In substantial renovations, often involving the addition of blocking for grab bars, the movement of the controls can be easily accomplished while the wall is disassembled. Many shower units will also require some addition of blocking to support the slide mounting bracket. The manufacturer's installation instructions should be followed to ensure that the unit is properly secured.

REFERENCE INDEX TO UFAS DOCUMENT

BATHTUBS

Primary References	UFAS page	Secondary References	UFAS page
4.20.1 General/Location	40	4.1 Scope & Technical Requirements for Bathing Facilities	5-6
		4.1.5 (3) Additions	11
		4.1.6 (3)(c)(i) Alterations	12
		4.1.6 (3)(c)(ii) Alterations	12
		4.1.7 Historic Preservation	14
		4.23.8 Bathing and Shower Facilities	44
4.20.2 Floor Space	40		
4.20.3 Seat	40	4.26.3 Tub & Shower Seats/ Structural Strength	45
4.20.4 Grab Bars	40	4.26 Grab Bars	45
4.20.5 Controls	42	4.27.4 Controls and Operating Mechanisms	45
4.20.6 Shower Unit	42		
4.20.7 Bathtub Enclosures	42		

INTRODUCTION

In addition to bathtubs, UFAS provides specifications for two other bathing fixtures, transfer showers and roll-in showers. The transfer shower contains a seat which allows users to sit while showering. The seat may be designed to fold up against the wall to allow users to stand while showering. The roll-in shower allows users to roll into the shower using a wheelchair. Additional features including grab bars, maneuvering space, appropriate controls, hand-held shower units, and minimal curbs for transfer showers, which make showers easier and safer to use for everyone, are also described in UFAS.

Transfer and roll-in showers which meet the UFAS specifications are fabricated from a variety of materials including, acrylic, plastic, and fiberglass. Several fixture manufacturers carry these molded units, which come complete with built-in grab bars and fixed or fold-up seats in the transfer showers. Custom-designed showers can also be constructed from tile or fiberglass panels to suit the requirements of a specific location.

In new construction, additions, and renovations (including historic properties), UFAS requires that, if tubs or showers are provided, then at least one accessible tub or one accessible shower must be provided. Some state codes are more stringent than UFAS and require both accessible tubs and showers if both are provided. Additional information on showers and bathroom layout can be found in Unit Five, Bathing Facilities and Shower Rooms.

BASIC DESIGN CONSIDERATIONS

TRANSFER SHOWER FEATURES

Transfer showers are a fixed size of 36 inches by 36 inches (inside dimension). It is the particular size of the stall in combination with the specific configuration of the seat and controls that makes the shower safe and easy to use. When properly designed and installed, these showers facilitate transfers from wheelchairs, allow seated people to sit comfortably in the corner with support from walls on two sides, provide grab bars for support when transferring or leaning forward to operate the controls, and include controls which are easy to use. Transfer showers can also be used for standing showers by ambulatory people if folding seats are provided.

Use of the 36" x 36" Transfer Shower

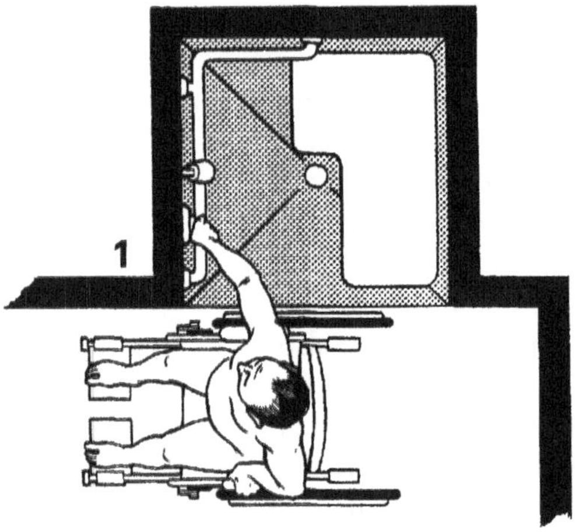

User pulls close to the controls which are easy to reach and tests the water temperature.

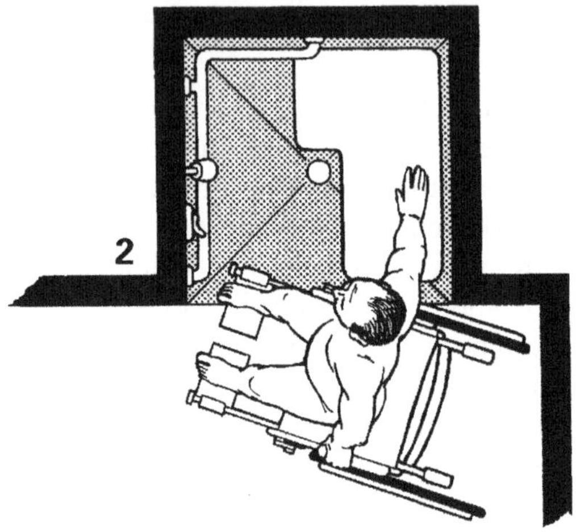

Because there is essentially no curb, the user can pull his wheelchair close to the seat. After removing the wheelchair armrest,

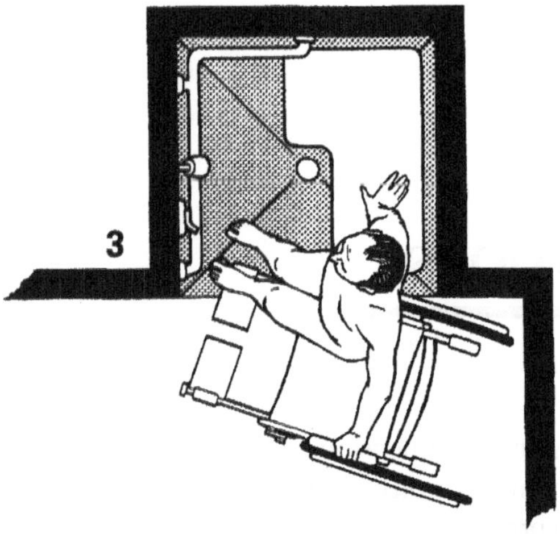

the user transfers from his wheelchair to the shower seat. Transferring is made easier and safer because the shower seat is generally mounted at the same height as the wheelchair seat.

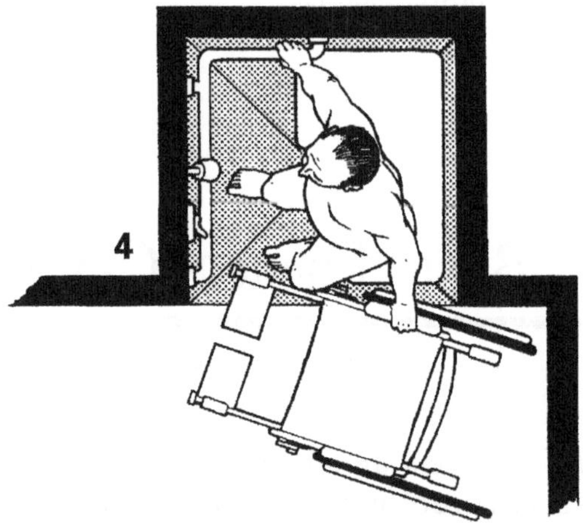

Using the grab bar for support, the user slides over to the corner where the shower walls provide lateral support. The size of the shower places the controls within easy reach. The grab bar provides support for those who cannot easily reach forward to operate the controls.

Wheelchair User

Use of the 36" x 36" Transfer Shower

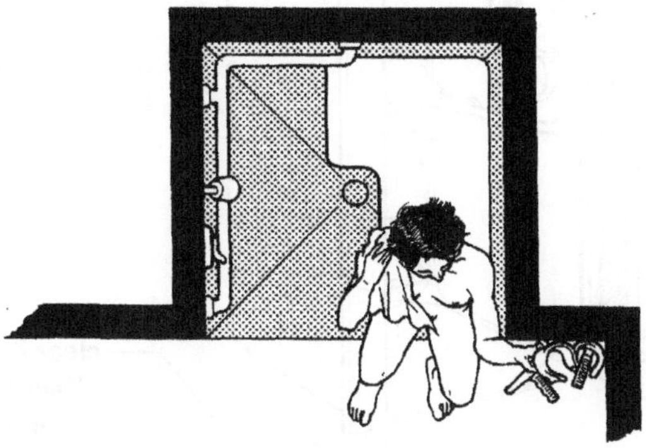

The seat in a transfer shower provides bathing ease for someone who walks with difficulty or who may not be able to stand to shower.

Crutch User

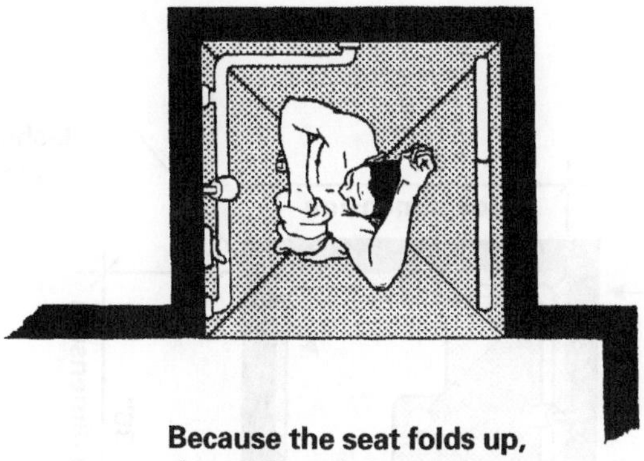

Because the seat folds up, the stall works as a conventional 36" x 36" shower stall.

Standing User

Floor Space. A transfer shower requires the clear floor space outside the shower to be a minimum of 36 inches by 48 inches. The 48 inch length is offset to one side to provide access to the shower seat for wheelchair users allowing them to align the edge of the wheelchair seat with the edge of the shower seat.

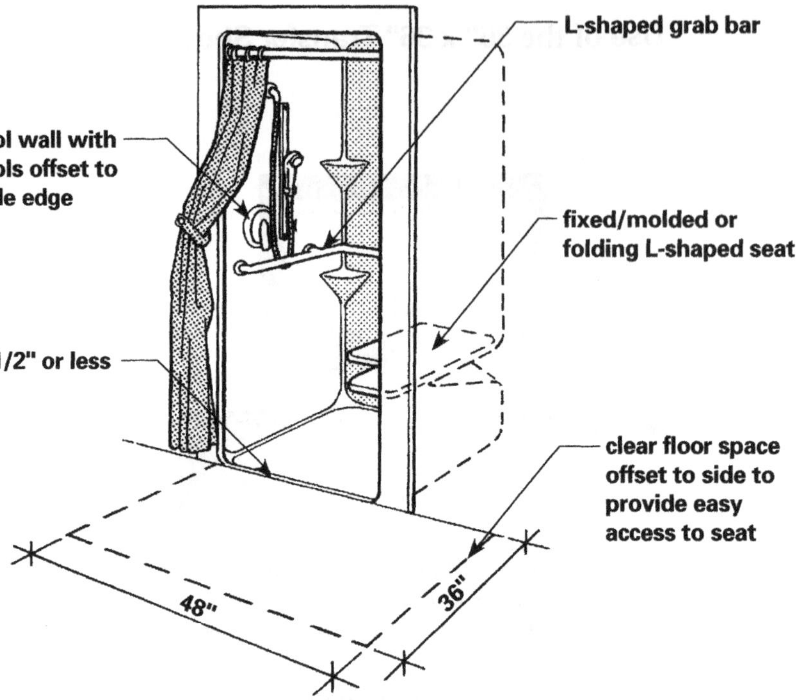

Maneuvering Space at Transfer Shower

PRACTICAL PLUS

Additional clear floor space forward of the control wall makes reach to the controls easier for wheelchair users. If space allows, the additional clear floor space should be 12 to 18 inches.

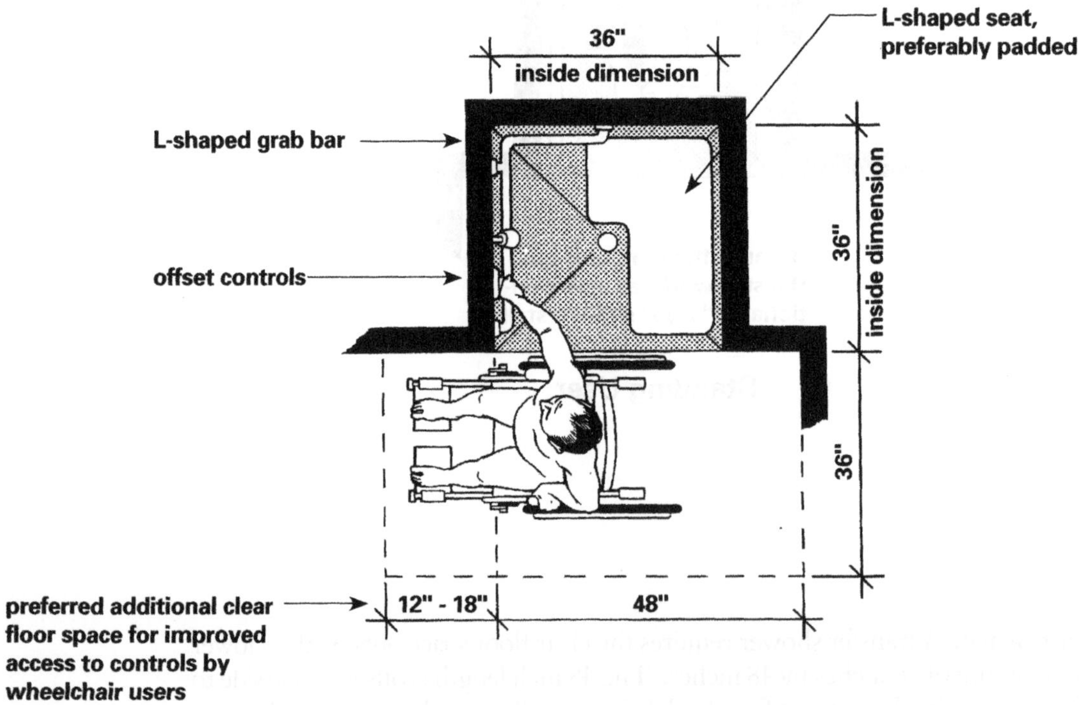

Additional Clear Floor Space

Grab Bars and Shower Seat. Grab bars must be provided on the wall of the shower stall next to and forward of the seat and along the wall directly across from the seat but never on the wall behind the seat. The seat can be fixed in place or designed to fold up against the wall. The seat must be 17-19 inches from the floor, extend the full depth of the shower stall, and be securely mounted on the wall across from the controls as shown in UFAS Figures 35, 36, and 37, pages 42 and 43. The grab bars and shower seat must comply with UFAS 4.26 Handrails, Grab Bars, and Tub and Shower Seats, page 45 (see Unit Three, Performance Specifications - Installation of Grab Bar Supports for more detail).

PRACTICAL PLUS

A separate vertical or vertical extension of the L-shaped grab bar, near the controls on the outside edge of the shower stall, can provide support for ambulatory users as they step into the shower. It may also serve to provide support to standing users who may be unsteady on their feet while showering.

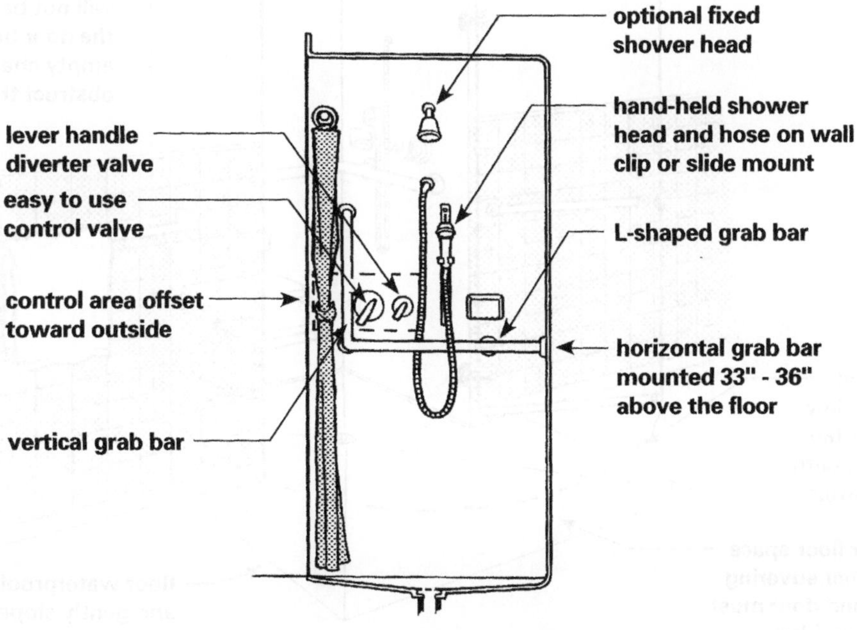

Additional Vertical Grab Bar Provides Support for Ambulatory User

Controls and Shower Unit. The controls must be located across from the seat and offset toward the outside of the shower. This location allows the controls to be conveniently operated from both inside and outside the shower. The shower unit must be usable both as a fixed shower head and as a hand-held shower. Although not required by UFAS, sometimes both fixed and hand-held shower heads are provided. In unmonitored or isolated facilities where vandalism is a consideration, a fixed shower head 48 inches above the floor may be used in lieu of a hand-held shower. If this option is implemented, it is best if a standard height shower head is also installed for standing people. All faucets and controls must be easy to operate without gripping or twisting.

Curbs and Shower Enclosures. ANSI and some state codes allow curbs of up to 4 inches on transfer showers. Because so many people with disabilities cannot lift their feet over curbs of this height, UFAS is more stringent and requires that curbs at transfer showers be no higher than 1/2 inch. Shower curtains are frequently provided as enclosures to help contain water and direct it back into the stall. Doors can sometimes be used but must swing clear 180 degrees to allow access to the controls and the seat. Additional clear floor space will also be required to provide proper maneuvering space at the door. Regardless of the enclosure used, it is best if the floor immediately outside the shower and the joint between the floor and fixture are sloped toward the drain and waterproofed to prevent damage to the floor surface and sub-flooring. In many cases the entire bathroom floor is waterproofed to prevent water damage from misdirected shower spray.

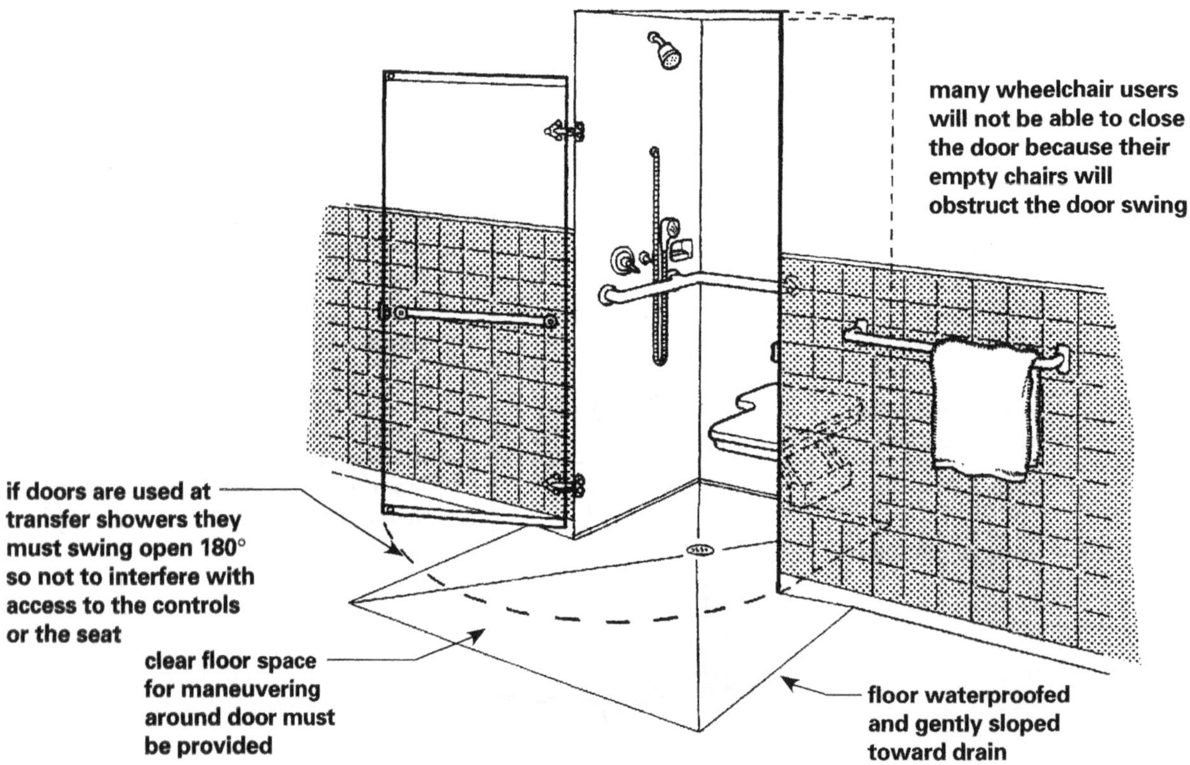

Hinged Door Shower Enclosure

PROBLEM EXISTING SHOWER STALL DOESN'T COMPLY

SOLUTION RENOVATE OR REPLACE EXISTING STALL

Traditional shower stalls, although they may be the appropriate size, generally lack several access features including grab bars, seats, and hand-held shower units. Many existing shower stalls also have a 3 - 4 inch curb, and some have partitions, doors, or other enclosures which obstruct access to the fixture. If the existing stall is a molded fixture, with appropriate clear floor space outside the shower stall, it can usually be removed and replaced with one of the multi-part, accessible stalls designed for installation in existing buildings.

If the existing stall was constructed on-site of tile or other material, then renovation will be more time consuming and expensive. Installation of grab bars, seat, and wall mount for the shower unit requires blocking in the walls. Removal of the curb will entail partial demolition of the floor. The amount of demolition required for this renovation is extensive, and in some instances, it may be more economical to rebuild the shower rather than attempt to salvage parts of the existing installation.

BASIC DESIGN CONSIDERATIONS

ROLL-IN SHOWERS

Like other UFAS bathing fixtures, roll-in showers can be used in a variety of ways depending upon the needs of the user. Roll-in showers are designed without curbs primarily to allow wheelchair users with special shower wheelchairs to roll directly into the stall. People can shower standing up as they would in any shower stall, and those who may have difficulty standing can sit on a portable shower chair. The minimum size roll-in shower occupies the same space as a standard tub and is often installed in a retrofit situation where a shower may be preferred over a tub.

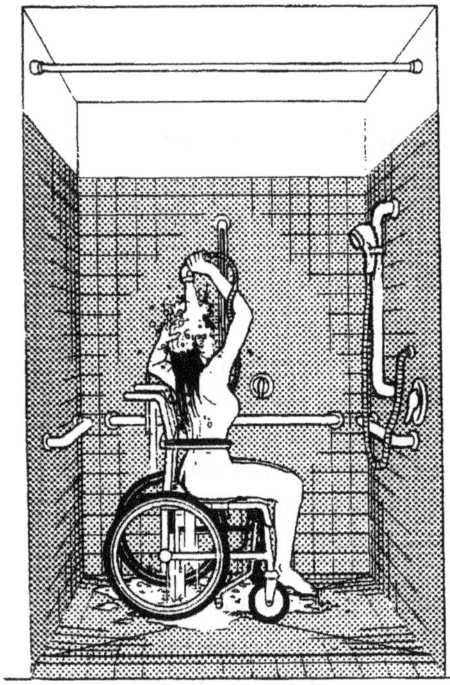

Roll-in showers provide enough space for people in wheelchairs to maneuver and enough space to have an attendant assist in the shower if necessary.

Portable seats can be placed in a roll-in shower for walking people who need to sit down to shower.

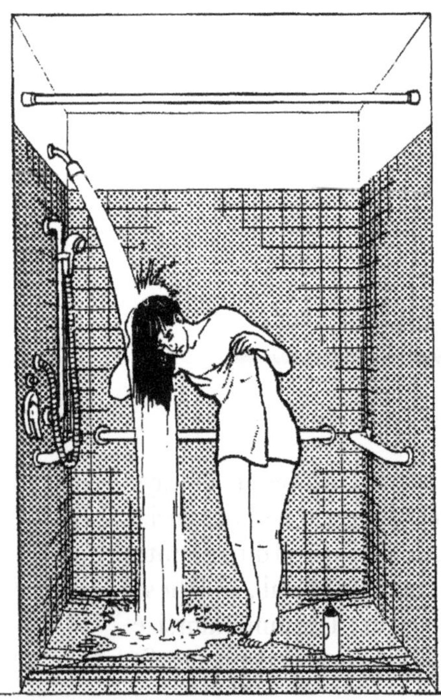

Roll-in showers can be used by non-disabled people in a conventional manner...

and they can be used by others for special purposes.

Use of A Roll-In Shower

Floor Space. Roll-in showers require a minimum clear floor space outside the shower of 36 inches by 60 inches. An adjacent lavatory can overhang the clear floor space provided that proper knee and toe space are allocated under the lav.

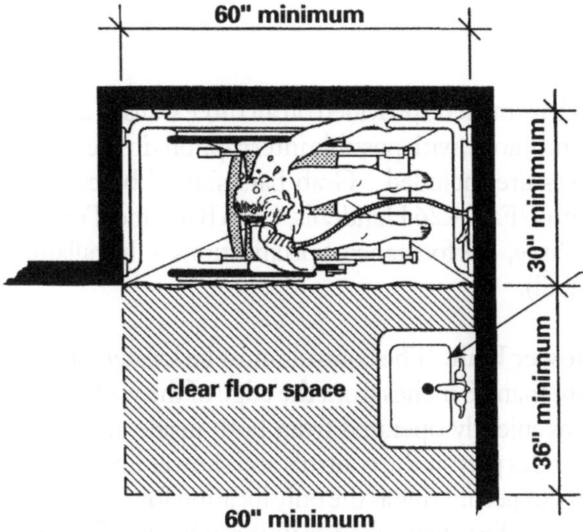

Maneuvering Space at Roll-In Showers

PRACTICAL PLUS

If possible, the controls for the shower should be mounted on the side wall of the shower away from a lav or a wall which may be flush with the wall of the shower. Inclusion of additional clear floor space parallel to the shower near the controls makes reaching the controls easier for people who use wheelchairs who may have difficulty leaning forward to operate the controls. The offset location of the controls and additional clear floor space makes it easier to regulate the water before entering the shower.

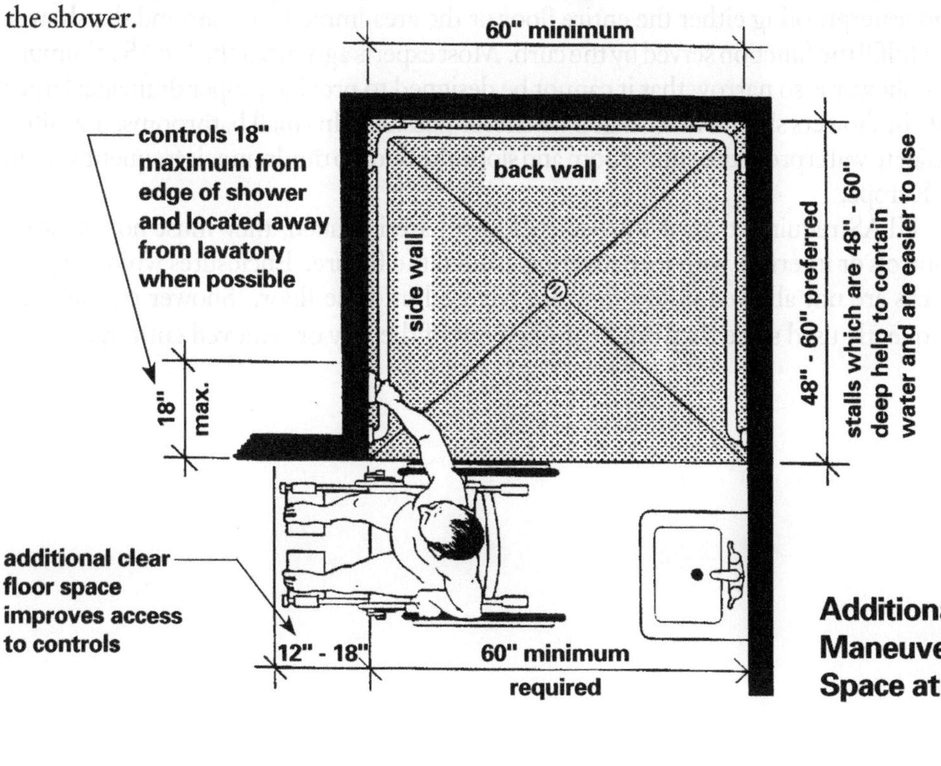

Additional Maneuvering Space at Roll-In Shower

Grab Bars. Grab bars must be provided on all three walls of a roll-in shower. The grab bars should be continuous, with possible interruptions in the corners if soap dishes or small corner shelves are included. Grab bars should be carefully selected and installed to comply with UFAS 4.26 Handrails, Grab Bars, and Tub and Shower Seats, page 45 (see Unit Three, Performance Specifications - Installation of Grab Bar Supports for more detail).

Controls and Shower Unit. The controls must be located on the side wall of the roll-in shower no more than 18 inches from the edge of the wall. This location allows the controls to be conveniently operated from both inside and outside the shower. ANSI and some state codes permit the controls and shower unit to be mounted on the back wall. UFAS does not permit this as the only location for the controls/shower unit, but a second auxiliary set of controls/shower unit can be installed on the back wall if desired.

The shower unit must be usable as both a fixed shower head and as a hand-held shower and, although not required, sometimes both a hand-held unit and standard height fixed head are installed. In unmonitored or isolated facilities where vandalism is a consideration, a fixed shower head 48 inches above the floor may be used in lieu of a hand-held shower. Although not required, many facilities also include a second fixed shower head mounted at standard height for use by standing people. All faucets and controls must be easy to operate without gripping or twisting.

Curbs and Shower Enclosures. Curbs to help contain water in the shower area are not permitted at roll-in showers. However, careful attention to the slope of the floor and waterproofing either the entire floor or the area immediately around the shower can fulfill the function served by the curb. Most experts agree that the UFAS minimum size shower is so narrow that it cannot be designed to provide proper drainage; larger roll-in showers should be installed whenever possible. In small bathrooms, it is often easier to waterproof the entire room and slope the floor to the drain as is frequently done in Europe.

UFAS requires that, if shower enclosures are included, they must not obstruct controls or interfere with maneuvering around the fixture. Enclosures which require tracks are not allowed unless they are recessed into the floor. Shower curtains are frequently used since they can be pushed out of the way or removed entirely.

PROBLEM — EXISTING TUB DOESN'T MEET USER NEEDS

SOLUTION — REPLACE TUB WITH ROLL-IN SHOWER

If the existing tub either doesn't comply with the UFAS requirements and/or can't be modified to meet the needs of the users, then it may be possible to replace it with a roll-in shower. This procedure will require extensive demolition and reconstruction of the walls, the floor, and the plumbing. A custom tile shower or a new multi-piece molded fixture with grab bars, appropriate shower unit, and controls can usually be installed in place of a standard tub. Regardless of the type and size of roll-in fixture used, careful attention must be paid to waterproofing all areas of the room which may be exposed to overspray from the shower.

PROBLEM — EXISTING GANG SHOWER DOESN'T COMPLY

SOLUTION — RENOVATE ONE STATION IN THE SHOWER TO CREATE ROLL-IN

Most gang showers can be renovated to make at least one station within the shower accessible. Many gang showers are open rooms without curbs or partitions to interfere with wheelchair access. If this is the case, then renovation will be limited to the installation of grab bars and an appropriate shower unit. In other situations, it may be necessary to remove a curb or reposition partitions which may interfere with the accessible route or the required clear floor space.

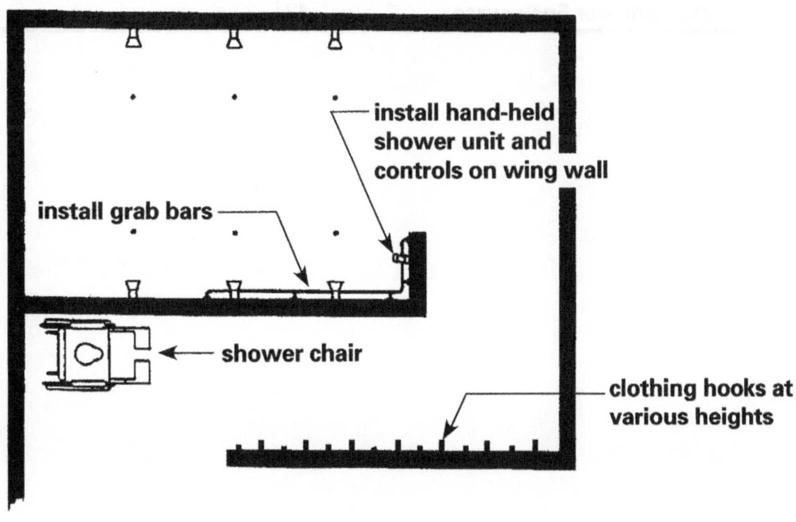

Gang Shower with Roll-In Station

REFERENCE INDEX TO UFAS DOCUMENT

TRANSFER AND ROLL-IN SHOWERS

Primary References	UFAS page	Secondary References	UFAS page
4.21.1 General/Location	42	4.1 Scope & Technical Requirements for Bathing Facilities	5-6
		4.1.5 (3) Additions	11
		4.1.6 (3)(c)(i) Alterations	12
		4.1.6 (3)(c)(ii) Alterations	12
		4.1.7 Historic Preservation	14
		4.23.8 Bathing and Shower Facilities	44
		A4.21.1 Shower Size Requirements/ Benefits	65
4.21.2 Size and Clearances	42		
4.21.3 Seat	42	4.26.3 Tub & Shower Seats/ Structural Strength	45
4.21.4 Grab Bars	42	4.26 Grab Bars	45
4.21.5 Controls	42	4.27.4 Controls and Operating Mechanisms	45
4.21.6 Shower Unit	42		
4.21.7 Curbs	43		
4.21.8 Shower Enclosures	43		

Introduction

The UFAS specifications for sinks are comparable to those for lavatories. Similar to lavatories, sinks must be designed and installed to provide adequate space for people to approach, maneuver about the fixture, and operate the controls easily. Suitable design and installation involves several features including the provision of appropriate clear floor space adjacent to an accessible route, sufficient knee space, a basin of appropriate depth, usable controls, and provision of a protective covering under sinks when waste and hot water lines are exposed.

Although access to all sinks is not required, there are many occupancies which install sinks for public and employee use. Sinks can be found in office kitchenettes, laboratories, classrooms, nursery/day care facilities, health care settings, laundries, and dining halls. Universally usable facilities should provide access to all elements and features whenever possible.

Basic Design Considerations

Design and Installation Requirements for Sinks

Mounting Height, Knee Space, Pipe Protection, and Clear Floor Space. UFAS requires that sinks be mounted with the counter surface or rim a maximum of 34 inches from the floor. Knee space that is at least 27 inches high, by 19 inches deep, and 30 inches wide must be provided under sinks. UFAS does not specify toe space as it does under lavs, although it is best if the drain and water supply pipes occupy as little of the knee space as possible.

The drain and water supply pipes should be insulated or a protection panel should be installed to prevent the wheelchair user's legs from coming into contact with hot or sharp objects. A clear floor space of 30 inches by 48 inches must be provided in front of the sink to allow for forward approach to the sink. A maximum of 19 inches of the required clear floor space may extend under the sink.

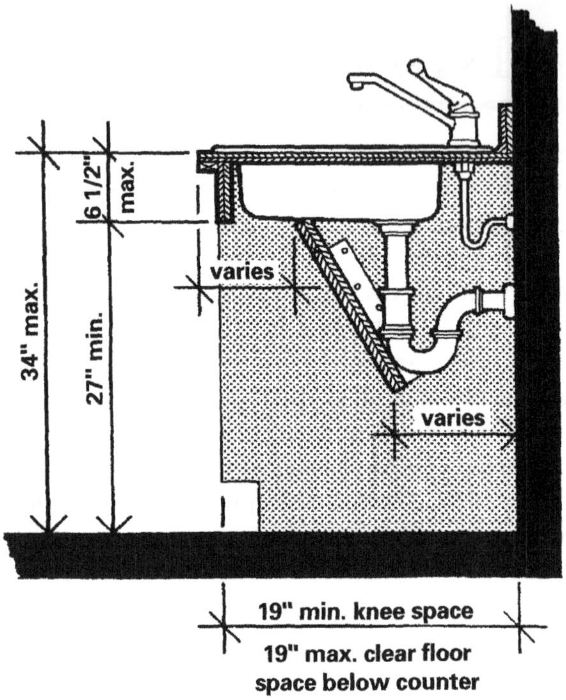

Knee Space at Sinks

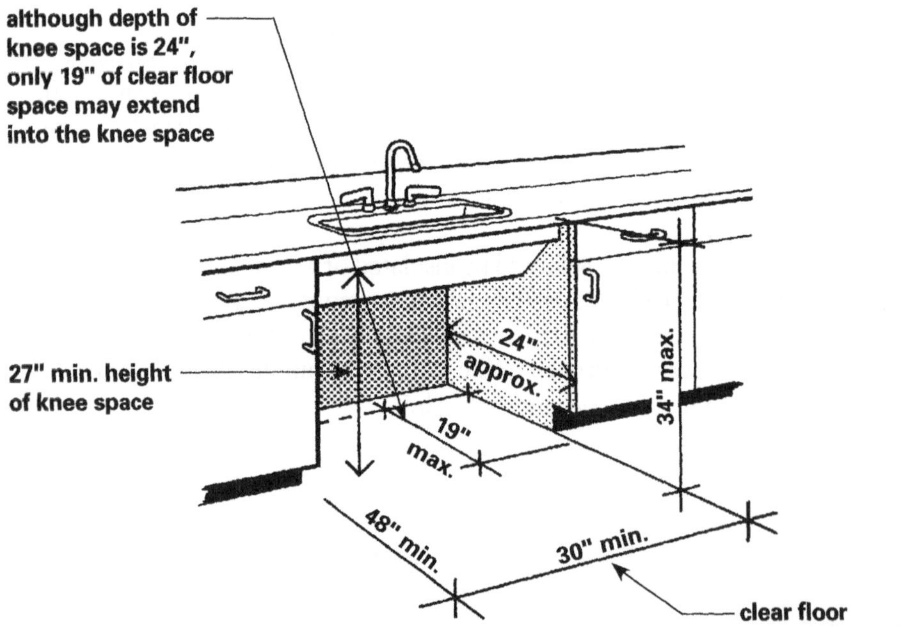

Maneuvering Space at Sinks

Depth of Sink. UFAS requires that the sink be no deeper than 6 1/2 inches. This requirement is designed to permit the installation of sinks which allow seated people to reach the bottom of the basin without difficulty. It is also helpful if the drain exits near the back of the basin to increase the available knee space under the sink.

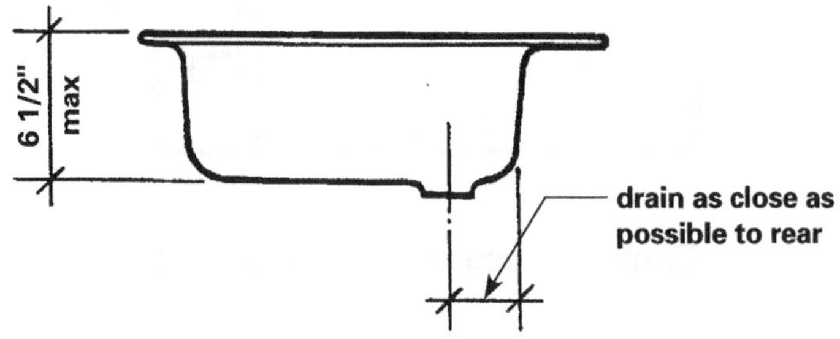

Sink Section

Faucets. UFAS requires that faucets comply with Section 4.27.4 Operation - Controls and Operating Mechanisms. Lever-operated, push-type, touch-type, or electronically controlled mechanisms are acceptable. At very large sinks it may be best if the controls are located to the side of the sink rather than the back to reduce the reach required. Spray hoses, frequently installed at sinks, are a very useful option.

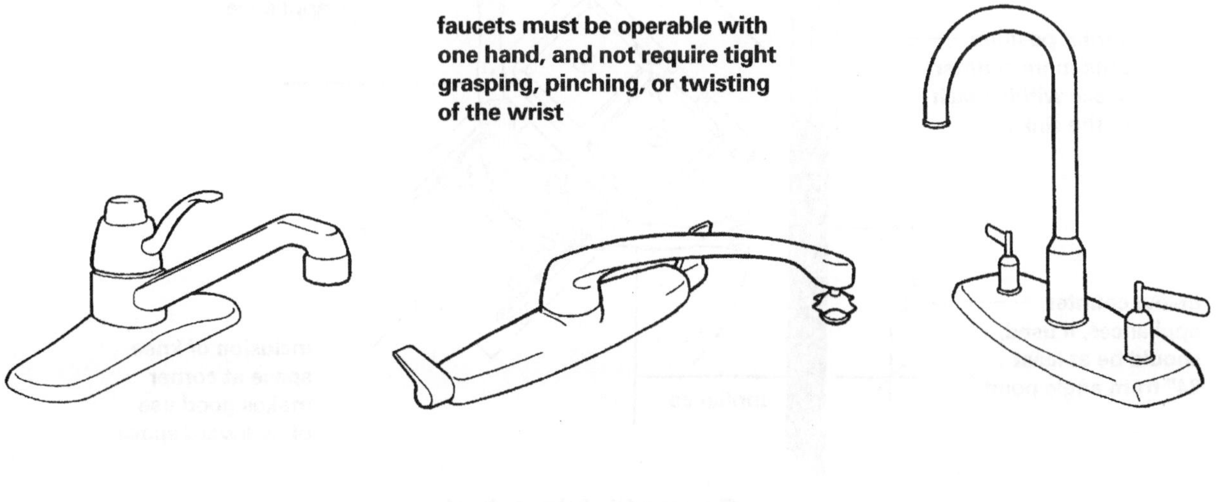

Acceptable Faucet Designs

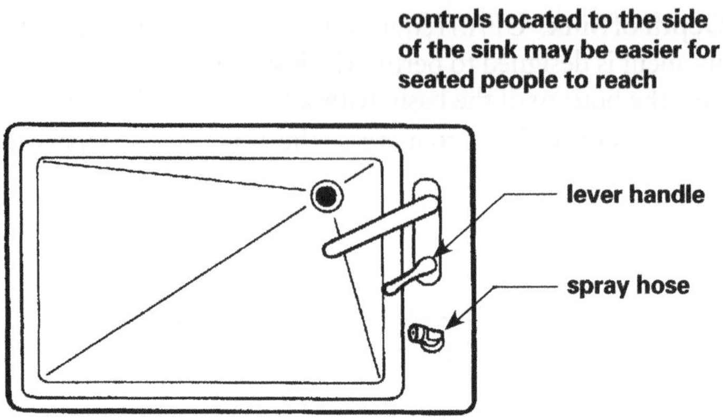

Controls Located to Side of Sink

Location. Sinks can be installed in counters in a variety of ways. It is best if some portion of the surrounding counter is installed at the same lowered height as the sink to provide an accessible work surface. Under-the-counter appliances, installed adjacent to the knee space for the sink, improve access to the appliance as well. However, because dishwashers and trash compactors are generally designed to be installed under standard height countertops the counter segment over built-in appliances will need to be approximately 36 inches.

Sinks can also be installed in the corner. This location takes full advantage of difficult to reach corner cabinet storage and puts more of the counter surface within reach. If under-the-counter appliances or storage units are installed, they should be located at least 24 inches away from the angled counter segment to allow ample space to open doors and/or drawers.

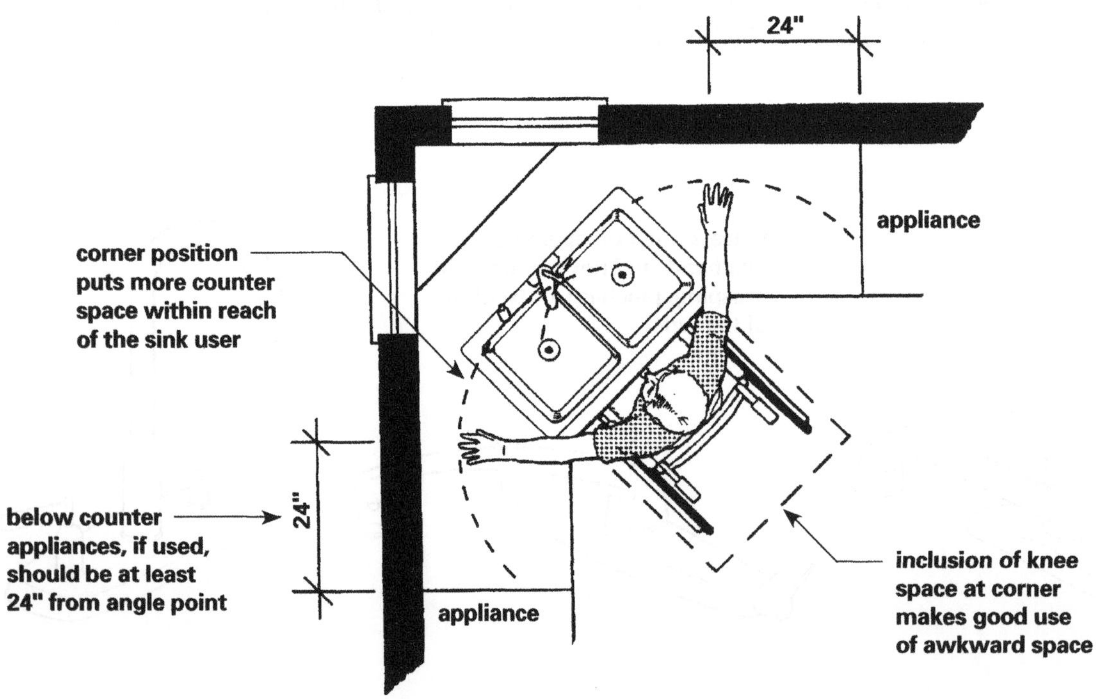

Corner Sink Installation

Types of Sinks. Double and triple sinks can be installed with knee space under only one sink, and the other sink(s) enclosed in a cabinet. This technique is useful when disposals or water filters are installed at the sink. The second/third sink may be deeper than the minimum 6 1/2 inches required by UFAS.

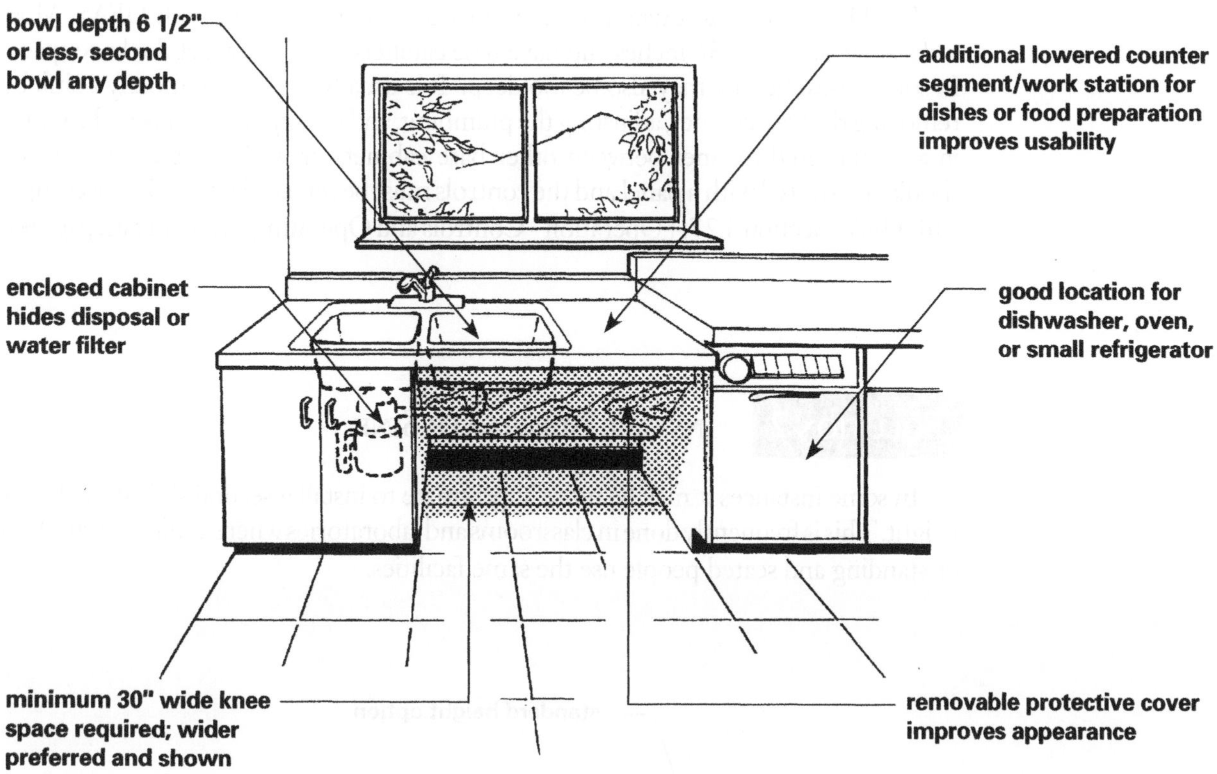

Double Sink with Single Knee Space

Utility sinks, because of the nature of their design, are not accessible. These sinks are typically 15 inches or more deep, eliminating the possibility of providing appropriate knee space. In addition, utility sinks are usually located in mechanical or utility rooms, spaces which are exempt from the UFAS requirements. However, it is possible to provide minimal access to these fixtures by providing a clear floor space parallel to the sink to permit a side reach.

PROBLEM — SINK DOESN'T COMPLY

SOLUTION 1 — MODIFY SINK

It is likely that most existing sink installations will not comply with UFAS. Most sinks are mounted at 36 inches and have base cabinets which obstruct the knee space. In some cases the sink may also be too deep. It is usually possible to modify a sink by removing the base cabinet, adjusting the plumbing, and rehanging the sink and counter in a cantilevered manner between other base cabinets or walls. The exposed pipes should be covered with a panel and the controls must be replaced if they do not comply with UFAS Section 4.27.4 Operation - Controls and Operating Mechanisms, page 45.

SOLUTION 2 — INSTALL ALTERNATE SINK

In some instances it may be more appropriate to install a second sink at the lower height. This is frequently done in classrooms and laboratories where adults and children or standing and seated people use the same facilities.

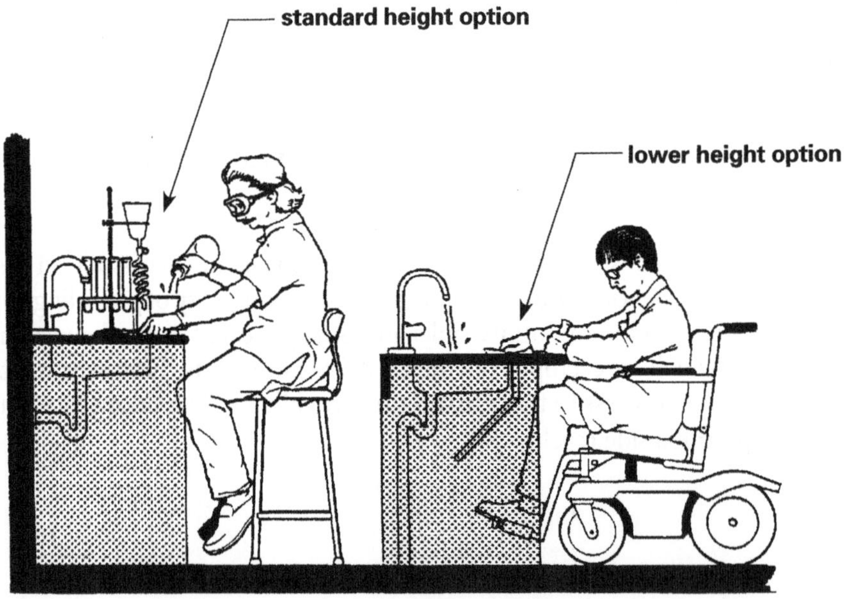

Install Alternate Sink at Lower Height

SOLUTION 3 INSTALL SINK IN ADJUSTABLE COUNTER

Several manufacturers produce sinks which can be adjusted to suit the height preferences of various individuals. These sinks have flexible drains and water supply lines which facilitate or permit adjustment up or down, either manually with a crank, or automatically with the assist of an electric motor. This option is more expensive but may be useful in settings with many users and limited space.

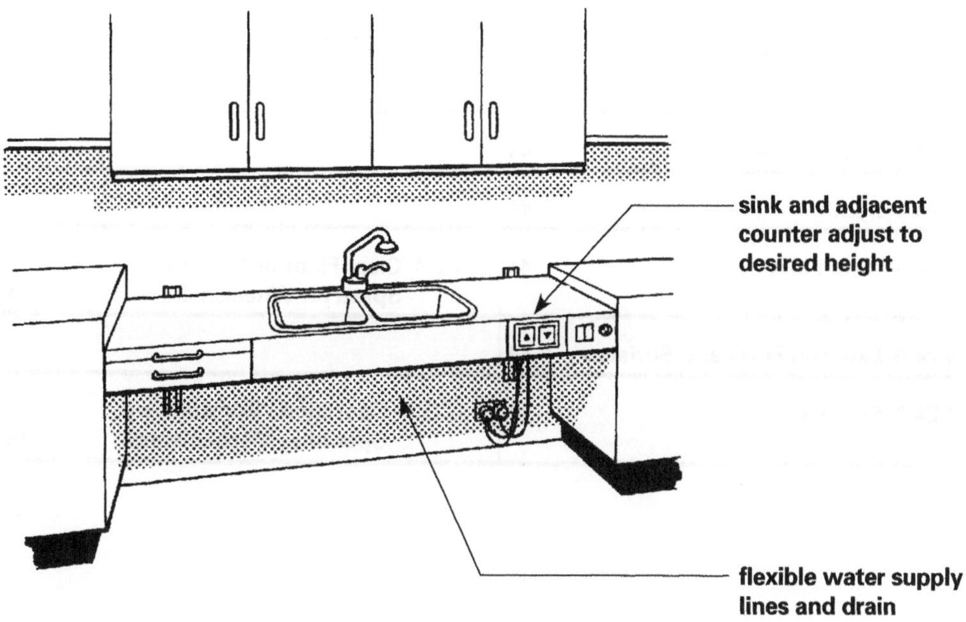

Manufactured Adjustable Sink and Counter

REFERENCE INDEX TO UFAS DOCUMENT

SINKS

Primary References	UFAS page	Secondary References	UFAS page
4.24.1 General	44	4.1 Scope & Technical Requirements 4.1.5 Additions 4.1.6 Alterations 4.1.7 Historic Preservation	5-6 11 12 13
4.24.2 Height	44		
4.24.3 Knee Clearance	44		
4.24.4 Depth	44		
4.24.5 Clear Floor Space	44	4.2.4 Clear Floor or Ground Space for Wheelchairs	14
4.24.6 Exposed Pipes and Surfaces	44		
4.24.7 Faucets	44	4.27.4 Operation - Controls and Operating Mechanisms	45

INTRODUCTION

Storage is an important part of most types of buildings. Whether in the home, an office, a store, or in an educational, medical, factory or industrial setting, well-designed functional storage improves both the aesthetic quality of the environment and the productivity of the occupants. Space designers and product manufacturers are constantly improving the usability of storage units and devices for use in a variety of settings. Most of these new storage options are modular and/or adjustable and can be configured to suit a variety of individual needs.

When storage facilities are furnished in an accessible space, UFAS requires that at least one of each type storage unit including cabinets, shelves, closets, and drawers be accessible. The accessible storage must be within the reach ranges specified by UFAS but additional storage may be provided outside these dimensions. Storage facilities which are not frequented by either the public or employees are not required to be accessible. In facilities scheduled for alteration, storage facilities in accessible spaces and other basic building elements should be considered high priority items.

BASIC DESIGN CONSIDERATIONS

ACCESSIBLE STORAGE DESIGN

UFAS contains a few very basic requirements for accessible storage, which for the most part, are the same as the unwritten principles followed by any good space designer. UFAS requires that clear floor space, 30 inches by 48 inches, which allows either a forward or parallel approach, be provided at accessible storage units. The height of the storage shall be within the reach ranges specified in UFAS Sections 4.2.5 Forward Reach and 4.2.6 Side Reach, page 15. The actual range will depend upon the direction of approach and whether the person must stretch over an obstacle to reach the desired item. Clothes rods shall be a maximum of 54 inches from the floor. Hardware should be easy to use and must comply with UFAS Section 4.27.4 Operation - Controls and Operating Mechanisms, page 45. These requirements apply to all aspects of storage facilities including drawers, cabinets, shelves and closets and they are described below in further detail.

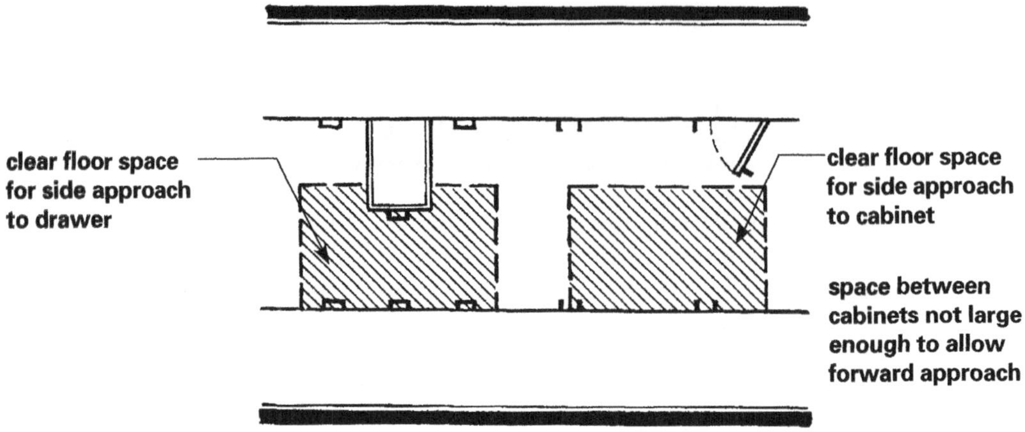

Maneuvering Space for Parallel Approach

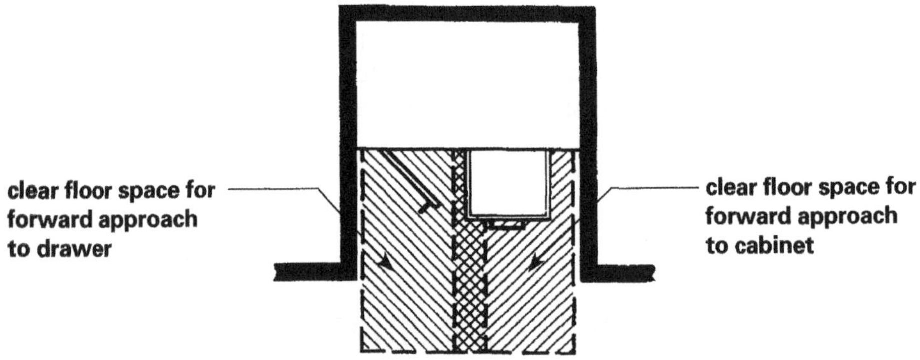

Maneuvering Space for Forward Approach

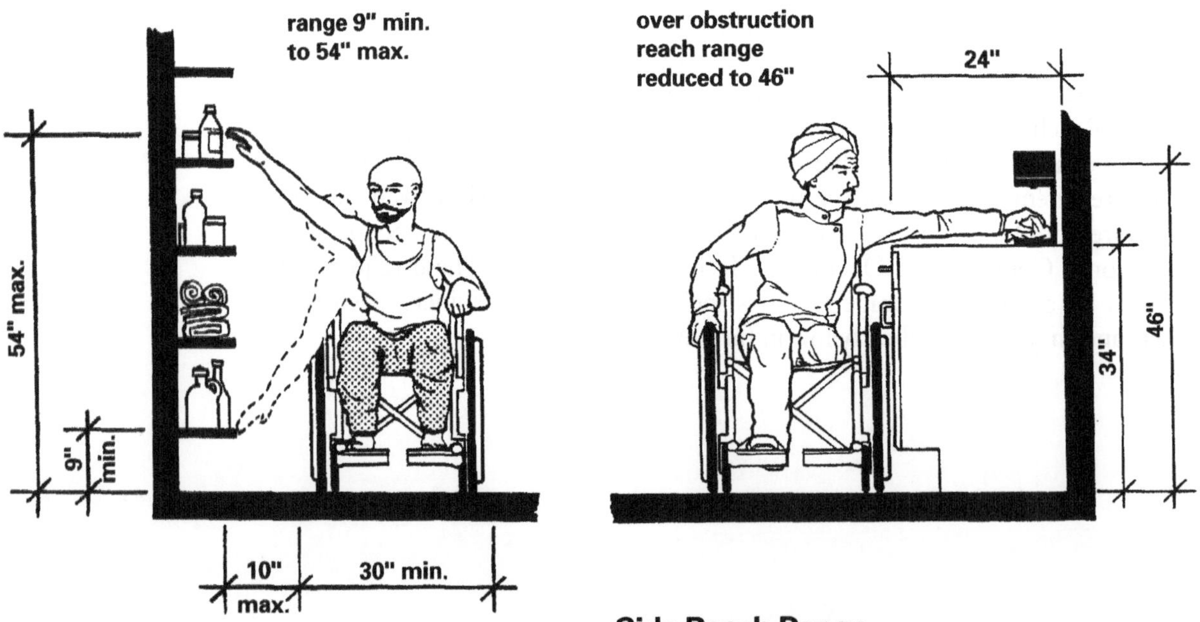

Side Reach Range

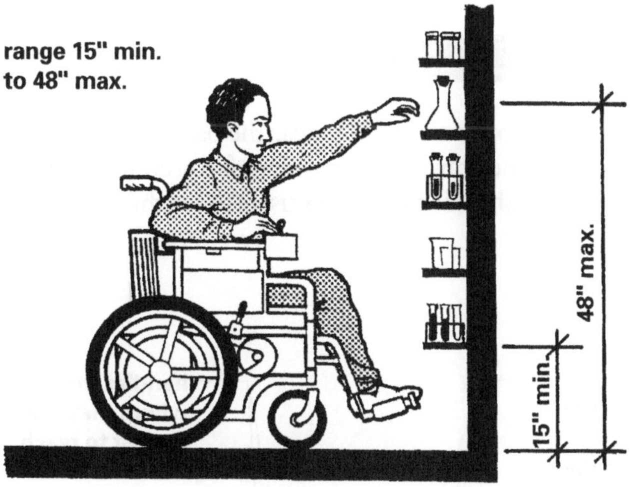

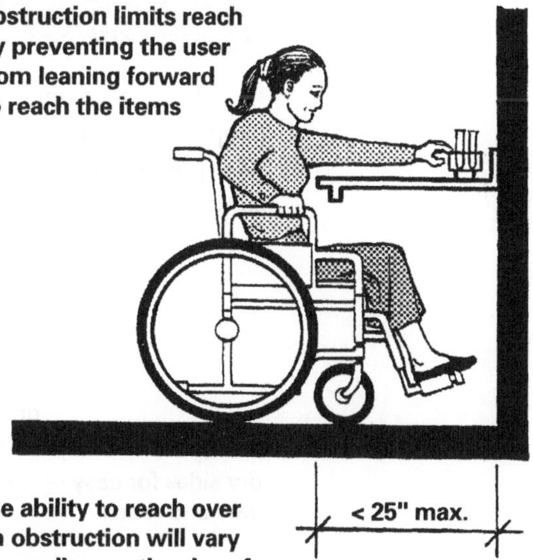

Forward Reach Range

Drawers. Drawers on easy-glide full extension slides are best for everyone. These drawers open their full length to expose the entire contents of the drawer. Office filing cabinets have long included this type of hardware and now other storage units have incorporated these slides. High quality slides make opening and closing the drawer easy and built-in stops prevent the drawer from falling forward. Loop-type handles are an excellent choice for hardware and should be mounted near the top edge of lower drawers and doors and near the bottom edge of upper drawers and doors to make them easier to reach.

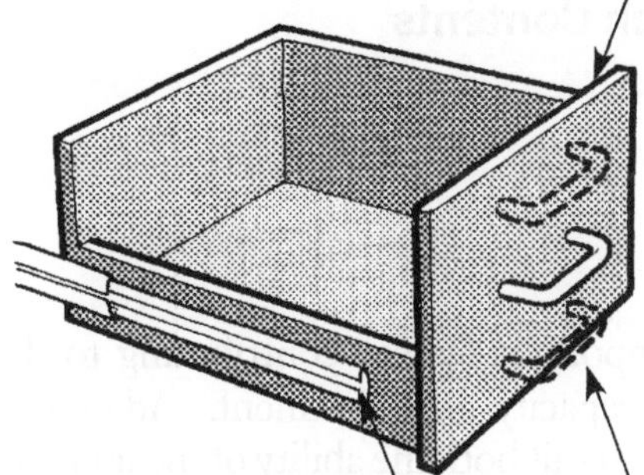

Full Extension Drawer on Slides

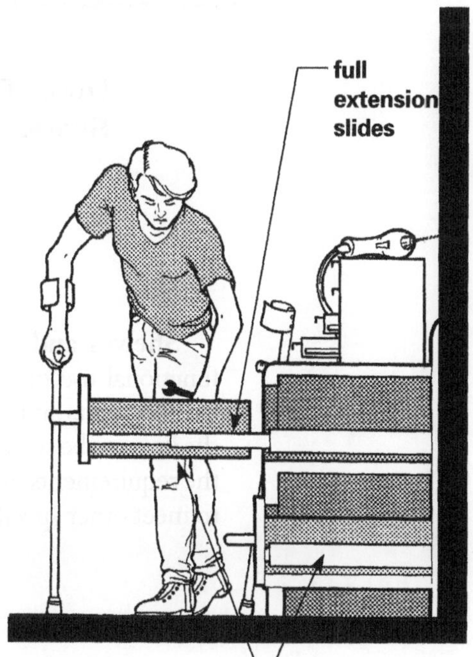

PRACTICAL PLUS

The sides of upper drawers can be lower than those near the base to allow seated people to see and reach the contents of the drawer. Several manufactured storage units incorporate drawers/baskets of wire mesh which also allow users to see the contents of all the drawers.

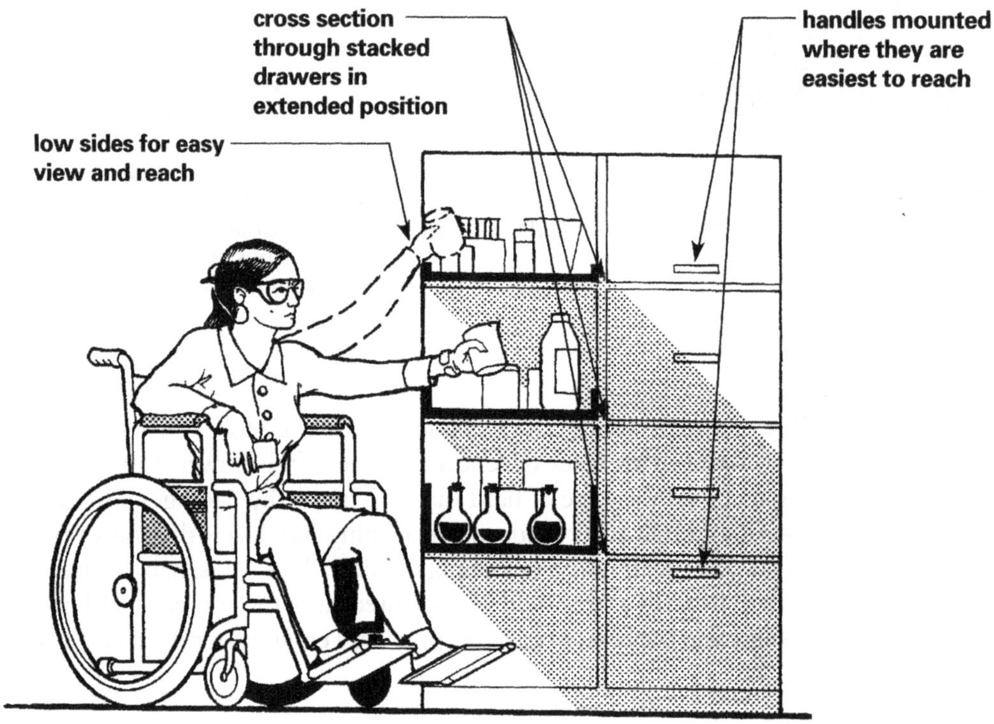

Upper Drawers with Lowered Sides Allow Seated Users to See and Reach Contents

Shelves and Closet Rods. The most important feature contributing to the functional use of any shelf or closet rod is its capacity for adjustment. Adjustable shelving units and closet rods can be configured to suit both the ability of the user and the items to be stored. There are many manufactured product options available to suit the requirements of virtually every conceivable setting. Custom units can also be built to meet other specific needs.

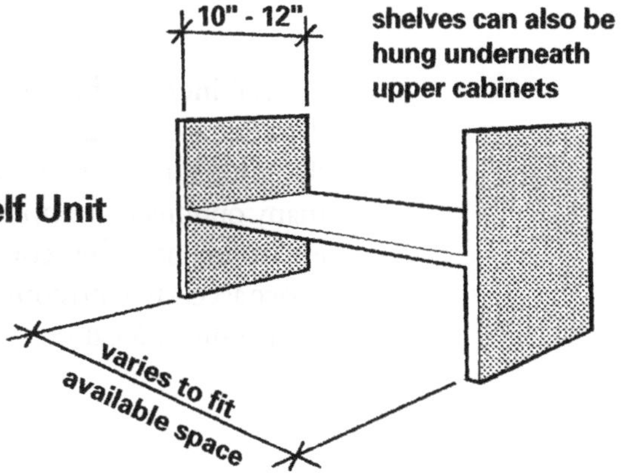

Free-Standing Countertop Shelf Unit

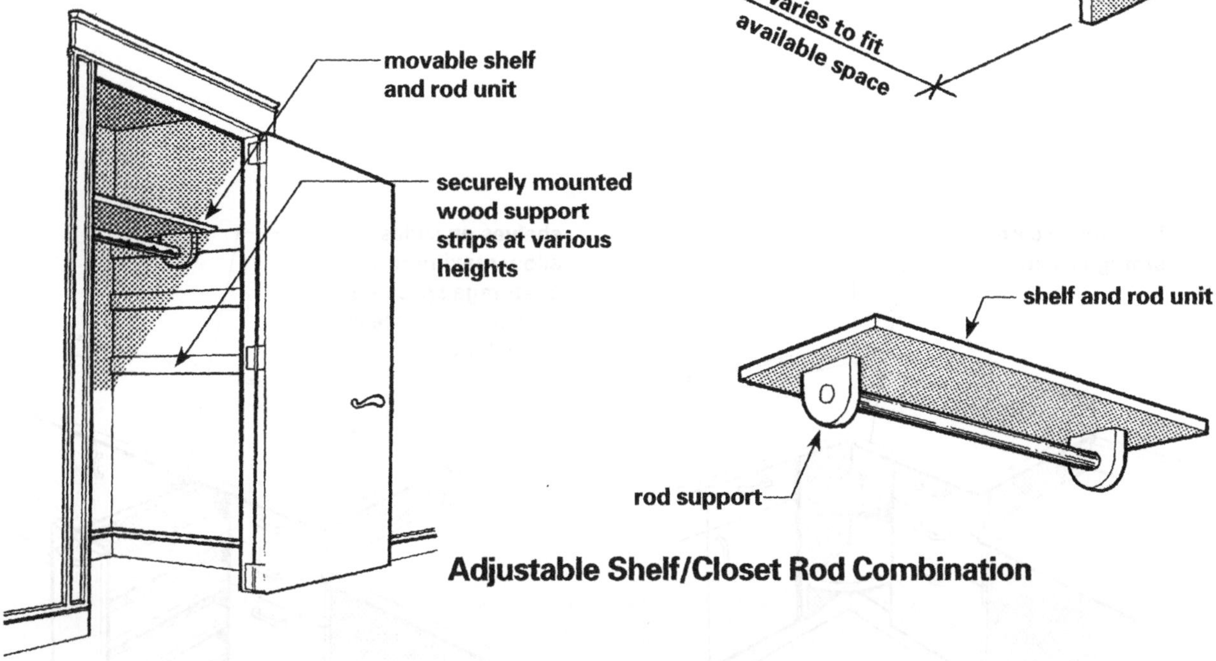

Adjustable Shelf/Closet Rod Combination

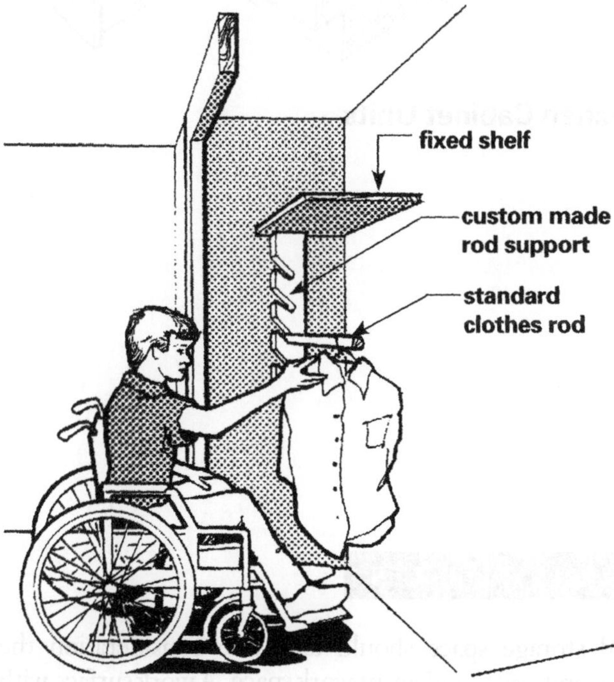

Adjustable Closet Rod with Fixed Shelf

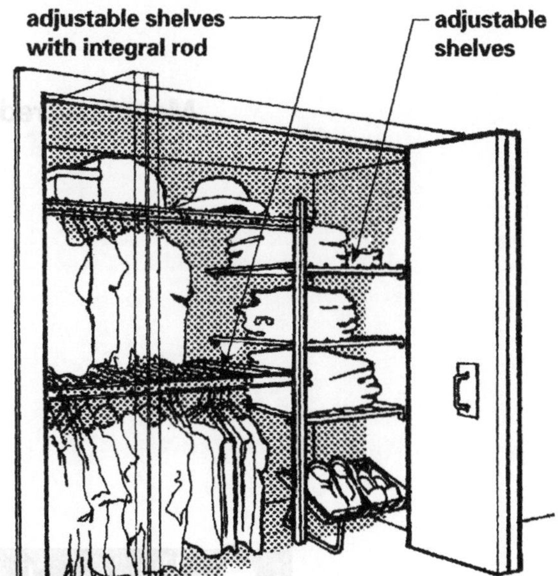

Commercially Available Ventilated Storage Unit

Cabinets and Carts. Cabinets of various types, which contain both shelves and/or drawers, are found in many settings. Built-in or movable specialty cabinets have been designed for use in various environments. Kitchen cabinets are now available with many options that improve use of difficult-to-reach storage spaces. Large corporate environments often contain sophisticated semi-automated filing systems which improve access to hard copy data. These filing systems bring all documents into easy reach from a single location.

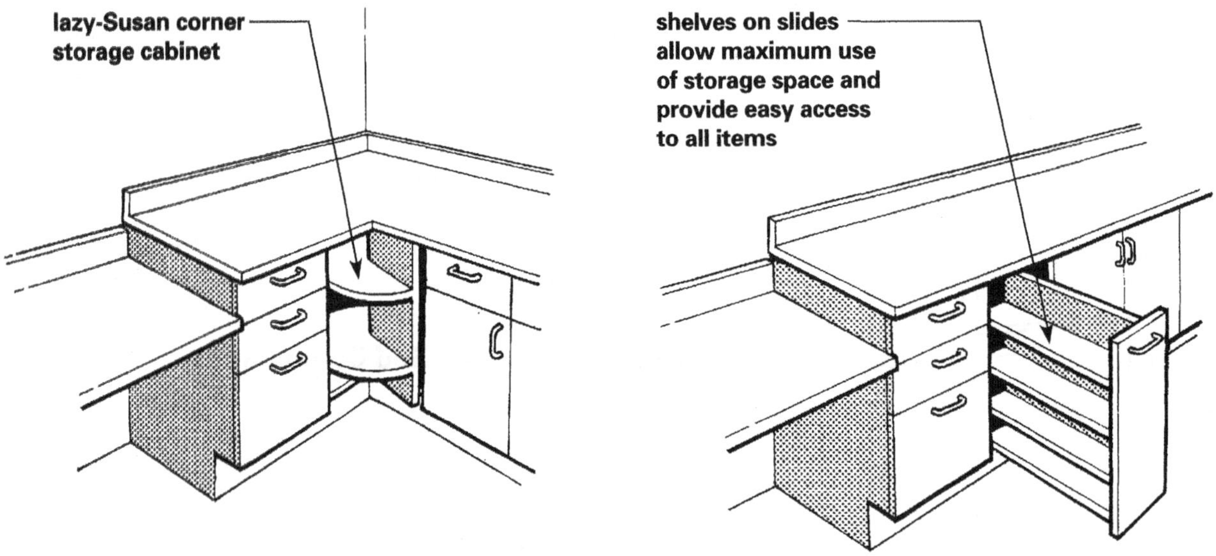

Manufactured Kitchen Cabinet Units

PRACTICAL PLUS

Design of frequently used storage space should take into consideration the relationship between the storage unit and the adjacent work space. A work surface with knee space, adjacent to the storage area, improves access and facilitates more immediate use of the stored item for all seated people. The knee space can be hidden behind retractable doors when not in use.

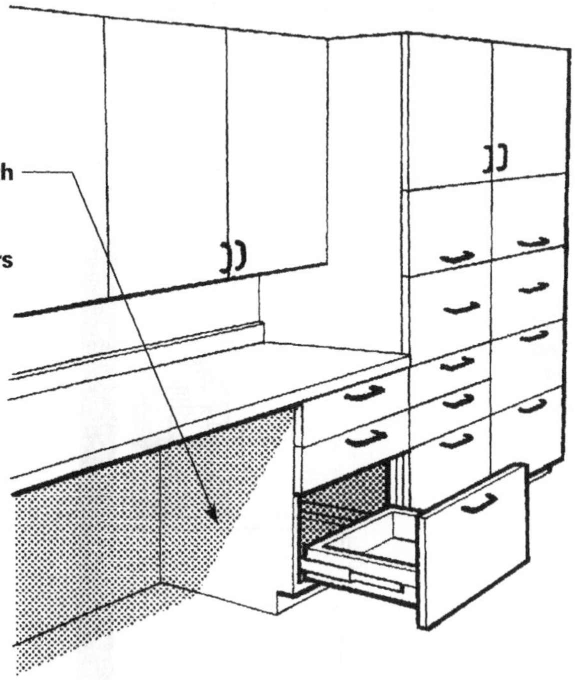

Adjacent Knee Space Improves Access to Storage

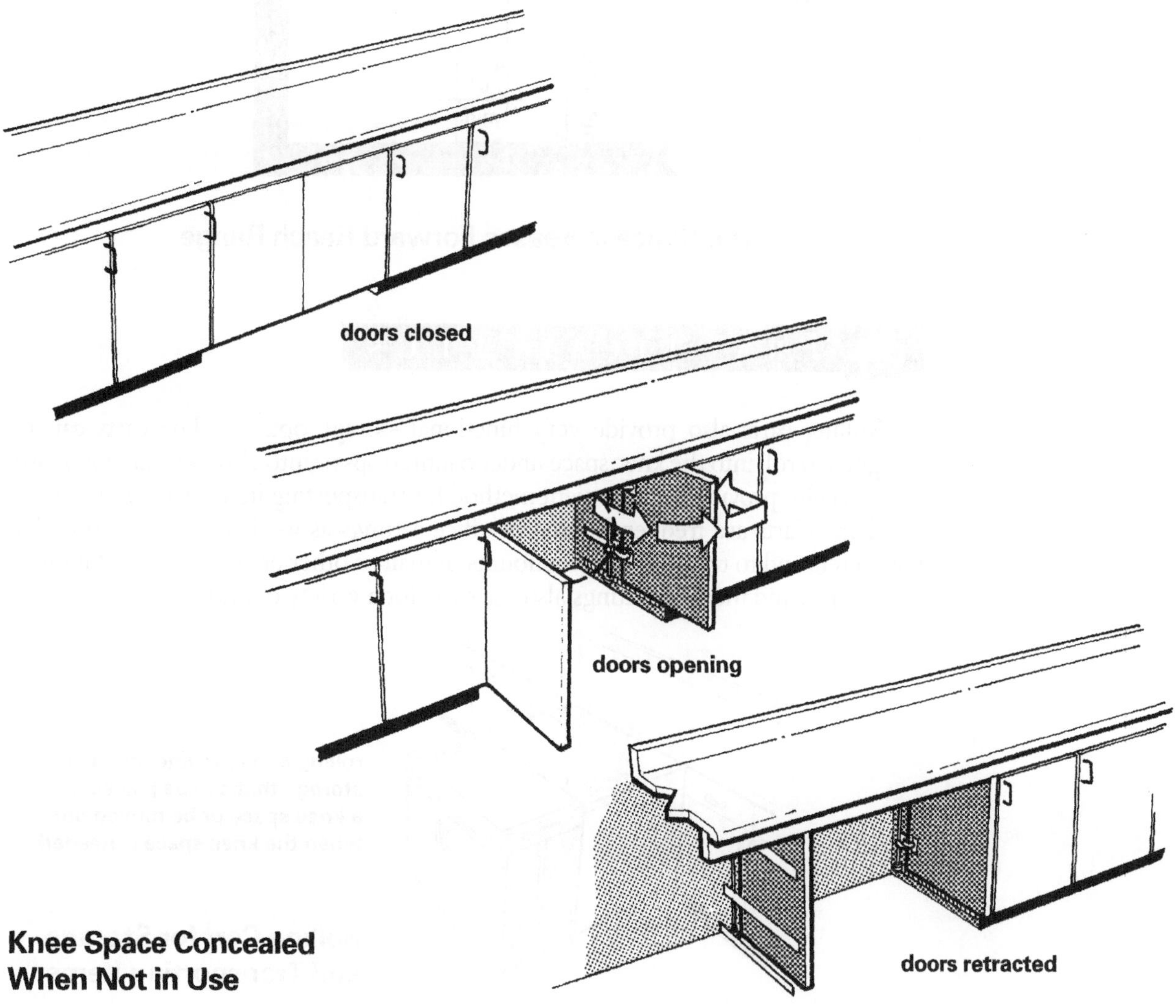

Knee Space Concealed When Not in Use

PRACTICAL PLUS

Toe space under cabinets improves forward reach to cabinets and shelves when full knee space cannot be provided. Although not required in UFAS, toe space is required by some state codes, usually in kitchens. Toe space should be at least 10 inches high by 6 inches deep to provide ample clearance for wheelchair footrests and user's feet.

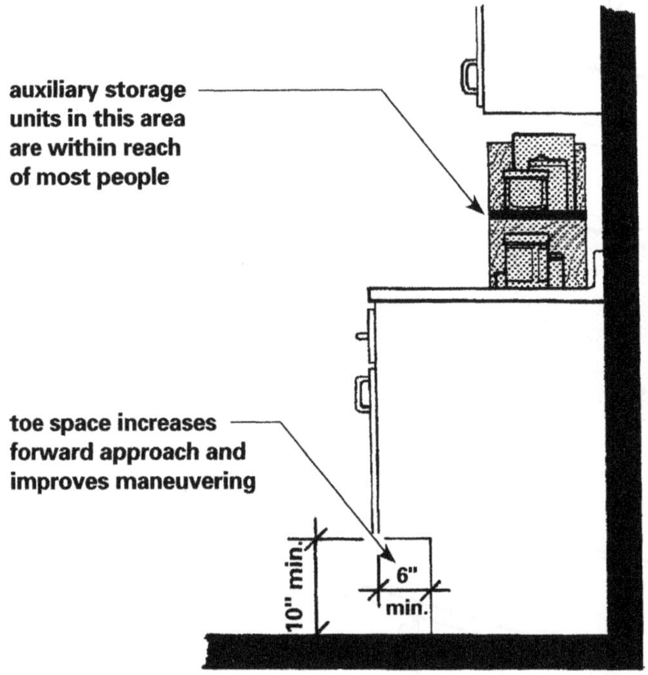

Toe Space Increases Forward Reach Range

PRACTICAL PLUS

Rolling carts also provide very functional storage options. The carts can be designed to roll into the knee space under countertops or into closets when not in use. The cart also provides a convenient method for transporting items from one place to another. Carts are frequently used in office settings as work surfaces for portable computers and to transport large amounts of mail or other documents. Restaurants, classrooms, and medical settings also use carts for a variety of purposes.

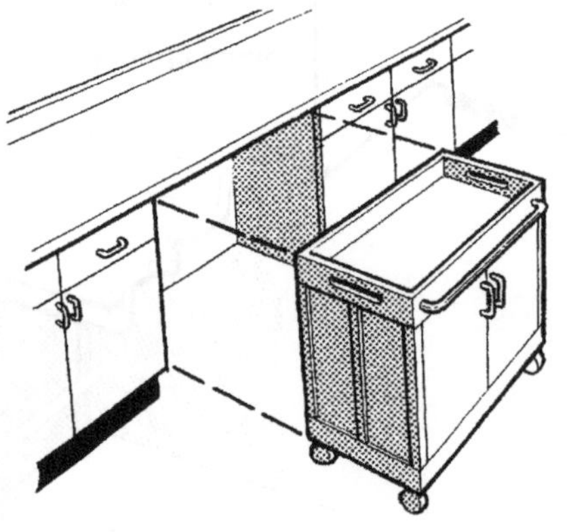

rolling carts provide movable storage that can be placed in a knee space or be moved out when the knee space is needed

Rolling Cart for Storage and Transporting Items

Closets. The single term "closet" is used to define a variety of very different sized spaces which serve the similar purpose of storage. For the purpose of this manual, closets will be defined in terms of the type of door. Closet doors either permit the user to enter the closet through a passage door, or the contents are reached from outside of the closet.

Shallow storage or clothes hanging closets should be designed such that their contents can be reached from outside the closet. When passage is not required, the doorway may be less than the 32 inches otherwise required. Single hinged doors to shallow closets should swing back 180 degrees to allow a close side or front approach. Doors to larger shallow closets should open the entire width of the closet, if possible, to eliminate dead space in the corners. Hinged pairs of doors and bi-fold doors should swing out of the way to allow full access to the closet contents.

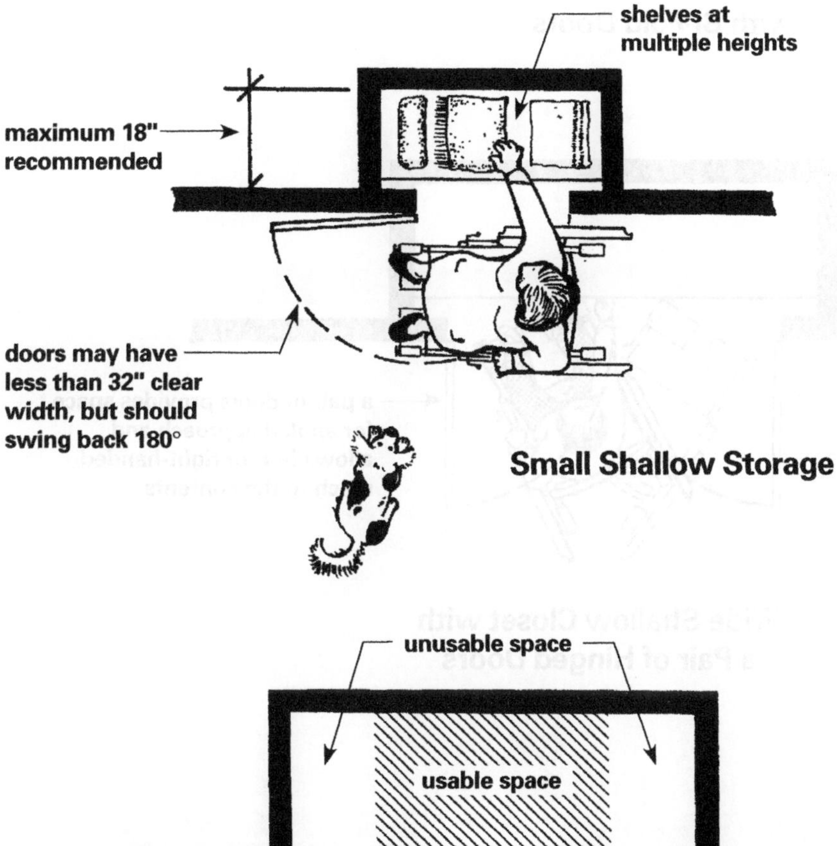

Small Shallow Storage Closet

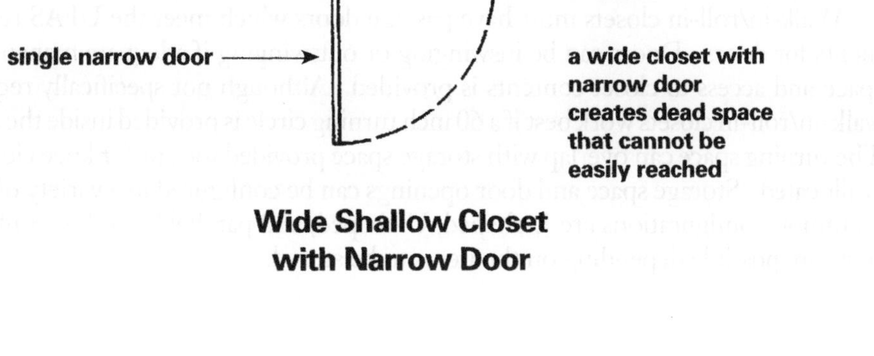

Wide Shallow Closet with Narrow Door

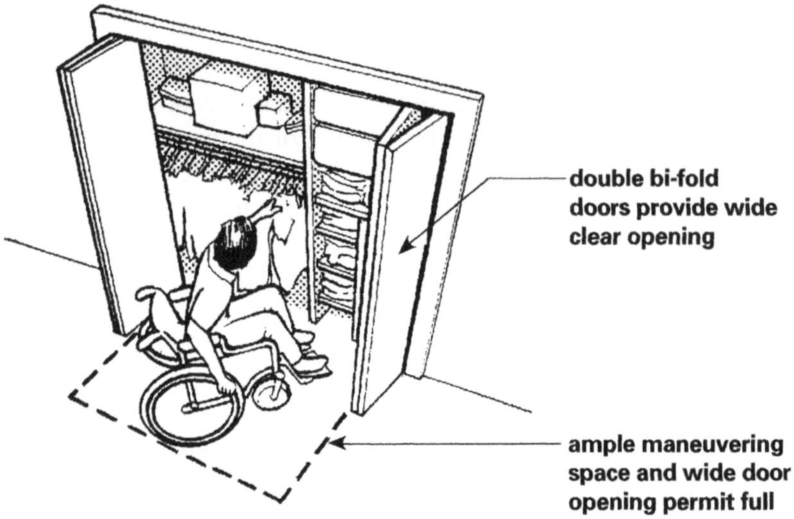

Wide Shallow Closet with Bi-Fold Doors

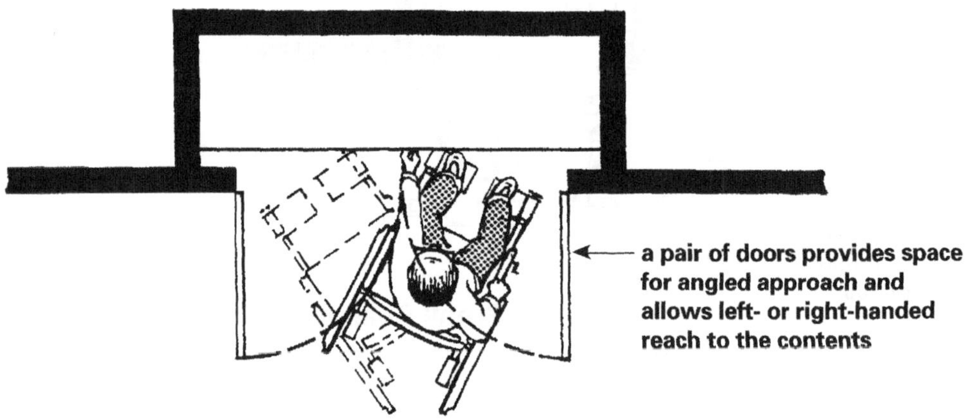

Wide Shallow Closet with a Pair of Hinged Doors

Walk-in/roll-in closets must have passage doors which meet the UFAS requirements for doors. Doors can be inswinging or outswinging if adequate maneuvering space and access to closet contents is provided. Although not specifically required, walk-in/roll-in closets work best if a 60 inch turning circle is provided inside the closet. The turning space can overlap with storage space provided toe and/or knee clearance is allocated. Storage space and door openings can be configured in a variety of ways. Common configurations are L-shaped, U-shaped, and parallel but other configurations are possible depending on the items to be stored.

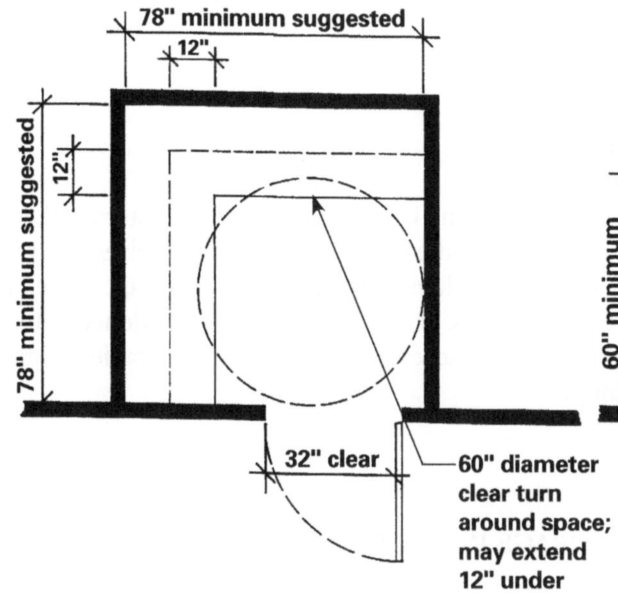

Walk-In/Roll-In Closet with L-Shaped Storage

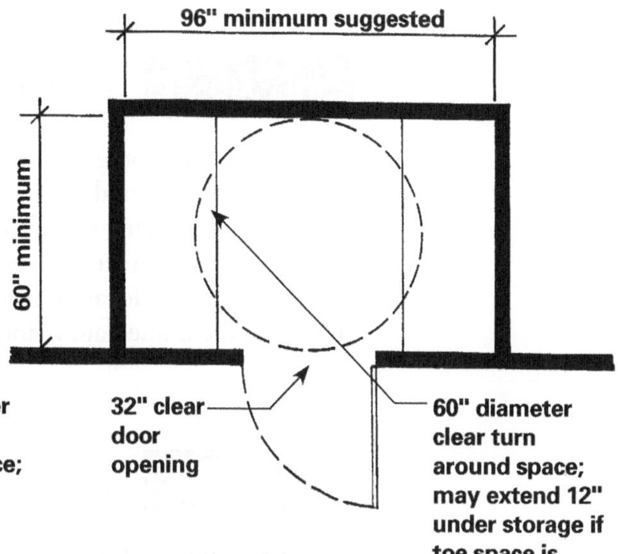

Walk-In/Roll-In Closet with Parallel Storage

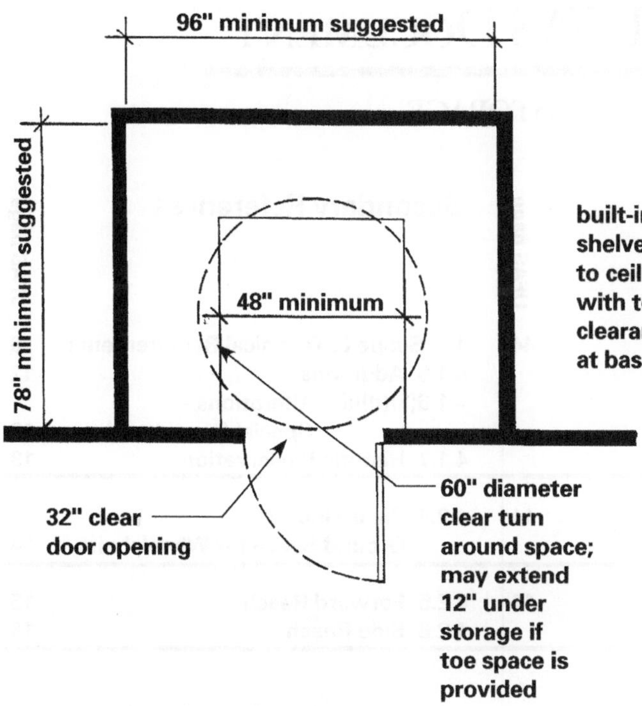

Walk-In/Roll-In Closet with U-Shaped Storage

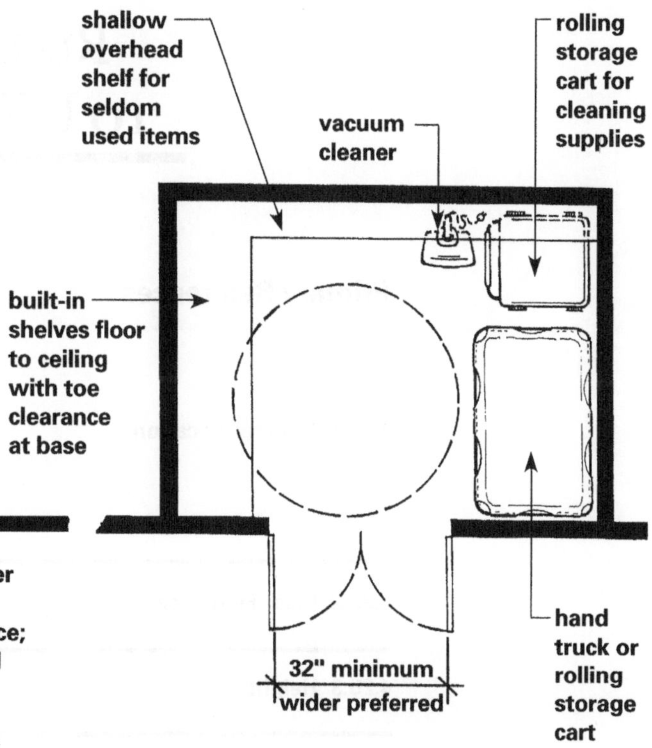

Walk-In/Roll-In Closet for Equipment Storage

PROBLEM — EXISTING STORAGE DOESN'T COMPLY

SOLUTION 1 — MODIFY STORAGE

If an existing storage unit doesn't meet the UFAS requirements for storage then it may be possible to modify all or part of it. If the storage unit contains shelves, drawers, or cabinets for storing specific equipment, then one of each type of storage should be modified to provide access to essential items. It is not necessary to provide access to all storage in a given location as long as the accessible storage is comparable to other storage in the immediate vicinity.

SOLUTION 2 — ADD STORAGE IN ACCESSIBLE LOCATION

If space allows, it may be possible to add a separate storage unit nearby. In some cases it may be necessary to relocate essential one-of-a-kind items to the accessible storage area so that these items are available to everyone. If new storage is installed it should be modular and/or adjustable to meet the needs of the individuals.

REFERENCE INDEX TO UFAS DOCUMENT

STORAGE

Primary References	UFAS page	Secondary References	UFAS page
4.25.1 General/Location	44	4.1 Scope & Technical Requirements 4.1.5 Additions 4.1.6(3)(d)(iii) Alterations - Special Consideration 4.1.7 Historic Preservation	6 12 12 13
4.25.2 Clear Floor Space	44	4.2.4 Clear Floor or Ground Space for Wheelchairs	14
4.25.3 Height	44	4.2.5 Forward Reach 4.2.6 Side Reach	15 15
4.25.4 Hardware	44	4.27.4 Operation - Controls and Operating Mechanisms	45

Introduction

The purpose of alarms is to provide notification of emergencies in a thorough and timely manner allowing all of the building's occupants to evacuate safely. Over the years, safety experts' definition of an "appropriate alarm" has changed as a result of research and development of new technology. Some life-safety code requirements were broad enough to encompass the new research findings, but others were (and still are) too narrowly defined to include or allow more effective alarm systems. Revisions and updates to these codes will eventually include the more stringent, more effective requirements.

UFAS requires that if emergency warning systems are provided then they shall include both visual and audible alarms. Health care occupancies and facilities with sleeping accommodations have unique requirements to accommodate the particular needs of the occupants. In facilities scheduled for alteration, appropriate alarms and other basic elements should be considered high priority items after other minimum requirements have been met, UFAS 4.1.6(3)(d)(iv), page 12. Additional information about alarms can be found in Unit Five, Egress.

Basic Design Considerations

Audible Alarms

UFAS requires that, fire alarms, if provided, shall produce a sound that exceeds the prevailing equivalent sound level in the space by at least 15 decibels or that exceeds by 5 decibels any maximum sound level with a duration of 30 seconds, whichever is louder. Sound levels should not exceed 120 decibels. Because many older people have difficulty perceiving frequencies higher than 10,000 Hz, UFAS suggests that alarms emit a lower frequency.

Audible alarms should produce signals which are easily distinguished from, and take precedence over, other audible signals used in the same facility. Pre-recorded or live voice evacuation instructions are also permitted by many codes. These messages are often used in conjunction with more traditional fire alarm evacuation signals.

PROBLEM AUDIBLE ALARM SIGNALS DON'T MEET REQUIREMENTS

SOLUTION SUPPLEMENT OR REPLACE EXISTING ALARMS

It may be possible to supplement the existing system with additional alarms that function within the parameters required. The product manufacturers should be contacted to make recommendations about adding to or upgrading the existing system. If modification is not possible, consideration should be given to replacing the system.

BASIC DESIGN CONSIDERATIONS

VISUAL ALARMS

In addition to the requirements that fire alarms produce an audible signal, in new construction UFAS requires that fire alarms produce a corresponding visual signal to alert those who are unable to respond to audible signals. In 1986-87 the Access Board sponsored research toward the development of requirements for visual alarms and signals that effectively alert hearing impaired individuals of fire and other emergencies. The findings of that study are available in a brochure titled, *Visual Alarms to Alert Persons with Hearing Loss*, which is available from the Access Board. The research indicated that the most effective visual signals for standard daytime conditions include the following features:

Type of Light: Xenon flash tube, high intensity strobe lamp
Color of Light: White (clear)
Flash Rate: 1-3 Hz (flashes per second)
Intensity: Minimum of 75 candela-seconds, maximum of 120
Flash Duration: Approximately one millisecond (0.001 second)

The composite visual signals produced by these alarms are bright enough to alert people nearby and safe enough to be viewed directly. Tests indicated that a visual signal of this type is capable of illuminating a rectangular room up to 1,000 sq.ft. Spaces which are divided into smaller areas or irregular shapes will require additional visual signals. The research also indicated that supplementary alarms, including illuminated flashing emergency exit signs and visual alarms mounted adjacent to emergency exits, were not effective as primary visual fire alarms. These supplementary alarms were of limited use because they did not provide notification in areas normally occupied (such as office space or rest rooms).

PROBLEM VISUAL ALARM SIGNALS DON'T MEET REQUIREMENTS

SOLUTION SUPPLEMENT OR REPLACE EXISTING ALARMS

In many cases it may be possible to supplement an existing audible-only alarm system with the addition of visual signal devices. However, because light does not travel around corners the way sound does, it is likely that buildings will require more visual signals than audible signals. Many alarm systems which combine both the audible and visual signal in the same signal device are available. Manufacturers or installers should be contacted directly regarding the specific use of their products.

BASIC DESIGN CONSIDERATIONS

AUXILIARY ALARMS

Smoke detectors with visual and audible signals and built-in transmitters/receivers can be installed on a permanent basis to communicate with the main fire alarm system. Portable units which utilize a standard 110 volt electrical cord are also available and are provided for hearing impaired guests at some hotels and motels. These units are not connected to the main alarm and are typically activated by built-in sound or smoke sensors.

REFERENCE INDEX TO UFAS DOCUMENT

VISUAL, AUDIBLE, AND AUXILIARY ALARMS

Primary References	UFAS page	Secondary References	UFAS page
4.28.1 General	45	4.1 Scope & Technical Requirements	6
		4.1.5 Additions	11
		4.1.6(3)(d)(iv) Alterations - Special Consideration	12
		4.1.7 Historic Preservation	13
4.28.2 Audible Alarms	45	A4.28.2 Audible Alarms	65
4.28.3 Visual Alarms	45	A4.28.3 Visual Alarms	65
4.28.4 Auxiliary Alarms	46	A4.28.4 Auxiliary Alarms	65

TACTILE WARNINGS

UFAS 4.29

INTRODUCTION

A tactile warning is defined in UFAS as a standardized surface texture applied to, or built into, walking surfaces or other elements to warn visually impaired people of hazards in the path of travel. Much research has been performed in this area to determine what type of surfaces are actually detectable and how these surfaces should be installed to facilitate safe use of a facility. The most recent research indicates that certain types of surfaces can indeed be reliably detected, and if properly installed, reduce the risk of accidents. At the present time, however, the only tactile warnings which UFAS requires are on handles of doors which lead to hazardous areas. An additional requirement is that the tactile warnings be used consistently throughout the facility.

BASIC DESIGN CONSIDERATIONS

TACTILE WARNINGS ON DOOR HANDLES

On doorways leading to hazardous areas, tactile warnings should be placed on the door handle hardware where the texture will be touched by anyone attempting to use the door. The distinctive texture should be applied by knurling or with an epoxy grit finish. Emergency exit doors should never have tactile warnings regardless of the risks which might be associated with their use, i.e., fire escape, stairs, etc.

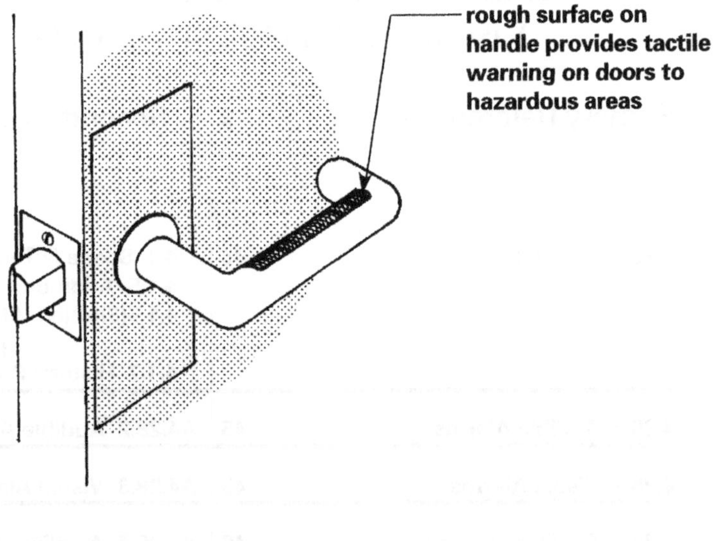

Knurled Door Handle

PROBLEM
NO USE OR INCONSISTENT USE OF TACTILE WARNINGS

SOLUTION
APPLY TACTILE WARNING

Determine which doors lead to hazardous areas of the facility and install tactile warnings. If existing tactile warnings are inconsistent, remove and replace with consistent warnings.

PRACTICAL PLUS

In addition to tactile cues, it is recommended that visual cues also be provided on doors leading to hazardous areas. Guide dogs are frequently trained to recognize and respond to visual cues, such as warning signs, caution stripes, etc.

PRACTICAL PLUS

Tactile warnings on walking surfaces (also called edge cuing) are useful on raised platforms, curbs, stairs, hazardous vehicular areas, and reflecting pools. Recent research indicated that variations in resilience, sound, and texture were detectable. Sound characteristics were the easiest to differentiate while textural changes were the most difficult to detect. However, because sound cues can be masked by other environmental noise, differences in resilience of materials appears to offer the most viable solution. Edge-cuing material should be at least 42 inches wide and securely installed along the rim of hazardous areas. For additional safety, the edge-cuing material should be lighter in color than the primary flooring and contrast with it. The edge-cuing material should also be slip-resistant and be able to withstand exposure to weather, moisture, or contaminants.*

* Refer to the report on *Transit Facility Design for Persons with Visual Impairments*, produced by the Architectural and Transportation Barriers Compliance Board (ATBCB), for more detailed information on selection and installation of effective edge cuing.

Edge Cuing on Platform

edge cuing should be lighter color which contrasts with primary floor color

platform edge

REFERENCE INDEX TO UFAS DOCUMENT

TACTILE WARNINGS ON DOORS TO HAZARDOUS AREAS/WALKING SURFACES

Primary References	UFAS page	Secondary References	UFAS page
4.29.1 General	46	4.1 Scope & Technical Requirements 4.1.5 Additions 4.1.6 Alterations 4.1.7 Historic Preservation	6 11 12 13
4.29.2 Tactile Warnings on Walking Surfaces *Reserved*	46		
4.29.3 Tactile Warnings on Doors to Hazardous Areas	47	A4.29.3 Tactile Warnings on Doors to Hazardous Areas	65
4.29.4 Tactile Warnings at Stairs *Reserved*	47		
4.29.5 Tactile Warnings at Hazardous Vehicular Areas *Reserved*	47		
4.29.6 Tactile Warnings at Reflecting Pools *Reserved*	47		
4.29.7 Standardization	47	A4.29.7 Standardization/Visual Cues	66

Introduction

Signage serves a variety of important purposes for all people and is found virtually everywhere in the built environment, on streets, sites, outside buildings, and inside buildings. Most buildings and facilities have signage systems which are used consistently throughout to provide direction to and information about various locations and services. Well designed signage systems save time and increase convenience for all people, particularly those with speech, cognitive, or hearing impairments who may have difficulty asking for and understanding directions. People with small children, people carrying packages or luggage, people using mobility aids, and people with limited stamina also find it frustrating to search for locations in poorly signed facilities.

Any or all of several types of information including letters and numbers, pictographs, logos, and other graphic images such as maps and floor plans of complex facilities may appear on a sign. Signs can be designed to be interpreted both tactilely and visually to provide direction and information. The content and length of messages on signs, use of color, lighting, and placement within the facility also contribute to the usability of a signage system. In some facilities, "audible" signage is incorporated to enhance the visual and tactile signage and often provides information which changes frequently such as arrivals and departures, closings, emergencies, etc.

Much has been written on the topic of signage and there are many theories about what works best. However, there are some basic principles upon which most experts agree regardless of individual professional preferences on some of the more controversial issues. UFAS addresses some of these basic principles in its requirements for signage.

UFAS requires that all signs throughout a facility comply with the specifications of 4.30 Signage. If signs are provided, all signs shall have character proportions within a specific width to height ratio to insure readability and shall have characters and symbols which contrast with the background of signs. If signage is provided that permanently identifies rooms and spaces (such as "Room 504", "MEN" or "WOMEN"), in addition, those signs must have raised sans serif characters within a specific size range and be mounted in a specific location at the height specified. The only exception to these requirements is for temporary signage at rooms and spaces, such as current occupant's name, provided the permanent room/space identification complies with UFAS. The signage included in additions to existing facilities must comply with UFAS and signage in the existing facility may need to be modified if accessible elements and spaces are located there. In alterations, including historic properties, where specific spaces are made accessible, the accompanying signage must also meet the UFAS requirements. When, in the course of alterations, the facility's signage is altered and signs are changed or added, they must comply. UFAS also requires that the international access symbol be displayed in certain locations; anytime the symbol is used, it must comply with the UFAS specifications.

BASIC DESIGN CONSIDERATIONS

LETTERS AND SYMBOLS

UFAS contains several requirements which affect the design of letters and symbols on signs. The purpose of these requirements is to produce signs which can be easily "read" tactilely and visually. The requirements are described in detail below:

Character Proportion. Letters and numbers on signs must have a width-to-height ratio between 3:5 and 1:1 and a stroke width-to-height ratio between 1:5 and 1:10. This requirement is designed to prohibit the use of very condensed or extended or extremely bold or light type faces.

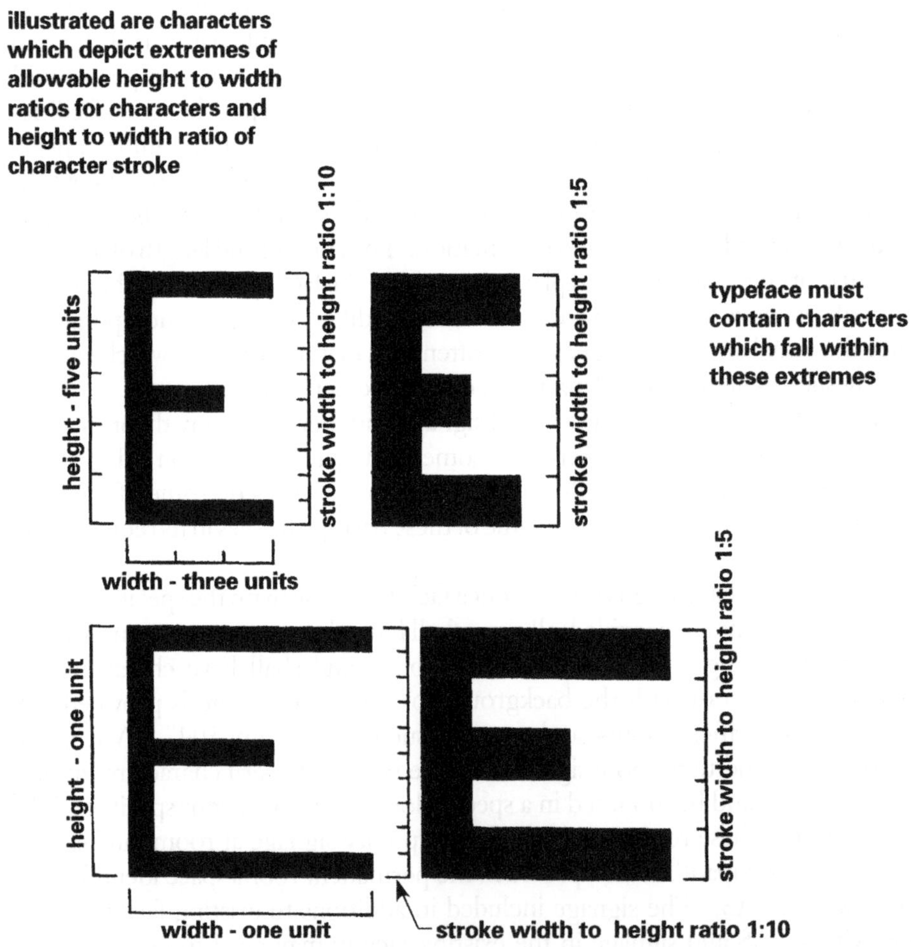

Character Proportion

Size and Type of Characters. Characters or symbols designed to be read tactilely must be at least 5/8 inches high but no larger than two inches. The type face must be a simple sans serif face devoid of flourishes and other excesses which make the characters difficult to decipher either visually or tactilely.

Helvetica

Avant Garde

Univers

Samples of Acceptable Type Faces

Raised Characters and Symbols. Letters and numbers on signs shall be raised 1/32 inch minimum to allow people to decipher information tactilely. Although some state codes allow either raised or incised characters, research has determined that raised characters, especially smaller sized characters, are easier to decipher. Raised characters are also easier to maintain since they do not become filled with dirt and grime.

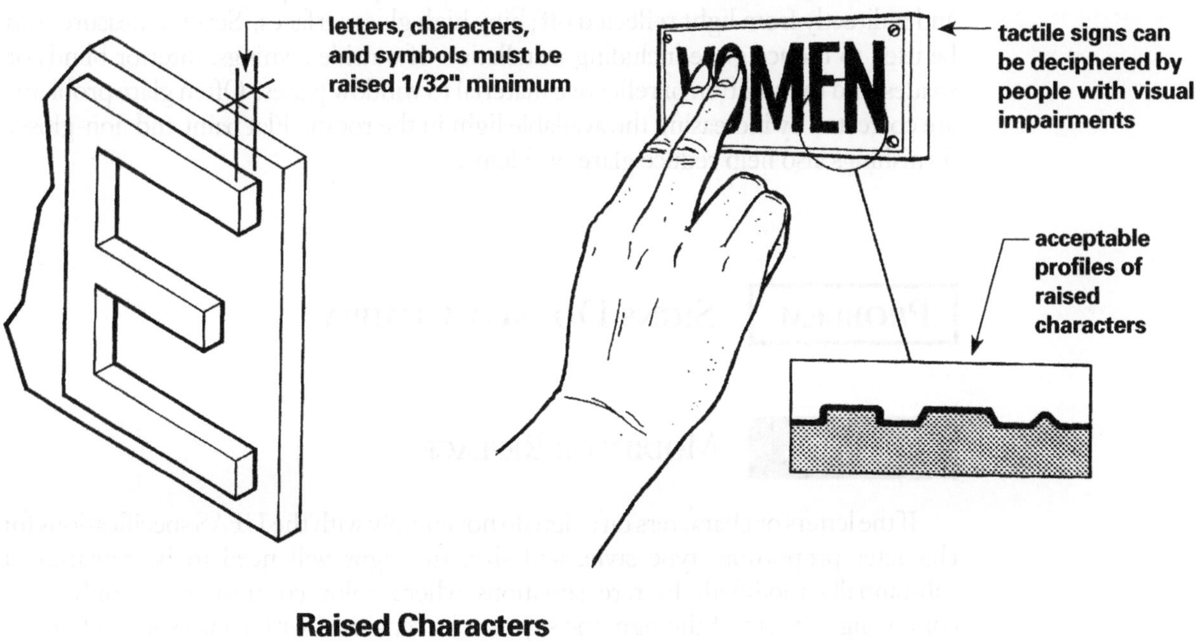

Raised Characters

Color Contrast. The characters or symbols must contrast with the background – either dark characters on a light background, or light characters on a dark background. Research has indicated that light characters on dark backgrounds are easier to read because the potential for glare is reduced by the dark background.

Contrast between Characters and Background

PRACTICAL PLUS

Braille characters are not required but are frequently included in signage systems. If included, braille characters should be incorporated in a consistent location on each sign throughout the signage system and to the left of standard characters. Braille characters do not take the place of tactile characters since many people with visual impairments do not read braille.

PRACTICAL PLUS

Matte finishes and appropriate lighting help reduce the problems created by glare. Glare can originate from several sources both directly from light fixtures and windows, and indirectly from light reflected off shiny high gloss surfaces. Several measures can be used to reduce glare including installation of outside awnings, interior blinds or shades, and the addition of reflective material to window panes. Often glare problems are corrected by increasing the available light in the room. Flat paint and non-glossy furnishings also help reduce glare problems.

PROBLEM — SIGNS DO NOT COMPLY

SOLUTION — MODIFY OR REPLACE

If the letters or characters on a sign do not comply with the UFAS specifications for character proportion, type style, and size, the signs will need to be replaced or substantially modified. In rare situations where color contrast is the only non-complying element of the sign, the sign can be repainted with contrasting colors.

BASIC DESIGN CONSIDERATIONS

LOCATION

Exterior Signage. Exterior signs may be used to indicate vehicular traffic flow, parking restrictions, danger zones, cross walks, visitor, employee, and delivery entrances, outdoor toilet facilities, phones, the name of the building, or a street address. At large complexes with multiple buildings, signage may also be installed at shuttle bus stops, various vendors, and street crossings.

The design considerations for exterior and interior signage are quite similar. One major difference is that exterior signage is often designed and placed such that it will be read from a distance. Signs which are not located on or adjacent to a pedestrian path must have characters and graphics large enough to seen from a distance. When characters must be larger and close approach to the sign is not intended, then it is not necessary for the characters to meet the two inch maximum or be raised as required in UFAS 4.30.4.

Signage that is designed to be read by pedestrians traveling along a path should meet the UFAS requirements. The signage should allow close approach but not interfere with pedestrian or vehicular traffic. Signage of this type can often be combined with exterior lighting fixtures and/or natural gathering locations on the site. Audio guides of campuses, transportation facilities, and other large public facilities provide another means of signage. Landmarks or unusual site features, indicated by the guides, provide important orientation cues for blind and visually impaired people. Outdoor speakers and audible cues are also used to relay information about specific site elements.

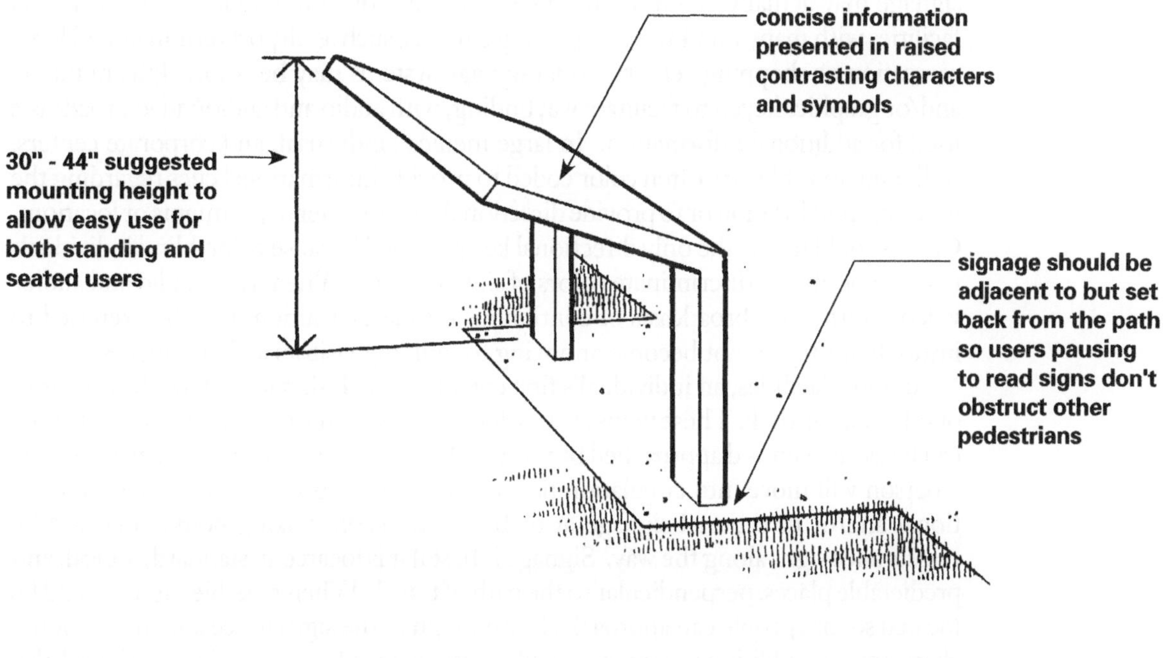

Exterior Sign Located to Side of Path

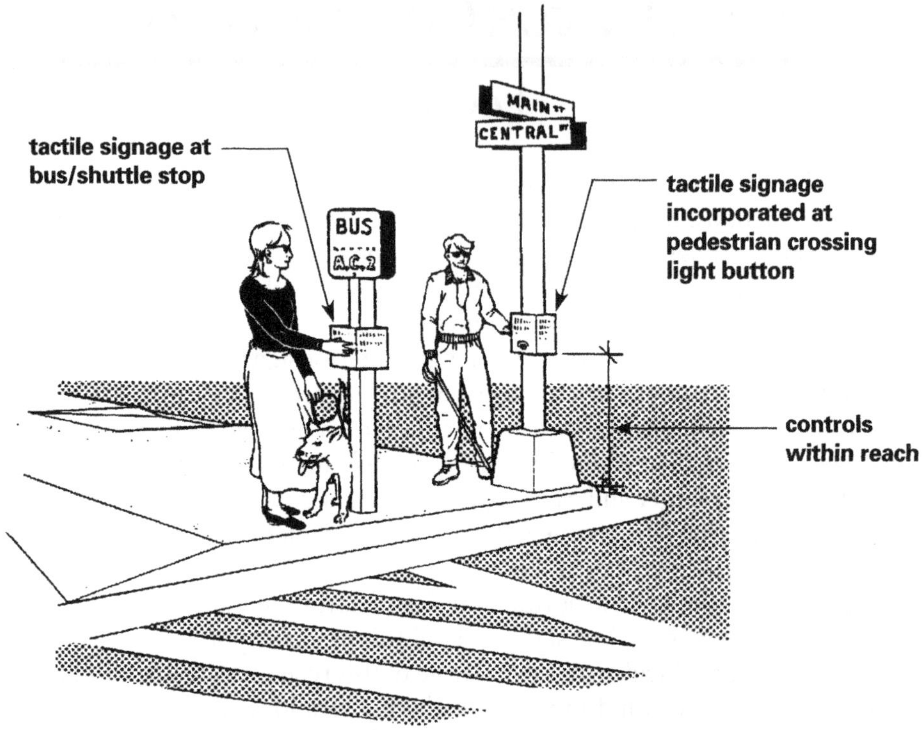

Tactile Signage at Crosswalk and Bus Stop

Interior Signage. Depending upon the complexity of the signage system, interior signage may actually begin on the site or the exterior of the building. In very large facilities with many buildings and parking garages, such as airport terminals and large recreation or shopping centers, visual signage systems may be color, alpha numeric, and/or graphics keyed to facilitate wayfinding, with audio and audio/video broadcasts used for additional information. In large medical, industrial, and corporate centers, walls and floor tiles are often color coded to provide informational cues regarding the user's current location or to provide directional cues to other departments or locations. Color should not be the only directional key provided because color-blind individuals may not be able to discriminate colors of similar value. When using audio and audio/video information broadcasts of continuous messages, caution must be exercised to insure that they do not become annoying to building visitors and employees.

In most facilities, an individual's first encounter with signage will be the directory or information desk. These items are best located close to the main entrance where they can be easily seen and approached by visitors. From the directory or information desk, a person will move into circulation paths which should provide additional informational and/or directional signage at or before decision making points followed by reassurance signs along the way. Signage is best if it is located in standard, logical, and predictable places, perpendicular to the path of travel. When possible, signs should be located so that people can approach close enough to the signs to see and make out the characters. In addition to helping people locate particular spaces, signage should also provide information about how to return to the lobby and the location of fire exits.

UFAS has only one general requirement for the location of signage–permanent interior signage must be located on the wall on the latch side of the door at a mounting height between 54 inches and 66 inches. UFAS specifies this location rather than the more traditional location on the door because doors are frequently left standing open, making it difficult or impossible to read the signage. Even more of a problem is the door flying open in the face of someone trying to decipher a door-mounted sign at close range. On double doors with latches in the center, signage is typically located to the right side of the door frame.

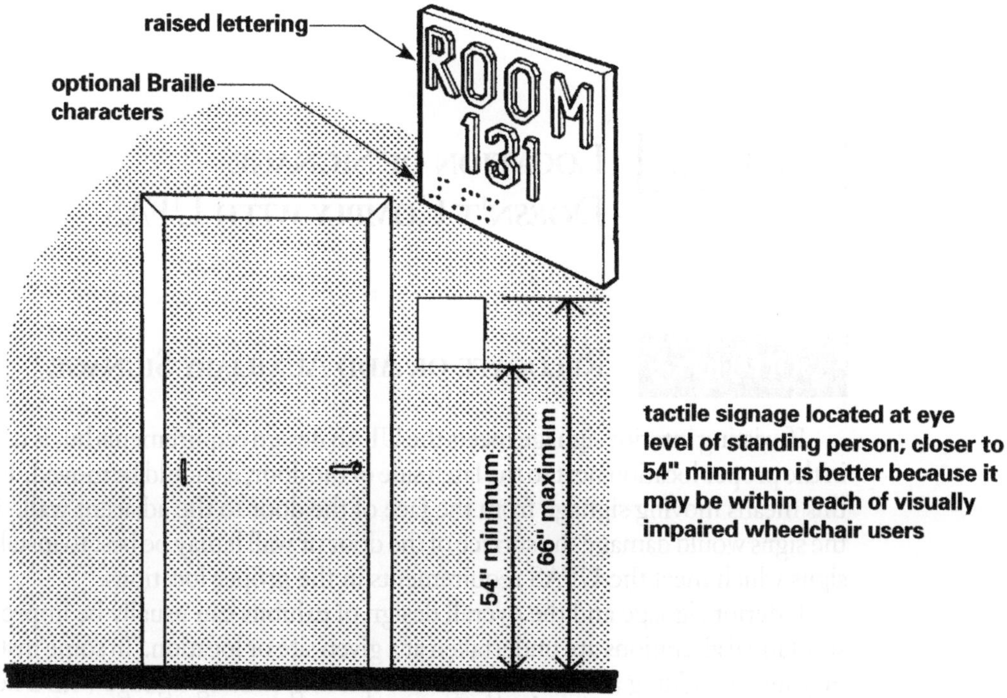

Sign Located to Latch Side of Door

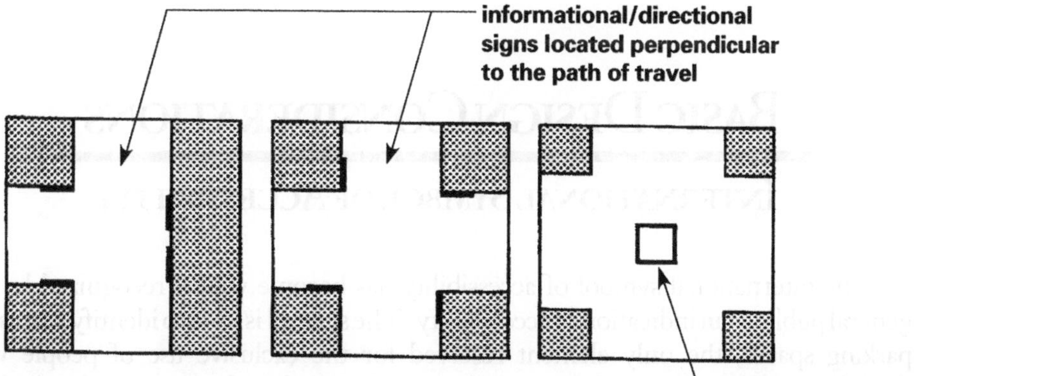

Signage Located in Standard, Logical, Predictable Places Perpendicular to the Path of Travel

Signage at Exhibits. UFAS makes a particular mention of signage included at exhibits in the scoping section on historic preservation. UFAS Section 4.1.7(2)(e), page 14, requires that all displays and written information, documents, books, etc. be located where they can be seen by a seated person, with exhibits and signage displayed horizontally no higher than 44 inches above the floor. Many people believe that 44 inches is too high for easily readable exhibits. Therefore, when possible the horizontal exhibit should be mounted so a seated person could look down upon it. Though included only in the historic preservation section of UFAS, these design suggestions hold true for all interior and exterior exhibit areas if they are to be universally usable, especially for young children and wheelchair users.

PROBLEM: LOCATION OF SIGNAGE DOESN'T COMPLY WITH UFAS

SOLUTION: RELOCATE OR ADD AUXILIARY SIGNAGE

If existing interior signage meets the UFAS design requirements but is not installed in the proper location next to the latch side of the door, it should be moved. Frequently this means moving signage from the face of the door to the adjacent wall. If moving the signs would damage the surface of the door or wall it may be best to install auxiliary signs which meet the UFAS requirements in the proper locations.

Exterior signage and the overall design of exhibits can usually be improved when substantial alterations are undertaken at a given site or location. In some instances this may involve adding auxiliary signage or replacing existing signage with a new system that meets the UFAS requirements.

BASIC DESIGN CONSIDERATIONS

INTERNATIONAL SYMBOL OF ACCESSIBILITY

The international symbol of accessibility has become widely recognized by the general public as an indication of accessibility. The symbol is used to identify accessible parking spaces, the only element reserved for the exclusive use of people with disabilities, and to indicate elements that are designed to facilitate use by disabled persons but which can also be used by the general public, such as telephones and toilet rooms. The access symbol is often used in combination with other graphics and text to provide more specific information for facility users.

UFAS requires that the international symbol of accessibility be displayed at parking spaces reserved for physically handicapped people, and at passenger loading zones, accessible entrances, and accessible toilet and bathing facilities. UFAS also states in the scoping section on historic properties, if it is determined that no entrance generally used by the public can be made accessible, then any unlocked entrance may be used provided that directional signs to the alternate entrance are installed. Many state codes are more stringent than UFAS, requiring that access symbols be posted on all accessible toilet rooms, at exits, and on building directories indicating the location of accessible facilities.

signs which combine pictograms/ graphics with words are easier to interpret since the message is reinforced in two distinct modes

Examples of Access Symbol Used in Signage

PRACTICAL PLUS

Research data analysis suggests minimum dimensions for the access symbol at various viewing distances. The pictogram symbol size appropriate for any situation may vary depending on the viewing conditions at a particular location.

Size	Location	Viewing Distance
2 1/2 inches	Interior	Up to 30 feet
4 inches	Interior	Greater than 30 feet
4 inches	Exterior	Up to 60 feet
8 inches	Exterior	Greater than 60 feet

PROBLEM ACCESS SYMBOL NOT INCLUDED ON SITE SIGNAGE AS REQUIRED

SOLUTION INSTALL ACCESS SYMBOL ON SIGNAGE

In most cases the symbol of accessibility can be incorporated into existing site signage as required by UFAS. Some state codes require that particular colors be used when displaying the access symbol. Other states allow the symbol to be incorporated into the design and materials used in other signage so long as the integrity of the symbol is maintained and the sign is legible. Most sign companies can provide both ready-made and custom signs which incorporate the access symbol.

REFERENCE INDEX TO UFAS DOCUMENT

INTERIOR AND EXTERIOR SIGNAGE

Primary References	UFAS page	Secondary References	UFAS page
4.30.1 General/Location	47	4.1 Scope & Technical Requirements 4.1.5 Additions 4.1.6 Alterations 4.1.7 Historic Preservation A4.30.1 General	5-6 11 12 13-14 66
4.30.2 Character Proportion	47	A4.30.2 Character Proportion	66
4.30.3 Color Contrast	47	A4.30.3 Color Contrast	66
4.30.4 Raised or Indented Characters or Symbols	47	A4.30.4 Raised or Indented Characters or Symbols	66
4.30.5 Symbols of Accessibility	47		
4.30.6 Mounting Location and Height	47		

INTRODUCTION

Public telephones are an important element installed in many buildings and outdoor locations. If telephones are to be universally usable they must be carefully installed to accommodate the needs of a variety of people, including children, wheelchair users, and others with visual or hearing impairments. Public phones should have features which are universally easy to use and operating instructions which are easy to understand, especially since phones are often used in emergencies.

If a public phone(s) is furnished or if a new phone(s) is added, either as a single unit installation or in a bank(s) of two or more phones, UFAS Section 4.1.2(16)(a), page 6, requires the following:

one or more single unit installations	one accessible phone/floor *
one bank	one accessible phone/floor *
two or more banks	one accessible phone/bank **

[In addition, at exterior phone installations only, if dial tone first service is not available, then a side reach telephone may be installed instead of the required forward reach telephone.]

*Accessible phones may be installed at 48 or 54 inches to accommodate either forward or side reaches.

**At least one public phone per floor must be 48 inches high to meet the requirements for a forward reach.

At both interior and exterior phone bank installations the accessible phone must be installed in proximity (either visual or with signage) to the bank. Although volume control switches may be installed on other public phones, at least one accessible public phone must also be equipped with a volume control switch. In facilities scheduled for alteration, telephones and other basic elements should be considered high priority items.

BASIC DESIGN CONSIDERATION

INSTALLATION REQUIREMENTS

UFAS contains several requirements which pertain directly to the installation of the phone. Basically these requirements insure that phones will be installed with ample maneuvering space for wheelchairs, their controls within reach, and positioned so as not to be hazards for blind or visually impaired or inattentive people.

Clear Floor or Ground Space. Similarly to other elements, UFAS requires that a 30 inch by 48 inch clear floor space be provided at phones to allow for a forward or parallel approach to the phone. Bases, enclosures, and fixed seats must not encroach on this maneuvering space or obstruct access to the phone in any way. Partial and full-length partitions can be installed to reduce noise provided they follow the requirements described in UFAS Figure 44, page 48. Some state codes also contain requirements for knee space under the telephone and/or shelf.

Protruding Objects. Telephones can be hazards for blind people when the phone or enclosure protrudes from the wall more than 4 inches. Telephones or phone enclosures with edges 27 inches or lower are detectable by cane and are less likely to pose hazards (see Unit Three and UFAS Section 4.4 Protruding Objects).

Mounting Height. UFAS requires that the highest operable part of the telephone be within the reach ranges specified in UFAS Sections 4.2.5, Forward Reach and 4.2.6 Side Reach, page 15. Although either a front approach or side approach is allowed at an accessible telephone, at least one public phone per floor must be configured to allow a forward approach and reach with the highest operable part no higher than 48 inches. An exception to this requirement is allowed at exterior phones. Even though dial-tone first service may not be available, accessible phones at exterior locations can be configured to allow a side approach and reach instead of the forward approach and reach. In this situation, the highest operable part, or coin slot, may be located no higher than 54 inches. (Dial-tone first service allows calls to be placed without inserting coins by dialing the Operator for assistance).

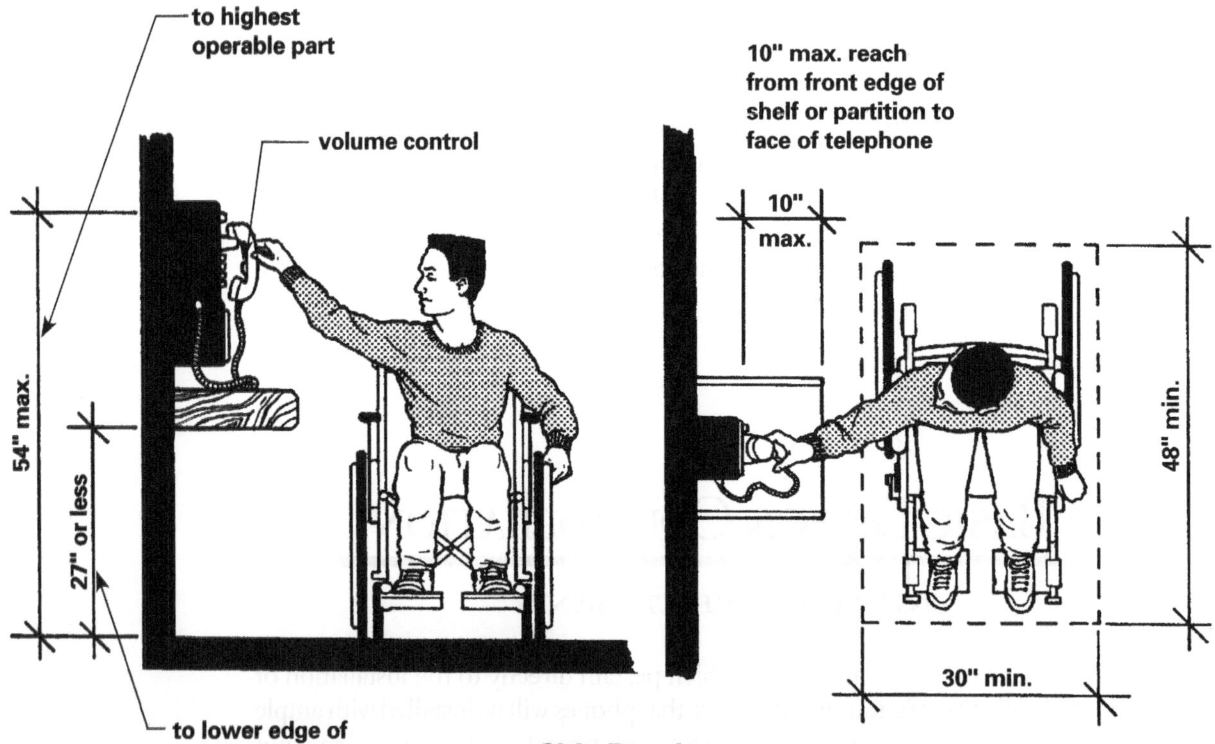

Side Reach

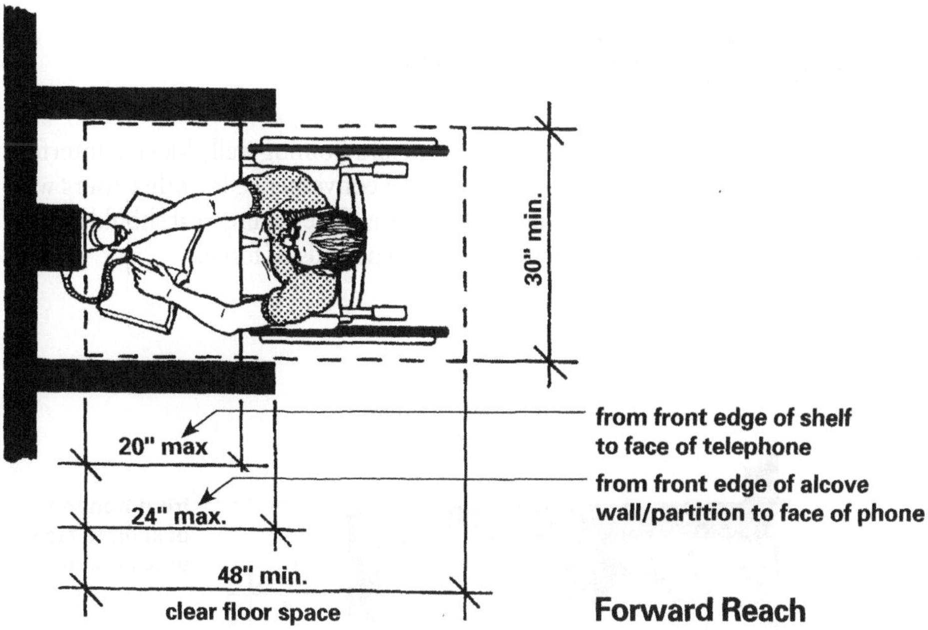

Forward Reach

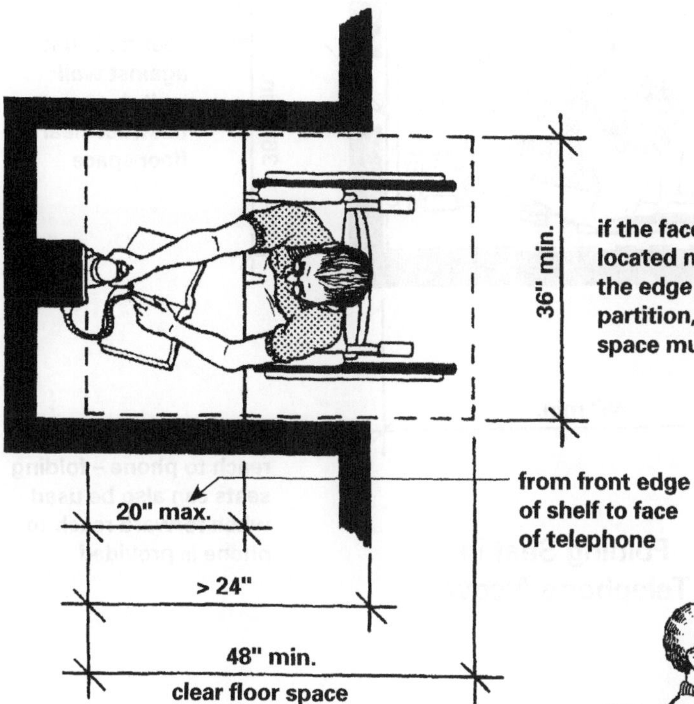

Forward Reach to
Phone in Alcove

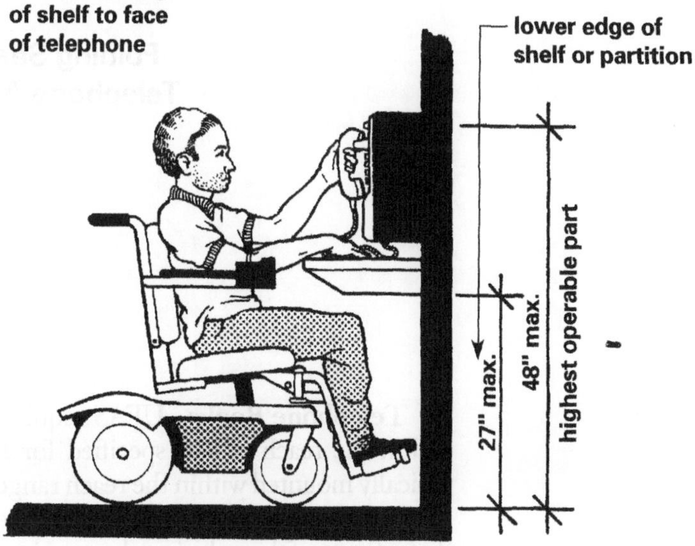

Forward Reach

PRACTICAL PLUS

A folding seat, mounted on either a partition or an adjoining wall, does not interfere with wheelchair maneuvering space but provides a convenience for other users who may prefer or need to be seated while using the phone. The folding seat should be easy to manage and securely mounted to withstand 250 pounds of force.

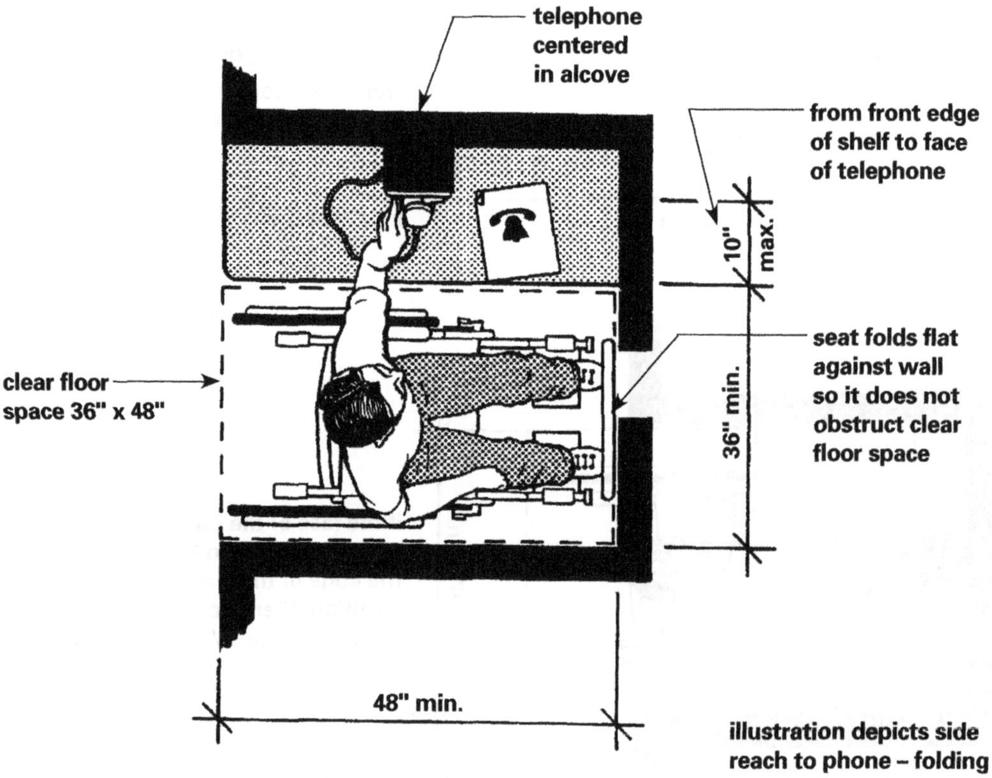

Folding Seat in Telephone Alcove

Telephone Books. UFAS requires that if provided, phone books must also be within the reach ranges specified for forward and side reaches. Phone books are typically mounted within the reach ranges specified for forward and side reach but are often tethered or permanently bound in difficult to handle devices designed to prevent theft. Some of these devices descend into the knee space below the phone and impede forward approach to the phone.

PRACTICAL PLUS

Phone books located on lowered tables or surfaces adjacent to the phone may be easier for many people to use. The lowered height makes access to the phone book easier and also provides a surface for note taking.

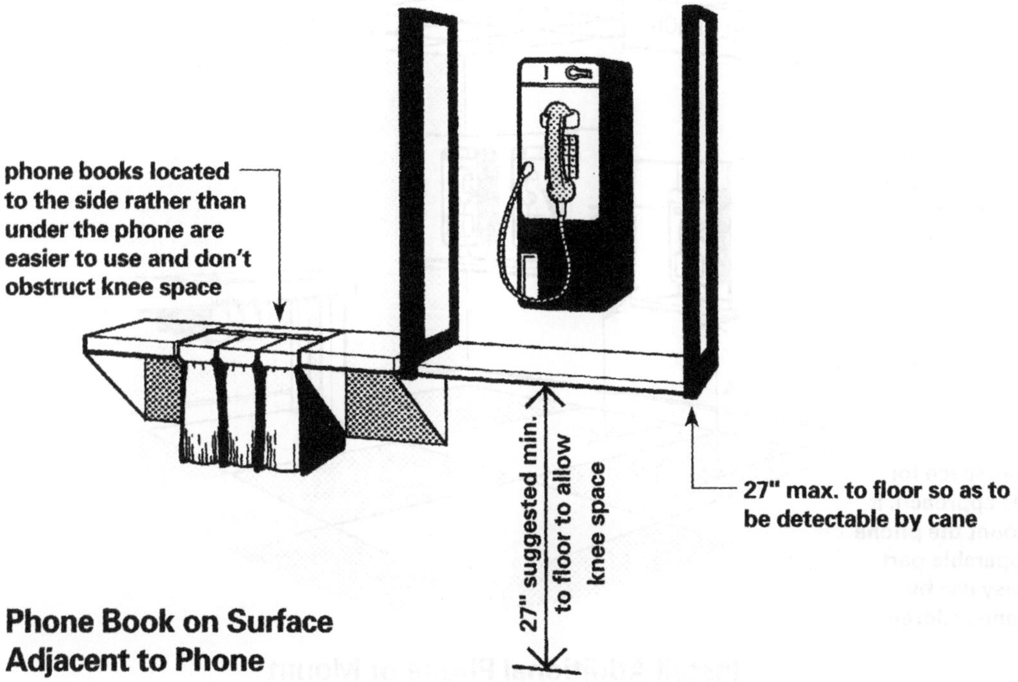

Phone Book on Surface Adjacent to Phone

PROBLEM TELEPHONE OPERATING CONTROLS TOO HIGH

SOLUTION LOWER EXISTING TELEPHONE OR ADD ANOTHER PHONE

If an existing telephone meets other UFAS design requirements, but the controls are too high to allow a forward approach to the phone then it may be possible to lower the phone. If space exists, it may be easier simply to install an additional phone nearby which meets all the UFAS requirements.

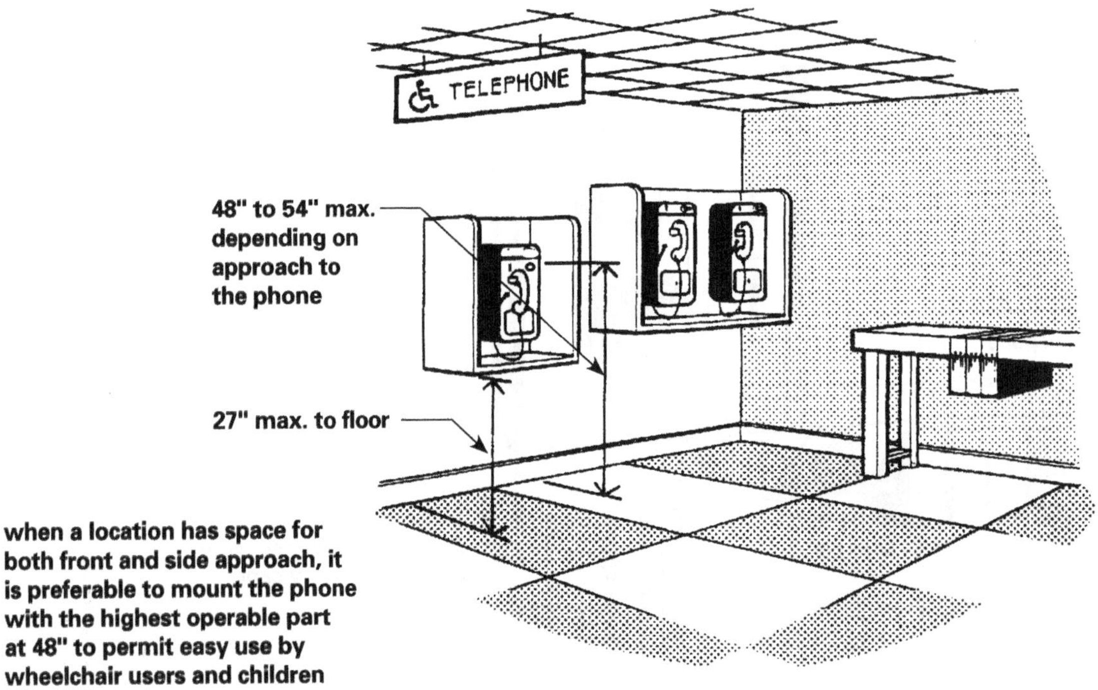

Install Additional Phone or Mount Existing Phone at Lower Height

PROBLEM TELEPHONE BOOTH OR PARTITIONS OBSTRUCT ACCESS TO PHONE

SOLUTION REMOVE OR RELOCATE PARTITIONS OR INSTALL ADDITIONAL PHONE

If all the existing telephones are enclosed in narrow partitions or have fixed seats which obstruct access to the phone, it will be necessary to modify the installation or install an additional phone. In some situations, it may not be desirable or possible to add another phone, and the existing partitions will need to be modified to comply with the UFAS clear floor space requirements to allow for a forward approach and reach.

BASIC DESIGN CONSIDERATION

TELEPHONE FEATURES

Several of the UFAS requirements for telephones pertain directly to the design of the phone. For a telephone to be accessible, the controls, cord length, receiver, and volume controls must be included as described in UFAS.

Controls. UFAS requires that push button controls be provided where service for such equipment is available. This service is currently available in most areas of the country with the exception of some small rural and remote areas.

PRACTICAL PLUS

It is helpful to have all controls and operating mechanisms designed so they are easy to use. Coin deposit and change return slots can be designed so that they facilitate use by persons with limited fine motor control. Instructions for use and the numbers on the key pad should be large, easy to read, and angled for the best viewing. When phones are located in dimly lit corridors or spaces there should be supplemental lighting added so controls and instructions are easy to see.

Cord Length. UFAS requires that the length of the cord from the telephone to the handset be at least 29 inches. This length allows the handset to be held to the ear comfortably by children and people who use wheelchairs.

Equipment for Hearing Impaired People. As a general rule, phones should be installed away from noisy locations which interfere with any user's ability to hear. In noisy environments, sound absorbing partitions can help deflect/absorb some of the noise which otherwise would make it difficult or impossible to hear.

UFAS requires that at least one of the accessible phones in a given location be equipped with a volume control switch which allows users to increase the volume of sound in the receiver. In addition to the volume control switch, UFAS requires that telephones be equipped with a receiver that generates a magnetic field. Many hearing aids rely on this electromagnetic field to operate the telephone pickup feature of the hearing aid which amplifies sound for the user. This feature is part of standard equipment currently being manufactured.

PRACTICAL PLUS

Telecommunication Devices for the Deaf also known as Telephone Display Devices (TDD) which can be installed in conjunction with standard pay phones are currently available. To operate the device, the user dials the phone in the traditional manner and places the handset in a holder. If the answering party responds with a TDD, a drawer containing the TDD keyboard opens and both people can begin conversing on the TDDs. When the conversation is finished, the handset is replaced, and the drawer closes.

If pay phone TDDs are not installed, it is helpful if pay phones have shelves below the phone to allow people to place personal portable TDDs close to the phone while completing calls. These shelves provide everyone with a functional surface for writing or resting parcels while using the phone.

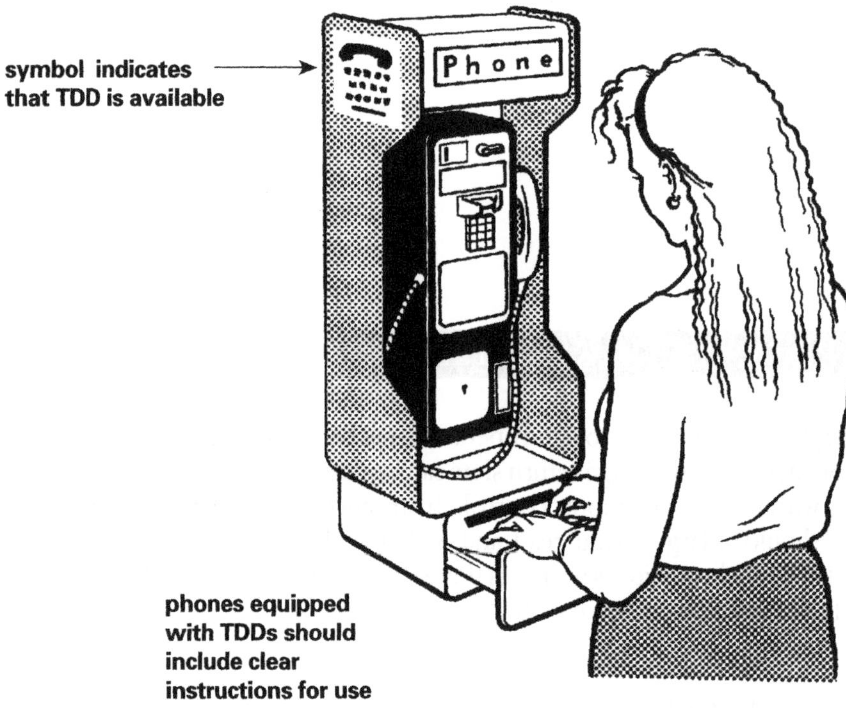

Pay Phone with Built-In TDD

PRACTICAL PLUS

When phones are equipped with either volume controls or TDDs it is helpful if signs and/or symbols are displayed which notify users which features are available. There are several symbols in use by phone companies which indicate that amplification features or TDDs have been installed.

PRACTICAL PLUS

Headsets with and without amplifiers or speaker phones can provide hands-free use of telecommunications equipment. These devices can be useful to people with mobility impairments both at home and at work. Many other functions, such as autodial and redial, are useful time saving features for everyone but are necessities for people with very limited use of their hands.

PROBLEM Existing Phones Don't Comply

SOLUTION Replace Phone or Install New Phone

If none of the existing phones has the features required by UFAS, at least one telephone per floor or bank should be replaced or an additional phone should be installed. In some instances the existing partitions provide ample maneuvering space and simply replacing the phone will be sufficient. If space allows, it may be possible to install an additional phone which meets all of the UFAS requirements.

Reference Index to UFAS Document

Interior and Exterior Phone Installations

Primary References	UFAS page	Secondary References	UFAS page
4.31.1 General/Location	47	4.1 Scope & Technical Requirements	6-7
		4.1.5 Additions	11
		4.1.6(3)(d)(v) Alterations - Special Consideration	12
		4.1.7 Historic Preservation	13
4.31.2 Clear Floor or Ground Space	47	4.2.4 Clear Floor or Ground Space for Wheelchairs	14
4.31.3 Mounting Height	47	4.2.5 Forward Reach	15
		4.2.6 Side Reach	15
		A4.31.3 Mounting Height	67
4.31.4 Protruding Objects	47	4.4 Protruding Objects	20
4.31.5 Equipment for Hearing Impaired	47	4.1.2(16) Public Telephones	6-7
		A4.31.5 Equipment for Hearing Impaired	67
4.31.6 Controls	47		
4.31.7 Telephone Books	47	4.2.5 Forward Reach	15
		4.2.6 Side Reach	15
4.31.8 Cord Length	48		

SEATING AND WORK SURFACES

UFAS 4.32

Introduction

Fixed seating and/or work stations are found in many spaces including, libraries, classrooms, restaurants, service agencies, conference centers, transportation terminals, and various places of employment. Access to well designed seating and work surfaces is important to all people regardless of whether the intended use is short term, infrequent, or long term. In most cases, accessible seating and work surfaces can be used by almost everyone.

When fixed or built-in seating, tables, or work surfaces are provided in accessible spaces, UFAS requires that five percent or at least one of each seating space, table, or work surface be accessible. If an addition is planned or a facility is scheduled for alteration, fixed or built-in seating, tables, or work surfaces and other basic elements should be considered high priority items.

Basic Design Consideration

Seating

UFAS contains several very basic requirements for seating and wheelchair maneuvering space which have broad applications for a variety of settings. UFAS requires that if seating spaces for wheelchair users are provided at tables, counters, or work surfaces, clear floor space, complying with Section 4.2.4 Clear Floor or Ground Space for Wheelchairs, page 14, must be allocated. Seating provided at tables, counters, and work surfaces, must also allow a knee space of at least 27 inches high, by 30 inches wide, and 19 inches deep. Clear floor space for approach to a table or work surface may not overlap knee space by more than 19 inches. UFAS Figure 45, page 49, illustrates some additional maneuvering clearances for approaches to built-in tables, counters, or work spaces.

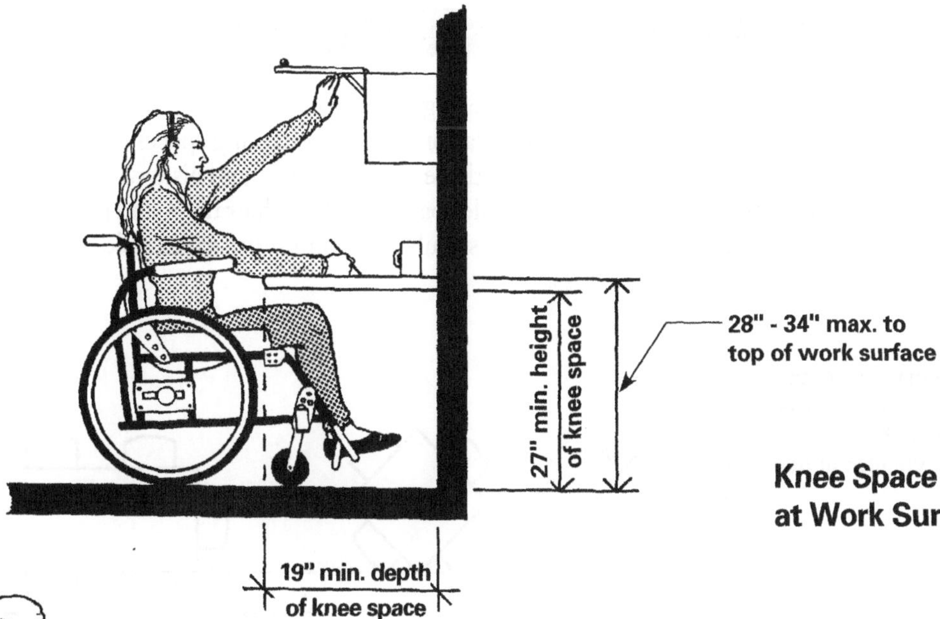

Knee Space at Work Surfaces

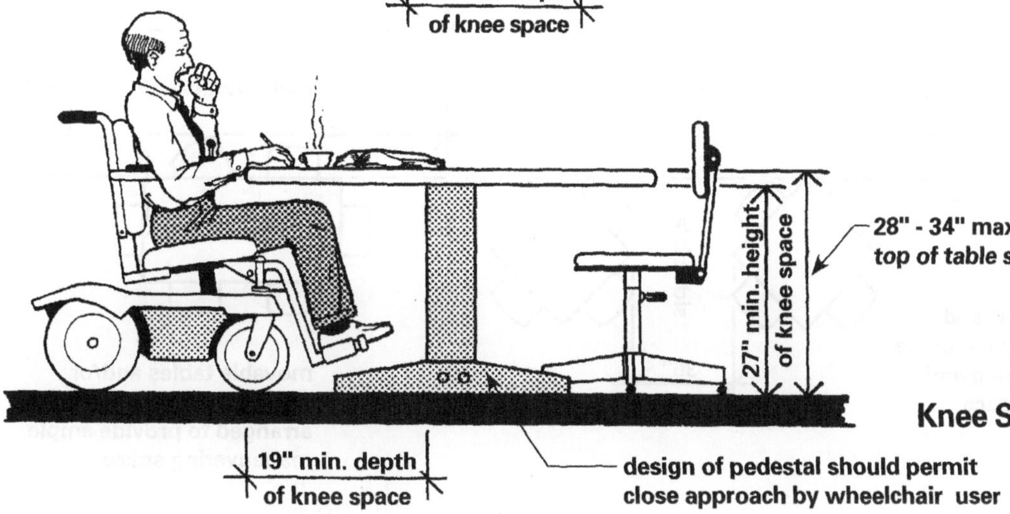

Knee Space at Tables

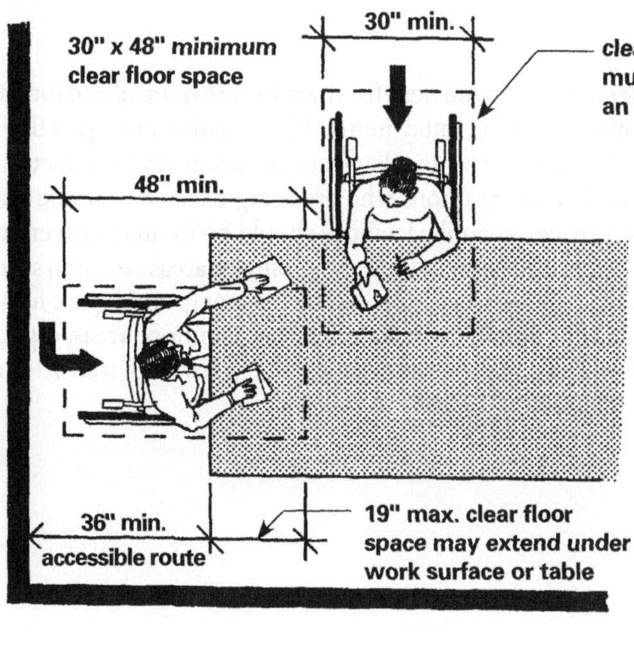

Clear Floor Space at Tables and Work Surfaces

PRACTICAL PLUS

In addition to the maneuvering clearances required in UFAS, several state codes contain additional recommendations for maneuvering spaces around fixed tables and chairs. At major access aisles, these codes recommend aisle widths between tables of 60 to 66 inches to provide ample space for wheelchair users and pedestrians to pass. If fixed chairs are installed, there should be a minimum access aisle of 36 inches to allow wheelchair users to pass.

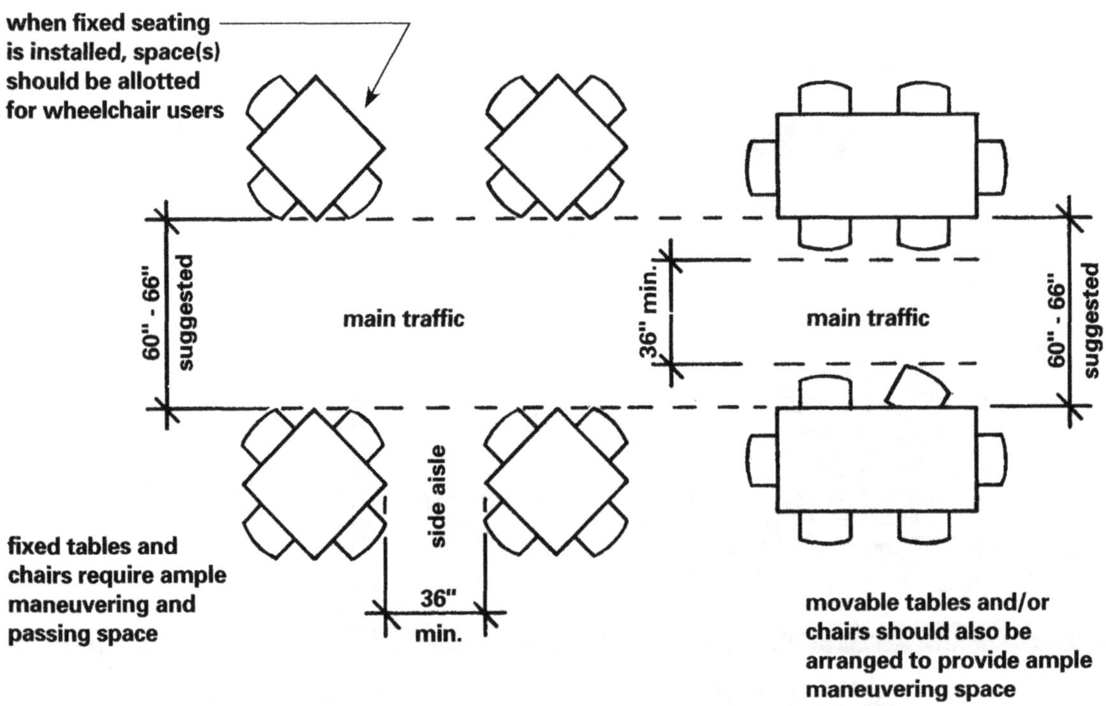

Maneuvering Space at Tables and Seating

The wheelchair spaces required near fixed seating are quite useful for parents with baby strollers and others carrying bulky items. Fixed seating and open floor spaces in these areas should be configured to allow conversation and interaction between wheelchair users and their companions who are using fixed or movable seating. Rest areas or conversation spaces in public facilities should be located adjacent to the flow of pedestrian traffic and within view of passersby. Similar areas are often seen outdoors in plazas, in parks, and on main streets. Open clear floor or ground space for wheelchair maneuvering and parking should be included in these outdoor areas, especially if the area provides shelter from inclement weather (i.e., covered transit stops, picnic pavilions, etc.).

PRACTICAL PLUS

Although UFAS does not provide any specific requirements for the design of chairs, or benches, there are several features which make seating safer and more comfortable to use. Chairs and benches with seats at 18 - 20 inches high and approximately 18 inches deep are best for most adults, while children prefer seats which better accommodate their body size. Chairs and benches with arms and backs provide support for a person while sitting and rising. A heel space of at least 3 inches under a chair or bench also facilitates rising from a seated position. Benches and chairs should be able to withstand at least 250 pounds of force.

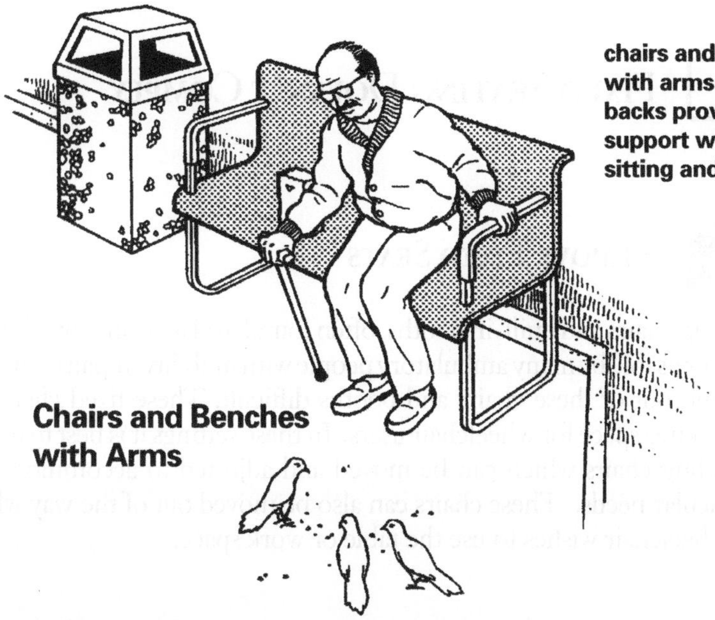

Chairs and Benches with Arms

PRACTICAL PLUS

When possible, outdoor furnishings should be located adjacent to an accessible route on a level, firm surface which provides ample maneuvering space. Outdoor furnishings should be designed so that water drains from all surfaces. Furnishings should be constructed of materials that do not splinter, peel, or retain excessive amounts of heat or dampness.

Wheelchair Accessible Picnic Table

PRACTICAL PLUS

In transportation terminals and on mass transit vehicles where space is limited, it may be possible to include folding seats which can be used when needed by passengers who prefer to be seated. When the folding seats are not in use the floor space is available for other passengers traveling with strollers, folding shopping carts, large parcels, luggage, or in wheelchairs.

PROBLEM FIXED SEATING DOESN'T COMPLY

SOLUTION REMOVE FIXED SEATS

Fixed swiveling chairs and built-in booths, often found in classrooms and fast food restaurants, are not usable by many ambulatory people with mobility impairments who find getting in and out of these chairs and booths difficult. These fixed chairs also obstruct access to knee space for wheelchair users. In these settings it is best to include several free-standing chairs which can be moved and adjusted to accommodate an individuals' particular needs. These chairs can also be moved out of the way when a person using a wheelchair wishes to use the table or work space.

BASIC DESIGN CONSIDERATION

TABLES AND WORK SURFACES

In addition to the knee space requirements described above, UFAS requires that the tops of tables and work surfaces be mounted between 28 and 34 inches. Work surfaces may include laboratory stations, study carrels, tables, typing stands, computer terminal stations, drafting tables, and other surfaces designed for the performance of specific tasks. The actual mounting height will depend on the individual's size and the type of work being performed. Both standing and seated people prefer different work heights for light detailed work and heavy manual work. UFAS Table A1, page 67, describes various mounting heights for work surfaces which are designed to be used by seated people.

PRACTICAL PLUS

There are some additional features not described in UFAS which make work surfaces easier and safer to use. Aprons or drawers, which often encroach upon the knee space below counters, should be designed and installed within the heights shown below. Tables and work surfaces with rounded edges and corners are safer for all people who may accidentally bump into the table when passing.

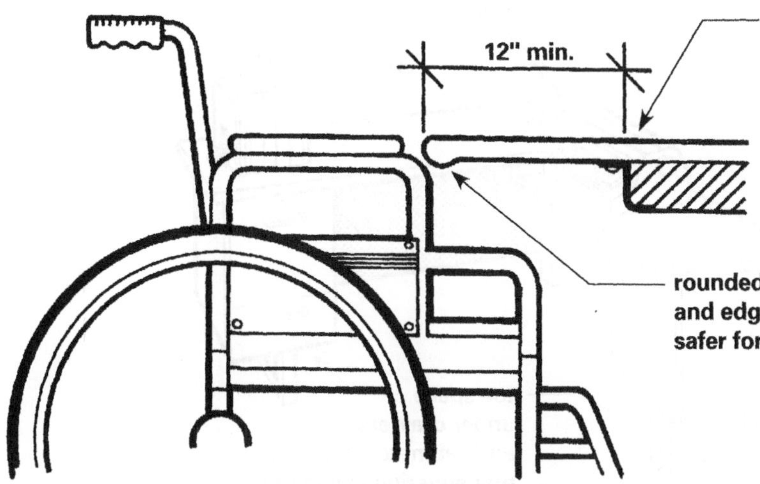

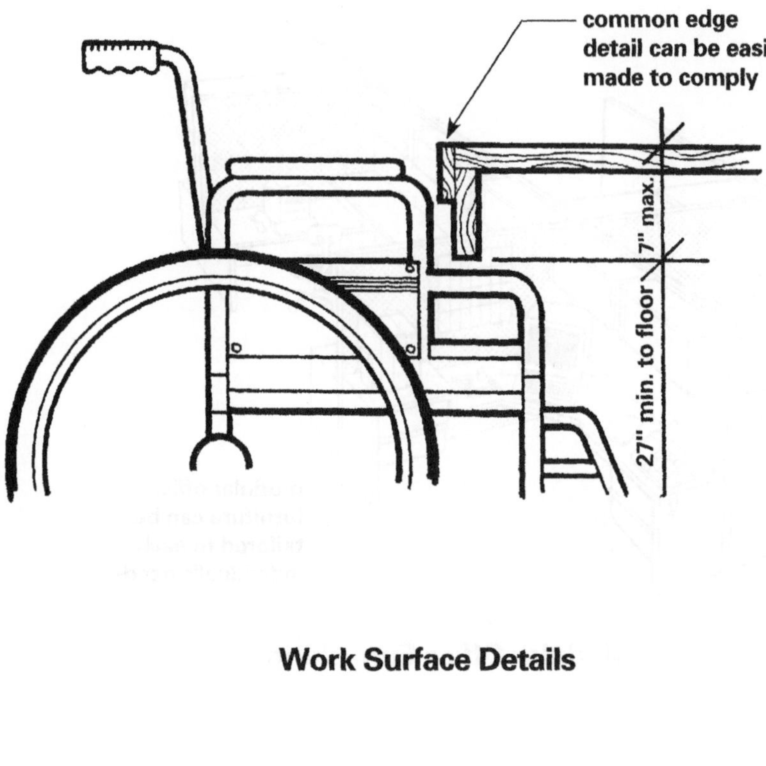

Work Surface Details

PRACTICAL PLUS

Work surfaces frequently have storage units either built-in or placed in proximity. Storage cabinets and/or drawers which provide toe clearance underneath improve maneuvering capability for people who use wheelchairs. The toe space occupies the difficult to reach space nearest the floor. Modular office furniture provides a number of options for installation of work surfaces and storage units.

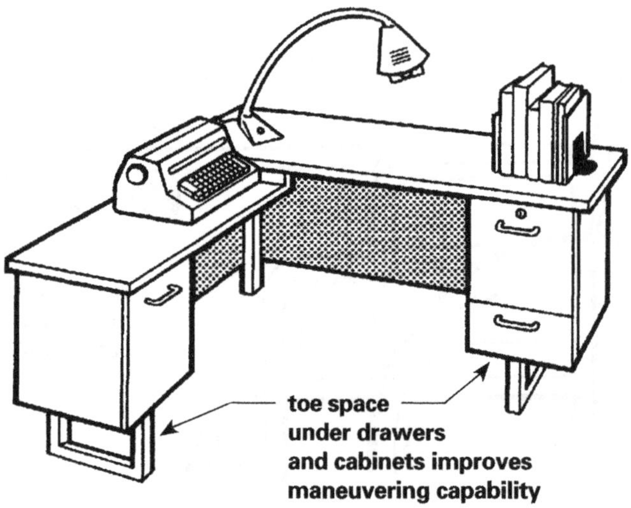

Toe Space Under Desk Drawers

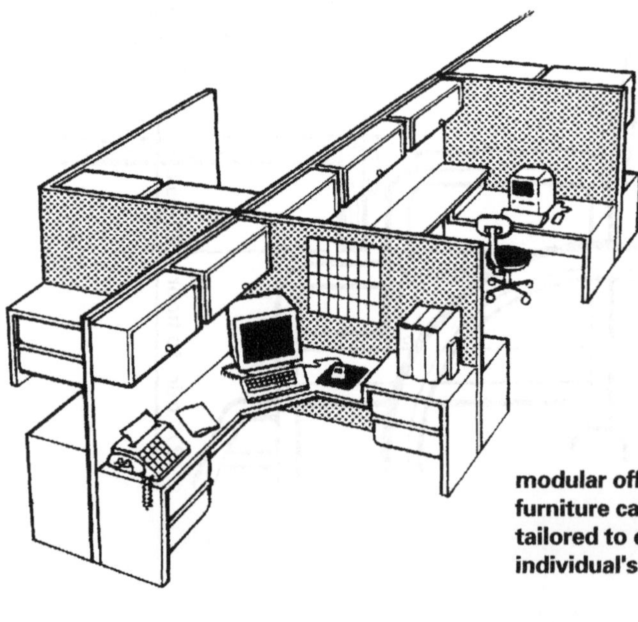

Modular Office Furnishings

PROBLEM WORK SURFACE IS MOUNTED TOO HIGH

SOLUTION 1 LOWER EXISTING SURFACE OR INSTALL ADJUSTABLE SURFACE

If possible, an existing surface should be permanently fixed at a lower height. However, if both standing and seated people must use the same work surface, it is best if the surface can be easily adjusted to suit both needs. Surfaces permanently installed at a compromise height don't work well for either the standing or seated person.

SOLUTION 2 INSTALL PULLOUT SURFACE

In some instances, it may be possible to install a pullout surface ("breadboard") which can be used by seated people. An appropriately sized surface and suitable hardware to hold the surface steady and support the weight required to perform the intended tasks must be considered. Use of the pullout surface should not obstruct the required maneuvering space or interfere with other pedestrian traffic.

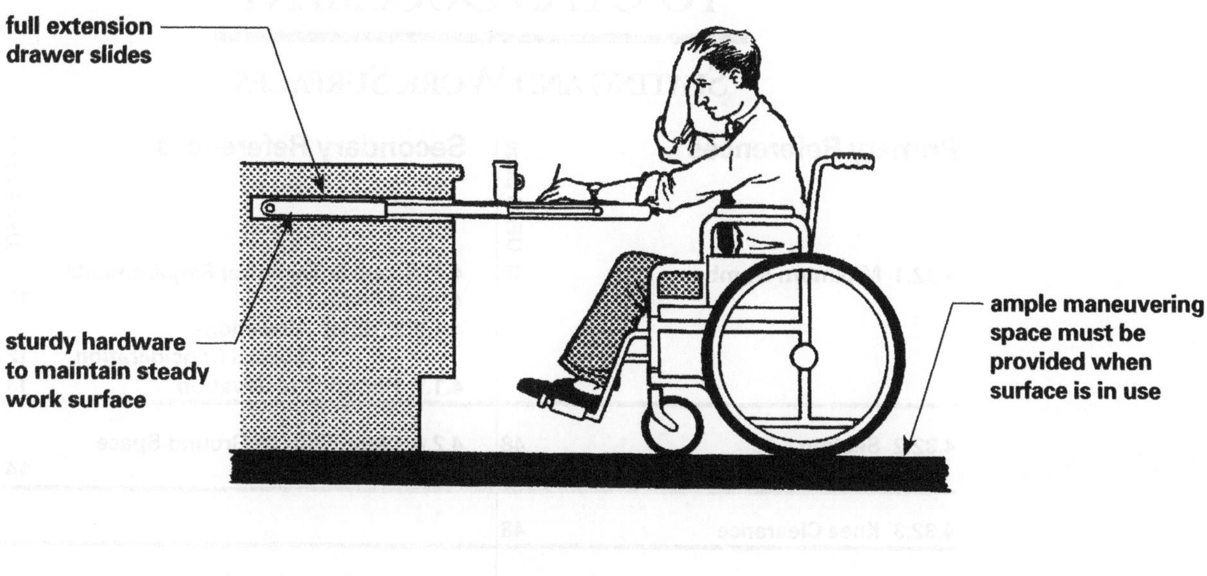

Install Pullout Surface

PROBLEM NO KNEE SPACE AT WORK SURFACE

SOLUTION REMOVE OBSTRUCTION

Work surfaces designed for standing people frequently have storage space underneath which obstructs knee space. It may be possible to remove some of the base cabinets, enclose and finish the exposed sides, and extend the floor finish into the knee space. In most cases the work surface, if designed for a standing person, will also need to be lowered to the maximum height of 28 - 34 inches to be usable by a seated person.

Remove Base Cabinets and Lower Work Surface

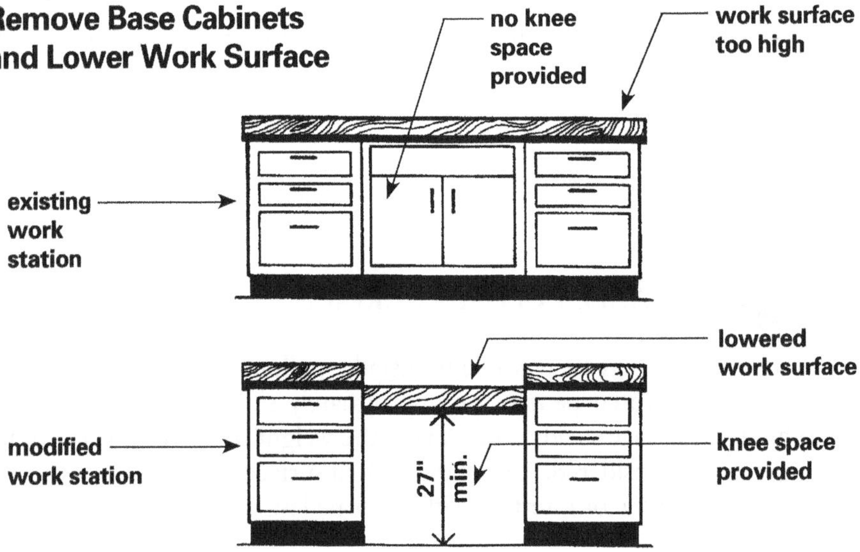

REFERENCE INDEX TO UFAS DOCUMENT

SEATING AND WORK SURFACES

Primary References	UFAS page	Secondary References	UFAS page
4.32.1 Minimum Number	48	4.1 Scope & Technical Requirements 4.1.5 Additions 4.1.6(3)(d)(vi) Alterations - Special Consideration 4.1.7 Historic Preservation	7 11 12 13
4.32.2 Seating	48	4.2.4 Clear Floor or Ground Space for Wheelchairs	14
4.32.3 Knee Clearance	48		
4.32.4 Height of Work Surfaces	49	A4.32.4 Height of Work Surfaces	67

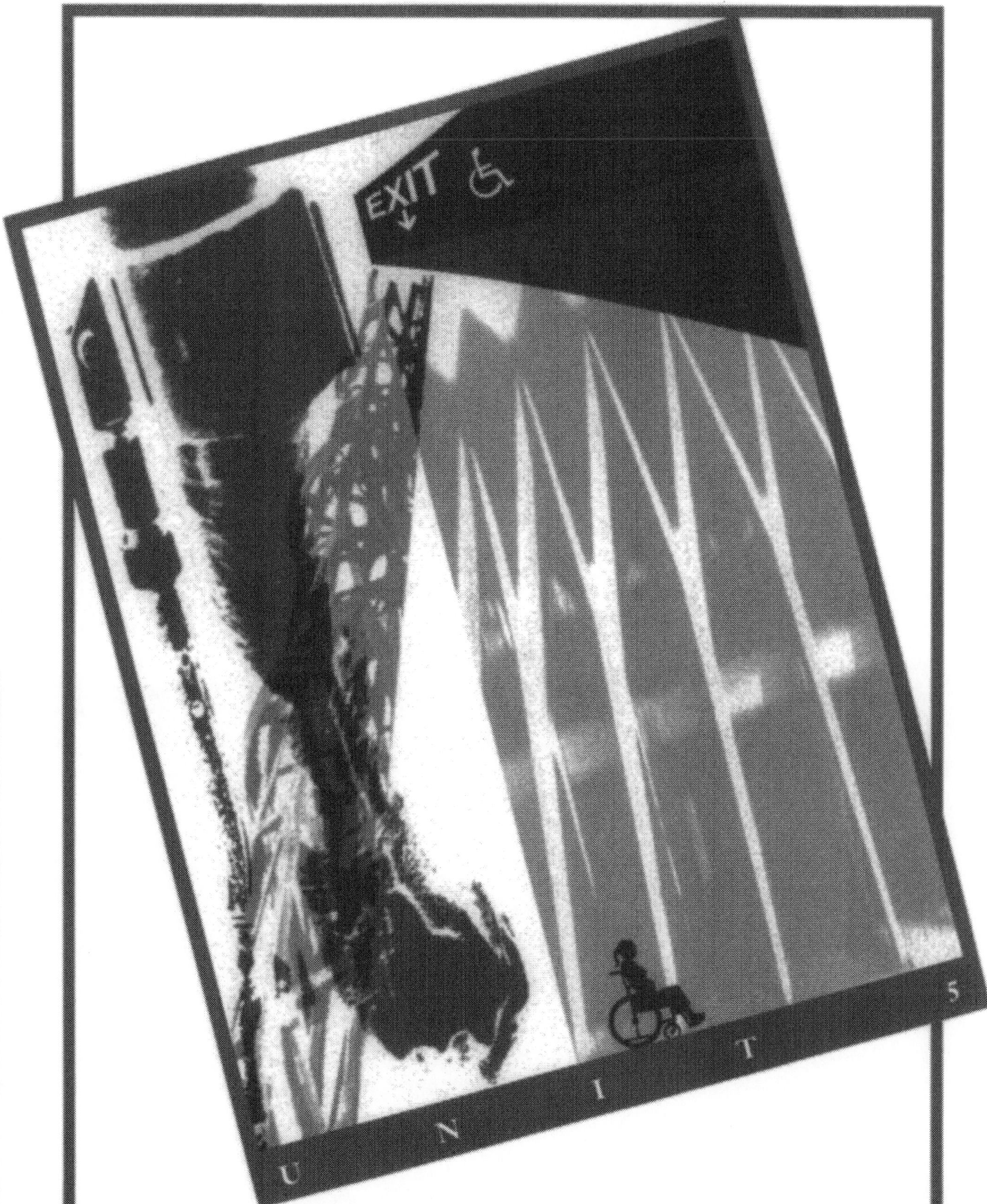
EXIT
U N I T 5

Technical Information
Modifications to Spaces

Overview

UFAS defines a space as "a definable area, e.g., toilet room, hall, assembly area, entrance, storage room, alcove, courtyard, or lobby." The organization of the *Retrofit Guide* departs from the UFAS definition of spaces only insofar as it characterizes spaces as "distinct spaces" and "occupancy specific spaces."

As discussed in Unit Three, information about "distinct spaces" is included in UFAS to further describe the properties that are peculiar to the functions these spaces are intended to serve. These sections rely heavily on cross-references to other sections, to insure that requirements for all elements and features of these distinct spaces are encompassed in the design.

Distinct Site and Building Spaces

UFAS identifies the following distinct site and building spaces commonly found in a variety of different facilities:

- **4.3.10 Egress/Safe Refuge**
- **4.6 Parking/Passenger Loading**
- **4.14 Entrances**
- **4.22 Toilet Rooms**
- **4.23 Bath/Shower Facilities**
- **4.33 Assembly Spaces**

Occupancy Specific Spaces

UFAS also contains several "spaces" sections which are set apart by occupancy-type for the purpose of clarifying access to elements and features which are specific to certain types of facilities. These "occupancy specific spaces" include:

- **5.0 Restaurants & Cafeterias**
- **6.0 Health Care**
- **7.0 Mercantile**
- **8.0 Libraries**
- **9.0 Postal Facilities**

What to Look For

The topic areas contained in Unit Five parallel the UFAS sections pertaining to spaces. The information on distinct site and building spaces is presented in a manner similar to that used in Unit Four, showing design considerations, related problems and solutions, and a reference index to the UFAS document (see sample layout pages 36 and 37). The occupancy specific type spaces will be presented in a slightly different manner, using comprehensive illustrations, annotated design solutions, and a reference index to the UFAS document.

EGRESS/SAFE REFUGE

UFAS 4.3.10

INTRODUCTION

Egress and life safety during an emergency are major concerns for all building occupants. UFAS contains little specific information on this topic because egress requirements are generally covered in building codes. However, life safety concerns become amplified when in the event of an emergency, building occupants are for some reason not able to accomplish evacuation without assistance. In any emergency, people have a broad range of needs but share a common need for information which will facilitate their ability to provide for their own safety as much as possible.

Much research has been completed in the area of life safety and egress and throughout the literature is a recurring trend which stresses interrelationships among several factors. Provision for life safety in any facility includes 1) building design, construction, use, and installation of protective devices and systems, 2) management and maintenance of the facility including the development and implementation of emergency plans, 3) various government institutions responsible for oversight of fire and safety codes and standards, and 4) integration of fire, rescue, and other specialized services to provide assistance in the event of an emergency. Of these safety issues, UFAS addresses building and facility design to provide accessibility.

Creation of a safe accessible facility begins during the development of the initial design of a new facility or during preliminary planning for substantial renovation of an existing facility. The design must provide for horizontal movement of all building occupants to areas of safe refuge and vertical egress for safe evacuation. The design must also include specification and installation of elements/materials which help manage a fire by reducing the spread of smoke, toxic fumes, and flames. Fire doors and walls, sprinkler systems, and flame retardant materials are often required in certain occupancies. Secondary power sources are sometimes required and often installed to allow independent operation of safety equipment in the event that the main source is lost.

The next step is to make every attempt to prevent an emergency from occurring and to make preparations to deal with an emergency should one occur. Safety drills, equipment checks, and training/instruction for building occupants should be completed and reaffirmed periodically. In any emergency, provisions must be made which allow occupants to 1) turn in an alarm, via an alarm pull box or phone, which notifies emergency personnel, 2) notify all occupants of the danger using sirens, flashing lights, or direct communication, and 3) provide information regarding the necessary evacuation procedure via audible and visual signals, public address announcements, or directly, through emergency personnel.

UFAS discusses egress in Section 4.3.10, page 19, under the broad topic of 4.3 Accessible Route. This section specifies that an accessible route which serves any accessible space or element must also serve as a means of egress or connect to a place of safe refuge. UFAS requires that these routes and places of refuge meet the requirements of the administrative authority having jurisdiction. Where building or life safety codes require more than one means of egress, then provisions must be made for more than one means of egress to be accessible. In multi-story buildings where at-grade egress from each floor is not possible, UFAS does permit the use of fire/smoke-proof horizontal exits and/or the provision of areas of safe refuge on each floor of the building.

BASIC DESIGN CONSIDERATION

ALARMS

Alarms serve a variety of purposes in emergencies and in most cases initiate a chain of events established to deal with the crisis. Alarms can be activated either manually, by an individual who becomes aware of a safety threat, or automatically, by smoke, heat, or other detectors. In addition to turning on audible and visual alarms, the activation of an alarm often causes automatic notification of emergency personnel, recapture of elevators, stairwell or elevator shaft pressurization, activation of emergency lighting, automatic closing of fire doors, initiation of automatic fire suppression systems, and automatic shut-off of ventilation, gas, and fuel supplies in the affected area.

All individuals must be able to activate and use emergency notification equipment for their own safety and the safety of all other building occupants. Each manual fire alarm station should be accessible, unobstructed, visible, of the same general type, and mounted on the marked exit route. The controls and operating mechanisms on alarms and emergency call boxes must be within reach and easy-to-operate. Additional information about alarms can be found in Unit Four, Alarms.

PROBLEM INAPPROPRIATE ALARM/ EMERGENCY CALL BOX

SOLUTION INSTALL PROPER ALARM/EMERGENCY CALL BOX

Often times it is possible to use existing equipment by remounting it at the appropriate height, performing minor modifications, or providing supplementary fixtures. If reuse is not possible, the alarm/emergency call boxes should be replaced.

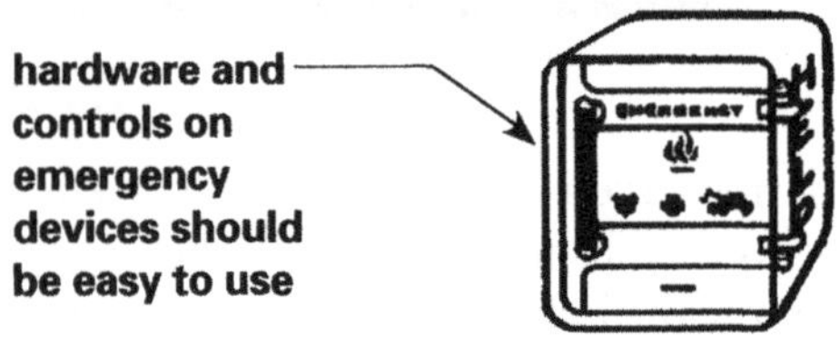

Emergency Call Box

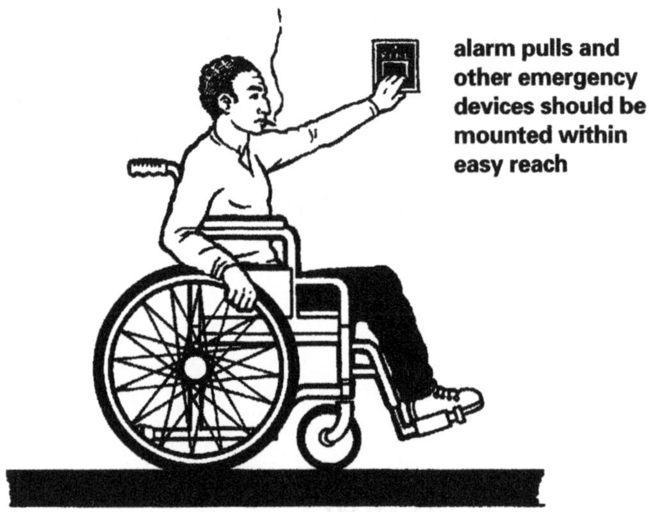

Alarm Switch

PROBLEM INAPPROPRIATE ALARM SIGNAL

SOLUTION INSTALL SUITABLE VISUAL AND AUDITORY ALARMS

An alarm signal should provide notice of a dangerous situation to all building occupants. In most cases, some combination of both visual and audible signals will be used to alert the building occupants. More detailed information about alarms can be found in UFAS Section 4.28 Alarms, page 45, and in Unit Four of this manual.

BASIC DESIGN CONSIDERATION

ACCESSIBLE ROUTE AS A MEANS OF EGRESS

As mentioned above, UFAS requires a means of egress be provided from all spaces which can be reached from an accessible route. An accessible "means of egress" provides a wheelchair accessible path of travel to an exit, exit enclosure, or an area of safe refuge. The requirements for an accessible route include a minimum path width, passing spaces, appropriate head room, proper surface textures, minimum slope, minimal changes in level, and accessible doors. Although stairs are not part of an accessible route, when designated for use as a means of egress, they should comply with UFAS specifications to improve safety for all users. More information about the specific requirements for an accessible route can be found in UFAS Section 4.3 Accessible Route, page 15; UFAS Section 4.13 Doors, page 33; and in Unit Four of this manual.

When planning for safe egress there are a number of issues which are generally addressed in the life safety codes. Some of these issues are the arrangement and number of required exits, the distance of travel to an exit, the number of people who can safely be discharged through a given exit, suitable illumination of the egress path, and signage to indicate the proper route, as well as to point out avoidable hazards. These critical issues become more complex for building occupants with various disabilities. For example, a blind individual who relies on auditory cues to facilitate mobility may become confused by the noise when a continuous audible alarm is used. A wheelchair user needs to know if the fire exit used by ambulatory occupants is the one intended for his/her use as well, or if alternate accessible exits are available and where they are located.

signs which incorporate universal symbols and text are generally easier to understand

Emergency Signage

Egress from spaces at grade level is usually easier to achieve using separated accessible entrances/exits along an accessible route which is all on one level. However, in most multi-story buildings, vertical passage between floors above and below grade is accomplished using an elevator as part of an accessible route. Unfortunately, for wheelchair users and others who cannot maneuver on steps, elevators are generally not available for egress during a fire.* A safe refuge area provides time (and, therefore, greater safety) to those building occupants who cannot use stairs.

* Under certain limited conditions, elevators are used for emergency evacuation purposes by trained emergency service personnel.

PRACTICAL PLUS

When possible, it is best if emergency signage includes information for wheelchair users and others who cannot use stairs. This is particularly true if the accessible means of egress is different from that used by other building occupants. Signage should indicate the route to follow, as well as the actual exit door(s).

Exit/Refuge Sign with Access Symbol

PROBLEM — PROVIDING AN ACCESSIBLE MEANS OF EGRESS

SOLUTION 1 — HORIZONTAL EXIT

Horizontal movement of large numbers of people can be accomplished more quickly and safely than vertical movement. Horizontal exits are formed by continuous fire walls and fire doors which divide a building into fire- and smoke-proof zones. Horizontal exits are designed to allow individuals to move from a dangerous area to a safe area in the same building or an adjacent building without changing levels. If the horizontal exit leads to an adjacent building with an elevator or walkway which provides street access, it may be possible for all building occupants to evacuate independently.

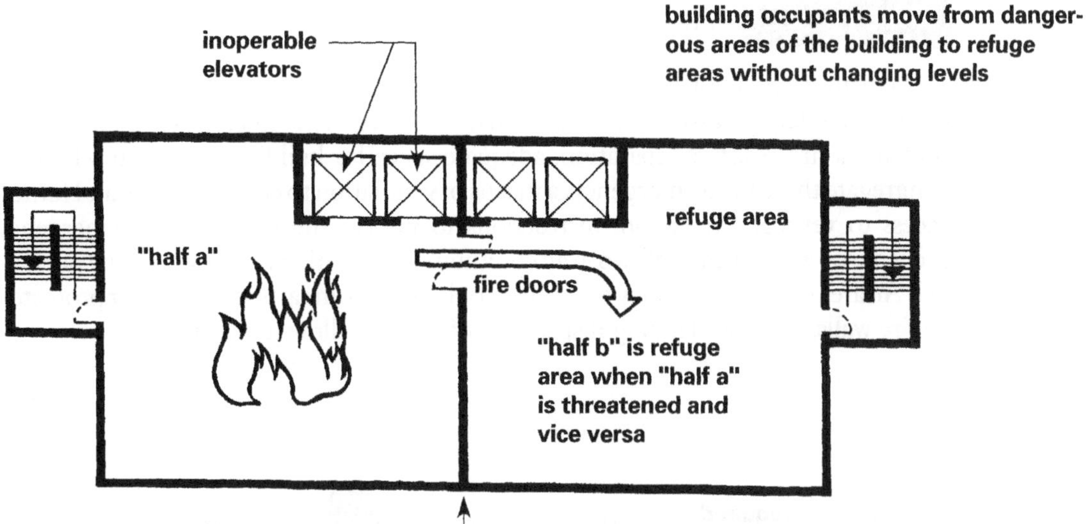

Because each "half" of the building is in essence a separate building, each half is an area of refuge for the other. If there is elevator service in each portion of the horizontal exit, the elevator in the non-threatened half may be used for evacuation.

Horizontal Exit To Provide Refuge Within Building

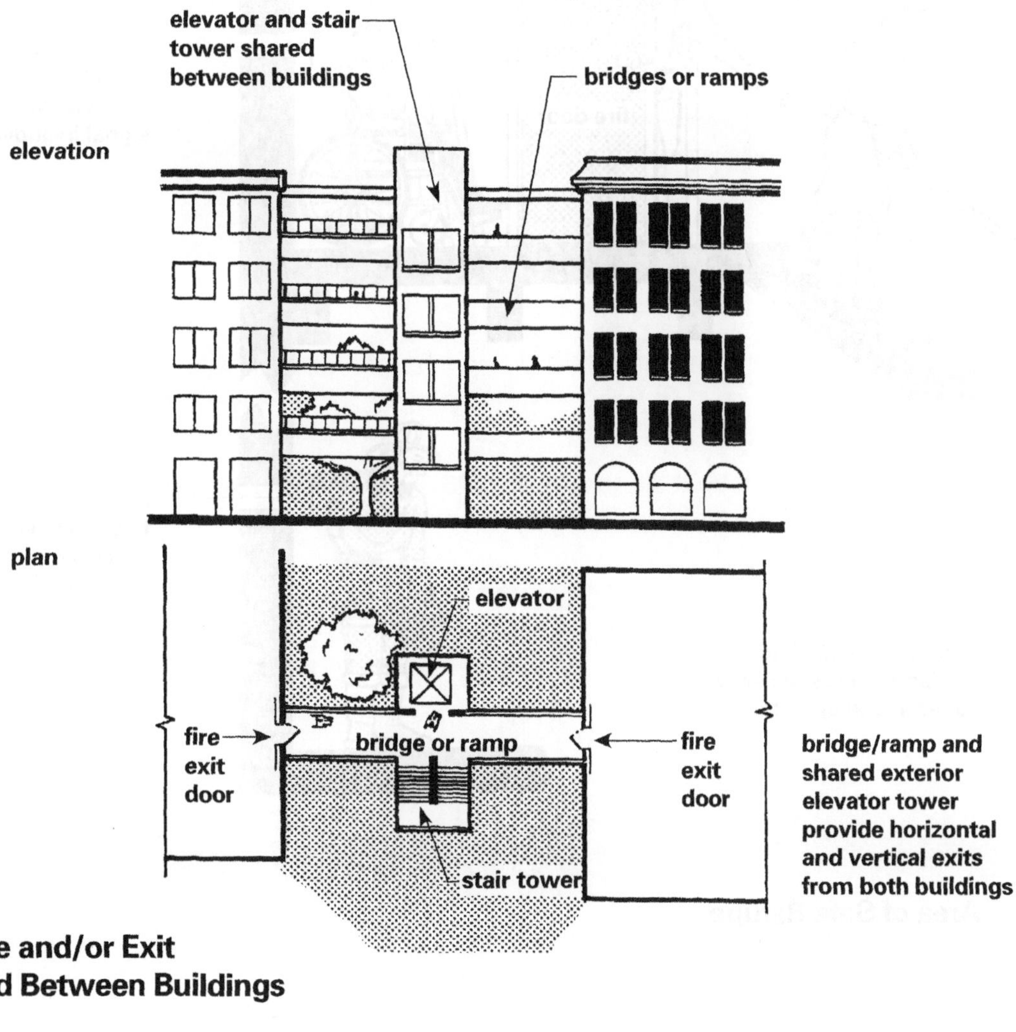

Refuge and/or Exit Shared Between Buildings

SOLUTION 2 AREA OF SAFE REFUGE

In many cases, a horizontal exit will lead to an area of safe refuge where individuals can wait in safety for assistance with evacuation. As a general rule, an area of safe refuge provides a fire-resistive separation, adequate space for building occupants who may congregate there in an emergency, a means of ventilation to control smoke and fumes, access to vertical circulation, instructions to inform the occupants of emergency procedures, and a means of two-way communication with emergency/rescue personnel. An area of safe refuge may be an elevator lobby, a compartment of a floor protected by fire walls, or a stair landing if space is sufficient to allow use of the stairs.

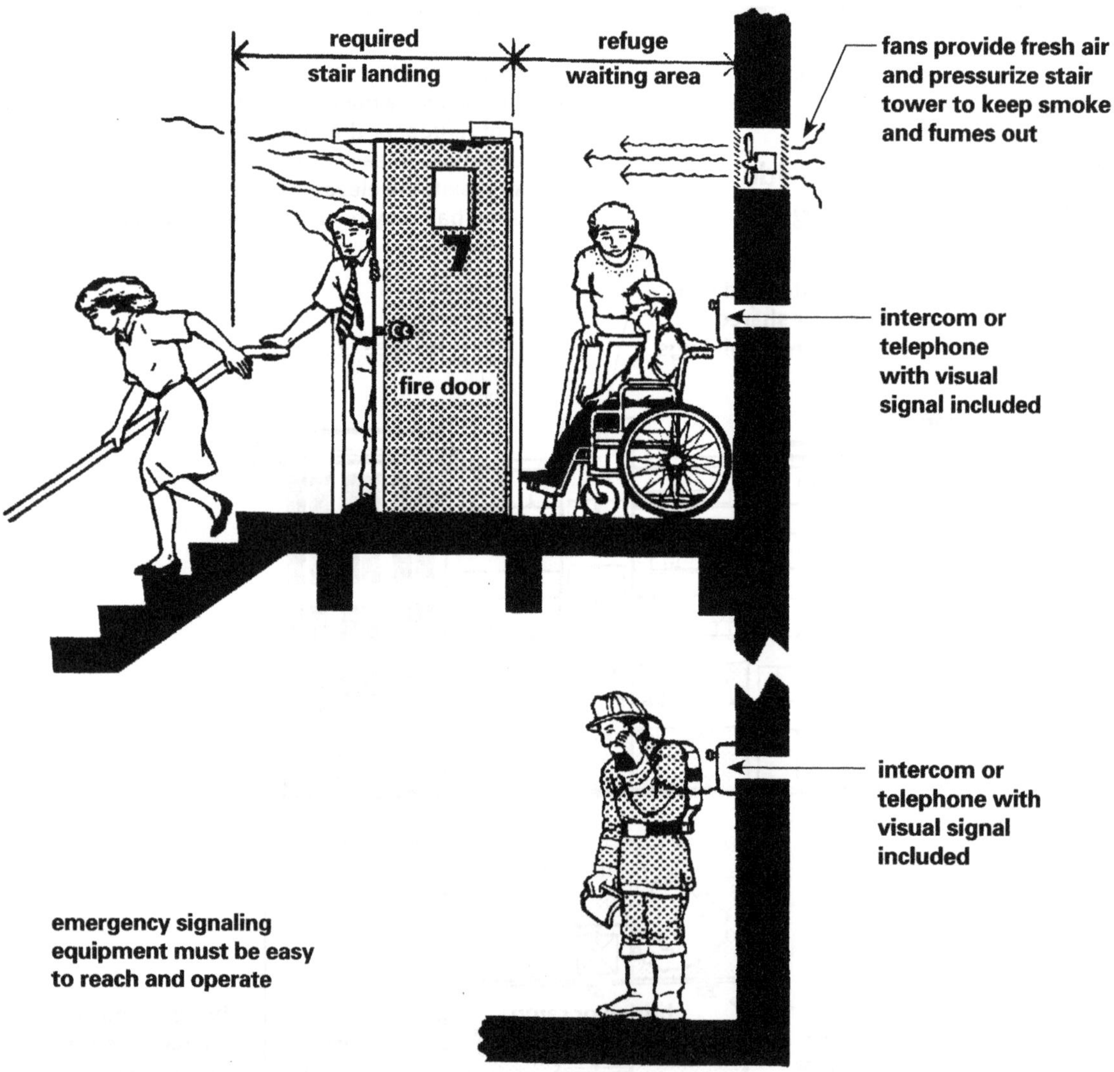

Area of Safe Refuge

Usually vertical circulation in areas of refuge is provided via stairs but in some circumstances it may be possible to include a "fire-safe" elevator also which can be used by emergency personnel for evacuation. "Fire-safe" elevators are specially enclosed and pressurized to prevent smoke and heat infiltration and are powered by a separate emergency power supply.

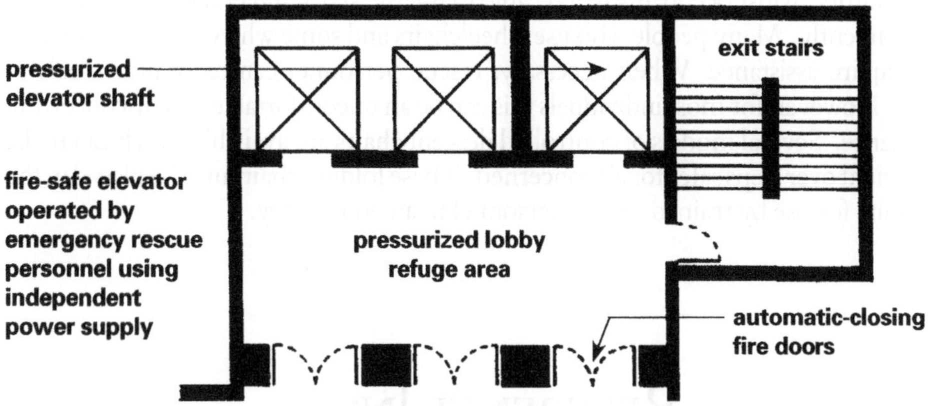

Safe Elevator

BASIC DESIGN CONSIDERATION

EMERGENCY MANAGEMENT PLAN

Section A4.3.10 in the Appendix to the UFAS document states that an emergency management plan for the evacuation of people with disabilities is essential in providing for fire safety in buildings where disabled people are residents or are regularly employed. An emergency plan should be developed jointly by facility management and local rescue/fire safety professionals working with each disabled individual to incorporate his/her needs and preferences. The plan should be shared with all building occupants, and safety checks and evacuation drills held on a regular basis. Follow-up reports which document weaknesses can provide an agenda for work sessions to develop better solutions. Evacuation drills provide an opportunity for the building occupants, facility managers, and the rescue personnel to determine the effectiveness of the emergency plan.

The effectiveness of most emergency plans hinges on the expectation that people will act in a reasonable manner having been informed about what to do in an emergency and being notified and informed of the crisis at hand. All building personnel should be well versed in proper safety procedures and be trained to provide assistance and give direction to visitors or others who may be unfamiliar with the facility. Some emergency plans may include specific duties for building supervisors or security personnel such as checking bathrooms, offices, and hallways, to insure or facilitate movement of all occupants to an area of safe refuge or building exit. The plan would also make provisions for individuals who have requested assistance either with notification of the emergency or with evacuation.

In many buildings, it will not be possible for the rescue squad to provide egress using the elevators. Most occupants will be able to use the stairs and evacuate the building independently. Many people who use wheelchairs and some who walk with difficulty will require assistance. When necessary, rescue personnel can carry individuals to safety. However, for most individuals this can be an uncomfortable and disconcerting experience. Several models of controlled descent chairs are available which can make movement over steps safer for all concerned. These folding chairs may be placed in the exit stairs for use by trained rescue personnel in an emergency.

REFERENCE INDEX TO UFAS DOCUMENT

AREAS OF SAFE REFUGE, HORIZONTAL EXITS, ALARMS, AND EMERGENCY MANAGEMENT PLANS

Primary References	UFAS page	Secondary References	UFAS page
4.3.10 Egress-General Information	19	4.1.2(7)(d) Scope & Technical Requirements	6
		4.1.5 Additions	11
		4.1.6 Alterations	12
		4.1.7 Historic Preservation	13
		4.3 Accessible Route	15
		A4.3.10 Egress - Emergency Management Plan	61

INTRODUCTION

Parking and passenger loading zones provide access to sites and facilities for people using various modes of private and public transportation. It is imperative that parking areas and passenger loading zones be well designed to provide a comparatively safe environment, especially given the inherent dangers in areas used by both pedestrians and vehicles. Everyone benefits when the safety requirements described in UFAS are implemented on a site.

People with disabilities use vehicles in much the same way as other drivers and passengers do. However, some drivers and passengers require special vehicle adaptations, such as hand controls and lifts, to facilitate use of standard vehicles such as cars, buses, taxis, and vans. It may also take longer for disabled people to enter and exit vehicles, especially when a lift or other assistance is required. For these reasons, special parking and passenger loading areas are earmarked for use by disabled persons. These designated parking spaces must be the ones closest to the entrance because many people with disabilities lack the strength and/or stamina to traverse long distances.

Special Adaptations and Use of Vehicles by People with Disabilities

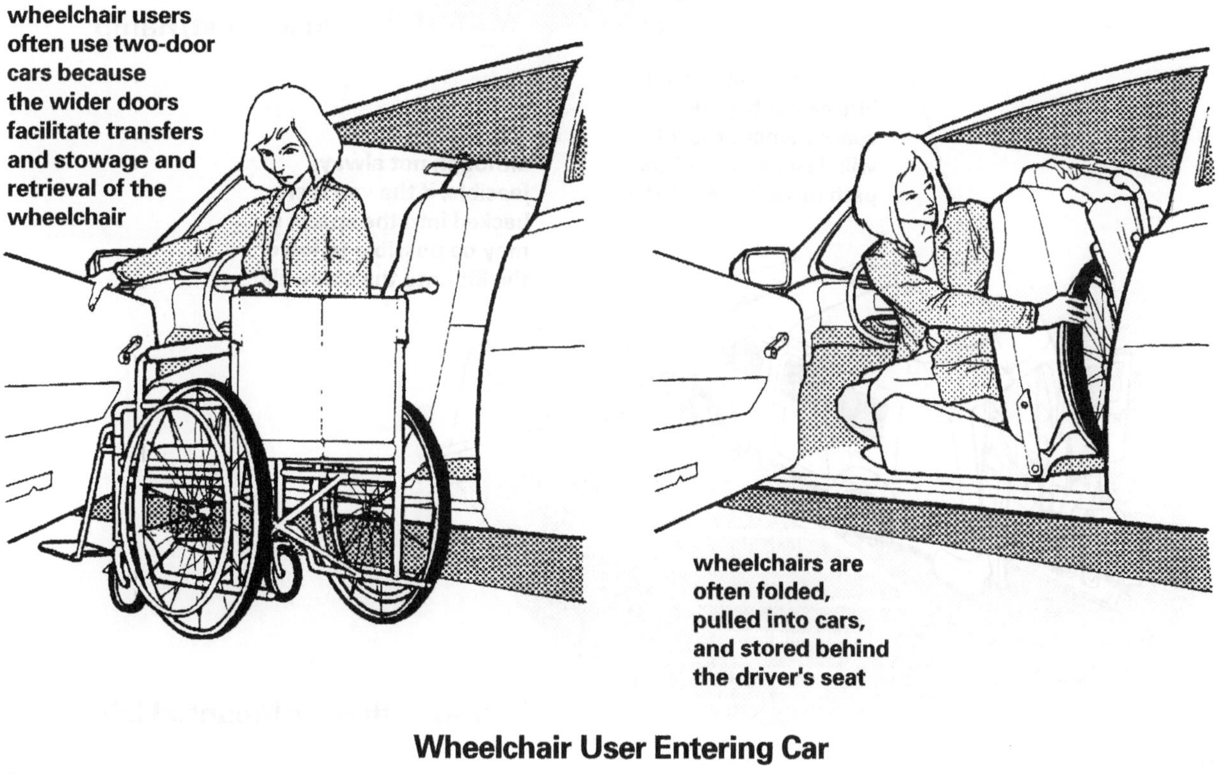

Wheelchair User Entering Car

Special Adaptations and Use of Vehicles by People with Disabilities

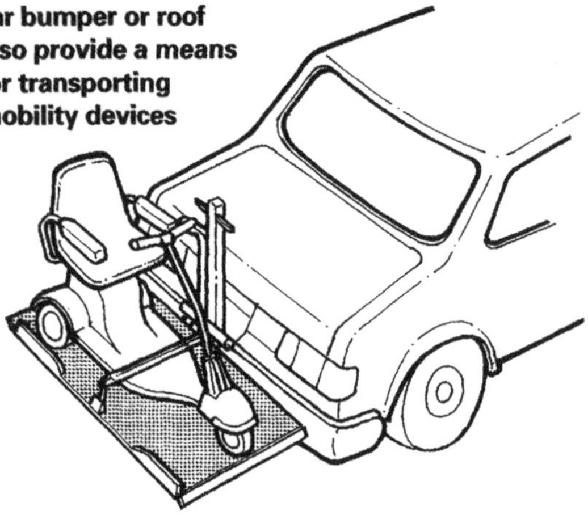

Car with Scooter Mounted on Back

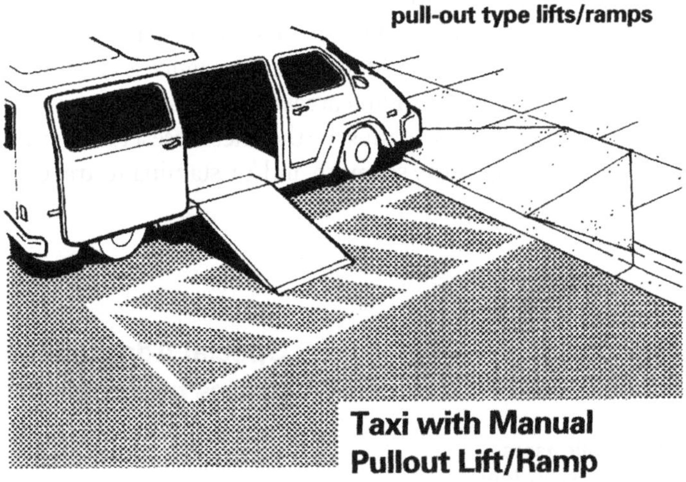

Taxi with Manual Pullout Lift/Ramp

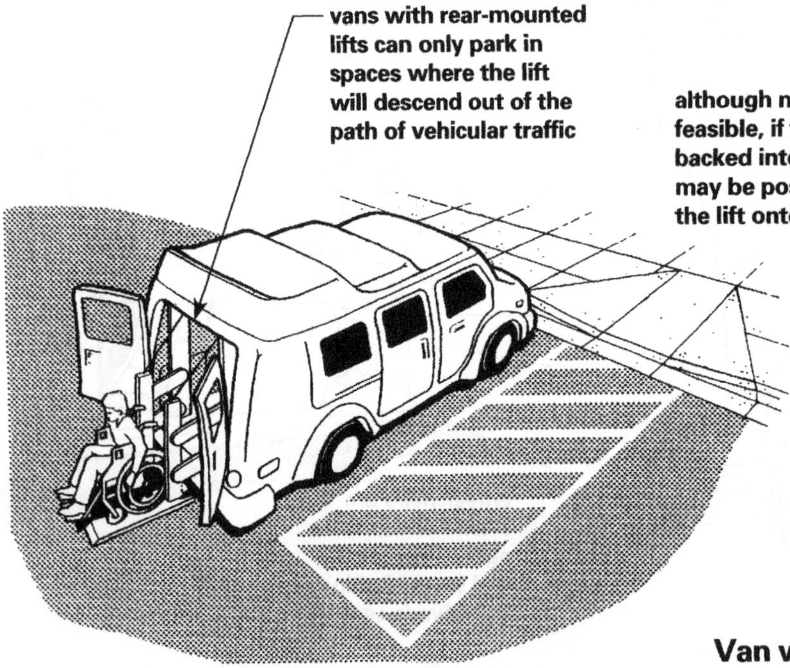

Van with Rear-Mounted Lift

Bus with Side-Mounted Lift

UFAS provides detailed scoping provisions regarding the required number of parking spaces per lot in Section 4.1.1(5), page 5. This section also includes several exemptions, additional requirements for parking spaces at various health care facilities, and states that, if provided, at least one passenger loading zone must comply with UFAS. If parking and passenger loading zones are added or altered, they must comply with the scoping and technical provisions for new construction. At facilities where alterations are planned, UFAS suggests that special consideration be given to the provision of accessible parking spaces and passenger loading zones. A few state and local codes have parking requirements which are more stringent than UFAS.

BASIC DESIGN CONSIDERATION

ACCESSIBLE PARKING SPACES

Parking facilities covered under the UFAS provisions include spaces in outdoor lots and interior/exterior parking garages for employees and/or visitors. Accessible parking spaces should be located in lots and garages to provide the shortest accessible path of travel to each building or adjacent street or sidewalk served by that parking area. Garages without elevators should include accessible parking on levels with accessible pedestrian paths. Parking spaces may be distributed among several parking lots if greater access is achieved, as in the case of a facility with a number of accessible entrances.

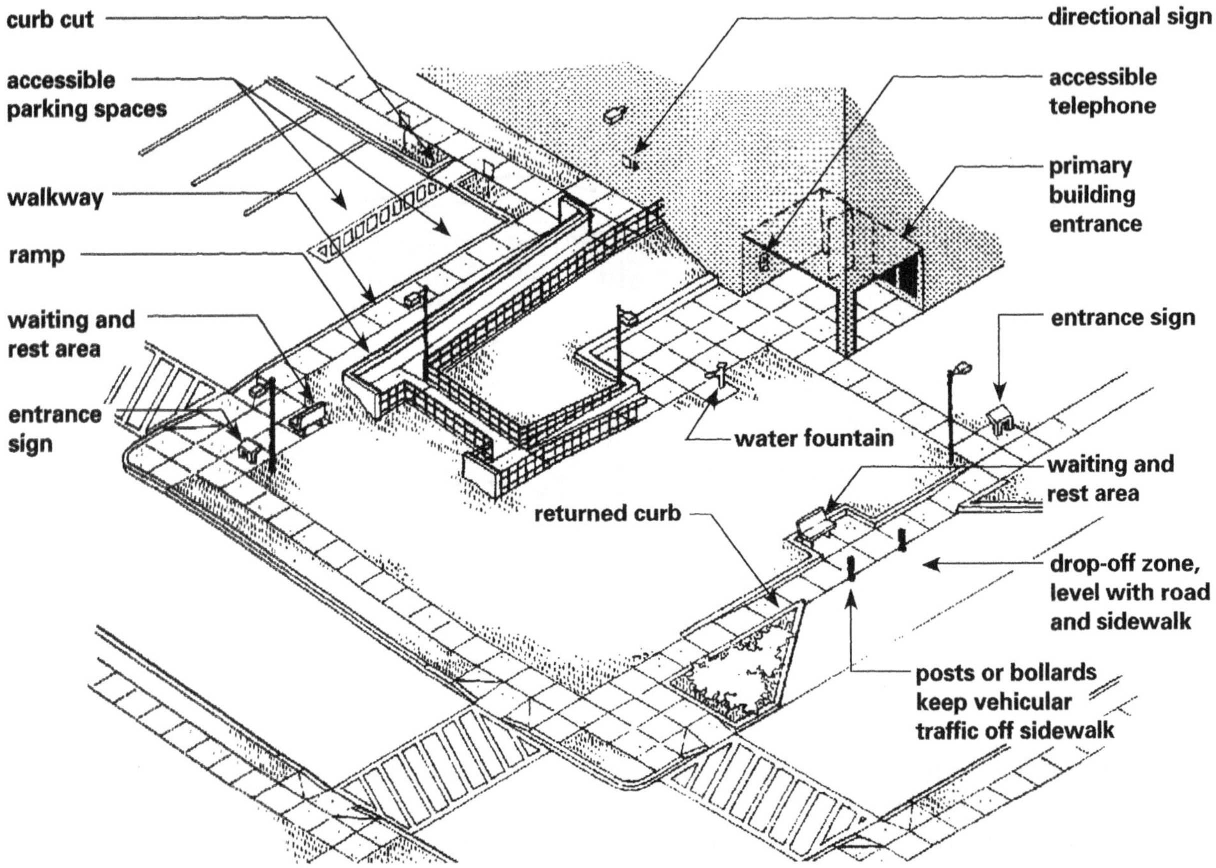

Location of Parking and Transit Stops

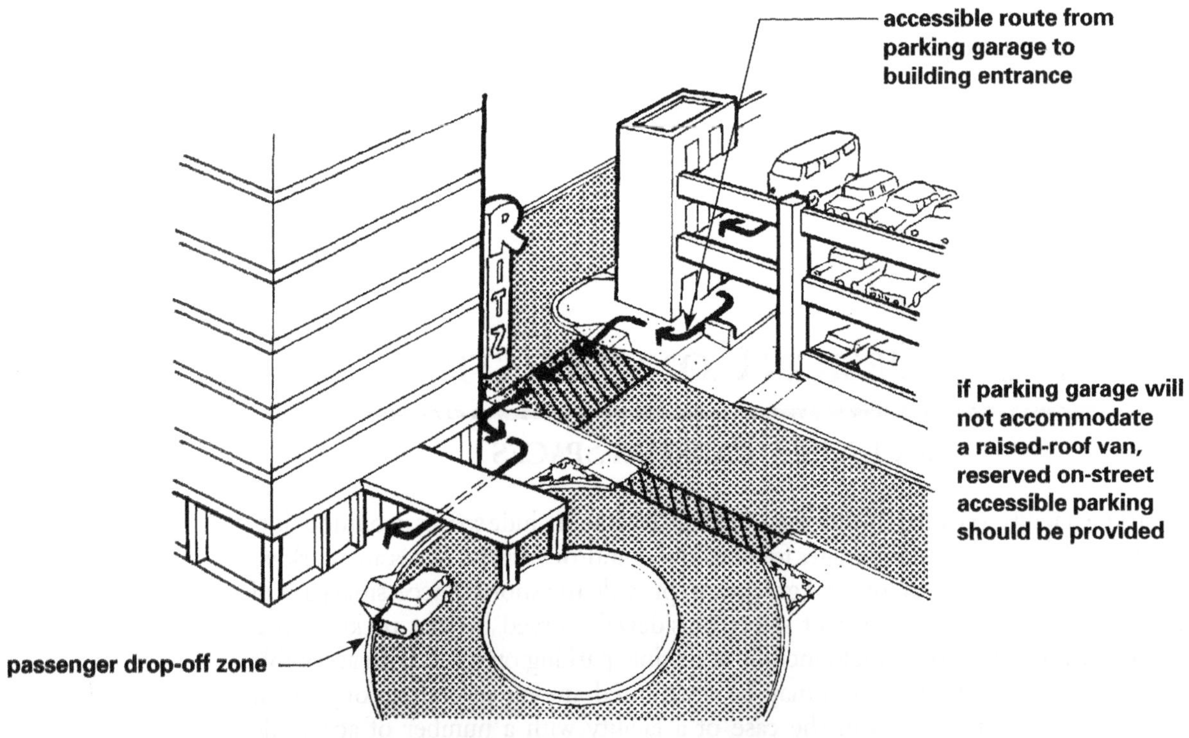

Parking Garage with Accessible Route(s)

UFAS requires that parking spaces be 96 inches wide with an adjacent access aisle 60 inches wide. "Wide" spaces without separate access aisles, permitted by some state codes, do not comply with UFAS. Although the wide spaces include access aisles, the aisles are not clearly marked and as a result are often obstructed by adjacent parked cars. UFAS requires that the access aisle be part of an accessible route and both the parking space and access aisle must be level, with a slope no greater than 1:50. Because both access aisles and parking spaces have a maximum slope of 1:50, built-up curb ramps which project into the access aisle are not allowed. Two accessible spaces may share one access aisle. Parked vehicles should not overhang and interfere with passage along accessible routes.

Many times accessible parking spaces will be located in areas which require users to cross vehicular traffic lanes. When this is the case, the accessible route (crosswalk) should be clearly indicated to inform both pedestrians and vehicle operators. Driveways, streets, and other vehicular lanes are not considered part of an accessible route when pedestrians and vehicles must travel in the same direction. If curbs, wheelstops, or other vehicle control measures are used, they should not obstruct pedestrian traffic.

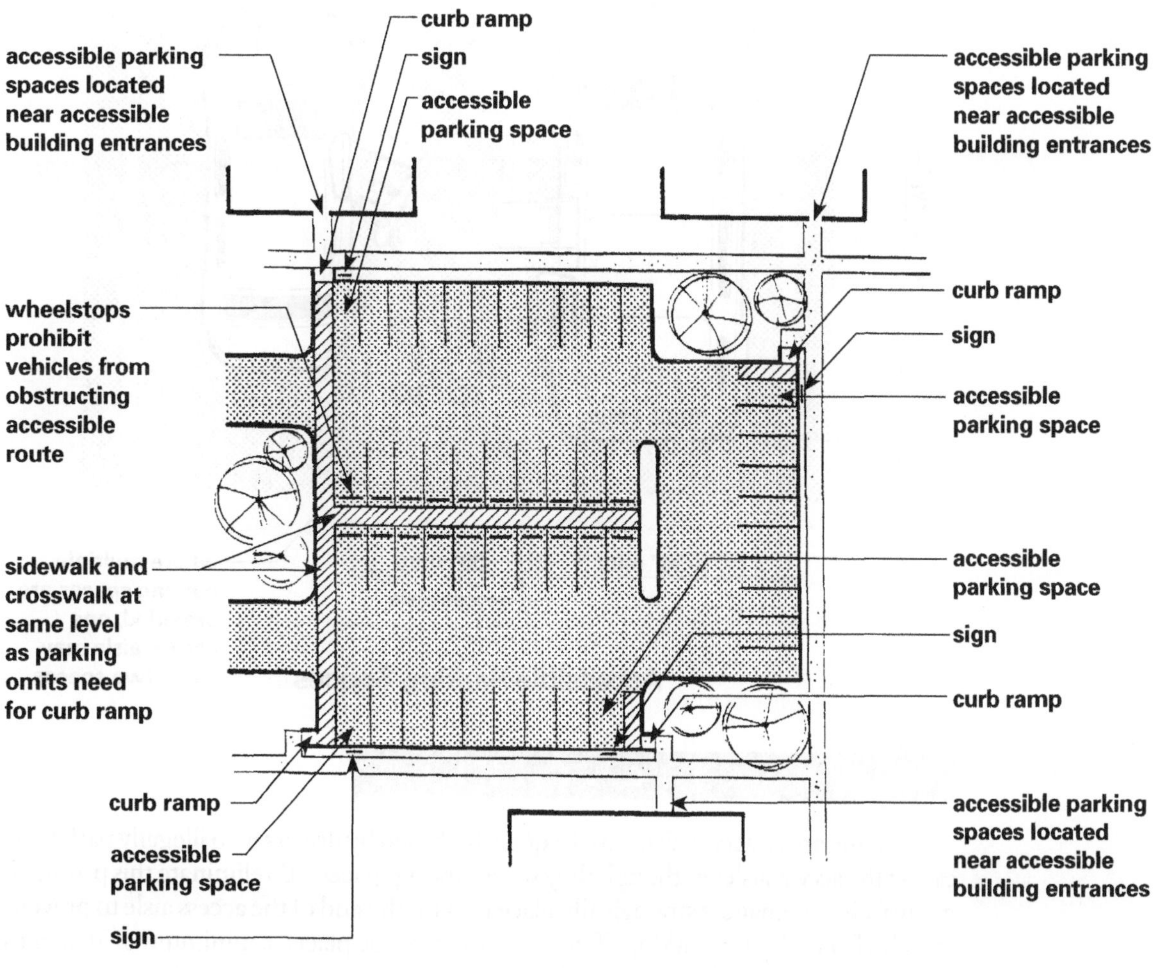

Parking Lot with Accessible Route/Crosswalk

Accessible parking spaces are the only elements exclusively reserved for use by people with disabilities. Signage displaying the International Symbol of Accessibility notifies all vehicle operators that spaces have been reserved for this purpose. UFAS requires that the signage be capable of being seen from the driver's seat and located so that a car parked in the space does not obstruct the view of the signage. The Department of Transportation Uniform Traffic Control Code and some state and local codes specify mounting heights for signage and should be consulted to ensure compliance. Access symbols painted on the surface of the parking space serve as auxiliary reminders but cannot be the only signage provided at the space. Painted symbols on the pavement are difficult to see at night and can become obscured by parked cars, snow and ice, and fluids leaked from vehicles.

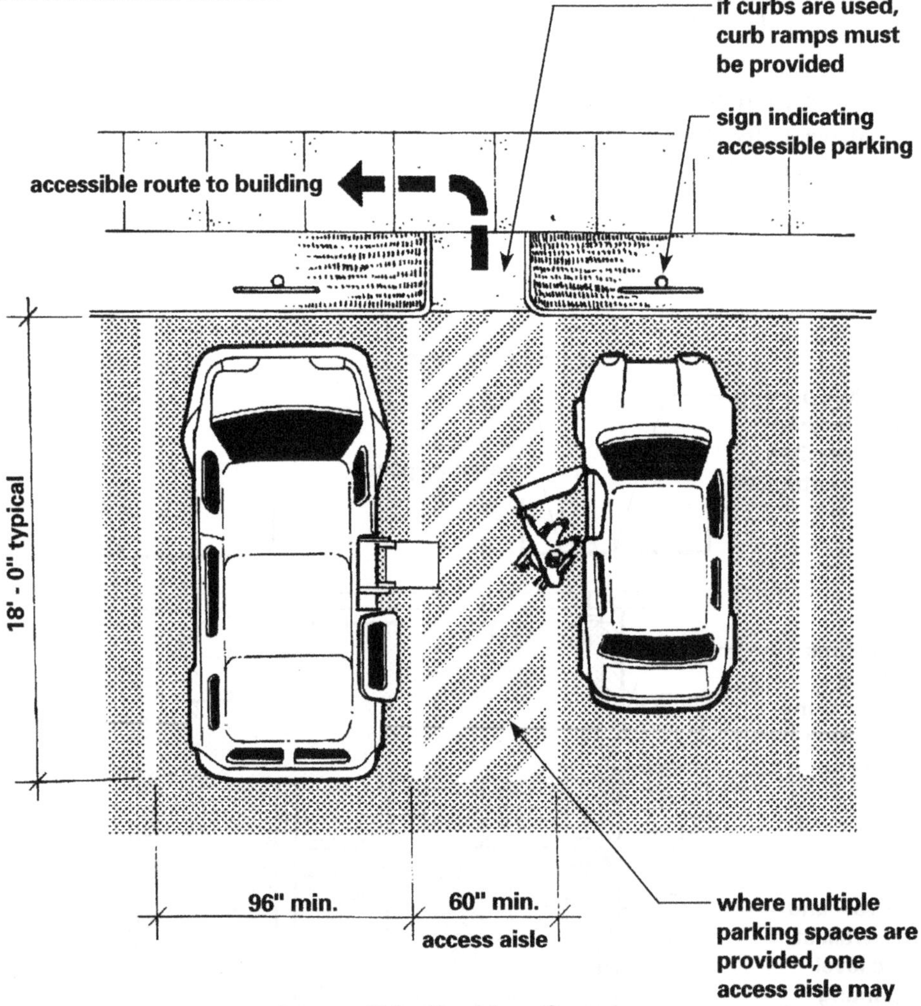

Accessible Parking Spaces

PRACTICAL PLUS

In some areas, access aisles are frequently abused by drivers who illegally park their cars in the access aisles as though they were parking spaces. To eliminate this problem, many facility managers strategically place posts at the end of the access aisle to prevent vehicles from illegally parking. The end posts must be placed a minimum of 36 inches apart to allow wheelchair passage. Posts must not obstruct maneuvering space in the access aisle or limit use of lifts or vehicle doors.

Although not specifically mentioned in the design requirements for UFAS, angled and parallel parking spaces are permitted as long as all the accessible parking space requirements are met. Angled and parallel parking spaces are frequently included on streets and in parking lots and access features can be easily incorporated in the design of these types of parking spaces. Some state codes include additional requirements which must be considered in the design of accessible, parallel parking spaces. In general, the requirements for parallel parking spaces are similar to those of passenger drop-off and loading zones.

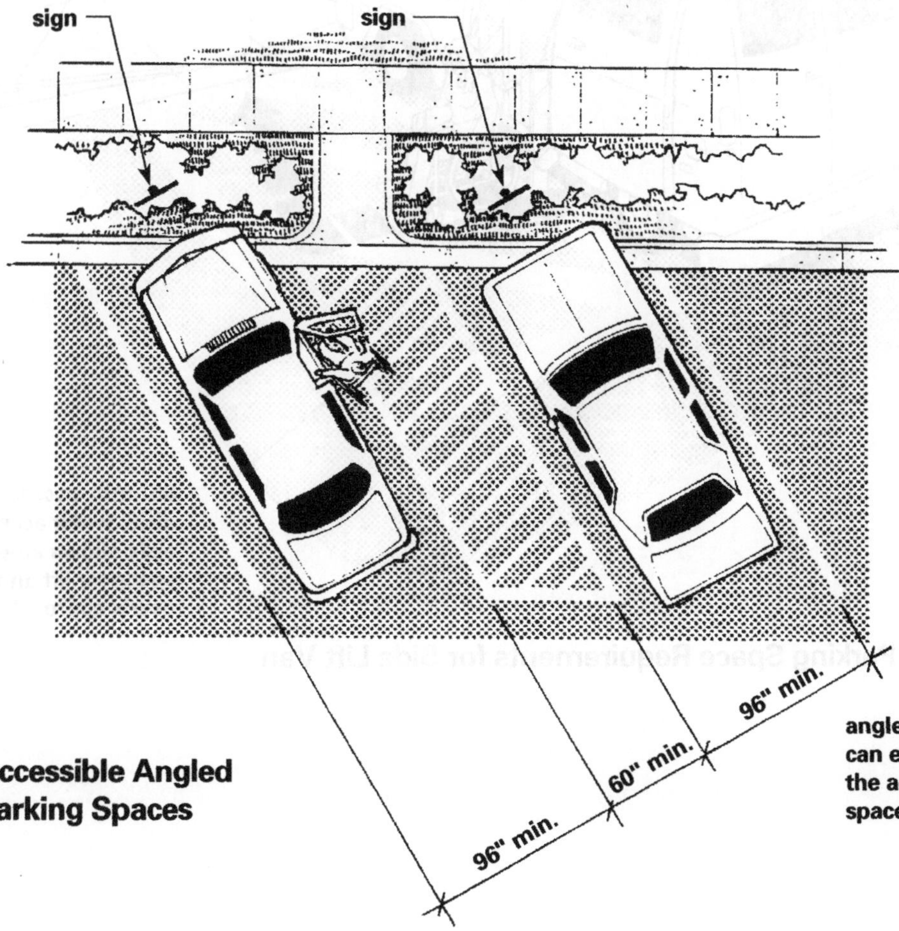

Accessible Angled Parking Spaces

If provided, access aisles for side lift vans must be 96 inches wide to allow full extension of the lift and maneuvering space for wheelchair users to approach or leave the lift. In garages a headroom clearance of at least 114 inches must be provided at van parking spaces and the vehicular route to and from the entrance/exit to the parking space. The extra headroom is necessary to accommodate the raised roofs frequently installed on accessible vans. Even though there are no UFAS scoping requirements for van spaces, if provided, they may be included in the total count of accessible parking spaces. Although van parking spaces are not required by UFAS, some states do require that a certain percentage of accessible parking spaces accommodate vans.

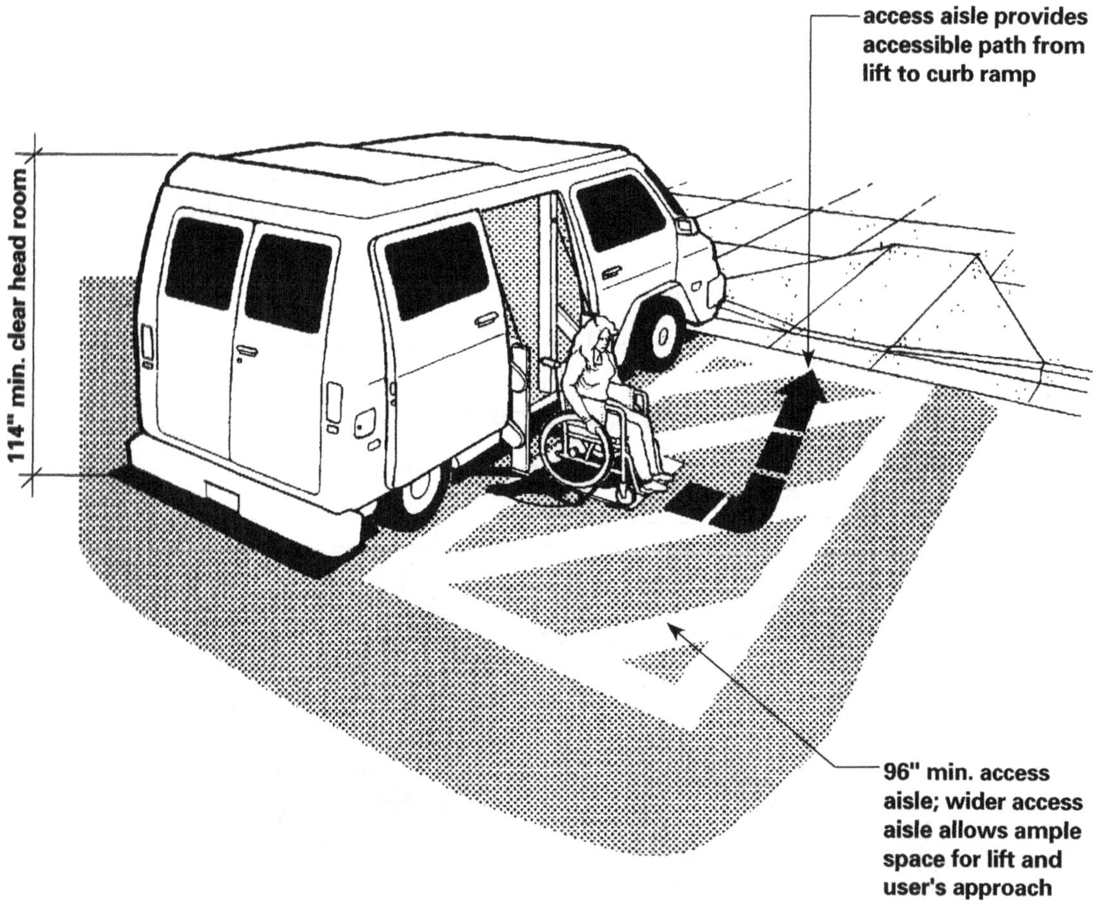

Parking Space Requirements for Side Lift Van

PRACTICAL PLUS

Van parking can easily be included at end-of-the-row spaces. The unlimited open area in this location provides ample maneuvering space for operating and approaching side lift vans. The access aisle must be clearly marked to prevent vehicles from illegally parking in this area.

Parking Space at End-of-Row for Side Lift Van

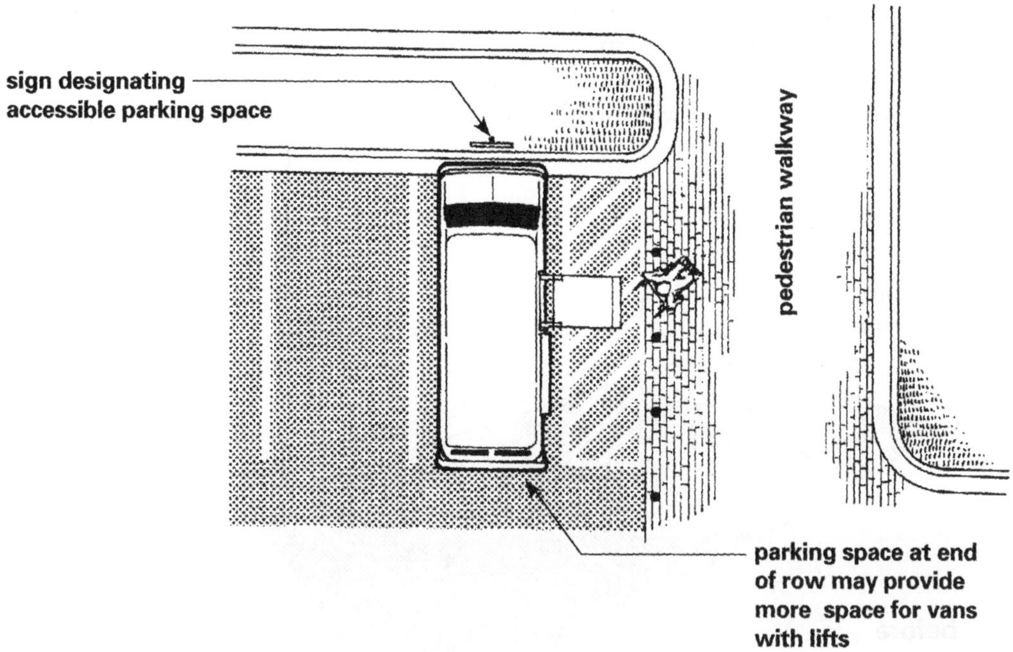

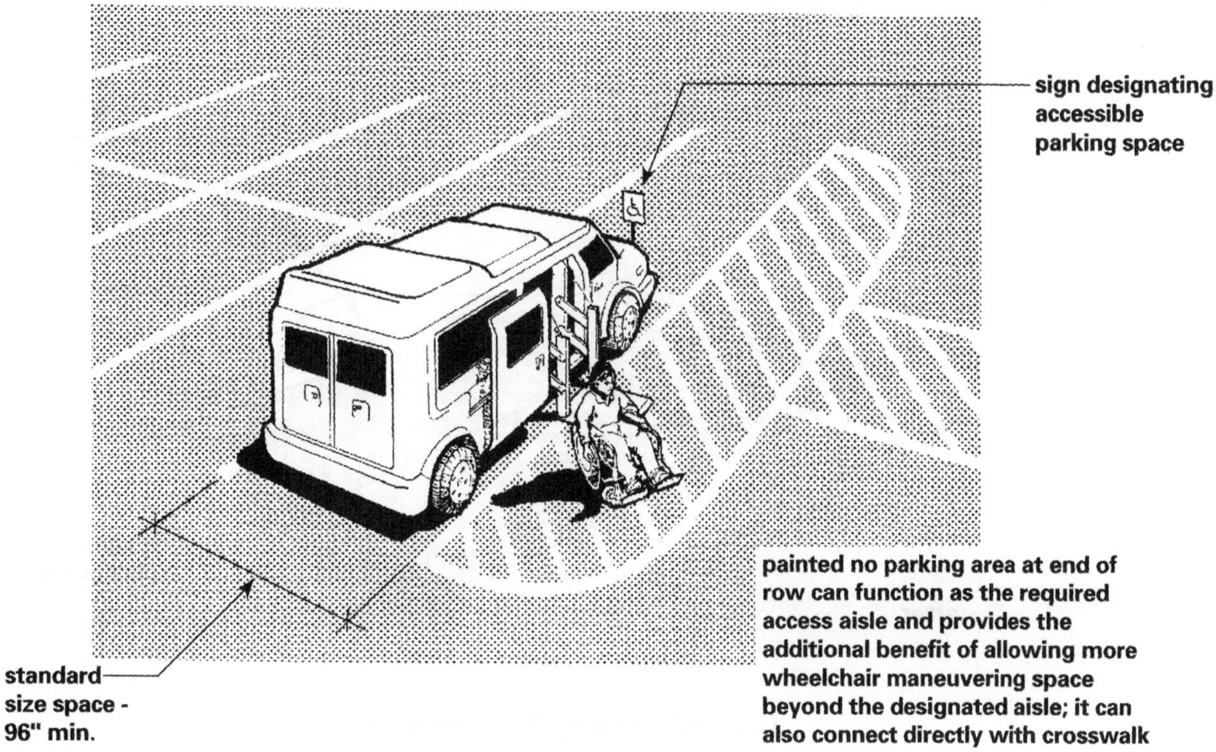

PROBLEM — NO ACCESSIBLE PARKING SPACES

SOLUTION — CONVERT STANDARD SPACES TO RESERVED SPACES

If the parking lot is located along an accessible route to the building entrance, or the route can be modified to provide access, then it is usually possible to convert existing spaces into spaces reserved for people with disabilities. Generally it takes three standard spaces to create two accessible spaces with a shared access aisle. The pavement markings indicating the location of the spaces and the access aisle will have to be repainted and signage will have to be installed. If the existing parking lot is sloped or the pavement is broken and uneven, it will also be necessary to resurface the spaces and access aisle.

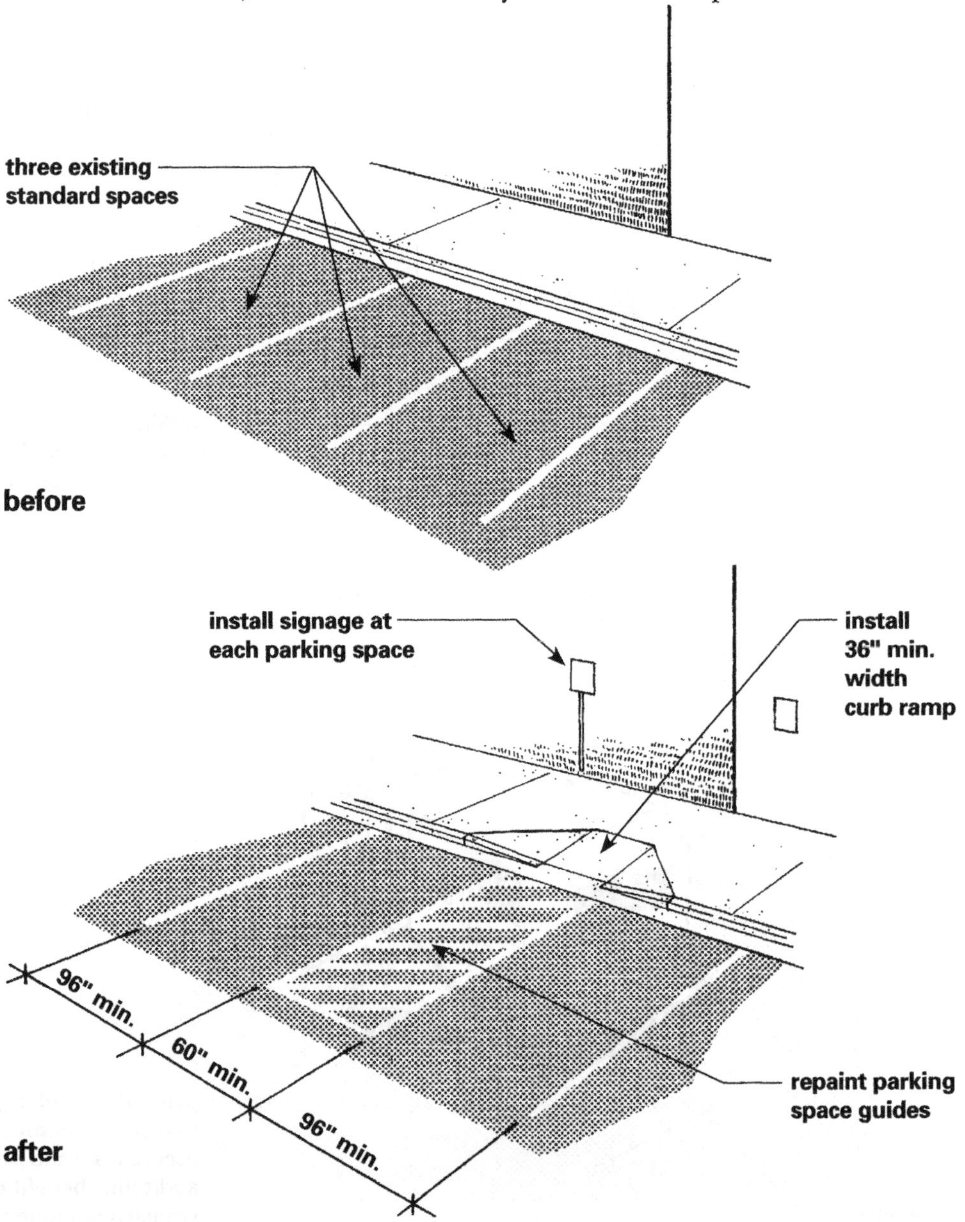

Convert Existing Parking Spaces

PROBLEM PARKED VEHICLES OVERHANG ACCESSIBLE ROUTE

SOLUTION INSTALL WHEELSTOPS IN PARKING SPACES

The overhang of a parked vehicle tends to obstruct a pedestrian path located directly in front of the parking space. This problem is true of parking spaces with and without curbs. When curbs are used as wheelstops, the pedestrian path must be wide enough to accommodate the accessible route and the overhanging vehicle. Or, another alternative is to place or locate the pedestrian path beyond a planting strip. If no curb is present then wheelstops or bollards should be installed to prevent cars from pulling into the pedestrian path.

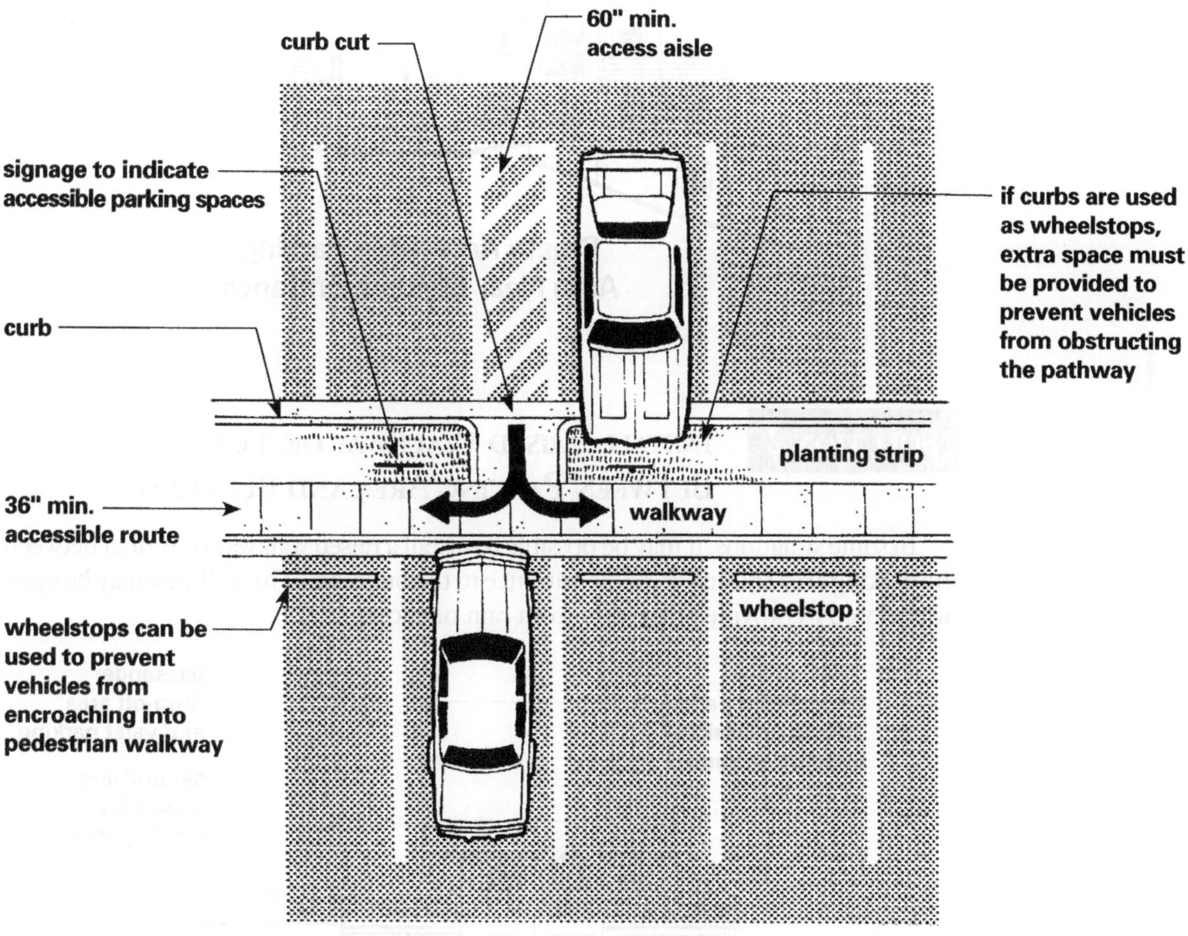

Curbs and Wheelstops Installed to Prevent Obstruction of Path by Overhanging Vehicles

PROBLEM PARKING AND BUILDING ENTRANCE LOCATED ON DIFFERENT LEVELS

SOLUTION 1 CREATE ACCESSIBLE PARKING AREA AT ENTRANCE LEVEL

When the general parking area is not located on an accessible route, if space allows, it may be possible to create a small accessible parking area near the entrance to the building. This area will often be located near the passenger loading zone if one is provided.

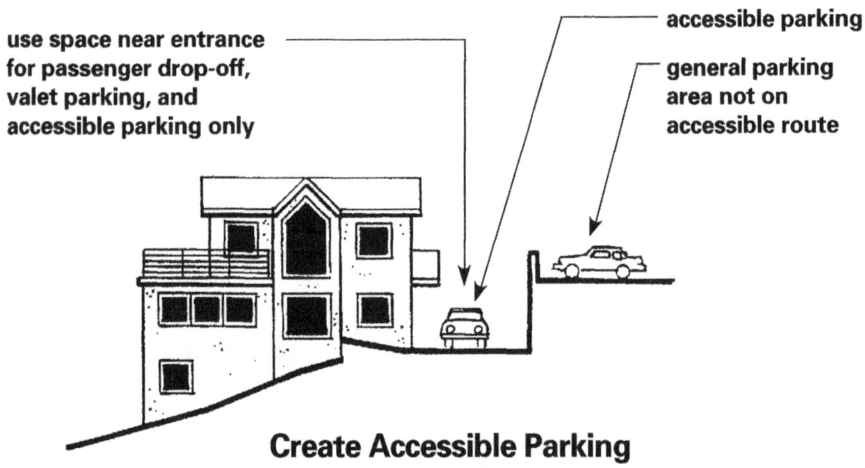

Create Accessible Parking Area Near Building Entrance

SOLUTION 2 INSTALL RAISED WALKWAY OR TUNNEL BETWEEN PARKING AREA AND BUILDING

In some situations, it may be possible to install a raised walkway or tunnel between the parking area and an accessible entrance to the building. The walkway may be open or enclosed to provide protection from rain or snow.

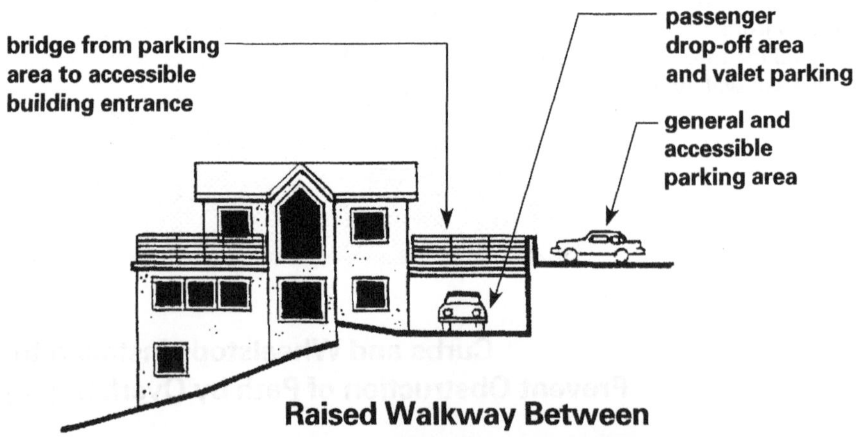

Raised Walkway Between Parking Area and Building

BASIC DESIGN CONSIDERATION

ACCESSIBLE PASSENGER LOADING ZONES

Accessible passenger loading zones must be located on an accessible route as close as possible to the nearest accessible entrance. It is also required that they have access aisles at least 60 inches wide and 20 feet long adjacent and parallel to the vehicle pull-up space. If curbs are used, at least one curb ramp must be included which connects the access aisle with an accessible route to the building entrance. Similar to accessible parking spaces, vehicle standing spaces and access aisles must have a slope no greater than 1:50.

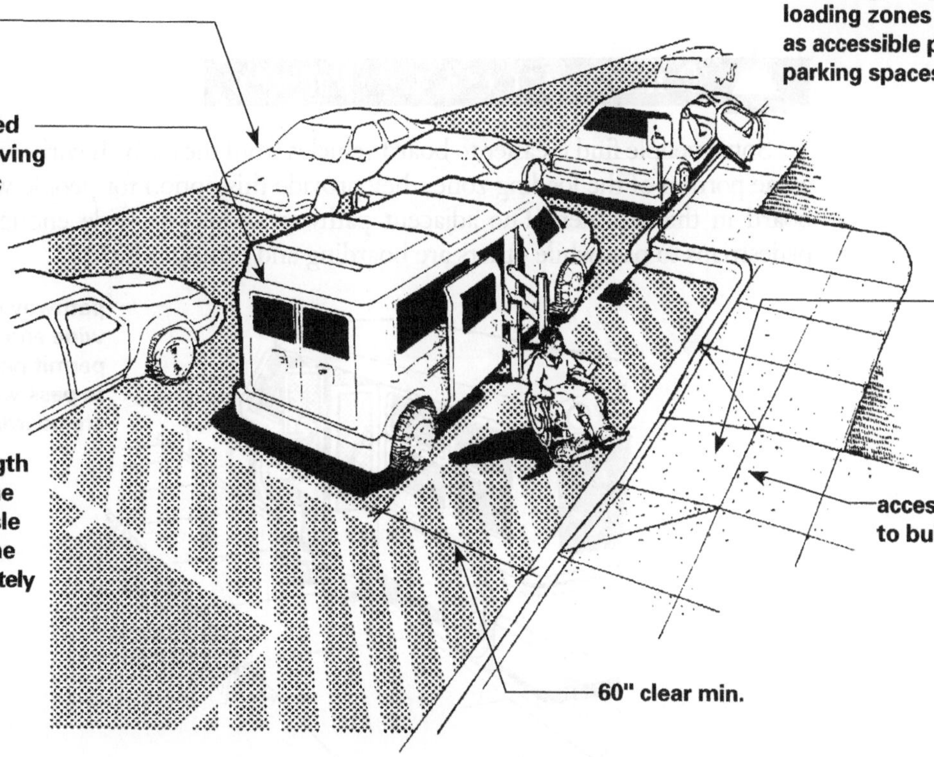

Features of Accessible Passenger Loading Zones

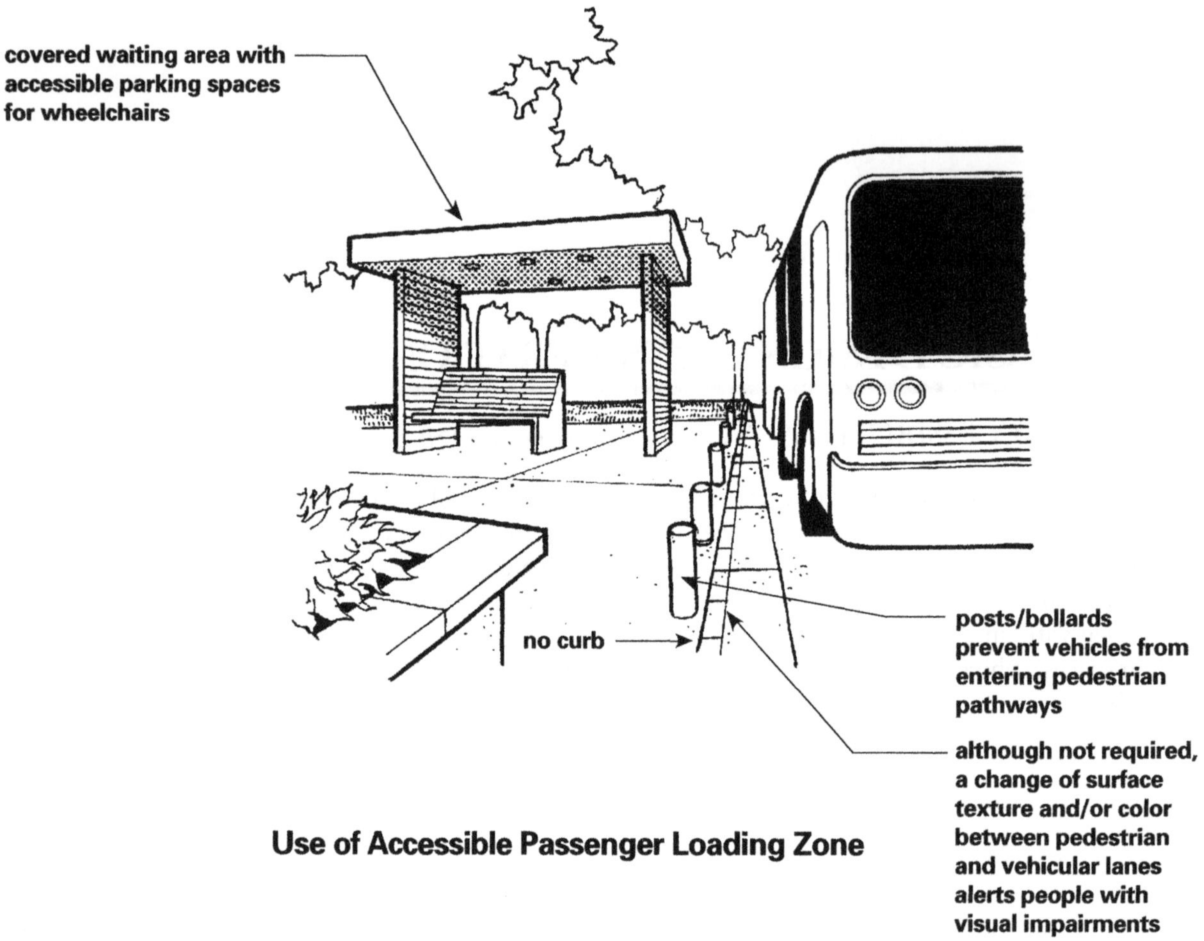

Use of Accessible Passenger Loading Zone

PRACTICAL PLUS

Some people find it easier to board vehicles from the curb. If curbs are used along some portion of the loading zone, they provide this option for people who prefer to board in this manner. The adjacent pathway should be wide enough to permit pedestrians to pass while others are boarding and exiting vehicles.

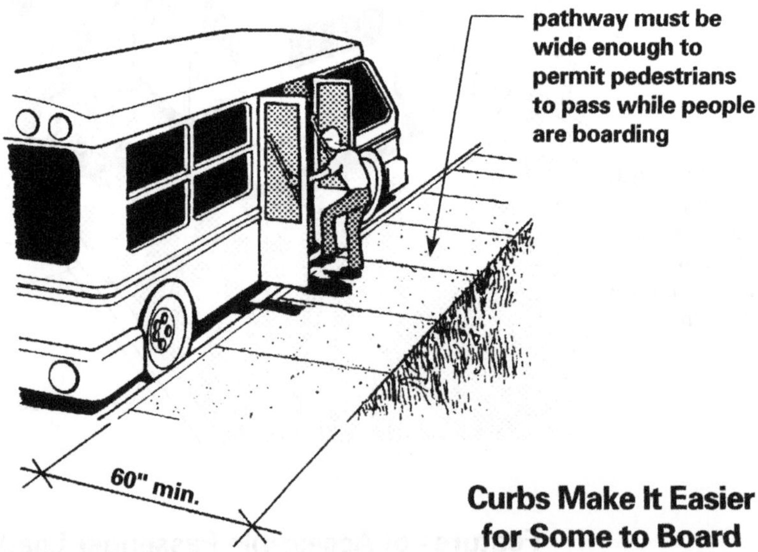

Curbs Make It Easier for Some to Board

If canopies, roof overhangs, or other overhead structures are included at passenger loading zones, they must provide a minimum clearance of 114 inches. The vehicle access route to and from the passenger loading zone and the site entrance/exit must also allow 114 inches of vertical clearance.

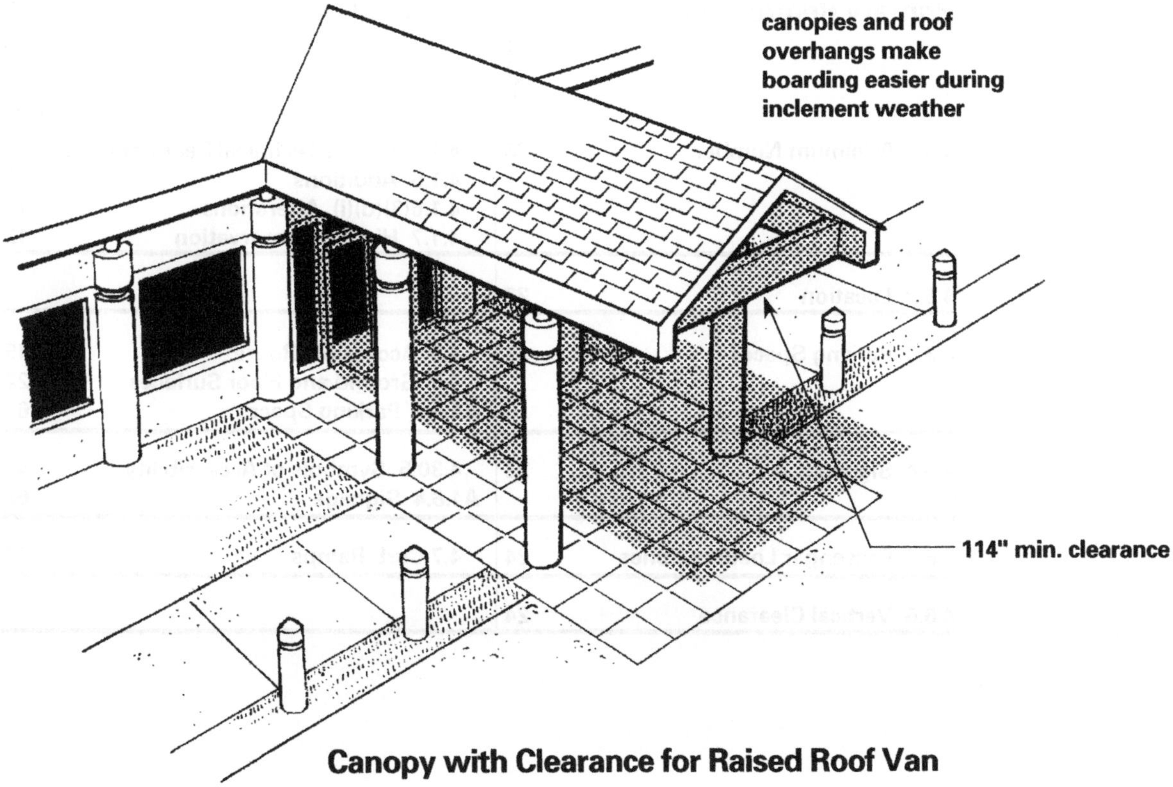

Canopy with Clearance for Raised Roof Van

PROBLEM PASSENGER LOADING ZONE NOT ACCESSIBLE

SOLUTION MODIFY AREA TO CREATE ACCESS

Passenger loading zones should be designed to be long enough to allow simultaneous use by more than one vehicle. As for width, the vehicle must be able to stop outside the lane of moving traffic and still have a 60-inch wide access aisle. If the width is insufficient, the passenger loading zone will have to be widened. Also, if the loading zone is not level or the pavement is uneven or broken, the area will have to be regraded and resurfaced. A curb ramp may also have to be installed to assure the availability of an accessible route.

REFERENCE INDEX TO UFAS DOCUMENT

PARKING AND PASSENGER LOADING ZONES

INTRODUCTION

UFAS defines an entrance as "any access point to a building or portion of a building or facility used for the purpose of entering. An entrance includes the approach walk, the vertical access leading to the entrance platform, the entrance platform itself, vestibules if provided, the entry door(s) or gate(s), and the hardware of the entry door(s) or gate(s)." UFAS further defines the principal entrance of a building or facility as "the main door through which most people enter."

Section 4.14 of UFAS provides minimum design requirements for entrances and uses UFAS Section 4.3 Accessible Route as a fundamental reference. Entrances are required to be part of an accessible route and must be connected by an accessible route to public transportation stops, accessible parking and passenger loading zones, public streets or sidewalks within the boundaries of the site, and to all accessible spaces and elements within the building. A service entrance must not be the sole accessible entrance to a building or facility unless it is the only entrance (i.e., garage, factory).

UFAS provides detailed scoping provisions for entrances included in new construction, alterations, additions, and historic properties. The provisions for new construction, which apply in all retrofit situations unless specifically exempted, require at least one principal entrance at each grade floor level. Also, when a building or facility has entrances which specifically serve transportation facilities, passenger loading zones, accessible parking facilities, taxi stands, public streets and sidewalks within the boundaries of the site, or accessible interior vertical access, then at least one entrance serving each function must be accessible. State and local building and fire codes also have requirements for egress which need to be considered when planning accessible entrances.

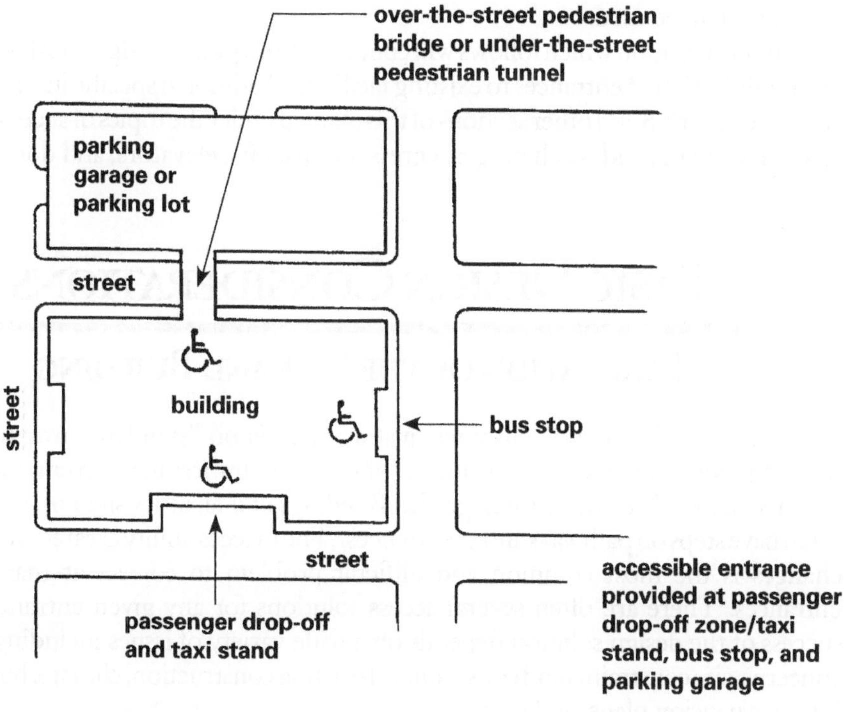

Accessible Entrances to Serve Various Functions

Accessible Entrance Each Grade Level

Entrances included in additions and alterations to existing buildings and facilities, including historic properties, must comply with the requirements for new construction outlined above with the following exceptions:

Alterations. In substantially altered buildings, at least one accessible entrance shall be provided. If other entrances are altered, they shall be made accessible.

Additions. If a new addition to a building or facility does not have an entrance, then at least one entrance in the existing building shall be made accessible and shall be connected by an accessible route to the new addition.

Historic Renovations. At least one accessible entrance used by the public shall be provided. If no entrance used by the public can comply, then access at any entrance not used by the public but left open (unlocked) with directional signs at the primary entrance may be used.

The information which follows will concentrate on global design considerations for thc modification of entrances to existing facilities. Additional specific information can be found in UFAS and other sections of this manual under the topics of accessible route, space allowances and reach ranges, egress, ramps, lifts, elevators, and doors.

BASIC DESIGN CONSIDERATIONS

EVALUATION OF THE SITE AND BUILDING

There is no "standard" entrance, just as there is no "standard" way to design a building. Some buildings have a number of steps at entrances to reach entry floor levels well above or below the finished grade. Buildings and facilities sited on steep terrain often have steps on pathways and at entrances. The inaccessibility created by these level changes is the most common and difficult problem to correct at many existing entrances. There are often several access solutions for any given entrance and the success of the design solution depends on a wide variety of issues including aesthetic concerns, site constraints and constraints of existing construction, climate, building use, future expansion plans, and cost.

The most desirable entrance features a level path/walkway (with a slope of 1:20 or less) to the building. Depending on the conditions at a given location, this solution is often possible even on very steep and uneven sites, using bridges or pedestrian connectors. When it is not possible to provide a level walkway, then some combination of vertical access arrangements must be made using ramps, lifts, and/or elevators. It is best if steps/stairs are used alongside a ramp for the convenience of people who prefer them and they are required for egress in the case of a lift or elevator.

All accessible entrances should display the International Symbol of Accessibility or signage which provides directions to the nearest accessible entrance. Accessible entrances that are not located at the main entrance of the building should be well lighted, easy to locate, and include interior signage that provides information similar to that provided at the main entrance.

PROBLEM — STEPS AT MAIN ENTRANCE

SOLUTION 1 — REGRADE ENTRY APPROACH

When the level change at an entrance approach is small, it is often possible to regrade the entrance and create a level walkway. Walkways have a slope of 1:20 or less.

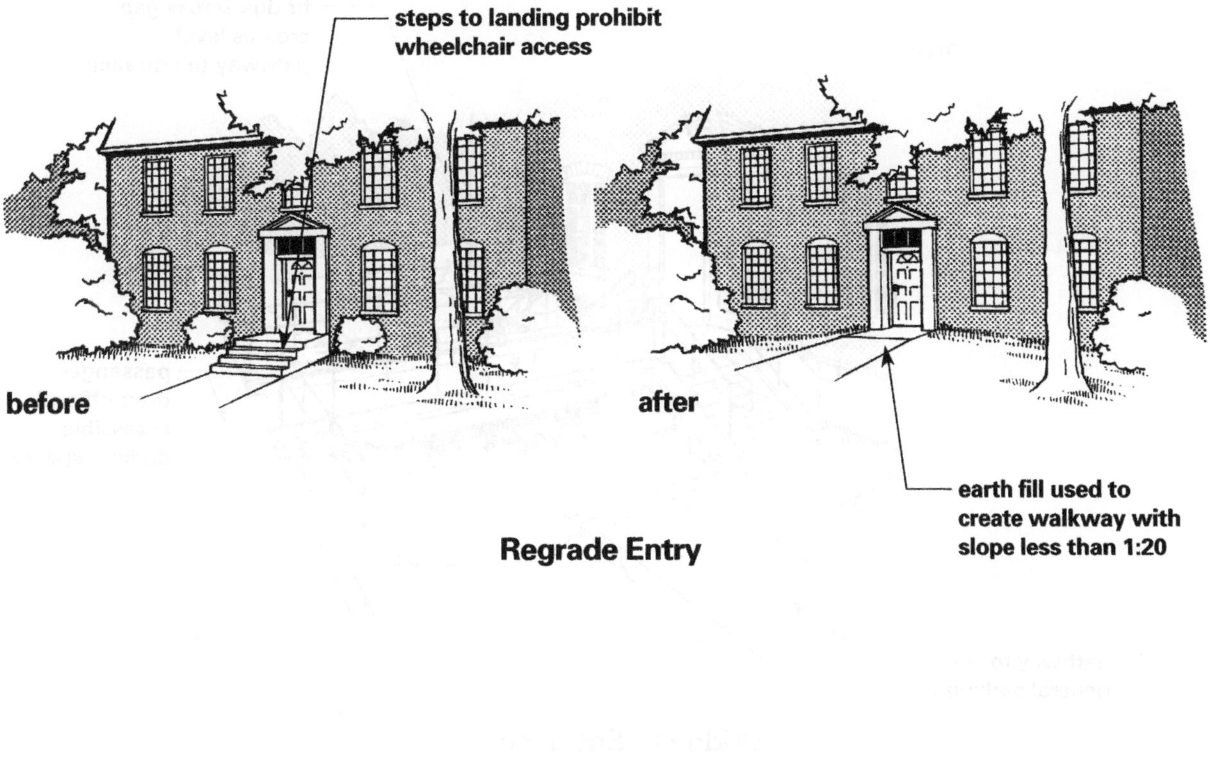

Regrade Entry

SOLUTION 2 USE BRIDGE TO SPAN GAP

When the existing terrain is uneven, it is often possible to use a bridge to span the gap from a location on the site to an entry on at least one level of the building. Handrails or walls should be used on the bridge to prevent users from slipping or rolling off the surface.

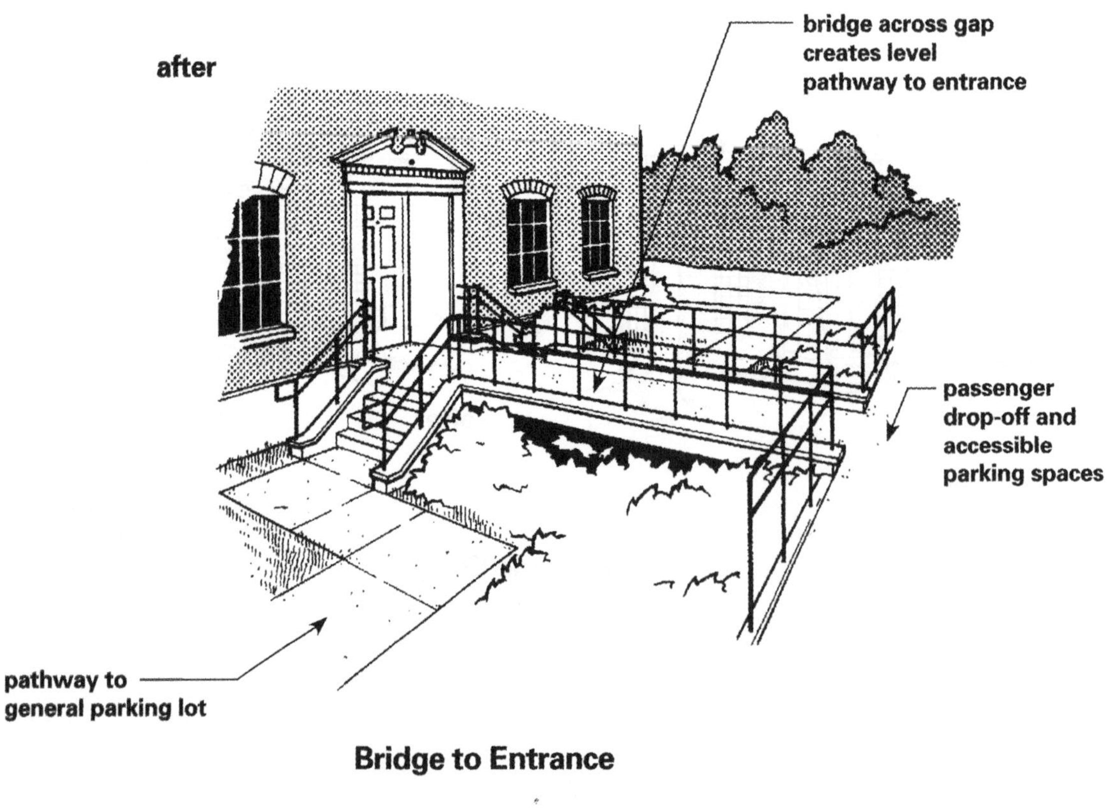

Bridge to Entrance

SOLUTION 3 USE RAMP IN COMBINATION WITH STEPS

When space allows, ramps can be used to gradually overcome vertical discrepancies. Ramps must meet the UFAS requirements and should be constructed of materials which are compatible with the existing structure. Steps should be included with ramps to give users the option of selecting the approach which best suits their needs.

Ramp Included with Steps

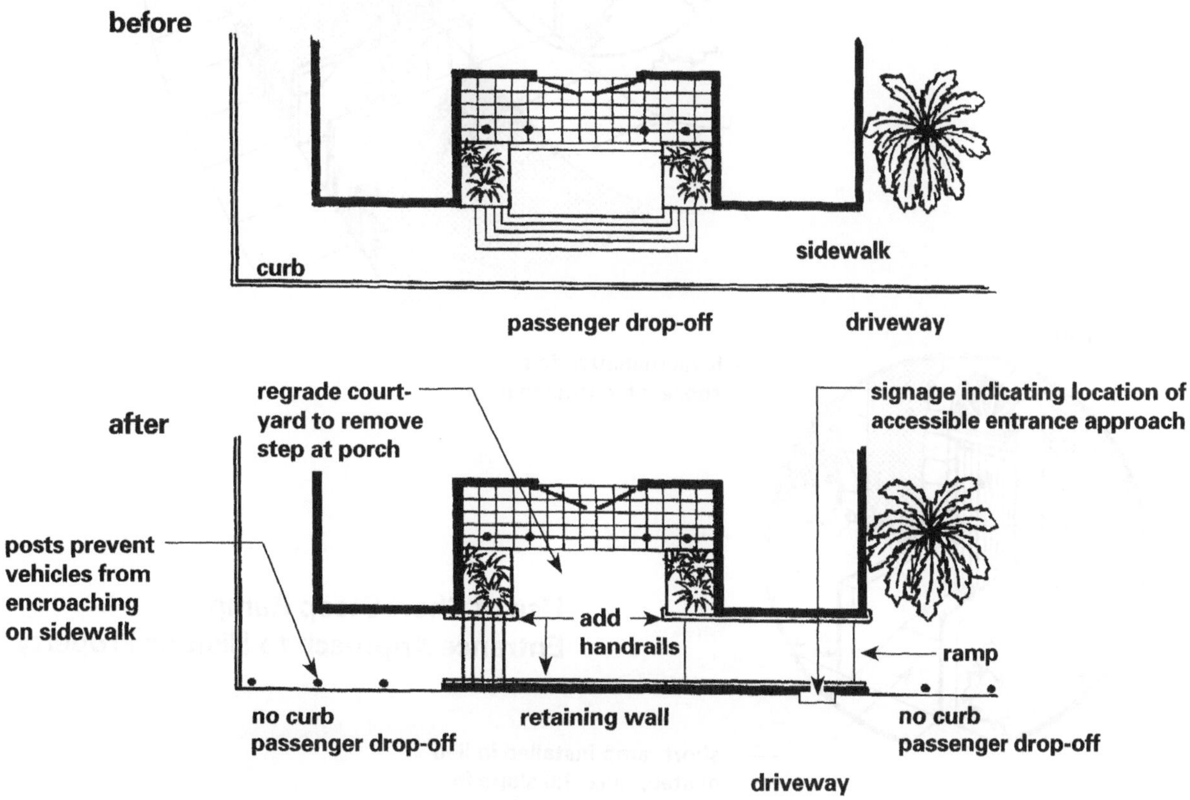

Reconfigure Approach to Entrance

In historic renovations, an existing entrance element, such as an approach walkway or path, may have a slope up to 1:6 for a run not to exceed 2 feet (UFAS 4.1.7(2)(a), page 14) but the requirement for level maneuvering space at the entrance door still exists. This exception to the general 1:12 ratio may be useful in modifications to historic buildings with moderate level changes at the entrance. Under certain circumstances other exceptions to the maximum slope of 1:12 may apply in facilities which are being altered (see Ramps for more detail).

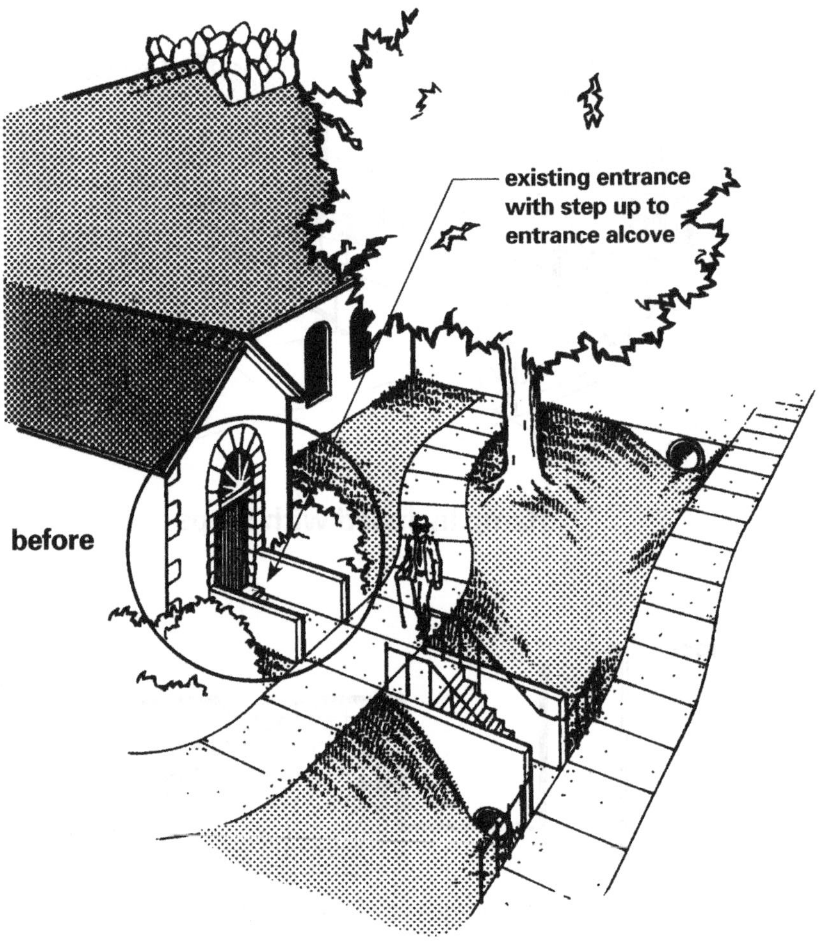

Use of Short Steep Ramp in Entrance Approach to Historic Property

Solution 4 Install Lift at Entrance

Often the existing site does not provide enough space for the installation of a ramp. If allowed by state or local codes, platform lifts may be installed to provide vertical access. Platform lifts are not a particularly reliable solution in high traffic areas where multiple users require assistance with vertical access.

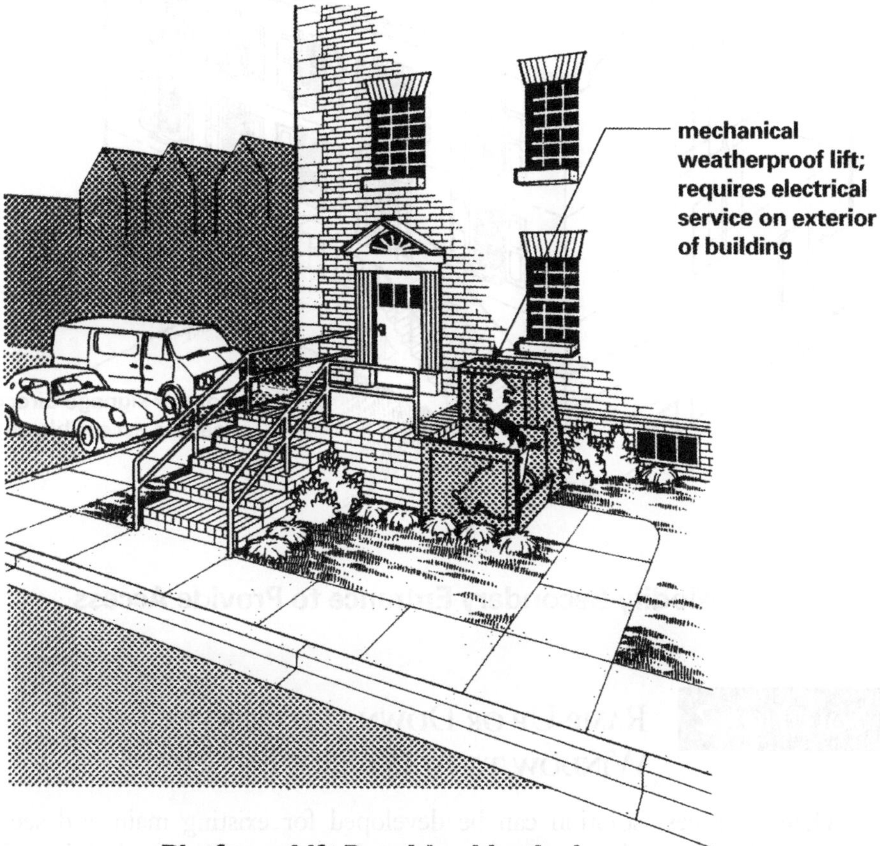

Platform Lift Provides Vertical Access When Space is Limited

Problem Not Possible to Provide Access at Main Entrance

Solution 1 Modify Secondary Entrance to Provide Access

When no access solution can be designed for the main entrance, then it is necessary to modify a secondary entrance for access. This entrance should provide easy access to all accessible interior spaces and amenities. When the principal entrance is inaccessible, directional signage should be placed such that it does not require "back tracking" by a person with a mobility impairment.

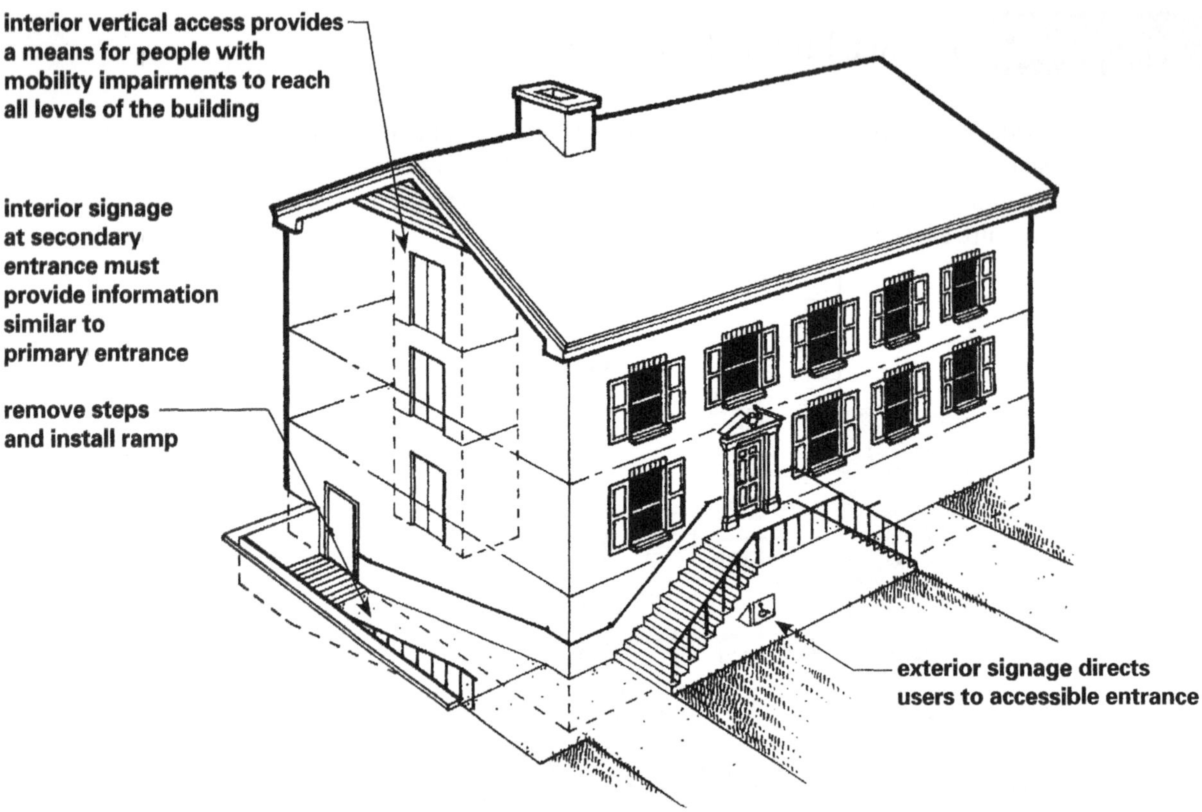

Modify Secondary Entrance to Provide Access

SOLUTION 2 RAMP UP OR DOWN AND CONVERT WINDOW TO ACCESSIBLE ENTRANCE

When no access solution can be developed for existing main and secondary entrances, then it may be necessary to create a new entrance to the building. This is frequently done by converting a window into a doorway. In some instances this can be accomplished using windows which are close to grade level in conjunction with a ramp to provide access to the new doorway.

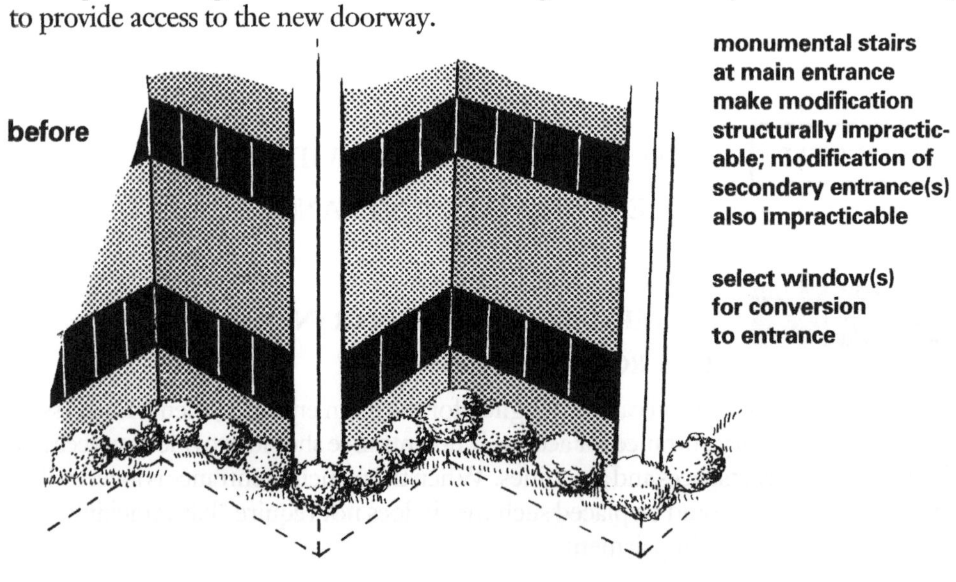

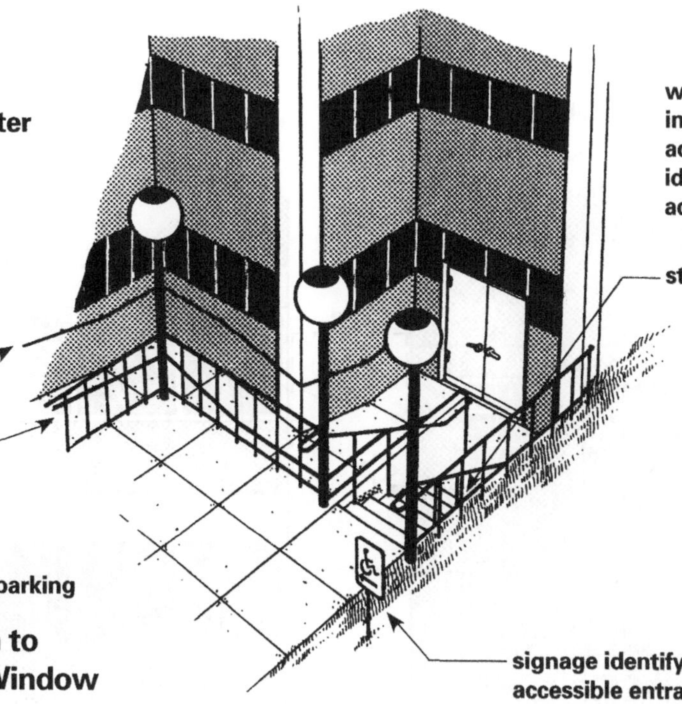

Ramp Down to Converted Window

SOLUTION 3 USE ELEVATOR IN ADJACENT BUILDING OR CONSTRUCT NEW TOWER

In some instances adjacent accessible buildings may be used to provide access to one or all levels of an inaccessible building. If two multi-story buildings are inaccessible it may be possible to construct a new tower with a dual door elevator which provides access to all floors in each building and includes a stop at grade level. This solution can also be used in single buildings (see Egress for more detail).

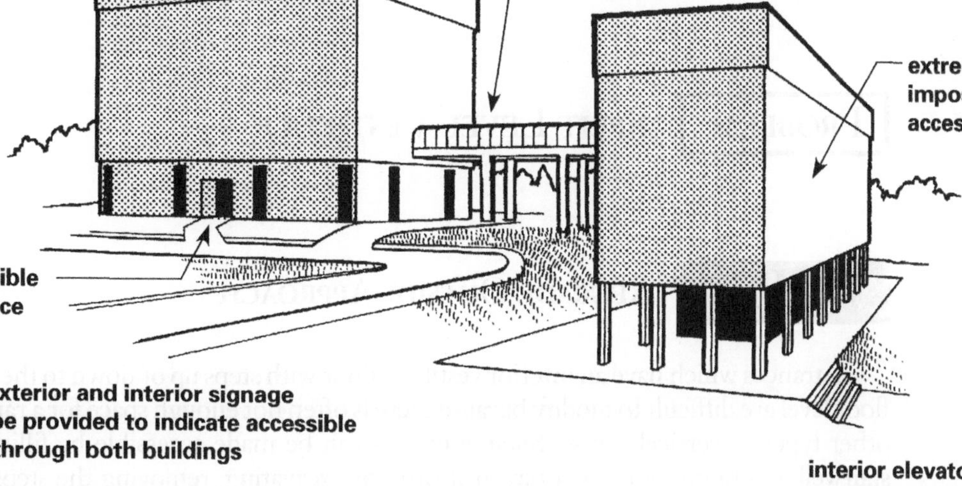

Elevator in Adjacent Building Provides Access

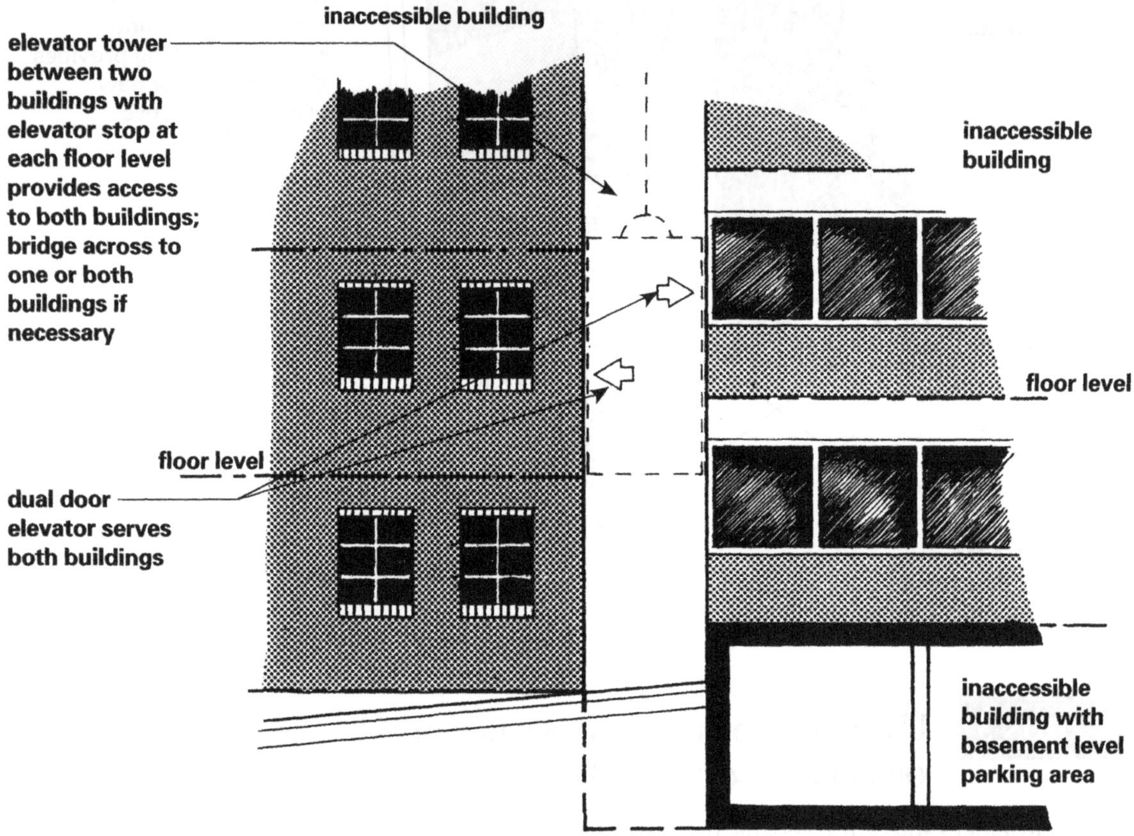

New Tower Provides Access to Two Buildings

PROBLEM — SPLIT LEVEL VESTIBULE

SOLUTION — REGRADE OUTSIDE APPROACH

Entrances which have an interior vestibule floor with steps up or down to the entry floor level are difficult to modify because there is often not enough space for a ramp or other types of vertical access. Such entrances can be made accessible by filling the stairwell and ramping up to a new platform; or excavating, removing the steps, and ramping down to a new platform.

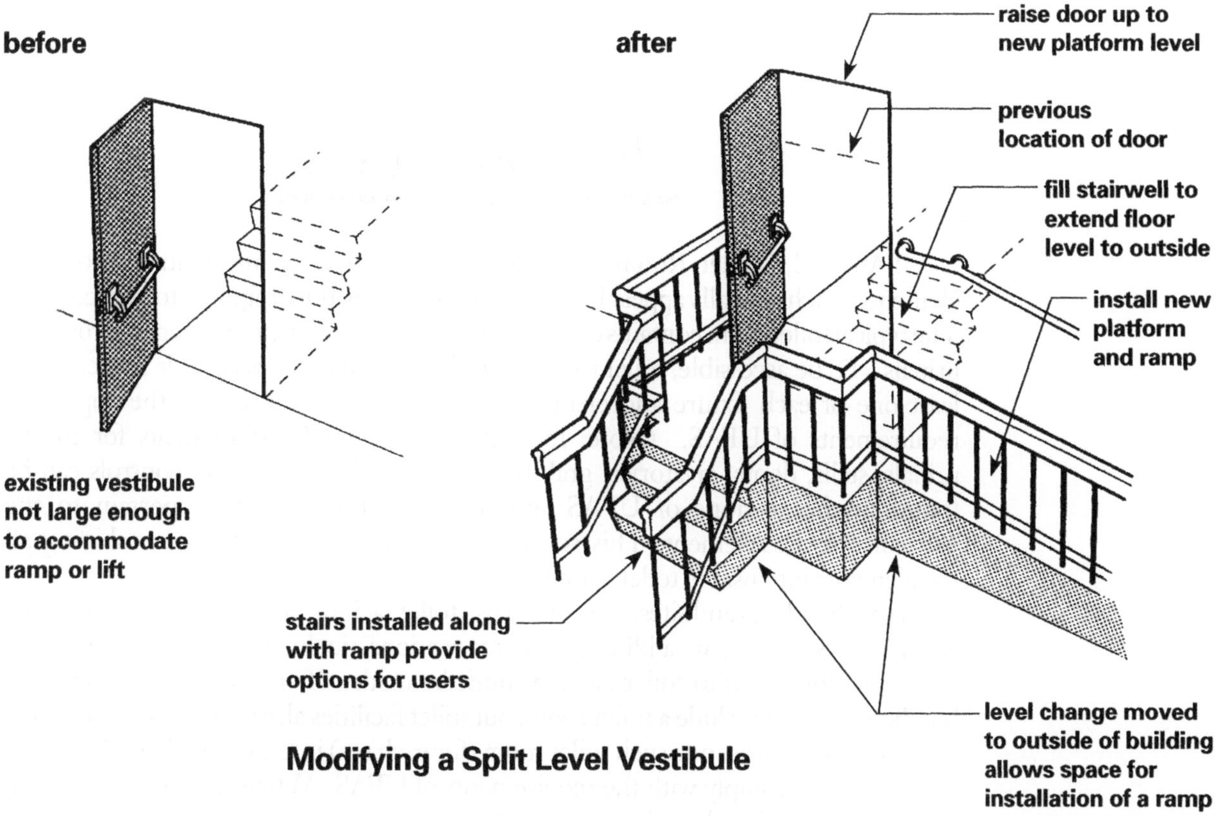

Modifying a Split Level Vestibule

REFERENCE INDEX TO UFAS DOCUMENT

ENTRANCES

Primary References	UFAS page	Secondary References	UFAS page
4.14.1 Minimum Number	36	**4.1.2(8) Scope & Technical Requirements**	6
		4.1.5(1) Additions	11
		4.1.6(3)(b) Alterations	12
		4.1.7 (2)(a & b) Historic Preservation	14
		4.3 Accessible Route	15
4.14.2 Service Entrances	36		

TOILET ROOMS

UFAS 4.22

Introduction

UFAS 4.22, Toilet Rooms, presents a compilation of information about the elements which typically appear in a toilet room and which are required to be accessible. The typical toilet room contains one or more lavatories, toilets, and, where appropriate, urinals. To be accessible, toilet rooms must be located on an accessible route, and at least one of each fixture and element provided must comply with the applicable requirements of UFAS. (Note: In-depth discussion of requirements for toilets, urinals, stalls, doors, lavatories, grab bars, mirrors, dispensers, and controls can be found in the sections of UFAS and the *Retrofit Guide* which pertain to the particular fixture/element. This section will focus on methods for combining all the elements into usable toilet rooms.)

In new buildings and sites, if common use toilet facilities are available, they must be accessible. Similarly, in additions and renovations (including historic structures), provisions for access to toilet facilities must be made. If an addition to an existing building does not include a toilet room, but toilet facilities already exist in the original building, then at least one such toilet room (for each sex) in the original building must be modified to comply with the requirements of UFAS. When retrofit construction involves substantial alteration, either one toilet room for each sex in the altered building or facility must comply, or at least one toilet room for each sex on each substantially altered floor must comply, whichever is greater. In alterations where it is not structurally practicable to modify the existing toilet facilities, a single accessible toilet room, usable by any person, may be added in the general location of the existing inaccessible toilets.

Basic Design Considerations

General Layout

The primary consideration in the layout of toilet rooms involves three aspects of maneuvering space requirements. The first space requirement concerns movement through the doorway and toilet room along an accessible route to gain access to specific elements such as toilets, lavatories, doors, and mirrors. The second space requirement concerns the clear floor space immediately surrounding the fixture/element which makes its use possible. The third space requirement is the provision of either a T-turn or 60 inch diameter space for the purpose of turning around. For instance, to ensure access to the toilet, UFAS provides specific requirements for an accessible route through the toilet room, an approach to the toilet stall, clear maneuvering space at the toilet fixture to facilitate transfers, and a turning space somewhere in the room to eliminate the need to back out. The accessible route, turning space, and maneuvering spaces at fixtures may overlap but should always be adjoining.

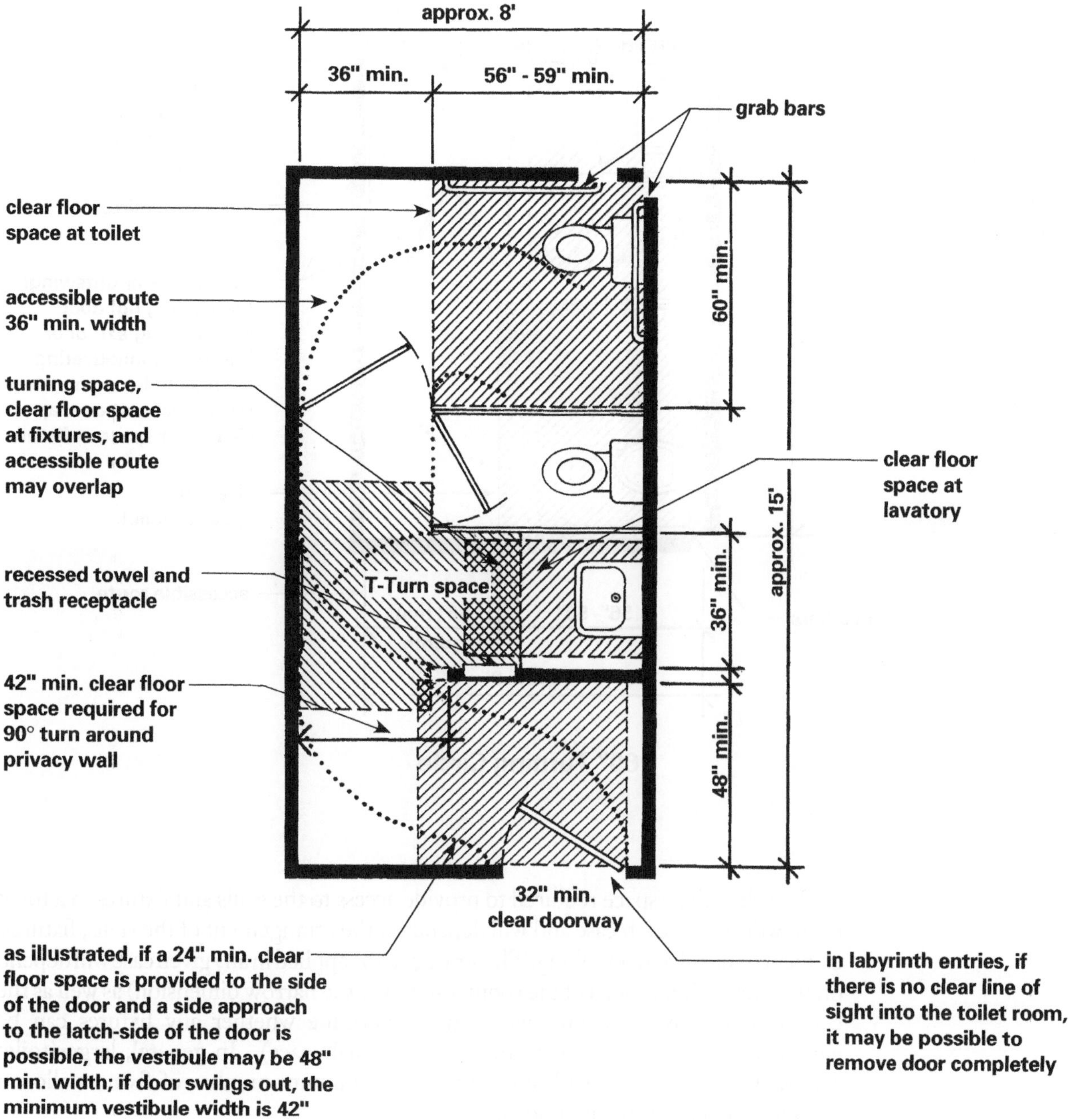

Toilet Room Showing Accessible Route, Turning Space, and Clear Floor Space at Fixtures

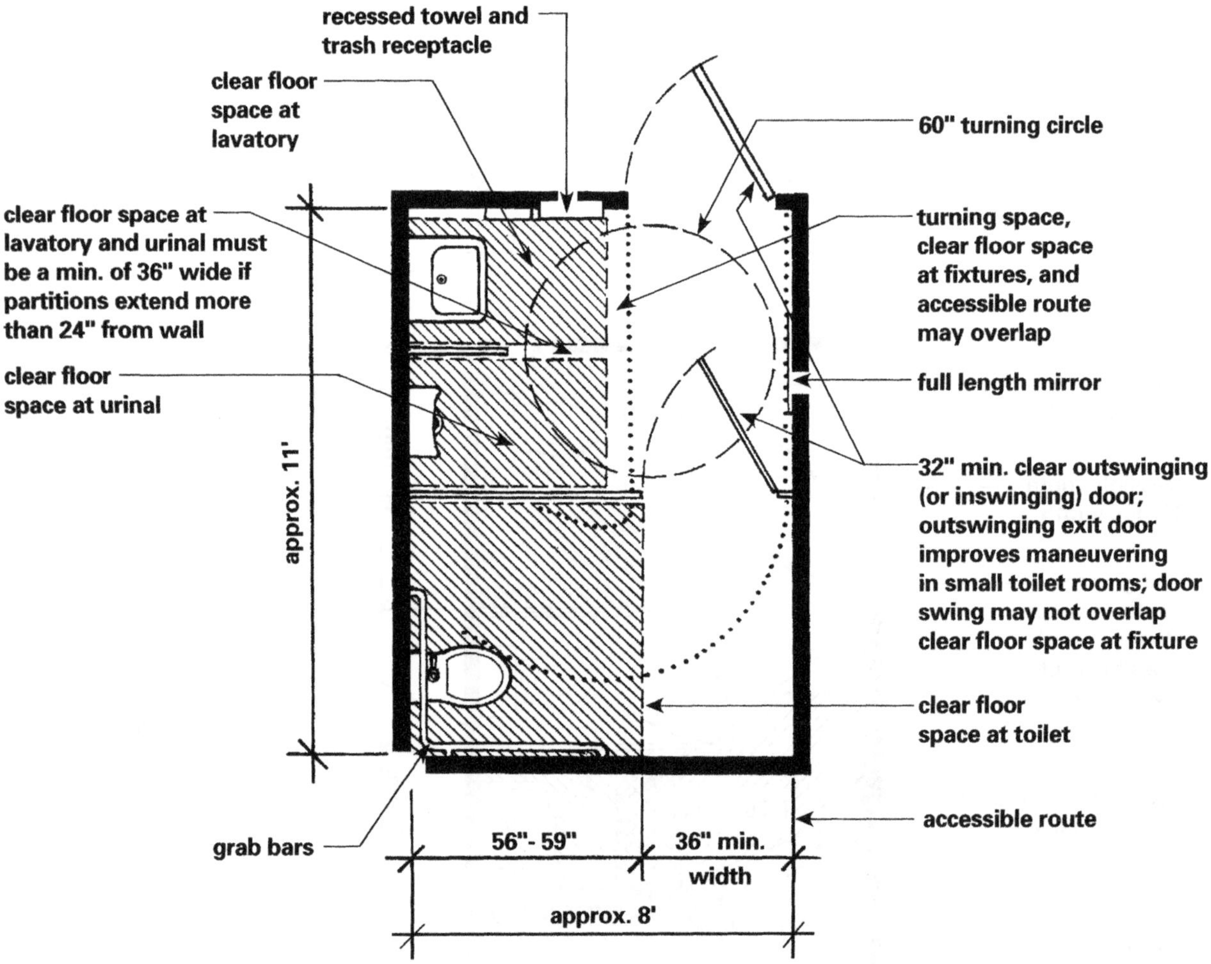

60" Turning Circle

The clear floor space required to provide access to the stalls and fixtures in a toilet room will vary in each case and will depend on the arrangement of the stalls, fixtures, elements, and related plumbing. The strategy to be applied in any given case will depend on the overall dimensions of the room (especially the narrow dimension) as well as the code required fixture count (which will determine whether any fixtures can be eliminated as part of a strategy to gain additional space). In general, larger toilet rooms and toilet rooms with more than the minimum number of fixtures allow a greater number of retrofit options.

PROBLEM INADEQUATE MANEUVERING SPACE LIMITS ACCESS TO FIXTURES

SOLUTION 1 REARRANGE, REMOVE, OR REPLACE ELEMENTS

Although wheelchair access to fixtures in a toilet room may not currently be provided, it is often possible to modify the existing space to provide access. Efficient use of the available space may involve a combination of many strategies, including reversing the swing of the door, moving or rehanging partitions, installing compact fixtures, and using recessed dispensers/receptacles. Even in small toilet rooms it is often possible to make significant improvements.

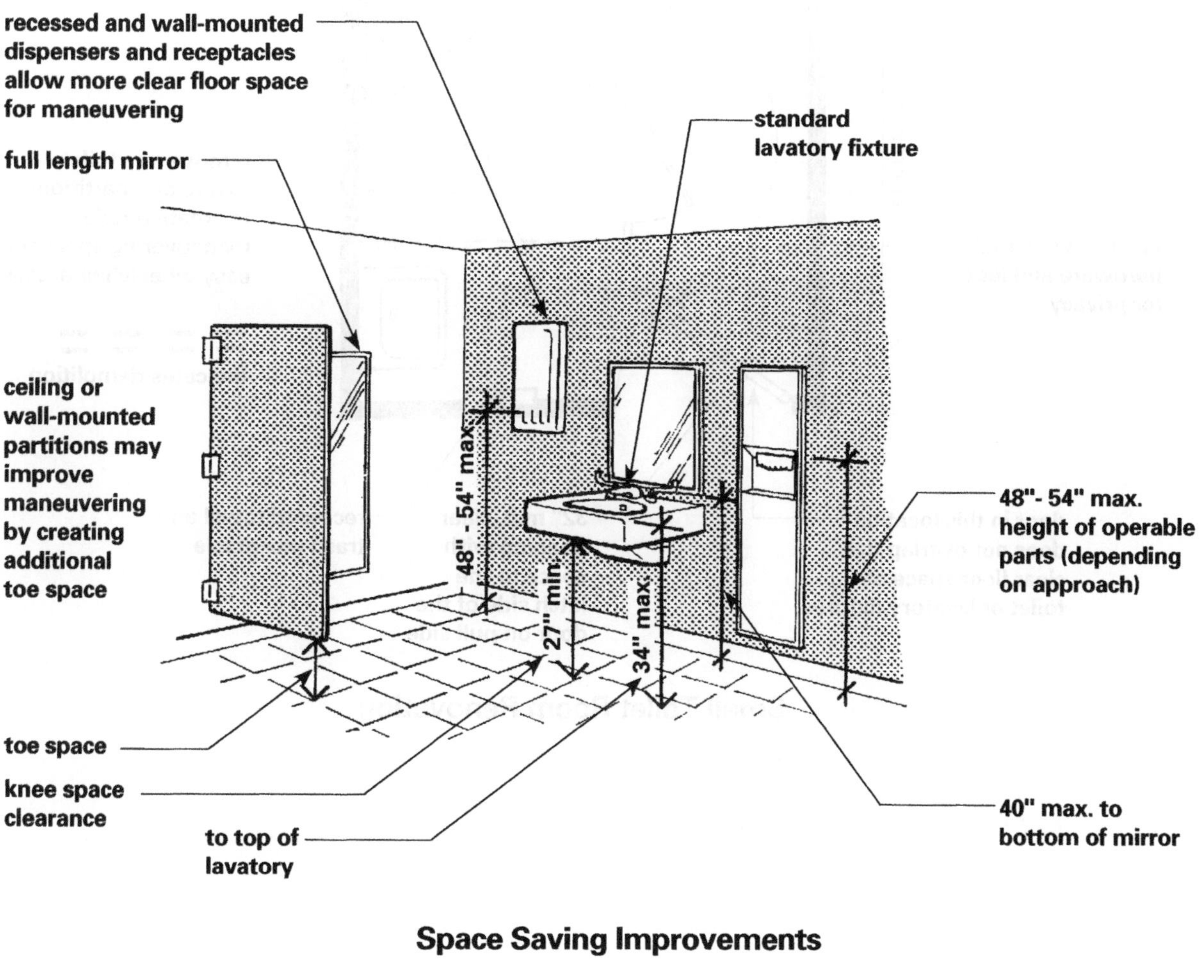

Space Saving Improvements

In most situations, provision of a UFAS 60 inch standard toilet stall is the most challenging issue. If the toilet room is wide enough (42 inches for an access aisle plus 56 inches or 59 inches for the UFAS standard toilet stall partition) to provide the necessary clear floor space and the number of toilets can be reduced by one, two existing toilet stalls can usually be converted into a single UFAS 60 inch standard stall. If access aisle space is limited, the two stalls at the end of the row can be converted into a single end-of-row standard stall. If renovation includes the removal of a fixture(s) it is important to maintain at least the code mandated minimum fixture count. In larger toilet rooms, it may be possible to maintain the fixture count by relocating one toilet and one lavatory.

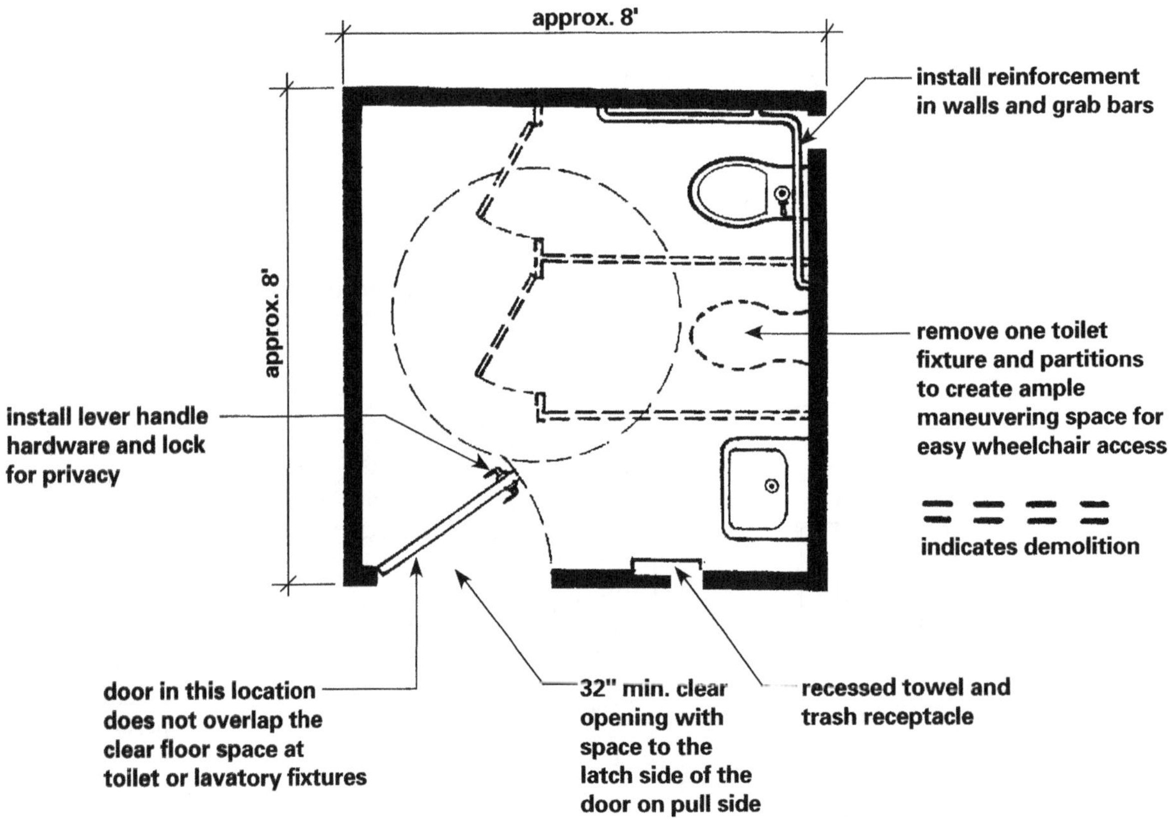

Small Toilet Room Renovation

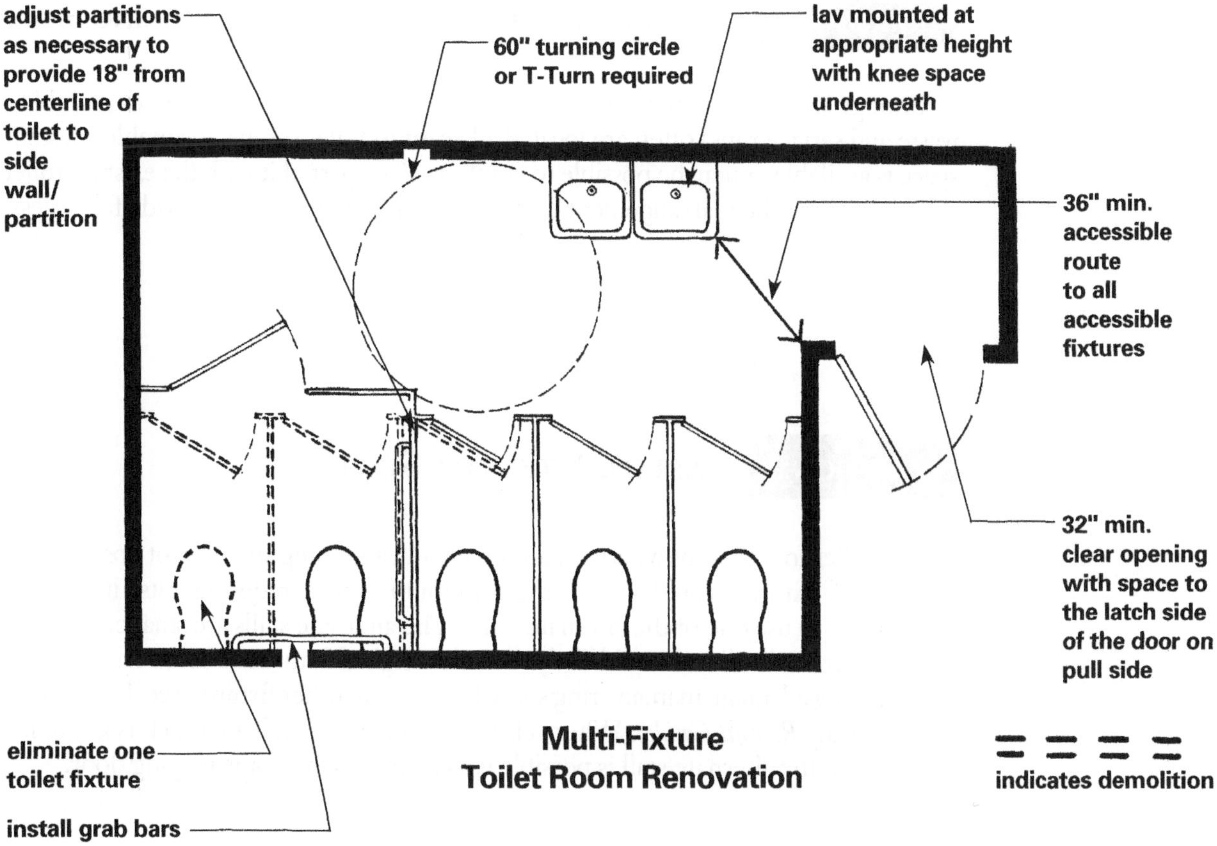

Multi-Fixture Toilet Room Renovation

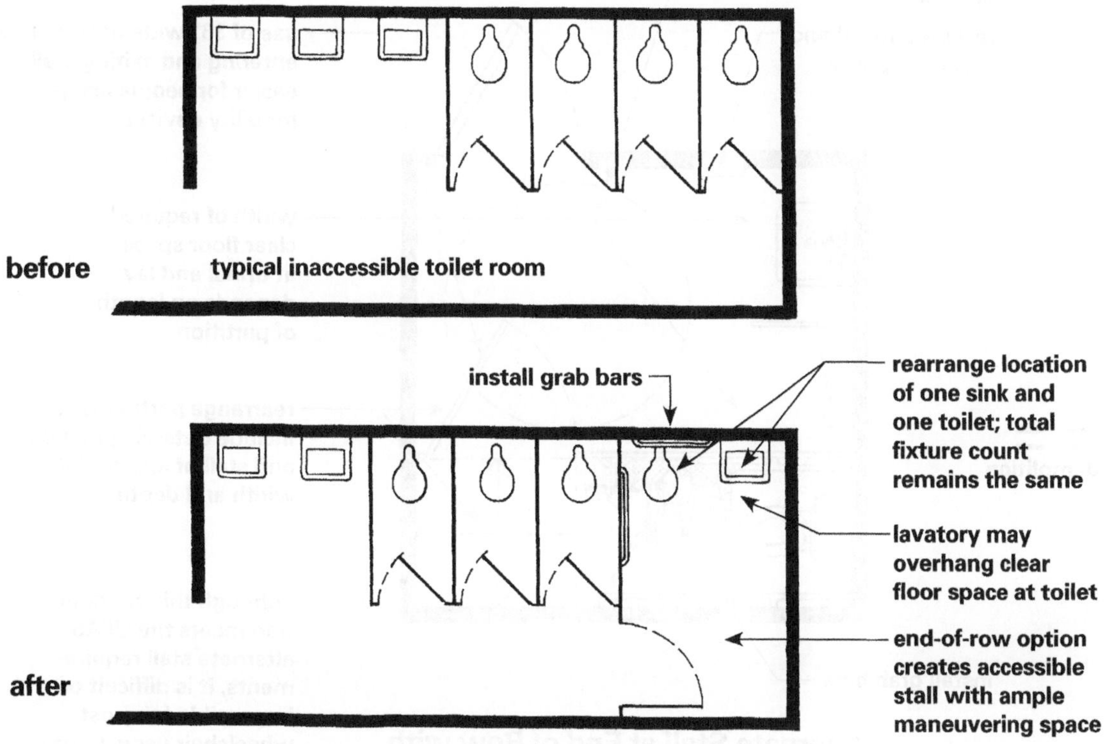

Multi-Fixture Toilet Room Renovation

SOLUTION 2 EXPAND TOILET ROOM INTO AN ADJOINING SPACE

Storage areas and janitors' closets (to take advantage of the shared use of plumbing waste and service runs) often are located adjacent to toilet rooms. If suitable adjacent space is available, it may be possible to combine all or part of it with the existing toilet room to permit the rearrangement of the toilet room fixtures and provide full access.

SOLUTION 3 INSTALL ALTERNATE STALL

In smaller toilet rooms where expansion into an adjoining space is not possible and removal of fixtures would violate the minimum fixture requirements, it may be appropriate to use one of the alternate stalls. The alternate stalls are smaller in width than the standard stall and would likely allow the original fixture count to be maintained while leaving adequate maneuvering space for access to other fixtures (see Toilet Stalls section of the *Retrofit Guide*). Where clear floor space for stall approach is limited, a variation on the alternate stall is possible using a full 36 inch outswinging door.

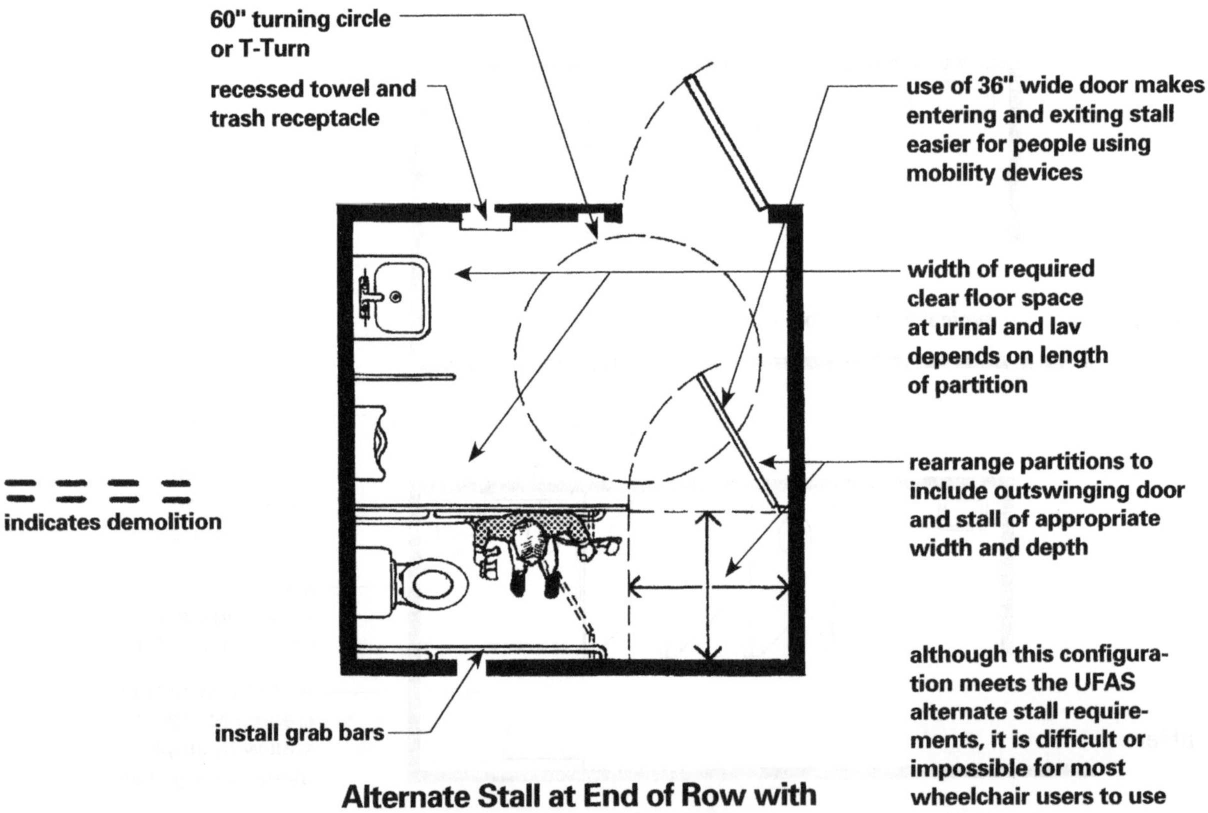

Alternate Stall at End of Row with 36 Inch Outswinging Door

PRACTICAL PLUS

The 60 inch wide standard stall and 36 inch wide alternate stall are designed to serve the needs of people with different abilities. The 60 inch stall is best for wheelchair users because of its additional maneuvering space and the 36 inch stall is best for people who have difficulty walking, being seated, and standing from a seated position. For this reason, it is best if a group toilet room includes both types of stalls.

before

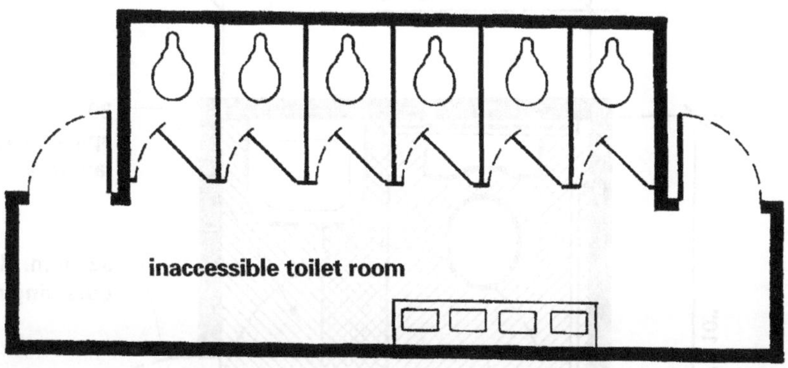

after

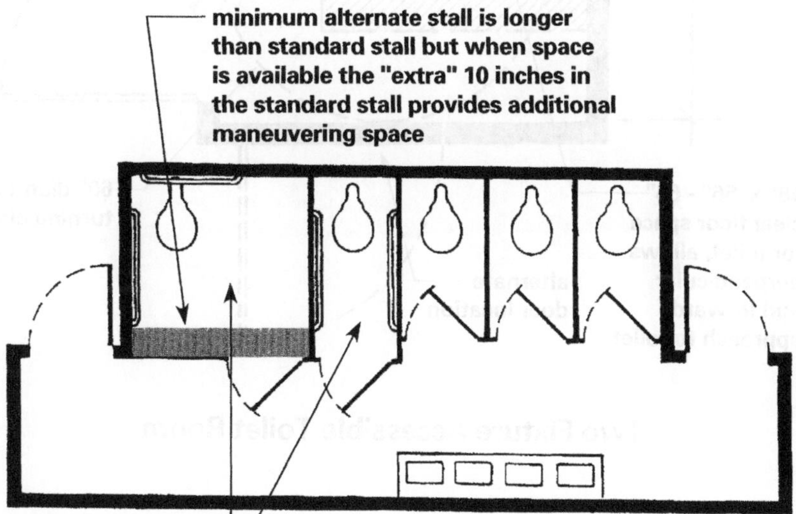

Include Both Standard and Alternate Stalls When Possible

SOLUTION 4 ACCESSIBLE TOILET ROOM OR UNISEX TOILET IN ALTERNATE LOCATION

When it is not practical to modify the existing toilet rooms, the best solution may be to install an accessible single-fixture toilet room or "unisex" toilet room in a nearby location. These toilet rooms are a functional alternative and often provide the best option for many people with disabilities. These toilet rooms are generally easier to use for both disabled people who require attendant help (especially when attendants and/ or spouses are of the opposite sex) and parents who must assist small children with toileting activities. The location of these toilet rooms should be clearly identified with appropriate signage.

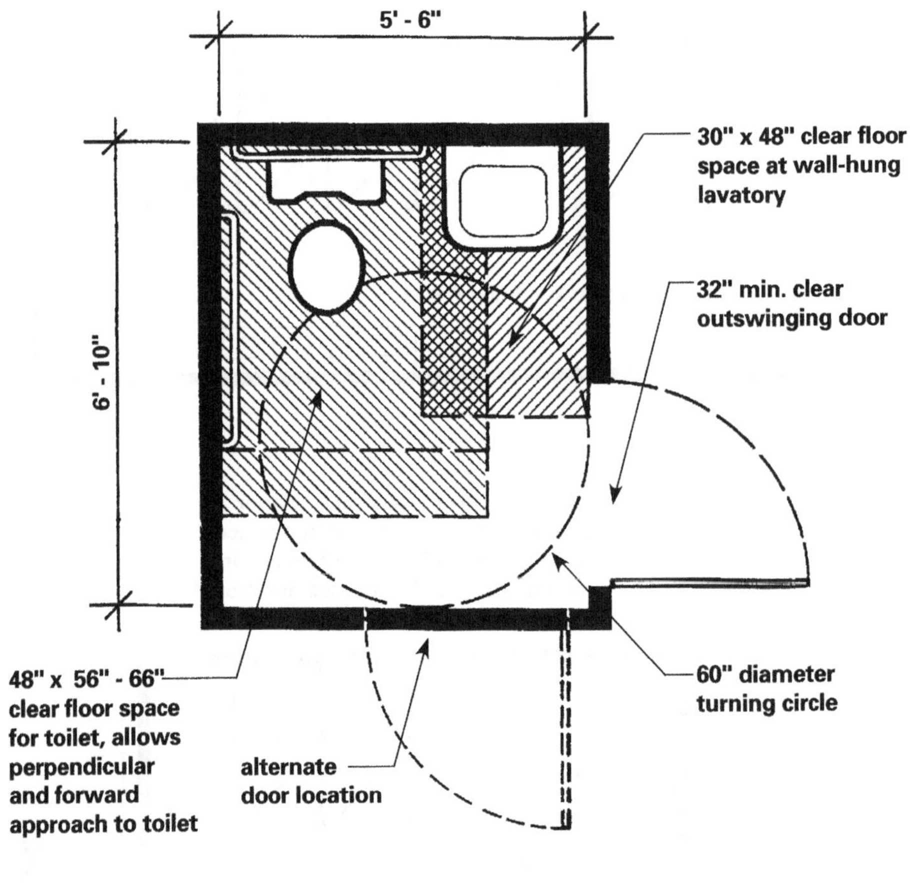

Two Fixture Accessible Toilet Room

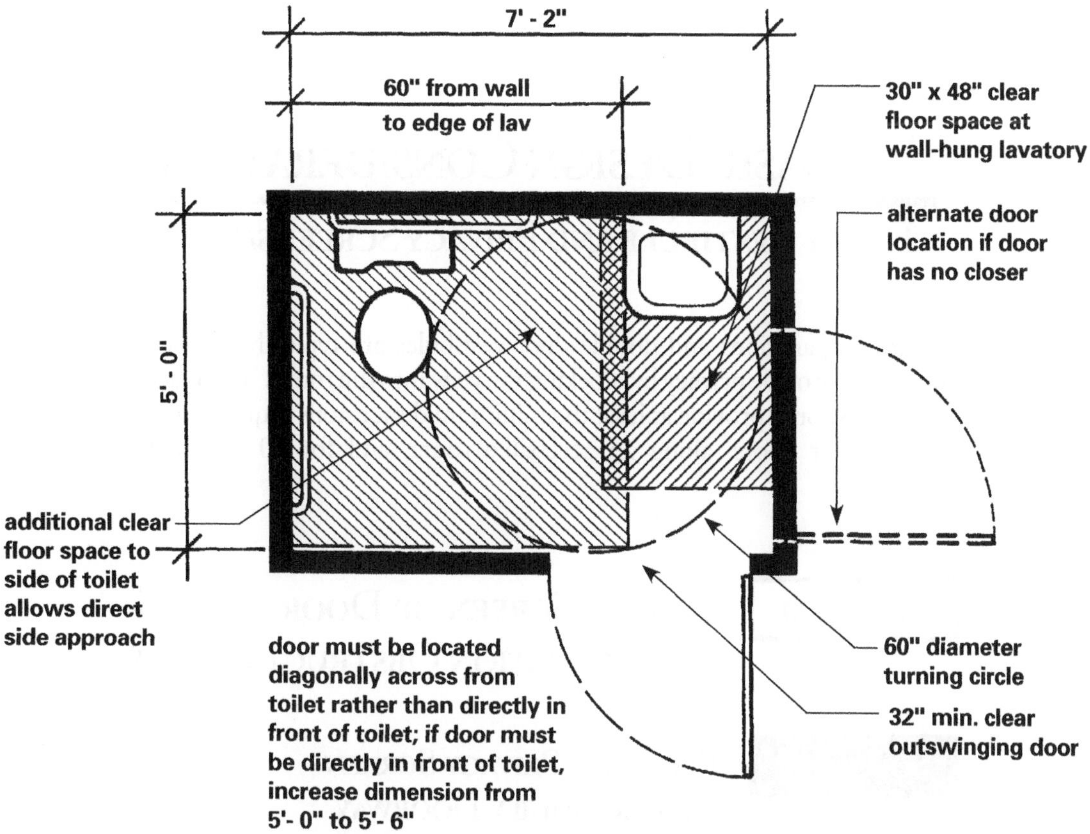

Two Fixture Accessible Toilet Room

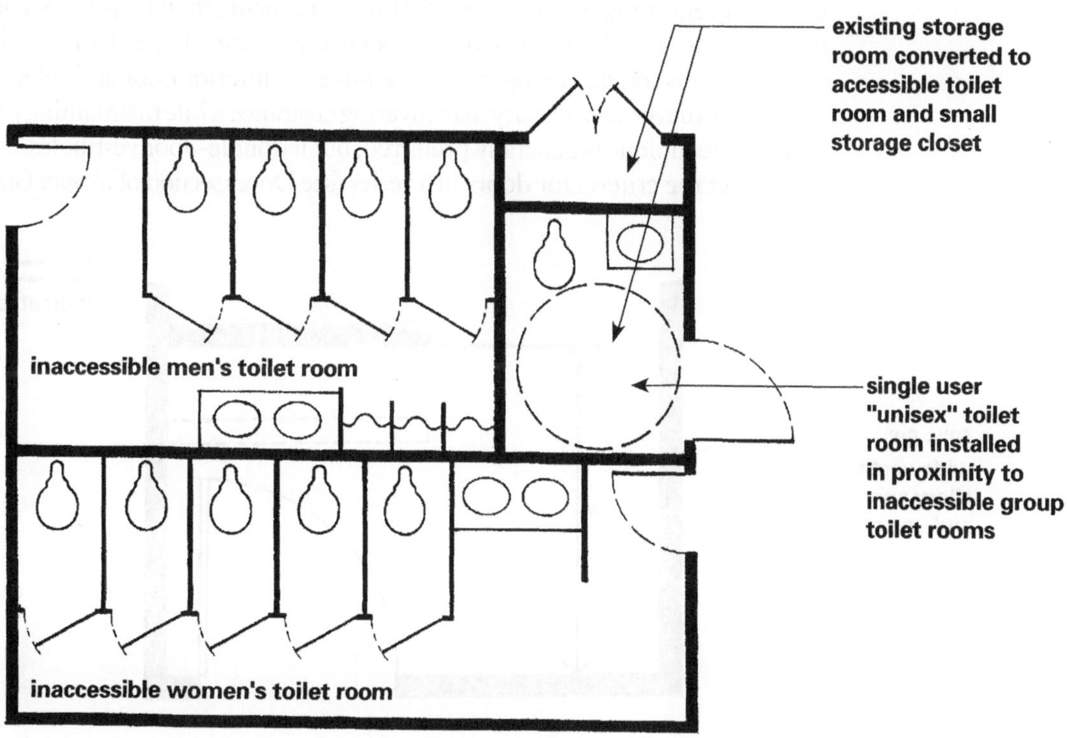

Unisex Accessible Toilet Room

BASIC DESIGN CONSIDERATIONS

ENTRY VESTIBULE AND PRIVACY SCREENS/PARTITIONS

Screens/partitions and double-door vestibules are typically used in public toilet facilities to provide privacy by blocking the view into the room. The placement of such partitions should provide at least the minimum dimensions required for maneuvering clearances at doors, along an accessible route, and for 90 degree turns around obstructions.

PROBLEM PRIVACY SCREEN OR DOOR CONFIGURATION OBSTRUCTS ENTRY

SOLUTION RELOCATE PRIVACY SCREEN AND/OR MODIFY DOORWAY

It may be possible to obtain the needed maneuvering clearances at toilet room entries by relocating privacy screen partitions, reducing their length, and/or modifying the doorway by relocating it or reversing the swing of the door. At double-door vestibules, it is sometimes possible to remove the interior door and relocate a privacy screen to achieve the necessary maneuvering clearance while maintaining privacy. This labyrinth technique is generally preferred, but if double-door vestibules are used they must meet the criteria for doors in a series (see Doors section of *Retrofit Guide*).

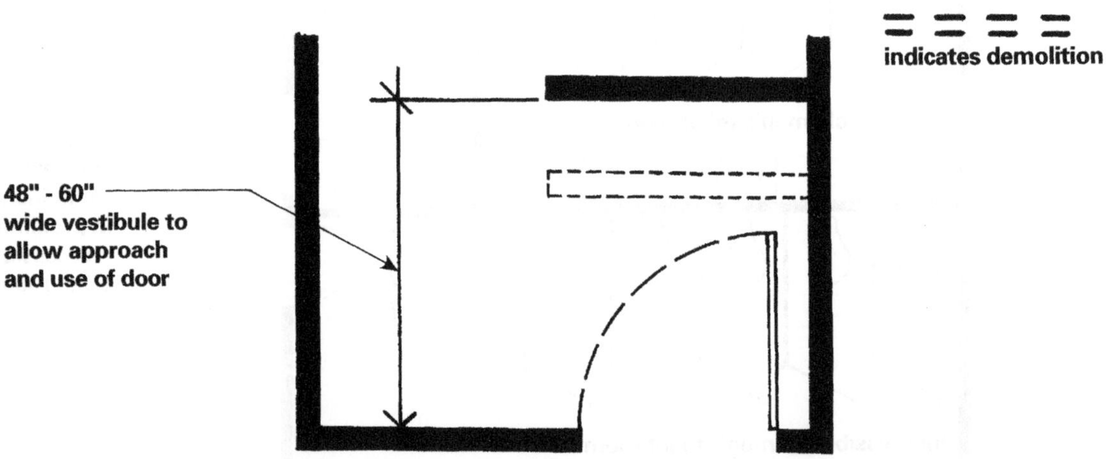

Move Partition to Provide Clear Floor Space at Door

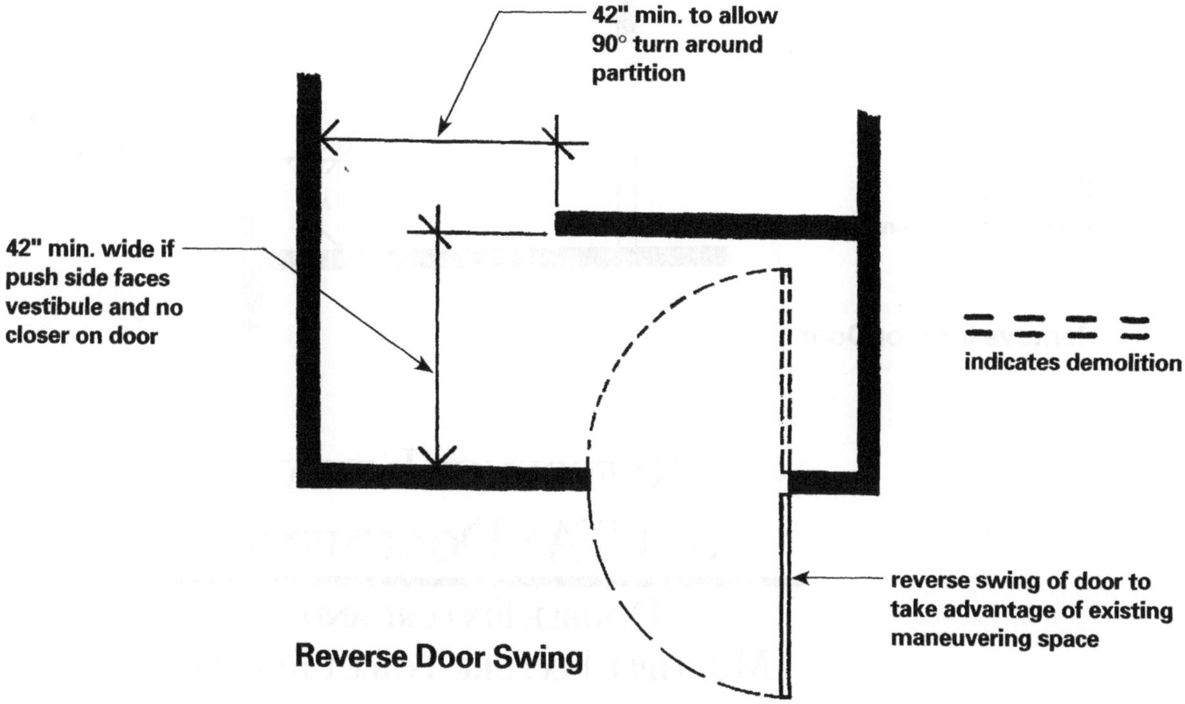

Reverse Door Swing

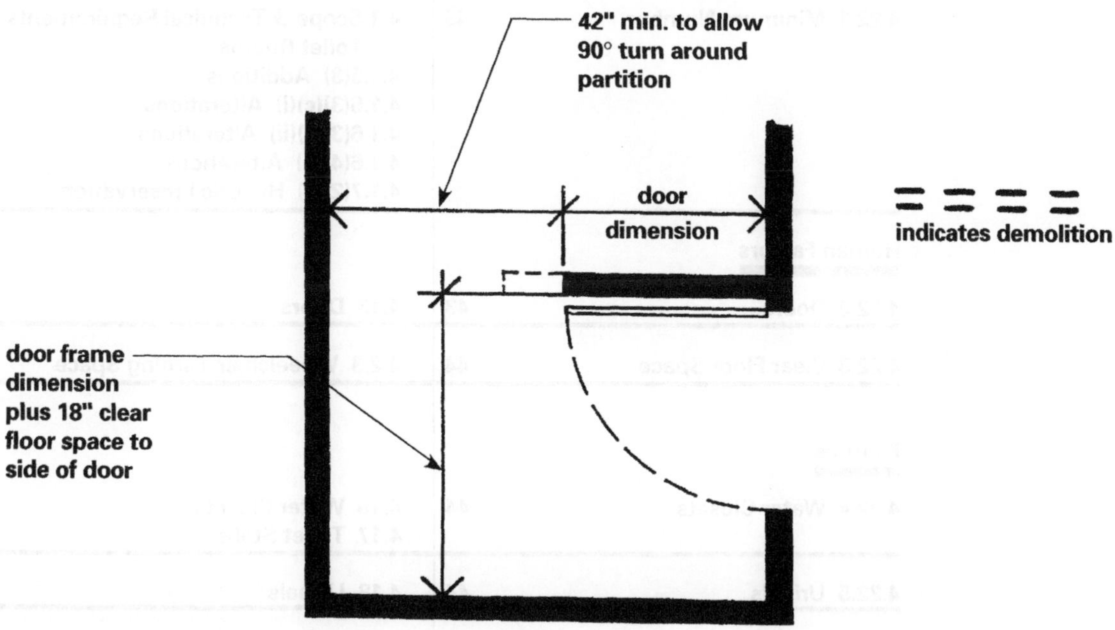

Shorten Partition to Allow 90° Turn Around Obstruction

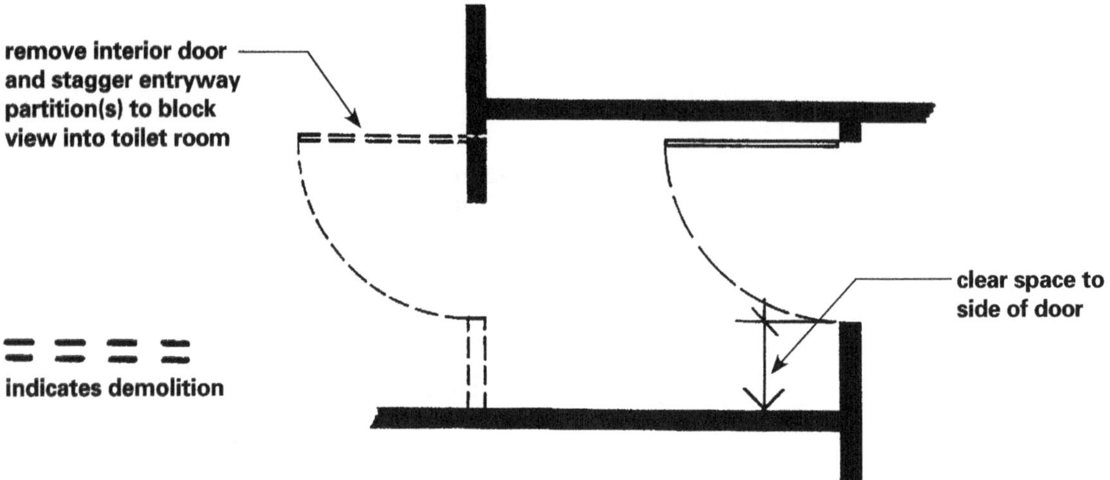

Remove Interior Door

Reference Index to UFAS Document

Double Fixture and Multiple Fixture Toilet Rooms

Primary References	UFAS page	Secondary References	UFAS page
Stall Types/Location			
4.22.1 Minimum Number	43	4.1 Scope & Technical Requirements for Toilet Rooms	5-6
		4.1.5(3) Additions	11
		4.1.6(3)(c)(i) Alterations	12
		4.1.6(3)(c)(ii) Alterations	12
		4.1.6(4)(e) Alterations	13
		4.1.7(2)(c) Historic Preservation	14
Human Factors			
4.22.2 Doors	43	4.13 Doors	33
4.22.3 Clear Floor Space	44	4.2.3 Wheelchair Turning Space	14
Fixtures			
4.22.4 Water Closets	44	4.16 Water Closets	37
		4.17 Toilet Stalls	38
4.22.5 Urinals	44	4.18 Urinals	40
4.22.6 Lavatories and Mirrors	44	4.19 Lavatories and Mirrors	40
4.22.7 Controls and Dispensers	44	4.27 Controls and Dispensers	45

BATH/SHOWER FACILITIES

UFAS 4.23

INTRODUCTION

Similar to the UFAS section on Toilet Rooms, UFAS Section 4.23, Bathrooms, Bathing Facilities, and Shower Rooms, presents a compilation of information about the elements and fixtures which typically appear in bathing/shower facilities and which are required to be accessible. A bathing/shower facility contains one or more showers or bathtubs, and often contains additional fixtures typically found in toilet rooms including lavatories, toilets, and urinals. To be considered accessible under the UFAS requirements, a bathing/shower facility must be located on an accessible route, and at least one bathtub or shower, and one each of all other fixtures/elements provided must comply with the applicable requirements of UFAS. (Note: In-depth discussion of requirements for toilets, urinals, stalls, doors, lavatories, grab bars, mirrors, dispensers, and controls can be found in the sections of UFAS and the *Retrofit Guide* which pertain to the particular fixture/element. This section will focus on methods for combining all the elements into universally usable bathing/shower facilities.)

In new buildings and sites, if common-use bathing/shower facilities are available, they must be accessible. Similarly, in additions and renovations (including historic structures), provisions for access to bathing/shower facilities must be made. If an addition to an existing building does not include a bathing/shower room, but bathing/shower facilities already exist in the original building, then at least one such bathing/shower room (for each sex) in the original building must be modified to comply with the requirements of UFAS. When retrofit construction involves substantial alteration, either one bathing/shower room for each sex in the altered building or facility must comply, or at least one bathing/shower room for each sex on each substantially altered floor must comply, whichever is greater. In alterations where it is not structurally practicable to modify the existing bathing/shower facilities, a single user, "unisex" bathing/shower facility may be included near the existing facilities.

BASIC DESIGN CONSIDERATIONS

GENERAL LAYOUT

As described in detail in the previous section on Toilet Rooms, the primary consideration in the layout of both toilet facilities and bathing/shower facilities involves three distinct but related aspects of maneuvering space requirements. The user must first be able to gain access to specific elements such as bathtubs, showers, toilets, lavatories, doors, and other elements by moving along an accessible route. Second, in order to be usable, each individual fixture/feature must have the required clear floor space which is adjacent to or overlapping the accessible route. Third, either a T-turn or 60 inch diameter space must be included in the room to allow users to turn around.

UFAS (1984) includes an exception to the turning space requirement for bathrooms/shower rooms with only one bathtub or shower, one toilet, and one lavatory; a 30 inch by 60 inch clear floor space may be used in lieu of unobstructed turning space. The three types of maneuvering spaces, the accessible route, the turning space, and the clear floor spaces at fixtures may overlap.

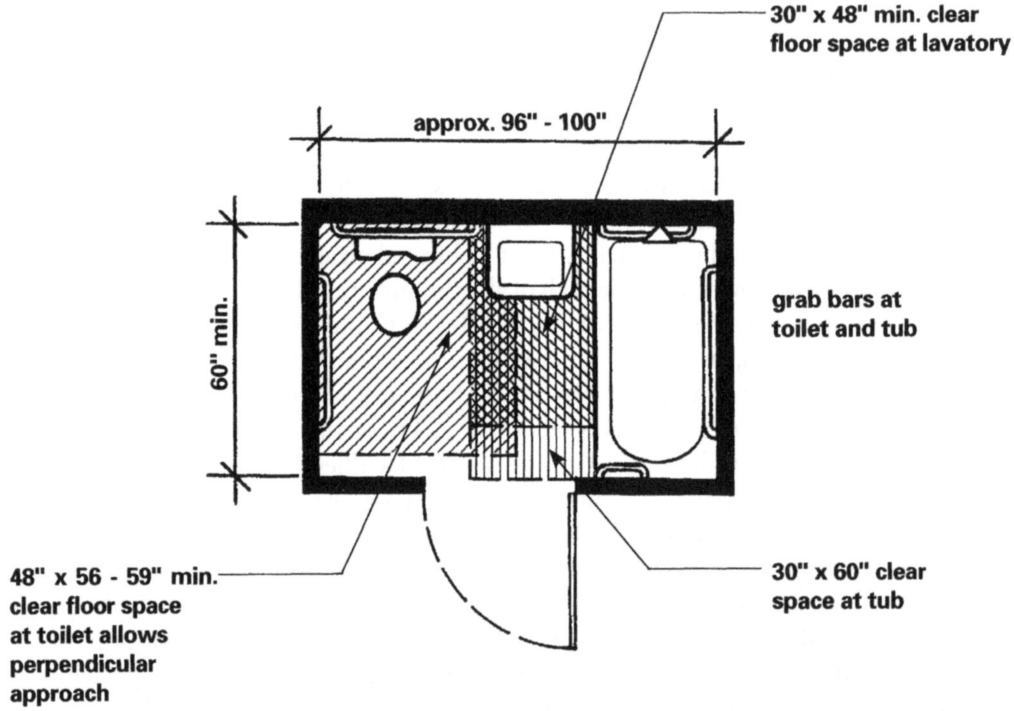

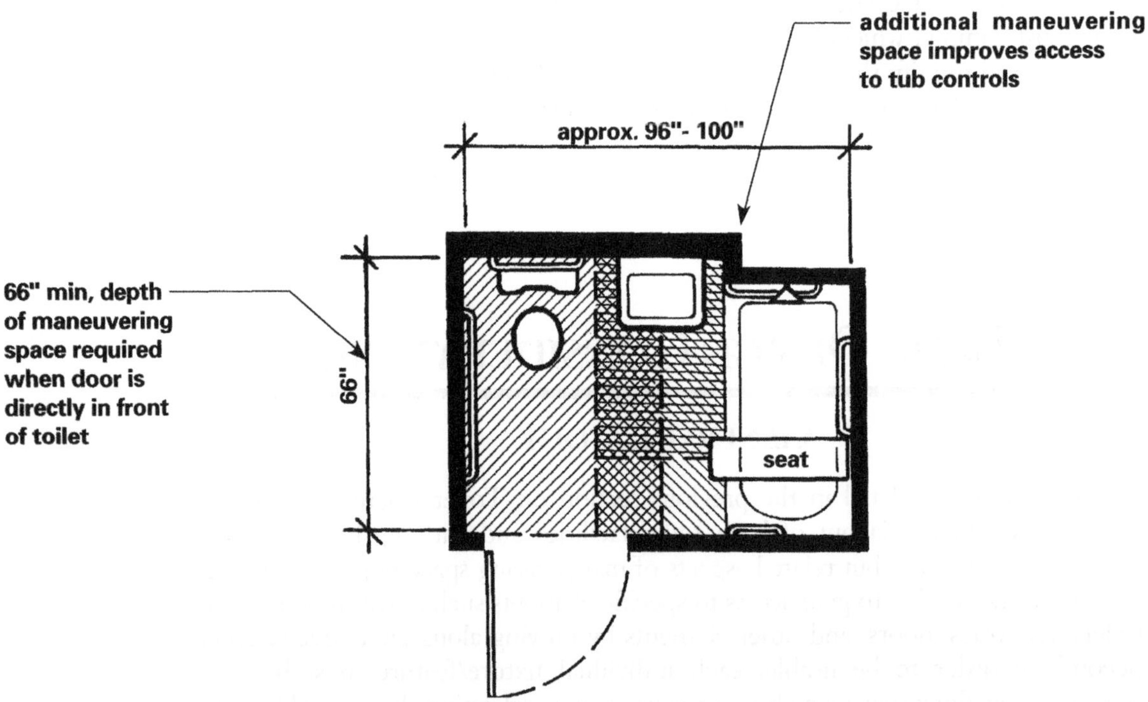

Single User Bathroom with Tub, Toilet, and Lavatory

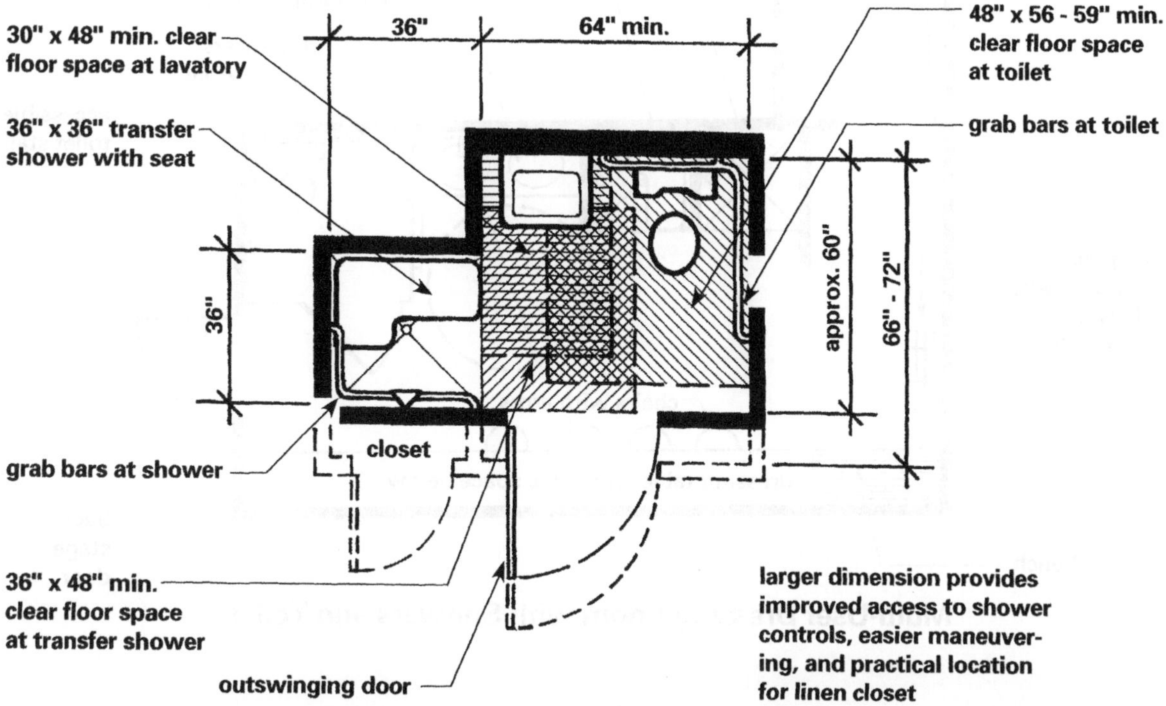

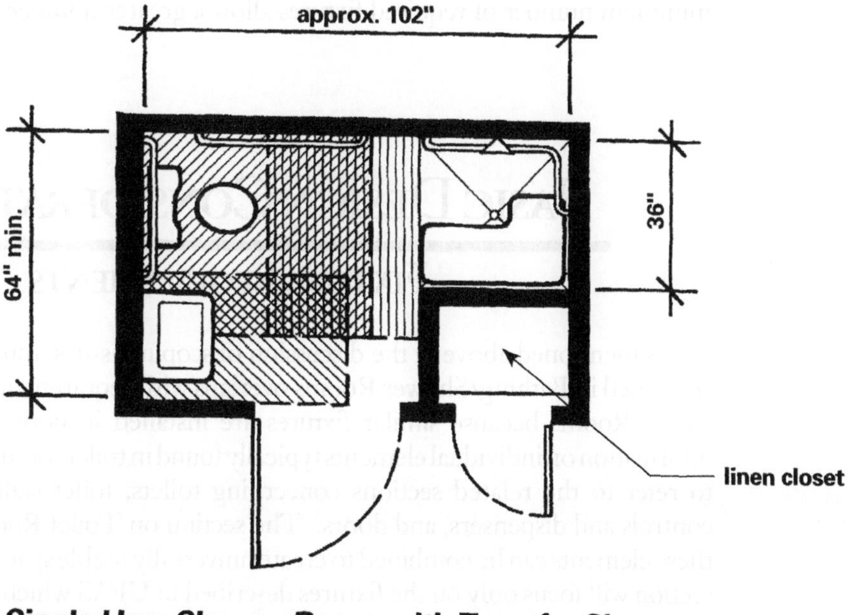

Single User Shower Room with Transfer Shower

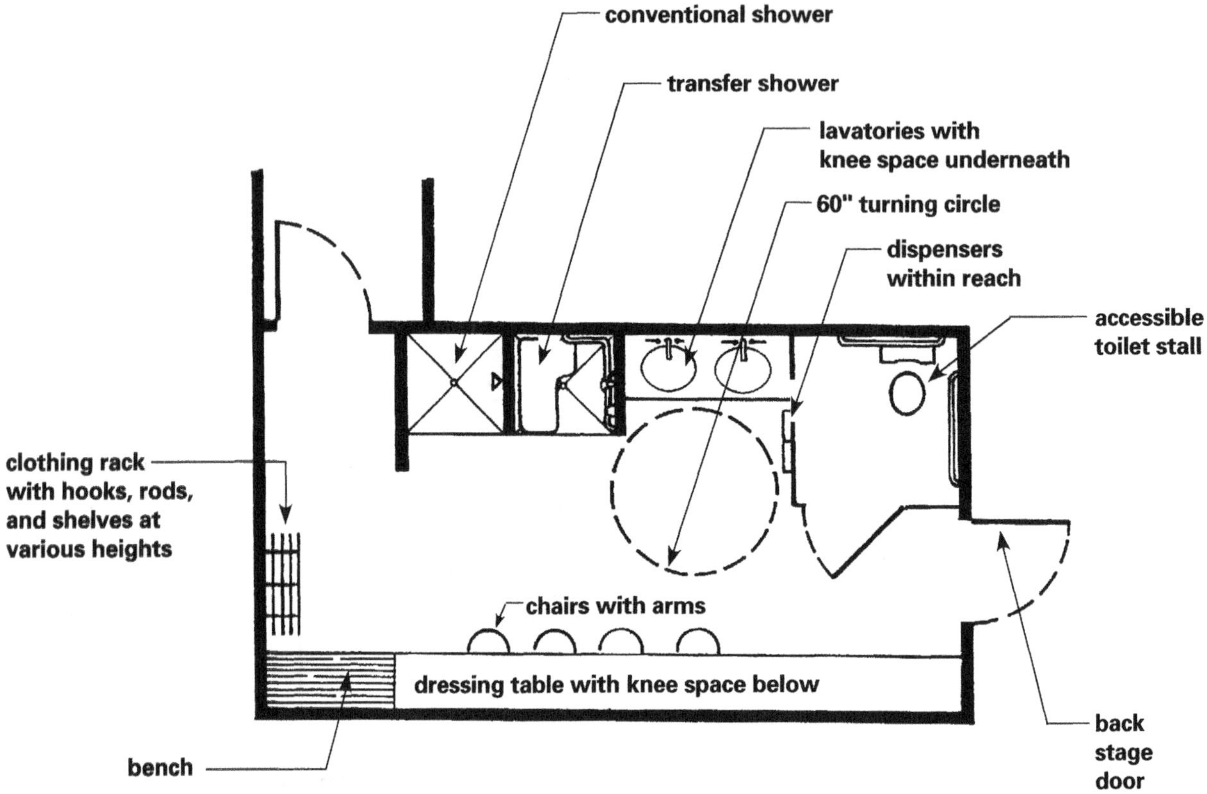

Multi-User Dressing Room with Showers and Toilet

Unless total demolition is planned, the existing arrangement of the fixtures, elements, and related plumbing will tend to dictate the range of possible options available in any retrofit situation As with toilet rooms, the strategy to be applied in any given case will depend on the overall dimensions of the room as well as the required fixture count. For these reasons, larger bathing/shower facilities with more than the minimum number of required fixtures allow a greater number of retrofit options.

BASIC DESIGN CONSIDERATIONS

FIXTURE REQUIREMENTS

As mentioned above in the discussion of scoping issues, much of the information contained in Bathing/Shower Rooms overlaps with requirements described earlier in Toilet Rooms because similar fixtures are installed in both spaces. For detailed information on individual elements typically found in toilet rooms, the user is requested to refer to the related sections concerning toilets, toilet stalls, urinals, lavatories, controls and dispensers, and doors. The section on Toilet Rooms describes how all these elements can be combined to create universally usable spaces. For simplicity, this section will focus only on the fixtures described in UFAS which are typically found in bathrooms and include bathtubs, showers, and medicine cabinets.

Bathtubs and Showers. UFAS requires that if bathtubs or showers are provided then at least one bathtub or one shower must be accessible. It is important to note that some state codes are more stringent than UFAS and require both an accessible bathtub and shower if both are provided. The selection of which type(s) of fixtures to include will depend on the needs of the users.

Medicine Cabinets. UFAS requires that if medicine cabinets are provided, at least one shall be located with a usable shelf no higher than 44 inches above the floor. Floor space which meets the requirements of 4.2.4 Clear Floor or Ground Space for Wheelchairs must also be included to ensure that the storage space is accessible to wheelchair users. Other more functional alternatives for bathing/shower room storage should be considered. Many disabled people have considerable amounts of medical and personal care items which need to be stored in or near the bathing/shower room. Shelves, drawers, and floor mounted cabinets can be designed to provide adequate and accessible storage for these items.

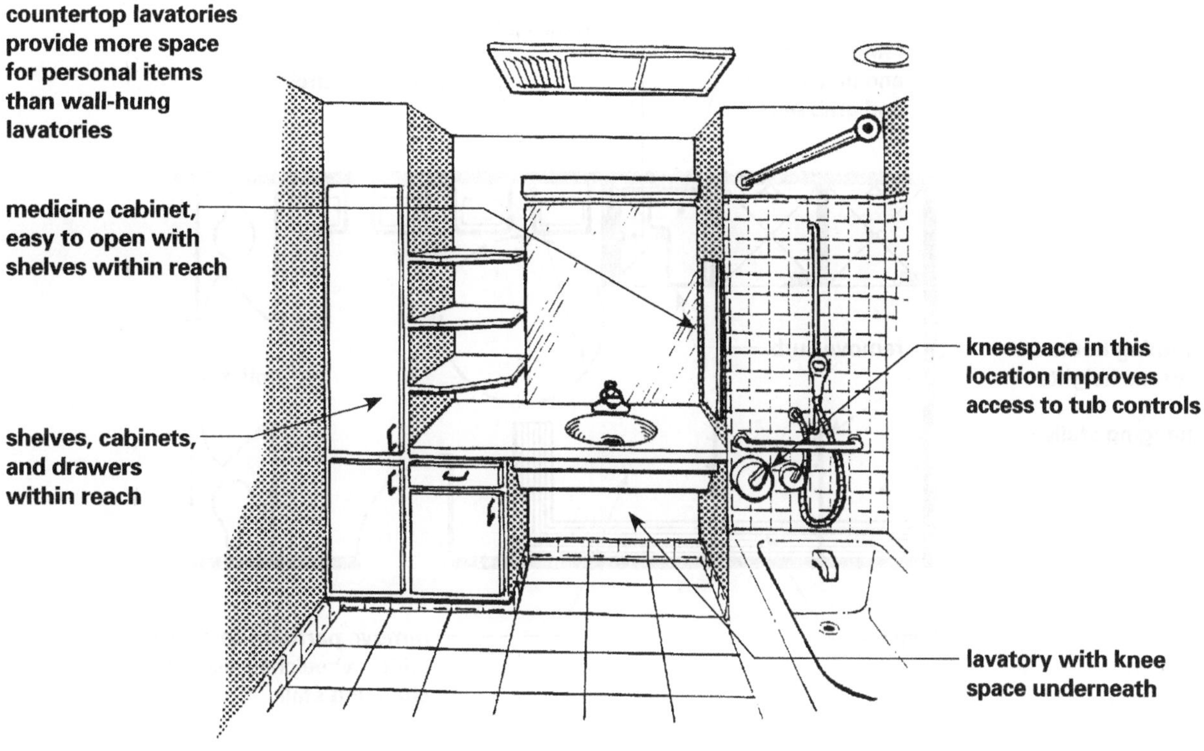

Storage Options for Bathing/Shower Rooms

PROBLEM ACCESSIBLE BATHTUB OR SHOWER NOT PROVIDED

SOLUTION 1 REARRANGE, REMOVE, OR REPLACE FIXTURES

It is often possible to modify the existing space to provide access to fixtures in a bathing/shower room. Efficient use of the available space may involve a combination of many strategies including reversing the swing of, or removing an entry or shower enclosure door, moving or rehanging partitions, relocating fixtures, and reinstalling fixtures so that the required clear floor spaces overlap.

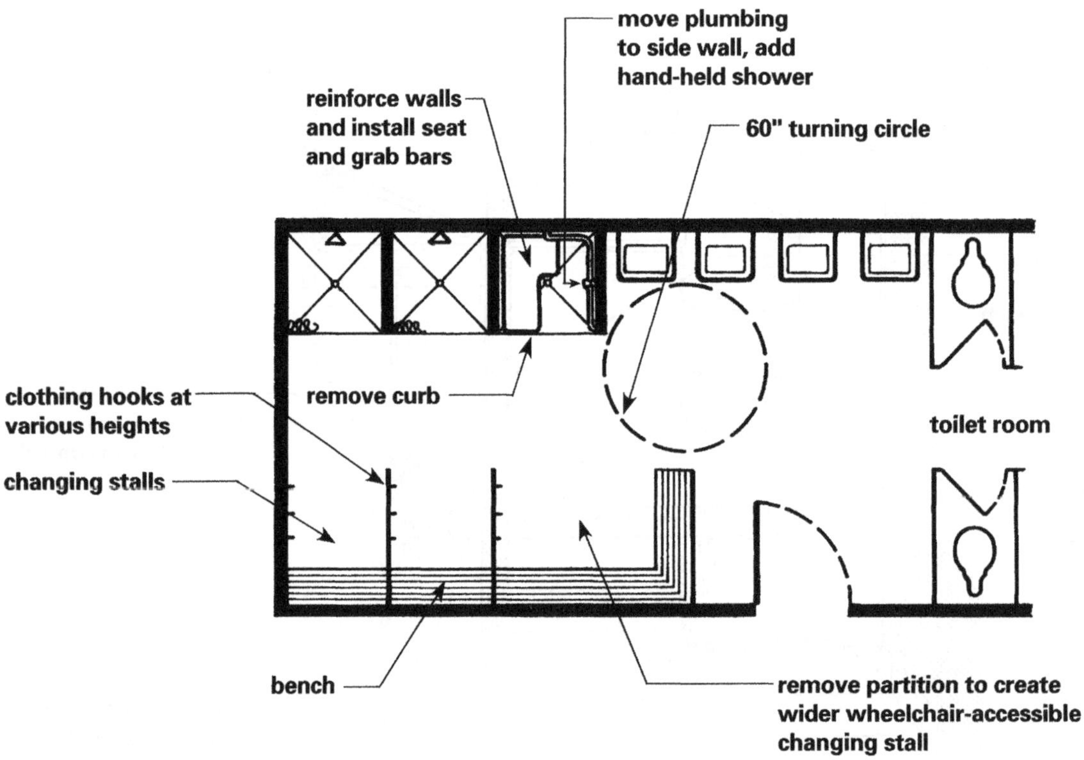

Conventional Shower Stall Replaced with Transfer Shower

before

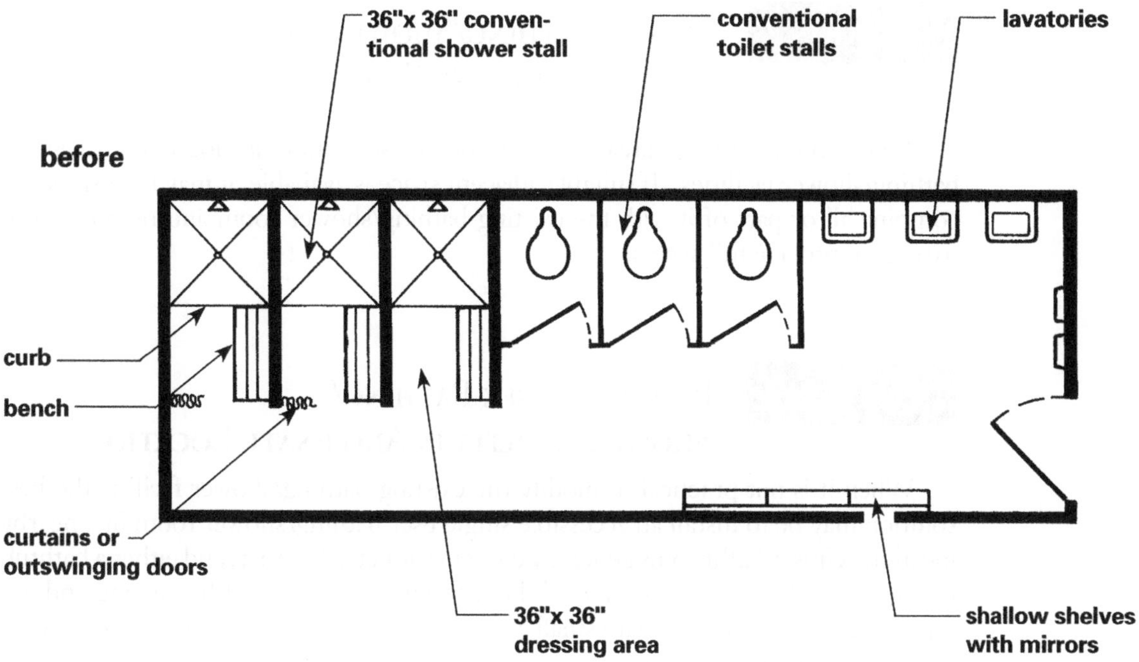

after

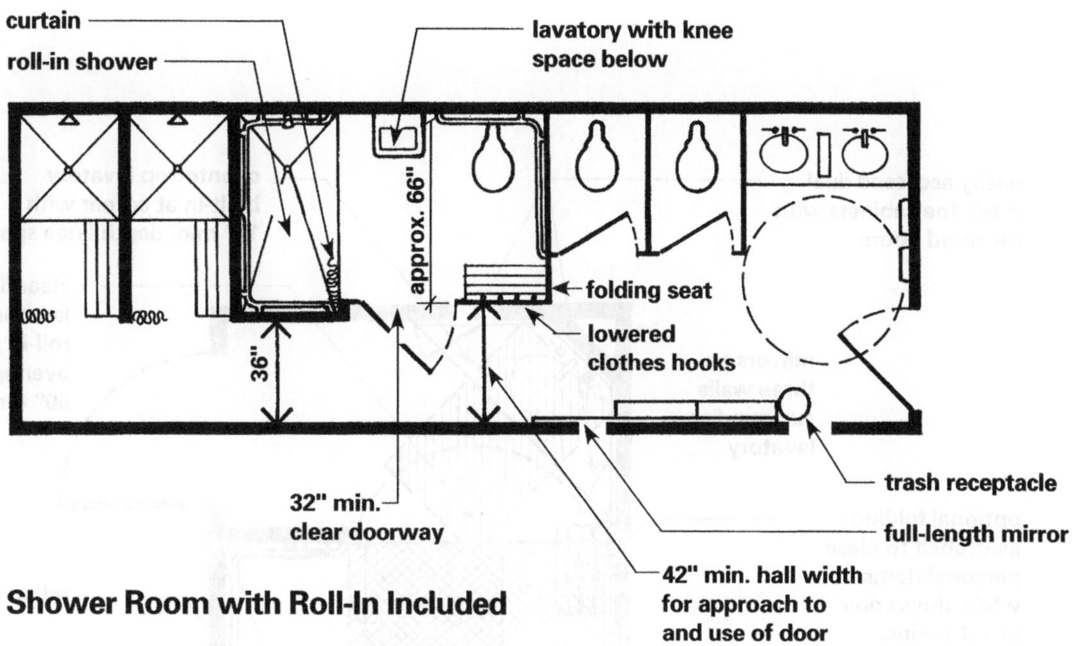

Shower Room with Roll-In Included

- switch locations of one lavatory and toilet
- remove curb, bench, and partitions
- waterproof floor and slope toward drain
- add hand-held shower unit, grab bars, mirror, and accessible toilet fixture
- add dual basin countertop lavatory with easy-to-reach dispensers
- add full-length mirror
- include some shelf segments at lower easy-to-reach and cane-detectable height

SOLUTION 2 EXPAND BATHING/SHOWER FACILITY INTO AN ADJOINING SPACE

Toilet rooms, storage areas, and janitor's closets often are located adjacent to bathing/shower facilities. If suitable adjacent space is available, it may be possible to combine all or part of it with the existing bathing/shower room and rearrange the fixtures to provide full access.

SOLUTION 3 INSTALL UNISEX BATHING/ SHOWER FACILITY IN ALTERNATE LOCATION

When it is not practical to modify the existing bathing/shower facility, the best solution may be to install an accessible single user bathing/shower room in a nearby location. Unisex bathrooms generally contain a toilet, a lavatory, and either a bathtub or shower and are fully accessible. These facilities can be used by anyone and are especially useful to parents with small children who need the extra space to assist with toileting, bathing, and dressing.

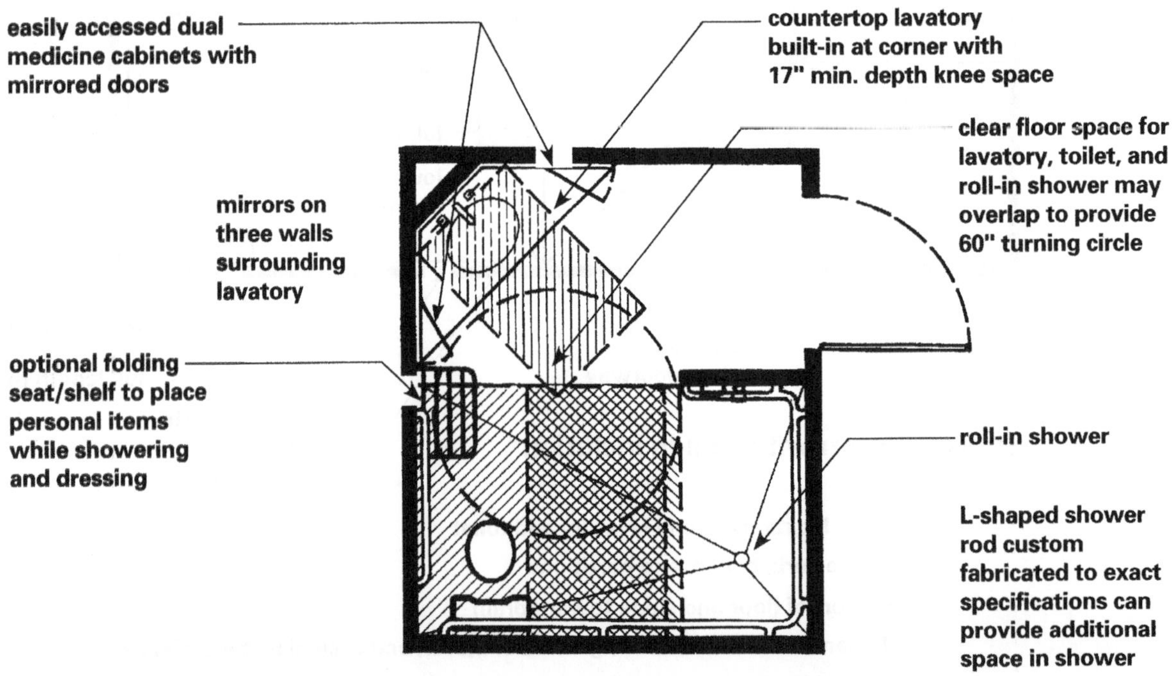

Single-User Unisex Shower Room with Roll-In Shower

PRACTICAL PLUS

In many instances it is possible to provide two accessible bathing options in one facility. Many state codes may require the provision of both a bathtub and a shower and some users can only bathe independently using a particular fixture. Multiple accessible bathing fixtures give users the option to select the fixture which most closely suits their individual needs.

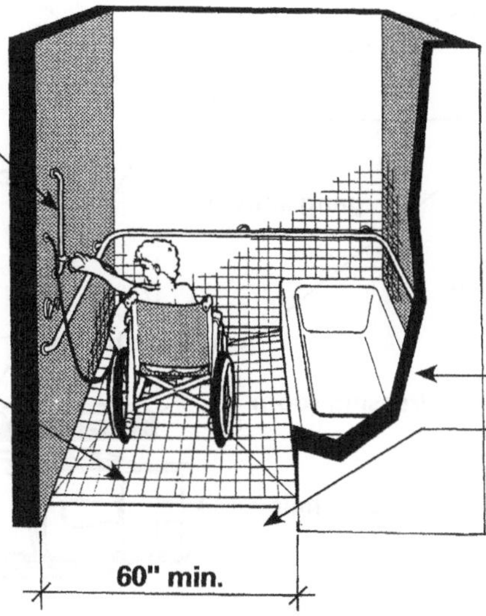

Combination Roll-In Shower and Bathtub

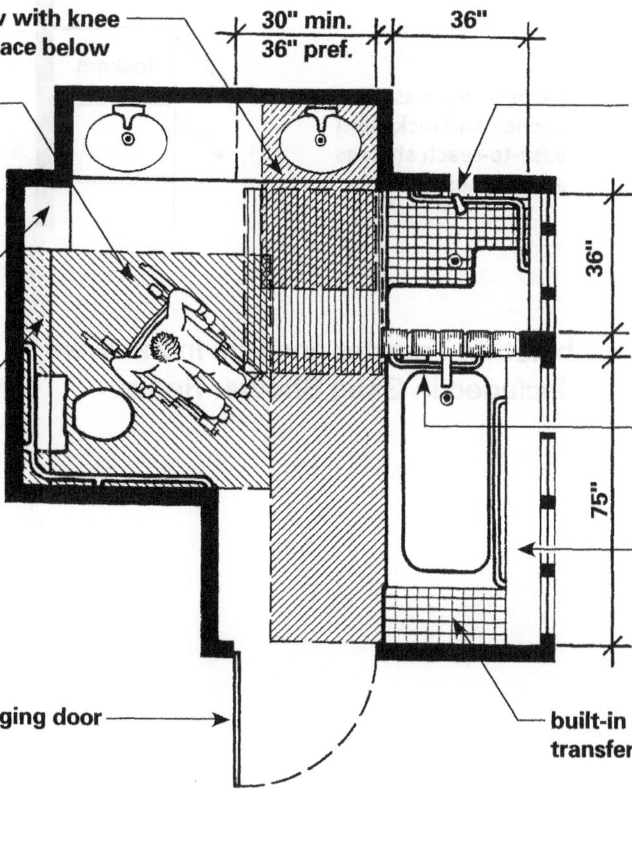

Combination Bathtub and Transfer Shower

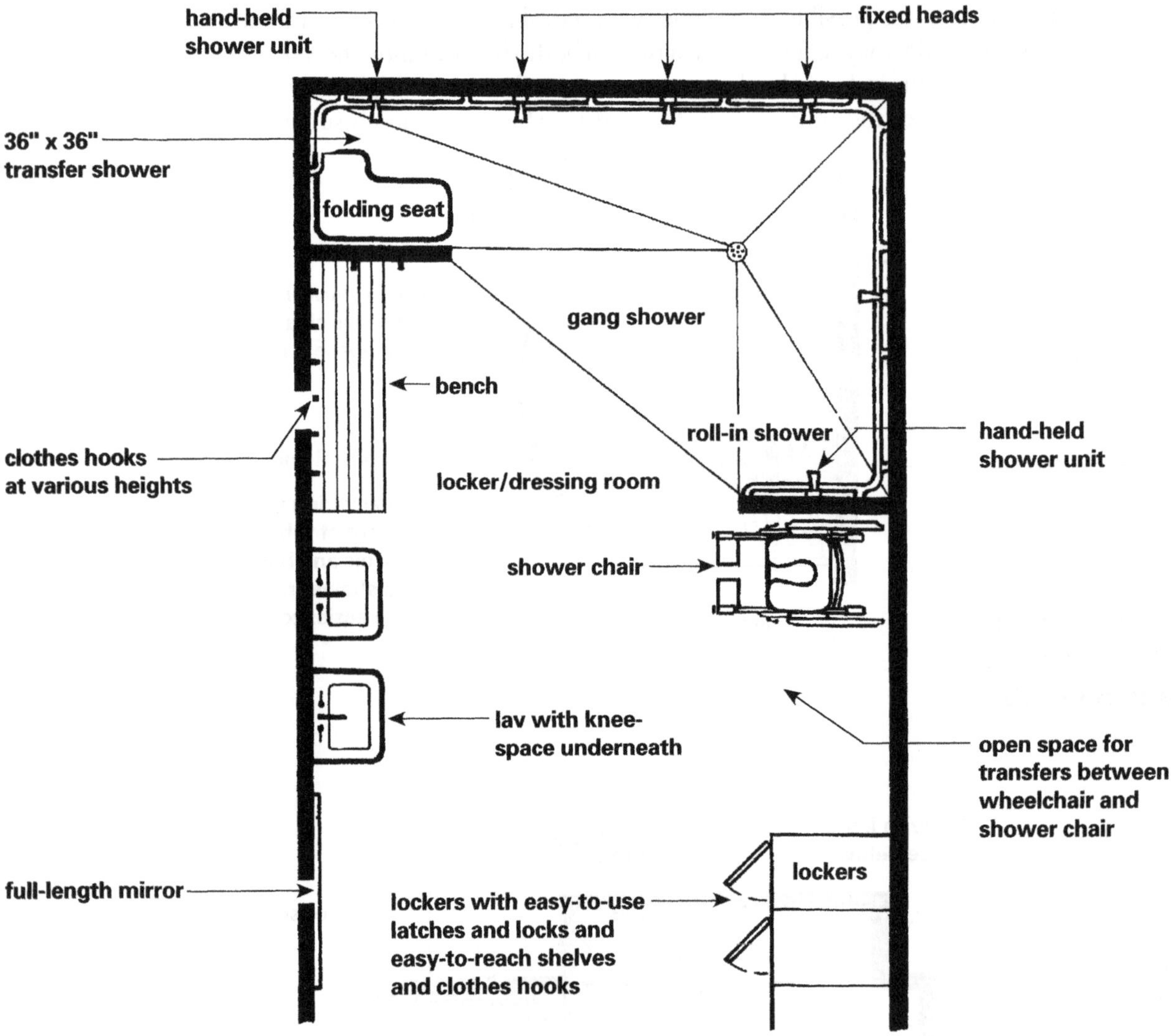

Combination Transfer and Roll-In Showers Included in Gang Shower Room

REFERENCE INDEX TO UFAS DOCUMENT

BATHROOMS, BATHING FACILITIES, AND SHOWER ROOMS

ASSEMBLY SPACES

UFAS 4.33

Introduction

"Assembly" is a type of occupancy classification used in UFAS and other building codes to describe facilities designed to accommodate large numbers of people. UFAS specifically defines assembly areas as "a room or space accommodating fifty or more individuals for religious, recreational, educational, political, social, or amusement purposes, or for the consumption of food and drink, including all connected rooms or spaces with a common means of egress and ingress." Assembly occupancies include a wide variety of facilities such as amusement parks, arenas, art galleries, auditoriums, bowling alleys, churches, courtrooms, drive-in theaters, tennis courts, libraries, restaurants, taverns, and television studios, to name just a few. UFAS further explains that areas such as conference rooms, which hold less than fifty people, would have to be accessible in accordance with other sections of the standard but would not have to meet all the criteria associated with assembly areas.

UFAS Section 4.1.2(18), page 7, includes a chart which indicates the number of wheelchair seating spaces which must be dispersed throughout an assembly area based on the total seating capacity. This section also describes the requirements for assistive listening systems in areas with and without audio-amplification systems. UFAS Section 4.1.6(4)(f), page 13, describes several exemptions permitted in structures which are being altered. In retrofit situations where it is structurally impracticable to disperse seating throughout the assembly area, seating may be located in collected areas as structurally feasible. These seating areas must be located on an accessible route that also serves as a means of egress. Additionally, in alterations where it is not feasible to alter all performing areas (stages, arena floors, dressing rooms, etc.) to be on an accessible route, then at least one of each type shall be made accessible.

Basic Design Considerations

Wheelchair Seating Spaces

Wheelchair seating spaces are required in assembly areas so that people using wheelchairs can attend events comfortably with their families and friends. UFAS Section 4.33, page 49, contains design information on the size and surface of wheelchair spaces and their location. Information on these features is described in greater detail below.

Size. UFAS describes the size of the wheelchair seating space based on the approach to the space. If forward or rear approaches to the spaces are required, then the wheelchair seating space must be a minimum of 48 inches by 66 inches. If a side approach is required then the wheelchair seating space must be a minimum of 60 inches by 66 inches. The larger clear floor area is required in order for the wheelchair user to turn into the space. Some state codes also have requirements for the size of wheelchair seating spaces and should be consulted to determine which is more stringent.

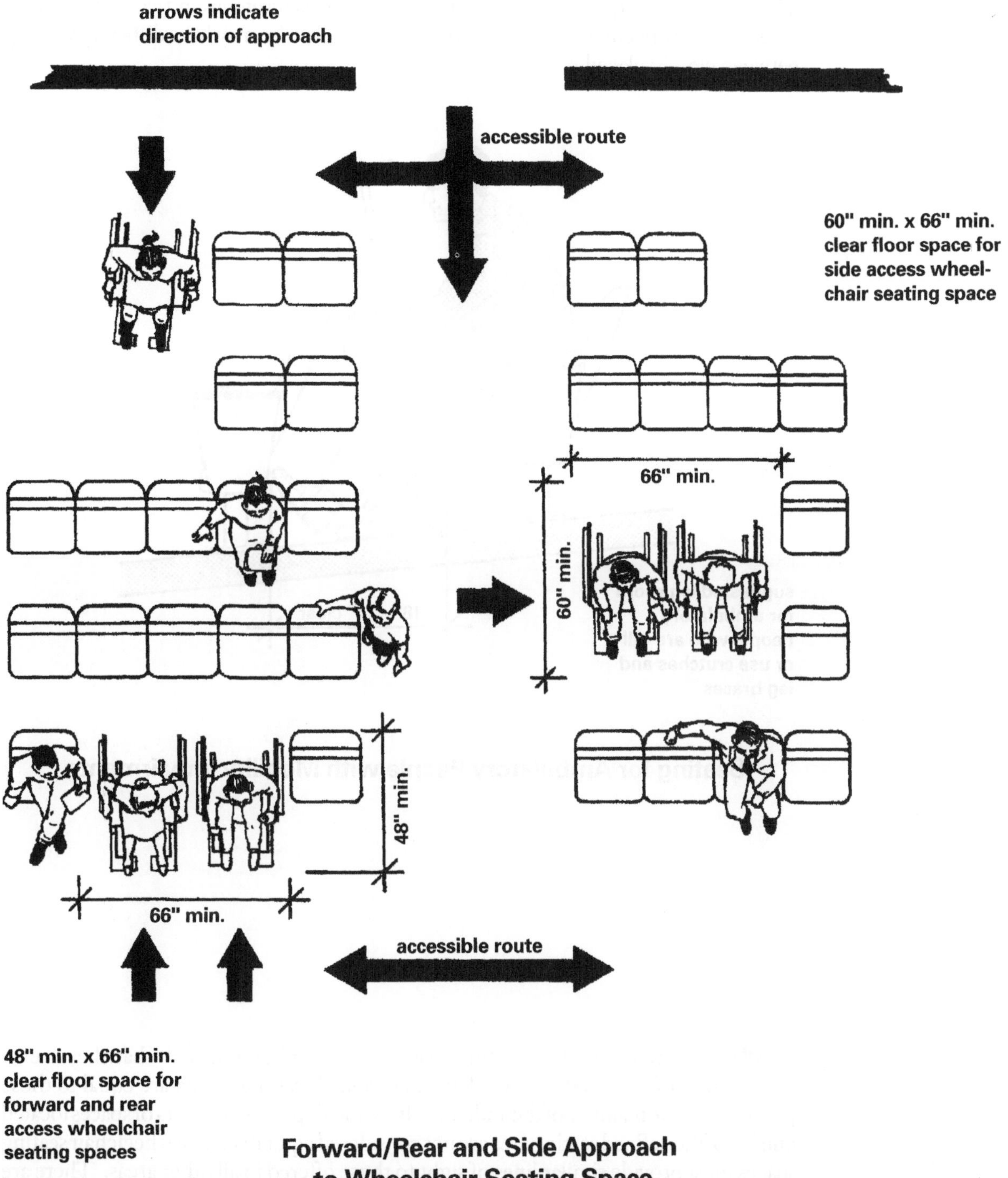

Forward/Rear and Side Approach to Wheelchair Seating Space

PRACTICAL PLUS

Some state codes include seating requirements for ambulatory people with mobility impairments. These codes typically require that a certain percentage of aisle seats allow between 18 inches and 24 inches between the back of one chair and the seat of another. This leg room is frequently necessary for people who use crutches and leg braces. These seats are also convenient for very tall people or people who may have difficulty walking between closely placed rows of seats.

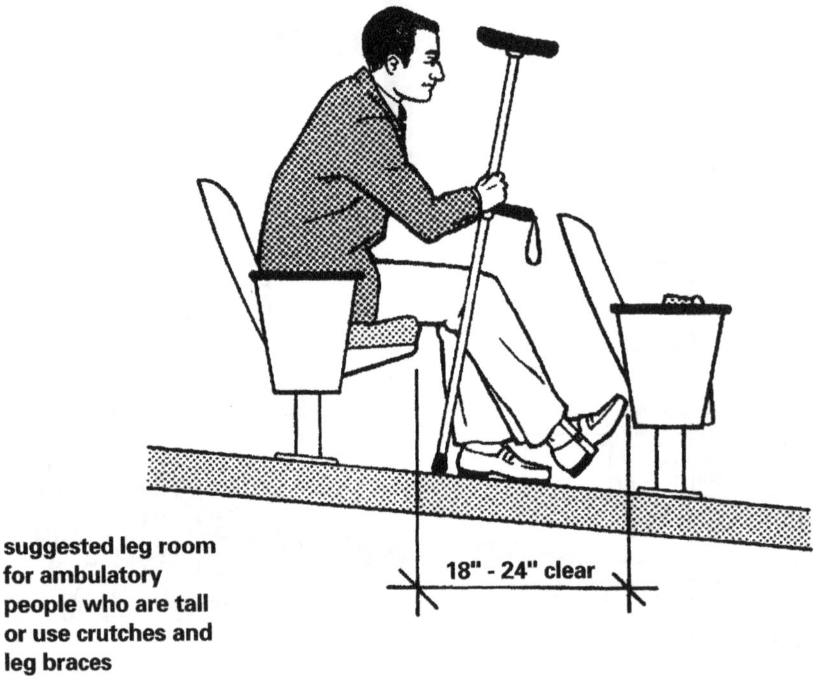

Seating for Ambulatory People with Mobility Impairments

Placement. Wheelchair seating spaces must be dispersed such that they are an integral part of any fixed seating plan and include locations which are equal to those provided for the majority of the audience. Individual spaces or clusters of spaces located outside of the defined seating area are not considered equitable. The wheelchair seating spaces must provide similar lines of sight to those offered in all other areas. There are two exceptions to the requirement that seating be dispersed: 1) viewing positions which are located in areas, such as bleachers and balconies, which have sight lines greater than five percent, and 2) other areas of existing facilities where it is structurally impracticable to disperse seating.

Wheelchair Seating Dispersed Throughout Seating Area

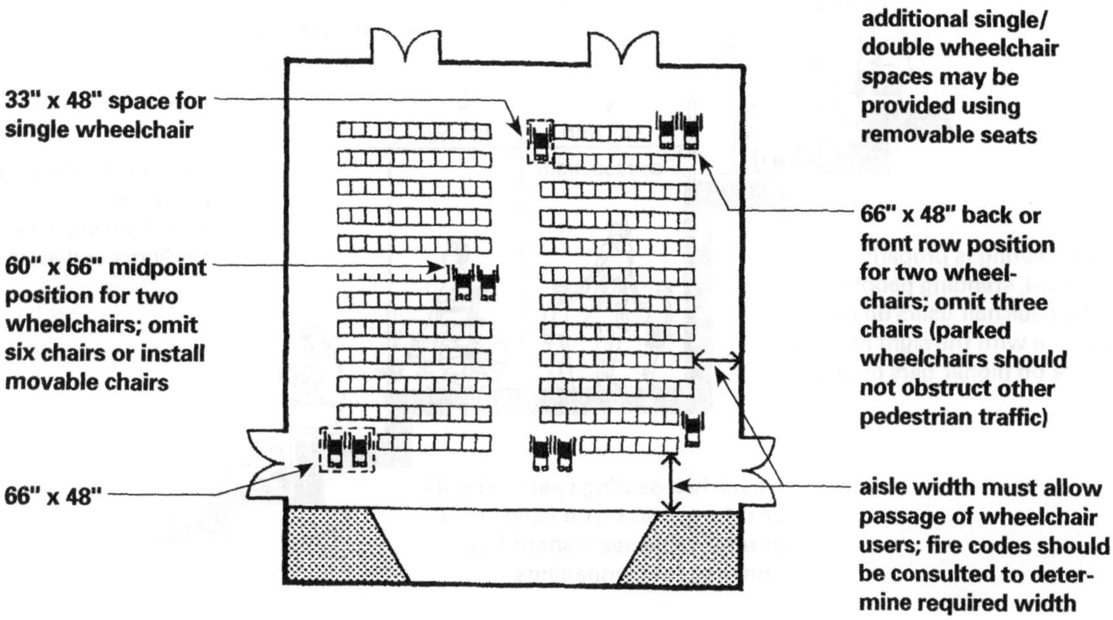

Theater Style Seating

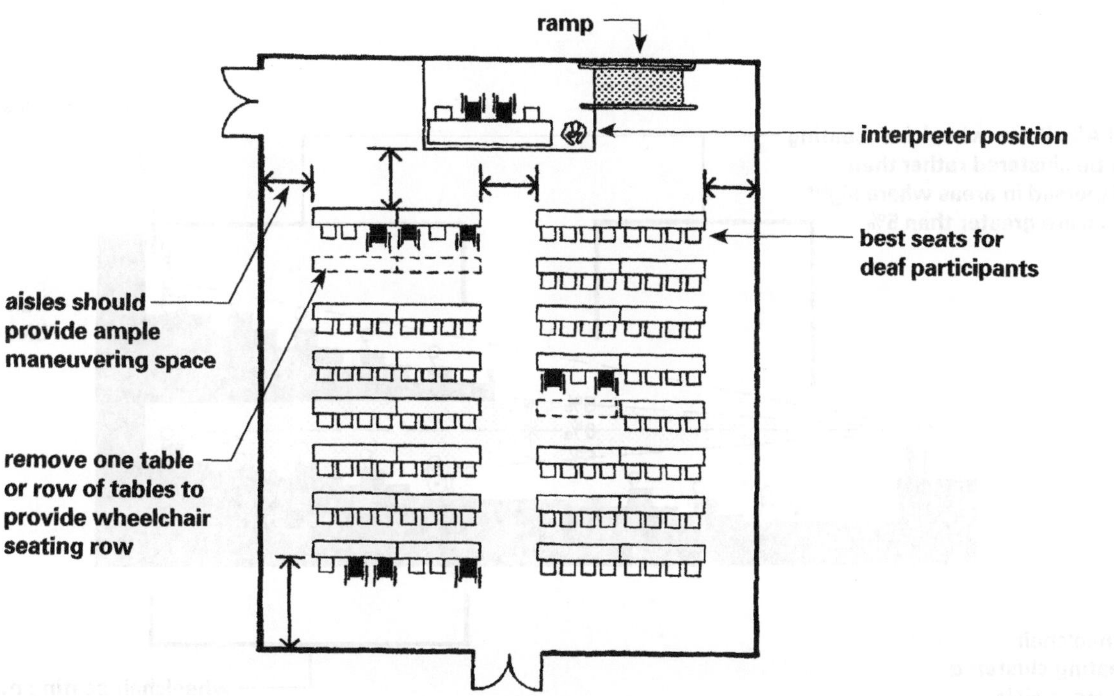

Classroom Style

Wheelchair Seating Dispersed Throughout Seating Area

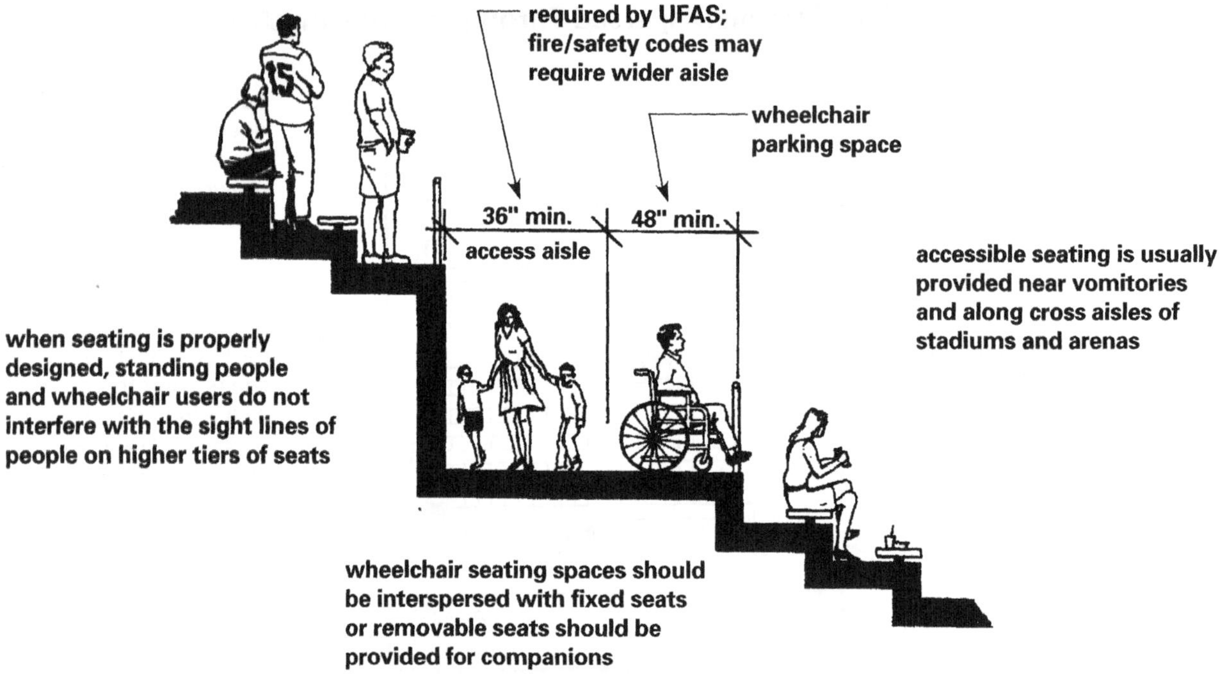

Stadium Style Seating

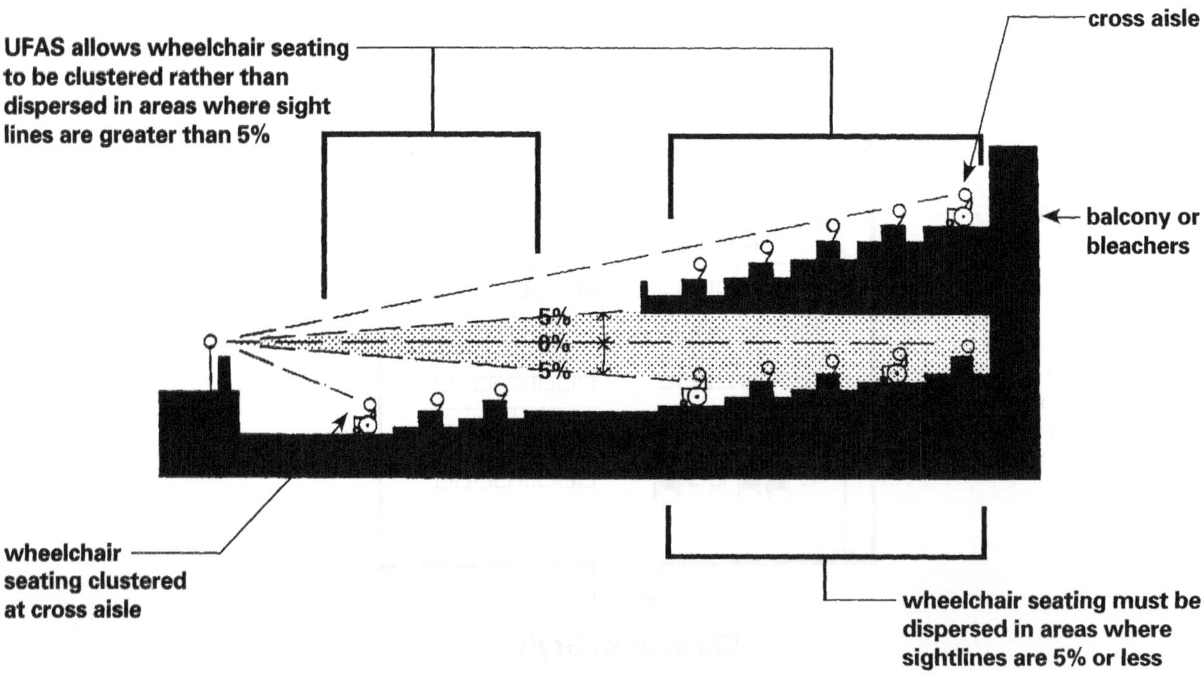

Wheelchair Seating Clustered in Some Areas

Wheelchair seating spaces must be on an accessible route that also serves as a means of egress in the event of an emergency. Most building/fire codes include formulas for determining the required width of main, side, and cross aisles based on the numbers of people projected to use a particular path in an emergency.

The wheelchair seating spaces required by UFAS are large enough to accommodate two wheelchairs. Some state codes specify a certain percentage of wheelchair seating spaces to accommodate one wheelchair. Although UFAS doesn't specifically describe single wheelchair spaces, it does require minimum "odd" numbers of seating spaces which may be designed for single users. Single spaces should be a minimum of 33 inches wide and either 48 or 60 inches long depending on the direction of approach and be dispersed throughout the viewing area.

The number of wheelchair seating spaces required in any given assembly area is based on the total seating capacity. UFAS Section 4.1.2(18)(a), page 7, describes the number of wheelchair seating spaces which must be included. State and local codes use a variety of different formulas to determine the number of wheelchair seating spaces and should also be consulted to determine the most stringent requirements. As with any facility, emergency evacuation plans for assembly areas should consider the safety of all patrons and employees.

Surfaces. UFAS requires that the surfaces of wheelchair seating spaces be stable, firm, and slip resistant in compliance with Section 4.5 Ground and Floor Surfaces, page 22. These surfaces must also be level to eliminate the need for wheelchair users to continually adjust their posture to compensate for an uneven surface.

PROBLEM — WHEELCHAIR SEATING SPACES NOT INCLUDED OR NOT DISPERSED

SOLUTION — INCLUDE WHEELCHAIR SEATING SPACES AS REQUIRED

If wheelchair seating spaces have never been included in the assembly area or were included but not dispersed, then steps should be taken to bring the area into compliance. Wheelchair seating spaces can be incorporated in lieu of traditional seating without much difficulty provided an accessible route can be furnished. If adjacent access aisles are wide enough, two wheelchair seating spaces can usually be substituted for three standard seats in the front and back row. If wheelchair seating spaces are incorporated in the middle of a seating section, generally six standard seats will need to be removed. It is often necessary to modify the floor area to make the seating space level or to provide an accessible route from the adjacent aisle to the seating space.

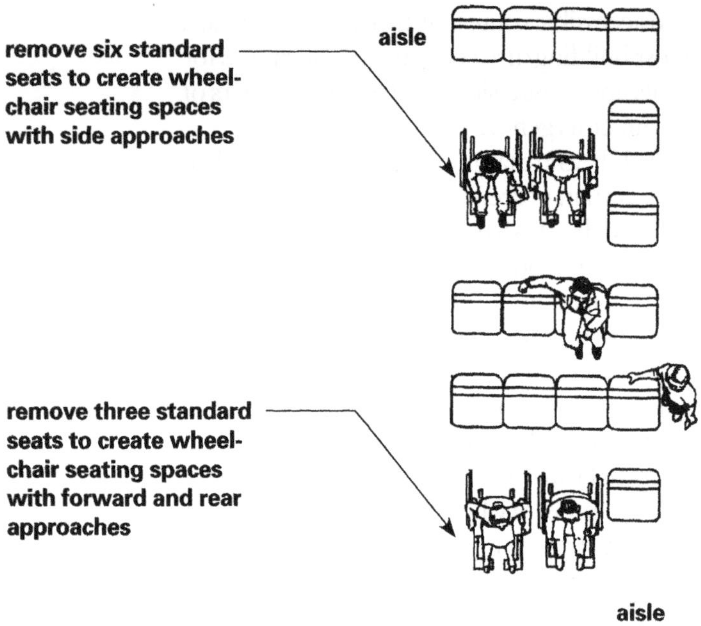

Remove Seats to Provide Wheelchair Seating Spaces

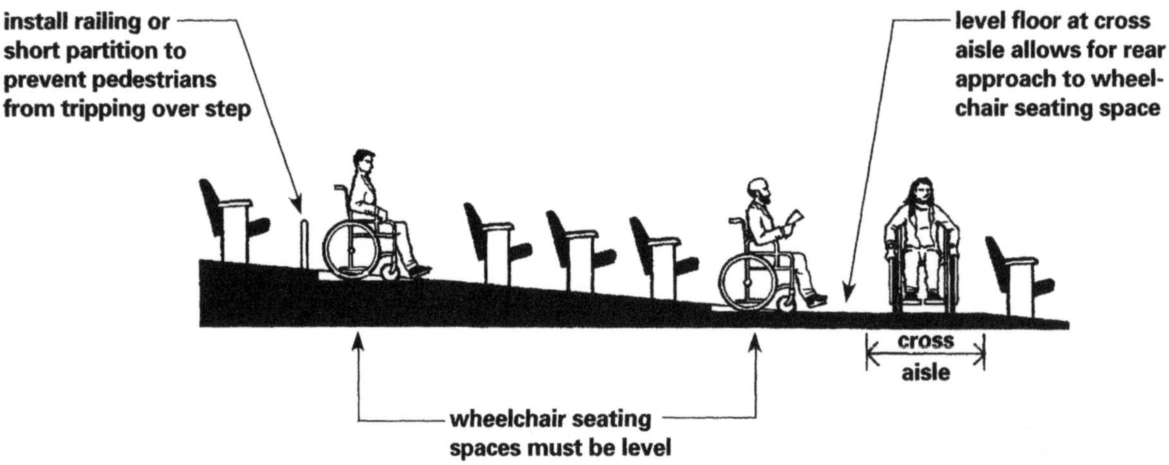

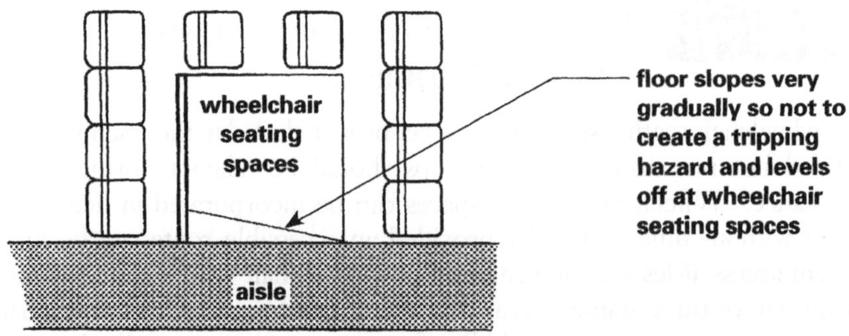

Modify Floor to Create Access Route from Aisle to Seating Space

PRACTICAL PLUS

Many facility operators install portable or removable seats which can be removed or installed depending on the needs of a particular audience. The seats can be stored in a nearby closet and removed or set in place by employees. If this technique is used, the facility management must develop a policy to insure that wheelchair users have equal access to seats for any given performance or event.

PRACTICAL PLUS

There are some design options which improve safe use of a facility even though it may be structurally impracticable to provide dispersed wheelchair seating spaces. Stepped aisles are dangerous for many people who have difficulty walking. These steps can be made safer by installing handrails on side aisles. Extra lighting on the steps and contrasting color strips make steps easier and safer to negotiate in low light situations.

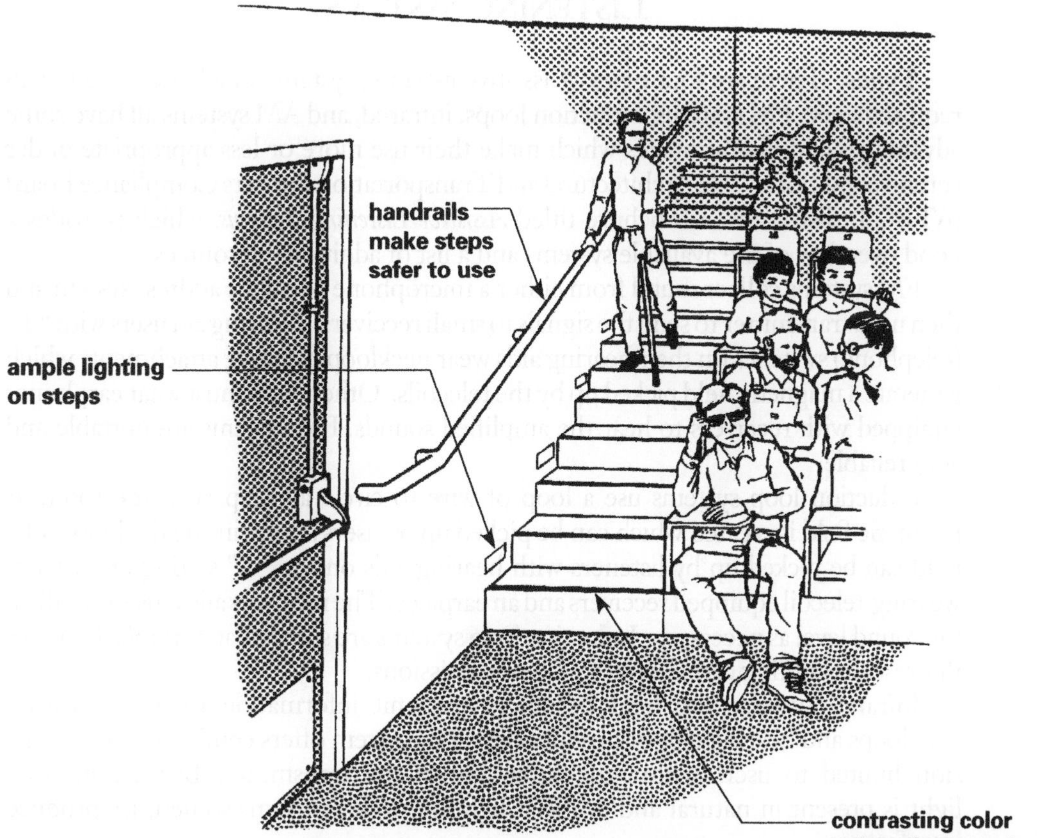

Seating Spaces Not Located on Accessible Routes Can Be Made Safer for All Users

BASIC DESIGN CONSIDERATIONS

ACCESS TO PERFORMING AREAS

UFAS also requires that an accessible route connect all wheelchair seating locations with performing areas, including stages, arena floors, dressing rooms, locker rooms, rehearsal rooms, and other spaces used by performers. In alterations, if it is structurally impracticable to alter all performing areas to be on an accessible route, then at least one of each type must be made accessible. The techniques used to make performing areas accessible will depend upon the layout of the existing facility. Ramps and lifts are frequently used backstage and side-stage to provide vertical access to the stage platform for heavy equipment, props, pianos, etc. Other topics in UFAS and the *Retrofit Guide* should be consulted for details on renovating specific features, elements, and spaces.

BASIC DESIGN CONSIDERATIONS

LISTENING SYSTEMS

Types. There are four types of assistive listening systems which meet the UFAS requirements. FM systems, induction loops, infrared, and AM systems all have some advantages and disadvantages which make their use more or less appropriate under certain conditions. The Architectural and Transportation Barriers Compliance Board (ATBCB) distributes a brochure titled *Assistive Listening Systems*, which provides a good overview of the available systems and a list of additional resources.

FM systems collect sound from either a microphone or public address system and then use a transmitter to send the signals to small receivers. Hearing aid users with "T" (telephone) switches on their hearing aids wear neckloop listening attachments which generate a magnetic field picked up by the telecoils. Other users must wear earphones equipped with receivers to hear the amplified sounds. FM systems are portable and very reliable.

Induction loop systems use a loop of wire to circle all or part of the room. A magnetic field is created which can be picked up by users sitting inside the loop. The field can be picked up by listeners with hearing aids on the "T" setting or by users wearing telecoil equipped receivers and an earpiece. The receivers allow users to adjust the sound level as necessary. Induction loop systems are somewhat portable, however fluorescent lighting can interfere with transmissions.

Infrared systems use light beams to transmit information to users wearing neckloops and hearing aids or headphones. The system offers confidential transmission limited to users within the sight line of the transmitter. Because infrared light is present in natural and artificial lighting, well lit rooms sometimes produce interference.

AM systems work in much the same way as FM systems. Users who wish to receive the transmission must wear neckloops and hearing aids or headphones. The sound quality of AM broadcasts is generally poorer than FM and as a result, these systems are rarely used.

Placement. If the listening system serves individual fixed seats, UFAS requires that those seats be located within a 50 foot viewing distance of the stage or playing area. At this distance viewers can distinguish facial expressions and pick up other small gestures which help them interpret the actions of the performers. In addition, sign language interpreters, frequently used to translate the speech of performers or speakers, can easily be seen from this distance.

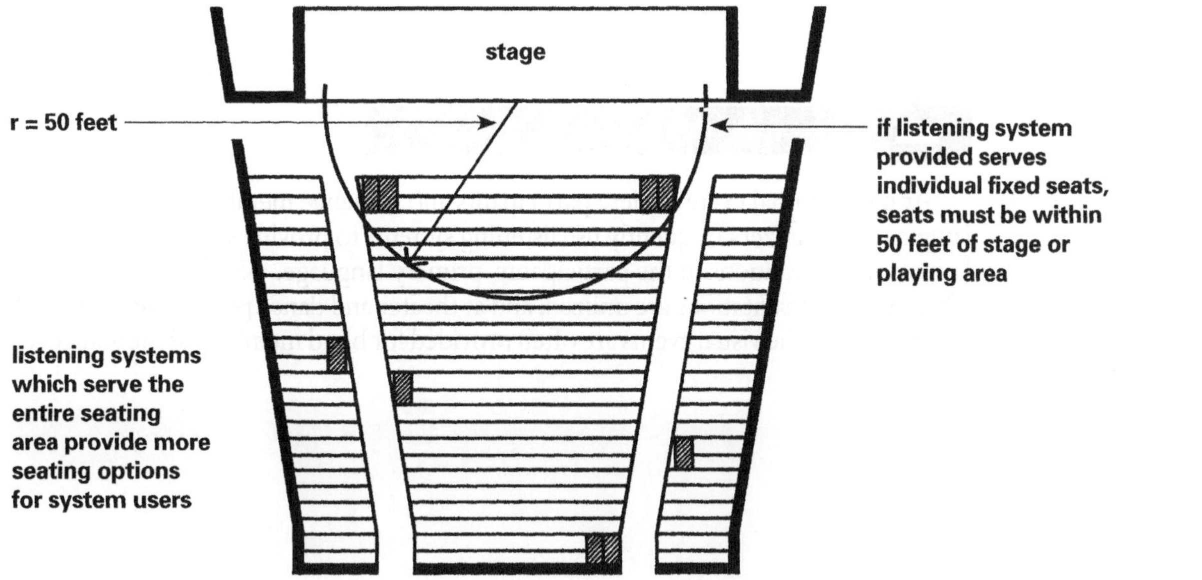

Location of Seats for Assisted Listening System

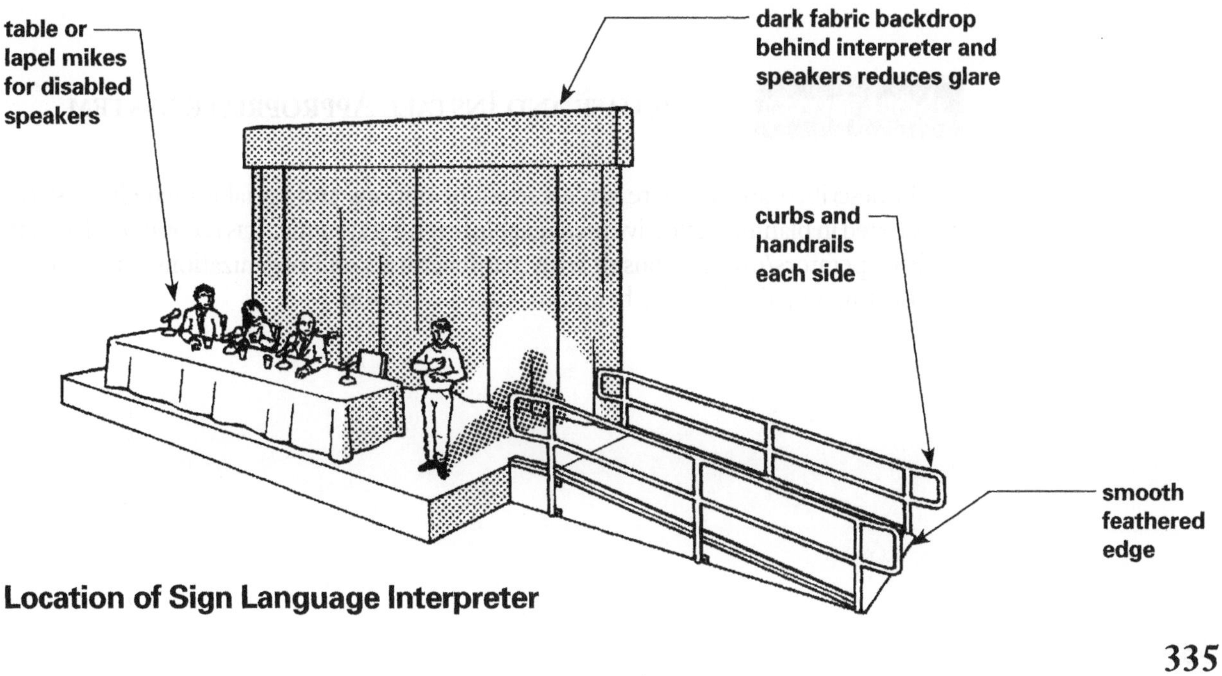

Location of Sign Language Interpreter

PRACTICAL PLUS

Because deaf people and those with hearing losses rely more heavily on their vision, it is imperative that ample lighting be provided. Back lighting and glare should be avoided whenever possible and ample natural lighting or artificial lighting should be arranged to avoid casting shadows. Particular attention should be given to visual displays, chalkboards, and interpreters.

Background noise from various sources should be reduced as much as possible. Ventilation and other mechanical equipment can be insulated to reduce interior noise. Landscaping and earth berms can also be used to buffer exterior noise.

PRACTICAL PLUS

At international events where participants and audience members speak different languages, organizers frequently use listening systems to provide simultaneous translations of presentations in the participants' primary language. Similarly, at meetings where visual presentations are utilized, and at theater and dance performances, verbal descriptions of the visual events are often provided for blind members of the audience.

PROBLEM — NO ASSISTIVE LISTENING SYSTEM INSTALLED

SOLUTION — PURCHASE AND INSTALL APPROPRIATE SYSTEM

As described above, there are a variety of options and variables which must be considered in planning effective manageable listening systems. It is recommended that facility operators/owners consult with manufacturers and organizations serving deaf and hearing impaired people before making a selection.

REFERENCE INDEX TO UFAS DOCUMENT

ASSEMBLY AREAS

Primary References	UFAS page	Secondary References	UFAS page
4.33.1 Minimum Number	49	4.1 Scope & Technical Requirements 4.1.5 Additions 4.1.6(4)(f)(i) Alterations 4.1.6(4)(f)(ii) Alterations 4.1.7 Historic Preservation	7 11 13 13 13
4.33.2 Size of Wheelchair Locations	49	A4.33.2 Size of Wheelchair Locations	67
4.33.3 Placement of Wheelchair Locations	49	A4.33.3 Placement of Wheelchair Locations	67
4.33.4 Surfaces	49	4.5 Ground and Floor Surfaces	22
4.33.5 Access to Performing Areas	49		
4.33.6 Placement of Listening Systems	49	A4.33.6 Placement of Listening Systems	67
4.33.7 Types of Listening Systems	49	A4.33.7 Types of Listening Systems	67

RESTAURANTS & CAFETERIAS

UFAS 5.0

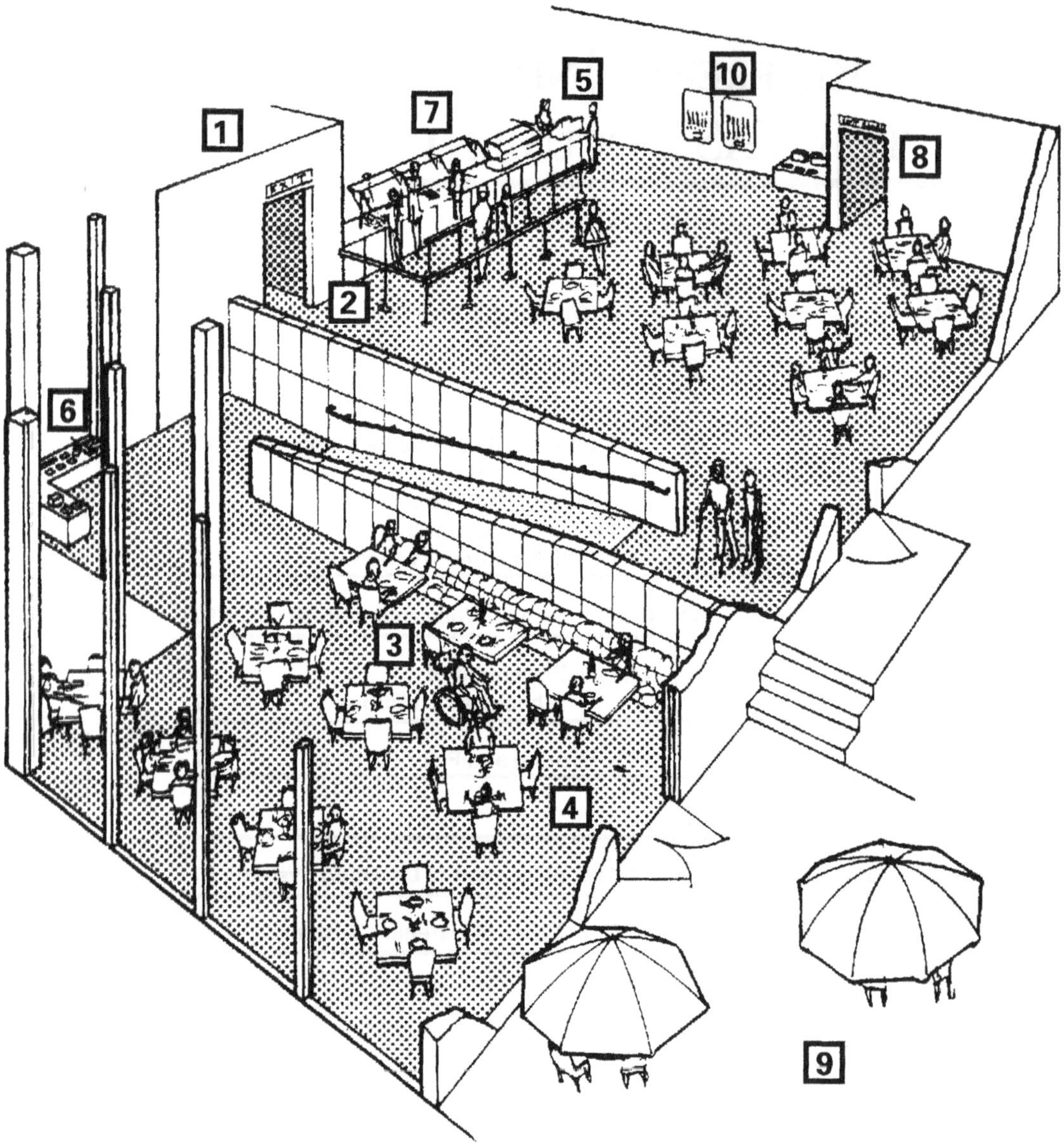

INTRODUCTION

Restaurants and cafeterias fall into the occupancy classification of "Assembly" and, therefore, must comply with the general accessibility requirements of UFAS when they undergo alterations. In addition to these requirements, UFAS Section 5.0 stipulates that: 1) five percent of the fixed seating and tables be accessible and, when practical, distributed throughout the facility; and 2) access to other levels, mezzanines, loggias, or raised platforms, is not required if the same services and atmosphere/character are provided in spaces located along an accessible route.

The design of specific components of restaurants and cafeterias including food service lines; tray slides; seating areas; self service shelves; dispensing devices; vending machines; and tableware, dishware, condiment, food, and beverage display shelves are also described in UFAS Section 5.0. These descriptions of specific components include references to related sections of the UFAS document including: 4.3 Accessible Route; 4.32 Seating, Tables, and Work Surfaces; 4.2 Space Allowance and Reach Ranges; and 4.27 Controls and Operating Mechanisms.

BASIC DESIGN CONSIDERATIONS

1 accessible entrances, toilet rooms, elevators, telephones, and parking required

2 food service lines with a preferred minimum width of 42 inches to allow space for patrons to pass (42 inches required if a person using a wheelchair must complete a switchback turn around crowd control standards/guides)

3 ample aisles required to provide access through fixed seating areas

4 adequate knee space and maneuvering space/clear floor space at fixed tables and fixtures required; recommended for movable tables and fixtures

5 tray slides and check-out counters no higher than 34 inches above the floor as required to facilitate use

6 self service shelves and/or dispensers mounted no higher than 54 inches or a maximum height of 46 inches when side reach over an obstruction is required

7 accessible work spaces for employees with disabilities recommended

8 clear signage indicating entrances, exits, and toilets required; signage indicating phones and other amenities recommended

9 accessible seating dispersed throughout facility; required in areas which offer different services, atmosphere, decor, views, etc.

10 if installed, vending machines must have reachable and usable controls

REFERENCE INDEX TO UFAS DOCUMENT

SEATING AND FOOD SERVICE IN RESTAURANTS AND CAFETERIAS

Primary References	UFAS page	Secondary References	UFAS page
5.1 General/Location	57	4.1-4.33 Scope and Technical Requirements	4
		4.3 Accessible Route	15
		4.32 Seating, Tables, and Work Surfaces	48
5.2 Food Service Lines	57		
5.3 Tableware Areas	57	4.2 Space Allowance and Reach Ranges	14
5.4 Vending Machines	57	4.27 Controls and Operating Mechanisms	45

INTRODUCTION

As described in UFAS, health care facilities include long-term care facilities, outpatient facilities, and general and special purpose hospitals. UFAS contains different scoping provisions for the various health care facilities but all institutional occupancies must provide access to common use, public use, or other areas which may result in the employment of physically handicapped persons. UFAS Section 4.1.4(9)(b), page 10, describes specific scoping requirements for patient bedrooms and toilets for the various types of health care facilities.

UFAS Section 6.0 includes specific design information regarding entrances to health care facilities, patient rooms, and patient toilet rooms. In addition to the specific design information provided, this section also references other portions of UFAS.

BASIC DESIGN CONSIDERATIONS

ENTRANCES

1 roof overhang or canopy, with ample vertical clearance, provides weather protection; required for at least one accessible entrance

2 required passenger loading zone, a minimum of 20 feet in length, incorporated at entrance

3 access aisle at least 60 inches wide required at passenger loading zone

4 level vehicle standing spaces and access aisle recommended

5 posts recommended in lieu of curb to separate pedestrian and vehicular traffic; change of material between sidewalk and driveway provides visual cue for drivers and pedestrians

6 clear signage required to indicate parking, crosswalk, entrance, etc.

7 handicapped parking spaces provided as required (based on type of health care facility)

8 covered waiting area for bus or shuttle recommended

Hospital Entrance

BASIC DESIGN CONSIDERATIONS

PATIENT BEDROOMS AND TOILET ROOMS

1 ample turning and maneuvering space around all fixtures and furnishings as required, especially at entrance

2 unobstructed aisle space between beds, between the side of bed and wall, and between the foot of bed and wall (or foot of opposing bed) as required

	one-bed room	two-bed room	four-bed room
side of bed and wall	36" min.	36" min.	36" min.
foot of bed and wall	42" min.	42" min.- 48" pref.	48" min.
between beds	NA	48" min.	48" min.

3 all doors with required maneuvering space and easy-to-use hardware (entry doors to acute care hospital bedrooms for in-patients exempted from requirement for clear space to side of door if door is at least 44 inches wide)

4 required maneuvering space around all fixtures in toilet rooms

5 various bathing fixture options recommended to suit patient needs

6 ample accessible storage for personal items recommended

7 telephones, water fountains, and other amenities accessible as required

8 tactile, easy-to-read permanent signage as required; straightforward temporary signage recommended

9 large picture windows for daylight and view of outdoors recommended

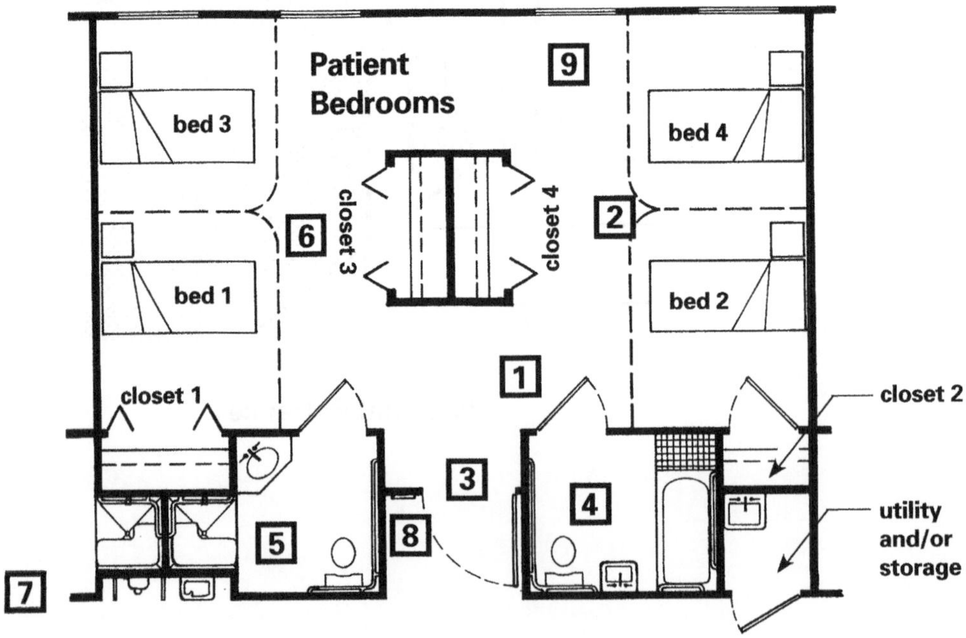

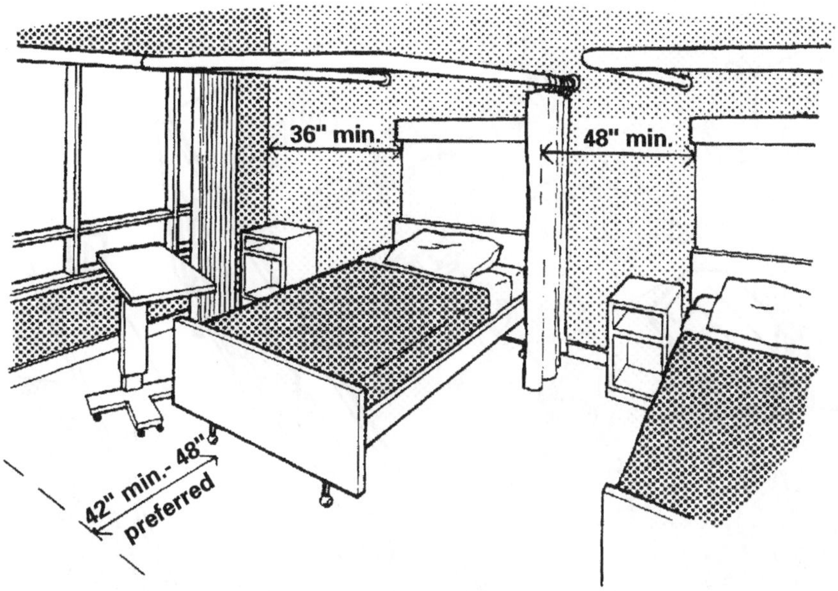

Patient Bedrooms

REFERENCE INDEX TO UFAS DOCUMENT

HEALTH CARE FACILITIES

Primary References	UFAS page	Secondary References	UFAS page
6.1 General/Location	57	4.1-4.33 Scope & Technical Requirements	4
		4.1.1(5)(e)(i-iii) Parking Spaces	5
		4.1.4(9)(b) Health Care Occupancies	10
6.2 Entrances	57	4.14 Entrances	36
		4.6.5 Passenger Loading Zones	24
		4.13.6 Maneuvering Clearances at Doors	36
6.3 Patient Bedrooms	57	4.2.3 Wheelchair Turning Space	14
		4.13 Doors	33
6.4 Patient Toilet Rooms	57	4.22 Toilet Rooms	43
		4.23 Bathing and Shower Facilities	44

MERCANTILE

UFAS 7.0

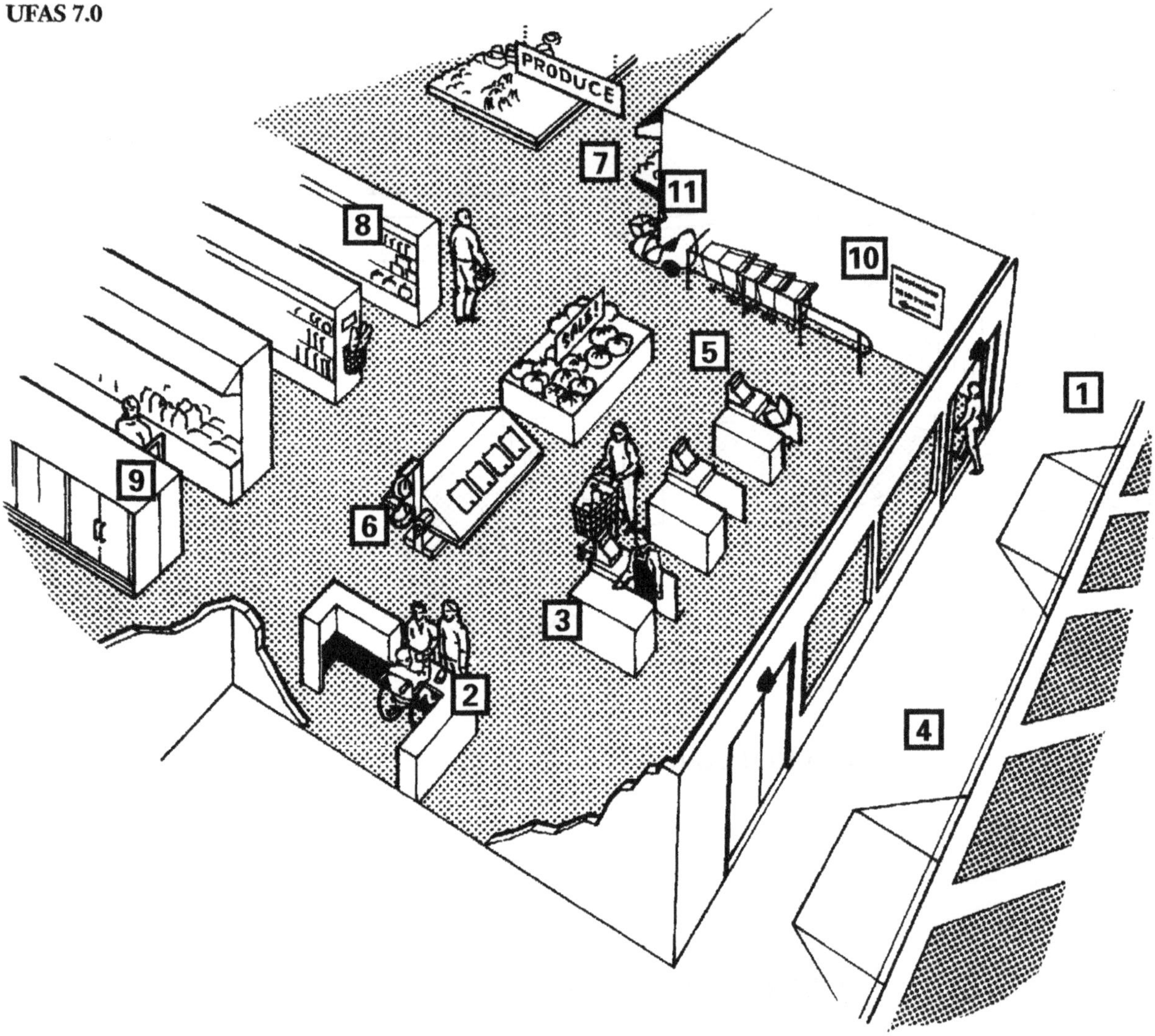

INTRODUCTION

Mercantile is a common occupancy classification, used in UFAS and other building codes, to describe "all buildings and structures or parts thereof, for the display and sale of merchandise, and involving stocks of goods, wares, or merchandise incidental to such purposes and accessible to the public." Department stores, drug stores, markets, retail stores, shopping centers, and sales rooms are listed in UFAS as examples of "mercantile" occupancies. UFAS requires access be provided to all areas for which the intended use will require public access or which may result in employment of physically handicapped persons.

UFAS Section 7.0 provides design information regarding several specific components of mercantile environments including service counters, check-out aisles, and security bollards. Specifically, where service counters exceeding 36 inches in height are provided for sales or distribution of goods to the public, a portion of the main counter or an auxiliary counter must be at 28 to 34 inches in compliance with UFAS 4.32.4 Height of Work Surfaces. At least one check-out aisle and adjacent counter shall be accessible and comply with UFAS 4.2.1 Wheelchair Passage Width with the counter height no higher than 36 inches. Security bollards or other devices installed to reduce the theft of shopping carts shall not obstruct access or egress for customers using wheelchairs.

BASIC DESIGN CONSIDERATIONS

MERCANTILE OCCUPANCIES

1 accessible entrances, toilet rooms, elevators, telephones, parking, and other features and spaces as required

2 service counter or portion of service counter as required at height usable by customers and employees who may use wheelchairs

3 at least one check-out aisle with ample passage space and counter no higher than 36 inches as required

4 entrance and exit must be free of bollards and other devices which obstruct wheelchair access and egress

5 clear passageways and aisles as required for easy maneuvering

6 self-service weigh stations and bulk food bins within easy reach recommended

7 bin-type and produce displays with knee space below recommended

8 display items stacked to allow easy reach from seated position recommended

9 in refrigerated sections, doors should have ample maneuvering space and loop handles or accessible hardware

10 signage indicating location of specific goods or departments, exits, toilets, phones, and other services recommended

11 battery-operated scooters for use by patrons who have difficulty walking are helpful but not required

REFERENCE INDEX TO UFAS DOCUMENT

MERCANTILE OCCUPANCIES

Primary References	UFAS page	Secondary References	UFAS page
7.1 General/Location	57	4.1-4.33 Scope & Technical Requirements 4.1.4(10) Mercantile Occupancies	4 10
7.2 Service Counters	57	4.32.4 Height of Work Surfaces	49
7.3 Check-Out Aisles	57	4.2.1 Wheelchair Passage Width	14
7.4 Security Bollards	57		

LIBRARIES

UFAS 8.0

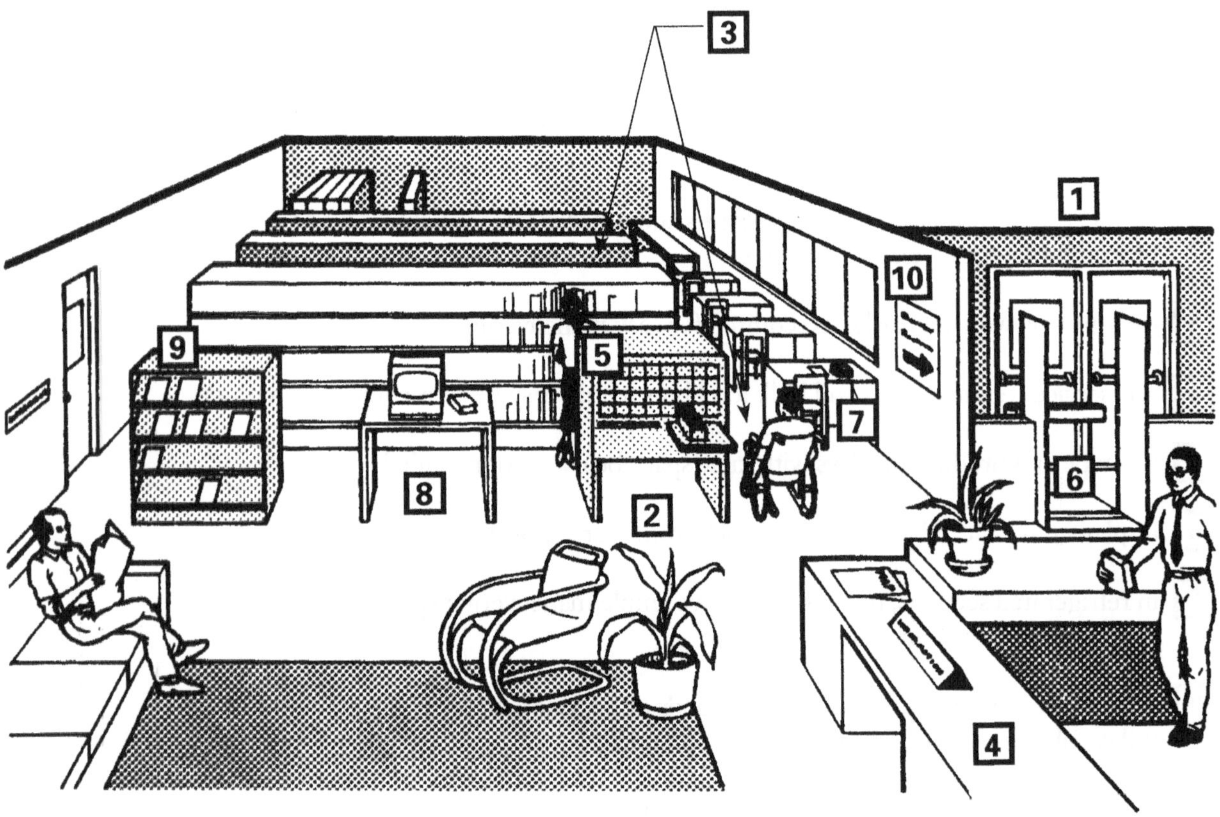

INTRODUCTION

Libraries fall into the occupancy classification of "Assembly" and, as a result, all areas of the facility intended for public access and areas where disabled people may be employed must meet the general requirements of UFAS. The design of specific components of libraries, including reading and study areas, checkout areas, card catalogs, and stacks are described in UFAS Section 8.0. These descriptions of specific components include 1) references to related sections of the UFAS document to insure that elements and features meet the proper requirements for accessibility, and 2) minimal scope requirements which specify that at least five percent or one each of these elements and features are accessible. In many situations independent access to all books and resources in a library would be prohibitively expensive and can be facilitated by staff members trained to provide assistance when necessary.

BASIC DESIGN CONSIDERATIONS

1. accessible entrances, toilet rooms, elevators, telephones, parking, and other features as required
2. adequate maneuvering space/clear floor space as required at fixtures and elements
3. access aisles between stacks 42 inches preferred minimum to allow space for maneuvering wheelchairs and book trucks; 36 inch minimum required
4. at least one checkout counter in each checkout area lowered to 32 - 34 inches for use by children and people who use wheelchairs
5. card catalog height of 48 inches preferred maximum; pull-out shelf or adjacent table should be mounted between 28 inches and 34 inches above floor
6. if installed, security gate must be accessible
7. knee clearance at a minimum of 5% of fixed seating, tables, and study carrels
8. computer terminals, microfiche readers, and other AV equipment should be located on accessible work surfaces with easy-to-operate controls
9. newspapers, current periodicals, and frequently used reference materials should be located within reach
10. large, clear signage for locating sections of the library, books in the stacks, and other elements/facilities such as phones, toilet rooms, elevators, etc. recommended

REFERENCE INDEX TO UFAS DOCUMENT

READING AND STUDY AREAS/CHECK-OUT AREAS/ CARD CATALOGS/STACKS

Primary References	UFAS page	Secondary References	UFAS page
8.1 General	58	4.1-4.33 Scope & Technical Requirements	4
8.2 Reading and Study Areas	58	4.2 Space Allowance and Reach Ranges	14
		4.3 Accessible Route	15
		4.32 Seating, Tables, & Work Surfaces	48
8.3 Check-Out Areas	58	4.13 Doors	33
		4.32 Seating, Tables, & Work Surfaces	48
8.4 Card Catalogs	58	4.2 Space Allowance and Reach Ranges	14
8.5 Stacks	58	4.3 Accessible Route	15

POSTAL FACILITIES

UFAS 9.0

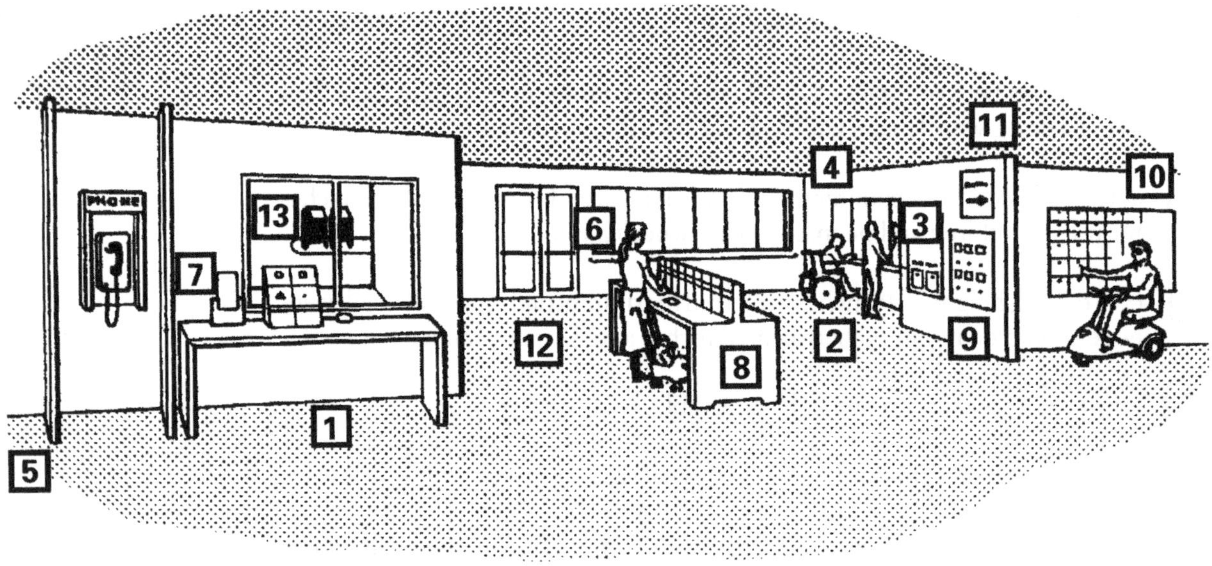

INTRODUCTION

Postal facilities are considered "Business" occupancies and as such must comply with the general access requirements for all areas of the facility intended for public access and areas where disabled people may be employed. There are no "exceptions" to these basic requirements and UFAS Section 9.0 lists some specific components including customer service counters, self-service postal centers, post office boxes, locker rooms, employee toilet rooms, water fountains, lunchrooms, lounges, attendance recording equipment, medical treatment rooms, emergency signals and switches, and controls which must also be made accessible.

Section 9.0 describes specific design considerations for post office lobbies, self-service postal centers, post office boxes, locker rooms, and attendance recording equipment. The descriptions of these components include 1) some minimal scoping information, five percent of all post office boxes must be accessible, and if writing desks are provided in the lobby at least one must be accessible; 2) design requirements for lobbies including specifications that clear passageways 48 inches in width be provided in front of customer service counters, all letter drops be installed within reach, all fixed partitions and handrails be installed to withstand 250 pound force, and self-service centers be easy to operate and have ample maneuvering space; 3) design requirements for locker rooms including specifications that clothing hooks and shelves in lockers be installed no higher than 48 inches, latches and locks on lockers be easy to operate, clear access aisles of 42 inches minimum be included in front of lockers, attendance recording equipment be installed no higher than 48 inches above the floor; and 4) references to related sections of UFAS (4.2 Space Allowance and Reach Ranges, 4.27 Controls and Operating Mechanisms, and 4.32 Seating, Tables, and Work Surfaces).

BASIC DESIGN CONSIDERATIONS

POST OFFICE LOBBIES

1 if provided, at least one writing desk with a work surface between 28 and 34 inches, ample knee space, and clear floor space to allow easy approach

2 required clear passageways a minimum of 48 inches wide in front of customer service counter to permit wheelchair maneuvering

3 letter and parcel drops must be within reach and easy to use

4 service counter at heights usable by customers and employees who may use wheelchairs recommended

5 if installed, fixed partitions must withstand a 250 pound force

6 if installed, handrails must be capable of withstanding a 250 pound force in any direction

7 self-service postal centers, including scales and adjacent work surfaces, must be mounted at an appropriate height and must provide clear floor space for easy maneuvering

8 brochures, pamphlets, and forms on racks within recommended reach ranges

9 self-service multi-commodity vending machines with coin return, selection buttons, and bill changers within easy reach, and with ample clear floor space for maneuvering required

10 at least five percent of post office boxes, of various sizes, located in the second or third set of modules, approximately 12 - 36 inches above the floor, with access aisles at least 66 inches wide

11 clear signage indicating exits, toilets, phones, and other services recommended

12 accessible entrances, employee toilet rooms, elevators, telephones, parking, and other features and spaces as required

13 drive-up outdoor mailboxes, accessible from driver's side of vehicle, although not required are a convenience for everyone

BASIC DESIGN CONSIDERATIONS

LOCKER ROOMS AND EMPLOYEE USE AREAS

1 lockers, intended for use by wheelchair users, must have clothing hooks and shelves which are easy to reach and latches/ locks which are easy to operate

2 unobstructed aisle space must be provided in front of lockers to provide easy access for wheelchair users

3 attendance recording equipment including time clock, card racks, and other work assignment logs installed no higher than 48 inches above the floor as required

4 counter at check-in area no higher than 36 inches above the floor as required

5 toilet rooms, lunchrooms, lounges, and medical treatment rooms accessible as required

6 emergency signals, switches, and controls within easy reach as required

7 telephones, vending machines, water fountains, and other amenities accessible as required

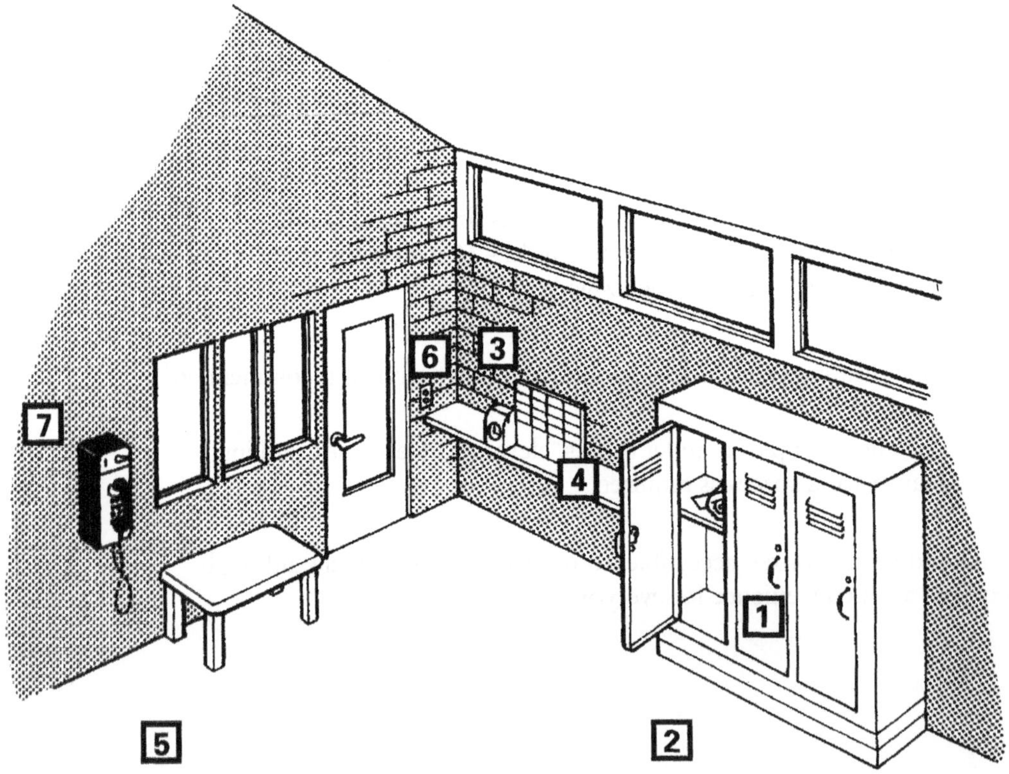

REFERENCE INDEX TO UFAS DOCUMENT

POSTAL FACILITIES

Primary References	UFAS page	Secondary References	UFAS page
9.1 General/Location	58	4.1- 4.33 Scope & Technical Requirements	4
9.2 Post Office Lobbies	58	4.2 Space Allowance and Reach Ranges	14
		4.32 Seating, Tables, and Work Surfaces	48
		A9.2 Post Office Lobbies	68
9.3 Self-Service Postal Centers	59	4.2 Space Allowance and Reach Ranges	14
		4.27 Controls & Operating Mechanisms	45
9.4 Post Office Boxes	59		
9.5 Locker Rooms	59	4.27 Controls & Operating Mechanisms	45
9.6 Attendance-Recording Equipment	59		

APPENDIX

Access Maryland. *Survey Guide and Survey.* Maryland: Author.

Adaptive Environments Center and Welch and Epp Associates. (1988). *Design for Access: A Guidebook for Designing Barrier Free State and County Buildings* (DCPO Contract No. 5887). Boston, MA: Division of Capital Planning and Operations, Executive Office of Administration and Finance, and the Office of Handicapped Affairs.

AIA Research Corporation and The Center for Fire Research of the National Engineering Laboratory, National Bureau of Standards. (1980). In B. M. Levin (Ed.), Fire and Life Safety for the Handicapped - Conference and Workshop Reports. Washington, DC: U.S. Government Printing Office.

American National Standards Institute, Inc. (1986). *American National Standard for Buildings and Facilities - Providing Accessibility and Usability for Physically Handicapped People* (A117.1). New York, NY: Author.

American National Standards Institute, Inc. (1979). *American National Standard for Power Operated Pedestrian Doors* (A156.10). New York, NY: Author.

American Society of Landscape Architects Foundation. (1974). *Access to the Environment, Volume 1* (HUD Contract No. H-2002-R). Washington, DC: Office of Policy Development and Research, Department of Housing and Urban Development and the Architectural and Transportation Barriers Compliance Board.

American Society of Landscape Architects Foundation. (1974). *Access to the Environment, Volume 2* (HUD Contract No. H-2002-R). Washington, DC: Office of Policy Development and Research, Department of Housing and Urban Development and the Architectural and Transportation Barriers Compliance Board.

American Society of Landscape Architects Foundation. (1974). *Access to the Environment, Volume 3* (HUD Contract No. H-2002-R). Washington, DC: Office of Policy Development and Research, Department of Housing and Urban Development and the Architectural and Transportation Barriers Compliance Board.

American Society of Landscape Architects Foundation. (1974). *Barrier Free Site Design* (HUD Contract No. H-2002-R). Washington, DC: U.S. Government Printing Office.

Applied Concepts Corporation. (1988). *Visual Signals Project - Guidelines and Advisory Standards: Recommendations and Cost Impact Analysis* (U.S. Department of Education Contract No. 300-86-0133). Washington, DC: U.S. Architectural and Transportation Barriers Compliance Board.

Applied Concepts Corporation. (1989). *Visual Alarms to Alert Persons with Hearing Loss.* Washington, DC: U.S. Architectural and Transportation Barriers Compliance Board.

Association of Physical Plant Administrators of Universities and Colleges. (1979). *Steps Toward Campus Accessibility*. Washington, DC: Author.

Ballantyne, D. S. (1983). *Accommodation of Disabled Visitors at Historic Sites in the National Park System* (Stock No. 024-005-00795-4). Washington, DC: U.S. Government Printing Office.

Barrier Free Environments, Inc. (1991). *The Accessible Housing Design File.* New York, NY: Van Nostrand Reinhold Company.

Barrier Free Environments, Inc. (1986). *Accessibility in Georgia: A Technical and Policy Guide to Access in Georgia.* Atlanta, GA: Georgia Council on Developmental Disabilities and the Georgia Division of Rehabilitation Services Client Assistance Program.

Barrier Free Environments, Inc. and Harold Russell Associates, Inc. (1980). *The Planner's Guide to Barrier Free Meetings.* Raleigh, NC: Authors.

Bell System (1981). *Telecommunications Services for Special Needs.* USA: Author.

Blasch, B. and Hiatt, L. (1983). *Orientation and Wayfinding* (Contract No. 300-82-0236). Washington, DC: U.S. Architectural and Transportation Barriers Compliance Board.

California State Accessibility Standards: Interpretive Manual. (1987). Sacramento, CA: The Office of the State Architect and the Department of Rehabilitation.

Cohen, U. and Hunter, J. (1981). *Access Information: Programming, Design, and Construction for Handicapped Persons* (Report No. R81-2). Milwaukee, WI: University of Wisconsin - Milwaukee, Center for Architecture and Urban Planning Research.

Construction Specification Institute. (1980). *Manual of Practice.* Alexandria, VA: Author.

Coons, M. and Milner, M. (Eds.) (1978). *Creating an Accessible Campus.* Washington, DC: Association of Physical Plant Administrators of Universities and Colleges.

Cotler, S. R. (1981). *Modifying the Existing Campus Building for Accessibility: Construction Guidelines and Specifications.* Washington, DC: Association of Physical Plant Administrators of Universities and Colleges.

Duncan, J., Gish, C., Mulholland, M. E., and Townsend, A. (1977, December). Environmental Modifications for the Visually Impaired: A Handbook. *Journal of Visual Impairment and Blindness.* New York, NY: American Foundation for the Blind.

Eisenberg, A. C. (1990, August). "ADA: New Challenges and Opportunities for Architects." *AIA Memo*, 33, 7-10.

Fishman, D. (1979). *Shopping Centers and the Accessibility Codes.* New York: The International Council of Shopping Centers.

Georgia Institute of Technology, College of Architecture. (1985). *Final Report: A Multidisciplinary Assessment of the Art of Signage for Visually Impaired Persons* (U.S. Department of Education Contract No. 300-83-0280). Washington, DC: U.S. Architectural and Transportation Barriers Compliance Board.

Gettings, R. M. and Katz, R. E. (1988). *Summary of Existing Legislation Affecting Persons with Disabilities* (Office of Special Education and Rehabilitative Services, U.S. Department of Education Contract No. 433J47700847). Washington, DC: U.S. Government Printing Office.

Goldman, C. D. (1983). Architectural Barriers: A Perspective on Progress. *Western New England Law Review, 5:465.* Springfield, MA: Western New England College, School of Law.

Hughes Associates, Inc. (1988). *Emergency Management Planning to Improve Safety for People with Disabilities: Guidelines for Facility Managers* (U.S. Department of Education Contract No. 300-87-0149). Washington, DC: U.S. Architectural and Transportation Barriers Compliance Board.

Hughes Associates, Inc. (1988). *Egress Procedures and Technologies for People with Disabilities: Final Report of a State-of-the-Art Review with Recommendations for Action* (U.S. Department of Education Contract No. 300-87-0149). Washington, DC: U.S. Architectural and Transportation Barriers Compliance Board.

Hughes Associates, Inc. (1988). *Review of Standards and Codes Plus Recommendations for Accessible Means of Egress: Prepared as Part of a Study of Egress Procedures and Technologies for People with Disabilities* (U.S. Department of Education Contract No. 300-87-0149). Washington, DC: U.S. Architectural and Transportation Barriers Compliance Board.

Information Development Corporation. (1985). *The System: Accessible Design and Product Information.* Raleigh, NC Author.

Johnson, B. M. (1979, December). "Accessible Pedestrian Systems for Those with Physical Disabilities." *Building Practice Note, Division of Building Research, National Research Council of Canada, 14.*

Jones, M. A. (1978). *Accessibility Standards Illustrated.* Chicago, IL: The Capital Development Board.

Karr, A. R. (1990, May 23). "Disabled-Rights Bill Instills Hope in Some, Brings Fear to Others." *The Wall Street Journal*, p. B1.

Kennett, E. W. (Ed.). (1982). *Proceedings of the 1980 Conference on Life Safety and the Handicapped* (NBS Grant # NB 80NADA 1058). Washington, DC: U.S. Department of Commerce, National Bureau of Standards.

Kirk, L. (1975). *Accent on Access.* McLean, VA: American Society of Landscape Architects Foundation.

Lifchez, R. (1979). *Getting There: A Guide to Accessibility for Your Facility.* Sacramento, CA: California Department of Rehabilitation, Technical Assistance Project.

Loversidge, R. D., Jr. (Ed.). (1978). *Access for All: An Illustrated Handbook of Barrier Free Design.* Produced for the Ohio Governor's Committee on Employment of the Handicapped. Columbus, OH: Special Press.

Lusher, R. H. (1989, July). "Making the Past Accessible." *The Construction Specifier,* p. 92-98.

Lusher, R. H. (1989). "Handicapped Access Laws and Codes." In J. A. Wilkes (Ed.),. *Encyclopedia of Architecture: Design, Engineering, and Construction, Volume 2,* (646-659). New York, NY: John Wiley & Sons, Inc.

Lusher, R. H. and Mace, R. L. (1989). "Design for Physical and Mental Disabilities." In J. A. Wilkes (Ed.),. *Encyclopedia of Architecture: Design, Engineering, and Construction, Volume 3,* (748-763). New York, NY: John Wiley & Sons, Inc.

Lynch, R.J. (1982). *Easy Access: A Digest of the Requirements of the New ANSI Standards.* Scottsdale, AR: Author.

Mace, R. L. (1976). *Accessibility Modifications: Guidelines for Modifications to Existing Buildings for Accessibility to the Handicapped.* Ralcigh, NC: Department of Insurance, Special Office for the Handicapped.

Massachusetts Easter Seal Society. (1980). *Access in the 80's: Problems & Solutions.* Boston: Author.

Milner, M. (1980). *Adapting Historic Campus Structures for Accessibility* (DHEW Contract No. 300-78-0288). Washington, DC: Association of Physical Plant Administrators of Universities and Colleges and the National Center for a Barrier Free Environment.

Milner, M. (1979). *Breaking Through the Deafness Barrier.* Washington, DC: Gallaudet College, Division of Public Services.

Milner, M. (1978). *Planning for Accessibility: A Guide to Developing and Implementing Campus Transition Plans* (Publication No. DHEW O-257-119). Washington, DC: U.S. Government Printing Office.

National Center for a Barrier Free Environment. (1978). *Opening Doors: A Handbook on Making Facilities Accessible to Handicapped People* (Contract No. B7B-5542). Washington, DC: Community Services Administration.

National Elevator Industry, Inc. (977). *Suggested Minimum Passenger Elevator Requirements for the Handicapped.* New York, NY: Author.

National Emergency Training Center. (1989, March). *Local Receive Site Coordination Guide: Meeting Special Needs of the Disabled in Evacuation and Sheltering Systems* (EENET No.1). Emmitsburg, MD: Federal Emergency Management Agency.

National Fire Protection Association, Inc. (1985). *NFPA 101 Life Safety Code.* Quincy, MA: National Fire Protection Association, Inc.

National Library Service for the Blind and Physically Handicapped. (1981). *Planning Barrier Free Libraries.* Washington, DC: The Library of Congress.

New Mexico Department of Education, Division of Vocational Rehabilitation. (1975). *Removing Architectural Barriers: An Illustrated Handbook of Chapter 41 of the 1973 New Mexico Uniform Building Code.* Santa Fe, NM: Author.

Newell, F. V. (1979). *How to Develop a Sign System.* Kansas City, MO: Best Sign Systems.

North Carolina State Building Code, Volume I-C, General Construction: Making Buildings and Facilities Accessible to and Usable by the Physically Handicapped. (1989) Raleigh, NC: Building Code Council and the North Carolina Department of Insurance.

Packard, R. T. (Ed.). (1981). *Ramsey/Sleeper Architectural Graphic Standards.* New York, NY: John Wiley & Sons, Inc.

Robinette, G. O. (Ed.). (1985). *Barrier Free Exterior Design: Anyone Can Go Anywhere.* New York, NY: Van Nostrand Reinhold Company.

Scott, B. H. (Ed.). (1985). *Book of Renovations.* Kansas City, MO: Mayor's Office on the Disabled, Kansas City, and Missouri Governor's Committee on Employment of the Handicapped.

Senate Committee on Environment and Public Works. (1979). *Architectural Barriers in Federal Buildings: Implementation of the Architectural Barriers Act of 1968* (Committee Print Serial No. 96-8). Washington, DC: U.S. Government Printing Office.

Small, R. and Allan, B. (1978). *An Illustrated Handbook of Barrier Free Design: Washington State Rules and Regulations.* Seattle, WA: The Easter Seal Society for Crippled Children.

Smith, W. D. and Frier, T. G. (1989). *Access to History: A Guide to Providing Access to Historic Buildings for People with Disabilities.* Boston, MA: Massachusetts Historical Commission.

State of Texas: Program for the Elimination of Architectural Barriers. (1989). Austin, TX: State Purchasing and General Services Commission.

Swedish International Development Authority and United Nations Centre for Human Settlements. (1983). *Designing with Care: A Guide to Adaptation of the Built Environment for Disabled Persons.* Austria: Author.

Sweet's Division. (1988). *Sweet's Catalog File: Products for General Building & Renovation.* New York, NY: McGraw-Hill Information Systems Company.

Templer, J., Lewis, D. and Sanford, J. (1983). *Ground and Floor SurfaceTreatments* (Contract No. 300-82-0236). Washington, DC: U.S. Architectural and Transportation Barriers Compliance Board.

The Section 3.7 Handbook: Building Requirements for Persons with Disabilities Including Illustrations and Commentary. (1984). Providence of British Columbia, Canada: Ministry of Municipal Affairs.

U.S. Architectural and Transportation Barriers Compliance Board. (1989). *Transit Facility Design for Persons with Visual Impairments.* Washington, DC: Author.

U.S. Architectural and Transportation Barriers Compliance Board. (1984, August 7). Uniform Federal Accessibility Standards. *Federal Register, 49 FR 31528.*

U.S. Architectural and Transportation Barriers Compliance Board. (1981, January 16). Minimun Guidelines and Requirements for Accessible Design. *Federal Register, 46 (11), 4270-4304*

U.S. Department of Housing and Urban Development. (1988). *Universal Design: Housing for the Lifespan of All People.* (Publication No. HUD-1156-PA). Washington, DC: Office of Intergovernmental Affairs.

Windham Southeast Supervisory Union. (1975). *Building Needs for the Handicapped.* Brattleboro, VT: Windham Southeast Supervisory Union.

Printed and bound by CPI Group (UK) Ltd, Croydon, CR0 4YY
16/09/2026
14963466-0001